Governance in a Global Economy

Governance in a Global Economy

POLITICAL AUTHORITY IN TRANSITION

Edited by
Miles Kahler and David A. Lake

PRINCETON UNIVERSITY PRESS

PRINCETON AND OXFORD

Copyright © 2003 by Princeton University Press
Published by Princeton University Press, 41 William Street, Princeton, New Jersey 08540
In the United Kingdom: Princeton University Press, 3 Market Place, Woodstock,
Oxfordshire OX20 1SY
All Rights Reserved

Library of Congress Cataloging-in-Publication Data

Governance in a global economy : political authority in transition / edited by Miles Kahler
and David A. Lake.
p. cm.
Includes bibliographical references and index.
ISBN 0-691-11401-3 (alk. paper) — ISBN 0-691-11402-1 (pbk. : alk. paper)
1. Corporate governance.   2. International business enterprises — Management.
3. International business enterprises — Government policy.   4. Globalization — Political
   aspects.   I. Kahler, Miles, 1949–   II. Lake, David A., 1956–
HD2741 .G688 2003
327.1 — dc21   2002042712

British Library Cataloging-in-Publication Data is available

This book has been composed in Sabon

Printed on acid-free paper. ∞
www.pupress.princeton.edu

1   3   5   7   9   10   8   6   4   2

CONTENTS

CONTRIBUTORS

JAMES A. CAPORASO is professor of political science at the University of Washington and current editor of *Comparative Political Studies*. Professor Caporaso has published articles in *International Studies Quarterly*, *American Political Science Review*, *International Organization*, *Review of European Integration*, as well as several other journals. He has written, coauthored, and edited numerous books, most recently *The Changing International Division of Labor*, *The Elusive State*, (with David Levine) *Theories of Political Economy*, and *Dilemmas of European Integration*.

BENJAMIN J. COHEN is Louis G. Lancaster Professor of International Political Economy in the political science department at the University of California, Santa Barbara. Professor Cohen is a specialist in international political economy. His current research focuses on the political and economic consequences of cross-border currency competition. His publications have addressed issues of international monetary relations, U.S. foreign economic policy, European monetary integration, developing country debt, and theories of economic imperialism. His most recent books include *In Whose Interest? International Banking and American Foreign Policy*, *Crossing Frontiers: Explorations in International Political Economy*, and *The Geography of Money*.

BARRY EICHENGREEN is George C. Pardee and Helen N. Pardee Professor of Economics, professor of political science, and director of Institute for European Studies at the University of California, Berkeley. Professor Eichengreen has published widely on the history and current operation of the international monetary and financial system. His books include *Toward a New International Financial Architecture*, *Globalizing Capital: A History of the International Monetary System*, *European Monetary Unification*, and *Golden Fetters: The Gold Standard and the Great Depression, 1919–1939*.

ZACHARY ELKINS is assistant professor of comparative politics at the University of Illinois, Urbana-Champaign. His research and teaching interests include comparative politics of developing nations, comparative political behavior, diffusion of political processes across nations, Latin American politics, and quantitative methods. He has received fellowships from the University of California's Institute on Global Conflict and Cooperation and the Ford Foundation for research in Brazil and Guatemala.

GEOFFREY GARRETT is vice-provost for International Studies and Overseas Programs and professor of political science at the University of California, Los Angeles. His current research focuses on the domestic effects of globalization around the world and on the dynamics of European integration. He is the author of *Partisan Politics in the Global Economy* and over forty articles in academic journals including the *American Political Science Review*, *Comparative Political Studies*, *European Journal of Political Research*, *International Organization*, *Journal of Theoretical Politics*, and *World Politics*. These works focus on numerous aspects of politics, economics, and law in market economies.

PETER GOUREVITCH is professor of political science at the University of California, San Diego. Professor Gourevitch is also the founding dean of the Graduate School of International Relations and Pacific Studies at the university, where he continues to serve on the faculty. He is past editor (with David Lake) of *International Organization*, a leading scholarly journal on international relations. His book, *Politics in Hard Times: Comparative Responses to International Crisis*, has been published in Spanish and Italian and soon will be available in Korean. Other publications focus on U.S.-Japan relations after the Cold War and international economic relations.

VIRGINIA HAUFLER is associate professor in the Department of Government and Politics at the University of Maryland. Her research focuses on the role of business in international politics and examines such topics as industry self-regulation, pressure groups and reputational effects, and business and conflict. Her books include *A Public Role for the Private Sector: Industry Self-Regulation in a Global Economy* (co-editor), and *Dangerous Commerce: Insurance and the Management of International Risk*. She is also active in the group Women in International Security (WIIS), which is dedicated to the advancement of women in international affairs careers.

MICHAEL J. HISCOX is John L. Loeb Associate Professor of the Social Sciences at Harvard University, where he is also a faculty associate at the Weatherhead Center for International Affairs. His current research addresses questions concerning factor mobility and structural adjustment within economies, trade adjustment assistance policies, the measurement of barriers to trade, determinants of foreign investment flows, and the size of nations. His most recent book is *International Trade and Political Conflict*.

MILES KAHLER is Rohr Professor of Pacific International Relations at the Graduate School of International Relations and Pacific Studies and director of the Institute for International, Comparative, and Area Studies at the University of California, San Diego. Professor Kahler is a specialist in international relations and international political economy. His edited and authored publications include *Legalization and World Politics*, *Capital Flows and Financial Crises*, and *International Institutions and the Political Economy of Integration*. From 1994 to 1996 he was Senior Fellow in International Political Economy at the Council on Foreign Relations.

ROBERT O. KEOHANE is James B. Duke Professor of Political Science at Duke University. He is the author of *After Hegemony: Cooperation and Discord in the World Political Economy*, for which in 1989 he was awarded the second annual Grawemeyer Award for Ideas Improving World Order. Other authored or coauthored works include *Power and Governance in a Partially Globalized World* (with Joseph S. Nye, Jr.), *Power and Interdependence: World Politics in Transition,* and *Designing Social Inquiry: Scientific Inference in Qualitative Research* (with Gary King and Sidney Verba). Between 1974 and 1980 he was editor of the journal *International Organization*. Keohane was also president of the International Studies Association, 1988–1989, and of the American Political Science Association, 1999–2000.

DAVID A. LAKE is professor of political science at the University of California, San Diego, and former research director for international relations at the University of California's Institute on Global Conflict and Cooperation. Professor Lake has published widely in international-relations theory, international political economy, and U.S. foreign policy. His most recent books include *Regional Orders: Building Security in the New World* (co-edited with Patrick M. Morgan), *Strategic Choice and International Relations* (co-edited with Robert Powell), *The International Spread of Ethnic Conflict: Fear, Diffusion, and Escalation* (co-edited with Donald Rothchild), and *Entangling Relations: American Foreign Policy in Its Century*.

LISA L. MARTIN is professor of government at Harvard University. Her major research interests involve international institutions and cooperation, domestic institutions and international cooperation, the international financial institutions, and the political economy of tourism. Her most recent book, *Democratic Commitments: Legislatures and International Cooperation*, focuses on the impact of legislative involvement on bargaining and implementation of agreements in the United States and the European Union.

WALTER MATTLI is associate professor of political science at Columbia University. His research interests include international political economy, international organization, international law, and Europe. He is the author of *The Logic of Regional Integration: Europe and Beyond*. He has also published articles on European legal integration, comparative regional integration, international commercial dispute resolution, transatlantic relations, and EU enlargement. In 2003 he was awarded the J. P. Morgan International Prize in Finance Policy and Economics by the American Academy in Berlin.

KATHLEEN R. MCNAMARA is associate professor of government at Georgetown University. Her areas of interest include international and comparative political economy, international organization, the European Union, and institutional and ideational theory. Professor McNamara is the author of *The Currency of Ideas: Monetary Politics in the European Union*. She has also written on the politics of central banking, globalization, and the role of ideas in policymaking.

JOSEPH S. NYE, JR., is Don K. Price Professor of Public Policy and dean of the Kennedy School of Government at Harvard University. He returned to Harvard in December of 1995, after serving as Assistant Secretary of Defense for International Security Affairs, in which position he won two Distinguished Service medals, and as Chair of the National Intelligence Council. Nye's most recent books are *The Paradox of American Power* and *Understanding International Conflicts*, now in its fourth edition.

JONATHAN RODDEN is associate professor of political science at the Massachusetts Institute of Technology. His research and teaching interests focus on the political economy of institutions. Professor Rodden's current work includes theoretical and empirical analyses of federalism in comparative perspective. He has recently published articles in the *Virginia Law Review*, *American Journal of Political Science*, and *European Union Politics*. He also led a collaborative project at the World Bank on fiscal discipline among state and local governments, which has resulted in an edited volume, *Fiscal Decentralization and the Challenge of Hard Budget Constraints*.

RONALD ROGOWSKI is professor of political science at the University of California, Los Angeles, where he specializes in comparative politics and political economy. His book *Commerce and Coalitions* explores how international trade shapes domestic political coalitions. In 1999, the American Political Science Association honored him by organizing a roundtable discussion to commemorate the tenth anniversary of its publication. His recent work considers how the design of electoral systems affects a nation's economic policies. He has also investigated globalization, capital mobility, and the sources of price differentials across national boundaries.

BETH A. SIMMONS is professor of government at Harvard University. Professor Simmons's current research focus is on the effects of international law and institutions on state behavior and policy choice. Her publications include *Who Adjusts? Domestic Sources of Foreign Economic Policy during the Interwar Years, 1923–1939*, winner of the 1995 American Political Science Association Woodrow Wilson Award for the best book published in the previous year in government, politics, or international relations. She has also published articles on international institutions in *International Organization* and *World Politics*.

PIETER VAN HOUTEN is lecturer in the Faculty of Social and Political Sciences (SPS) and a teaching fellow at Churchill College at the University of Cambridge. His dissertation, "Regional Assertiveness in Western Europe: Political Constraints and the Role of Party Competition," received the William Anderson Award for the best doctoral dissertation completed and accepted in 1999 or 2000 in the field of state and local government, federalism, or intergovernmental relations from the American Political Science Association.

ACKNOWLEDGMENTS

THE EDITORS and authors thank the University of California's Institute on Global Conflict and Cooperation, and especially its director, Peter Cowhey, for its generous financial support of this project. Without IGCC's sponsorship, this project and publication would not have been possible. We are also indebted to Marissa Sanders and Katy Vicknair of the IGCC for organizing the working group conferences. Lynne Bush, IGCC's senior editor, has overseen the production of this volume with her usual efficiency, skill, and good cheer.

In addition to the authors represented in this volume, we acknowledge the participation of Daniel Gitterman and Lawrence Saez in all phases of the project. Their contributions were important for the development of the project and its findings. In addition, Judith Goldstein, Stephan Haggard, Scott Kastner, Mikhail Klimenko, Barbara Koremenos, Stephen Krasner, Skip Lupia, David Mares, Stephanie Mc-Whorter, Angela O'Mahony, Robert Powell, Kal Raustiala, Chad Rector, James Shinn, and Richard Steinberg participated in one or more of the meetings of the working group and provided helpful comments on the project and on early drafts of the papers.

We are grateful to Charles Myers at Princeton University Press for his support throughout the publication process and his wise counsel to the editors.

Chapter 1

GLOBALIZATION AND GOVERNANCE

Miles Kahler and David A. Lake

Contemporary debate over globalization casts its political effects as both revolutionary and contradictory. In a "power shift" of historic proportions (Mathews 1997), some analysts claim that we are entering an age of the "virtual state" (Rosecrance 1996). Globalization, they argue, drains political authority from nation-states, long the dominant form of political organization in world politics. The state's monopoly of familiar governance functions is ending as governance migrates down to newly empowered regions, provinces, and municipalities; up to supranational organizations; and laterally to such private actors as multinational firms and transnational nongovernmental organizations (NGOs) that acquire previously "public" responsibilities. In this view, globalization not only transfers the location of governance, it also forces a convergence of state institutions and policies. In exercising their residual authority, states are constrained to look and act alike. Although a transfer of governance to subnational units may increase democratic accountability, these governance changes and the accompanying pressures for convergence are more often seen as a threat to the ability of societies to chart their own democratically determined courses.

Skeptics contest each of globalization's alleged effects. National governments jealously guard many traditional spheres of governance, particularly defense, criminal justice, and immigration. Rather than promoting new forms of political organization, groups who demand self-determination define their claims as possession of a nation-state. If the nation-state is a beleaguered and ineffectual fossil, its enduring popularity at the dawn of the new millennium is baffling. A skeptical view of deregulation regards the award of enhanced authority to private actors as partially or wholly offset by public intervention in new areas such as environmental or consumer protection. In Seattle, Washington, D.C., and Genoa, new transnational political movements protest a deregulated and integrated international market. Although some press for reformed and transformed international institutions, others, somewhat paradoxically, rely on national governments for policy change or urge those governments to withdraw from pro-market international organizations (O'Brien et al. 2000).

Sorting through these contradictory claims requires careful definition of globalization and governance, identification of the range and dimensions of variation in both, a preliminary survey of changes in governance that appear to result from increasing globalization, and a theoretical frame for examining more systematically the links between globalization and governance. We begin these tasks of definition, identification, and explanation in this introductory chapter. The authors in the volume build on the common definitions developed here. They also share a common baseline: an increase in globalization that sets the last four decades apart from both an earlier era of globalization (the decades before 1914) and the period of economic disintegration produced by depression and world war.

Collectively, the chapters in this volume find that the effects of globalization on governance are more complex and contingent than many observers claim. Globalization exerts a profound effect on economic and political life. Important shifts in the locus of governance have occurred in all three directions — downward, upward, and laterally. Some measure of convergence can be observed. These trends are neither universal nor uniform, however. Variation occurs from issue-area to issue-area. As Benjamin J. Cohen describes in chapter 6, authority over monetary policy has in some cases been delegated to other governments and to regional entities. In international financial regulation, however, Barry Eichengreen (chapter 7) confirms the persistent dominance of national authorities. Some important political effects appear unrelated to the advance of globalization. Pieter Van Houten (chapter 5) argues that international economic integration has not been an important influence on demands for increased regional autonomy in Europe. Walter Mattli (chapter 8) and Virginia Haufler (chapter 9) contend that private forms of governance, of growing importance, are often dependent on national political authorities for their effectiveness. In addition, although governments appear to converge on policies of economic openness, there appear to be few pressures for convergence on other policies — and, as Ronald Rogowski (chapter 10) argues most forcefully, few good theoretical reasons for expecting such convergence. Finally, as James Caporaso (chapter 14) and Robert Keohane and Joseph Nye (chapter 15) note, there are multiple forms of accountability. Although traditional mechanisms of democracy may not apply at the international level outside of the European Union, other means of monitoring and constraining authorities remain important.

General conclusions about the changing nature of global political authority remain elusive. The chapters that follow demonstrate that neither globalization nor governance is homogenous. Rather, international economic integration — itself differentiated and uneven — is producing a new fabric of global governance that displays many variations and shadings.

To explain this diversity, the authors adopt an explicitly actor-oriented and political theory of globalization. Globalization is often portrayed as an inexorable, impersonal set of market forces that compels passive states to comply with its dictates—an environmental constraint that states ignore only if they are willing to be left behind in the new global competition. Existing theoretical accounts are largely functionalist or efficiency-based. In contrast, the authors in this volume emphasize globalization's effects on governance through political actors. Globalization changes the policy preferences of some actors, increases the bargaining power of others, and opens new institutional options for still others. For modern actors, the most important effect of globalization often lies in its effects on other political actors, their strategies, and the institutional settings in which they interact. In this way, we seek to reintroduce agency and choice into the story of globalization.

GLOBALIZATION AND GOVERNANCE: DEFINITION AND VARIATION

Globalization Defined

Globalization is often defined expansively as networks of interdependence that span intercontinental distances (Keohane and Nye 2000a, 105). As such, the term incorporates a host of profound changes in world politics: growing political linkages at the global level, erosion of local space and time as structures of economic life, and homogenization of social life through global standards, products, and culture. Typically, these broad trends are attributed to radically reduced communication and transportation costs. Conceived in this way, globalization is an umbrella term, covering a wide variety of linkages between countries that extend beyond economic interdependence. No single volume could coherently examine how globalization, thus defined, affects governance.[1] Equally important, this broad definition includes elements of governance within it, and thus risks confounding the two crucial variables of this study.

We therefore focus on a central aspect of globalization: economic integration at the global level. The reduction of barriers to economic exchange and factor mobility gradually creates one economic space from many, although that process remains far from complete. Most economists and most authors in this volume adopt this meaning. Although he attaches profound systemic significance to globalization, Thomas Friedman (1999, 7–8) also adopts this meaning when he defines globaliza-

---

[1] For a more comprehensive overview, however, see Nye and Donahue (2000).

tion as "the inexorable integration of markets, nation-states and technologies to a degree never witnessed before — in a way enabling individuals, corporations and nation-states to reach around the world farther, faster, deeper and cheaper than ever before." This definition has an important, if implied, political dimension, as well. Although facilitated by lower communication and transportation costs, globalization rests on the decisions of national governments to open their markets to others and to participate in a global economy. It is this political dimension, we argue, that is crucial for understanding globalization and its effects on governance.

Several chapters in this volume focus on "Europeanization" as what Caporaso (chapter 14) calls the "leading edge" of globalization. Economic integration displays important regional variations. Through what is clearly a politically driven process, Europe has traveled farthest in opening national economies to goods and factor flows between neighbors. The supranational institutions of Europe, which encouraged economic integration and were deepened by it, are in certain respects unique. As Kathleen McNamara (chapter 13) points out, however, European integration is a "most likely case" for investigating globalization's effects on governance. For this reason, Europe serves as a central case in several chapters that follow.[2]

Variation in Globalization

Those who define globalization broadly often portray its changes as revolutionary and unique, incomparable to any previous historical period. Economic historians, endorsing the narrower definition of global economic integration, beg to differ. They do not view globalization as either an inexorable trend or as a sharp rupture that divides contemporary history from the past. Instead, historians find substantial variation in economic globalization over the past century, as well as similarities between the present and the decades before 1914. For many, that earlier era represents a level of integration that has been surpassed only recently, if at all. Sachs and Warner (1995), for example, portray the contemporary global economy as reestablishing a process of integration that had been disrupted in midcentury by decades of war and depression.

Claims of comparability between globalization then and now are in turn qualified by more detailed investigation of the pre-1914 world economy. Simple measures of gross economic flows and other standard measures of economic integration may not capture the greater "depth and diversity" of trade and capital market integration today (Irwin

---

[2] For a similar treatment of Europeanization as globalization, see Weber (2001).

1996, 45). Manufactures play a much larger role in trade and a larger share of the economy, particularly services, is exposed to international competition today (Baldwin and Martin 1999; Bordo, Eichengreen, and Irwin 1999). Capital markets also differ. Short-term capital flows are far more important than they were before 1914; the enormous contemporary foreign exchange market did not exist in the earlier period.[3] In addition, borrowing by the private sector and by financial institutions, particularly in the then-emerging markets, was far less important than long-term public borrowing for infrastructure development (Bordo, Eichengreen, and Irwin 1999; Obstfeld 1998). Foreign direct investment is strikingly different in the two periods. Investment by multinational corporations before 1914 was typically in the agricultural and mining sectors through freestanding companies; multinational investment today is more likely to be in manufacturing and to display the characteristics of the global factory — parceling out production chains across jurisdictions (Feenstra 1998; Prakash and Hart 2000, 2). An ability to disaggregate the production process across national borders was far more difficult in the technological conditions of a century ago.

On the other hand, labor was clearly more globalized in the pre-1914 era. Indeed, levels of labor migration were "staggering by modern standards" (Baldwin and Martin 1999). Migration flowed from Europe to the United States and other territories of settlement; it also flowed among colonial and quasi-colonial territories, expanding Chinese populations in Southeast Asia and Indian populations in the Caribbean and Pacific islands. At the same time, immigration provided the first evidence of backlash against globalization, as restrictions were first imposed in the United States and elsewhere during the 1880s (O'Rourke and Williamson 1999, chap. 10; Williamson 1998).

One critical difference underlies this more nuanced and disaggregated portrait of old and new globalization: information. Although trade in goods was spurred by falling ocean transport costs in both periods, radical and persistent reductions in the costs of cross-border communication are far more significant in the second. These cost reductions shrink the information asymmetries that had hindered development of more diverse and transparent international capital markets before 1914 (Bordo, Eichengreen, and Irwin 1999). They also open novel techniques of organizing production across borders, whether integrated vertically in global factories or through looser cross-border production networks (Borrus, Ernst, and Haggard 2000). Sharply reduced communication costs and technological innovation also affect cultural integration through

---

[3] Mauro, Sussman, and Yafeh (2001) find that the co-movement of spreads across emerging markets is higher today than in the period 1870–1913.

trade in digitized images, absent before 1914. The costs of cross-border political organization have also declined, although transnational politics — women's suffrage, peace, labor rights — first flourished at the turn of the last century (Keck and Sikkink 1998).

Globalization before 1914 differed from contemporary globalization. The intervening decades, however, brought a sharp retreat from globalization of all kinds. Between 1914 and 1945, the global economy disintegrated. Barriers to capital mobility — suspension of the gold standard and imposition of foreign exchange controls — increased during the Great Depression of the 1930s. International capital mobility reached its lowest point during World War II and the immediate postwar years (Obstfeld and Taylor 1998, 381). Trade protectionism, which had existed in pre-1914 Europe and America, also intensified and spread during the years of depression and war. Relatively closed trading blocs, typically based on colonial empires, became the new norm. Restrictions on immigration proliferated, strangling the previously robust movement of labor (O'Rourke and Williamson 1999, 185–86).

After 1945, this trend toward closure gradually reversed itself among the industrialized countries. Beginning in the 1950s, the rich countries removed exchange controls, reduced tariffs and other trade barriers through multilateral negotiations, and, as the postwar boom tightened labor markets, relaxed restrictions on immigration. A shift to flexible exchange rates in the early 1970s led to a gradual removal of capital controls. By the 1980s, economic integration in the industrialized world met or surpassed the levels seen before World War I.

Globalization, however, required the embrace of economic openness by developing and formerly socialist economies, as well. This integration occurred later and remains less complete; its results were also more controversial. Although some developing countries had pursued international economic integration since independence, most distanced themselves from liberalized trade and financial flows after 1945. Only in the last two decades of the twentieth century did policies of economic openness gain global popularity. In chapter 11, Beth Simmons and Zachary Elkins examine alternative explanations for this remarkable shift toward liberalization. On a number of measures, integration of developing and transitional economies into global trade and financial systems has been striking. The share of developing countries in world trade grew from 23 percent in 1985 to 29 percent in 1995; thirty-three developing countries replaced relatively closed trade regimes with open trade regimes in the same decade (IMF 1997, 72–73). Capital flows to developing countries increased dramatically after the debt crisis of the 1980s. Those flows, with the exception of foreign direct investment, were subject to equally marked disruptions in the wake of financial crises that continued to affect emerging markets during the 1990s (Kahler 1998). Labor migration also grew during these decades, although never reaching the heights of the late nineteenth century. The new migration, however, like trade and investment, broke with a strictly North-South pattern, producing "the globalization of international migration" (Castles and Miller 1993; see also Sassen 1998, chaps. 2–4).

Globalization has varied across the twentieth century. Each of the authors investigates the latest turn to globalization, which occurred in the second half of the century, as a central independent variable that may account for changes in governance. Although this common understanding of globalization is shared by the authors, several qualifications should be noted. Globalization remains uneven across markets for capital, goods, and labor, economic sectors, and regions. Even among the industrialized countries, where integration is deepest, globalization has not created a borderless world or the end of geography. Capital mobility in the highly integrated financial markets in Europe and the United States is still much lower than it is within national economies (Obstfeld 1995). Border effects are also powerful in international trade: political units within a national economy still trade more intensively than units across national borders (Helliwell 1998). In measuring the advance of globalization, the benchmark is all-important: the world is more globalized than it was three decades ago, but national economies, at least in the industrialized world, remain far more integrated than the global economy.

Governance Defined

Like globalization, governance can be conceived broadly or narrowly. Most generally, the Commission on Global Governance (1995, 2) defines its subject as "the sum of the many ways individuals and institutions, public and private, manage their common affairs. It is a continuing process through which conflicting or diverse interests may be accommodated and cooperative action may be taken." Similarly, Keohane and Nye (2000b, 12) define governance as "the processes and institutions, both formal and informal, that guide and restrain the collective activities of a group." As such, governance is nearly synonymous with patterned social interaction, similar to Grotian conceptions of international regimes (Krasner 1983, 10). Governance can also be understood more narrowly as that subset of restraints that rests on authority, where authority itself is a social relationship in which "A (a person or occupant of an office) wills B to follow A and B voluntarily complies" (Scheppele and Soltan 1987, 194). In other words, governance is characterized by decisions issued by one actor that a second is expected to obey.[4] Most of the papers in this volume focus on this narrower meaning of governance as a set of authority relationships.

Under either conception, however, governance is not government (Young 1999). Many social and political units—among them families and clans, firms, labor unions, alliances, and empires—govern social interactions and can possess authority, at least in regard to their members. Nation-states assert sovereign authority and claim a monopoly over the legitimate use of force, but they represent only one type of governance structure. Corporations, NGOs, international standard-setting bodies, and many other entities all act authoritatively within the global system.[5] In other words, all can contribute to international governance.

In investigating the effects of globalization, three analytic dimensions of governance are particularly important: centralization or dispersal of the sites of governance (across levels of governance or between public and private governance); the degree to which governance ultimately responds to the wishes of those who are governed, the dimension of democratic accountability; and convergence or divergence among the forms of governance and their policy products. We discuss each of these dimensions in turn.

As the chapters in part 1 discuss, governance varies according to the centralization of authority. Authority can be highly concentrated—vested in a single, hierarchical entity with claims to exclusive jurisdiction, as in totalitarian national states or the transnational Roman Catholic church. Governance can also be widely dispersed among individual nodes exercising only limited jurisdiction. Exemplars are the United States and Switzerland—decentralized federal states with large spheres of private activity. Understanding this dimension of governance requires identification of the site(s) or location(s) of authority. More sites of authority produce a more decentralized system. International anarchy—a

---

[4] Scheppele and Soltan refer to this as the paradigmatic definition, which they contrast with their own alternative. Three characteristics of authority are worthy of note in our discussion of governance. First, power may be a foundation of authority, but authority does not itself rely upon the exercise of coercion (Peters 1967, 92–94). Second, although the claim to authority may need to be justified by appeals to divine right, tradition, popular support, and so on, A's authoritative commands do not themselves need to be justified. This distinguishes authority from moral or scientific commands (ibid.). Finally, the strength of authority is measured by the maximum divergence between A's command and B's preferences under which B will still comply voluntarily. A is weak when it is limited to willing only that which B would do anyway. At the same time, authority is never without limit. There is always some command that A could issue that B would defy. On authority, see Friedrich (1958) and Pennock and Chapman (1987).

[5] For a typology of governance structures at the public-private intersection, see Börzel and Risse (2001).

system of sovereign states — consists of actors without any overarching authority and, thus, constitutes a highly decentralized governance structure. Subsidiarity, a term that originated in the European Union, implies a normative bias toward decentralized governance. Governance at the level closest to the ultimate principals — the electors in a democracy — is preferred (CEPR 1993). Another term for such decentralized systems is multilevel governance (see Hooghe and Marks 2001).

Sites of authority are often difficult to identify, since modern governance structures are typically composed of chains of delegated authority with, at each level, more or less "agency slack" (see Kiewiet and McCubbins 1991).[6] When not carefully monitored, authority that is delegated can be "lost" — transferred, permanently if unofficially, to agents. Delegations and transfers of authority can be observationally equivalent, and thus it can be difficult to distinguish who has authority in complex patterns of governance. This is a central question in the literature on the European Court of Justice, for instance (Alter 1998). Unless mechanisms of oversight are carefully crafted and vigilantly maintained, even democratically elected legislators may begin to act on their own interests rather than those of their constituents. In such cases, whether authority is actually vested in citizens or their representatives can be hard to discern.

Debates over globalization's effects on governance often hinge on the same distinction between delegated and transferred authority.[7] When states create international dispute-settlement procedures, for instance, they may delegate authority to the new entity, allowing it to act on their behalf only so long as decisions are compatible with their interests, or, more rarely, they may transfer previously sovereign powers to an entity that can now expect compliance with its rulings. Globalization may lead to greater delegation of authority to a greater range of entities, but

---

[6] Authority is also hard to identify for a second reason. In equilibrium, voluntary and coerced compliance can be observationally equivalent. In relations between the strong and weak, the former often need not utter explicit threats to compel the desired behavior by the latter. The weak appear to follow the wishes of the strong of their own accord. In such unequal relationships, the power to coerce is latent but nonetheless central to the observed behavior. Only when subjugated peoples test their chains by trying to escape, protest, or rebel do their shackles become evident. If the strong are powerful enough, the weak seldom want to test their limits, but their compliance is strictly a function of constraints. Since coercion does not appear to play a significant role in contemporary changes in governance, even as a latent force, we do not develop this second measurement problem.

[7] Delegation and transfers of authority are best described by close, detailed study of institutional rules and practices, on the one hand, and careful attention to out-of-equilibrium behavior such as when agents attempt to exercise "too much" slack, on the other. In American politics, this is phrased as delegation versus abdication. For close institutional analyses, see Kiewiet and McCubbins (1991) and Lindsay (1994).

states may still retain the ability to revoke this authority at will. States would then remain dominant political actors. On the other hand, if globalization is producing real transfers of authority from states to other types of units, a fundamental change in world politics may be underway.

As indicated in the chapters in part 3, the question of delegation is closely related to the second dimension of governance, democratic accountability. Broadly defined, accountability can be understood as the slack between the principals and agents. The addition of democracy raises a further question, namely, to which principals are the agents responsible? Democracy is an ambiguous and contested term, particularly when applied outside the confines of domestic politics. Nearly all definitions of democracy have at their core the idea of rule by the people. Such a standard has in turn three requirements: the members of a particular group — or those compelled to comply with the rules and norms of a group — have the ability to communicate their preferences to those who act on their behalf, insure that their preferences are weighed equally in the formulation of policy, and remove leaders who fail to satisfy at least a majority of the members (Dahl 1971, 2).

Whether such a benchmark can be applied to international governance is a controversial issue. In chapter 15, Keohane and Nye argue that democracy stops at the boundaries of the nation-state; accountability, on the other hand, does not. Caporaso (chapter 14), drawing on the experience of European integration, claims that democratic standards may be applied to the institutions produced by economic integration. Although democratic accountability is most contentious in contemporary debates over global institutions, such as the World Trade Organization (WTO) or the International Monetary Fund (IMF), its applicability to other nonstate actors is central in assessing global governance. In some NGOs, for example, leaders or boards of directors appoint their own successors. Members may choose to exit the organization, but otherwise they have little voice. Other NGOs take a more classically democratic form, and members elect the leadership. Although the growth of NGOs is often taken to imply a more vibrant transnational civil society, their emergence need not imply greater democracy in practice. Once again, the meaning of democratic accountability outside the context of national politics is at issue.

A third and final dimension of governance — convergence or divergence in forms of governance and in resulting policies — lies at the center of globalization debates. This topic is taken up in part 2 of this volume. Globalization may not "hollow out" the core governance functions of states, but it may produce nation-states alike in institutions and policies. Critics of globalization contend that competitive economic pressures will produce institutional and policy homogeneity over time in a direction favored by the most mobile factor of production — footloose capital. It is further assumed that these mobile capitalists will prefer lax regulation and less government intervention. In this view, the welfare state is placed at risk, and governments are no longer free to adopt policies that respond to the needs of their societies, calling into question their own democratic accountability. Conversely, globalization may produce a competition in regulatory stringency — a race not to the "bottom" but toward "best practice" (Guillén 2001; Vogel 1995). Similarly, Rogowski (chapter 10) claims that globalization provides incentives for divergence in governance and policy, not increasing homogeneity, a position supported by the general findings of Peter Gourevitch (chapter 12) and McNamara (chapter 13). Both the facts — whether convergence in governance and policy has taken place — and the explanation — whether the pattern of convergence or divergence is explained by globalization — are a central part of the investigation that follows.

Globalization and Variation in Governance

These dimensions of governance — centralization, democratic accountability, convergence — changed in identifiable directions during the pre-1914 and post-1945 eras of global economic integration. The similarities and differences in governance across the two periods provide an initial and incomplete test of the political consequences of globalization.

Rather than political fragmentation, which has produced nearly two hundred sovereign units in today's global system, large-scale units dominated world politics and the international economy in the decades before World War I. These states and empires were reluctant to delegate powers to international institutions, but were often decentralized internally. Political integration before 1914 occurred through territorial annexation (the United States, Russia), extension of hierarchical imperial or quasi-imperial relationships (Britain and the other European colonial powers), and creation of large federal states (Canada, Australia). By 1914, a highly integrated capitalist economy was populated by relatively large political units. Economic and political integration increased in tandem (see Lake and O'Mahony 2002).

This outcome is anomalous in light of models, discussed in the following section of this chapter and subsequent chapters, that associate an open world economy with political fragmentation and a bias toward smaller political units. Globalization appears to produce incentives for large-scale territorial governance in one era and not in the other. Three explanations can be offered for this divergence. Peripheral societies in the earlier period were at times unable to maintain the level of gover-

nance required for successful economic integration. When economic exchange produced political turbulence, outside powers extended their
control (Hopkins 1973). Capture by particular interests or sectors that
demanded more intensive, territorial, or compliant governance best explains other cases of territorial expansion. Finally, military competition
rather than globalization may have driven government policy. After
1945, these motivations for direct governance of other political units
faded. In addition, governance costs increased over the century, both in
the capacity of populations to resist unwanted alien rulers and the expected level of public-goods provision.

A second key difference in governance between the two periods was
the scarcity of international institutions with substantial delegated authority before 1914. Governments created narrowly defined functional
organizations related directly to spillovers from economic integration
(e.g., the International Telegraph Union), as well as several currency
unions. The degree of delegation to these institutions was low, however.
National and imperial polities with large internal markets may have
reduced the need for delegation upward to international institutions.
Today, of course, international organizations proliferate, but as Cohen
(chapter 6), Eichengreen (chapter 7), and Mattli (chapter 8) suggest,
they have acquired, at best, modest new authority.

Despite these differences, the two periods of globalization share a
common bias toward decentralized governance by subordinate units.
Care must be taken in measuring centralization of governance. Many
federations are shams, whatever their constitutional outlines, and, as
the chapters to follow indicate, different dimensions of decentralization
can move in conflicting directions. Nevertheless, nearly all successful
federations, with the exception of the United States, were constructed in
the late nineteenth century. Although created through amalgamation,
rather than devolution from an existing state, these were genuine federations with significant powers vested in subnational units. Even the British Empire, largest of the era, was characterized by substantial decentralization. Arguments over subsidiarity — the appropriate assignment of
governance functions to different levels — were a constant in intraim-
perial relations (Davis and Huttenback 1986). Today, significant devolution has appeared across the advanced industrialized states and beyond
(documented in Hooghe and Marks 2001, esp. 191–212; and Jun and
Wright 1996). Michael Hiscox (chapter 3), Geoffrey Garrett and Jonathan Rodden (chapter 4), and Van Houten (chapter 5) examine the
scope of contemporary decentralization and its connection to globalization.

Democratic accountability, a second dimension of governance, creates
a sharp distinction between the integrated world of a century ago and
the globalized world of today. Both the location of governance and pol-

icy convergence were influenced by this difference. Before 1914 governments did not respond to the median citizen in their societies, since that individual was often denied the vote (women and often a large share of the male population). Limited democracy was coupled with a large award of governance to the private sector that permitted accommodation to the demands of globalization. In addition, the standard for government policy was radically different: few believed that the government had broad responsibilities in economic management. By the late twentieth century, governance was shifting toward a more circumscribed public domain (or a least one that is defined differently), but the contemporary benchmark is a level of government activism set at midcentury during a period of economic closure.

Weak democratic accountability before 1914 permitted policy capture by economic interests, which created both policy divergence and convergence. Policy was not consistently supportive of economic opening. Tariff policy after 1870 shifted toward increased protection of agriculture and manufacturing in every European country except Britain and Denmark (O'Rourke and Williamson 1999, chap. 6). The most important instance of strong policy convergence was the gold standard, which was supported by domestic commitments and institutions and reinforced by the central place of Britain in the midcentury international economy as well as by the network externalities of a common currency standard (Eichengreen 1996, chap. 2). Convergence in other domains, such as corporate governance, occurred much more slowly, if at all, even in fundamentals such as accounting standards (Bordo, Eichengreen, and Irwin 1999). This was, of course, the era when different models of capitalist industrialization first became salient (see Gerschenkron 1962). Nonetheless, policy convergence may have been less important to global economic integration in an era when the scope of government regulation was far narrower than it would become in the twentieth century.

Policy credibility under the gold standard may have benefited from an absence of democratic governance, since "the workers who suffered most from hard times were ill positioned to make their objections felt" (Eichengreen 1996, 31). On the other hand, the failure of pre-1914 national or international governance to address the distributional consequences of economic integration undermined the globalized system. Political backlash was created that supported international economic closure in the 1920s and beyond. The rise of working-class representation and universal suffrage weakened efforts to reestablish the gold standard and closed the world to large-scale migration well before the crises of the Great Depression and World War II (O'Rourke and Williamson 1999).

From 1914 to 1945 the double crisis of war and depression brought economic disintegration and heightened the centralization of governance functions and political authority at the level of the nation-state. The New Deal in the United States; Hitler's *Gleichshaltung*, which eliminated the federal character of Germany; Stalinism in the Soviet Union; Peronism in Argentina; and Vargas's *Estado Novo* in Brazil were all exemplars of this trend. Delegation of governance functions to international and regional institutions was also arrested in the decades of economic closure. Although the League of Nations system had created a number of new international organizations, few functioned as designed.

In the latter half of the twentieth century, economic integration resumed among the industrialized economies and within the Soviet bloc with modest delegation of authority to international and regional institutions. Post-1945 international institutions also remained tightly constrained until currency convertibility and trade liberalization fostered growing economic openness. Economic liberalization and the creation of a European common market reduced pressures for further political amalgamation. In the rest of the world, economic disintegration and then globalization witnessed the creation of large numbers of small-scale polities, in striking contrast to the earlier era of globalization. Before the 1990s, efforts at economic integration within the developing world uniformly failed; large federations that succeeded the colonial empires seldom survived. Nation-states remained the principal political units in the international system. Renewed economic integration after 1980, however, produced a wave of regional institution building. Unlike the earlier generation of regional institutions, these were delegated a modest increment of authority by their members. Developing countries also markedly increased their level of participation in global economic institutions in the last decades of the twentieth century.

Under conditions of policy-induced economic disintegration, the developing world after 1945 was hostile to any model of governance other than the sovereign (little delegation to international or regional institutions), centralized (little devolution to subnational units) nation-state. In the industrialized world, however, successive waves of devolution accompanied growing economic integration. Fiscal centralization peaked around 1950 (Oates 1999). Beginning in the 1970s, regional governments, some based on ethnic cleavages, were created in the industrialized countries, and devolution first took hold outside the industrialized world.

Economic disintegration in midcentury had been accompanied by both a failure of market-driven policy convergence and a decline in democratic accountability. Economic closure was enacted in part to permit a wide array of policy experiments in the face of depression and international insecurity. Existing variants of capitalism were transmogrified into even more extreme forms of fascism and communism. That permissive environment continued after 1945 among the developing countries. The industrialized economies, on the other hand, began to converge on a model of "embedded liberalism" (Ruggie 1982) that combined liberal external policies and interventionist internal policies in support of international economic integration, while retaining different models of capitalism (Gourevitch, chapter 12) and considerable freedom of action in fiscal policy (McNamara, chapter 13). This policy mix enabled democratic governance and economic openness to coexist in a stable equilibrium that had been beyond reach before 1914. Such convergence as occurred owed more to the policy preferences of the dominant power and to international institutions than it had before 1914, but those factors did not stop the spread of socialist economic planning, import-substituting industrialization, and capital controls throughout much of the world. The reasons for global policy convergence on full international liberalization after 1980 remain controversial, as Simmons and Elkins describe in chapter 11.

This examination of globalization's effects on changes in governance over the past century highlights at least one anomaly — economic integration has been associated with both large– and small-scale political units. Globalization also appears to be associated with changes in the other dimensions of governance. Economic integration appears to favor political devolution within nation-states and modest delegation to international institutions. The decades of economic closure at midcentury saw the greatest concentration of governance functions at the level of the nation-state. Policy convergence, limited though it is, has occurred under conditions of economic integration, but it has appeared in different domains and has resulted from a variety of political and institutional dynamics. Finally, democratic accountability, that bright line that separates the two eras of globalization, has ambiguous consequences that are reflected in contemporary debates over globalization. Governments that are more accountable for the economic welfare of their electorates can construct a sounder political foundation for international economic integration. On the other hand, policies that support globalization may not be able to withstand the backlash produced by its distributional consequences and readily expressed in democratic polities.

Explaining the Effects of Globalization on Governance

This initial probe of globalization and governance has produced many interesting questions and puzzles, but it is not itself an explanation. Contemporary scholarship, in turn, has yielded only a partial, un-

systematic, and ultimately inconclusive body of theorizing on the relationship between globalization and governance. In this section, we review functionalist and efficiency-based theories commonly found in economics and then outline an actor-oriented, strategic-choice framework
that lends a measure of coherence to the existing literature and directs
further inquiry. We do not offer a single, comprehensive theory of globalization's effects on governance. In subsequent chapters, each author
contributes to an ongoing theory-building enterprise. Our purpose here
is to provide a general framework that can unify the specific theories
offered and open up a new and distinctive line of theorizing on globalization.[8]

Economic Explanations

Most existing theories of globalization and governance are, in one form
or another, functionalist or efficiency-based. Functionalism explains
outcomes by their anticipated effects. Efficiency-based explanations expect outcomes to trend toward those that produce the greatest utility; in
most cases, this is assumed to be equivalent to the greatest net wealth
and to entail a heavy reliance upon market exchange. These models
dominate popular and economic discussions of globalization, which
tend to see international markets as "forcing" states to put on what
Friedman (1999) has called the "golden straitjacket"—a set of neoliberal policies that expand international openness, limit the role of the
government in managing the economy, and cede full rein to private initiative and investment. Even more scholarly works—including the mag-
isterial work of Held et al. (1999), a study that echoes many of the
more nuanced conclusions of this volume and recognizes that states retain a large measure of choice even within a globalized economy—
nonetheless see globalization as changing the costs and benefits of alternative actions in an environment to which states, through a political
process that is left unstated, necessarily respond.

In most functionalist accounts, globalization tends to produce an upward shift in the site of governance to the regional and the supranational levels. Efforts to solve transnational problems (cross-border spillovers) generate a process of expanding supranational authority, of which
the European Union is the exemplar (Haas 1958; Keohane and Hoffman 1991; Mattli 1999). Solving one transnational problem can also
change the incentives of the parties in a second area through issue linkages or through the self-interested actions of politicians in the new su-

---

[8] This framework draws heavily upon Lake and Powell (1999) and the essays within
that volume.

pranational entities. Pressures for yet greater expansions of international authority steadily build and eventually lead to new forms of governance. This approach awards a central role to both regional institutions behaving strategically and domestic interests, governmental and nongovernmental, that may forge transnational alliances to forward their goals (Mattli and Slaughter 1998). Earlier functionalist models emphasized the value to problem-solving governments in transferring governance functions to regional and global institutions under conditions of economic integration. Current models of "neofunctionalism" further complicate the calculus by increasing the number of relevant governmental and nongovernmental actors. In this volume, Lisa Martin (chapter 2) finds that externalities and economies of scale in the tourism industry may be large at first, promoting larger decision-making units within and between states. Over time, however, they appear to contract, creating incentives for decentralization. Martin demonstrates that, even in functionalist terms, globalization does not lead only to upward shifts in governance.

Efficiency-based explanations are similar in structure: governance responds to shifting costs and benefits of market integration. In this vein, economists have devised a series of models in which the size and shape of states are expected to conform with the least costly means of delivering goods and services to constituents.[9] In a series of related models that have received wide attention, Casella and Feinstein (1990), Alesina and Spolaore (1997), Bolton and Roland (1997), and Alesina, Spolaore, and Wacziarg (2000) posit a trade-off between the benefits of economic integration, in the form of lower transaction costs within a single market, and the costs of political integration, particularly policies less reflective of individual preferences. When barriers to international trade are high, the benefits of national economic integration are relatively large. In those circumstances, states have an incentive to expand their internal market by increasing the area and population they control. When barriers to international trade fall, the benefits of national economic integration decline, relative to other political goals, and the state can be expected to shrink. According to these models, increased international economic openness may explain increased demands for regional autonomy in the advanced industrialized states: with a single European market and an integrated global economy, for instance, Catalans, Scots, and other regional groups no longer need their current national markets. Van Houten (chapter 5), however, finds little evidence for this direct link between globalization and regional assertiveness in Europe.

[9] These models are well described by Martin (chapter 2) and Hiscox (chapter 3). See also Marks and Hooghe (2000).

In addition to predictions about the sites of governance, economic approaches also suggest that globalization affects democratic account-ability. Unfortunately, the predictions of these models sometimes con-flict. Functionalist and efficiency-based models often posit limited op-tions for states: delegation of authority to supranational entities, which may or may not be democratic, or delegation to private actors (firms or even NGOs). Such delegation implies a decline in state capacity — the ability of governments to control their own fates — and accountability, as faceless bureaucrats satisfy the dictates of international markets rather than the preferences of local citizens. At the same time, many efficiency models predict that global integration reduces the benefits of large nation-states and enhances pressures for smaller-scale units that will provide public goods closer to the ideal points of their citizens. In addition, smaller-scale units are more likely to allow improved monitor-ing and control of agents by their citizen-principals, enhancing account-ability. These models leave aside one key determinant of accountabil-ity — institutional variation.

Finally, most claims that globalization induces convergence in gover-nance and policies — Friedman's golden straitjacket — are also based on assumptions of competition and efficiency. A benign version of the com-petitive process, as envisaged by Charles Tiebout, permits diverse bun-dles of public goods to be produced for mobile voters (consumers) or firms, a view echoed by Rogowski in chapter 10. Critics of globalization view convergence in a less favorable light, arguing that international markets drive countries to become more similar in structure or policy. Although this may elevate countries to adopt best practices, even in the area of social policy, more often these competitive pressures are ex-pected to induce lower levels of national regulation than are desired by the voters of any country. Although seldom specified precisely, these models are based on strategic behavior among governments that may be more attuned to (or captured by) particular interests, rather than na-tional electorates. Firms in such models, highly sensitive to differences in national policy regimes, increase their bargaining power vis-à-vis governments by using a credible threat to exit the national jurisdiction.

These economic explanations for variation in governance display three shortcomings. First, their predictions do not always match the empirical regularities that are found in the history of globalization. They tend to imply uniform changes in governance when actual pat-terns are more varied. In addition, large-scale political units during the late nineteenth century run counter to models predicting an association between economic openness and reduced scale of units. Assignment of governance functions often does not match these models either: it is difficult to explain the Common Agriculture Policy of the European

Union, for instance, on the basis of efficiencies in the production of public goods or the scope of externalities. Immigration, which can have large externalities, remains largely in the hands of national policymakers, even in the European Union.

Second, explanations based on these models are typically underdetermined. Each highlights a need that is compatible with alternative governance structures and, therefore, each falls short of explaining the particular institutions that are actually observed. Scale economies, for instance, are a necessary part of nearly all explanations of unit size and form. The benefits of pooling resources and efforts with others provides a strong incentive to create and maintain larger units. At the same time, scale economies can be realized in many different ways, including the cooperative efforts of separate and independent units, long-term partnerships like alliances or customs unions, confederations and supranational institutions that "pool" sovereignty, or hierarchies in the form of states and empires (Lake 1999a). The joint maximization of tax revenues on trade does not require a unitary, integrated state, only that the local jurisdictions coordinate their extractions and distribute the revenues according to some agreed-upon rule. Similarly, convergence on best practice or the lowest common denominator (via a "race to the bottom") are both consistent with increased competition, but functionalist accounts cannot predict which of these divergent paths will be taken. Economic explanations are powerful, but they often point to multiple institutional solutions.

Finally, the conception of politics that lies at the core of these models is underdeveloped. Groups or states may demand changes in governance, but actors do not always get what they want. Even casual observers of politics know that the most efficient institution is not always adopted. Missing from functionalist and efficiency-based explanations are actors with competing interests and an understanding of how they aggregate or bargain over those interests. A persistent theme across nearly all of the chapters in this volume is that globalization is an important environmental change that is affecting states, even as its influence and constraints are mediated by national politics and institutions. Surmounting the limitations of functionalist approaches requires a shift from problems and solutions to actors and their strategic environment.

Political Explanations

To paraphrase the famous Prussian military strategist, Carl von Clausewitz, we begin from the premise that governance is politics by other means. As is now well known, economic integration produces distributive outcomes that favor some groups and disadvantage others. Those economic changes are sometimes apparent to all participants; in other cases, they are prospective and uncertain. In light of those changes, political actors will form distinct preferences over policy: in the first instance, policies toward globalization itself (more or less economic opening); in the second, policies to redistribute the benefits of globalization. Since institutions shape the politics of choice and the outcomes observed, concerned parties will attempt to align governance structures with their interests. That is, the politics of designing, building, and overturning institutions of governance at all levels is really about policy choices. Thus, debates about supranationalism, decentralization, the respective roles of public and private sectors, and accountability are often struggles over institutions that will produce results favoring some groups or interests at the expense of others. Contests over governance are contests over policy. As a result, we can use many of the tools of strategic choice to explain governance debates and choices (see Lake and Powell 1999). We begin with the preferences of actors, and then turn to institutions as mechanisms for aggregating preferences and structuring bargains.

[handwritten margin note: extending beyond national authorities or limits.]

Preferences

Globalization as international economic integration has relatively predictable effects on the policy preferences and interests of political actors.[10] Globalization may also homogenize preferences across countries, with important implications for national loyalties and bargaining between states. Finally, globalization creates new actors with distinct preferences over governance and the international policy agenda.

Globalization leads to a more efficient use of resources by expanding international markets — permitting greater specialization and a more extensive division of labor — and breaking down local monopolies. Wealth creation occurs at both the global and the national levels. Such arguments for global economic integration restate the traditional economic case for free trade in goods and free flows of factors of production (capital, human capital, labor) across national boundaries. Although there may be winners and losers within each country, as well as painful adjustment costs when economic actors shift from less profitable to more profitable activities, the potentially large aggregate benefits of globalization open up the possibility of Pareto-improving, compensatory bargains within (and between) countries. Both aggregate benefits and particular costs associated with globalization motivate group conflict.[11]

---

[10] On preferences, strategies, and choices, see Frieden (1999).

[11] For a more skeptical view of globalization, or at least the way it has been implemented through international organizations, see Stiglitz (2002).

Aggregate benefits of globalization are distributed across groups within countries in predictable ways, creating relatively clear lines of cleavage within societies.[12] Using the Stolper-Samuelson theorem, for instance, Rogowski (1989) has demonstrated that free trade will generally increase the welfare and political power of abundant factors of production and decrease the welfare and political power of scarce factors of production, creating broad, class-based cleavages within societies. When assets are specific to particular occupations, on the other hand, the interests of the factors employed in that sector will be determined by the net trade position of the industry — capital and labor within the steel industry, for instance, will favor similar trade policies. Factor-mobility across occupations within countries has varied systematically in the past, thereby creating distinct political eras characterized by internationally induced cleavages (Hiscox 2001).[13] In this volume, Rogowski most clearly exemplifies this mode of analysis; he develops a model in which capital and labor struggle for control over policy and examines the effect of increased capital mobility on policy outcomes. The distributive implications of globalization also play a central role in the arguments of Hiscox (chapter 3), Garrett and Rodden (chapter 4), and — at the industry level — Mattli (chapter 8).

Winners and losers from globalization will pursue their interests into the political arena. Losers will seek to impede greater integration, if possible, or press winners to share their gains through redistributive policies.[14] Winners, on the other hand, will seek to solidify integration and retain as much of the gains as possible. The outcome of this struggle depends crucially upon the initial starting point — although winners become more politically powerful, they may still remain a minority force — and on the political institutions in which they compete. Nonetheless, economic theory can be used to identify the distributional consequences of globalization, at least to a first approximation, and to help us identify how increased economic integration is likely to affect the preferences and interests of important groups within society. This is a working hypothesis more or less central to nearly all of the chapters in this volume.

As their interests change, groups may seek to move governance functions to the regional or global level, on the one hand, or to private

---

[12] Frieden and Rogowski (1996) summarize the literature. Garrett (2001) looks at both intra— and international distributional issues. Robinson (2000) argues that the impact of globalization on inequality depends upon the nature of prior institutional and political equilibria.

[13] On the distributive effects of globalization, see Garrett (2001), Robinson (2000), and Scheve and Slaughter (2001). On the effects of international capital mobility on interests, see Frieden (1988) and Haggard and Maxfield (1996).

[14] On who protests against globalization, see Lichbach and Almeida (2001).

harsh/grating a shrill·

hands, on the other, depending on which forum promises to be most conducive to the realization of their interests. This is a form of the "institutional capture" argument, a point stridently made by opponents of globalization in their criticism of existing global institutions and the privileged access that they are alleged to offer to corporate interests. More broadly, actors will try to shape governance institutions to reflect their changing preferences.

Simple political economy models of this kind carry a complete accounting for preferences only so far. As many of the papers in this volume demonstrate, actors may have significant political preferences that cannot be captured in a simple pro- or antiglobalization dimension. Eichengreen (chapter 7), for instance, finds that although both developed and developing countries want to stabilize financial markets, they want to do so for different reasons and in very different ways. Often of greater interest are the preferences of actors over both a wider range of policies and the site where policy will be made. Consider the choice between closure and harmonization. Although opponents of globalization are sometimes attacked as disguised protectionists, arguments for harmonization may provide an alternative to closure that can reduce politically potent fears of regulatory competition while maintaining high levels of economic openness. (In certain domains, the European Union has pursued a course of harmonization within wider or narrower parameters, while allowing national policy choices to dominate in others.) Harmonization can also be a policy chosen by the proponents of globalization, aiming to level domestic policy differences that impede cross-border exchange (Kahler 1996).

Models of convergence as well as delegation of governance to private-sector actors depend on assumptions regarding actor preferences. Critics of globalization argue that footloose capital prefers self-regulation and a shrunken role for the state. The conditions under which the beneficial model of jurisdictional competition is transformed into an undesirable collective movement toward regulatory laxity are also based in part on assumptions regarding the policy preferences of firms. Both benign and malign models rely on firms (or holders of capital) that are mobile and sensitive to variation in regulatory conditions across jurisdictions. Pressures toward regulatory laxity are built on an assumption that firms uniformly desire less stringent regulation. Yet, such an assessment requires empirical verification. Since regulatory regimes are very likely to reflect in part the interests of those regulated, it is important to take into account both the costs and benefits of regulation from the point of view of the firm. Both Mattli (chapter 8) and Gourevitch (chapter 12) challenge the notion that firms always and everywhere prefer less to more regulation. Haufler (chapter 9) finds an increasing trend toward increased industry self-regulation in response to transnational political pressure.

Globalization may have a second effect on preferences beyond the responses of winners and losers to greater market integration: a homogenization of tastes. Often portrayed as an inexorable force eroding traditional and local cultures, globalization may also create or reinforce certain norms across societies, such as market competition or democracy. Equally significant for the models of governance considered here, preferences for public goods, such as education, social regulation, or sound legal systems may also become more similar across national borders. Such homogenization in normative preferences and preferences over public goods, if it occurs, could sharply reduce the trade-off between more centralized and efficient policy, on the one hand, and the demand for policies that reflect localized preferences over public goods on the other. Martin (chapter 2), for example, shows that child-sex tourism, once a subject with differing national preferences and standards of acceptability, is slowly being outlawed as a result of transnational normative pressure. More broadly, Simmons and Elkins (chapter 11) examine the influence of social emulation on the adoption of surprisingly similar policies of financial liberalization. → *To try to equalize by imitation*

In addition to its distributive effects on existing political actors, globalization may also increase the number of actors with preferences over particular policies and governance structures. As economic integration expands, new groups are mobilized into politics because of transnational spillovers, including environmentalists, consumers, and other activists who are increasingly concerned with not only where, but also how, goods are produced. Haufler (chapter 9) examines how transnational environmental groups have mobilized opinion and led reputationally sensitive firms to regulate their own environmental practices (see also Arts 1998). Martin (chapter 2) shows how the issue of child-sex tourism became both globalized and politicized.

These new actors often have preferences over governance that are difficult to explain using a simple political-economy logic. For example, many NGOs that favor social regulation (environmental, labor, and consumer protection) in the United States often prefer the national level of policymaking to either subnational (state) or international policy arenas. Those preferences can change over time, however, and according to issue-area. State governments were at one point the laboratories of regulatory experimentation for such groups, and many held great hopes for institutions such as the International Labor Organization and still mobilize in favor of international environmental regimes. As in the case of corporations that favor economic integration, the probability that a particular institutional arena will amplify political influence and reduce that of one's opponents is clearly a central calculation. Predicting choice of forum may be difficult, however, when institutions themselves are the subjects of political conflict.

Institutions

Institutions aggregate the preferences of actors into policies and, when preferences conflict, set the rules of conflict resolution through bargaining. This holds for groups within countries and states within the international arena. As Rogowski (1999) has shown, institutions affect policy bias, the credibility of commitments, the coherence and stability of policy, the mobilization and projection of power, and — over the longer term, at least — the strategic environment of the actors themselves.[15] As a result, institutions may be decisive in determining observed policy outcomes. In general, we understand better the effects of institutions in stable democracies, where scholars have devoted substantial attention to institutional differences and their policy consequences (Cox 1997; Shugart and Carey 1992; Tsebelis 2000). Even in relatively "thin" institutional settings, where few rules of aggregation exist and actors are more dependent on "unrestricted" bargaining, or those cases in which institutions themselves are open to renegotiation (as in many international governance debates), bargaining is conditioned by the existing institutional environment (see Gourevitch 1999).

One prominent effect of institutions on the link between globalization and governance is their amplification or dilution of policy preferences. In this volume, Martin (chapter 2), Van Houten (chapter 5), and Gourevitch (chapter 12) all find that existing domestic political institutions strongly condition the effects of globalization on governance. Even if globalization influences policy preferences in predictable ways, its effects are mediated by political institutions. In chapters that emphasize preferences, institutions also play an important, if implicit, role. In the models of both Rogowski (chapter 10) and Garrett and Rodden (chapter 4), groups are formally treated as bargaining over policy, but they are actually embedded in institutions that aggregate their preferences (i.e., determine the bargain) and which are assumed to remain fixed as globalization increases. Eichengreen (chapter 7) shows how different institutions — the IMF, the Basle Committee of Banking Supervisors, and others — developed different diagnoses and solutions to the financial crisis of 1997–1998. These different viewpoints followed from their institutional mandates. Institutions exert a profound effect on the choice

---

[15] On the long term effects of institutions, see Kahler (1999).

of governance structures, including the site of governance, the convergence of national structures, and the accountability of decision makers.

In influencing the sites of governance, globalization strengthens political actors favoring economic openness; those actors, in turn, will design institutions to ensure that their preferences are translated into policy. If a dominant political coalition favors economic openness and creates institutions to enhance the credibility of such policy commitments, a backlash against globalization may only change those policies with difficulty or after considerable delay. For example, the gold standard, a major prop for international economic openness before 1914, was embedded in national legislation that created barriers to change. American populists discovered its domestic resilience in their protests during the late nineteenth century. Regional trade agreements, such as the North American Free Trade Agreement (NAFTA) have served a similar institutional purpose for those promoting economic opening against domestic opposition in the 1990s. On the other hand, more decentralized institutions, which may have been created for other purposes entirely, can impede the program of economic opening that is promoted by internationalists (Verdier 1998). Cutting against the conventional wisdom that globalization necessarily hollows out the state, Mattli (chapter 8) argues that new international standards-setting bodies—established by transnational firms with global markets—have actually served to strengthen national standards organizations. In shifting negotiations over standards to the international level, corporations have transformed many national bodies from "talk shops," where national firms largely worked out standards between themselves, into more vibrant actors that now represent their industries in international forums.

Governance institutions may also be chosen to enhance policy credibility over time. For example, national governments that lack a convincing track record of stable economic policy (or worse, possess a long record of volatile policies) will suffer from a credibility deficit with external investors. These perceptions may be reinforced by domestic political instability. Under such conditions, institutional rather than simple policy choice may be required, including national institutions that add policy credibility (independent central banks) and regional and global institutions (EU or WTO) that bind governments and their successors through treaty obligations. Such external obligations are reinforced when negotiated with richer or more powerful neighbors, a significant motivation for Mexico's accession to NAFTA (Mansfield and Milner 1999). Cohen (chapter 6) argues that the decision to adopt a regional currency is often motivated in part by concerns for macroeconomic stability and the need to enhance credibility. Decentralization or federalism may be an alternative means of enhancing government policy commitments through institutional constraints. Barry Weingast (1995) has argued that "market-preserving federalism" provides a means for governments to commit credibly to rules that sustain a market economy. The key is replacing a monopoly over economic policies at the center with jurisdictional competition that stimulates "a diversity of policy choices and experiments" (Montinola, Qian, and Weingast 1995).

Finally, institutions affect the site of governance directly. For example, democratic political institutions are predicted to produce smaller political units under globalization than authoritarian governments. Following the economic models described earlier, as trade expands and the benefits of a national market decline relative to those of an international market, voters will elect to form separate states that more closely reflect their preferences.[16] Since separatists in each region do not internalize the negative externalities of secession (lost benefits of economic integration) imposed on others, democratic voters will tend to produce too many states (relative to a benign social planner) (Alesina and Spolaore 1997; Bolton and Roland 1997). Augmenting and providing a political dimension to these more functionalist accounts, Martin (chapter 2) argues that countries with federal institutions are more likely to decentralize control over tourism policy. Countering this argument, however, Garrett and Rodden (chapter 4) find that globalization may lead to a centralization of fiscal policy within states. By allowing for both federalism and compensatory transfers between regions, they expect not secession, but side payments from the regions of the country that benefit from unity to those that lose. These transfers, in turn, enhance the fiscal role of the central government, the one unit that can credibly enact such transfer payments.

Institutions also figure prominently in analysis of globalization's effects on the dimensions of political accountability and convergence. Confusion arises in defining accountability itself, which can describe the principals (the electorate as a whole or a narrower set of interests) or the relationship between the principals and their agents (degree of agency slack); Keohane and Nye (chapter 15) discuss competing conceptions of accountability, Caporaso (chapter 14) argues that whether the European Union is interpreted as a parliamentary democracy, a regulatory state, or a rights regime has important implications for our understanding of the extent of accountability and transparency. Any trade-off between globalization and democratic accountability, if such a trade-off exists, is highly dependent on institutional design.

Critics of globalization see a stark trade-off between efficiency or

---

[16] Conversely, these models predict that as preferences become more homogenous, the size of the state will increase to capture further benefits of an internal market.

credibility, on the one hand, and accountability, on the other. Globalization induces (corporate) pressure for upward transfer of key governance functions to regional and international institutions that are alleged to be weakly accountable. External demands for policy credibility lead to an enhanced role for institutions, national and supranational, that can avoid democratic oversight of their policymaking. More optimistic observers of globalization emphasize increased demands for transparency that are best served by, and strengthen, democratic oversight. In challenging collusive institutional arrangements at the national level, global economic actors and multilateral institutions may in fact increase accountability. Many argued that this could be one consequence of the Asian economic crisis, but Eichengreen (chapter 7) shows that multiple institutions, each with its own agenda, as well as the unwillingness of developed countries to restrain financial markets, stymied some proposed reforms. Martin (1999) suggests that the creation of strong legislative-oversight committees in some European parliaments actually strengthened both efficiency and accountability. As the site of governance changes under the influence of economic integration, more compensatory measures may appear at the national level.

In arguments about the scope and degree of convergence under conditions of globalization, institutional assumptions interact with changes in preferences described earlier. Pressure for greater laxity in regulatory regimes, for example, depends on national governments that are responsive to firms and their threat of exit, expressed or tacit (but see Rogowski, chapter 10). As governments move further away from the preferences of their electorates, this model is more likely to be transformed. Distance from the electorate's preferences, in turn, is highly dependent on political institutions. Finally, for regulatory competition toward laxity to take place, governments must behave strategically vis-à-vis the policy choices of other governments. What limited empirical evidence exists on this point (all from within national federal systems), suggests that strategic behavior is dependent on issue-area.[17] It may also depend on institutions — federal, regional, or global — that discourage competitive behavior.

If the struggle over governance is, at its core, a struggle over policy, then the preferences of the actors and the rules of existing institutions will be important determinants of these conflicts and their outcomes. The voices and policy preferences heard within the IMF will depend upon group interests articulated through national political institutions and then negotiated in accord with the current rules of the institution. We expect such "normal politics" to comprise the majority of cases of

---

[17] These arguments are elaborated in Kahler (1999).

governance change in international politics. In these cases, the tools available to political scientists can be very useful in explaining the strategies and choices of the actors and the outcomes observed. On the other hand, actor preferences may be conflicted and diffuse and, on a particular issue, the winners and losers from alternative policies may not be known precisely in advance. Decisions may also be reached in an environment where no clear rules of governance exist. In these cases, political norms and philosophies about what is "right" or "just" may be more influential and outcomes themselves less easily explained (Gourevitch 1999, 156–59).

It is precisely because important, politically powerful groups dislike outcomes produced by existing institutions that governance becomes contested. Since *who* gets to decide and *how* decisions are reached matters, the site and nature of authority becomes an object of political conflict. Knowing what the conflict is about, whose interests are at stake, and how existing institutions shape political competition can help us understand where governance gets sited, how accountable the governors are, and to whom they are accountable. Together, a focus on the preferences of actors and the institutions within which they struggle provide the foundation for a political theory of globalization and governance.

OUTLINE OF VOLUME

The chapters that follow are organized into three broad sections, each focusing on a dimension of governance identified above. Some of the more important findings of each paper have been highlighted above in context. Here, we simply note how the individual chapters fit together.

Part 1 addresses the changing location of governance. Beginning with economic theories, Martin (chapter 2) examines the role of political institutions and social norms and assesses one internationalized industry, tourism, that is also a prime mover of globalization.

Hiscox (chapter 3), Garrett and Rodden (chapter 4), and Van Houten (chapter 5) then analyze the links between globalization and political decentralization—or the transfer of authority to subnational levels of governance. Like Martin, Hiscox begins with economic theories but emphasizes the distributive effects of globalization—its tendency to create winners and losers—and tests propositions on the relationship between site-specific assets and demands for political decentralization. Contrary to conventional wisdom, Garrett and Rodden predict and find strong evidence for greater fiscal centralization with globalization. Van Houten also challenges the link between globalization and decentralization; he finds no relationship between imports and exports as a percentage of regional GDP and what he calls regional assertiveness.

Cohen (chapter 6) and Eichengreen (chapter 7) examine forces for supranational governance in the areas of money and finance, the leading edge of globalization. Cohen outlines the trend toward currency regionalization and assesses the role of various economic and political factors driving the creation of currency hierarchies. Eichengreen analyzes the proposals for financial reform in the wake of the East Asian financial crisis and efforts to regulate the highly leveraged hedge funds considered by many to be primary contributors to that crisis. He finds limited movement toward supranational governance here, and outlines the principal impediments.

Mattli (chapter 8) and Haufler (chapter 9) examine moves toward private governance. Mattli surveys the growth of private industry standards and the complex interplay of public and private actors in setting industry regulations. Highlighting the role of transnational pressure groups, Haufler examines the trend toward industry self-regulation with respect to the environment. Together, they suggest that public authority remains important despite the growth of private sites of governance.

Part 2 takes up issues of convergence within the global economy. Simmons and Elkins (chapter 11) find a significant convergence in policies on financial liberalization within regions and among countries that share the same dominant religion. Although acknowledging the important role of economic competition and domestic political institutions, they attribute these effects in part to social emulation. Conversely, Rogowski (chapter 10), Gourevitch (chapter 12), and McNamara (chapter 13) see globalization as entailing a logic of specialization and divergence. Rogowski develops a formal model of policy choice under capital mobility and predicts that, under a broad range of conditions, countries are likely to adopt more dissimilar, rather than similar, stances toward capital. Gourevitch argues that corporate governance structures are embedded into larger organized and liberal market economic systems, that these market systems have differing advantages and disadvantages, and that both are consistent and can flourish within a global economy. McNamara, in turn, examines fiscal policy in Europe in the run-up to monetary unification. In this most-likely case for convergence, where states needed to harmonize policy to sustain a unified currency, she finds that although each country brought their fiscal deficits under control, as required, they did so in very different ways. Although globalization does constrain states in some ways, it also allows them considerable room to maneuver within the international economy.

The chapters in Part 3 address problems of democratic accountability within a globalized economy. Keohane and Nye (chapter 15) address different types of accountability. Arguing that traditional conceptions of democratic accountability that rely upon direct electoral representation are not the only means of constraining power, they show how hierarchy, legal rules, reputations, and markets also create forms of accountability and can be used in a global economy both to give publics more influence on policy and to enhance the legitimacy of international governance. Like McNamara, Caporaso (chapter 14) takes Europe as a test case for arguments about the effects of globalization. After surveying issues of governance within the European Union, he probes different conceptions of accountability — one based on democracy and transparency, a second on rights — and traces how demands for greater accountability have grown with the deepening of market integration.

In the concluding chapter, we return to the themes of the volume, summarize key findings of the collection, and suggest issues for future research.

Globalization and Changing Locations of Governance

Chapter 2

THE LEVERAGE OF ECONOMIC THEORIES
Explaining Governance in an Internationalized Industry

Lisa L. Martin

THIS VOLUME studies globalization, herein defined as the reduction of barriers to economic exchange and factor mobility that create economic integration.[1] As the density of transactions across international borders increases, patterns of governance shift. Functions formerly performed by national governments may move up to regional or global institutions; they may also move down to subregional or local levels. Economic theories offer predictions about variations in the level of governance. They begin from a normative perspective, identifying the most efficient level of governance for activities with particular characteristics. This normative literature becomes the source of positive hypotheses by introducing the assumption that institutional change responds to the demands of economic efficiency. The first section of this chapter reviews economic theories of decentralization. These theories point to three factors as key to patterns of governance. First, the level of governance should rise (i.e., move up from the local or national level) as the externalities associated with economic activities rise. Second, the level of governance should move down (e.g., toward the local level) as the heterogeneity of individual tastes and attributes increases. Third, greater economies of scale encourage a higher level of governance.

To the extent that globalization generates externalities or economies of scale, therefore, we expect the level of governance to rise, with regional and global organizations becoming more influential. We see this pattern in many economic issues today. On the other hand, issues that are not characterized by high externalities or economies of scale and where people have diverse tastes may come to be governed on lower levels. Globalization is unlikely to have a constant effect on all the factors that influence the choice of governance level. We thus need to direct our attention to both change over time and continuing variation across issues in order to test economic explanations of governance.

[1] My thanks go to David Singer for research assistance, and to participants in the globalization and governance conference, particularly Peter Gourevitch, Miles Kahler, and David Lake, for comments on previous drafts.

While political models of governance are less extensively developed than economic models, I suggest a simple institutionalist expectation about governance. As new issues come on the agenda, the institutions used to govern them will reflect the structure of existing institutions. Where strong centralized governments or supranational institutions exist, they will take on responsibility for policy. In federal systems, policy will be made at the state or provincial level. Interesting dynamics arise when economic and institutional demands are in tension with one another, leading to conflict and inefficiency in policymaking.

To explore these questions, this chapter focuses on a sector of huge economic significance, but insufficient political analysis: tourism. Tourism has been little studied by political scientists, but as an international economic activity it has tremendous importance for many states and is often highly politicized. Tourism presents interesting variation in the outcome variable of governance. For example, some national governments are active in developing tourism policy, while others leave these efforts to local or regional authorities. Some efforts at international-level governance are also evident. At the same time, when we disaggregate the issue-area of tourism, we find substantial variation in the potential explanatory factors. Some issues and regions exhibit notable economies of scale, or externalities, while others do not; development of the tourism industry over time also presents variation in these variables.

This chapter therefore looks at a number of aspects of the tourism industry. It finds that economic and institutional variables act as predicted, especially when we are considering the economic aspects of tourism. When considering the social aspects of tourism, however, the increasing activity of nongovernmental organizations (NGOs) seems at least as important. While the evidence presented in this chapter is not a systematic test of hypotheses, patterns emerge that encourage further study. The chapter draws on the secondary literature on tourism, and is exploratory in nature. It surveys available evidence on patterns in tourism. This approach is appropriate for a little-studied area of political economy and allows for a survey of a range of explanatory variables.

The chapter begins with a brief summary of economic and institutional theories about levels of governance. It then introduces the topic of tourism policy. It goes on to consider three aspects of tourism in more depth: governance of marketing and tourism regulation within countries; international efforts at governance; and attempts to control child-sex tourism.

ECONOMIC AND INSTITUTIONAL MODELS OF GOVERNANCE

Economists and political economists working on decentralization, integration, and federalism have developed a series of models that specify the optimal level of governance. These models take very different forms. In spite of this diversity, the models converge on three factors — externalities, heterogeneity, and economies of scale — as key to explaining the most efficient level of governance. This section reviews some of the relevant economic literature. The baseline economic hypothesis is that patterns of governance will reflect optimal economic choices. I also suggest a simple institutional model of governance. This model predicts that governance of tourism will reflect existing policymaking institutions, as the mechanisms for governing a new issue-area will draw on established institutional assets.

Charles Tiebout developed an early model of decentralization that continues to influence modern analyses (Tiebout 1956). His approach assumed labor mobility and emphasized the benefits of decentralization that resulted from competition among subnational governments to attract labor and capital. As in more recent models, the role of governments is to provide local public goods. In the tourism sector, local public goods take a number of forms. One is the intensity of regulation of the industry — whether it is allowed to grow unchecked or subject to government oversight. Another is the type, if any, of government assistance provided to the sector. While most economic actors would likely prefer government support, they differ on the type of support they desire. Areas catering to different clientele will vary greatly on this spectrum, depending on factors such as geography or the segment of the market targeted. Thus the demand for local public goods will differ depending on location, stage of development of the industry, and related factors.

Decentralization allows local governments to provide specialized public goods. If the population is heterogeneous in its demand for public goods, the ability to choose among a variety of goods provided by governments is valuable. Centralized provision would not allow expression of this heterogeneity of demand. Thus, as long as economies of scale are not too large, decentralization is optimal because it allows for matching between tastes and public goods. Another classic version of this argument is known as Oates's Decentralization Theorem (Oates 1972). This theorem focuses on the trade-off between externality or spillover effects and the costs of "one size fits all" solutions resulting from centralized provision. Like Tiebout, Oates argues that decentralization is preferable in the absence of countervailing pressures such as externalities. These two basic models outline the tension that has been elaborated in more recent work. Increasing externalities or economies of scale produce pressures for centralization, tending to increase the optimal level of governance. Increasing heterogeneity in the demand for local public goods, such as government provision of marketing targeted at a specific niche, will produce pressures for decentralization, decreasing the optimal level of governance.

Recent work has introduced more sophisticated political economy elements to models of decentralization. The Tiebout and Oates models assume a benevolent central planner. Political economy models endogenize the choice of the level of decentralization. Alberto Alesina and Enrico Spolaore (1997) use a spatial model to examine the relationship among economic integration, heterogeneity, and decentralization. They come to the conclusion that economic integration can encourage the decentralization of policymaking in other issue-areas. Economic integration leads to supranational decision making on economic issues, for the usual reasons related to externalities. This dynamic means, however, that the state is no longer necessary as the source of economic policy. Therefore, citizens will find it preferable to have public goods provided on a smaller scale so that they can choose a local public good closer to their ideal point. For example, if citizens exhibit diverse demands over the degree to which government imposes limitations on tourism for environmental-protection reasons, economic integration can lead to devolution to allow specialization in the provision of these goods. These models adopt the assumption of interjurisdictional heterogeneity, a crucial assumption because it provides the demand for decentralization.

The economic literature on issues such as federalism and decentralization is quite diverse, and this summary has been brief and selective. Nevertheless, it suggests convergence in the factors that are likely to determine the level of decentralization — that is, the level at which governance occurs. An important factor encouraging central government policymaking is the level of externalities. If transaction costs are not negligible (i.e., the Coase solution is difficult to arrange and enforce), decentralized policymaking in the presence of externalities can be inefficient. The obvious example is environmental spillovers. If localities make policy, but do not internalize the environmental costs of their policies, efficiency demands a more centralized pattern of decision making. This logic leads to the hypothesis that we should see more centralized patterns of governance in issues that involve substantial externalities.

Economies of scale should also have significant influence on the level of governance. Economies of scale refer to the changing marginal cost of providing a service or good. When economies of scale are low, there is little benefit to producing a good on a large scale. But when they are high, the marginal cost of producing an additional unit of the good falls as the total amount of the good produced increases. In this case, efficiency would dictate producing on a large scale, which in the case of the provision of public goods would imply national– or supranational-level governance. Economies of scale may be substantial at some stages of the tourism-development process, for example in providing basic infrastructure such as transportation and power. Once the basic infrastructure is in place, the efficient scale of ongoing activities declines. We could therefore expect something of a life cycle in the pattern of central government involvement in the tourism industry, with large-scale government intervention in the early stages, less when tourism is firmly established. Overdevelopment of the tourism industry could later lead to government re-regulation, as it steps in to address externalities created by each locality increasing its provision of tourism services without consideration of the overall effect on the environment. When we consider issues such as marketing of tourist destinations, some economies of scale likely exist, prohibiting efficient provision by very small localities. Economies of scale in marketing are likely not so great, however, that they provide a substantial impetus for large-scale international cooperation.[2]

Consideration of economies of scale and externalities therefore produce pressures for centralization. In contrast, centralized provision of public goods is inefficient when tastes over these goods are heterogeneous. This logic leads to a third hypothesis: heterogeneity should lead to more decentralized patterns of governance. Globalization, with its decrease in transaction costs and increase in mobility of factors, might encourage more centralized policymaking on economic issues. If, however, tastes over other kinds of policies remain diverse — some are willing to pay for high levels of environmental protection, others put little value on this good — constituents will demand decentralized decision making.

Political models of the level of governance are less fully developed than economic models. While political analysts generally suggest that "bargaining" or "coalition dynamics" will influence governance, these dynamics have not been specified to the degree necessary to provide refutable hypotheses about variation in levels of governance. To provide a start toward a more testable model, here I suggest a simple institutional mechanism.

A central question is how existing institutions will influence governance of a particular issue-area. One straightforward proposition is that governance of any specific issue will tend to reflect broader institutional structures that are already in place when that issue becomes the subject of government policy. That is, as tourism becomes an issue for government concern, an institutionalist would expect that governance of tour-

---

[2] It may be interesting to speculate about how globalization could have changed economies of scale in marketing. Decreased communication costs, particularly those afforded by the Internet, are likely to have made very small-scale marketing (such as that by individual hotels) affordable. Thus, along this dimension, globalization could produce pressure for decentralization and perhaps privatization.

ism will reflect the general structure of the government. Federal systems will deal with tourism in a federalist manner, leaving primary responsibility for policymaking at the state or provincial level. Centralized systems will deal with policy at the center. When strong regional or supranational institutions, such as the EU, exist, they will take on some responsibility for policymaking in this new issue.

The hypothesis that governance of tourism will reflect broader governmental institutions follows directly from either a historical or rational institutionalist perspective. Historical institutionalism focuses on path dependence and the ways that patterns of behavior will tend to replicate themselves. This perspective would lead us to expect that policymaking structures in new issues would build on existing structures, so that we would see a great deal of continuity in institutions. The same pattern can be derived from a rational institutionalist perspective, concentrating on the calculation of costs and benefits. Rational institutionalists take into account the costs associated with constructing new institutions, risk aversion of those who would need to construct them, and the transactions-cost savings associated with using existing institutions. These factors all lead us to expect that institutions for dealing with new issues will build on existing institutions. Thus an institutionalist would expect that the governance structure for tourism policy will look similar to that for general policymaking.

We therefore have straightforward propositions from economic and institutionalist viewpoints. One interesting question, which will prove to be important in some of the cases discussed later in the paper, is what to expect when economic and institutionalist dynamics are in tension with one another. For example, consider a situation where economies of scale exist (perhaps the early stages of tourism development), leading to a demand for centralized government involvement. But assume that the country concerned has a federal structure, so that there are no strong centralized institutions on which to build. Where would we expect policy to be made? Since there is no particular reason to expect either economic or institutional considerations to trump the other, the answer is indeterminate. We can, however, make one prediction in this instance: that there will be significant tension and inefficiency regarding tourism policy, regardless of the level at which it ends up being made. If the central government takes on responsibility for policy, it may lack the capacity and authority to be effective. But if policy remains on the local level, the economies of scale necessary to provide initial infrastructure will not be realized. Thus, we would expect continuing conflict over tourism policy when economic and institutional dynamics push in opposite directions. The remaining sections of this paper will introduce the policy issues associated with the tourism industry, then ask about the explanatory leverage provided by these economic and institutional models of governance.

THE POLITICAL ECONOMY OF TOURISM: AN INTRODUCTION

Political scientists have rarely paid serious attention to tourism policy. In the substantial literature on tourism, dominated by sociologists, anthropologists, and the occasional economist (Sinclair and Stabler 1997; Tribe, 1995), a few calls for political scientists to take the subject seriously have appeared, to little effect (Matthews and Richter 1991; Richter 1983b). These authors make a number of points, all valid: that tourism as an activity has substantial political implications; that governments use tourism for political ends; that tourism policy often leads to conflicts between local and central governments; and that, in economic terms, it is difficult to exaggerate the importance of tourism to many states.

One can identify some possible reasons for the neglect of this issue-area by political scientists. Tourism is rarely recognized as a sector or industry in standard national accounts such as the balance of payments. Calculating tourism receipts is tricky, since it involves making choices about exactly which activities count as tourism, what percent of restaurant and taxi receipts are attributable to tourism, and so forth. In fact, one of the major activities of international organizations concerned with tourism is to develop standard methods for estimating tourism receipts and related statistics. Another reason can be attributed to those few political scientists who have studied tourism. Their work has tended to be heavily influenced by dependency theory (for example, see Mowforth and Munt 1998; Pérez 1974; Turner 1976). While some of the issues raised by dependency theory — such as whether tourism generates endogenous growth, cultural degradation often associated with tourism, or the dominance of multinational corporations (MNCs) in many tourist locations — have validity, the lack of social-scientific standards in this work has limited its impact.

Serious study of tourism is well-justified, however. One justification is substantive in that tourism raises a number of the central issues associated with globalization — fear of homogenization of cultures, the growing importance of trade in services, and so on. Economic justifications are also abundant. By some accounts, tourism is now the largest industry in the world, and the largest export sector. These figures are of course sensitive to the definition of tourism. The OECD, using a fairly restrictive definition of tourism, concludes that it is the second-largest service sector in international trade, following only banking (1991, 5). There is little doubt that tourism is the lifeblood of many countries, with some small states depending on it for more than 50 percent of their GDP. Even for large states tourism can be surprisingly important—it accounts for 14.8 percent of French, 16.1 percent of Italian, and 12.8 percent of British GDP (World Travel and Tourism Council 1999c). Even in the United States, tourism accounts for 12.1 percent of GDP (World Travel and Tourism Council 1999b). It accounts for one of the top three sources of revenue in most states in the United States (Richter 1983b, 314), and was the largest services export in the 1980s, according to one calculation (Richter 1989, 3). Tourism is "an extremely important dimension of globalisation: between 1950 and 1991, international visitor movements increased almost twenty-fold from 25 million to 450 million" (Faulkner and Walmsley 1998, 2).

Tourism also has economic attributes that make it an attractive industry for many countries. It directly generates foreign exchange, attractive to governments facing balance-of-payments difficulties. Once past the initial, relatively capital-intensive stage of building hotels and infrastructure, it is a labor-intensive industry, generating substantial employment (Tisdell 1998, 10). The World Travel and Tourism Council (WTTC) claims that more than 8 percent of all jobs worldwide depended on the tourism industry in 1999. Another estimate credits tourism for a third of trade in services for developing countries, and 25 percent of trade in services worldwide (Edgell 1990, 9).

Tourism is also a rapidly growing industry, thanks to declining transportation costs, increasing disposable incomes in the developed world, and increases in leisure time. The World Tourism Organization, the major intergovernmental organization focused on tourism, estimates an annual average growth rate of tourism receipts from 1980 to 1997 of 8.72 percent worldwide (World Tourism Organization 1999, 14). (In the tourism literature, the World Tourism Organization is called the WTO. The World Tourism Organization is housed in Madrid, and its Spanish acronym is OMT. The official acronym agreed in discussions with the World Trade Organization is WTO-OMT. I will use this acronym.) Another estimate puts the average annual growth rate in the 1980s at 9.6 percent, the fastest growing sector of world trade during that decade (Laws, Faulkner, and Moscardo 1998, 2). The Asian financial crisis of the late 1990s temporarily slowed the rate of tourism growth, but growth rates were estimated at 4.7 percent in 1999 (World Travel and Tourism Council 1999a). While growth is unlikely to remain at these exceptionally high levels, there is little doubt that tourism is an economically attractive industry and of vital importance for many states. It accounts for something in the neighborhood of half of employment in many Caribbean countries, for example (World Travel and Tourism Council 1999d).

Tourism is also the focus of political and social conflict. Volumes have been published on its negative social, cultural, and environmental effects. I look at one of these consequences, child-sex tourism, in more detail in a later section. On the environmental side, the tourism industry faces a dilemma (Briassoulis and van der Straaten 1992). It is precisely the environment (natural or "built") that attracts tourists. Yet too much success in attracting tourists can severely degrade the environment (see Green and Hunter 1992). Concern about this issue has led to the development of concepts such as "sustainable tourism" and "ecotourism." Environmental concerns are exacerbated by the fact that tourist flows are concentrated both spatially and seasonally.

Social and cultural conflicts associated with tourism have received extensive scholarly and popular attention, and are closely associated with globalization. One way to approach this issue is to see tourism as the commodification of local culture, religion, and arts. Alternatively, central governments, like China's, often worry that the introduction of tourists into a local setting will lead to discontent and "contamination" of the local culture. Authors discuss how exposure to rich Western tourists creates recognition of "relative deprivation" and new demands for income and consumption (Robinson 1999, 1). David Edgell writes that "(a)ll too frequently there are complaints that tourism generates pollution, crowding, crime, prostitution, and the corruption of the language, culture, and customs of some local populations" (1990, 71). He also notes the range of government policies that constitute barriers to the tourism trade, including limits on foreign exchange, departure and entry taxes, and subsidies to domestic providers of tourism services (1990, 53).

Governments face conflicts created by the economic incentives associated with tourism and the social problems that it threatens to exacerbate. They have numerous policy choices to make: how heavily to regulate tourism, whether to devolve or privatize tourism policy, and whether to participate in regional and international efforts to cooperate on tourism issues. The way in which tourism policy fits into broader economic and social policies varies across countries. Studying the role of tourism in economic development strategies, Zhen-Hua Liu concludes that developing countries see it as primarily an economic activity with social consequences, while developed countries tend to see it as primarily a social activity (1998, 27). Those studying the conflict between economic and social incentives also note that multinational corporations play a major role in tourist development, raising the usual set of concerns about their activities.

The rest of this chapter will apply the hypotheses specified above to various issues within tourism. First, we expect that the level of governance should increase as externalities do. This suggests that when spill-over effects are low we will see few pressures for international-level governance. In general, tourism affects only the immediate environment. Externalities do sometimes emerge, however. Examples noted below include overdevelopment of the tourism industry within some "mature" destinations or the environmental consequences of massive cruise-ship traffic. We would therefore expect to see pressure in the former case for the central government to limit excessive development by localities, and for regional cooperation to regulate the cruise industry.

We also expect pressures for a higher level of governance when economies of scale are high. One interesting trend is changes over time as tourism in a particular destination is developed. Initial development requires provision of infrastructural goods that exhibit large economies of scale, suggesting extensive central government intervention. As the industry becomes established, economies of scale are not so obvious, and government intervention should decrease (until the externalities argument noted in the previous paragraph sets in). Economies of scale are also likely to explain spatial variation. Very small or underdeveloped destinations can realize economies of scale in marketing by banding together. Larger and highly developed destinations can realize economies of scale without such centralization.

Pressure for decentralization should reflect heterogeneity in demand for the provision of local public goods. It is important to clarify that the variable here is the *type* of local public good at stake. We are not asking simply whether the tourist industry wants government support—nearly all actors do, in order to increase their rents. We are instead asking about the form of local public goods. Two examples are infrastructure and marketing. Destinations with geographic heterogeneity (beaches versus ski slopes) will demand different types of infrastructure. Similarly, destinations that are catering to the mass-tourism market will demand different patterns of government regulation than those targeting the luxury or ecosensitive market. The segment of the market targeted will also produce heterogeneity in the demand for the type of marketing. We expect that greater heterogeneity will lead to more decentralization.

Finally, the institutional hypothesis suggests that governance structures for tourism should mirror those for policymaking in general. This explanatory variable is relatively easy to measure. Federal countries should show a greater tendency to decentralize tourism policy than centralized governments. Regions with relatively strong international organizations should be more likely to cooperate on the international level. The following sections consider empirical evidence relevant to these hypotheses. I first turn to the issue of marketing and regulation on the national level, then to international efforts on these same dimensions. I then focus on one issue where there has recently been growing international activity and efforts to regulate, child-sex tourism. Cases have been chosen based on the availability and quality of the existing secondary literature.

COUNTRY-LEVEL VARIATION IN GOVERNANCE
OF REGULATION AND MARKETING

States exhibit a great deal of variation in their approach to governing the regulation and marketing of tourism. Some national governments are active and interventionist, while in other nations policies are made at a lower level of governance. Trends across time are also apparent. National governments are often interventionist in the early years of tourism development, but the pattern recently has been toward decentralization and privatization, at least in established tourist destinations. This section argues that the patterns are largely consistent with the pressures of economic factors discussed above. Governance in tourism is also strongly conditioned by the federal structure of states, however. At times economic and institutional imperatives contradict one another, leading to ineffective and incoherent policies.

Interesting variations emerge across countries in their approach to governance. Nearly all countries have a National Tourist Organization (NTO) or National Tourist Administration (NTA).[3] These bodies are usually responsible for marketing and promotion. Some go beyond these functions to engage directly in the regulatory process and direct flows of resources to localities. The powers of local or provincial governments to adopt independent policies vary substantially.

The following overview suggests a number of generalizations. The major economic factor determining patterns of governance is economies of scale. When the tourist industry is new or small, central governments tend to have more authority, since they are more likely to be able to generate resources on the necessary scale to have an impact on the world market. Externalities within countries appear limited, so that they do not exercise much pressure toward an aggressive central government policy. At times, however, the central government will play a more active role in order to prevent economically or environmentally destructive competition among localities; externalities in these situations do become high enough to encourage government action. Patterns over time are also evident. The trends toward decentralization and privatiza-

---

[3] Generally, NTOs have more autonomy from the central government and tend to involve more private representation than NTAs.

tion are widespread. The absence of strong externalities combined with increasing intensity of tourism fits this pattern, as increased intensity means that economies of scale can be realized at low levels of governance. Heterogeneity of preferences for local public goods then encourages moving to these lower levels.

Economic pressures thus work as anticipated. Institutions also exert influence, however. Federal states tend to have more decentralized tourist governance. In the early stages of development, economic pressures are often overwhelming. But when they are not, it is difficult to sustain governance patterns in tourism that do not match those within the state more generally. Attempts to import models of tourism governance from federal to centralized systems, for example, have not worked effectively.

The most systematic analysis of tourist policies has been in Western Europe. The pattern of decentralization over time holds here. One author finds that "many Western European governments have devolved state involvement to the regional and local levels" (Hall 1994, 25). France, for example, fits this pattern. French tourist policy, while never very aggressive, was in the hands of the central government until the early 1980s. The 1982 Decentralization Act enhanced the power of local authorities and led to more local initiatives and a strengthened role for regional councils (Tuppen 1991, 205). Paris still controls most of the funding for tourist policy, but municipal councils have the right to sanction or refuse tourist-related building projects. Few localities, however, have been willing to exercise this right and forgo the economic benefits of increased tourism.

Other than the trend over time, the other major pattern within Western Europe is the dominance of domestic institutional structures in determining governance patterns within the tourism sector. Put simply, federal states tend to have highly decentralized governance patterns in this sector. Tourism policy is no different than any other economic policy in this respect. Colin Michael Hall finds that "(f)ederal structures will have a major impact on the relative importance attached to tourism development by the various levels of government" (1994, 26). Along with other analysts, he argues that extreme decentralization is suboptimal, leading to the overdevelopment of the industry and no effective control of policy. Thus, when tourism is a highly-developed industry, externalities arise in the form of a classic "prisoners' dilemma." Each locality has incentives to maximize the number of tourists visiting, but the overall effect is to degrade as a destination the country as a whole.

Hall cites Switzerland, Germany, and Austria as examples of this dilemma. All three states have federal structures and so have been slow to respond to economic pressures to centralize. Switzerland has gone furthest in centralization, as it has faced the greatest overdevelopment of the industry. Traditionally its tourist governance was highly decentralized, in keeping with its domestic institutions in general. In the 1970s and 1980s, however, the Swiss central government began to play a more active role in coordinating cantonal policies. Externalities considerations motivated this change. An oversaturated tourist sector, combined with intense competition among cantons, was degrading the value of the overall tourist product. As one expert writes, in "a devolved political economy it is, of course, difficult for small communal councils to prevent the goose from laying one too many golden eggs" (Gilg 1991, 150). A case study focusing specifically on Austria finds an almost total lack of central direction and substantial variation across provinces in their approach to tourism (Zimmerman 1991). Germany exhibits a similar pattern (Schnell 1991). "Tourism has never attained a very prominent position at the federal level in Germany, with few explicit policies on tourism being formulated and no separate ministry or department of tourism being established" (Pearce 1992, 75). The pattern of decentralized governance in federal systems holds outside Europe, as well, with the United States having a weak central program and strong programs at state or substate levels (Richter 1983b, 319).

When clear national policies for tourism do exist in the OECD, they generally focus on promotion and marketing. Governments adopt some measures that could limit tourist flows, such as exchange controls, customs regulations, travel-documentation requirements, and local equity participation for firms in the industry. But the thrust of government intervention has been to develop the tourist industry, through building accommodations (as in the early years of Greek tourist policy; see Leontidou 1991; and Chiotis and Coccossis 1992) or providing infrastructure. The OECD, in a comprehensive study of measures that could be perceived as obstacles to tourism, concluded that "(i)nternational tourism in the OECD area is, by comparison with other service sectors, remarkably free from protectionist and discriminatory practices" (OECD 1991, 12).[4] As decentralization has proceeded, most rural regions and cities have now developed their own tourism policies. There is a pattern to the functions that different levels of government take on. Promotion of international tourism is primarily the responsibility of the central government, while localities concentrate on the domestic market and direct provision of services.

One exception to the rule that the structure of tourism governance mimics that of domestic political institutions appears in the United Kingdom. The United Kingdom has long devolved tourist policy to the

---

[4] It is worth noting that the OECD only came to this conclusion after deciding to omit civil aviation, a highly regulated market, from its definition of tourism.

regions, even during periods of centralization of other economic policy functions (Shaw, Greenwood, and Williams 1991). The Development of Tourism Act of 1969 established a British Tourist Authority and three national tourist boards in England, Scotland, and Wales; Northern Ireland had long had its own tourist board. "Effective policy-making in UK tourism is left to sub-state agencies which, in other fields, would only be charged with the task of policy implementation" (Shaw, Greenwood, and Williams 1991, 183). This outcome seems anomalous; there is no obvious economic reason that would account for the United Kingdom's distinction.

The case of Ireland reinforces the importance of broader political institutions. In the spirit of decentralization that swept Europe in the 1980s, the Irish central government encouraged the formation of regional tourist organizations in spite of the fact that such an intermediate tier of government did not exist in the Irish system (Pearce 1992, 185). While these organizations have persisted, they have led to a great deal of unresolved conflict since they do not fit neatly into the more general scheme of governance. In contrast, in Spain, with its strong regional institutions, decentralization of tourism authority has worked well, leading to reduced conflict, increased profits, and increased respect for the environment (Barke 1999, 260). The Netherlands presents an interesting and somewhat distinctive pattern. Elsewhere, decentralization generally came as an initiative from the top. In the Netherlands, however, the impetus for the creation of provincial tourist organizations came from the local — not provincial or central — level (Pearce 1992, 185). Economies of scale played a role in this development. The Dutch tourism industry is highly developed, so that very low-level governance could still achieve economies of scale; thus, localities wishing to express their diversity of preferences over local public goods pushed for more authority. In sum, the evidence from the OECD countries supports the conclusion that "functional" factors and domestic institutions explain the pattern of governance (Pearce 1992, 185–86).

Outside the OECD, systematic studies of tourism policy are rarer. Linda Richter undertook a comparative study of tourism politics in ten Asian countries in the 1980s (1989). This study suggests that the generalizations drawn from the OECD carry over to the Asian context, although for most of the countries there mass tourism is a newer experience.

One Asian country with a long history of tourism is India. The Indian case supports the claim that tourism policy is decentralized in federal systems. Richter considers Indian tourism policy a success, generating revenue without destroying local cultures. She attributes much of this success to "a federal system that allowed states to pursue their own, often very innovative, approaches to tourism and remain somewhat apart from the vagaries of national politics" (Richter 1989, 103); this is in line with arguments that decentralization allows for experimentation and reflection of heterogeneity. "Tourism organization very clearly reflects the federal character of the country" (Richter 1989, 114). She also finds that the division of responsibilities between center and province is similar to that in Europe, with the center concentrating on international tourism and the states on local recreation. Domestic tourism is shared between the two levels. In South Asia more widely, Richter finds that "(s)pecific tourism organization has . . . come to reflect both overall governmental patterns and an apparent tendency on the part of most of the countries to pattern national tourism organization on the Indian model" (Richter and Richter 1985, 205). Pakistan presents something of an exception. Although tourism is legally decentralized, in line with its federal structure, in practice provincial programs are nearly nonexistent (Richter and Richter 1985, 208).[5]

Richter's study of China also shows a similarity to trends in Europe, in that decentralization has increased over time (Richter 1983a, 404). As in most of Europe, this process was part of a general movement to decentralize decision making. Provinces responded to the increased room to maneuver by developing their own strategies to attract tourists. The center (the China International Travel Service) periodically reasserts its authority, however, leading to conflict. Other Asian cases worthy of note include Myanmar, where a government tourism campaign led to a tenfold increase in tourism from 1992 to 1995 (Mowforth and Munt 1998, 315). In Bali, with a highly developed tourist industry, the government has turned to trying to balance economic benefits and negative impacts on the island. For example, the government changed its strategy (with United Nations Development Program [UNDP] assistance) from focusing on a "tourist ghetto" to creating sixteen centers of tourism development around the island (Mowforth and Munt 1998, 313–14).

Turning to Latin America, a WTO-OMT Commission for the Americas report on tourism legislation (WTO Commission for the Americas 1995) presents evidence consistent with these patterns of governance. Tourism policy in Latin American countries has been broadly similar; but there is some evidence of increasing differentiation over time as the tourist sector becomes more developed. Initially, the state played a large

---

[5] As a note, the Maldives presents an interesting case of a government struggling to balance economic and cultural incentives. The government set aside thirty uninhabited islands for the development of predominantly European tourism. The government hopes that this "enclave" strategy will both bring in foreign exchange and allow it to prevent the contamination of its Muslim population with European customs (Richter and Richter 1985, 214).

role in developing the tourism industry throughout the region, and private actors were excluded from policymaking. "Centralization and intervention" were the rule, for example with governments mandating "authorised price systems" (WTO Commission for the Americas 1995, 3). Over time, private agents have come to play a larger role, although the state often continues to regulate the entry of new operators.[6] During the 1980s, continuing intervention combined with rapid development of the sector and entry of private actors led to an unworkable degree of complexity in regulations and bureaucracy, hurting the competitiveness of Latin American tourism. The early 1990s saw a turn away from government intervention toward liberalization and an even greater role for private agents. New awareness of environmental considerations, however, raises the potential for a turn back to government intervention.

The report on legislation in the Americas provides further support for two patterns noted above: the strong explanatory role of federalism and the trend toward decentralization over time. It notes that "the tourism Administrations in the federal states . . . sometimes carry out more duties than the Central Administration" and that "local Administrations are increasingly important," especially in issuing licenses (WTO Commission for the Americas 1995, 7). Rules to restrict tourist movements are only evident in areas with an undeveloped tourism industry; other restrictions on movement, such as stringent visa requirements, have largely disappeared. Regulation of accommodation and travel agencies, in contrast, continues to draw government attention, and the transport sector remains highly regulated. These trends are what we would expect for a tourist industry in the early stages of its development, where economies of scale are best achieved at a high level of governance.

This survey reveals preliminary support for a number of propositions. Patterns of governance seem broadly consistent with the economic pressures of scale, externalities, and heterogeneity. For example, one report concludes that the interaction of heterogeneous demands for local public goods and economies of scale indicates that "small countries are able to organize themselves more effectively as tourism destinations," while in "the larger States, decentralization often seems to be a good basis for tourism policy" (WTO/CEU-ETC Joint Seminar 1997, 20). The same report illustrates the argument about heterogeneity creating demands for decentralization by arguing that it is easier to market small islands

---

[6] One motivation for public and national-level governance is the enforcement of cartels. While I have not considered this motivation in this paper, it may deserve more attention. It would be interesting to explore whether supranational governance might have the same motivation.

with "a well-defined destination-related experience" than more hetero-geneous destinations such as "a sophisticated highly developed river valley in Austria or a mountain valley in Switzerland or Bavaria" (WTO/CEU-ETC Joint Seminar 1997, 11).

At the same time, economic factors leave substantial variation unex-plained, and sometimes confront anomalies such as the suboptimal level of centralization in federal states with highly developed tourism sectors. Institutional factors are thus related to patterns of governance. Change over time is also apparent, with decentralization and privatization be-coming more common. These trends are consistent with the view that increased tourism intensity allows economies of scale to be achieved at a low level of governance, which in turn allows heterogeneity of prefer-ences to be expressed. Only when the tourist industry reaches a satura-tion point do externalities loom large enough to encourage national governments to again become interventionist.

INTERNATIONAL GOVERNANCE

Supranational governance, in the strict sense, is not a major factor in tourism. While movement toward regulation of trade in services is tak-ing place within the WTO and could come to have significant implica-tions for tourism, currently there is little supranational regulation. Insti-tutionalized cooperation at the regional and global levels is common, however. Dozens of intergovernmental organizations exist that are spe-cifically focused on tourism. Two of the most active are the Caribbean Tourist Organization (CTO) and the Pacific Asia Travel Association (PATA). Bilateral tourism treaties are also common. The United States has negotiated approximately ten since the early 1980s, with countries including China, Mexico, Egypt, and the former Yugoslavia. These treaties commit each country to encourage tourism by allowing tour operators to establish operations in their country. Regional economic agreements such as NAFTA have implications for tourism through a number of their provisions (Smith and Pizam 1998).

In addition, the major regional economic organizations have commit-tees or other bodies devoted to tourism. ASEAN has an ASEAN Tour-ism Association, encourages coordination among ASEAN NTOs, and organizes numerous events to promote the ASEAN region as a tourist destination. The EU currently has a Tourism Unit within DG XXIII (Enterprise Policy, Distributive Trades, Tourism, and Cooperatives) that also promotes activities such as the European Year of Tourism in 1990. The OECD has been active, for example by publicizing lists of regula-tory impediments to travel among OECD countries, and has established a Tourism Committee (OECD 1997). The OAS has been a slow starter, perhaps because tourism accounts for a relatively small percentage of regional GDP in Latin America (5.6 percent, ahead only of South Asia). But it has now created an Inter-Sectoral Unit for Tourism, which seems to have ambitious plans for regional promotion of tourism. On the global level, the WTO-OMT is active in collecting tourism data, publishing studies on tourism issues, developing standard procedures for tourism accounts, and so on.

As these examples suggest, the major function of international institutions dealing with tourism is promotion of the industry. Some, like the OECD, go beyond marketing to develop recommendations for policy changes. A survey of international efforts in this area provides support for the emphasis on heterogeneity of demands for local public goods, as states that see themselves as having a similar tourist product and catering to the same market tend to have the most active regional organizations. Externalities also work as expected. Externalities within the tourism industry, other than the usual competitive pressures, rarely spill far across international borders. Thus, as predicted, supranational governance is limited. On the few occasions where cross-border externalities emerge, so do attempts to organize governance at a level above the state. Economies of scale, however, are more often the motivation for international cooperation. Small states with limited marketing budgets, such as small Caribbean nations or the thirteen members of PATA, and that are relatively homogeneous are the most likely to join forces. In addition, relatively strong organizations like the EU or OECD are likely to be the most active in developing tourism policies. The patterns found on the national level thus repeat themselves on the international level.

Studies of the role of the EU in tourism policy often begin by asking whether the EU actually has a tourism policy. In spite of the existence of the Tourism Unit, the answer is unclear. The reason may lie in heterogeneity — the diversity of the European tourism industry, and its mix of public and private ownership, makes central regulation unlikely. The strongest argument in favor of a supranational tourism policy likely favors not the EU level, but a regional level, such as the Mediterranean. One study of Greek tourism policy, for example, concludes that the "problems and opportunities which Greece faces with regard to tourism are, to a great extent, problems common to many other southern European and Mediterranean countries" (Chiotis and Coccossis 1992, 142). Even though an EU-wide tourism policy does not seem to match the scale of the problems, the flexibility and depth of EU structures lead to demands that it take a more active role in this sector. This finding echoes that about the importance of federal structures on the domestic level: overarching institutional structures channel tourism policy in ways that are sometimes in tension with economic demands.

Even without a specific policy, many EU activities have substantial implications for tourism within the Union. The most significant is probably the Structural Funds, used to promote development of rural and backward regions in the EU. The Structural Funds have led to the development of ambitious tourism projects. Other policies that have direct implications for tourism include the completion of the single market, EMU, transport, taxation, free movement of people, and competition policy (European Commission 1996). The EU recognized the economic importance of tourism by issuing a declaration in July 1992 stating that it was appropriate to take actions in this area, and beginning to work with Eastern European and Maghreb countries to promote certain types of tourist enterprises.

In an attempt to devote more attention to tourism, the commission published a paper in 1986 on "community action in the field of tourism." This paper led the council to adopt a range of measures, including promotion of certain types of tourism and collection of standardized information. Perhaps most significantly, it moved to harmonize package travel, promoting competition in this segment of the market across national borders. These measures suggest that the EU sees its major role as limiting the externalities that could arise from unregulated competition among national-level tourism policies. The institutional structure of the EU probably encouraged the commission to turn its attention to tourism in the first place; once focused on the issue, externalities worked as expected to explain where the commission decided to take action. The EU also encourages cooperation among NTOs and occasionally develops marketing strategies for the EU as whole. As the EU moves toward a common transport policy, tourism will become a more central issue.

The OECD's Tourism Committee is primarily engaged in data collection, presenting annual reports of tourist flows and receipts worldwide. This activity is driven by recognition that increasing competition from East Asia and the Pacific threatens segments of the tourist industry in OECD countries. Annual meetings of "senior policymakers in the tourism area" take place within the committee (OECD 2000a). It also issues occasional reports on OECD-member tourism policies, both to encourage liberalization and to help members improve competitiveness (2000c). The 2000 report notes "the increasing role played by local/regional authorities in the design and implementation of tourism policies" (2000b). The OECD has improved data collection procedures and developed macroeconomic indicators for tourism. It intends to begin discussions with nonmember countries, giving some credence to fears expressed by developing countries that they will come under pressure from the North to adopt higher public health and safety standards in areas relevant to tourists, perhaps in the next round of GATS negotiations (2000a). For example, Kenyan officials express concern about an EU Consumer Protection Law that could prevent tour operators in the EU from booking trips to countries that do not adopt EU minimum standards (World Tourism Organization 1994, 201).

The Americas have been relative laggards in using regional organizations to coordinate tourism policies (WTO Commission for the Americas 1995, 8). International governance issues relevant to the Americas include NAFTA and efforts at regional cooperation in the area most dependent on tourism, the Caribbean. Tourism did not receive a separate chapter in the NAFTA agreement, but is covered in sections dealing with trade in services, financial and telecommunications investments, and temporary entry of persons (Smith and Pizam 1998, 17).

Economies of scale, relative homogeneity, and heavy dependence on tourism have led to more intense interest in regional cooperation within the Caribbean. "By aggregating resources to tackle problems that are regional in scope, functional cooperation, both among the states and at other public and private levels, seems to be the key to future economic survival" (Holder 1996, 146). Regional cooperation here supports the claim that cooperative efforts among NTOs "are largely driven by perceived scale economies in marketing and market research" (Pearce 1992, 197). The Caribbean Tourism Organization (CTO), with thirty-two member states, has been relatively active. For example, it has taken on one of the major new economic and environmental problems in the region, the explosive growth of the cruise ship industry. In 1994 it issued a report outlining the negative effects of cruise ships on the environment, such as waste discharge. As the cruise ship industry is one of the few areas in tourism where substantial externalities across national borders are obvious, international cooperation in this area supports the idea that externalities influence patterns of governance. Cruise ships also raise major revenue problems, as the cruise lines are skillful at playing states off against one another to gain favorable tax treatment.

The CTO has also developed regional marketing strategies, as many of its members have marketing budgets that are too small to have much of an impact on their own. Private actors, such as American Airlines, have contributed funds to these regional efforts. The CTO also worries about anticipated GATS negotiations, which it sees as having major implications for tourism, but for which its members are not well prepared. The biggest fear is having to allow international providers of tourism services to displace domestic providers.

One final regional effort worth mentioning is ASEAN. ASEAN formalized cooperation on tourism with establishment of a subcommittee in 1976. Because of the growth of tourism in ASEAN countries in the first half of the 1990s, this sector has received more attention recently. A 1995 "plan of action on ASEAN cooperation in tourism" specified sustainable tourism development, preservation of cultural and environmental resources, provision of transportation and infrastructure, easing immigration procedures, and human resource development as priorities for regional cooperation (ASEAN 1998). The plan specifically calls for development and promotion of ASEAN as a "single and collective tourism destination" (ASEAN 1998, sec. II.8.a).

On the global level, there is one major intergovernmental organization devoted to tourism, the WTO-OMT. The WTO-OMT was established in 1975, and its membership overlaps strongly with that of the WTO. It includes about 150 affiliate members from the private sector. The WTO-OMT holds numerous conferences and issues reports on topics such as sustainability and environmental implications of tourism. Its agenda is straightforwardly protourism. It has promulgated a "global code of ethics for tourism" (World Tourism Organization, 1999a). The WTO-OMT's most influential activities are likely its development of accounting standards and data collection efforts.

The WTO-OMT Business Council has been deeply concerned with the problem of taxation of tourism (WTO Business Council 1998). As economic theory would lead us to expect, this global organization concerns itself with externalities issues. In particular, it argues for harmonization of taxation rates across countries, arguing that lack of harmonization creates unfair competitive advantages. Other externalities issues have occupied the WTO-OMT's attention, such as differing food-safety standards that have led some European countries to warn their citizens against traveling to certain destinations (Regional Conference for Africa and the Mediterranean 1991).

The United Nations has a number of organs that deal with tourism-related issues. As discussed in the next section, the problem of child-sex tourism has engaged a number of UN bodies. The environmental consequences of tourism, under the heading of sustainable development, have also attracted UN attention. A series of background papers and meetings have focused on the issue of "sustainable tourism," suggesting ways in which workers in the tourism industry could be better integrated into policymaking structures and possible industry initiatives to further environmental protection (see summary of the dialogue at http://www.un.org/esa/sustdev/tsout.htm). It is not obvious, however, that these meetings, which took place with some intensity in 1999, will encourage much follow-up activity or steps toward actual governance.

Overall, supranational governance of tourism is limited. Existing regional organizations have turned to the issue but have taken few steps toward actual regulation. They concentrate on data collection and dissemination. Only the highly institutionalized structure of the EU has explicitly moved toward setting policy; however, even these steps are tentative. The limited nature of cross-border externalities limits the demand for supranational governance; instead, keeping governance at the national or subnational level allows expression of diverse preferences. Only when economies of scale exert strong pressures for international cooperation, as in the case of the very small states of the Caribbean, do we see more active regional bodies. Economic considerations thus shape governance patterns as expected; some influence of existing institutional structures is also evident.

CHILD-SEX TOURISM

Global governance on tourism issues is in its infancy. One developing area of global governance is child-sex tourism. This issue illustrates the potential for international efforts to influence domestic legislation, when international concern is high and well-organized lobbying groups exist, even as it challenges economic theories of governance. The issues examined so far in this chapter were largely economic in nature — marketing, economic consequences of excessive tourism, and so on. Child-sex tourism, while having economic implications, has gained worldwide attention because of its social implications. A survey of governance efforts in this area suggests that economic theories provide little explanatory leverage.

To summarize, the governance pattern is roughly as follows. A global agreement exists that can be used to address child-sex tourism, in the form of the Convention on the Rights of the Child. Within the last few years, a number of tourist-sending states have passed legislation that allows for prosecution of individuals who engage in child-sex tourism after they return to their home country. These laws have extraterritorial reach, since they are intended to prosecute individuals for actions carried out in other countries, and which may or may not be illegal in the country where they occurred. A number of countries have also reached bilateral memoranda of understanding. NGOs are the major force leading to adoption of these laws and growing awareness of the problem of child-sex tourism. The overall picture is therefore hard to classify neatly in terms of governance. National-level legislation predominates, yet it has extraterritorial reach, and is often justified on the basis of enforcing commitments to global agreements. Private actors — NGOs — are more important than governmental actors in explaining the actions taken.

Concerns that tourism promotes prostitution have a long history. These concerns became acute as mass tourism to Southeast Asia flourished in the 1980s and 1990s. Especially troubling was the prevalence of child prostitution in Thailand, the Philippines and other countries in the region. Thailand was estimated to have between 30,000 and 50,000 child prostitutes in 1993, and the Philippines 75,000 in 1997 (Anonymous 1998). The International Labor Organization (ILO) published a major report on prostitution in Southeast Asia in 1998. It found that the "sex sector" in Asia is "effectively internationalised" as a large part is driven by demand from international travelers (International Labor Organization 1998, 1). A March 2000 conference in the Philippines, focusing on the issue of trafficking in people for purposes of prostitution, estimated that 250,000 Asians are bought and sold every year (Anonymous 2000).

In the Philippines, sex tourism emerged in the 1970s as Marcos made development of the tourism industry a top priority. "Prostitution houses" sprouted, and the "number of 'hospitality women' in Manila issued with health certificates jumped from about 1,700 in the early 1980s to more than 7,000 in 1986" (Ofreneo and Ofreneo 1998, 103). The mid-1980s marked something of a turning point, as sex tourism "achieved such a high profile that it provoked a concerted protest from women's groups in the Philippines, Japan and other Southeast Asian countries. As a result, there was an appreciable decline in overtly organized sex tourism, which was replaced with semi-underground and more covert forms of sex tourism" (Ofreneo and Ofreneo 1998, 103).

Thailand also exhibits the pattern of a peak, then fall-off, in organized sex tours for foreign visitors (Boonchalaksi and Guest 1998, 136). Analysts differ on the contribution that tourists make to prostitution in Thailand. Some claim that the industry is much larger than can be explained by foreign demand, and that the attention to tourism as a contributor follows only because foreign sex tourists tend to be highly concentrated and visible. Others argue that public "policy concerning prostitution is formulated and implemented with an eye to its effect on tourist arrivals, rather than on the larger segment of the sex industry catering to the domestic market" (Bishop and Robinson 1998, 98). The Thai government has been active in promoting tourism in general, and some have charged it with taking actions that encourage sex tourism, such as minimizing the threat of AIDS (Boonchalaksi and Guest 1998, 137). The Thai government has taken a tougher line in recent years, however, especially on child prostitution. In contrast, some provincial governments continue explicit government support for sex tourism. A similar situation may hold in Indonesia, where municipal governments encourage the development of massage parlors, nightclubs, and strip-tease clubs in order to attract tourists (Lim 1998, 183). In recent years, countries outside Southeast Asia, including some in Central America and Africa, have begun to attract child-sex tourists.

International attention to the problem of child-sex tourism has been magnified by the actions of a well-organized NGO, ECPAT (originally End Child Prostitution in Asian Tourism, now End Child Prostitution and Trafficking). ECPAT has organized congresses on the sexual exploitation of children and works with countries on implementing programs to end child prostitution. It publishes regular reports on the progress of national plans (for example, see http://www.ecpat.net/eng/Ecpat—inter/ projects/monitoring/online—database/countries.asp?arrCountryID-173). Its work feeds into that of IGOs such as the UN, ILO and PATA. ECPAT has successfully raised awareness of this issue and stimulated high-level discussions. For example, a UN Commission on Sustainable Development meeting in April 1999 ended up spending a great deal of time on the issue of sex tourism (as well as environmental issues) (United Nations Commission on Sustainable Development 1999).

One of ECPAT's most conspicuous successes came in the passage of Australian legislation to prosecute Australians who promote or engage in child-sex tourism, the Crimes (Child-Sex Tourism) Amendment Act of 1994. This act led, in 1996, to what was apparently the world's first legal prosecution of a man charged with being a promoter of sex tourism (Hall 1998, 87). The extraterritorial reach of the proposed law raised some questions in Australia. The sponsor of the bill argued that it "was a substantial contribution to the development of international institutional arrangements surrounding children's rights" (Hall 1998, 91). Debate also focused on the issue of enforceability, and collection of proof continues to be a problem (Parliament of Australia 1994). It is interesting to note that no representatives of the tourism industry testified in the lengthy debates. The contribution of ECPAT to the passage of this bill was substantial. ECPAT had concentrated its lobbying activities on Australian politicians for several years, and many speeches in parliament made direct reference to ECPAT.

ECPAT has engaged in similar campaigns in other countries, with impressive legislative results. As of October 1999, twenty-four countries had passed or amended criminal laws to apply to sexual crimes committed against children abroad (International Tribunal for Children's Rights, 68).[7] Some countries, including Australia, France, and the United States, have engaged in prosecutions under these laws; in others, the status of implementation remains unclear. Targets of the laws include both individuals who engage in sexual activity with minors abroad and

[7] These states are: Australia, Austria, Belgium, Canada, China, Denmark, Finland, France, Germany, Iceland, Ireland, Italy, Japan, the Netherlands, New Zealand, Norway, Portugal, Spain, Sweden, Switzerland, Taiwan, Thailand, the United Kingdom, and the United States.

tour operators who organize trips for the purpose of sex with children. These national laws with extraterritorial reach, stimulated by lobbying efforts and international conferences (such as a prominent one in Stockholm in 1996; see World Congress against Commercial Sexual Exploitation of Children 1996), represent the major response thus far.

In the United States, additional lobbying efforts have focused on working with the military and the major airlines. U.S. military forces are often stationed in areas characterized by child prostitution; indeed, some blame these forces for stimulating such activity in the first place (Williams 1997, 154). Lobbying of the airlines has focused on attempting to convince them to publicize the U.S. laws under which those engaging in child-sex tourism could be prosecuted when they return to the United States, and to show a video with warnings about child-sex tourism. While these efforts have had some success elsewhere — Air France shows such a video on its flights to Southeast Asia — American airlines have refused to cooperate. Attempts to pass legislation that would require action by the airlines have also failed.

National-level legislation has limited effectiveness. In particular, difficulties collecting evidence and sometimes extraditing individuals for prosecution have arisen. Addressing these problems would require multilateral commitments or bilateral cooperation. Thus far, while numerous discussions of possible multilateral mechanisms have taken place, the practical emphasis has been on bilateral memoranda of understanding (MOUs) between tourist-sending countries and those countries where child-sex tourism takes place. For example, the United Kingdom and Australia have both reached MOUs with the Philippines that provide for cooperation between law-enforcement agencies, economic assistance, immigration controls, and other forms of government consultation. Germany is reportedly pursuing similar agreements.

NGOs, while happy to see bilateral and national measures appearing, stress the superiority of potential regional or global commitments. Child-welfare initiatives already exist at the regional and global levels, so the emphasis has been on including sexual exploitation in this agenda. Thus far, however, regional results have been limited. The EU claims that it is taking steps to prosecute EU citizens who travel abroad for purposes of child-sex tourism. But these efforts seem to be carried out through national legislation, as discussed above; for example, Britain has announced that it will alert countries when a known British pedophile is traveling to them.

On the international level, the Convention on the Rights of the Child is seen as the primary example of "hard law" that directly confronts the sexual exploitation of children. "Soft law" in the form of action programs by UN bodies including the ILO, UNICEF, and the UN Commission on Human Rights has also proliferated in the 1990s. This combination of hard and soft law provides justification for national-level legislation with extraterritorial reach, and enhances the effectiveness of NGO efforts on the national level. The WTO-OMT has been quietly active on this issue, although it has not given it much publicity. Interpol has set up a Standing Working Party on Offenses Committed against Minors, with groups established in 1993 to focus on specific law enforcement issues (Muntarbhorn 1995, 5).

What are the implications of emerging efforts to combat child-sex tourism for governance patterns? The dominant role of NGOs and national-level legislation with extraterritorial reach stands out. Regional efforts are minimal; bilateral efforts are so far sporadic, but perhaps gaining momentum. Global-level conventions and other statements have proliferated, and provide support for national efforts. But economic theory does not seem to provide a great deal of leverage on governance patterns; levels of social concern and the organizational capacities of NGOs matter more. We can, perhaps, identify a role for externalities, in that the functional demands of attempting to enforce extraterritorial laws require cross-border cooperation. Efforts in this direction are emerging, and calls for greater efforts are common. Whether such functional demands will eventually lead to greater supranational governance remains an open question.

This issue suggests that the range of applicability of economic theories of governance may be limited. When we study an issue where the policy issue concerns social relations rather than economic considerations, economic theories do not appear to provide much leverage. Concepts of externalities and economies of scale do not describe well the concerns that are giving rise to efforts at governance for the problem of child-sex tourism. Institutional theories have somewhat more power, as existing international organizations are providing a focus for governance efforts. The impetus behind the early policymaking efforts in this area comes from nongovernmental entities, however, and theories that focus on their motives, organization, and power are likely to prove more powerful here (Keck and Sikkink 1998).

Summary

This review of governance in the tourism industry suggests the following generalizations. When dealing with aspects of tourism that have primarily economic implications, economic theories of governance perform well. The predictions of economic models are largely met when considering the organization of marketing of tourism and regulation of its economic aspects. The level of cross-border externalities is generally low, leading to little demand for international-level governance. When obvious externalities do arise, as in the case of cruise ships in the Caribbean, international governance emerges. Externalities also work as expected within states, as national governments in highly developed, mature destinations will sometimes step in to limit overdevelopment of the sector.

The influence of heterogeneity in demands for local public goods on patterns of governance is strong. Attempts to impose unified governance on heterogeneous tourist destinations, whether within countries or on the international level, have not gone far. There is an interesting interaction between level of tourist industry development and heterogeneity: when the industry is highly developed, even modest levels of heterogeneity lead to widespread devolution. We can interpret this effect as having to do with economies of scale, which are the other major economic factor explaining governance patterns. Small, resource-strapped destinations are most likely to band together for promotion purposes; government intervention is most likely to provide infrastructure. We therefore see a life cycle in governance of the tourism industry. In the early stages of development large-scale investments are needed, creating substantial economies of scale and national-level government intervention. Devolution tends to occur as the industry becomes more developed and economies of scale can be achieved at lower levels. When the development of tourism is very intense, the national government may again intervene, for reasons related to externalities.

Domestic political institutions, particularly federalism, also provide explanatory leverage. Federal states, as a rule, have devolved governance structures in tourism. The cases in which governance in tourism and broader political institutions differ widely are those in which tourism governance is conflictual and not effective. Overall, governance of the economic aspects of tourism seems to reflect functional factors such as economies of scale and heterogeneity, and domestic political institutions. Determining which of these sets of factors explains more variation, and how they might interact, will require more systematic collection of evidence across a much larger set of cases.

When we turn to the social aspects of tourism, the picture gets more complex, with economic theories providing less leverage. The social aspect of tourism considered here has been child-sex tourism. We find a complex and conceptually challenging pattern, with a global convention, national-level legislation with extraterritorial reach, some bilateral agreements, and extensive NGO activity. This issue demonstrates that international-level governance of a sort is possible in tourism when the demand on the part of well-organized actors is strong enough. Overall, economic theories of governance perform well when applied to the economic aspects of tourism, but when we consider social issues such as child-sex tourism, these models provide little explanatory leverage.

Chapter 3

POLITICAL INTEGRATION AND DISINTEGRATION IN THE GLOBAL ECONOMY

Michael J. Hiscox

Two opposing trends appear to be chipping away at the foundations of the modern state system from different sides.[1] Both trends involve pressure for a relocation of decision-making authority away from the state—a change in the location or site of governance, to use the terms applied by Kahler and Lake in chapter 1. On one hand, states have been delegating more responsibility over decision making "upwards" to supranational institutions at global and regional levels. The political integration in Europe over the past three decades is the most prominent example, of course, but there has been a more widespread, recent trend toward regional integration and the strengthening of rule-making powers of international institutions such as the World Trade Organization (WTO) and the International Monetary Fund (IMF). On the other hand, recent years have also witnessed a great deal of political decentralization within states and a trend toward the devolution of decision-making powers "downwards" to subnational political units. One manifestation of this is the recent decomposition of the former Soviet Union and Yugoslavia, which led to the creation of new, smaller states in Eastern and Central Europe. There has also been a more general growth in the strength of regional autonomy movements (in Spain, Britain, Italy, and Canada, for instance), and greater devolution of important government functions from national to local levels (in the United States and Britain, for example).

There are plausible reasons for thinking that both, seemingly counterpoised, trends may have been accelerated by "globalization"—that is, by growing economic integration in the international system (to use the narrower definition of the term favored by Kahler and Lake in chapter 1). According to one prominent line of thought, as the world's economies have become more closely woven together it has become more

---

[1] Originally prepared for the Conference on Globalization and Governance, University of California, San Diego, La Jolla, CA, March 2001. I would like to thank the reviewers, the conference participants, and especially Miles Kahler, David Lake, Bob Powell, Jonathan Rodden, and Pieter van Houten, for helpful comments and suggestions.

difficult for states to effectively pursue key policy objectives, like dealing with economic recession, financial crisis, and environmental problems, without coordinating their actions with those of other states at some supranational level. The demand for political integration or supranational forms of governance may thus have increased substantially with globalization. On the other hand, as another set of scholars has pointed out, globalization has also made smaller political units more economically viable, since trade between nations can substitute more easily for trade within nations and the size of the internal market is less important for national wealth. If smallness confers benefits — in the shape of policies tailored more closely to the preferences of citizens — this argument suggests that globalization may have encouraged new demands for political devolution and disintegration from subnational groups.

I do not attempt to synthesize, or mediate between, these two different types of arguments here. Instead I want to investigate an entirely separate channel through which globalization can generate greater support for both political integration *and* disintegration in different contexts — by altering the distribution of income across (and within) political units. Regional differences in incomes within nation-states have long been considered crucial in the politics of secession (Gourevitch 1979). We know from standard trade theory, meanwhile, that globalization can have profound effects on incomes in different local economies, as well as on the way income is distributed within those economies. To date, however, no one has connected these different issues to examine the broad effects of globalization on political demands for changes in the location or site of governance.

Taking an explicitly actor-oriented approach, like other chapters in this volume, I begin with a simple formal model of the provision of public goods. The model reveals that the benefits of political integration (relative to disintegration) for individuals in different political units depend critically upon differences in incomes and income distributions in those units — and these can be altered significantly by globalization. In essence, where globalization has variegated or heterogeneous effects on incomes across a set of political units it will raise the redistributive stakes associated with political integration among them, while reducing the mutual benefits of integration. In such cases, globalization can be expected to encourage demands for political disintegration or, equivalently, to diminish support for political integration. The converse of this also holds: where globalization has a homogenizing effect on incomes across a set of political units, it will tend to make political integration more likely — in effect, it will make political integration more closely resemble a positive-sum rather than a zero-sum game between the median voters in the different political units. This hypothesis is tested in a rudimentary fashion using evidence on political decentralization in fifty-six nations during the 1980s and 1990s.

Research on Globalization and Political (Dis)Integration

Perhaps the first major line of thinking about the effects of globalization on political integration has roots in the political science literature on economic interdependence and the creation of international regimes. Cooper (1972) examined the way interdependence among industrial economies undermined the effectiveness of national policies and suggested that one rational response would be for states to coordinate economic policymaking. A similar theme emerged in Keohane and Nye's (1977) landmark study of interdependence, and in Keohane's later work on international regimes (1982, 1984). The underlying idea is that, with greater globalization, uncoordinated national policies generate more and larger negative externalities (in the form, for instance, of inefficiently low levels of environmental and financial market regulation), thus making it more attractive to relocate decision making to supranational levels to internalize these externalities and Pareto-improve welfare. Testing this argument is particularly difficult for the obvious reason that it involves measuring externalities (which, by definition, are not priced in any market) and how they are affected by globalization.

A very different type of argument, which suggests a very different relationship between globalization and institutional change, has appeared in the recent political-economy literature on the optimal size of nations.[2] The basic approach taken in these studies is to make the size of political units endogenous to decisions about the provision of public goods. Models by Casella and Feinstein (1990), Wei (1991), Alesina and Spolaore (1997), Alesina, Spolaore, and Wacziarg (2000), and Bolton and Roland (1997) all focus on the apparent trade-off between the economic benefits of large nations and their political costs — the latter assumed to follow from an increased heterogeneity among voters in preferences over policy and thus a larger difference gap between the equilibrium national policies and the policies preferred by subnational groups. Critically, the economic benefits of political integration are assumed to be increasing in barriers to international exchange, since internalizing more trade within a national market will lower transaction costs more dramatically when barriers to international trade are high. Thus these models predict that globalization makes political decentralization and secession more attractive to local or regional subnational groups. As evidence in support of this argument, Alesina, Spolaore, and

[2] For a review, see Bolton, Roland, and Spolaore (1996).

Wacziarg (2000) point out that the number of nations in the international system has varied with overall trade openness (the average ratio of imports plus exports to GDP) between 1870 and the present. When average openness was decreasing, from 1870 to the 1920s, the number of countries was slowly falling. After World War II, rising openness was matched by rapid growth in the number of nations.[3]

The results produced by these models rest on several very questionable assumptions. One key assumption is that policy preferences of citizens are more heterogeneous in large nations than in small nations. There actually seems to be very little clear evidence supporting this premise, and no compelling logic.[4] Indeed, Hiscox and Lake (2002) report that ethnic and religious fractionalization among citizens, a commonly applied indicator of heterogeneity in voter preferences, is not at all strongly or significantly related to the size of nations. A second, related assumption is that the heterogeneity of preferences among citizens in different political units is itself unaffected by the processes of globalization. This may be missing the forest for the trees when it comes to analyzing the effects of globalization—it is the potentially homogenizing effect of globalization that lies at the heart of a great deal of popular antiglobalization sentiment and has been discussed at great length by commentators interested in the extent to which globalization is synonymous with "Americanization" and the destruction of cultural distinctions (Friedman 2000). While there are alternative views (e.g., Huntington 1993), and I am not aware of any empirical studies that actually gauge the effects, it is easy to see that, if the flow of information and ideas across national borders has a homogenizing effect on the preferences of citizens over consumption of public (and private) goods, this is a simple route via which globalization may have made political integration more attractive and feasible.

But the assumption used in recent models that I want to take issue with most directly here is the assumption that incomes in different political units are also exogenous to globalization. It seems especially clear that globalization can have a large impact on incomes and income distributions in different local economies. Indeed, a large body of international economic theory is focused on these very issues, with studies concentrating on how trade openness has differential effects on growth and incomes across nations, across regions within nations, and even across

---

[3] One problem with this evidence, of course, is that openness is famously endogenous to size.

[4] In terms of the median preference distance from the median voter, a small jurisdiction split into different ethnic or religious groups, for instance, might be far more polarized than a larger jurisdiction with the same "extreme" groups, but a larger population of "moderates."

different classes and sectors within regions.[5] To date, however, this connection has been overlooked in the literature on globalization and political integration. Gourevitch (1979) long ago emphasized the importance of regional income disparities in the politics of secession, and this theme has been reiterated in formal analyses recently (e.g., Bolton and Roland 1997; Fearon and van Houten 2002), but these arguments have not been linked to the debate about the effects of globalization on political integration. In all of the formal models that examine the impact of globalization, incomes and income distributions are treated as exogenous.[6] This chapter will examine the way in which globalization can affect decisions about the structure of governance by altering incomes and income distributions in different political units.

A MODEL OF THE PROVISION OF PUBLIC GOODS

The model developed here draws heavily from formal approaches taken by Alesina and Spolaore (1997) and Bolton and Roland (1997). Consider a political unit or jurisdiction, J, of population size s, and assume that there is no mobility into or out of the jurisdiction.[7] This jurisdiction may be regarded as a nation itself or as a province or regional unit within a nation. The citizens of the jurisdiction, indexed by i, have quasi-linear preferences over private consumption, c, and a publicly provided good, g:

$$U_i = c_i + G_i(g) \qquad (3.1)$$

where G $(\cdot)$ is a concave and increasing function. Assume that public goods cannot be targeted to specific individuals or groups, but must be provided identically to all citizens (this fits with the classic definition of public goods as nonexcludable). Assume that taxes cannot be targeted either, and that government spending is financed by taxing each citizen's income, y_i, at common rate, t. This assumption is more restrictive, but is not crucial for the results below. Relaxing it to allow for more or less progressive taxation, for instance, would actually accentuate the basic

---

[5] For general reviews of the literature and evidence on these various issues, see Dollar and Kraay (2001) and Garrett (2002).

[6] In fact, Alesina and Spolaore (1997) assume that per-person incomes are identical across all individuals in each nation and differ across nations only as a linear function of size.

[7] Relaxing this assumption would allow individuals with similar preferences to "sort" themselves into separate communities. The classic reference is Tiebout (1956); see also Benabou (1993); Epple and Romer (1991); and Rubinfield (1987). Allowing for this kind of mobility in the model elaborated here would have the effect of reducing all incentives for decentralization.

findings but would make the analysis much less tractable.[8] Private consumption is equal to disposable income:

$$U_i = (1 - t)y_i + G_i(g) \tag{3.2}$$

The government's budget constraint can be written in terms of population averages as:

$$ty = Q(g) \tag{3.3}$$

where $Q(\cdot)$ is an increasing cost function. The standard assumption, for which there is empirical support, is that the long-run average cost of public goods provision is decreasing in scale.[9] To keep things simple here, assume that costs take the following basic form:

$$Q(g) = qg \tag{3.4}$$

where q measures marginal costs ($q > 0$).

Now we can write:

$$U_i = y_i - qg + G_i(g) \tag{3.5}$$

Using (3.2) and (3.3), we can rewrite this as:

$$U_i = (y - qg) [(y_i - y)/y] + (y - qg) + G(g) \tag{3.6}$$

where y is mean income per capita.

To keep things simple on the demand side, all individuals have identical tastes in the consumption of public goods:

$$G(g) = -k(g_0 - g)^2 \tag{3.7}$$

where g_0 is the ideal amount of the public good everyone would like to consume, and k measures satisfaction from consumption of g relative to other consumption ($k > 0$). This specification establishes that there is diminishing utility in the consumption of the good and allows us to easily define equilibrium policy in terms of provision of g. By holding tastes constant across individuals we are setting aside the well-known results linking preference heterogeneity in an electorate with underprovision of public goods (e.g., Alesina, Baqir, and Easterly 1999; Easterly and Levine 1997).

Substituting (3.6) into (3.5) and solving for the level of public spending, g_i^*, that maximizes the utility of the ith voter yields:

$$g_i^* = g_0 - q (1/2k) (y_i/y) \tag{3.8}$$

[8] The assumption is thus adopted routinely in formal models of public goods provision: see for instance, Alesina, Baqir, and Easterly (1999), Alesina and Spolaore (1997); and Persson and Tabellini (2000).

[9] See Alesina and Spolaore (1997). For evidence, see Easterly and Rebelo (1993).

To solve for the political equilibrium here we can follow the tradition of applying the median-voter theorem (e.g., Alesina and Spolaore 1997; Bolton and Roland 1997; Alesina, Baqir, and Easterly 1999).[10] We thus derive the amount of the public good provided in equilibrium:

$$g^* = g_0 - q \ (1/2k) \ (y_m/y) \qquad (3.9)$$

where y_m is the income of the median voter. Since income is distributed unequally, so that median income is less than average income $(y_m < y)$, it is clear from equation (3.9) that the size of government is increasing in the skewness (inequality) of the income distribution. This result fits with the conclusions reached by Meltzer and Richards (1981) in their classic treatment of the effects of income distribution on the size of government programs.[11] Since each citizen receives the same amount of the public good (and values it equally) but richer citizens bear a greater tax burden (in absolute terms), provision of greater amounts of the good involves larger redistribution from richer to poorer citizens.

Now consider the potential for political integration. Allow that voters in the jurisdiction, J, must decide whether to support enlargement of the size of the political unit in which decisions about the provision of the public good are made; that is, whether to support political integration with another unit (call it H) that will create a larger jurisdiction (call it F). Historical approximates of such decisions can be located in the pre-federation politics of several countries (e.g., the United States, Canada, and Australia) and, in a more attenuated form perhaps, in the recent experiences of nations joining the European Union. The key question is when will a majority in J support the creation of F? But notice that answering this question in our simple median-voter framework also tells us about the potential for political disintegration; that is, it also tells us when a majority in J will support the preservation or continuation of F if we start from the slightly different, but analytically equivalent, premise that the larger unit, F, already exists and J is identifiable within F as a potentially autonomous political unit. Again, there are many examples of such decisions about whether to remain in (or secede from) political unions both in the histories of the established federations (e.g., in

---

[10] While this locates us in the realm of democratic politics, note that the solutions extend to cases in which governments require majority support from limited subsections of the population (or "selectorates"), which are set apart from the larger population in terms of certain characteristics (most likely, income). In these cases, equilibrium policy will be set according to the preferences of the median member of the selectorate.

[11] Empirical evidence for this relationship is much less clear: see Persson and Tabellini (2000). The complication here likely involves the identity or position of the median voter in different types of democratic and less-than-democratic regimes.

the antebellum South in the United States) and in recent political debates over regional autonomy in Britain, Canada, and elsewhere.

The simplest approach here is to compare the utility derived by the
median voter in J from policy set in J with that same voter's utility when
policy is set in the larger unit, F. To do this we substitute from (3.9) into
(3.6) for each of the equilibria. The difference between the utility of the
median voter (in J) when policy is set in F rather than J is:

$$\Delta U_m = (y_{m*} - y_m) + qg_0 \left(\frac{y_m}{y} - \frac{y_{m*}}{y_f} \right) + \frac{q^2}{2k} \left(\frac{y_{m*} y_{mf}}{y_f^2} - \frac{y_m^2}{y^2} \right)$$

$$+ \frac{q^2}{4k} \left(\frac{y_m^2}{y^2} - \frac{y_m^2 f}{y_f^2} \right)$$

(3.10)

where y_{m*} represents the income of this median voter in the enlarged
jurisdiction, and y_f and y_{mf} are the mean and median incomes in F, respectively. Notice that the technology of production for the public good is
taken to be identical across units and is not altered by political integration.
And to keep the focus on incomes, I have assumed that individuals in both
units have identical consumption preferences — thus we are setting aside
the issues, raised in the previous section, of whether preference heterogeneity is increasing in jurisdictional size and whether preference heterogeneity is itself endogenous to the processes of globalization.

Since we have imposed no restrictions upon incomes (or income distributions) in the development of the model thus far, this result is very
general and now requires some careful elaboration. We can evaluate the
key comparative statics here by focusing on the most interesting scenarios. The three critical features of each scenario are: (a) whether incomes and income distributions differ between J and H in the absence
of political union; (b) whether the formation of F itself changes incomes
and income distributions in J and H, and; (c) whether globalization
affects these first two issues.

Scenario 1: Globalization Reduces the Income
Benefits of Political Integration

First, imagine the simplest scenario in which incomes and income distributions are identical in J and H and the formation of the large political
unit, F, has identical "lifting-all-boats" effects on the incomes of individuals in both units. In this case it is easy to see that $y_m/y = y_{m*}/y_f$
$= y_{mf}/y_f$ and so, from equation (3.10), $\Delta U_m = (y_{m*} - y_m)$. This is the
scenario examined by Alesina and Spolaore (1997). Here the benefits of
political integration just depend upon the extent to which the creation
of a larger internal market increases individual incomes; the baseline

assumption is that incomes are an increasing function of the size of the internal market, since there are efficiency gains from incorporating more productive assets into one integrated economy.[12] The relationship between size and income, however, can be affected by globalization. The greater are the barriers to international trade, the more important is the size of the domestic market as a determinant of per capita incomes. In this case it is easy to see that globalization, by reducing barriers to trade, reduces incentives for political integration that are associated with the efficiency effects of size: in terms of the results, the gain in income for the median voter in J, $y_{m*} - y_m$, is decreasing in globalization. This is the standard Alesina-Spolaore result. But it is now easy to see that it is very much a special case in which no differences are permitted in incomes or income distributions across political units. Since globalization is known to have profound effects on incomes in local economies, we want to relax this assumption.

Scenario 2: Globalization Affects the Size of the "Regional Transfers" Problem

Consider instead a scenario in which we allow differences in incomes in J and H. For simplicity, assume that the formation of F itself has only negligible effects on individual incomes in each unit ($y_{m*} = y_m$).[13] Manipulation of (3.10) now yields:

$$\Delta U_m = y_m \left\{ qg_0 - \frac{q^2}{2k} \frac{y_m}{y} \right\} \left[\frac{1}{y} - \frac{1}{y_f} \right] \tag{3.11}$$

where we know the second term (in braces) must be positive for $g > 0$. Thus, whether integration imparts benefits or costs for the median voter in J is simply a function of the final term in (3.11): integration will be beneficial as long as average income is lower in J than in H (and thus F); it will be costly if income is higher in J than in H. This is the so-called regional-transfer effect: richer regions will oppose integration because it results in a tax-revenue transfer to poorer regions (Bolton and Roland 1997).

---

[12] Alesina and Spolaore actually assume that income is simply a linear function of total human capital in each nation (distributed uniformly over the world) and hence size. This is obviously an extreme assumption. It seems very difficult to maintain that the efficiency effects of creating the large market always outweigh the distributive effects. Indeed, trade economists generally assume that the opposite is the case when considering the income effects of trade liberalization. To the extent that the formation of F affects incomes (on this, see the next note), it might actually hurt the median voter in J if, for example, that voter drew income primarily from an asset or factor of production that was more abundant in H than in J.

[13] This is not such an extreme simplification since economic ties are typically quite close between neighboring political units (those likely to consider integration) regardless of general levels of globalization.

How might this be affected by globalization? Clearly, if globalization accentuates income disparities between political units (perhaps because they are differently endowed with productive resources valued differently in world markets) it will raise the distributional stakes associated with integration: median voters in different units can expect to give or receive larger regional transfers, depending upon whether they are located in richer or poorer areas. The importance of the world oil market for Norway since the 1970s, and its opposition to inclusion in the European Union, provides a recent case in point. Other Scandinavian economies, experiencing less success in world markets in the 1970s and 1980s, were much more disposed to favor inclusion in the EU. Or, going back further in history, consider the success of the southern, cotton– and tobacco-exporting states in the United States in the antebellum era, and their demands for greater autonomy and threats of outright secession. The reopening of Atlantic trade routes after the Napoleonic Wars spurred rapid economic growth in the South in the 1820s and 1830s and accentuated the distributional conflicts inherent in political integration with the sluggish manufacturing economies of the North.

Scenario 3: Globalization Affects the Size of the "Preference-Distance" Problem

Finally, we can allow for the possibility that globalization affects not just incomes in different political units, but also the way income is distributed. Consider a scenario in which there are no differences in average incomes between J and H ($y = y_f$), but there are differences in income distributions. Again setting aside any effects of integration on individual incomes ($y_{m^*} = y_m$), we can manipulate (3.10) to yield:

$$\Delta U_m = -\frac{q^2}{4k}\frac{1}{y^2}(y_m - y_{mf})^2 \tag{3.12}$$

Clearly, any difference in the distribution of incomes between the political units translates into a cost for the median voter in J when considering political integration. If income is distributed more equally in J than in H ($y_m > y_{mf}$) this cost results from policy in F providing for "too much" spending on g (and hence too much redistribution between richer and poorer taxpayers) compared to what the median in J prefers; if income in J is less equally distributed than in H political integration provides for "too little" government spending in the eyes of the median voter in J. This is the cost of integration examined by Bolton and Roland (1997), and it is quite similar in flavor to the analysis of "preference distance" in models that focus on heterogeneity in tastes for consumption of public goods (e.g., Alesina and Spolaore 1997).

Again, there is a clear link to be made here between these calculations about political integration and the effects of globalization on incomes. Where globalization has made income distributions more similar among a set of political units it should (all else being equal) reduce opposition to integration; and the converse should also hold. Empirical examples are rather difficult to assess, however, since there is much academic debate about the effects of globalization on income inequality. One broad implication of the famous Stopler-Samuelson (1941) theorem is that the expansion of international trade in recent years has actually increased income inequality in labor-scarce industrial economies (by lowering real wages relative to returns on more abundant factors of production) and reduced income inequality in labor-abundant developing nations (Wood 1994).[14] If this is correct, globalization may have actually helped to reduce opposition to various forms of political integration between industrial and developing nations by shrinking the differences between income inequality (and hence median preferences over the provision of public goods). The growing willingness among the original EU members to consider the inclusion of Southern and Eastern European nations in the 1980s and 1990s is consistent with this logic, although there were obviously many other forces at work.[15]

According to the simple model elaborated above, it seems clear that if globalization has a substantial impact on incomes and income distributions within and among nations (as highlighted in scenarios 2 and 3 above) it will also have a major impact on decisions about political integration and disintegration. There appears to be some evidence that these effects are important in particular cases; the effects of globalization on relative incomes in different political units, and hence on the "regional-transfers" problem (scenario 2), seem especially salient.

In the next section I examine cross-national data to test, in a very preliminary way, for the effects of globalization on demands for political disintegration or decentralization within existing nations. I focus on testing one proposition in particular: to the extent that recent globaliza-

[14] The empirical evidence is more mixed, and debates surrounding it are contentious. See Choksi, Michaely, and Papageorgiu (1991), Krueger (1978), and Robbins (1996). For a review, see Davis (1996).

[15] Even setting aside other political motivations for European "enlargement," it is quite likely that the average income effects described in scenario 2 may have outweighed the inequality effects described here (as globalization has arguably accelerated growth rates most rapidly in many of these developing nations). Another possible example of the importance of income-distribution effects, however, is the continued British opposition to further European integration. The fear of importing "socialism" from the EU has long been a concern for the British (see Bolton and Roland [1997], 101), and the salience of this issue may well have increased as income inequality rose much more rapidly in Britain in the 1980s and 1990s than in the other core members of the EU, due at least in part to increased exposure to international market forces.

tion has had the effect of making incomes less similar across regional units within a nation, all else being equal, it will have increased incentives to demand greater regional autonomy in the provision of public goods. This follows clearly from scenario 2 above and requires the least extreme simplifying assumptions: it allows that income levels can differ substantially across regions within nations (the Alesina-Spolaore approach does not), while assuming that regions within nations are reasonably well integrated economically and tend also to have similar income distributions. Since the key variables for the analysis are quite difficult to measure quantitatively using available data, and the empirical work that has been done on related questions to date has been very limited, the analysis is treated as a very preliminary approach to the issue rather than as any type of definitive test.

EVIDENCE: GLOBALIZATION, REGIONAL INCOMES, AND POLITICAL DISINTEGRATION

To proceed here we need some measure of the demands for political disintegration by subnational groups, in the form of pressure for devolution, for instance, or secession. These types of demands, and their intensity, are extremely difficult to measure cross-nationally. Perhaps the best available measure is the degree of support for region-based political parties used by van Houten (chapter 5) and Fearon and van Houten (2002). Unfortunately, this measure is only available for a very narrow set of advanced economies. The proxy measure I have used here for demands for disintegration in a broad set of developed and developing economies is the amount of change in political institutions granting more power to subnational political units. The underlying assumption is that pressures for disintegration or decentralization of decision-making authority are likely to translate into some actual expansion in the authority and autonomy of subnational governments, and this will be reflected in institutional changes.

A real problem here is that the simple model developed in the previous section does not generate any predictions about institutional outcomes (that is, the equilibrium allocations of political authority across local and national governments that should be expected under different conditions). To provide such predictions we would need to add to the framework an explicit model of the bargaining that takes place between political units over whether (and under what terms) integration is to take place or continue.[16] The comparative statics examined above just

---

[16] For a bargaining model of this type that emphasizes the role of regional parties, see Fearon and van Houten (2002).

indicate when demands for disintegration by median voters in different political units will be higher or lower. The assumption made for conducting the empirical analysis that follows is that any bargains reached among such median voters are more likely to involve decentralizing institutional changes when demands for political disintegration from some of those voters grow more intense (this could be because the institutional changes are themselves part of bargains that forestall outright secessions, or because they signify failures to reach agreements on other terms — involving fiscal transfers, for example — that might have satisfied voters seeking change).[17]

The measure of institutional change is derived from the World Bank's *Database of Political Institutions* (Beck et al. 1999), which provides data on institutions for 177 nations for the period between 1975 and 1997. The database includes a variable indicating whether state and provincial governments are locally elected: coded as 0 if neither the state executive nor the state legislature are locally elected; 1 if the executive is appointed, but the legislature is elected; and 2 if they are both locally elected. I have used changes in this score over time as a measure of shifts in the authority of subnational units vis-à-vis the national government.[18] Clearly this is a crude measure of shifts in political authority and does not capture the multitude of ways in which authority over policy can be devolved from national to subnational governments. Nevertheless, since such devolution presumes locally responsible subnational governments, this does seem to capture some basic variation that is central to the issue of decentralization or disintegration. Similar data are available on the local election of municipal governments for a reasonable number of nations from 1985.

Tables 3.1 and 3.2 report the data. Overall, there is a trend toward devolution between 1980 and 1997: the average change in the state government election score was 0.18 (see table 3.1); the average change in the score for municipal governments was 0.15 (see table 3.2). There is also some interesting variation across nations, however, in the extent

---

[17] In the bargaining model developed by Fearon and van Houten (2002), credible threats of secession produce transfers from the "center" to the region to keep the nation together and only rarely is secession an equilibrium outcome.

[18] The database includes other variables of interest. One of these is a dummy variable indicating the existence of autonomous regions in a nation. This seems a little extreme, however, for our purposes here (it classifies Montenegro as one such region in Yugoslavia, for instance, but not Northern Ireland or Scotland in the United Kingdom). More interesting is another dummy variable indicating whether states and provinces have authority over taxing, spending, or legislating. Unfortunately, there is a vast amount of missing data for this variable (and the coding rule is not entirely clear), so I have not relied upon it here.

TABLE 3.1
Local Election of State and Provincial Governments, 1980–1997

Nation	1980	1997	Change
Argentina	0	2	2
Australia	2	2	0
Austria	2	2	0
Belgium	1	2	1
Benin	1	2	1
Bulgaria	2	2	0
Brazil	1	2	1
Canada	2	2	0
Switzerland	2	2	0
China	2	2	0
Colombia	1	2	1
Germany	2	2	0
Denmark	2	2	0
Spain	2	2	0
Guyana	0	2	2
Italy	2	2	0
Japan	2	2	0
Sri Lanka	0	2	2
Madagascar	2	2	0
Mexico	2	2	0
New Zealand	2	2	0
Philippines	2	2	0
North Korea	2	2	0
Uruguay	0	2	2
United States	2	2	0
South Africa	1	2	1
Albania	1	1	0
Côte d'Ivoire	1	1	0
Congo	1	1	0
France	1	1	0
Ghana	0	1	1
India	1	1	0
Iceland	1	1	0
Israel	1	1	0
Mozambique	1	1	0
Malaysia	1	1	0
Netherlands	1	1	0
Panama	0	1	1
Senegal	1	1	0
Sweden	1	1	0
Venezuela	1	1	0
Afghanistan	0	0	0

TABLE 3.1
Continued

Nation	1980	1997	Change
Bolivia	0	0	0
Brunei	0	0	0
Bhutan	0	0	0
Cameroon	0	0	0
Costa Rica	0	0	0
Cuba	0	0	0
Dom. Rep.	0	0	0
Finland	0	0	0
Gabon	0	0	0
Hungary	0	0	0
Indonesia	0	0	0
Lesotho	0	0	0
Maldives	0	0	0
Nigeria	2	0	−2
Portugal	2	0	−2
Saudi Arabia	0	0	0
El Salvador	0	0	0
Swaziland	0	0	0

Source: World Bank 2000.
*Score: 0 = no local elections; 1 = legislature; 2 = legislature and executive.

to which change occurred. It is not surprising that there is very little change in the Western democracies, where state and municipal governments were already locally elected as of 1980, and in the stable non-democracies, where no governments are actually elected. Among other nations, however, there have been some substantial changes. It should be noted that there are far fewer shifts in the election scores for municipal governments (table 3.2), perhaps due to the abbreviated period for which data are available.

The aim is to test whether these measures of demands for political disintegration are affected by globalization—specifically, by the impact of globalization upon relative incomes in different regions within each nation. Measuring changes in regional incomes is itself a very difficult task. In the best study to date, van Houten (chapter 5) has gathered detailed economic data on regions in six Western European economies. As far as I am aware, however, no data are currently available on regional income disparities for a large set of more diverse nations. To proceed here we are forced to improvise. I make the assumption that regional incomes are affected more diversely by exogenous changes in world market prices when export income is tied more directly to owner-

TABLE 3.2
Local Election of Municipal Governments, 1985–1997

Nation	1980	1997	Change
Bolivia	0*	2	2
Nicaragua	0	2	2
Benin	1	2	1
Colombia	1	2	1
Canada	2	2	0
Switzerland	2	2	0
China	2	2	0
Costa Rica	2	2	0
Germany	2	2	0
Denmark	2	2	0
Dom. Rep.	2	2	0
Spain	2	2	0
France	2	2	0
United Kingdom	2	2	0
Guyana	2	2	0
Honduras	2	2	0
Hungary	2	2	0
Ireland	2	2	0
Iceland	2	2	0
Italy	2	2	0
Japan	2	2	0
Libya	2	2	0
Sri Lanka	2	2	0
Madagascar	2	2	0
Mali	2	2	0
Mauritius	2	2	0
Norway	2	2	0
New Zealand	2	2	0
Papua, N.G.	2	2	0
North Korea	2	2	0
Tunisia	2	2	0
Turkey	2	2	0
United States	2	2	0
Venezuela	2	2	0
Vietnam	2	2	0
Yugoslavia	2	2	0
Chile	0	1	1
Guinea	0	1	1
South Korea	0	1	1
Laos	0	1	1
Albania	1	1	0
Botswana	1	1	0

TABLE 3.2
Continued

Nation	1980	1997	Change
Côte d'Ivoire	1	1	0
Cuba	1	1	0
Jordan	1	1	0
Mozambique	1	1	0
Netherlands	1	1	0
Poland	1	1	0
Afghanistan	0	0	0
Angola	0	0	0
Bangladesh	0	0	0
Belize	0	0	0
Cent. Af. Rep.	0	0	0
Eq. Guinea	0	0	0
Guatemala	0	0	0
Kuwait	0	0	0
Lebanon	0	0	0
Morocco	0	0	0
Malta	0	0	0
Malawi	0	0	0
Nigeria	0	0	0
Saudi Arabia	0	0	0
Senegal	0	0	0
Singapore	0	0	0
Chad	0	0	0
Egypt	2	0	-2
Zaire	2	0	-2

Source: World Bank 2000.
*Score: 0 = no local elections; 1 = legislature; 2 = legislature and executive.

ship of location-specific resources. The idea here is that the greater the degree to which export wealth is generated by geographically concentrated resources, the greater the potential that globalization will magnify interregional income disparities. Depending upon their particular resource endowments, some regions will do much better from exposure to world markets than others. As a basic measure of the importance of location-specific resources in each economy, I have used the share of ores and metals and agricultural raw materials exports in total exports.[19]

[19] Using shares of these types of exports in total GDP produces substantively identical results in the analysis that follows, since the two types of measures are very highly correlated, but data on trade flows are somewhat more complete and reliable than GDP data so I have relied upon them here.

TABLE 3.3
Primary Commodity Exports as Percent of Total Exports, 1980–1997

Nation	Agricultural Raw Materials	Oreas and Metals	Total
Chad	66.75	0.00	66.75
Chile	9.44	53.83	63.28
Mali	62.29	0.29	62.57
Papua, N.G.	10.23	50.23	60.46
Zaire	3.00	54.50	57.50
Bolivia	5.89	42.28	48.17
Peru	3.89	43.22	47.11
Guyana	2.00	40.25	42.25
Cent. Af. Rep.	25.00	13.29	38.29
Paraguay	38.11	0.00	38.11
Jordan	0.63	35.06	35.69
Afghanistan	29.75	0.25	30.00
Australia	11.00	17.06	28.06
New Zealand	20.44	5.00	25.44
Zimbabwe	7.83	16.67	24.50
Morocco	2.72	21.33	24.06
Ghana	5.50	17.33	22.83
Albania	11.50	10.50	22.00
Cameroon	15.11	6.11	21.22
Uruguay	19.67	0.39	20.06
Malaysia	16.44	3.50	19.94
Cote d'Ivoire	18.40	0.00	18.40
Canada	9.17	8.44	17.61
Nicaragua	16.12	1.00	17.12
Benin	15.00	1.50	16.50
Senegal	3.92	12.23	16.15
Egypt	9.78	5.83	15.61
Finland	11.06	3.50	14.56
Brazil	3.50	10.56	14.06
Mozambique	9.86	3.71	13.57
Bulgaria	3.00	10.50	13.50
Iceland	0.89	11.78	12.67
South Africa	3.67	8.93	12.60
Philippines	3.33	8.56	11.89
Norway	2.11	9.50	11.61
Indonesia	6.59	4.59	11.18
Pakistan	11.00	0.17	11.17
Sweden	7.44	3.44	10.89
Sri Lanka	9.60	1.13	10.73
Poland	2.83	7.83	10.67
Madagascar	4.13	6.07	10.20

TABLE 3.3
Continued

Nation	Agricultural Raw Materials	Oreas and Metals	Total
Thailand	6.89	3.28	10.17
Kenya	6.76	2.65	9.41
Bhutan	7.00	2.20	9.20
Bangladesh	9.11	0.00	9.11
Guatemala	8.06	0.44	8.50
Turkey	4.28	4.00	8.28
Portugal	6.39	1.67	8.06
Honduras	4.67	3.33	8.00
India	2.78	5.00	7.78
Austria	4.33	3.39	7.72
United States	4.06	2.89	6.94
Romania	3.22	3.44	6.67
Netherlands	3.83	2.78	6.61
Hungary	2.63	3.75	6.38
El Salvador	3.72	2.33	6.06
Belgium	1.61	4.33	5.94
Congo	5.30	0.60	5.90
Maldives	4.50	1.33	5.83
Mexico	1.33	4.44	5.78
Singapore	3.72	2.00	5.72
China	3.33	2.25	5.58
Argentina	3.83	1.72	5.56
Angola	0.00	5.50	5.50
Colombia	5.22	0.22	5.44
Venezuela	0.00	5.33	5.33
Denmark	4.00	1.11	5.11
Spain	1.94	3.00	4.94
Israel	3.06	1.83	4.89
France	1.83	2.67	4.50
Costa Rica	3.61	0.72	4.33
United Kingdom	1.00	3.11	4.11
Switzerland	1.00	3.06	4.06
Germany	1.00	2.56	3.56
Tunisia	1.00	2.28	3.28
Ireland	1.67	1.50	3.17
Belize	2.38	0.00	2.38
Italy	1.06	1.11	2.17
Ecuador	1.67	0.44	2.11
Japan	0.94	1.06	2.00
South Korea	1.00	1.00	2.00
Panama	0.50	1.33	1.83

TABLE 3.3
Continued

Nation	Agricultural Raw Materials	Oreas and Metals	Total
Malawi	1.69	0.00	1.69
Malta	0.17	0.78	0.94
Kuwait	0.24	0.53	0.76
Dom. Rep.	0.07	0.50	0.57
Mauritius	0.47	0.00	0.47
Saudi Arabia	0.00	0.31	0.31
Nigeria	0.22	0.00	0.22

Source: World Bank 2000.

The data are compiled from the World Bank's *World Development Indicators* for the years between 1980 and 1997. Table 3.3 reports a summary of these measures for the sample of nations for which there is data on changes in political institutions.

History (or, at least, historical anecdote) suggests that this approach is not unreasonable. Demands for greater political autonomy and secession among southern U.S. states in the antebellum era were fueled by the economic success of southern agriculture (especially cotton and tobacco growers) in world markets. Tensions over separatism in Canada have always been exacerbated by regional disparities in the effects of increased trade, which have tended to enrich grain producers and mining industries in the West relative to manufacturers in the East. In Australia, federation was thrown into doubt early in the twentieth century by threats of secession from Western Australia, the most successful exporter of primary commodities among the colonies. Other types of variables affect regional wealth, of course, but many of these (including regional endowments of labor and capital) are more endogenous to market forces.

There is some question about the degree to which globalization has affected producers of agricultural and mineral commodities over the past few decades. Barriers to trade in agricultural commodities have proved quite durable, although there has been some progress toward liberalization in recent years. At the opposite end of the spectrum, trade in mineral products has actually been very open for many years. Still, there is good reason to believe that world markets have become more integrated over time in both sectors as global transportation and communication costs have fallen, making it easier to connect producers and consumers of these commodities in a wider range of locations and thus increasing elasticities of both supply and demand. And a wave of trade liberalization has swept developing nations since the 1980s, due at least in part to powerful exogenous pressures, increasing the growth potential of these exporting sectors.

The approach taken to the analysis here just involves relating the measures of demands for political disintegration across nations to this basic measure of the sensitivity of regional incomes to globalization. The first dependent variable is the change in the categorical variable indicating the degree to which state governments are locally responsible between 1980 and 1997 (from table 3.1). The second dependent variable is the sum of the change in this variable between 1985 and 1997, and the corresponding variable indicating local election of municipal governments (from table 3.2). I have used the sum of changes in both municipal and state election scores here in order to allow for more variation in the dependent variable while still incorporating the evidence on municipal-level changes. The key explanatory variable is the total share of ores and minerals and agricultural raw materials exports in total exports for periods corresponding with the measurement of each dependent variable. We expect that, since this variable is associated with the degree to which regional incomes will be differently affected by globalization, it will be positively related to pressure for political disintegration in recent decades.

Controls are included in the estimations to account for other characteristics of nations that may plausibly be associated with political disintegration (or demands for it). These controls include measures of population and land area, which we may expect to be positively associated with pressure for devolution or secession if it is true that larger nations are likely to include citizens with more heterogeneous preferences over consumption of public goods (pace Alesina and Spolaore 1997). The level of democracy is included since any type of institutional change may be more likely in more democratic systems.[20] Table 3.4 reports summary statistics for all the variables used in the analysis.

Table 3.5 reports the results from the analysis of changes in the local accountability of state and provincial governments between 1980 and 1997. The first specification includes the basic controls along with the state election score for 1980 (since we expect highly "devolved" systems will not be able to shift further along the scale). As expected, both area and level of democracy have a positive effect on devolution, while population and real income do not appear to have significant effects. The

---

[20] Data on area, population, and real GDP per capita are from the World Bank's World Development Indicators. The measure of democracy is the Polity III democracy score minus the autocracy score (Jaggers and Gurr 1999).

TABLE 3.4
Descriptive Statistics

Variable	Obs.	Mean	Std. Dev.	Min.	Max.
State election score 1980	69	0.91	0.84	0	2
State election score 1985	77	0.96	0.83	0	2
State election score 1997	77	1.04	0.87	0	2
Change in state score 1980–1997	67	0.18	0.67	−2	2
Change in state score 1985–1997	76	0.09	0.29	0	1
Municipal election score 1985	41	1.46	0.78	0	2
Municipal elections score 1997	43	1.63	0.69	0	2
Change in municipal score 1985–1997	40	0.15	0.43	0	2
Total change in election scores 1985–1997	40	0.25	0.63	0	2
Area (million sq. km)	79	0.95	2.13	0.00	9.32
Population (million), 1980–1997	79	47.9	156.0	0.2	1,110
GDP per capita (US $000), 1980–1997	76	8.65	10.9	0.14	42.6
Democracy score	71	1.57	7.07	−10	10
Primary commodity exports (% exports), 1980–1997	72	12.93	12.0	0.22	60.7
Agricultural raw materials (% exports), 1980–1997	72	6.68	7.41	0	38.1
Ores and metals exports (% exports), 1980–1997	72	6.25	9.96	0	47.6

second specification includes the measure of the sensitivity of regional income differences to globalization (the importance of primary commodity exports). As anticipated, this measure has a significant positive effect on devolution. That the substantive effects are quite sizeable is clear if we calculate the predicted probabilities that a nation with no local elections for state government in 1980 ended up granting local elections for both state legislatures and executives by 1997 (with all other variables set to means). With primary commodity exports of 0 percent (roughly, the mean level minus one standard deviation), the probability of such devolution is only 10 percent; with primary com-

TABLE 3.5
Change in Local Election of State and Provincial Governments, 1980–1997

	Specifications		
	(1)	(2)	(3)
State election score 1980	−1.56***	−1.58***	−1.58***
	(0.62)	(0.65)	(0.68)
Log population	−0.11	0.17	0.18
	(0.29)	(0.34)	(0.34)
Log area	0.30*	0.41*	0.41*
	(0.24)	(0.21)	(0.21)
Log GDP per capita	−0.06	0.16	0.17
	(0.26)	(0.30)	(0.31)
Democracy score	0.10*	0.14*	0.14*
	(0.06)	(0.06)	(0.06)
Total commodity exports (%)		0.06**	
		(0.02)	
Agricultural raw materials exports (%)			0.07
			(0.06)
Ores and metals exports (%)			0.06***
			(0.02)
N	56	54	54
Log likelihood	−38.59	−35.66	−35.66
Threshold 1	−4.47	−0.57	−0.51
	(4.34)	(5.21)	(5.23)
Threshold 2	1.10	5.28	5.31
	(4.19)	(5.23)	(5.28)
Threshold 3	2.50	6.81	6.88
	(4.21)	(5.28)	(5.32)

Note: Ordered logit. Dependent variable: Change in Election Score (see table 3.1).
Standard errors in parentheses.
*$p < .1$, **$p < .05$, ***$p < .01$.

modity exports of 24 percent (the mean plus one standard deviation), the probability of this change is 34 percent. If we include separate measures for the importance of agricultural raw commodity exports and exports of ores and metals (the third specification), the results suggest that it is the mining sector that exerts the most influence on political demands.

Table 3.6 reports the results of the analysis of changes in the local accountability of municipal as well as state and provincial governments between 1985 and 1997. Again, the first specification just includes the basic control variables, and again area and democracy have the anticipated effects. The second and third specifications introduce the explana-

TABLE 3.6
Change in Local Election of Municipal and State Governments, 1985–1997

	Specifications		
	(1)	(2)	(3)
State election score 1985	−0.09	−0.39	−0.37
	(0.74)	(0.90)	(0.91)
Municipal election score, 1985	−1.16*	−1.28*	−1.21*
	(0.63)	(0.68)	(0.72)
Log population	−0.09	0.28	0.29
	(0.30)	(0.42)	(0.42)
Log area	0.47*	0.55*	0.56*
	(0.26)	(0.39)	(0.34)
Log GDP per capita	−0.41	−0.30	−0.29
	(0.31)	(0.35)	(0.35)
Democracy score	0.14*	0.19**	0.18*
	(0.07)	(0.09)	(0.09)
Total commodity exports (% exports)		0.07**	
		(0.03)	
Agricultural raw materials exports (%)			0.07
			(0.6)
Ores and metals exports (%)			0.06**
			(0.03)
N	54	48	48
Log likelihood	−30.55	−21.37	−21.36
Threshold 1	−10.96	−6.14	−6.18
	(6.07)	(7.58)	(7.58)
Threshold 2	−4.42	2.06	2.08
	(5.58)	(7.21)	(7.19)
Threshold 3	−3.88	2.95	2.97
	(5.58)	(7.25)	(7.23)

Note: Ordered logit. Dependent variable: Sum of Change in Election Score for State and Municipal Governments (see table 3.2).

Standard errors in parentheses.

$*p < .1$, $**p < .05$, $***p < .01$.

tory variables of interest. Total primary commodity exports and, specifically, exports of ores and metals, again have significant positive effects on the extension of local electoral control over state and municipal governments between 1985 and 1997.

It is worth noting here that in separate research on civil wars, Collier and Hoefler (2000) have discovered that the importance of primary commodity exports has a large and significant positive effect on the probability of the occurrence of internal war in a nation. They argue that this is linked to the incentives of rebel leaders: such leaders are more likely to organize internal revolts when there are more "lootable" resources for the taking.[21] The argument I have outlined above suggests an alternative or additional interpretation: to the extent that civil conflicts reflect demands for greater regional autonomy or secession (and not outright revolution), the Collier-Hoefler results may in part be reflecting regional disparities in incomes within nations and how they affect incentives for political disintegration versus integration. Since ethnic groups are typically concentrated by region within nations, such considerations may overlap with ethnicity-based grievances.

CONCLUSIONS AND IMPLICATIONS

The analysis above suggests a number of avenues for further research. It reveals that, at a very general level, globalization may have several and contradictory effects on support for political integration (including supranationalism and regionalism) and political disintegration (including devolution, secession, and perhaps even civil conflict). Previous arguments have highlighted the way globalization can reduce the income-enhancing effects of political integration (e.g., Alesina and Spolaore 1997), or how globalization can magnify the cost-reducing effects of political integration (e.g., Cooper 1972). I have focused instead upon the effects of globalization on relative incomes (and income distributions) in different political jurisdictions. The simple formal model of the provision of a public good shows that the benefits of political integration for individuals in different political units depend upon differences in income levels (and income inequality) between those units—and these differences can be altered significantly by globalization. To the extent that globalization has variegated (rather than homogenizing) effects on incomes across political units, it makes it less likely that political integration will be supported by electoral majorities in those units. The overall lesson from the analysis is that, as Kahler and Lake (chapter 1) have emphasized, the effects of globalization are far more complex and contingent than is often claimed.

Other chapters in this volume have addressed very similar issues from slightly different angles. Garrett and Rodden (chapter 4) examine evidence indicating that, across a broad set of countries, greater trade openness is associated with more fiscal centralization rather than decentralization. They attribute this finding primarily to the impact that greater exposure to world markets has on incentives to improve capaci-

---

[21] Fearon 2002 has also discussed the importance of (internationally) valuable natural resources in explaining the duration of civil wars.

ties for macroeconomic stabilization and interregional risk sharing, both managed at the national level. But they also point out that different regions within nations may be advantaged and disadvantaged by globalization, and heightened redistributive conflicts between these regions and central governments can generate greater fiscal centralization (as central governments "buy off" potential breakaway regions to keep the nation together). This argument seems quite consistent with the approach I have taken in this chapter, focusing on how globalization may affect the magnitude of the "regional-transfers" problem and thus demands for political disintegration (reflected empirically in decentralizing institutional changes). Together, I think these two chapters point to the need for a more fully elaborated model of the bargaining that creates and preserves integrated political entities; a model that takes into account the key dimensions over which such bargains can be struck (including formal institutional powers for making different types of policies at different levels as well as explicit fiscal transfers from central governments to regions).

Van Houten's excellent analysis of demands for regional autonomy in Western European nations (chapter 5) helps to buttress this case by revealing the variety of different types of autonomy demands made by regional actors. He finds no clear quantitative evidence that regions that are more exposed to globalization (in terms of their dependence upon imports and exports), or more likely to succeed in world markets (measured by productivity levels), make greater demands for autonomy, but he does point to some qualitative evidence that globalization may have increased redistributive conflicts between regions. One possible reason for the general divergence in our findings, apart from the measurement issues, is that in the advanced economies of Western Europe, region-specific assets are likely far less important as determinants of export income than in the developing nations I have examined in this chapter. Improved data on regional incomes in developing nations, and how they are affected by exposure to international markets, will hopefully resolve this issue more definitively in the future.

Finally, it should be noted that I have relied upon a very simple model of the provision of public goods in order to explore the different ways in which globalization, by affecting regional incomes, can alter incentives to change the location or site of governance. My main aim was really to take issue with previous treatments of political integration that assume regional incomes (and the differences between them) are exogenous to globalization. The model is meant only to clarify some of the key determinants of the relative attractiveness of political integration (and disintegration) to individual voters. In developing a fuller model of the way individual preferences are translated into political bargains it is

clear that more careful attention should be paid to institutional variables that affect the political costs of making regional demands. Indeed,
van Houten (chapter 5) shows that institutional features of the political
landscape in Western European nations (in particular, the strength of
regional political parties) can have powerful effects on demands for regional autonomy.

Chapter 4

GLOBALIZATION AND FISCAL DECENTRALIZATION

Geoffrey Garrett and Jonathan Rodden

The international integration of markets and the decentralization of authority within nation states are two defining trends of the contemporary era.[1] A popular speculation is that globalization has caused a downward shift in the locus of governance by reducing the economic costs of smallness and allowing localities and regions with distinctive preferences to pursue their own political and economic strategies (Alesina and Spolaore 1997; Bolton and Roland 1997). This chapter analyzes these claims by examining the location of *fiscal* authority within states. Using a large cross-country data set composed of expenditure and revenue decentralization data for the 1980s and 1990s, it demonstrates a rather striking relationship: international market integration has actually been associated with fiscal centralization rather than with decentralization.

There are several potential explanations, but we propose a straightforward argument for the globalization–fiscal-centralization nexus that rests on perceptions of uncertainty and risk. First, macroeconomic conditions are perceived to be more volatile in more globally integrated countries (pace Rodrik 1998). Second, regional demands for insurance against asymmetric shocks increase with international market integration (following Persson and Tabellini 1996a,b). Thus, one should expect decentralized actors to prefer both more macroeconomic stabilization and more interregional risking sharing under globalization, and both objectives are better served via centralized fiscal arrangements than by decentralized ones.

It is important to note, however, that fiscal centralization does not imply the centralization of all authority — it may even be consistent with

[1] We thank conference participants and UCSD, MIT, the Midwest Political Science Association, and the American Political Science Association, along with the following individuals for helpful comments: Carles Boix, Kelly Chang, Lucy Goodhart, Michael Hiscox, Pieter van Houten, Miles Kahler, David Lake, Richard Locke, Ben Lockwood, Robert Powell, Ronald Rogowski, Beth Simmons, and Richard Steinberg. Nancy Brune and Andrew Youn provided excellent research assistance. Geoffrey Garrett gratefully acknowledges financial support from the Carnegie Foundation's Globalization and Self-Determination grant to Yale University.

increased local discretion in choosing leaders, regulating the environment and economy, or spending centrally generated funds. For example, funds for regional assistance in the EU are generated centrally (via national VAT revenues), but administered at the subnational level. Similarly, Scottish devolution has entailed more Scottish self-governance without the decentralization of taxation away from London. We leave these issues to others (see chapters 3 and 5, in the present volume) and focus on fiscal decentralization.

Our measure of fiscal decentralization is simple: the subnational (combined state and local) share of total public sector expenditures. This measure has the advantage of being available on a yearly basis for a large number of countries around the world. Furthermore, it has been used in previous studies that do not address globalization (e.g., Oates 1972; Panizza 1999), allowing us to replicate and extend their results. While it does not capture the decentralization of tax autonomy, it does provide a comparable measure of the share of total public sector resources that pass through the hands of subnational officials.[2] Table 4.1 provides an overview of countries for which yearly expenditure data have been available for most of the last two decades.[3] Averages for the period from 1982 to 1989 and for 1990 to 1997 are shown in the first two columns. This cut-off is useful because several countries underwent transitions to democracy in the late 1980s, and, by all accounts, global economic integration has increased substantially since 1990. The countries displayed in table 4.1 demonstrate a good deal of variation in vertical fiscal structure. They range from heavily decentralized Canada and the United States, in which more than half of all government expenditure takes place at subnational levels, to countries like Paraguay or Thailand, where subnational governments undertake less than 10 percent of total expenditure.

For our purposes, the right-hand column in table 4.1 is the most important. It shows that fiscal decentralization was by no means a universal phenomenon in the 1990s. Some countries—in fact, nearly half of the

[2] For a discussion of the costs and benefits of this and other measures of decentralization, see Rodden (2003a).

[3] All public finance data are taken from the IMF *Government Finance Statistics Yearbook*, various years. Most of the averages shown in table 4.1 are for the entire period specified, but, because of missing data, some of the averages reflect slightly shorter periods. Note that intergovernmental transfers are not removed from the numerator (total subnational expenditures). This would be inappropriate because, as discussed in Rodden (2003a), the IMF's distinction between grants and own-source local taxation is quite misleading if used in cross-national analysis. It is necessary, however, to subtract grants from the denominator (combined central, state, and local expenditures) to avoid double-counting the grants in the expenditures of the central and subnational governments.

TABLE 4.1
State and Local Share of Total Government Expenditure

	1982–1989 Average	1990–1997 Average	Change
Peru	0.10	0.25	0.15
Mexico	0.12	0.26	0.14
Spain	0.23	0.36	0.13
Brazil	0.29	0.41	0.12
Argentina	0.35	0.44	0.09
Bolivia	0.14	0.21	0.07
Guatemala	0.04	0.10	0.05
Nicaragua	0.03	0.08	0.05
United States	0.48	0.53	0.05
Israel	0.10	0.14	0.04
India	0.46	0.49	0.03
Luxembourg	0.15	0.17	0.02
France	0.17	0.19	0.01
Indonesia	0.12	0.13	0.01
Austria	0.33	0.34	0.01
Norway	0.34	0.35	0.01
Portugal	0.08	0.09	0.01
United Kingdom	0.28	0.29	0.01
Ireland	0.28	0.29	0.01
Bulgaria	0.19	0.19	0.01
Germany	0.45	0.45	0.00
Kenya	0.05	0.04	0.00
Thailand	0.07	0.07	−0.01
Belgium	0.12	0.12	−0.01
Philippines	0.09	0.08	−0.01
Iceland	0.24	0.23	−0.01
Denmark	0.55	0.54	−0.01
Canada	0.67	0.65	−0.02
Netherlands	0.32	0.30	−0.02
Australia	0.52	0.50	−0.02
New Zealand	0.12	0.10	−0.02
Paraguay	0.04	0.02	−0.02
Botswana	0.06	0.03	−0.03
Sweden	0.40	0.37	−0.03
Finland	0.45	0.41	−0.04
South Africa	0.26	0.22	−0.04
Switzerland	0.59	0.55	−0.04
Malaysia	0.19	0.15	−0.04
Italy	0.30	0.23	−0.07
Nigeria	0.54	0.46	−0.07
Romania	0.20	0.11	−0.09
Zimbabwe	0.21	0.12	−0.09

Source: GFS.

sample—became more centralized. But on the other hand, some countries — most notably Brazil, Mexico, Peru, and Spain—considerably decentralized expenditures between the 1980s and 1990s (by more than 10 percent of total expenditures). The question is whether and how these differences are related to the extent of international market integration in these countries.

The remainder of the paper is divided into six sections. The second section begins with a general overview of the literature on fiscal decentralization and then elaborates arguments proposing a link between globalization and decentralization. We develop our alternative hypothesis that globalization should promote fiscal centralization in section three. Our empirical tests of these contending perspectives are presented in sections 4 (based on cross-section averages) and 5 (using time-series cross-sectional data). Section 6 discusses the findings, draws out some broad lessons, and maps out an agenda for further research. Section 7 offers a brief summary of the findings.

GLOBALIZATION AND DECENTRALIZATION: THE CONVENTIONAL VIEW

The key intuition of fiscal federalism theory is that the benefits of decentralization are positively correlated with the (geographic) variance in demands for publicly provided goods (Musgrave 1959; Oates 1972). Although the political process through which demands for decentralization are transformed into policy is not made explicit, this line of argument maintains that excessively centralized systems in large, heterogeneous countries will face overwhelming pressure to decentralize, lest they fall apart through secession or civil war.[4]

The new literature on globalization and decentralization provides a simple extension of this approach. Alesina and his collaborators examine a basic trade-off between the benefits of large jurisdictions and the costs of heterogeneity (Alesina and Spolaore 1997; Alesina and Wacziarg 1998). The benefits of size derive from scale economies in taxation, common defense, internal free trade and the decreasing per capita cost of nonrival public goods. But large size comes at a cost: the difficulty of satisfying a more diverse population.[5] As in the Musgrave-

---

[4] A newer literature revisits the relationship between heterogeneity and the normative case for decentralization from a political-economy perspective that explicitly attempts to model government behavior. Inman and Rubinfeld (1997) and Lockwood (2002) examine the costs of centralization from a distributive politics perspective and highlight the importance of legislative bargaining and legislative rules. Besley and Coate (1999) consider costs of centralization associated with strategic voting for delegates to the central legislature.

[5] Bolton and Roland (1997) emphasize a related trade-off. In their model, the benefits of coordination and economies of scale are traded off against the benefits of setting tax

Oates formulation, sufficiently high levels of heterogeneity generate demands for decentralization or even secession. One of the original claims made in the new literature is that globalization reduces the costs of — and hence increases the supply of — decentralization. According to Alesina and Spolaore (1997, 1041), "a breakup of nations is more costly if it implies more trade barriers and smaller markets. On the contrary, the benefits of large countries are less important if small countries can freely trade with each other. Concretely, this result suggests that regional political separatism should be associated with increasing economic integration."

But many countries might stop short of breaking up. Instead of seceding, regionally distinct groups with strong preferences might opt for a fiscal decentralization scheme. As Bolton and Roland (1997, 1057–58) contend, "any benefits of decentralization that might be obtained in a world with several nations may also be achieved within a unified nation by replicating the administrative structure of the world with several nations and implementing a suitable degree of decentralization of authority among the regions."

In the globalization era, not only citizens, but investors, as well, might prefer decentralization. Weingast's (1995) "market-preserving federalism" — directly applied to the context of globalization by McGillivray and Jensen (2000) — argues that fiscal decentralization, by forcing governments to compete for mobile capital, creates incentives for politicians to provide market-friendly policies. Moreover, fiscal decentralization found the favor of the World Bank and IMF in the late 1980s and early 1990s, creating an additional external demand for decentralization in some developing countries. If these arguments are correct and central governments are interested in pleasing investors and multilateral lending agencies, they may face incentives to devolve fiscal authority to subnational governments.

GLOBALIZATION AND INCENTIVES FOR FISCAL CENTRALIZATION

We have no quarrel with important elements of the conventional wisdom about globalization and decentralization. Economic integration seems to increase the credibility of secession threats in countries with concentrated minority groups (e.g., Russia) or high levels of income inequality between regions (e.g., Italy). When there is sufficient will to hold the country together, it may well be possible to forestall secession by instituting a decentralization program that allows regions to pursue

---

rates and determining redistributive transfers locally in societies with heterogeneous income levels across regions.

distinctive economic and political strategies (as in Belgium). Central governments might introduce local elections, set up regional parliaments, enhance the constitutional protections of subnational governments, or improve their representation in the central government (Scotland and Wales). The central government might loosen its regulation and oversight of subnational governments, transform conditional grants into block grants, and allow local governments greater freedom over local schools and cultural institutions.

Such devolution need not translate, however, into a shift of fiscal resources into the hands of local governments. On the contrary, we believe that it is more likely for the relationship to go in precisely the opposite direction — globalization will lead to the centralization of public expenditures (and even more so, taxation), while simultaneously enhancing the political autonomy and discretion of subnational officials.[6]

The conventional view has overlooked an important benefit of centralized fiscal arrangements. Larger fiscal units are more effective at risk sharing — pooling economic resources to provide insurance for regions adversely affected by unexpected asymmetric economic shocks (Persson and Tabellini 1996a). Thus all regions — whether rich and poor, or dominated by the ethnic majority or a minority group — might benefit from fiscal centralization because they cannot predict ex ante which of them will be hit by negative shocks or when this will happen. Globalization is widely perceived not only by scholars, but also by citizens, to increase volatility and hence aggregate economic risk (Rodrik 1997; Scheve and Slaughter 2001); thus it also increases the aggregate social utility of automatic interregional tax-transfer insurance schemes. According to Atkeson and Bayoumi (1993, 91), "Integrated capital markets are likely to produce large flows of capital across regions or national boundaries. However, they are unlikely to provide a substantial degree of insurance against regional economic fluctuations, except to the extent that capital income flows become more correlated across regions. This task will continue to be primarily the business of government."

More specifically, the pooling of risk via national insurance schemes can only be the business of the central government, which alone has the authority over tax rates and the geographical distribution of expenditures to make such schemes work. Among other factors, capital market imperfections prevent regional and local governments from being able to provide such insurance themselves (von Hagen 1998). In fact, subna-

---

[6] Data limitations make it very difficult for us to test our argument directly on taxation. We would, however, expect globalization to be associated not only with higher levels of fiscal centralization in general, but also with an increasing mismatch between more centralized taxation and more decentralized spending.

tional spending is often procyclical — severely so in many developing countries (IADB 1997).

Regional specialization is another likely consequence of economic integration (Krugman 1991). As regions become more specialized, they become increasingly vulnerable to the vagaries of global markets, and hence have fewer incentives to "go it alone" by relying on themselves to provide insurance. Citizens in small, vulnerable export-oriented jurisdictions with relatively undiversified economies, such as newly formed "export clusters" in the Brazilian and Indian states, might not be enthusiastic about fiscal decentralization if it implies a smaller fiscal role for the central government.

There is considerable evidence that interregional risk-sharing insurance and more permanent interregional fiscal redistribution are prominent features of several federations, including the United States. Sachs and Sala-i-Martin's (1992) influential early study of the United States may well have overestimated the magnitude of inter-state redistribution (see von Hagen 1998). Nonetheless numerous subsequent studies have found evidence of significant interregional insurance and redistribution in response to asymmetric shocks not only in the United States, but also in Canada, France, Germany, and the United Kingdom.[7]

The logic of fiscal centralization for the purpose of interregional risk sharing holds in countries where regional business cycles are not highly correlated. Thus this argument is most plausible in large, diverse countries. Even in smaller countries, however, if globalization increases aggregate risk, voters may demand increased provision of stabilization by the central government. The traditional fiscal federalism literature argues that fiscal stabilization can only be successful if firmly under the control of the central government. Except perhaps for very rare cases like those of the U.S. states and Canadian provinces (even these are debatable), fiscal stabilization is not likely to be successful at lower levels of government.

Although risk sharing and redistribution are distinct in theory, they blend together in practice. Persson and Tabellini (1996a,b) point out that under the realistic assumption that some regions have more favorable output distributions than others, nominal risk-sharing schemes will have long-term redistributive consequences. Indeed, many of the recent empirical studies designed to assess the short-term "insurance" quality of intergovernmental transfers find stronger evidence of outright long-term regional redistribution in response to asymmetric shocks (e.g., Kletzer and von Hagen 2000). That is, regions that suffer negative

---

[7] For literature reviews, see von Hagen (1998), Kletzer and von Hagen (2000), and Obstfeld and Peri (1998).

shocks are subsequently favored in the distribution of transfers and become more dependent on transfers in the long term. Although not previously seen in such a light, this evidence is consistent with the literature
on globalization and the compensation of "losers" from free trade. The
compensation literature argues that globalization might lead to larger
government because, in order to assemble a stable political coalition in
favor of free trade, it may be necessary for those who benefit from free
trade explicitly to "buy off" those who lose with a more extensive
safety net or other redistributive transfers (Garrett 1998b).

When protectionist barriers fall and capital constraints are lifted in a
country, it is often not difficult to predict some of the winners and losers
ex ante. Some of the losers are often regionally identifiable, and to the
extent that the affected regions are represented in the central legislature
or capable of undermining the regime's support coalition, it may be
necessary to pay them off with increased transfers in order to obtain
their political support for the move to freer trade. Other things being
equal, this would lead to a larger spending role for the central government vis-à-vis subnational governments.

Increased spending pressure on the central government might come
not only from regions who fear volatility and the loss of jobs associated
with globalization, but turning the logic of Alesina and Spolaore on its
head, it might also result from the demands of ethnic minorities. To the
extent that some large, diverse countries like Canada, India, Russia, and
Indonesia are able to stay together in spite of demands for secession,
globalization might only increase the costs of staying together. Secession
threats from a region with distinct preferences may not be credible in an
autarchic world, but perhaps such threats gain credibility in a world of
free trade. Consider the importance of potential trading partners in bol-
stering the credibility of exit threats made by Estonia, Quebec, the
Slovak Republic, or oil-rich Russian republics, or the importance of the
European Union to Scottish and Basque independence movements.

These newly credible exit threats might be a useful bargaining chip in
negotiations over the distribution of central government spending. To
the extent that there are benefits to the rest of the country from keeping
breakaway regions in the union (e.g., maintaining a larger risk-sharing
pool), the rest of the country may be willing to send disproportionately
large transfers to such regions to buy their cooperation (Fearon and van
Houten 1998). Knowing this, of course, such regions face incentives to
amplify their threats. This is a familiar story in post-Soviet Russia (Triesman 1999) and modern India. Even if subnational governments end
up gaining autonomy and spending more, this effect may be overwhelmed by the larger spending role of the central government. If the

central government wishes to use public spending to "buy" the loyalty of voters in would-be breakaway regions, it might try to spend the money directly rather than through general-purpose transfers to regional governments. Alternatively, the central government may decide to beef up its spending on the military and internal security forces in order to quell the threat of regional violence. Either of these possibilities might lead to fiscal centralization.

In sum, our general point is that even if one accepts the Alesina-Spolaore and Bolton-Roland arguments about the effects of globalization on the break-up of nations, it is inappropriate to argue that fiscal decentralization within an existing country is a halfway house to secession.[8] Indeed, we believe the opposite is likely to be true. In order to hold onto political power and perhaps even forestall secession, the national government may have to centralize fiscal policy so as to deliver benefits (in the form of risk sharing and outright fiscal redistribution) to risk-averse groups, especially those in would-be secessionist localities.[9]

ANALYSIS OF CROSS-SECTION AVERAGES

This section examines the relationship between international market integration and the centralization of fiscal policy using data from a cross-section of countries around the world. We start out by conducting separate analyses of the two periods displayed in table 1: 1982–1989, and 1990–1997. The cases are selected based on the availability of sufficient data on the dependent variable — subnational expenditure as a share of total public sector expenditure. These data are derived from the IMF's *Government Finance Statistics Yearbook*. Higher scores on the dependent variable denote more decentralization.

The independent variables follow from the discussion above. First, to test arguments about size and heterogeneity, we include the natural logs of *area* (square kilometers) and average *population*. The basic model also includes the log *of GDP per capita* in inflation-adjusted U.S. dollars, since Oates (1972) and Panizza (1999) find that wealthier countries demonstrate higher levels of decentralization.[10] Following Panizza

---

[8] This view also drives part of the empirical analysis of Hiscox (chapter 3 in the present volume).

[9] Of course these arguments are complicated by the fact that within countries, different regions are likely to have different preferences over levels of risk sharing and redistribution according to their output distribution. These issues will be discussed in greater detail below.

[10] All of the above are taken from the World Bank *World Development Indicators*, 2000.

(1999), we also include a measure of *ethnic fractionalization* as a proxy for preference heterogeneity.[11]

Next, we include averages of Gurr's twenty-point measure of *democracy*.[12] According to Panizza (1999) and Alesina and Spolaore (1997), if geographically dispersed heterogeneous preferences over public goods are taken as a given, a rent-seeking authoritarian government that can rule without consent might be more willing and able to suppress demands for decentralization than a democratically elected counterpart.[13]

We also include a simple dummy variable for political federalism.[14] Above all, federal systems are distinct from unitary systems in that they provide formal or de facto veto authority to regional politicians over all or some subset of federal policy decisions. In most cases this is accomplished through special constitutional protections and amendment procedures and an upper house that disproportionately represents the regions. All of these factors should allow subnational officials to bargain for larger shares of the public sector's resources. It is also possible that some of the variation in fiscal decentralization will be explained by urbanization rates if demands for local government services are higher in urban areas. Thus we include a variable that measures urban population as a share of the total.[15]

The next group of variables addresses globalization using two simple measures. We use *trade/GDP* ratios to capture the international integration of national goods and services markets.[16] Second, *capital account openness* is a dummy variable from the IMF's annual Exchange Arrangements and Exchange Restrictions describing whether countries impose significant restrictions on capital account transactions (coded as "0") or not ("1" = open). This is a simple way to measure interna-

---

[11] We use the standard "ethnolinguistic fractionalization" (ELF) index used by other authors, even though we are quite skeptical about this variable. Originally published in the Atlas Narodov Mira (1964), it is included in Taylor and Hudson (1972), and reflects the likelihood that two randomly drawn people will be from different ethnic groups. The variable is fraught with conceptual and measurement problems, and is very likely out of date (Laitin and Posner 2000). We include it in order to replicate Panizza (1999).

[12] The source is the Polity 98 data set.

[13] Regional elites have also played important roles in the protests and negotiations that have led to democratic transitions. In new democracies, decentralization is often an attractive political strategy for reelection-seeking politicians who wish to build or consolidate local bases of support (O'Niell 2000).

[14] This variable is taken from Rodden (2002). Cases are coded as federal if they feature constitutional protections for states and state-based representation in an upper chamber of the legislature.

[15] The source is the World Bank, *World Development Indicators*, 2000.

[16] Ibid.

tional capital mobility that is available for all IMF members on an annual basis.

Finally, we include two public finance variables calculated from the GFS. First, it seems possible that decentralization might be more advanced in countries with larger public sectors, so we include a control for the average overall scale of government spending as a portion of GDP. Finally, we consider the possibility that decentralization is little more than a thinly veiled attempt by central governments to "offload" central government deficits onto state and local governments by increasing subnational expenditure responsibilities without a corresponding increase in revenues. This is a common complaint among critics of fiscal decentralization in a wide variety of contexts ranging from Latin America and Africa to the United States. In order to control for this in the cross-section regressions, we include the central government's average fiscal balance as a percentage of revenue.

Findings

The results from the regressions on the first period (1982–1989) are presented in table 4.2, and the results from the second period (1990–1997) are presented in table 4.3. First, we estimate a basic model using the variables that have been analyzed by others, along with the urbanization variable. As expected, countries with larger *area* are significantly more decentralized. In addition, countries with higher *GDP per capita* are more decentralized. *Population* and *urbanization* have no effect on decentralization in any of the estimations, so we drop them from subsequent analysis.[17] We do the same for ethnic fractionalization, which, contrary to the findings of Panizza (1999), was also not significant in any of our estimations.[18] The main findings of previous studies hold up, however — decentralization is positively correlated with *area* and *wealth* in both the earlier and later periods. They also survive the inclusion of several control variables not included in previous studies.

Next, we add the two institutional variables. *Democracy* has the expected positive sign in both the earlier and later periods, though it is only significant in the earlier period. This is not surprising, given that,

[17] We have also included another variable — defense expenditures as a share of total spending — but, as it did not affect the results presented here and did not approach statistical significance, we do not include it.

[18] There are several potential reasons for the divergence with the earlier finding. Panizza (1999) uses single-year observations, and, of the three years considered, the coefficient for ethnic fractionalization was only significant for 1985. Moreover, the sample is slightly different.

TABLE 4.2
Determinants of Expenditure Decentralization, 1982–1989

Dependent Variable: State and Local Expenditure as Share of Total Government Expenditure (Average)

	(1) Coef.	(1) S.E.	(2) Coef.	(2) S.E.	(3) Coef.	(3) S.E.	(4) Coef.	(4) S.E.	(5) Coef.	(5) S.E.
Basic variables										
Area (log)	0.037	0.017**	0.029	0.01**	0.049	0.02**	0.052	0.013***	0.037	0.021*
Population (log)	0.004	0.02								
GDP Per Capita (log)	0.148	0.037***	0.055	0.03*	0.110	0.02***	0.082	0.032***	-0.0092	0.031
Ethnic Fractionalization	0.001	0.001								
Urbanization	-0.001	0.002								
Institutional variables										
Democracy			0.010	0.004***					0.010	0.003***
Federalism			0.088	0.05*					0.060	0.052
Globalization variables										
Trade/GDP					0.019	0.107			-0.103	0.10
Open capital accounts					-0.006	0.054			0.046	0.046
Public Finance variables										
Total Expenditure/GDP							0.287	0.187	0.454	0.154***
Central Balance/Revenue							0.136	0.115	0.210	0.10**
Constant	-1.57	0.392	-0.686	0.32	-1.388	0.40	-1.255	0.305	-0.309	0.427
R^2	0.44		0.58		0.46		0.46		0.69	
N	40		42		41		42		41	

*$p \leq .10$, **$p \leq .05$, ***$p \leq .01$.

TABLE 4.3

Determinants of Expenditure Decentralization, 1990–1997

	Dependent Variable: State and Local Expenditure as Share of Total Government Expenditure (Average)									
	Coef.	S.E.	Coef.	S.E.	Coef.	S.E.	Coef.	S.E.	Coef.	S.E.
Basic variables										
Area (log)	0.036	0.02**	0.02	0.01	0.041	0.019**	0.044	0.013***	0.008	0.015
Population (log)	0.019	0.02								
GDP Per Capita (log)	0.075	0.04**	0.048	0.03*	0.070	0.028**	0.093	0.035***	0.041	0.036
Ethnic Fractionalization	0.0004	0.001								
Urbanization	0.001	0.002								
Institutional variables										
Democracy			0.005	0.01					−0.001	0.005
Federalism			0.193	0.04***					0.198	0.039***
Globalization variables										
Trade/GDP					−0.045	0.094			−0.079	0.067
Open capital accounts					0.056	0.059			0.051	0.041
Public Finance variables										
Total Expenditure/GDP							0.148	0.237	0.301	0.186
Central Balance/Revenue							−0.476	0.20**	−0.339	0.164**
Constant	−1.271	0.415	−0.515	0.30	−0.885	0.432	−1.26	0.30	−0.394	0.375
R^2	0.37		0.58		0.37		0.51		0.74	
N	38		41		41		41		41	

$*p \leq .10$, $**p \leq .05$, $***p \leq .01$.

after many successful transitions to democracy, the later period demonstrates less variation across countries. Thus it appears that democracy is positively correlated with decentralization, but the pooled time-series analysis below provides a much better test. Second, the *federalism* variable clearly accounts for a good deal of cross-national variation in fiscal decentralization. As expected, state and local governments are responsible for a much larger share of public spending in formally federal systems. This finding is especially strong in the later period.[19]

Next, we add the globalization variables. Capital account openness and trade had no significant effects on decentralization in either period in any specification. Thus we find no support using cross-section averages for either the conventional wisdom or our alternative argument. This is not very surprising, however, since globalization and decentralization are processes that unfold over time within countries. We must exploit the time-series cross-section data before discarding these arguments.

Finally, we add the public finance variables. The coefficient for *total government expenditure* (as a share of GDP) is positive in each estimation, and even significant in the full model for the earlier period, but it is not significantly different from zero in the later period. Thus, if anything, we have tentative evidence that countries with larger public sectors tend to be more decentralized.

The coefficients for *central government balance* are difficult to interpret. Like globalization, the offloading argument is a dynamic one; thus it is difficult to come up with clear predictions about cross-section averages. During the 1980s, there appears to have been a positive relationship between central government fiscal balance and levels of decentralization, but during the 1990s, countries with large central government deficits tended to be significantly more decentralized.

Similar models were also estimated using state and local share of total government *revenue*, and the results were virtually identical to those presented here. The main results were not affected by case-wise deletion, revealing that the results are not driven by any individual cases. Additionally, since the dependent variable has a lower limit of 0 and an upper limit of 1, we also estimated all of the models presented in tables 4.2 and 4.3 using Tobit, and the results were virtually identical.

In sum, the cross-section analysis finds reasonable support for the

---

[19] Note that this does not mean that states and provinces are less dependent on transfers from the central government. Our spending variable does not distinguish between expenditures funded by own-source revenue and those funded by transfers. Rodden (2002) shows that subnational units in federal and unitary systems display, on average, similar levels of reliance on transfers from higher-level governments.

most important findings of Oates (1972) and Panizza (1999) that larger and wealthier countries tend to be more decentralized. Previous findings regarding *ethnic fractionalization* do not hold up, but, as we have noted, the quality of the data is extremely low. Moreover, there is additional support in the cross-section data for Panizza's (1999) finding that more democratic countries tend to be more decentralized. In addition, federal countries are more decentralized.

POOLED TIME-SERIES ANALYSIS

Table 4.4 presents our regression analysis of spending and revenue decentralization using panel data, comprising observations for forty-seven countries for the period 1978–1997. The panel specification is important in this context because some of the independent variables of interest have changed considerably in the past twenty years. Most notably, many countries in our sample have democratized, expanded their trade with the rest of the world, and opened their capital accounts. In any case, decentralization is a dynamic rather than static concept; thus the empirical specification presented in this section is a significant improvement over previous studies that use cross-section averages or single-year observations. We have used a variety of different estimation techniques with largely similar results, and table 4.4 reports the results of a conservative approach — regressions using panel-corrected standard errors, taking into account the unbalanced nature of our panels. We include lagged dependent variables and dummy variables for all countries (fixed effects) to take into account variations over time and cross-national variations that should not be attributed to any of our independent variables.[20]

The first thing to note about the regression estimates is that patterns of decentralization were sticky over time (the coefficients on the lagged dependent variables were around .7 and highly statistically significant). Furthermore, the battery of country dummy variables (not reported) was highly significant (the null hypothesis of common intercepts for all countries can be rejected with extremely high levels of confidence). In general, the patterns of parameter estimates were very similar for both spending and revenue decentralization. For convenience, we therefore concentrate on the spending equation (the first column of table 4.4), though we must compare both equations in order to interpret the effects of the central government's fiscal balance.

---

[20] The presence of a lagged dependent variable can bias the fixed-effects estimator even if the error term is not correlated over time. But in panels where the time-series dimension is long (as is the case here), the bias is rather small.

TABLE 4.4
Determinants of Expenditure and Revenue Decentralization

	State/Local Expenditure Share		State/Local Revenue Share	
Dependent Variable	Coef.	P.C.S.E.	Coef.	P.C.S.E.
Basic variables				
Lagged dependent variable	0.679	0.06***	0.73	0.06***
Area (log)	0.006	0.01	0.003	0.01
GDP per capita (log)	0.005	0.01	0.01	0.01
Institutional variables				
Democracy	0.001	0.0004**	0.001	0.001
Federalism	0.084	0.02***	0.078	0.02***
Globalization variables				
Trade/GDP	−0.032	0.01***	−0.02	0.01*
Open capital accounts	−0.005	0.003*	−0.007	0.004*
Public finance variables				
Total expenditure/GDP	−0.019	0.02	−0.005	0.02
Lagged central balance/ Revenue	−0.052	0.02***	0.035	0.01***
Central balance/Revenue	0.096	0.02***	−0.031	0.01***
R^2	0.99		0.99	
Countries	47		48	
Years	1978–1997		1978–1997	
N	564		576	

*$p \leq .10$, **$p \leq .05$, ***$p \leq .01$.

OLS with panel-corrected standard errors. Fixed effects with constant suppressed. Coefficients for country dummies not shown.

Control Variables

Let us begin with the basic control variables. It is not surprising that *area* does not enter significantly since fixed effects are included. In contrast with previous studies and the simple cross-section results presented above, we detect no relationship between *GDP per capita* and decentralization over time within countries. Not surprisingly, countries with formal federal political structures tended also to be fiscally more decentralized. Consistent with normative views about democracy, more democratic countries tended to be more decentralized (though this effect was not significant in the revenues equation). We also estimated models including the index of *ethnic fractionalization*, population, urbanization, and defense expenditures. None of these approached statistical significance, and none affected any of the results reported in table 4.4, so we do not report them here.

The results provide evidence that decentralization should not only be understood as a response to demands of voters and investors, but also as a strategic attempt by central governments to shift deficits onto subnational governments. Both the level and the lagged level of the central government's surplus (deficits are negative numbers) as a percentage of revenue are included in the regressions. By including the lagged level, we attempt to control for trends and isolate short-term dynamics. It is important to note that the coefficients for central government balance are statistically significant, but have the opposite sign in the expenditure and revenue equations. Controlling for the previous year's level, higher surplus levels (i.e., lower deficits) are associated with *higher* subnational expenditure and *lower* subnational revenue. Note that the models control for fluctuations in GDP and overall government expenditure. Other things being equal, improvements in the central government's fiscal stance are associated with larger shares of total public sector expenditure taking place at the subnational level, but smaller shares of total public sector revenue flowing to state and local governments. Thus improvements in central government finances seem to be achieved, at least in part, on the backs of state and local governments. These results dovetail with frequent complaints of "offloading" or "unfunded mandates" around the world, but they are merely suggestive. Considerable further analysis is needed. The rather straightforward OLS model presented here is not an optimal way to address the dynamics of strategic deficit shifting.[21]

Globalization

For present purposes, the most interesting parameter estimates concern the two globalization variables. Put simply, countries that were more exposed to *trade* and that had *open capital accounts* had more centralized fiscal systems. This is wholly inconsistent with the logic of the Alesina-Spolaore or Bolton-Roland arguments, both of which hold that decentralization is a compromise on the way to secession, made more likely by globalization because of the reduced costs of small size in open markets. It is, however, completely consistent with our argument about responding to risk.

---

[21] Future work might use an error-correction set-up with dynamic panel estimation techniques to examine the relationship between central and subnational deficits (see Arellano and Bond [1998]). Such analysis might consider more carefully the opposite causal relationship, as well—subnational governments are often able to shift their own deficits onto the central government (Fornasari, Webb, and Zou 1999; Rodden 2002).

In order to check the robustness of these results, we have used a variety of additional estimation techniques. Similar results were obtained using AR1 correction rather than a lagged dependent variable. A model with a lagged dependent variable and no fixed effects yielded a similar result for trade, but the coefficients for "openness" fell below traditional levels of statistical significance. We also estimated the model in first differences, and estimated an "error-correction" model using both first differences and lagged levels of the independent variables. We also included a panel of year dummies. These models yielded similar results for trade, though, again, the statistical significance of the coefficient for "openness" is sensitive to the model specification. In general, the coefficients are slightly larger and less sensitive in the "expenditure" equations. In every single equation, however, the signs for trade and openness are negative, and both are significant in most.[22]

Of course we should not overestimate the magnitude of these effects — especially for openness. The coefficient of −0.005 on the open capital account variable in the spending equation, for example, suggests that removing all significant restrictions on capital account transactions only increases the state and local share of total expenditure by .5 of 1 percent of total government spending. The "trade" results are somewhat more impressive, however. In the same equation, a 10 percent increase in trade as a share of GDP (a typical year for Malaysia, or roughly the increase in Canada over the last five years) is estimated to have reduced the state and local share of expenditures by .32 percentage points. Moving from the United States or Brazil, where trade is on average around 20 percent of GDP, to Belgium, where it is around 120 percent, one finds a 3.2 percent increase in the central government's share of expenditures.

DISCUSSION

It is commonly assumed that globalization has had two effects on political systems around the world. On the one hand, globalization has reduced the minimum efficient scale of politics, resulting in the proliferation of nations. On the other hand, globalization has also been associated — on the same logic — with fiscal decentralization within na-

[22] When one or more of the control variables is dropped (including *GDP per capita*, *area*, and *total expenditures*, none of which ever attains statistical significance), the trade and openness variables are highly significant using either dependent variable and virtually all estimation techniques. We also obtain higher levels of significance for trade and openness when using a larger data set of over sixty countries, but we do not include these additional countries here because the GFS only provides very limited, non-overlapping-year coverage.

tions. We do not wish to debate the merits of the first proposition, but the empirical analysis above calls into question the globalization-decentralization nexus. We have discovered a modest but robust, highly significant relationship between trade integration and expenditure centralization.

One might respond that this finding is wholly consistent with the Alesina-Spolaore argument because globalization has facilitated secession and the creation of new sovereign states. If the impetus for secession were heterogeneity within old national boundaries, both new states and what remains of existing states would be more homogenous than the polyglots that preceded them. Given the increased homogeneity of preferences in all states after secession, there would be less reason to decentralize authority in any of them. This argument relies on asserting that globalization has been causally implicated in cataclysmic events such as the end of African colonialism in the 1960s and the break-up of the Soviet Union. No political boundaries, however, changed in any of the countries in our study during the period we analyze. Thus there must be another explanation for the fiscal centralization we observe.

We have argued that globalization, by increasing perceptions of aggregate and region-specific risk within countries, might actually undermine the credibility of regional exit threats and create powerful new demands for fiscal centralization. Decentralization of taxation increases economic competition among regions, and all else being equal, this is likely to result in smaller government — and hence less cushioning of adverse economic shocks through fiscal policy. In more integrated economies, these shocks are perceived to be larger and less predictable, exacerbating the demands for governmental redistribution of wealth and risk. Regional governments know that centralized fiscal systems are likely to deliver the most stabilization and fiscal redistribution in favor of their citizens. Moreover, we have argued that the central government may get more involved in regional redistribution as a way of placating regions that stand to lose from trade integration.

Undoubtedly there are some regions for which globalization has raised the costs of fiscal centralization. The median voter in a relatively wealthy region is likely to prefer a more decentralized fiscal system than the median voter in a poor region (Bolton and Roland 1997), and the median voter in a persistently disadvantaged region will prefer less insurance than the median voter in a more productive, diversified region (Persson and Tabellini 1996b). Indeed, in accordance with the logic of Bolton and Roland (1997) and Hiscox (chapter 3 in the present volume), the Italian North and the wealthy German states like Baden-Württemberg and Bavaria are growing increasingly weary of paying into centralized risk-sharing and redistribution schemes that benefit others. They prefer fiscal decentralization, and apparently are willing to push hard for it. There is no guarantee, however, that they will win. As we have argued, the stakes have also been raised for the poorer, less diversified, or smaller and more vulnerable jurisdictions (e.g., Sicily, Saarland, and Bremen) whose residents believe they have more to fear in a world of integrated markets (Rodden 2003b).

Moreover, there is considerable support for our argument in the evolution of the European Union. In the 1985 deal to complete the internal market, the member states agreed to introduce a new system of development assistance to poorer regions of Europe. The 1992 Maastricht treaty that set the European Union on the course to the creation of the euro was accompanied by a large increase in this development assistance. The combination of Maastricht and the euro render Europe the closest example we have of a completely open international market. But its creation generated risks, particularly for less well-off areas. As a result, the *central* EU budget was expanded considerably to pay for these fiscal transfers. Of course, the EU's budget is still only a tiny portion of European output. Our argument predicts that, in the future, demands for a larger EU fiscal authority will grow appreciably.

Of course, the EU's budget has been the subject of considerable debate and acrimony among member governments in recent years, and strife over the renegotiation of intergovernmental fiscal contracts is growing in other countries ranging from Brazil, Argentina, and India to Germany and Canada. The fault lines are the same — poor and vulnerable jurisdictions desire increased risk sharing and redistribution while wealthy or well-positioned jurisdictions desire less. This fact is consistent with both the conventional wisdom about increased credibility of exit threats and our countervailing argument about increased perception of risk. But neither the existing literature nor our chapter provide a satisfactory positive theory of the conditions under which the wealthy or poor regions are likely to win these battles. The next step in a positive theory of globalization and the vertical movement of fiscal authority is a more careful examination of (1) the geographical distribution of risk, and (2) the political institutions through which such battles are fought.

First, consider some simple demographic facts. Regional income disparities within countries around the world are often staggering, and in developing countries especially, regional inequality is on the rise (Shankar and Shah 2000). Poor regions almost always vastly outnumber the wealthy, and small rural jurisdictions are very frequently overrepresented in legislatures (Samuels and Snyder 2001). In most developing countries, the lion's share of economic activity is concentrated in only one or two "urban giants" (Ades and Glaeser 1995; Henderson 2000). Unless the relatively wealthy (often urban) jurisdictions can threaten to bring down the regime through riots or credibly threaten to secede, there are few reasons to expect that vastly outnumbered wealthy regions can defeat the poor regions who prefer higher levels of risk sharing and redistribution.

To better understand the conditions under which globalization leads to fiscal centralization or decentralization, it is necessary to examine more carefully the institutions through which regions are represented in the central government's decision-making process. For example, at one extreme, a country like Israel has no territorial aspect to representation and policymaking at all—it is a unitary system with one national electoral district and an integrated national party system. At the other extreme are Brazil and the European Union, federations in which small states are vastly overrepresented in both chambers of the legislature, and political parties do little to create incentives for cross-jurisdiction cooperation. Fiscal policies in the latter type of system are more likely to be chosen through a process of regional intergovernmental bargaining than simple majority rule (Cremer and Palfrey 1999). Persson and Tabellini (1996a) hypothesize that this type of intergovernmental bargaining will lead to lower levels of centralized insurance than systems where risk-sharing schemes are chosen by majority rule with one-person–one-vote.

The European Union provides a good example of the importance of representation schemes in mediating battles over risk sharing and redistribution. In contrast to other federations, the EU has not developed a full-blown centralized risk-sharing scheme to rival other large federations (notwithstanding its innovations with respect to fiscal support for poorer regions). Under the current, highly confederal configuration, however, the creation of such a system would require the consent of every state, including the wealthy states that are net contributors. It would be much more difficult for wealthy states to rebuff demands for greater risk sharing and redistribution, however, if, for example, the European Parliament, using a simple majority-decision rule, had exclusive authority over fiscal policy.

Future research might build from our findings, drawing on more refined institutional arguments to pinpoint the demographic and institutional conditions under which demands for more centralized risk sharing overwhelm demands from wealthy states for greater fiscal decentralization. Such studies might try to improve on the blunt measure of fiscal decentralization used in this chapter. Detailed cross-national data for a large number of countries on the size, conditionality, and distribution of intergovernmental transfers would be extremely helpful. Additionally, improved efforts should be made to conceptualize and measure political decentralization across countries.[23]

Our arguments about risk sharing and redistribution may or may not be the driving force behind the observed relationship between trade integration and fiscal centralization. We have also addressed the argument that globalization leads to decentralization by enhancing the credibility of secession threats of ethnic and linguistic minorities. While this seems plausible, we point out that the price would-be secessionist regions demand to stay within the federation might result, if anything, in fiscal centralization. Of course our empirical results do not prove this conjecture. These arguments should only apply in countries with regionally concentrated groups with distinctive preferences who make secession threats that are taken seriously. In the vast majority of our cases, however, such groups either cannot easily be identified, or their exit threats would not viewed as credible by the central government. The best way to examine arguments about exit threats and fiscal (de)centralization is to limit the analysis to a smaller group of countries where such concentrated groups exist and their threats are taken seriously (see, e.g., van Houten's chapter in the present volume; Fearon and van Houten 1998).[24] Future work might build on the framework of Triesman (1999) and use disaggregated regional, fiscal, political, and demographic data to examine the interaction of trade, exit threats, and distributive politics in such countries.

SUMMARY

Along with chapters 3 and 5 in the present volume, this chapter departs from previous studies of globalization and shifting locations of governance by considering not only a binary choice between secession and staying together, but also the distinct possibility of (de)centralization within countries. It also contrasts the likely effects of globalization on political and fiscal authority. The conventional wisdom that globalization strengthens the credibility of regional autonomy movements and puts pressure on central governments to cede *policy* control and *political* autonomy to local officials is quite plausible, though van Houten (chapter 5 in the present volume) finds no evidence of this in his Euro-

[23] For a good start, see Henderson (2000). For an overview of other attempts, see Rodden (2003a).

[24] It is worth noting that when we estimate the model presented in table 4.4 including only the cases from our data set in which secession threats seemed reasonably credible—Belgium, Canada, India, Indonesia, Italy, Spain, and the United Kingdom—the "trade" coefficient was negative, similar in magnitude, and significant at the 10-percent level.

pean sample. But this chapter has argued that globalization may also encourage regions that choose to stay within countries to push for fiscal arrangements that better mitigate market risk for citizens within their borders. Consistent with this argument, the data analyzed above suggest that increased trade integration is associated with mild fiscal centralization.

While this finding presents an interesting challenge to a common hypothesis, it is probably most useful as an invitation to further research. Along with chapters 3 and 5, this chapter moves toward a richer understanding of the relationship between globalization and the vertical distribution of authority within countries. Future studies should continue to distinguish between globalization's effects on political and fiscal decentralization, and explore more carefully the varieties of each. These chapters also point toward several mediating factors that deserve more rigorous analysis, including the distribution of income and risk across jurisdictions, and the roles of constitutions, legislative rules, and partisan incentives.

Chapter 5

GLOBALIZATION AND DEMANDS FOR REGIONAL AUTONOMY IN EUROPE

Pieter Van Houten

THE GLOBALIZATION LITERATURE often links globalization to secessionist or autonomy demands.[1] For example, Giddens (1999, 13) states that
"local nationalisms spring up as a response to globalizing tendencies, as
the hold of older nation-states weakens." Similarly, Micklethwait and
Wooldridge (2000, xviii, 156) assert that "globalization has often
helped awaken old nationalist or fundamentalist impulses" and that
"political separatism has been . . . linked to globalization." Apparently,
"the 'globalization' of markets goes hand in hand with political separatism" (Alesina, Spolaore, and Wacziarg 2000, 1294). Although widespread, this view has rarely been subjected to conceptual and empirical
scrutiny. What are the possible mechanisms by which globalization induces political separatism and autonomy demands? How can these be
tested empirically? Is there evidence for the alleged link between globalization and subnational pressures for changes in governance structures?
This chapter begins to address these questions. While the previous two
chapters by Hiscox (chapter 3) and Garrett and Rodden (chapter 4)
focused primarily on *actual patterns* of political and fiscal decentralization, this chapter focuses exclusively on *subnational pressures* for
decentralization.

Such pressures are one possible channel through which globalization
constitutes a challenge to nation-states. In general terms, global economic and social developments appear to make it increasingly difficult
for these states to deliver the goods and services on which their legitimacy ultimately depends.[2] Kahler and Lake (chapter 1) indicate that
states are, in fact, challenged on various dimensions. One element relates to the "vertical" distribution of authority between levels of government, where there are pressures from above (supranational organiza-

[1] I am grateful to Miles Kahler, David Lake, Michael Hiscox, Jonathan Rodden, Paolo
Dardanelli, Bonnie Meguid, and participants at the "Globalization and Governance" conferences and the 2001 APSA meeting for comments and suggestions on earlier drafts of
this chapter.
[2] Holton (1998) provides an overview of the academic debates on these developments,
while Friedman (2000) gives a good indication of the public debates.

tions) and below (subnational units). While the existence of these challenges is hardly contested, however, their consequences are very much in dispute. As this volume shows, it has become increasingly clear that the effects of globalization on governance structures are subtle and multifaceted. Our best hope for understanding these developments is to focus in detail on its various elements. This chapter does this for subnational demands for decentralization.

Specifically, this chapter focuses on the possible relation between processes of globalization and/or European integration and regional autonomy demands in Western Europe. The dual pressures on the state are nowhere more salient than in Europe. On the one hand, European integration has transferred a number of significant competencies to the European level. On the other hand, some states have broken up (Soviet Union, Yugoslavia, and Czechoslovakia), while powers have been devolved in several others (e.g., Spain, Belgium, United Kingdom, and France). Moreover, demands for further devolution are present in many countries. The slogan "Europe of the Regions" (Delamaide 1994; Loughlin 1996; Nijkamp 1993) captures the possible result of these developments, although skepticism about its prospects is widespread (Anderson 1990; Le Galès and Lequesne 1998). We need more detailed empirical analyses of various aspects of these developments to move beyond such general claims.

This chapter makes two contributions. First, it reviews the existing literature on the relation between globalization (and European integration) and regional autonomy demands, identifying several possible mechanisms and testable hypotheses. This provides a useful agenda for empirical research on these issues. Second, it makes a start with such research through a brief discussion of the evolution of autonomy demands in Western Europe in recent decades, as well as an analysis of contemporary autonomy demands for a sample of eighty-three regions in six countries. The conclusions from this analysis are rather skeptical about the impact of globalization on regional assertiveness. It certainly has played a role in changing and reinforcing demands in assertive regions, but there is little evidence that it has induced an overall rise in autonomy demands. Moreover, in this sample, it cannot account for variation in autonomy demands across regions, once other economic, cultural, and political factors are controlled for. The evidence suggests that political institutions such as political parties and party systems are crucial mediating factors. I conclude that our attention to politics is crucial to understand the challenges to nation-states, and that these challenges may be weaker than is often suggested.

The first section of the chapter defines globalization and its relation to European integration. The second section reviews the literature on the link between globalization and subnational autonomy demands, while the third section presents alternative hypotheses. The fourth section critically evaluates the claim that globalization and European integration have induced an overall increase in regional assertiveness. The fifth section presents the results of a synchronic empirical test of the hypotheses, and discusses their implications for an understanding of the effect of globalization on governance structures. The conclusion speculates about wider applications of this chapter's arguments.

GLOBALIZATION AND EUROPEAN INTEGRATION FROM A SUBNATIONAL PERSPECTIVE

Globalization is a term that currently pervades social science and public discourse. In its broadest use, it is simply a label for a whole array of contemporary economic, social, and cultural processes. This understanding of globalization makes it difficult to assess its social and political impact, including its effects on governance structures. A narrower conceptualization of globalization is analytically more useful. Following the other contributions in this volume, I interpret globalization as a process of economic integration, in which "[t]he reduction of barriers to economic exchange and factor mobility gradually creates one economic space from many" (Kahler and Lake, chapter 1 in the present volume).

The literature has focused much attention on the distinction and relation between globalization and (supranational) regionalism, as exemplified by regional trade blocs such as NAFTA, MERCOSUR, and, most prominently, the European Union (e.g., Fawcett and Hurrell 1995; Mansfield and Milner 1997). Whereas our definition of globalization emphasizes the gradual formation of one global economic space, these developments suggest the formation of several economic spaces. One of the central issues in the literature is the extent to which these two processes are compatible, and whether supranational regionalism is a stepping stone or an impediment to globalization. From a global perspective, these are important questions, which justify the distinction between the two processes.

Seen from a subnational perspective, however, this distinction begins to fade. For political and economic actors operating at the subnational level, both globalization and regional integration imply the formation of a larger economic space and the reduced relevance of the national state as a regulatory regime. In fact, in the case of Western Europe, the economic dimension of European integration and globalization are two sides of the same coin, with European integration being an especially advanced form of globalization (Kahler and Lake, chapter 1; McNamara, chapter 13). Indeed, most foreign trade of European regions takes place within the European Union, and European integration has caused significant changes in the economic regulatory framework for regions, reducing the influence of the national state. Therefore, this chapter not only focuses on the relation between globalization and regional autonomy demands, but also on possible relations between European integration and such demands. Of course, European integration differs from the more general process of globalization in its extensive supranational institutional structure (Verdier and Breen 2001). This institutional dimension can have additional effects on autonomy demands, as I will indicate below.

GLOBALIZATION, EUROPEAN INTEGRATION, AND REGIONAL AUTONOMY DEMANDS

Connections between globalization and local/subnational developments have been identified in various fields and contexts. For instance, the importance of local factors for economic performance in the international economy is now widely recognized (Porter 1998; Scott 1998; Storper 1997). Similarly, the impact of globalization on cities is an important theme in urban sociology and geography (Eade 1997; Le Galès and Harding 1998; Sassen 1994; Sellers 2002). Claims about a connection between globalization and pressures for political decentralization and autonomy are also widespread. As with many alleged political implications of globalization, however, these claims are rarely spelled out clearly. The literature on regions and European integration is more specific (e.g., Lynch 1996) but has similar shortcomings.

In this section, I provide explicit formulations of the possible links between globalization and regional autonomy demands. It is possible to discern four mechanisms by which globalization and European integration may have an impact on regional autonomy demands. I will describe these mechanisms, and derive testable hypotheses from them. Some of these hypotheses refer to predicted changes over time and can only be evaluated in a diachronic framework, while other hypotheses refer to variation across regions and can be evaluated in a cross-sectional framework. Thus, this section provides an extensive agenda for empirical research on the link between economic integration (globalization and European integration) and regional autonomy demands.

The first mechanism indicates that *regional autonomy demands can result from a negative response to globalization*. Regional assertiveness, then, is the result of opposition to the intrusion of global economic forces, and the cultural and social effects that are perceived to accompany it. Regional autonomy demands can be part of a "backlash" against globalization, in which groups reinforce their cultural and local traditions to protest or shield themselves against this process (Barber 1996; Castells 1997; Friedman 2000; Micklethwait and Wooldridge 2000; Tossutti 2002). To the extent that such a backlash occurs in Western Europe, however, it is reflected in the programs of populist right-wing parties and rarely takes the form of territorially concentrated protests and demands for more regional powers to provide protection against globalization. As a possible exception, Beirich and Woods (2000) suggest that this mechanism can explain the continued success of the Northern League in Italy, arguing that many party supporters are industrial workers and craftsmen who fear the effects of globalization on their work and life, and support the party because it promises to protect local communities and identities.

Similarly, this mechanism is rarely mentioned in the literature on subnational implications of European integration. Keating (1998, 163) indicates that a "rejectionist regionalism" (opposing European integration) occurred in many regions in the 1970s but has now mostly disappeared. On the other hand, Hooghe (1995a, 161–63) suggests that Euro-skepticism still plays some role in Flemish nationalist circles in Belgium.

If this first mechanism operates, regional autonomy demands will increase over time, and occur in regions that are most exposed to aspects of globalization, such as international trade, foreign direct investment, American economic and cultural influence, or immigration of foreign workers.

The second mechanism indicates that *globalization and regional integration can provide new "opportunity structures"* for regional actors to further their interests against national states. This mechanism is at the heart of the idea that globalization weakens and challenges nation-states, and, thus, increases and legitimizes "bottom-up" pressures on existing state structures (Keating 1997, 1998; Williams 1997). Castells (1997, 42–50) argues that this dynamic is operating in Catalonia, where regional movements attempt to use changing global circumstances to carve out more opportunities for self-government within the Spanish state.

This mechanism is prominent in the European integration literature, summarized by the idea that developments at the European level may allow regions to "by-pass" the nation-state (Keating and Hooghe 1996; Lynch 1996, 12). As Hooghe and Marks (2001, 91) indicate, "[c]entral states have lost control over major areas of decision-making; new opportunities have been created for regional mobilization; . . . and peripheral nationalists have been confronted with a new context in which they have had to reevaluate their strategies and goals." More specifically, European integration may have led to an increase in regional mobilization and demands through the involvement of regions in the planning and implementation of regional policies (Ansell, Parsons, and Darden 1997; Hooghe 1996; Hooghe and Marks 2001; Jeffery 2001; Taylor 1995), the provision of institutional channels for direct regional participation at the European level (Hooghe 1995b; Hooghe and Marks 1996, 2001), and the provision of a new forum and rhetoric for regional movements to express cultural grievances (Keating 1995; Kellas 1991; Laitin 1997; Sharpe 1993; Wright 1998). Indeed, virtually all regionalist parties and politicians now seem to support European integration (De Winter and Cachafeiro 2002). It is worth noting, however, that this process is not an unequivocally positive good for them. If a region has limited powers, European integration can be one of the instruments to improve this. If, however, a region has considerable powers, then European integration and the development of state-like structures at the European level may erode these powers. This idea of European integration as a double-edged sword for regions deserves more attention.

This logic predicts a rise in regional assertiveness over time. Thus, the acceleration of the economic and institutional dimensions of European integration since the mid-1980s (after the Single European Act and the Maastricht treaty) should have led to a rise in regional assertiveness. As a corollary synchronic hypothesis, regions already possessing the institutional capacity to utilize these opportunities are most likely to voice autonomy demands (Marks et al. 1996).

The third mechanism points to a more indirect effect of globalization and European integration. In a world of national economies and tariff barriers, efficiency considerations favor the existence of large states; however, *under conditions of increased economic integration, smaller geographical units become more viable, and threats of secession more credible.* Even regional politicians and movements not interested in independence may then make secessionist claims to secure concessions from the center. This mechanism plays a prominent role in a developing political economy literature on secession and (dis)integration of states (Alesina and Spolaore 1997; Alesina, Spolaore, and Wacziarg 2000; Bolton and Roland 1997; Fearon and Van Houten 2002; Hiscox, chapter 3). Alesina, Spolaore, and Wacziarg (2000) present the fact that the number of states in the international system correlates with international trade openness as evidence for the operation of this mechanism.

The literature on European integration hints at this mechanism when it states that European integration has reduced the importance of nation-states and thus makes it easier to pursue autonomist or secessionist aspirations. For example, Keating (1998, 163) indicates that "minority nationalist movements note that European integration has reduced the cost of national independence, and propose simply to join the list of member states," while De Winter (1998, 221) notes that "European integration has made the calls for independence of ethnoregionalist parties more realistic." On the whole, however, this mechanism has not been explored in much detail in the literature on European integration. As an exception, Dardanelli (2001) shows that European integration was a relevant factor in the increase in support for devolution of powers to Scotland between the 1979 and 1997 referenda. European integration took away the fear of the costs of Scottish independence, which was seen by many voters as the likely long-term consequence of devolution.

In short, this mechanism predicts that regional assertiveness will be more frequent and stronger if economic integration increases.

The final mechanism specifies that *regional politicians may demand more competencies to be able to adequately respond to new imperatives in an integrated economy*. Globalization and regional integration create an economic environment in which local and regional factors become increasingly important for economic success, and national policies can provide less insurance to negatively affected territories. As a result, regional political actors have an incentive to obtain more policy instruments to shape economic and industrial policies. In principle, all regions face these incentives. Economic theory indicates that reducing trade barriers and increasing trade flows will, in the long term, lead to greater specialization and benefit all regions (Rogowski, chapter 10). Moreover, if national governments can provide less protection against global economic forces, then all regional politicians will have few options left other than trying to take more matters in their own hands. This reasoning predicts an overall rise in regional autonomy demands. This logic is flawed, however. First, globalization may not reduce the capacity of states to provide welfare policies (Garrett 1998a). Second, politics evolves around short-term considerations, and only already internationally competitive regional economies will initially flourish in a more integrated economy. Politicians in less competitive regions will face incentives to avoid responsibility for potentially disappointing short-term economic results, and thus refrain from demanding more powers from the national level. Therefore, this mechanism primarily predicts that the most economically competitive regions will be the most assertive.

The increased importance of local factors in a global economy has received considerable attention in the literature on business economics and economic geography. Michael Porter's influential study points to the importance of a strong "home base" for industrial performance in the international economy: "[t]he more competition becomes global, ironically, the more important the home base becomes" (Porter 1998, 614). He indicates that these principles also apply to regional economies

(1998, 158). Other authors have elaborated on these ideas (Amin and Thrift 1994; Hilpert 1991; Ohmae 1995; Scott 1998; Storper 1997). Industries competing in a global economy, so the argument goes, require highly flexible inputs and labor skills. Small and medium-sized companies embedded in regional economic networks and complemented by regionally designed stimulation policies and investments in infrastructure are in the best position to be successful. This provides incentives for regional politicians to demand more control over policy instruments.[3] Most of this literature ignores such political implications, although Scott (1998, 148) indicates that, "a collective consciousness of local identity and a will to act seem clearly to be on the rise in regional communities throughout the more developed parts of the worlds." Some political scientists are more explicit about this, however, and argue that this process leads to an increase in subnational demands for certain competencies (Keating 2001; Scharpf 1994). Deeg (1996) shows that globalization has led to increased competition between German regions, and spurred demands for more regional control over economic and industrial policies, especially among the richer regions.

The European integration literature also contains variations of this argument (Färber 1996; Keating 1995; Kurzer 1997). Most concretely, European regulation has reduced the ability of national states to protect and support regional economies. As Färber (1996, 32) argues, "European law prohibits national, regional, and local governments from intervening by special subsidies . . . or quantitative trade restrictions and measures with equal effects." As a result, "European regions . . . need autonomous competencies and instruments to manage their economic problems" (Färber 1996, 35). Kurzer (1997) argues that European integration has led to an increase in territorial tensions in Belgium, as a result of stronger economic competition between regions for investments.

This section has discussed various possible mechanisms linking globalization and European integration to regional autonomy demands, and derived testable hypotheses for these mechanisms. Some of these hypotheses address developments over time, predicting a rise in regional assertiveness with increasing economic integration and institutionalization of a European polity. Other hypotheses focus on variation across regions. These predict that regional autonomy demands are most likely in regions most exposed to aspects of globalization such as international trade, foreign direct investment, American economic influence, or inter-

---

[3] Anecdotal evidence from Belgium supports this. The Flemish employers organization (VEV) appeals to exactly this logic (with references to the arguments by Porter, Ohmae, and others) to demand more fiscal and economic instruments for the region (interview with Jan Van Doren, VEV, Antwerp, 20 October 1998).

national migration, and in the most economically competitive regions. The second part of this paper takes a first cut at evaluating these hypotheses.

Alternative Hypotheses

Globalization is, of course, not the only possible determinant of regional autonomy demands. In fact, several cultural, economic, and political factors have been hypothesized to influence the emergence and strength of such demands. This section provides a brief overview of these factors.

Cultural factors (distinctive linguistic, ethnic, or religious regional characteristics) play a prominent role in many explanations of regional autonomy demands. Given the frequent cultural appeals by regional protagonists and the remarkable resilience of culturally distinct regions, this is not surprising. Some authors claim that ethnic and cultural ties override other political ties, and are sufficient to explain the occurrence of regional movements (e.g., Connor 1994; Esman 1977a; Smith 1995). While most analysts disagree with this essentialist view, a number of other explanations consider cultural differences at least necessary for regional autonomy demands. That is, only regions with "ethnic potential" (Gourevitch 1979) are presumed to be assertive.

Variation in assertiveness between regions with ethnic potential may depend on *economic* conditions. On the one hand, some scholars argue that *relatively poor* regions are most likely to give rise to regional assertiveness. For example, Hechter (1975) claims that secessionism occurs if a "cultural division of labor" between a disadvantaged and culturally distinct peripheral region and the center, resulting from processes of industrialization and modernization, serves to mobilize regional protest. Rokkan and Urwin (1983) and Horowitz (1985), albeit in different contexts, concur. On the other hand, and more frequently, others argue that *relatively rich* regions are most likely to exhibit regional assertiveness. Gourevitch (1979) hypothesizes that autonomy demands will develop in regions that are economically strong, but lack political power. Several other analyses make similar claims (e.g., Bookman 1992; Harvie 1994; Nairn 1977). Thus, the existing literature indicates two opposing hypotheses on the role of economic factors.

A few contributions have pointed to *political* factors as determinants of regional assertiveness.[4] For example, Newman (1996) argues that the development of regional policies in the 1960s and 1970s spurred minor-

---

[4] References to "politics" are common in the literature on regionalism. However, this is usually treated as synonymous with "contingent" or "nonpredictable" (see, for example, Keating [1998]). Attempts to explicitly theorize about political factors are rare (van Houten 2000).

ity nationalism in a number of European countries (cf. Keating 1988), while differences in the nature of democratic decision-making processes between countries (cf. Meadwell 1991) are also important. These arguments effectively point to the importance of *country-specific* factors in explaining variation in regional assertiveness.

All arguments discussed so far focus primarily on the variation between assertive and nonassertive regions (that is, on whether autonomy demands occur at all). It is assumed that regional autonomy demands will always be as strong as possible, subject only to "external" constraints, such as the strength of the center or limits to popular identification with regional interests.

Considerable variation in demands exists, however, in assertive regions with similar economic and cultural characteristics. To explain this variation, I have formulated a distinctly political explanation, which focuses on the impact of *regional party systems* (van Houten 2000). Regional politicians demanding increases in regional autonomy attempt to introduce or maintain a territorial cleavage in politics. That is, they attempt to obtain "inclusive" voter support (support that cuts across other cleavages) by appealing to regional interests, defined in opposition to the center. Demands for more fiscal and social welfare powers (demands that significantly challenge the existing organization of the state), which, if granted, would force regional politicians to take positions on socio-economic matters, can undermine such an electoral strategy. The reason is that such demands will make other, intraregional cleavages more salient again. The impact of this dilemma is conditional on the nature of party competition in a region. If a regional politician competes against nationally organized parties, incentives to mobilize heterogeneous and inclusive voter support are large, and demands for tax powers consequently less likely. On the other hand, if a regional politician competes mostly against regionally organized parties, such incentives are smaller (a claim to be the primary representative of the region is less persuasive in this situation). A territorial cleavage has now been institutionalized in the political system, however, increasing its salience for the population and framing many issues. Making strong demands will then become a necessity for most parties in order to be seen as credible political forces in the region. Thus, demands are hypothesized to be strongest if there are several regionally organized parties, even if most of them are not traditionally "regionalist."

This brief review provides several alternative hypotheses that need to be included in order to evaluate the relative explanatory power of the globalization arguments. It should be noted that it may be difficult to empirically distinguish globalization effects from other economic effects. Relatively rich or poor regions may experience political mobilization for domestic reasons (e.g., to decrease or increase transfers to other regions), or as a result of processes of globalization (e.g., to take advantage of its strength in the international economy, or to protest against further economic marginalization). The second part of the chapter attempts to make such distinctions.

GLOBALIZATION AND A GENERAL RISE
IN REGIONAL AUTONOMY DEMANDS

At the heart of the arguments about the role of globalization and European integration is the claim that they have induced a rise in regionalist activity in recent decades. The consensus in recent writings on Western European regionalism is indeed that regional autonomy movements and demands have become more frequent. This alleged "rise of regional Europe" (Harvie 1994) has, as far as I know, not been subjected to comprehensive empirical tests, however. In this section, I question this conventional wisdom, although more definitive answers will have to await further research. This is not to deny that some changes have taken place in the nature of regional autonomy demands in recent decades, and that globalization and European integration have played a part in this. I argue, however, that these developments have mostly been confined to already assertive regions.[5]

A general rise in regionalist activity in recent decades cannot be taken for granted as a self-evident fact. Subnational regionalism is by no means a new phenomenon. As Keating (1998, 11) notes, "Regions and regionalism have a long history in Europe. Regions predated the rise of nation-states and helped shape the emergence of the state system. They constituted an obstacle to centralized state and nation building over centuries, and remained as an element in the politics of states." Studies by Stein Rokkan and his collaborators on the role of territorial identities and cleavages in processes of state formation in Western Europe make clear that regional protests and autonomy demands have always been a prominent feature of Western European politics, although with varying strength and frequency (Rokkan and Urwin 1982, 1983).

In the immediate decades after World War II, regionalism was mostly declining, as the expansion of the welfare state helped to consolidate nation-states. In the 1960s and 1970s, a revival of regionalism occurred, which has been attributed to the reemergence of cultural and ethnic grievances (Esman 1977b) and the further extension of the welfare state (Keating 1988; Newman 1996). The logic of the latter claim is

---

[5] Sorens (2002a, b) reaches a similar conclusion. He finds that globalization cannot account for cross-sectional variation in secessionist parties, but has induced a rise in support for already existing parties.

that central governments, through their territorial policies and decentralization of some economic policies, provided regional movements with policies and institutions around which to mobilize. This wave of regionalism declined again in the 1980s, but did not disappear. This fluctuation of the emergence and success of regionalist movements is a reminder that the evolution of regionalism in the postwar period has not been a linear process. Comparative analyses of the electoral results of regionalist parties confirm the existence of large variations across time and place in the success of these parties (De Winter 1998; Gordin 2001).

Neither of the attributed causes of the rise of regionalism in the 1960s and 1970s is directly related to globalization or European integration. Therefore, if there is a rise in regionalism induced by these processes, it must be a more recent phenomenon. The most obvious indicator of a possibly new regionalist dynamic is the emergence of demands for state restructuring in formerly non-assertive regions. Examples are several Northern Italian regions, Rhône-Alpes in France, and Baden-Württemberg in Germany (Harvie 1994). The most salient instance of a new regionalist movement is the Northern League in Italy. This party originated as a confederation of separate regional parties, and became prominent in Italian politics in the early 1990s. Globalization and European integration played some role in the emergence and rise of this party. European and global economic developments have reduced the reliance of regions on the centralized Italian state (Golden 2001), and the Northern League explicitly supports European integration to emphasize this point. The Northern Italian regions are among the richest and most competitive regions in the global and European economy, and businesses and politicians would like to exploit this. Furthermore, some of the support for the Northern League seems to come from workers and craftsmen who fear the consequences of globalization and look to this party to protect local culture and practices (Beirich and Woods 2000). Thus, in this case the link between economic integration and regional autonomy demands is a complex combination of the first, third, and fourth mechanisms discussed above.

Usually neglected, however, is the fact that there are also several regions which have hosted regional autonomy movements in the postwar period, but are now relatively nonassertive (Le Galès 1998, 260). Examples are Sicily and South Tyrol in Italy (Finkelstein 1998; Katzenstein 1977), and regions such as Brittany and Alsace in France (Brustein 1988). It depends on the balance between these two opposing developments whether it is possible to declare a "rise of regional Europe." Pending more detailed research, my tentative conclusion is that there has been at most a very moderate increase in manifestations of regional assertiveness in Western Europe. This calls into question some of the arguments about the impact of globalization and European integration on political separatism.

But what about the *nature* of autonomy demands? Has this changed in recent decades, possibly as a result of globalization? Keating (1998, 2001) strongly argues along these lines, and states that " the European state is undergoing profound changes, its authority and powers challenged by continental integration, the advance of the market and a panoply of effects subsumed under the term globalization," which has "encouraged a new regionalism, defined not merely in relation to the state but also in relation to the market and the continental regime" (1998, ix). Similarly, Harvie (1994) points to the emergence of a "bourgeois regionalism," in which economic motives dominate. Empirical research on regions such as Catalonia and Scotland supports these assertions.[6]

A central tenet of mainstream Catalan nationalism is the combination of a desire for autonomy and a lack of enthusiasm for independence. This has often created difficulties for the nationalist movement in its dealings with the Spanish state (Keating 2001, 158). In recent years, it has increasingly embraced global and European developments to get around these difficulties. For Catalan nationalists, European integration "provides a series of opportunities for policy influence, coalition-forming and building transnational networks," and "gives credibility to Catalan arguments that sovereignty can be divided and shared" (Keating 2001, 197).[7] Catalan nationalism now fully endorses free trade and European integration. Although much of its strive for autonomy still concerns bilateral relations with the Spanish state, this increasingly outward-looking perspective has transformed the Catalan nationalist movement. Here, globalization and European integration are linked to (changes in) autonomy demands through the second and third mechanisms identified earlier.

Nationalism in Scotland has developed along similar lines. The Scottish National Party was opposed to European integration and free trade in the 1970s, but has now completely reversed its position, and aims for "independence in Europe" (Keating 2001; Lynch 1996). The operating mechanisms linking economic integration to autonomy demands are the same as in Catalonia. Scottish political actors increasingly try to exploit new opportunities at the supranational level, and support for devolution and autonomy has increased because European integration may have reduced the anxiety among large parts of the population about the possible consequences of devolution and independence (Dardanelli 2001).

---

[6] See Lynch (1996) as an example of similar research on several other regions with nationalist movements.

[7] See Roller (1999) and Nagel (2001) for an overview of Catalonia's activities in this respect.

These examples suggest that globalization and European integration have indeed changed and reinforced autonomy demands in certain regions (De Winter and Cachafeiro 2002). Separatism plays a diminishing role, and is replaced by concerns among regionally assertive politicians about the competitiveness of regional economies in the European or global economy. Most examples used in this line of research come, however, from regions with a long history of regionalism (such as Catalonia, Scotland, and Flanders), which are not representative of most European regions (Tomaney 2000). There is no evidence that these developments constitute a general and uniform trend. Thus, sweeping claims about a general rise in regional assertiveness in Western Europe need to be qualified.

GLOBALIZATION AND CONTEMPORARY VARIATION IN REGIONAL AUTONOMY DEMANDS

As indicated earlier, the arguments about the links between economic integration and regional autonomy demands suggest several hypotheses about expected variation across regions. This section tests these hypotheses on a sample of eighty-three regions in six Western European countries. This analysis is distinctive because of its unit of analysis (regions) and its explicit focus on regional *demands* for autonomy. Most existing evaluations of theories of separatism and decentralization use indicators based on *outcomes* and for countries (see, for example, Garrett and Rodden, chapter 4; Hiscox, chapter 3; Tossutti 2002). These theories focus on bottom-up pressures for changes in the territorial structure, however, and do not address the conditions under which these demands will result in actual policy and constitutional changes (Garrett and Rodden, chapter 4). Furthermore, aggregate indicators for countries can mask important variation and developments at the subnational level. Therefore, a focus on demands from subnational political actors provides a more direct evaluation of the arguments discussed in the first part of this chapter. Enough data exist for Western European regions to make a preliminary evaluation possible. In this section, I will describe the data and indicators, and present the main results of the analysis. Thereafter, I discuss the implications of these results for the claims about a link between economic integration and demands for changes in governance structures.

Data and Coding

The dataset consists of regions in six Western European countries: Belgium, France, Germany, Italy, Spain, and the United Kingdom.[8] These countries are all member states of the European Union, and (with the

[8] For a more detailed discussion and analysis of the dataset, see van Houten (2001).

exception of the English regions in the United Kingdom) have regions with democratically elected legislatures. Moreover, all have experienced regionalist activity of some form in the postwar period, indicating that the territorial structure of the state has more than just administrative significance. A *region* is defined as the administrative level immediately below the national state. Excluding the regions in which the country capitals are located (the "centers"), this gives a total of eighty-three regions. I will first describe the indicator for regional autonomy demands (the dependent variable), and then discuss the measures used to evaluate the globalization and alternative hypotheses.

REGIONAL AUTONOMY DEMANDS

For a useful analysis of variation in regional assertiveness, it is necessary to distinguish between different types of demands. I distinguish here between demands for *spending powers* (autonomy to make expenditure decisions) and demands for *taxing powers* (autonomy to make both expenditure and revenue decisions) (van Houten 2000). Demands for taxing powers constitute a significant challenge to existing state structures, while demands for spending powers typically do not. Thus, the underlying criterion for coding demands is the extent to which they constitute a challenge to the existing organization of a state. If regional politicians or parties with some political credibility and electoral support have advocated (in the 1990s) granting more powers and autonomy to the region, I ask the following questions:

- Who makes the demands — regional politicians affiliated with parties that participate in the regional government ("governing" politicians), or politicians from parties in the regional opposition ("oppositional" politicians)?
- Do the demands include demands for taxing powers, or are they restricted to demands for spending powers?

Demands made by governing politicians are a greater challenge than demands by oppositional politicians. Governing politicians have more political responsibilities and accountability, so their demands are more meaningful. The answers to these questions provide an indicator of regional assertiveness with the following values:

- HIGH: Governing politicians demand taxing powers.
- MEDIUM: Oppositional politicians demand taxing powers, or governing politicians demand spending powers.
- LOW: Oppositional politicians demand spending powers.
- NONE: No autonomy demands.

The MEDIUM category groups together two different scenarios, because it is ambiguous which constitutes a larger challenge to a state. In the

TABLE 5.1
Regions with Various Levels of Regional Assertiveness

Low	Medium	High
Aquitane (F)	Wallonia (B)	Flanders (B)
Brittany (F)	Alsace (F)	Basque Country (S)
Languedoc-Rousillon (F)	Corsica (F)	Northern Ireland (UK)
Provence-Alpes-Côte d'Azur (F)	Rhône-Alpes (F)	Scotland (UK)
North Rhine-Westphalia (G)	Baden-Württemberg (G)	
Sardinia (I)	Bavaria (G)	
Tuscany (I)	Hessen (G)	
Balearic Islands (S)	Emilia-Romagna (I)	
Canary Islands (S)	Friuli-Venezia Giulia (I)	
Valencia (S)	Liguria (I)	
North-West (UK)	Lombardy (I)	
	Piedmont (I)	
	Trentino-Alto Adige (I)	
	Val d'Aosta (I)	
	Veneto (I)	
	Catalonia (S)	
	Galicia (S)	
	Navarre (S)	
	Northern (UK)	
	Wales (UK)	

Total number of regions in sample: 83 (Belgium: 2; France: 21; Germany: 15; Italy: 19; Spain: 16; United Kingdom: 10).

case of differences between regional parties or politicians, I code for the *maximum* level of assertiveness in the region. Table 5.1 lists the regions with LOW, MEDIUM, and HIGH levels of assertiveness (the other forty-eight regions are not assertive).

INDICATORS FOR THE GLOBALIZATION HYPOTHESES

A direct indicator for a region's exposure to the international economy would be the volume of foreign direct investment (FDI). "Since," however, "data on FDI are usually collected at a national level, analysis of the regional incidence of investment is . . . not possible" (European Commission 1999, 116). A less direct, but straightforward and frequently used, measure of exposure to globalization is the volume of foreign trade (Garrett and Rodden, Chapter 4; Verdier and Breen 2001). Thus, a first "globalization variable" is the volume of exports and imports of a region, measured as percentage of regional GDP.[9] Although

[9] Sources: statistical agencies of Germany (www.statistik-bund.de), Italy (www.istat.it),

correlated to other economic indicators such as relative GDP per capita (a correlation coefficient of 0.46) and regional GDP (0.27), the variable is sufficiently distinct to allow for a test of the impact of globalization on autonomy demands, independent of other economic factors. Other publicly salient elements of globalization are the "Americanization" of economy and society, and increases in migration flows. This analysis does not include indicators of links between regions and the American economy, but this is an area worth exploring in future studies. As a proxy for migration flows, I use the number of foreign citizens in a region (as percentage of the regional population).[10]

One of the hypotheses suggests that, under conditions of globalization, regions with competitive economies will exhibit regional assertiveness vis-à-vis national states. *Competitiveness* is a multifaceted concept, which is hard to quantify in a single indicator (European Commission 1999; Porter 1998); however, a crucial element of economic competitiveness is productivity (Porter 1998). I include several simple measures of the productivity of a regional economy: gross value added (GVA) per capita, and absolute and relative (compared to the average of the whole sample) GVA per employed person (cf. Pinelli et al. 1998).[11] These three measures are strongly correlated, and GVA per employed person is used in the analysis. This measure is not too strongly correlated with relative regional GDP per capita (0.53) and regional GDP (0.44), and can be used as a separate variable.

OTHER INDEPENDENT VARIABLES

Several other variables are included to test and control for alternative explanations of autonomy demands. First, the main *cultural* variable is the presence or absence of a (historical) regional language that differs from the language spoken at the center; the more distinct the two languages (based on linguistic criteria), the larger the cultural difference is coded to be (Laitin 2000, 148–49). This indicator only partially captures cultural or ethnic differences, but its main advantage is that, unlike many existing measures, it is relatively independent of the outcome

---

United Kingdom (www.statistics.gov.uk), and Basque Country (www.eustat.es); the French Ministry of Foreign Trade (www.commerce-exterieur.gouv.fr); and the Belgian National Bank (www.nbb.be). The data are for the most recent available year (between 1995 and 1999).

[10] Source: Eurostat's CRONOS database.

[11] Sources: Eurostat (1996), Eurostat's REGIO database (not available for the former East German regions). These measures are problematic in several ways. First, they are only rough measures of economic competitiveness. Second, the quality of some of the data is suspect. In particular, the values of the indicators for the United Kingdom are implausibly low, although results of the analysis do not significantly change if the United Kingdom regions are left out. Consequently, the results of this part of the analysis are very tentative.

to be explained (regionalist and secessionist activity) (Fearon and van Houten 2002).

Second, I include three *economic* variables, which previous work has shown to be significant determinants of regional assertiveness (Fearon and van Houten 2002; van Houten 2001): regional GDP per capita relative to the national average, total regional GDP, and overall GDP of the country.[12] In addition, I test for a possible effect of direct European subsidies to a region.

Third, an indicator for the configuration of regional party systems, which reflects the electoral importance of regional and national parties, is included as the main *political* variable. A *regional party* is defined as a party that nominates candidates for elections in a strict subset of the regions of a state (typically just one), and explicitly, albeit not necessarily primarily, refers to this subset.[13] This includes parties such as SNP in Scotland, PNV in Basque Country, CSU in Bavaria, CVP or VLD in Flanders, and the Northern League in several Northern Italian regions. It excludes parties that aim to be national but occasionally fail to run candidates in a particular district or region. Based on a sample of election results and secondary sources (Dupoirier 1998; Fitzmaurice 1996; Hartmann 1997; Hearl, Budge, and Pearson 1996), I code regional party systems as follows:

1. Only national parties: nationally organized parties generally receive more than 95 percent of the regional vote in elections.
2. National parties dominate regional parties: nationally organized parties receive the majority of regional votes (between 50 and 95 percent) in elections, regionally organized parties the minority (5–50 percent).
3. Regional parties dominate national parties: regionally organized parties receive the majority (50–95 percent) of votes, nationally organized parties the minority (5–50 percent).
4. Only regional parties: regionally organized parties receive more than 95 percent of regional votes.

This coding scheme is independent of the *number* of regional parties in the party system. Empirically, however, the (relatively few) cases in category 4 tend to consist of a large number of such parties, distinguished by their position on nonterritorial issues. On the other hand, the cases in category 3 (and some of those in category 2) tend to have dominant regional parties. Moreover, there is not a perfect correspondence between regional assertiveness and regional party systems. Some

---

[12] Sources: Eurostat (1996), Eurostat's REGIO database. These data are for 1995.

[13] Thus, a party does not need to consider itself "regionalist" to be coded as regional. It does, however, need to be self-consciously organized as "non-national."

cases of high assertiveness (e.g., Basque Country) do not entirely consist of regional parties, while a number of regions (e.g., Andalucia) have regional parties that do not make autonomy demands. Finally, country dummies are included to control for any remaining country-specific factors, and to provide a preliminary test of some of the general political explanations.

Findings

Table 5.2 presents the main results of the statistical analysis. These are ordered probit estimates, with levels of regional assertiveness as dependent variable. Models (1), (2), and (3) show the results directly relevant for the globalization hypotheses. Model (4) includes only the variables that were consistently significant in various model specifications; this model is used to illustrate the substantial effects of some of these variables. Model (5) includes only regions with *some* level of assertiveness in order to analyze cross-regional variation in specific demands.

These analyses indicate that globalization has no direct impact on variation in regional assertiveness. Model (1) shows that the volume of imports and exports is not significantly correlated to levels of regional assertiveness, when regional and country GDP and relative GDP per capita are included, and language differences and the configuration of the regional party systems are controlled for. Similarly, model (2) indicates that the percentage of foreigners in a region is not significantly related to regional autonomy demands. Thus, this sample provides no direct support for the hypothesis that those regions most exposed to globalization will be the most assertive.

The data on productivity show a similar, albeit slightly more nuanced, picture. The indicators for regional competitiveness come close to conventional levels of significance in some model specifications. Model (3) in table 5.2 shows, however, that gross value added per worker is not statistically significant if certain other variables are included. Nonetheless, this is an area in which further research (with more extensive productivity data, and better indicators of regional competitiveness) will be fruitful.

In contrast, the findings provide support for several of the other hypotheses. First, the analysis indicates that culturally distinct regions are more likely to be assertive. The variable indicating the presence of a distinct regional language is consistently significant in models (1)–(4). To get a sense of the effect of this variable, consider the (hypothetical) example of a region with a relative GDP of 94 percent, a GDP of about 26 billion ECU in a country with a GDP of 800 billion ECU, and regional parties obtaining a minority of votes in elections. Without a dis-

TABLE 5.2
Ordered Probit Estimates for Levels of Regional Assertiveness

Variables	Coefficients (standard errors)				
	(1)	(2)	(3)	(4)	(5)
Language difference	2.76* (0.78)	2.70* (0.78)	2.34* (0.78)	2.59* (0.77)	1.22 (0.90)
Relative GDP per capita	0.020* (0.0075)	0.014 (0.0074)	0.020* (0.0089)	0.017* (0.0070)	0.012 (0.012)
Log of regional GDP (mECU)	0.70* (0.20)	0.57* (0.18)	0.60* (0.18)	0.59* (0.18)	0.24 (0.23)
Country GDP (billion ECU)	−0.0012* (0.00040)	−0.0012* (0.00051)	−0.00018 (0.00052)	−0.00081* (0.00039)	0.00023 (0.00064)
Regional party system	0.99* (0.25)	0.90* (0.26)	1.13* (0.29)	0.94* (0.25)	1.00* (0.35)
Exports and imports (% of GDP)	−0.012 (0.0086)				
Foreigners (% of population)		0.077 (0.058)			
Gross value added per employee			−0.037 (0.025)		
Threshold 1	10.19 (2.13)	8.41 (2.02)	9.00 (1.99)	9.11 (1.94)	5.75 (2.68)
Threshold 2	10.85 (2.16)	9.06 (2.05)	9.66 (2.02)	9.75 (1.97)	8.31 (2.93)
Threshold 3	13.21 (2.35)	11.49 (2.27)	12.22 (2.28)	12.16 (2.20)	
N	83	83	78	83	35
Log likelihood	−55.9	−56.0	−55.1	−56.8	−23.6
Chi^2	66.3	66.3	62.3	64.5	18.1

Models (1)–(4): 4 levels of assertiveness (none, low, medium, high). Model (5): 3 levels of assertiveness (low, medium, high).
*$p \leq .05$.

tinctive regional language, the predicted likelihood of no assertiveness, a low level of assertiveness and a medium level of assertiveness (according to model [4] in table 5.2) is respectively 43 percent, 25 percent, and 32 percent. If this region were to have a highly distinctive language, these odds are 11 percent, 17 percent, and 68 percent. Second, various economic factors have an impact on the likelihood of regional autonomy demands. Relatively rich regions (regions with a high relative GDP per capita) are more likely to be assertive than relatively poor regions. Moreover, regional GDP is positively related to levels of assertiveness, while country GDP is negatively correlated to autonomy demands. Larger regions have better prospects to deliver public goods to the population, which makes claims for autonomy or independence more credible. Similarly, opportunity costs of such claims are smaller if the region is part of a relatively small or poor country. Thus, both variables are indicators of regional bargaining power vis-à-vis the center (Fearon and van Houten 2002). Third, none of the country dummies were significant, indicating there are no remaining country-specific factors that have a systematic impact on levels of regional assertiveness. Similarly, the amount of European subsidies received by a region was not significant, so direct financial benefits from European integration are not systematically related to levels of assertiveness.

Finally, the hypothesis about the role of party competition finds support in this analysis. After controlling for cultural and economic variables, the composition of the regional party systems still has a discernible impact on regional assertiveness. The party variable is consistently statistically significant in models (1)–(4). Importantly, and consistent with the argument presented in the previous section, model (5) in table 5.2 shows that this is the only variable that can account for variation among assertive regions. None of the cultural or economic variables can help us explain variation in the *type* of autonomy demands. Table 5.3 illustrates the effect of the party variable. Even for a region with relatively "favorable" conditions for strong autonomy demands (a relative GDP per capita of 110 percent, a GDP of about 60 billion ECU in a country with a GDP of 650 billion ECU, and a highly distinctive regional language), it depends on the configuration of the regional party system whether the most likely level of assertiveness is medium or high.

Discussion

This analysis of regional autonomy demands in six Western European countries finds no support for the idea that globalization is a *direct* determinant of these demands. Neither the indicators for regional exposure to globalization (import and export volume and number of foreign citizens) nor the measure of "fitness" to compete in the international economy (productivity of the regional economy) have a clearly significant impact on regional autonomy demands, once other factors are controlled for.

Although it raises serious doubts about many existing arguments suggesting a link between globalization and regional autonomy demands,

TABLE 5.3
Party Competition and Predicted Levels of Assertiveness (Percentages)

Level of Assertiveness	Regional Party Competition			
	(1)	(2)	(3)	(4)
None	17	3	0	0
Low	21	8	1	0
Medium	60	77	58	24
High	2	12	41	76

Based on model (4) in table 5.2; language difference: high; regional income per capita: 110; log(regional GDP): 11; country GDP: 650.

we cannot conclusively infer the absence of such a link from this analysis. First, the statistical analysis focuses only on cross-regional variation in autonomy demands. As argued earlier, it is plausible that globalization and European integration have changed the nature, if perhaps not the frequency, of autonomy demands over time. Since, however, some of the proposed mechanisms by which economic integration can affect autonomy demands imply an expected relation between globalization and cross-regional variation in demands, the statistical analysis at least calls into question the validity of these mechanisms. More research, especially with more fine-grained globalization indicators, is necessary to further evaluate the relative importance of the various mechanisms. This chapter has formulated an agenda for such research by identifying the possible mechanisms linking globalization and autonomy demands, and indicating how these can be tested.

Second, globalization and European integration may have other *indirect* effects on autonomy demands. Hiscox (chapter 3) argues persuasively that globalization can affect regional income and inter- and intraregional income distributions. These changes, in turn, may increase (or decrease) subnational pressures for changes in governance structures. The data used in this chapter cannot directly test these arguments, but do raise doubts about their applicability to Western Europe. The proxy used by Hiscox for interregional income distributions, the relative importance of primary commodity exports (see table 3.4, chapter 3), is only very weakly correlated with the actual data on income differentials between regions in my sample. In the postindustrial societies of Western Europe, it is perhaps unlikely that the globalization effects emphasized by Hiscox are very relevant, and his arguments are more convincing for countries with a higher dependence on agriculture and natural resources. Nevertheless, Hiscox's assertion, discussed in more detail by Garrett and Rodden (chapter 4), that globalization may have increased the stakes in redistributive conflicts between regions does find some resonance in Western European cases. In particular, the increase in demands for more competencies and less interregional financial solidarity by regions in Northern Italy and Southern Germany suggest the plausibility of this claim. Redistributive conflicts are mediated by political processes and institutions, however. To put it simply, such conflicts are only politicized when political actors decide to do so (Fearon and van Houten 2002). We need to complement economic arguments with a political theory to better understand this indirect effect of globalization (Garrett and Rodden, chapter 4; Kahler and Lake, chapter 1). Moreover, it is worth emphasizing that, as Garrett and Rodden show, redistributive conflicts between regions do not always lead to decentralization. Equally important is that demands arising from such conflicts can vary significantly in their nature (from demands only for spending powers to demands for far-reaching fiscal autonomy), with implications for pressures on existing governance structures. Again, we need a political theory to comprehend these implications.

Indeed, the most important conclusion of this chapter's analysis is that any possible influence of globalization on autonomy demands is mediated by political factors. As with other arguments linking economic factors to regional autonomy demands, the globalization arguments fail to recognize this, and suffer from a functionalist bias (Kahler and Lake, chapter 1; Kohler-Koch 1996). They assume that economic imperatives will inevitably give rise to political action and consequences. This chapter has shown that this is misguided. More positively, the demonstrated impact of party competition on levels of assertiveness indicates a particular mechanism through which economic and cultural factors are filtered.

Elsewhere, I provide further evidence for these claims through detailed case studies (van Houten 2000). In Flanders, arguably the most assertive region in contemporary Western Europe, the nature of party competition exacerbated autonomy demands in the 1990s. In an attempt to deal with particular cultural conflicts in Belgium in the late 1960s and early 1970s, Belgian national parties split into regional parties. Initially, this appeased the conflicts, and most involved politicians had no intentions of escalating autonomy demands. This was precisely what happened in the 1990s, however, when new economic and social issues appeared on the political agenda. Many political issues (such as industrial policy, social welfare, and reforms of the criminal justice system) are now discussed in territorial terms, and virtually all political parties demand regional fiscal autonomy and more control over economic and social policies. Although the population is ambivalent about these developments, the perceived competition with strongly regionalist parties for marginal voters, and the inability (as a result of the structure of the party system) to appeal to voters in other regions has induced this behavior on the part of all mainstream parties. As a result, subnational pressures have made the Belgian state increasingly fragile.

On the other hand, in Catalonia, a region with a long history of regionalism and cultural and economic conditions similar to those of Flanders, regional politicians long refrained from making strong demands for taxing powers. One of the reasons for this was the close competition between regional and national parties in the region, which forces the main regional parties to appeal to a broad spectrum of voters. Demands for fiscal autonomy are likely to undermine this strategy, and have been mostly avoided. As a result, the Spanish state is under significantly less pressure than the Belgian state. Similarly, the nature of party competition is an important determinant of the type of demands made by the Bavarian government for reforms of the German federal system, making it unlikely that this government will strongly push for an increase in regional fiscal autonomy in Germany.

The arguments and findings on the crucial role of party politics resonate with other analyses of the impact of globalization (e.g., Boix 1998; Garrett 1998a), and are consistent with the actor-centered framework laid out by Kahler and Lake (chapter 1).[14] Globalization creates pressures and incentives for political actors to change governance structures, but electoral and party competition are important intervening factors, which will either reinforce or dampen autonomy demands. Thus, party systems are one of the institutions to be considered in this general framework.

But what explains the configuration of regional party systems in a region? Are these perhaps endogenous to economic and cultural conditions, including globalization? There is no doubt that cultural and economic factors are relevant determinants of regional party systems, but they can only account for a limited amount of the observed variation (Roller and van Houten 2002).[15] Moreover, while political parties in Western Europe certainly face challenges and are forced to adapt to new circumstances (Donovan and Broughton 1999; Pennings and Lane 1998), party systems have proven to be remarkably resistant to fundamental changes (Lipset and Rokkan 1967; Mair 1997). There are no strong reasons to believe that this is changing. At certain "critical junctures" major changes occur, as happened in Belgium in the late 1960s, but

[14] In contrast to Garrett and Boix, however, I focus on the role of the organizational structure of parties rather than party ideology.

[15] An analysis of the dataset with regional party system as dependent variable reveals that language difference and regional share of GDP (regional GDP divided by country GDP) are statistically significant variables, but leave much variation to be explained. The various globalization indicators are not statistically significant.

these become institutionalized and resist further changes. While party systems have become more complex in recent years, this has not led to major changes in the territorial organization and focus of the main parties. Therefore, it is reasonable to take these party structures as given, and analyze (as this chapter did) how they mediate or neutralize globalization effects.

Summary

This volume shows that the impact of globalization on governance structures is heavily contested, and that much detailed empirical research is needed before more general conclusions can be reached. The last three chapters, although not reaching a clear consensus in their conclusions, make important progress in understanding the effects of globalization on decentralization. This chapter has focused on a specific aspect of this—demands for subnational autonomy. It has identified various possible mechanisms linking globalization to regional autonomy demands, and has derived hypotheses from these mechanisms. A first preliminary empirical evaluation, consisting of a brief assessment of developments over time and a cross-sectional empirical analysis of regions in six Western European countries, found only limited support for these hypotheses. Globalization and European integration have changed the nature of autonomy demands in already assertive regions, but there is no clear evidence for a general rise in autonomy demands or for an important role played by globalization in accounting for variation in demands across regions. Other cultural and economic factors, as well as political institutions (in particular the nature of party competition), are more relevant determinants of regional assertiveness. It will be interesting to see if further empirical research confirms this conclusion.

A first implication of these findings is the necessity of distinguishing between different types of demands for autonomy and decentralization. Autonomy demands are not uniform across cases, and show considerable differences, for example, in the extent to which they include demands for fiscal decentralization. "Pressures from below" for decentralization do not necessarily include demands for the transfer of fiscal powers. This may be a further reason for the negative relation between globalization and fiscal decentralization found by Garrett and Rodden (chapter 4). A second, and more general, implication is that globalization may not be as strong a challenge to existing state structures as is often assumed (cf. Wright 1998, 45). Its general impact on regional autonomy demands is not as strong as many claim. Furthermore, to the extent that it does induce autonomy demands, such demands only challenge state structures in certain instances, namely, if they include demands for autonomy on fiscal autonomy. Due to political considerations this is often not the case. Finally, the conclusions of this chapter may have implications for broader issues. The argument about the role of party competition is based on the idea that politicians will try to avoid responsibility over issues that cut across cleavages reflected in the existing party system. This can give incentives to transfer "unwanted" competencies to other levels of government. This reasoning suggests that the structure of party competition will be an important factor in any transfer of competencies, including transfers to private bodies or supranational organizations. Surprisingly, comparative research on party attitudes and actions toward European integration is still limited (e.g., Hix 1999a; Marks and Wilson 2000). Such research is a promising test ground for wider applications of this chapter's arguments.

In sum, this chapter makes a case for the inclusion of political parties as a crucial institution in a positive theory of changes in governance structures. Economic globalization may create pressures on the "vertical" distribution of governance functions, but these institutions will mediate and constrain the incentives of political actors to actually bring about changes.

Chapter 6

MONETARY GOVERNANCE IN A WORLD
OF REGIONAL CURRENCIES

Benjamin J. Cohen

One of the most remarkable developments in the world economy at the dawn of the new millennium is the rapid acceleration of cross-border competition among currencies — what I have elsewhere called the *deterritorialization* of money (Cohen 1998).[1] Circulation of national currencies no longer coincides with the territorial frontiers of nation-states. A few popular monies, most notably the U.S. dollar and the euro (succeeding Germany's deutsche mark, the DM), have come to be widely used outside their country of origin, competing directly with local rivals for both transactions and investment purposes. The origins of this development, which economists call "currency substitution," can be found in the broader process of globalization, which, for the purposes of this volume and following Kahler and Lake (chapter 1), may be understood to refer to economic integration at the global level. The result is a fundamental transformation in the way money is governed. Where once existed *monopoly*, each state claiming absolute control over the issue and circulation of money within its own territory, we now find something more like *oligopoly*, a finite number of autonomous suppliers, national governments, all vying ceaselessly to shape and manage demand for their respective currencies. Monetary governance, at its most basic, has become a political contest for market loyalty, posing difficult choices for policymakers.

Among the alternative policy choices available to governments today, an option that is attracting increasing attention is replacement of national currencies with a *regional* money of some kind. Currency regionalization occurs when two or more states formally share a single money or equivalent. Broadly speaking, two main variants are possible. First, countries can agree to merge their separate currencies into a new joint

[1] This essay has benefited from comments by other contributors to this collective project and especially by the editors, Miles Kahler and David Lake. Special thanks, as well, to Jeffrey Chwieroth, Eric Helleiner, Barbara Koremenos, and Richard Steinberg for valuable insights and suggestions. The research assistance of Tom Knecht is gratefully acknowledged.

money, as members of Europe's Economic and Monetary Union (EMU) have done with the euro. This is *currency unification*, a strategy of alliance. Alternatively, any single country can unilaterally or by agreement replace its own currency with an already existing money of another, an approach typically described as full or formal *dollarization*.[2] This variant, a more subordinate strategy of followership, has long been official policy in a miscellany of tiny enclaves or microstates around the world, from Monaco to the Marshall Islands, as well as in Panama and, for many years, Liberia, and was more recently adopted by Ecuador and El Salvador, each of which now uses America's greenback in place of its own former currency.

The emergence of regional currencies can be regarded as a logical corollary of the intense competitive contest among monies — a Darwinian struggle where, ultimately, only the fittest may survive. Among informed observers today it is rapidly becoming conventional wisdom that the number of currencies in the world will soon decline.[3] The only question is: What will the resulting population of monies look like? Scholars are just beginning to explore this critical issue.[4]

Not all local currencies will disappear, of course. Even in today's globalizing world, many states remain determined to preserve some semblance of their traditional monetary sovereignty. But the range of countries likely to choose the regional option, in one form or another, is certainly great enough to raise significant questions for the future of monetary governance. Currency regionalization, in contrast to a strictly national money, implies an upward shift in the delegation of formal authority. Monetary sovereignty is either *pooled* in a partnership of some sort, shifting authority to a joint institution like the European Central Bank (ECB), or else *surrendered* wholly or in part to a dominant foreign power such as the United States.[5] Many governments thus are faced with a tricky tripartite choice: traditional sovereignty, monetary alliance, or formal subordination. How will they decide?

The aim of this chapter is to provide the first building blocks for a

---

[2] The adjectives "full" or "formal" are frequently added to distinguish this policy choice from the market-driven process of currency substitution, which in the past was also often popularly labeled dollarization (now unofficial or informal dollarization). Dollarization, of course, does not necessarily require the dollar. Some other currency, such as the euro or yen, may also be chosen to replace a country's currency.

[3] See, for example, Alesina and Barro (2001); Dornbusch (2001); Fischer (2001); and Rogoff (2001).

[4] See, for example, Alesina and Barro (2002).

[5] The distinction between pooling and surrender of sovereignty, which is generic to the question of how to organize political authority, is of course a familiar one in political science and is used in a variety of contexts — in analyzing differences between confederal states and empires, for instance.

positive theory of currency regionalization. In the spirit of the actor-oriented framework outlined by Kahler and Lake (chapter 1), the analytical focus here is the state—specifically, central decision makers responsible for currency policy. The working assumption is that economic globalization is driving policymakers to reconsider their historical preference for strictly national money. The question is: What delegation of authority is most likely to emerge in individual countries? What conditions are most likely to influence the choice among available options?

The chapter is organized as follows. I begin in the first section with a brief look back at the dramatic transformation of global monetary relations that has occurred in recent decades—a period during which many governments, finding it increasingly difficult to sustain the market position of uncompetitive national currencies, have begun to reflect instead on the possibility of a regional currency of some kind.[6] The second section then highlights the considerable leeway available in designing alternative forms of either currency unification or dollarization, while the third section identifies key factors that can be expected to dominate the calculations of rational policymakers in thinking about the choices before them. Taking all factors into account, it is clear that for many states traditional sovereignty will remain the preferred option. But taking account of possible variations in the degree of regionalization, it is also clear that for many other countries some form of monetary alliance or subordination could turn out to be rather more appealing.

Can individual state preferences be predicted? The fourth section surveys the empirical record, looking at countries that have rejected regionalization, as well as those that have embraced it. Comparative analysis suggests that outcomes will depend most on country size, economic linkages, political linkages, and domestic politics. The relevance of these variables is then illustrated with some brief case studies in the fifth section. The sixth section concludes the chapter with a few generalizations about the future of monetary governance in a world of regional currencies.

THE NEW GEOGRAPHY OF MONEY

That the global monetary environment has been greatly transformed in recent decades is undeniable. A half-century ago, after the ravages of the Great Depression and World War II, national monetary systems—with the notable exception of the United States—were generally insular and strictly controlled. Starting in the 1950s, however, barriers separat-

---

[6] The discussion in the beginning of the first section—on deterritorialization and governance—is necessarily condensed and is based on arguments presented at greater length in Cohen (1998).

ing local currencies gradually began to dissolve, first in the industrial world and then increasingly in many emerging-market economies, as well. Partly this was the result of an increased volume of trade, which facilitated monetary flows between states. But even more it was the product of intense market competition, which, in combination with technological and institutional innovation, offered an increasingly freer choice among currencies. Currency substitution widened the range of opportunities for a growing number of actors at all levels of society.

Deterritorialization and Governance

Most scholarly attention has been paid to the remarkable growth in recent decades of capital mobility, reflected in a scale of international financial flows unequaled since the glory days of the nineteenth-century gold standard. The high level of capital mobility today is commonly cited as one of the most visible artifacts of contemporary globalization. But these flows are just part of the story of money's growing deterritorialization. A focus on capital mobility, emphasizing integration of financial markets, highlights only one of the standard functions of money: its use as a store of value. In fact, the interpenetration of monetary systems today has come to be far more extensive, involving *all* of the functions of currency—not just money's role as a private investment medium but also its use as a medium of exchange and unit of account for transactions of every kind, domestic as well as international. Cross-border currency competition means much more than capital mobility alone.

Deterritorialization is by no means universal, of course—at least, not yet. But it is remarkably widespread. Krueger and Ha (1996) estimate that foreign currency notes in the mid-1990s accounted for twenty percent or more of the local money stock in as many as three dozen nations inhabited by at least one-third of the world's population. In all, as much as one-quarter to one-third of the world's paper money supply is now located outside its country of issue. Most currency substitution is concentrated in Latin America, the Middle East, and republics of the former Soviet Union, where the dollar is favored; or in East-Central Europe and the Balkans, where the DM traditionally predominated. By a different measure, focusing on foreign currency deposits rather than paper money, the International Monetary Fund identifies some eighteen nations where, by the mid-1990s, another state's money accounted for at least thirty percent of broad money supply.[7] The most extreme cases,

---

[7] Baliño, Bennett, and Borensztein (1999). Broad money supply (M2) is defined to include all coins and notes in circulation, demand deposits (checking accounts), and all other "reservable" deposits (time-deposits).

with ratios above 50 percent, included Azerbaijan, Bolivia, Croatia, Nicaragua, Peru, and Uruguay. Another thirty-nine economies had ratios approaching 30 percent, indicating "moderate" penetration.

The implications of deterritorialization for monetary governance are only beginning to be understood. For specialists in open-economy macroeconomics, who typically focus narrowly on capital mobility, the significance of recent developments lies mainly in implications for the choice of exchange-rate regime. Traditionally, the exchange-rate issue was cast in simple binary terms: fixed versus flexible rates. A country could adopt some form of peg for its currency or it could float. Pegs might be anchored on a single currency or a basket of currencies; they might be formally irrevocable (as in a currency board) or based on a more contingent rule; they might crawl or even take the form of a target zone. Floating rates, conversely, might be managed or just left to the interplay of market supply and demand. More recently, the issue has been recast—from fixed versus flexible rates to a choice between, on the one hand, contingent rules of any kind and, on the other, the so-called corner solutions of either free-floating or some form of monetary union. Today, according to an increasingly fashionable argument known as the bipolar view or two-corner solution, no intermediate regime can be regarded as tenable (Fischer 2001). Owing to the development of huge masses of mobile wealth capable of switching between currencies at a moment's notice, governments can no longer hope to defend policy rules designed to hit explicit exchange-rate targets. The middle ground of contingent rules has in effect been "hollowed out," as Barry Eichengreen (1994) memorably put it.

But that too is just part of the story. In reality, more is involved here than simply a choice of exchange-rate regime. At its most fundamental, what is involved is nothing less than a challenge to the long-standing convention of national monetary sovereignty. Once we look beyond capital mobility alone to the broader phenomenon of currency competition, we see that in many areas of the world the traditional dividing lines between separate national monies are becoming less and less distinct. No longer are most economic actors restricted to a single currency—their own home money—as they go about their business. Cross-border circulation of currencies, which had long been common prior the emergence of the modern state system, has dramatically reemerged, resulting in a new geography of money. The functional domains of many monies no longer correspond precisely with the formal jurisdiction of their issuing authority.

Currency deterritorialization poses a critical challenge because governments have long relied upon the advantages derived from formal monetary monopoly to promote their conception of state interest. In fact, five main benefits are derived from a strictly territorial currency: first, a potential reduction of domestic transactions costs to promote economic growth; second, a potent political symbol to promote a sense of national identity; third, a powerful source of revenue (seigniorage) to underwrite public expenditures; fourth, a possible instrument to manage the macroeconomic performance of the economy; and finally, a practical means to insulate the nation from foreign influence or constraint. But all of these gains are eroded or lost when a government is no longer able to exert the same degree of control over the use of its money, by either its own citizens or others. Instead, in a growing number of countries, policymakers are driven to compete, inside and across borders, for the allegiance of market agents—in effect, to sustain or cultivate market share for their own brand of currency. The monopoly of monetary sovereignty yields to something more like oligopoly, and monetary governance is reduced to little more than a choice among marketing strategies designed to shape and manage demand.

Broadly speaking, for affected states, four strategies are possible, depending on two key considerations—first, whether policy is defensive or aggressive, aiming either to preserve or promote market share; and second, whether policy is unilateral or collective. These four strategies are:

1. *Market leadership*: an aggressive unilateralist policy intended to maximize use of the national money, analogous to predatory price leadership in an oligopoly.
2. *Market preservation*: a status-quo policy intended to defend, rather than augment, a previously acquired market position for the home currency.
3. *Market alliance*: a collusive policy of sharing monetary sovereignty in a monetary union of some kind, analogous to a tacit or explicit cartel.
4. *Market followership*: an acquiescent policy of subordinating monetary sovereignty to a stronger foreign currency via a currency board or full dollarization, analogous to passive price followership in an oligopoly.

Of these four, a strategy of market leadership is of course generally available only to governments with the most widely circulated currencies, such as the dollar, euro, or yen. For the vast majority of states with less competitive monies, decision making is limited to the remaining three—a tricky, tripartite choice.

The Basic Question

The basic question is plain. What constraints on national policy are states willing to accept? Should policymakers seek to sustain their traditional monetary sovereignty (market preservation)? Or, alternatively, should they countenance delegating some or all of that authority upward, either to the joint institutions of a monetary union (market alliance) or to a dominant foreign power (market followership)? A former president of the Argentine central bank put the point bluntly (Pou 2000, 244): "Should a [country] produce its own money, or should it buy it from a more efficient producer?" Buying money from a more efficient producer necessarily implies a degree of regionalization in monetary affairs.

Many states, for the present at least, appear resolved to continue producing their own money. They would prefer to keep the national currency alive, no matter how uncompetitive it may be. Monetary sovereignty can be defended by tactics of either persuasion or coercion. Persuasion entails trying to sustain demand for a currency by buttressing its reputation, above all by a public commitment to credible policies of "sound" monetary management. The idea is to preserve market confidence in the value and usability of the nation's brand of money — the "confidence game," as Paul Krugman has ironically dubbed it (Krugman 1998a). Coercion means applying the formal regulatory powers of the state to avert any significant shift by users to a more popular foreign money. Possible measures range from standard legal-tender laws, which specify what money creditors must accept in payment of a debt, to limitations on foreign currency deposits in local banks and even to the extremes of capital controls or exchange restrictions. Both floating and contingent exchange-rate rules are consistent with a strategy of market preservation.

A desire to continue producing a national money is understandable, given the historical advantages of a formal monetary monopoly. But at what cost? As currency competition accelerates, tactics of persuasion or coercion become increasingly expensive. Growth and employment may have to be sacrificed, more and more, in order to keep playing the confidence game; widening distortions in the allocation of resources may be introduced by controls or restrictions. The costs of defending monetary sovereignty are real, a direct result of the transformation of the global currency environment. And as they continue to mount, the alternative of buying from a more efficient producer becomes increasingly appealing — or, at least, less unappealing. Not surprisingly, therefore, in a growing number of countries more attention is being paid today to the corner solution of monetary union, in the form of either formal dollarization or currency unification.

In Latin America, for example, the idea of dollarization has become a topic of intense public debate since Argentina's former President, Carlos Menem, spoke out in its favor in early 1999. Likewise, in East-Central Europe and the Mediterranean, "euroization" increasingly is touted as a natural path for countries with close ties to the European Union (EU) or hopes of one day joining the EU. Should more governments decide to go the route of dollarization, emulating the recent examples of Ecuador and El Salvador, it is not too difficult to imagine the gradual emergence of two giant monetary blocs, one centered on the United States and one on EMU's "Euroland." (Eventually a third bloc could also coalesce around the Japanese yen, though not any time soon.) As one observer has predicted, "By 2030 the world will have two major currency zones — one European, the other American. The euro will be used from Brest to Bucharest, and the dollar from Alaska to Argentina — perhaps even in Asia. These regional currencies will form the bedrock of the next century's financial stability."[8]

Much will depend, of course, on the policies adopted by the market leaders, which could significantly alter the relative costs and benefits of followership as contrasted with strategies of either market preservation or alliance. Unfortunately, these policies cannot be easily predicted. On the one hand, monetary leadership can yield substantial benefits, both economic and political. Economic gains include additional opportunities for seigniorage as well as an enhanced degree of macroeconomic flexibility. Politically, an international currency may yield dividends in terms of both power and prestige. The prospect of such benefits could lead the United States and Europe (and/or Japan) to offer explicit incentives to the potential dollarizer, especially if, as I have suggested elsewhere (Cohen 2000b), active competition for market share breaks out among the market leaders. But, on the other hand, there are also considerable risks in monetary leadership, including, in particular, policy constraints that could be imposed by pressures to accommodate the needs of followers. Such risks might prompt Washington and others to seek to discourage rather than encourage formal adoption of their currencies.

Absent material incentives to dollarize, some governments might instead prefer to look to the idea of currency unification, a less subordinate form of monetary union on the model of EMU. One long-standing currency union, the CFA Franc Zone, already exists in Africa; another, the Eastern Caribbean Currency Union (ECCU), functions smoothly in the Caribbean; and since the Maastricht treaty in 1991, which set the timetable for EMU, prospects for more such alliances have been discussed in almost every region of the world.[9] EMU is clearly viewed as a test case for a strategy of pooling, rather than surrendering, monetary sovereignty. If Europe's experiment comes to be seen as a success, it could have a powerful demonstration effect, encouraging similar initia-

[8] Beddoes (1999, 8). See also Eichengreen (1994); Hausmann (1999a,b) and Mundell (2000).

[9] These include prospects in Asia (Eichengreen and Bayoumi 1999), Africa (Honohan and Lane 2001), Latin America (Levy Yeyati and Sturzenegger 2000), Australia-New Zealand (Grimes and Holmes 2000), and even between the United States and Canada (Buiter 1999).

tives elsewhere. Alongside two (or three) major currency zones, a variety of new joint currencies in addition to the euro could also eventually come into existence.

Scenarios of currency regionalization, therefore, seem not only plausible, but even likely — indeed, arguably for many states the most reasonable outcome to be expected from today's accelerating deterritorialization of money. At present there are more than 170 central banks in the world, as compared with fewer than twenty a century ago; and more than one hundred currencies that formally float more or less freely. Can anyone really believe that such a polyglot universe represents a stable equilibrium? "Convergence on regional monies is a no-brainer," writes Rudi Dornbusch (2001, 242). The logic of competition suggests that many governments could eventually yield to the market power of more efficient producers, replacing national monies with regional currencies of some kind. Regionalization of the world's monies has happened before, in medieval Europe and again during the nineteenth century, as Eichengreen and Sussman (2000) remind us. Obviously, it can happen again. For Ricardo Hausmann, formerly chief economist of the Inter-American Development Bank, the process has an almost historical inevitability about it: "National currencies are a phenomenon of the twentieth century; supranational currencies are the solution of the future" (Hausmann 1999b, 96). That formulation may be a bit too deterministic. Nonetheless, there is little doubt that alongside national monies a new geography of regional currencies is beginning to emerge as a by-product of globalization.

Degrees of Regionalization

The question is: What might that new geography look like? For individual countries a wide range of scenarios is possible, depending on the *degree* of regionalization involved. Whichever strategy a government is considering, whether alliance or followership, considerable leeway exists for variations of design along two key dimensions. These dimensions are institutional provisions for (1) the issuing of currency and (2) the management of decisions. Examples of currency regionalization have differed dramatically along each dimension, providing policymakers a rich menu. A guide to this diversity is provided in appendix 6A, which contains a complete listing of all cross-border currency arrangements presently in existence among sovereign states.

Currency Issue

The highest degree of currency regionalization is of course when a single money is used by all participating countries. That is the way dollarization works in many of the small enclaves and microstates that have eschewed any currency of their own, such as Micronesia and Liechtenstein (table 6A-1).[10] That is also the way it works in a case of currency unification such as the ECCU, which shares the Eastern Caribbean dollar, and of course Europe's EMU. But a single money is by no means universal in regional currency arrangements. Relationships, in practice, may involve not one money but two or more bound together more or less tightly — an exchange-rate union.

Though the idea might seem counterintuitive, parallel circulation of two or more monies is in fact fully consistent with formal dollarization. Two currencies, for instance, has long been the case in Panama, where token amounts of locally issued coins (Panamanian balboas) circulate freely alongside the greenback at a fixed rate of exchange. Ecuador and El Salvador, too, are expected to maintain limited circulation of their own currencies even with formal dollarization, as do Kiribati and Tuvalu in the Pacific (table 6A-2). Local coins also used to be issued by several independent enclaves in Europe, such as San Marino and Andorra, prior to the introduction of the euro. In all of these cases, which may be labeled *near-dollarized* countries, the foreign currency dominates domestic money supply but falls short of absolute monopoly — a somewhat lower degree of dollarization.

Even lower on the scale is a *currency board*, such as has long existed in Brunei, Djibouti, and Hong Kong. With a currency board, the home money continues to account for a large, if not dominant, part of domestic money supply. In principle, though, issue of the local money is firmly tied to the availability of a designated foreign currency — usually referred to as the anchor currency. The exchange rate between the two monies is rigidly fixed, ostensibly irrevocably (an exchange-rate union); both currencies circulate as legal tender in the dependent country; and any increase in the issue of local money must be fully backed by an equivalent increase of reserve holdings of the anchor currency. During the 1990s new currency boards were established in a number of economies, including most notably Argentina, Bulgaria, Estonia, and Lithuania (table 6A-3). All of these arrangements still continue in operation except for Argentina's, which collapsed in early 2002.[11]

---

[10] I include here only politically sovereign entities, excluding all monetary arrangements with scattered dependent territories left over from the era of colonialism. In most cases, dependent territories make exclusive use of the currency of the "mother" country. These include the external dependencies of Australia, Denmark, France, New Zealand, Norway, the United Kingdom, and the United States. Exceptions include, inter alia, Bermuda, the British Virgin Islands, and the Turks and Caicos Islands, all of which use the U.S. dollar though they are territories of the United Kingdom.

[11] For a discussion of factors leading up to the collapse of Argentina's currency board, see Pastor and Wise (2001).

The lowest degree of dollarization is a *bimonetary* relationship, where legal-tender status is extended to one or more foreign monies, but without the formal ties characteristic of a currency board. Local money supply is not dependent on the availability of an anchor currency, and the exchange rate is not irrevocably fixed. Bimonetary relationships exist in a diverse range of states, from Bhutan to the Bahamas (table 6A-4).

Parallel circulation of two or more currencies is also consistent with a strategy of monetary alliance, as several present and past examples demonstrate (table 6A-5). Closest in spirit to a single money is today's CFA Franc Zone, born out of France's former colonial empire in Africa, which combines two separate regional currencies for West Africa and Central Africa, each cleverly named to preserve the CFA franc appellation, plus one national currency, the Comorian franc (CF) for the Comoros. Together the two regional groups comprise the *Communauté Financière Africaine* (African Financial Community). Technically each of the two regional currencies is legal tender only within its own region and managed by its own regional central bank. But the arrangement is very strict in the sense that it makes no allowance for any change of the exchange rate between the two CFA francs, and circulation between the two regions is not at all uncommon.

Essentially similar were two notable exchange-rate unions established in late nineteenth-century Europe—the Latin Monetary Union (LMU), which grouped together Belgium, France, Italy, Switzerland, and Greece; and the Scandinavian Monetary Union (SMU), comprising Denmark, Norway, and Sweden. The LMU was created in 1865, the SMU eight years later. The purpose of both was to standardize existing gold and silver coinages on the basis of a common monetary unit—in the LMU, the franc, and in the SMU, the krone (crown). Within each group, national currencies and central banks continued to exist. The separate currencies circulated freely at par, and no changes of official rates were even contemplated until the breakdown of the gold standard during World War I, which ultimately led to formal dissolution of both unions in the 1920s.

A less symmetrical, albeit comparably strict, model was provided by the Belgium-Luxembourg Economic Union (BLEU), which lasted nearly eight decades from 1922 until absorbed into EMU in 1999. Separate national monies were issued by each government, as in the LMU and SMU; but only one, the Belgian franc, enjoyed full status as legal tender in both states. The Luxembourg franc was limited in supply by a currency board–type arrangement and was legal tender only within Luxembourg itself. The arrangement was quite binding. Only once, in 1935, was there ever a change in the exchange rate between the two francs (subsequently reversed during World War II).

At the opposite extreme is the so-called Common Monetary Area (CMA) combining the Republic of South Africa — a sovereign state for decades — with two former British colonies, Lesotho and Swaziland, and South Africa's own former dependency, Namibia (formerly the United Nations trust territory of South West Africa). The origins of the CMA go back to the 1920s when South Africa's currency, now known as the rand, became the sole legal tender in several of Britain's nearby possessions, including Basutoland (later Lesotho) and Swaziland, as well as in South West Africa, previously a German colony. But following decolonization, an arrangement that began as an early example of dollarization based on the rand has gradually been transformed into a much looser scheme representing a much lower degree of regionalization, as each of South Africa's partners has introduced a distinct currency of its own. Today the CMA encompasses no fewer than four national currencies, only one of which, the rand, is legal tender outside its country of issue. The rand circulates legally in Lesotho and Namibia — both of which can now be described as bimonetary countries — but no longer in Swaziland. The rand serves as anchor for South Africa's three neighbors, but each government formally retains the right to change its own exchange rate at will.

Decision Making

Provisions for the delegation of decision-making authority may be equally varied, whether we are speaking of dollarization or currency unification. The logic of a regional currency, by analogy with national money, would seem to call for a single central agency with strong supranational powers — the highest possible degree of regionalization — and indeed that is the case in several instances. Microstates like Micronesia or Liechtenstein, totally without any money of their own, naturally cede all powers to the central bank of the country whose currency they use. The relationship is strictly *hierarchical*, with no assurance at all that the dependent state's specific views will be taken into account when monetary decisions are made. Likewise, both the ECCU and EMU have created joint institutions (respectively, the Eastern Caribbean Central Bank and the ECB) with exclusive authority to act on behalf of the group. Monetary sovereignty is fully pooled on a principle of *parity*, officially a relationship of equals.[12] But these are by no means the only possibilities. Other examples exist to demonstrate how formal powers may be more decentralized, reducing the degree of regionalization involved.

---

[12] Von Furstenberg (2000) characterizes these as, respectively, "uncooperative unilateral monetary unions" and a "multilateral sharing model of monetary union."

Most unusual is the CFA Franc Zone, with its two subregional central banks — a case of shared or dual supranationality. More common is the persistence of national monetary authorities with more or less symmetrical rights and responsibilities. The greater the degree of symmetry, the weaker is the element of supranationality.

Closest in spirit to a single central authority is the sort of highly asymmetric relationship characteristic of near-dollarized countries like Panama or Ecuador. A national monetary agency exists but without significant powers. Somewhat less demanding is a currency-board relationship, as in Hong Kong today or Luxembourg under BLEU, where local authorities may retain a significant degree of discretion depending on how the rules are written. A currency-board relationship is inherently asymmetrical, plainly favoring the central bank of the dominant partner, but need not be entirely one-sided. And yet less demanding are bimonetary relationships of the sort that exist in countries like the Bahamas and Bhutan. Least demanding is a wholly decentralized model of the sort practiced in the nineteenth century's LMU and SMU, where monetary management remained the exclusive responsibility of the members' separate central banks. Though in each case there was one central bank that could be said to enjoy disproportionate influence (the Banque de France in the LMU, the Swedish Rijksbank in the SMU), powers within each bloc were in principle symmetrical. The element of supranationality was minimal. The same principle of decentralization, implying a minimal degree of regionalization, is also characteristic of the CMA today.

Costs and Benefits

With such a rich menu to choose from, how will governments decide among the three broad options of market preservation, alliance, or followership? At issue are potential benefits and costs, both economic and political. Rational policymakers must take five key factors into account, all of which can be expected to vary systematically with the form and degree of currency regionalization under consideration.

Economic Factors

On the economic side, three factors stand out. These are implications for (1) transactions costs; (2) macroeconomic stabilization; and (3) the distribution of seigniorage.[13] The first of these three factors argues

---

[13] Not surprisingly, these three factors dominate discussions by economists. See, for example, Alesina and Barro (2002).

clearly for currency regionalization in some form. The remaining two can be expected to reinforce a preference for market preservation.

As compared with a world of separate territorial monies, currency regionalization has one unambiguous benefit. That is a reduction of transactions costs—the expenses associated with search, bargaining, uncertainty, and enforcement of contracts. When diverse local monies are replaced by a single regional currency, whether via monetary union or dollarization, there is no longer a need to incur the expenses of currency conversion or hedging in transactions between participating economies. Trade, as a result, could be increased substantially—by as much as a factor of three, according to empirical estimates by Andrew Rose—generating considerable efficiency gains.[14] This is the standard economic argument for monetary integration.

Indeed, nothing demonstrates the power of economies of scale more than money, whose usefulness is a direct function of the size of its functional domain. The larger a currency's transactional network, the greater will be the economies of scale to be derived from its use—what economists call money's "network externalities." Ceteris paribus, this factor implies a preference for the biggest currency regions possible. At the extreme, network externalities would be maximized if there were but a single currency in circulation everywhere—one global money.

Related to this factor are three other efficiency gains that also enhance the appeal of currency regionalization. First is a reduction of administrative costs, since individual governments will no longer be obliged to incur the expense of maintaining an infrastructure dedicated to production and management of a separate national money. That saving would of course be of most interest to poorer or more diminutive sovereignties because of the diseconomies of small scale involved in monetary governance. Second, as a supposedly irreversible institutional change, currency regionalization could also establish a firm basis for a sounder financial sector—a benefit that would be of particular value to states that previously have not enjoyed much of a reputation for price stability or fiscal responsibility. Finally, with regionalization there could be a substantial reduction of interest rates for local borrowers in countries that have not yet succeeded in establishing a solid credit rating in international financial markets. All of these gains represent additional transactions-costs savings and, as such, carry the same implied preference for the biggest currency regions possible.

---

[14] Rose (2000). Though frequently challenged, Rose's results have been consistently confirmed by other studies, as Rose (2002) demonstrates in a comprehensive analysis.

Because of the power of economies of scale, savings will be substantial for even a low degree of regionalization. Marginal benefits will diminish with successively higher degrees of regionalization.

MACROECONOMIC STABILIZATION

Counterbalancing regionalization's efficiency gains, however, which are all of a microeconomic nature, is a potentially serious cost at the macroeconomic level: the loss of an autonomous monetary policy to manage the aggregate performance of the economy. This is the standard economic argument *against* monetary integration. Individually, governments give up control of both the money supply and exchange rate as policy instruments to cope with domestic or external disturbances. The more shocks there are likely to be and the more they can be expected to be asymmetric between economies, the greater will be the disadvantage of a single regional money. Ceteris paribus, this factor thus implies a preference for *avoiding* currency regionalization to the extent possible — just the reverse of the transactions-cost factor. As Krugman has written, the challenge "is a matter of trading off macroeconomic flexibility against microeconomic efficiency" (Krugman 1993, 4).[15]

On balance, the loss will be least onerous for countries that have already experienced substantial erosion of monetary autonomy owing to the growing deterritorialization of money. The greater the degree of informal currency substitution that has already occurred — reflecting a local currency's lack of competitiveness — the greater is the degree of constraint imposed even now on a government's ability to manage macroeconomic conditions; this is precisely the circumstance that is leading increasing numbers of countries to look for a more efficient producer of money. Indeed, the loss of autonomy might even be welcomed in some countries where past abuses of a monetary monopoly have led to persistent price instability or even hyperinflation. Currency regionalization in some form, by tying the hands of policymakers, may be seen as the only way to restore a reasonable degree of monetary stability. Conversely, the loss of policy flexibility will be felt most acutely in more insulated states that still enjoy a measure of monetary autonomy.

---

[15] Readers will recognize a more-than-passing familiarity of this trade-off to the central tension identified by Charles Tiebout and others interested in the optimal level of governance in world affairs — a tension between scale economies and externalities, on the one hand, which argue for larger units and greater centralization of authority; and on the other hand, heterogeneity of preferences, which argues for the reverse. Scale economies and externalities are at the heart of the efficiency gains offered by currency regionalization, while macroeconomic flexibility is valued precisely because of the persistence of national differences. But that is not the only trade-off implicated in currency regionalization, as the discussion will make clear, and may not even be the most salient. Functionalist Tiebout-type models are too narrow to capture all of the elements of the policy choices involved.

Comparing degrees of regionalization, it is evident that relatively little autonomy is sacrificed in bimonetary relationships or relatively symmetrical alliances like the CMA. Both money supply and the exchange rate can still be changed should circumstances warrant. The impact on policy flexibility, at the margin, will rise significantly with successively higher degrees of regionalization.

THE DISTRIBUTION OF SEIGNIORAGE

A final economic issue involves seigniorage — the spending power that accrues from the state's ability to create money. Technically identified as the excess of the nominal value of a currency over its cost of production, seigniorage in the modern era derives from the difference between the interest-free liabilities of the central bank — cash in circulation — and the interest earned on the central bank's counterpart assets. It is, in effect, a pure profit attributable to the central bank's traditional position as a monopolist. In absolute terms seigniorage may not be very large, amounting to just a small fraction of a percent of GDP. But as the equivalent of a supplemental source of finance for government expenditure, it is apt to be considered of substantial value — a privilege not to be abandoned lightly.

Ceteris paribus, this factor, too, implies a preference for avoiding currency regionalization to the extent possible. With any form of regional currency, a certain amount of seigniorage profit will by definition be diverted elsewhere, going to either a joint institution or a dominant foreign power. Here also relatively little is sacrificed when the degree of regionalization is low. A bimonetary relationship or even a currency board keeps a national currency in circulation, permitting retention of some measure of seigniorage revenue; the same is true of a decentralized monetary union, as well. But here again the impact, at the margin, will rise significantly with successively higher degrees of regionalization, unless provisions can be agreed upon to compensate governments for interest earnings forgone. One precedent for such compensation is provided by the CMA, where the South African government makes annual payments to Lesotho and Namibia according to an agreed-upon formula for seigniorage-sharing, in order to encourage continued use of the rand. Another is provided by EMU, where net profits of the ECB are distributed proportionately to each of the member central banks.

Political Factors

On the political side, two factors stand out. These involve issues of (1) social symbolism and (2) diplomatic influence. Both also can be expected to reinforce a preference for market preservation. In fact, each goes to the heart of the fundamental purpose of the state in world politics: to permit a community to live in peace and to preserve its own social and cultural heritage.

SOCIAL SYMBOLISM

Money has long played a powerful role in politics as a symbol to help promote a sense of national identity. As Eric Helleiner (1998) has noted, a territorial currency, enjoying sole place as legal tender within the political frontiers of the state, serves to enhance popular patriotism in two ways. First, because it is issued by the government or its central bank, the currency acts as a daily reminder to citizens of their connection to the state and oneness with it. Second, by virtue of its universal use on a daily basis, the currency underscores the fact that everyone is part of the same social entity—a role not unlike that of a single national language, which many governments also actively promote for nationalistic reasons. Both aspects help explain why so many governments are still determined to stick to monetary strategies of market preservation, keeping their currencies on life support no matter how uncompetitive they may have become. Such behavior is not at all irrational insofar as value continues to be attached to allegiance to a distinct political community.

Once in place, a territorial currency can also take on a psychological life of its own in defiance of all economic or political logic. Indeed, it is difficult to overestimate the emotional attachment that most communities come to feel for their monies—even monies that have clearly failed the test of market competition.

The symbolic role of money would obviously be compromised by regionalization in any form, whether via dollarization or currency unification. Ceteris paribus, therefore, this factor, too, would appear to imply a preference for avoiding currency regionalization to the extent possible. Here also, however, relatively little is sacrificed when the degree of regionalization is low. Even with a currency board or decentralized monetary union a national currency is preserved, thus continuing to provide a basic symbol to help sustain a society's sense of community. It is only at the highest degrees of regionalization—full or near-dollarization or something like EMU or ECCU—that the full impact of this factor will be felt.

DIPLOMATIC INFLUENCE

Money has also long played a role as an instrument of diplomatic influence. Indeed, as Jonathan Kirshner has written, "Monetary power is a remarkably efficient component of state power . . . the most potent instrument of economic coercion available to states in a position to exercise it" (Kirshner 1995, 29, 31). Money, after all, is, at its most basic, simply command over real resources. If a nation can be threatened with a denial of access to the means to acquire vital goods and services, it is clearly vulnerable in geopolitical terms.

This factor, too, implies a preference for avoiding currency regionalization to the extent possible. Monetary sovereignty enables policymakers to avoid dependence on some other source for their purchasing power. In effect, government is insulated from outside influence or constraint in formulating and implementing policy. Conversely, that measure of insulation will be compromised by any form of dollarization or currency unification. Again, the sacrifice is relatively modest when the degree of regionalization is low, since exit costs will be correspondingly limited. So long as national currency remains in circulation, with some degree of decentralization of decision making, room exists for a restoration of monetary sovereignty to escape painful diplomatic coercion. But here again the impact, at the margin, will rise significantly with successively higher degrees of regionalization.

MAXIMUM ACCEPTABLE REGIONALIZATION

Taking all five factors into account, two implications become clear. First, it is evident why so many states appear resolved to continue producing their own money. A regional currency's saving of transactions costs, on its own, would seem unlikely to outweigh the considerable negatives implied: the losses of macroeconomic flexibility, seigniorage, a social symbol, and political insulation. In effect market preservation — defense of national monetary sovereignty — is a government's default strategy.

Second, it is evident why there is such wide variation in the design of regional currencies. Lower degrees of regionalization help to alleviate of some of the perceived disadvantages of an upward shift of authority. The considerable leeway for variations of design offers more opportunity to accommodate the interests of individual participants.

Is there, then, some degree of regionalization that will encourage more governments to depart from their default strategy? At the risk of oversimplifying a highly difficult decision, the key elements for rational policymakers can be reduced to a two-dimensional diagram comparing the cost of market preservation with the costs of either an alliance strategy or a followership strategy, as in figure 6.1.

Along the horizontal axis of the figure are alternative degrees of regionalization, ranging from the lowest forms at the left (e.g., a bimonetary system, or something like the CMA) to the highest at the right (e.g., pure dollarization, or something like the EMU). In principle one should distinguish not one but two metrics for regionalization, corresponding to the two separate dimensions involved — institutional provisions for currency issue and decision making. But in practice such an approach

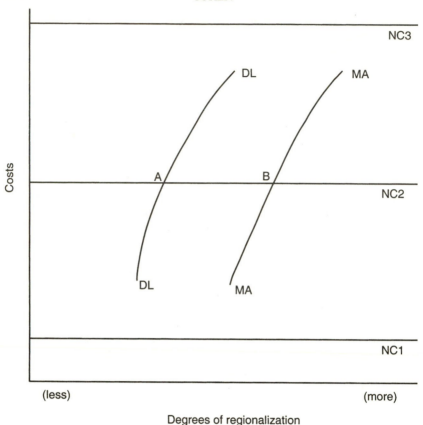

Figure 6.1. Choice Diagram

would only complicate the analysis with little promise of additional insight. For the heuristic purposes of this essay, it is sufficient to collapse the two dimensions into a single scale that may be read from left to right as a rough measure of the share of formal authority delegated upward from the individual state.

On the vertical axis are total costs as perceived by a nation's policymakers. Begin with the cost of maintaining a strictly national currency (NC). NC may be represented by a horizontal line, since the estimated cost of a national currency is invariant to the degree of regionalization. The height of the line, low or high, will vary considerably from country to country reflecting differences in the cost of a default strategy of market preservation. Overall, for most states, it is clear that the height of NC is dramatically rising owing to the growing deterritorialization of money. Indeed, it is this upward movement that is the driving force connecting globalization and currency regionalization. As currency competition grows, the net benefits of monetary sovereignty are correspondingly reduced. Where a half-century ago most governments might have faced a line as low as *NC1*, today they may be confronted with lines as high as *NC2* or even *NC3*.

Curves *DL* and *MA* represent the net costs of, respectively, dollarization and monetary alliance. Each is a composite of the five factors just outlined — microeconomic efficiency gains, which decline at the margin with successively higher degrees of regionalization; and the losses of macroeconomic flexibility, seigniorage, social symbolism, and political insulation, all of which are a rising function of the degree of regionalization. Though it is manifestly difficult, a priori, to assign specific weights to each of these five factors, the overall direction of the relationship is clear. The greater the share of formal authority that is delegated upward, the higher is the estimated net cost as compared with a national currency. For any single country, the maximum acceptable degree of currency unification is represented by point *A*, where the cost of preserving a national currency equals the cost of the least demanding form of a followership strategy. By similar reasoning, the maximum acceptable degree of monetary alliance is point *B*.

The positions of *DL* and *MA* relative to *NC* will vary considerably from country to country, yielding diverse outcomes. For some, the cost of maintaining a national currency may already have become so elevated that it is now somewhere in the neighborhood of *NC3*, where there is no point of intersection with either *DL* or *MA*. Even the strictest form of monetary alliance or dollarization would thus be an acceptable option. By contrast, for others the position of *NC* might still be closer to *NC1*, below both *DL* and *MA*, making neither regionalization strategy acceptable in even its most diluted form. For some, *DL* might lie below *MA*, making some form of dollarization acceptable (*A*); for others, *MA* might lie below *DL*, resulting in just one point of intersection (*B*) where monetary alliance is the preferred option; and for yet others, *DL* and *MA* could lie close together, making the choice between dollarization and monetary alliance especially difficult.

The key question is: What determines the relative position of the three curves for any given country? Therein lies the core of a positive theory of currency regionalization.

DETERMINING STATE PREFERENCES

At issue are state preferences. The more we know about what it is that influences policymakers' estimates of prospective benefits and costs, the easier it will be to predict preferences and therefore the delegation of authority that is ultimately likely to emerge in individual countries. Although policymakers can be expected to vary the weights they attach to particular gains or losses, depending on each state's individual circumstances, study of the empirical record does reveal some reasonably consistent patterns of behavior. Three conditions seem especially influential in determining strategic choices: (1) country size; (2) economic linkages; and (3) political linkages. In addition, domestic politics must also be assumed to play a key role.

The Empirical Record

There are limitations to the empirical record, of course. We do have an abundant population of states committed to one form of currency regionalization or another, as appendix 6A shows: some eighteen fully dollarized or near-dollarized economies, seven currency boards, ten bimonetary systems, and thirty-seven countries in a total of four different monetary unions, adding up to nearly a third of all sovereign entities in the world. This would certainly seem a large enough sample to look for meaningful patterns of behavior. But it is also evident that relatively few of these arrangements are the product of calculated decisions by fully independent governments. The majority, in fact, grew out of relationships that originated in colonial times or in United Nations trusteeships. These include most of the fully dollarized and near-dollarized economies listed in tables 6A-1 and 6A-2 as well as three of the four monetary unions listed in table 6A-5 (all but EMU). In all such cases it was currency regionalization that was the default position, not some form of exclusive national currency.

Moreover, the empirical record is at best only an *indirect* indicator of preferences, since government choices are rarely fully unconstrained. In most cases it must be assumed that observed relationships are the outcome of strategic interactions and bargaining rather than unilateral decision making.

Nonetheless much can be learned, despite such limitations. Path dependency may be pervasive, but governments were not, after all, *compelled* to preserve inherited arrangements. A decision *not* to abandon a regional currency can tell us as much about preferences as a decision to adopt one. Moreover to this sample we may add other governments that, once given the opportunity, *did* in fact abandon a regional currency. These cases, too, tell us something about government attitudes. One instructive set of precedents is offered by the host of Third World countries that, once decolonization began after World War II, rapidly chose to abandon colonial-era currency boards for independent national monies. These also include the interesting case of the East African shilling, a joint currency shared by Kenya, Tanzania, and Uganda, which notably failed to outlive decolonization. Other precedents are provided by the successor states of recently failed federations—the former Soviet Union, Czechoslovakia, and Yugoslavia—nearly all of which chose to establish monies of their own in one form or another as soon as they gained their independence.

Likewise, choices may not be unconstrained, but outcomes may still be interpreted as evidence of revealed preference. The difficulty of inferring preferences from outcomes is a familiar one in social-science methodology but is generally not considered an insuperable barrier to analysis, so long as observations are handled with caution.

So what does the record tell us?

Country Size

One thing the record tells us is that country size clearly matters, at least for the world's smallest states. Of all the economies that were fully or near-dollarized until recently, the largest was Panama, with a population of less than three million. Most are truly tiny enclaves or microstates. Small size also dominates among nations that have adopted currency boards or bimonetary systems and is an accurate description of the members of both the ECCU and CFA Franc Zone. One safe bet, ceteris paribus, is that the smaller an economy's size—whether measured by population, territory, or GDP—the greater is the probability that it will be prepared to surrender the privilege of producing a money of its own.

The logic is simple. Smaller states are least able to sustain a competitive national currency. The NC curve is already greatly elevated. Conversely, these are the economies that stand to gain most from a reduction of transactions costs. Whether in the form of dollarization or currency unification, some degree of regionalization offers both enhanced network externalities and lower administrative costs. Moreover, since in most cases these countries are also inherently vulnerable in political terms, less importance is likely to be attached to the risks that go with dependence on some other source for their purchasing power. Indeed, advantage may be seen in the protection that could be offered by association with either a powerful patron or a local partnership. Hence either DL or MA, or both, may fall below NC, encouraging governments to abandon strategies of market preservation.

How small must a state be? Until recently, regionalization seemed the preference of only the poorest and most diminutive specks of sovereignty around the globe. The threshold was very high. But as globalization has gradually elevated the NC curve, even bigger nations, as we know, have begun to join in, such as Ecuador and El Salvador. The threshold is clearly shifting downward, increasing the number of potential candidates.

Size, however, by no means explains all. Obviously there are many small states that have elected *not* to go the route of regionalization — at least, not yet. These include many former colonies and trust territories, as well as most of the successor states of recently failed federations, which even today remain intent on preserving, to the extent possible, the privileges of a national monetary monopoly. Small size per se is by no means a sufficient condition to predict the choice of strategy. Conversely, there are also some larger nations that have indeed chosen to delegate monetary authority elsewhere, most notably Bulgaria, Estonia, and Lithuania, with their currency boards, and the members of EMU. Small size is not a necessary condition, either.

Economic Linkages

Another condition that appears to matter, not surprisingly, is the intensity of economic linkages between nations. Many of the countries that make use of a popular foreign currency have long been closely tied to a market leader economically. This is especially true of the numerous dollarized or bimonetary systems in the Caribbean and Central America, as well as the several dollarized enclaves of Europe and the Pacific. Likewise, we know that nearly a half-century of deepening integration preceded the start of EMU. Another safe bet, ceteris paribus, is that closer economic bonds will also increase the probability that a government will be prepared to surrender the privilege of producing its own money.

Here again, the logic is simple. Economies that are already closely linked would, because of the efficiency gains involved, appear to be natural candidates for a regional money of some kind. Linkages might operate through trade, as is evident in the European Union, or through financial relationships developed from formal or informal currency use. The higher the level of interaction, the more we would expect to see both greater savings of transactions costs and closer convergence of economic activity. If relations are mostly concentrated on a market leader, lowering the DL curve, some form of dollarization might prevail. This especially would be the case in countries where currency substitution has now become widespread, as in Latin America or East-Central Europe. Conversely, if links are closer within a group of neighboring states — say, as a result of a common integration project like the EU — MA would be lowered, making currency unification more likely.

It is clear, however, that this condition, too, on its own is neither necessary nor sufficient for predictive purposes. Both Mexico and Canada are more closely tied to the United States than most other Hemispheric economies, yet to date each remains firmly committed to defending its traditional monetary sovereignty. Conversely, both the ECCU and CFA Franc Zone continue to thrive despite an absence of much reciprocal trade, while successor states of recently failed federations have mostly preferred to produce their own national monies in spite of the previously close integration of their economies. Economic linkages alone are rarely decisive. The reason is that they bear on only two of the five factors of interest to rational policymakers: the trade-off between microeconomic efficiency and macroeconomic flexibility. Governments are undoubtedly sensitive to such considerations, but not exclusively.

Political Linkages

A third condition that appears to matter is the intensity of political linkages between nations, whether formal or informal. Ties may take the form of a patron-client relationship, often descended from a previous colonial or trusteeship association; or they may be embodied in a network of cooperative diplomatic arrangements, possibly institutionalized in a formal alliance. Whatever the form, the influence of such ties is unmistakable — in currency groupings that have failed, as well as those that have survived.

On the negative side, I have already mentioned the several monetary unions that broke up in recent decades: in East Africa following decolonization, as well as in the former Soviet bloc following the end of the Cold War. We also know that many former dependencies of the old imperial powers, once granted independence, quickly rejected dollarization or colonial-era currency boards in favor of a money of their own. Plainly, in all of these cases, governments were motivated by a desire to assert their newfound rights and prerogatives as sovereign states; in other words, to *reduce* political linkages. Conversely, in the monetary unions that survived decolonization (ECCU and CFA Franc Zone), as well as in EMU and CMA, inter-state ties have always been stronger; and the same is true of most of today's dollarized entities, as well, which have long been accustomed to a hierarchical relationship with the source of their money. These are cases where governments are *least* interested in a reduction of political linkages.

Thus a third safe bet, ceteris paribus, is that closer political bonds, too, will increase the probability that a government will be prepared to surrender the privilege of a national money. The logic is that political linkages reduce two of the key costs associated with regionalization — the loss of a social symbol and the increase of vulnerability to outside influence. For states with already close ties to one of the market leaders, this means a lower *DL* curve, making some form of followership relatively more attractive. Candidates might include many of the countries of Latin America, ever in the shadow of the United States; or numerous economies of the former Soviet bloc, Mediterranean basin, or sub-Sahara Africa, with their close links to Europe. Likewise, for states already engaged in a common integration project, such as Mercosur in South America or the Association of Southeast Asian Nations (ASEAN), political linkages lower the *MA* curve, making a strategy of monetary alliance seem an increasingly natural choice.

Here again, however, as with size or economic linkages, the condition is rarely decisive, since it, too, bears directly on only a subset of the factors of interest to policymakers. Djibouti, for example, has a currency board that has always been based on the dollar despite the absence of any direct relationship with the United States. Israel, conversely, has expressly rejected dollarization in spite of its close ties to Washington (Cohen 1998, 38). Political linkages, too, on their own, are neither necessary nor sufficient for predictive purposes.

Domestic Politics

Finally, what of domestic politics? The material interests of specific constituencies are systematically influenced by what a government decides to do with its money. State strategies thus are bound to be sensitive to the interplay among domestic political forces, as well as the institutional structures through which interest-group preferences are mediated.

Unfortunately, no studies yet exist that directly probe the role of domestic interest groups in currency regionalization. Strong hints, however, are provided by a related literature focusing on the wave of financial liberalization that swept emerging-market economies in the 1980s and 1990s.[16] Though details differ from country to country, it is clear that critical constituencies benefited measurably from the integration of local financial markets into the growing structure of global finance, including in particular big tradable-goods producers, banks and other financial-services firms, and large private asset-holders — those that Jeffrey Frieden (1991a, b) refers to as "integrationist" interests. Exporters and importers, as well as domestic banks, gained improved access to loanable funds and lower borrowing costs; the owners and managers of financial wealth were freed to seek out more profitable investments or to develop new strategies for portfolio diversification. Most of these integrationist interests, research reveals, were active in

---

[16] Notable examples include Auerbach (2001); Haggard, Lee, and Maxfield (1993); Loriaux et al. (1997); Maxfield (1990); Pauly (1988).

lobbying policymakers to reduce or eliminate past restraints on capital mobility. Extrapolation from this literature suggests that many of these same powerful constituencies are likely to favor currency regionalization, as well, since a regional money offers the same advantage of financial openness. These are the actors who will benefit most from the anticipated reduction of transactions costs; for them, the *DL* and *MA* curves appear lower than they do to others. And they are not the type of actors who are apt to be shy about promoting their own interests.

Much rests, therefore, on the degree of political influence exercised by such groups as compared with other domestic constituencies, such as producers of nontradables and workers, who might oppose abandoning a national currency — "anti-integrationist" forces who feel they would benefit more from preservation of some measure of monetary autonomy. Integrationists' degree of influence, in turn, will be a function of domestic institutions and political structures. The issue is the extent to which government decision making is insulated from the pressures of such groups. How much attention is paid to their specific preferences and demands? This is less a matter of formal regime type than of practical access to the corridors of power. The greater the relative influence of integrationist interests, the more probable it is that policymakers will be prepared to delegate monetary authority elsewhere. This seems another safe bet, again ceteris paribus.

ILLUSTRATIONS

Generalization is of course difficult when no single variable can be considered either necessary or sufficient to forecast behavior. A parsimonious predictive model is simply not possible. Nonetheless, much insight can be gained by looking at all relevant conditions together in the context of specific cases. Two brief comparisons serve to illustrate the value of such an analytical approach.

Argentina versus Ecuador

Consider first Argentina and Ecuador, a pair of states that, as indicated, have chosen strategies of market followership — but to significantly different degrees and with very different outcomes. Argentina moved first, in 1991, when it adopted a currency board tied firmly to the dollar. Subsequently, following former President Menem's expression of interest, the idea of full dollarization was considered but ultimately rejected by the government of Menem's successor, Fernando de la Rúa, even before the currency board's eventual collapse. Ecuador, by contrast, decided in 2000 to adopt the dollar formally, leaving only token amounts of its own previous currency in circulation. What explains the difference in the degree of regionalization attempted by the two countries?

In two key respects, the pair are quite similar. Each state has strong economic linkages with the United States, particularly through currency substitution. At the end of 1999, the dollar accounted for some 56 percent of total bank deposits in both Argentina and Ecuador.[17] And each is close to the United States politically, long accustomed to Washington's leadership role in the Western Hemisphere. In terms of figure 6.1, both conditions suggest a lowered DL, helping to explain why each country might have been predisposed to dollarization in some form.

But in two other respects, the pair are quite dissimilar. One obvious difference is size. Whereas Argentina, Latin America's third largest economy, is a middle-income emerging market with a fair amount of industry, Ecuador is much smaller in territory and population and far less developed economically. The other difference has to do with domestic politics, which since the late 1980s have been rather more open and pluralistic in Argentina than in Ecuador. In Ecuador, particularly in the crisis circumstances prevailing in early 2000 when the dollarization decision was taken, few opportunities existed for opposition to mobilize against the new currency strategy. Integrationist forces were able to dominate decision making. In Argentina, by contrast, anti-integrationist forces are much better organized and represented politically, creating a more level playing field. The first contrast suggests a more elevated NC curve for Ecuador, raising the maximum acceptable degree of regionalization as compared with Argentina. The second suggests a higher DL curve for Argentina, lowering the maximum acceptable degree of regionalization as compared with Ecuador.

Hence we should not be surprised by the differing outcomes in the two cases, following President Menem's remarks in 1999. At the very time that Ecuador embraced full dollarization, unilaterally delegating all of its monetary authority to Washington, Argentina was holding out for a better deal, preferably in the form of a bilateral treaty of monetary association with Washington. If the nation was to surrender what remained of its historical monetary sovereignty, proud Argentinians wanted to be seen as partners with the United States, not a mere dependency. When Washington politely declined, Buenos Aires decided to remain instead with its less demanding currency board, until even that degree of commitment proved impossible to sustain.

Eastern Caribbean versus East Africa

A second instructive comparison is between the Eastern Caribbean and East Africa, two regions that have had strikingly different experiences

---

[17] Confidential source. In addition, substantial amounts of U.S. bank notes can be assumed to be in circulation in both countries.

with strategies of market alliance. Each region inherited a common currency from its former colonial master, Great Britain, upon receiving independence in the 1960s — respectively, the West Indian dollar (now the Eastern Caribbean dollar) and the East African shilling. But whereas the Eastern Caribbean Currency Union, as indicated, has functioned smoothly for decades, its East African equivalent, the East African Community (EAC), fell apart almost as soon as the British left the scene. First the East African shilling was replaced by separate national currencies in a looser exchange-rate union; and then in the mid-1970s even the exchange-rate union was abandoned as all three constituent members extended exchange restrictions to each other's money. The contrast between outcomes in the two regions could not be greater. Again, we may ask what explains the difference.

In fact, similarities between the two cases are considerable. The economies in both regions are among the smallest and poorest in the world. For all of them, the cost of preserving a strictly national currency is undoubtedly high (a greatly elevated NC). There is also relatively little difference between the regions in the intensity of economic linkages within each group or, so far as one can judge, in the political influence of integrationist interests. On all of these counts we would not expect much variance in the degree of regionalization elected by the two groups.

But the two cases do differ significantly along the political dimension, where postcolonial ties proved to be far more durable in the Eastern Caribbean than in East Africa. In the EAC, as I have noted elsewhere (Cohen 2000a), decolonization left little feeling of solidarity among the three constituent members, despite their legacy of common services and institutions. Much more influential was a pervasive sensitivity to any threat of encroachment on newly won sovereignty, which raised the perceived cost of currency unification (elevating MA). Once independent, each was more concerned with building national identity than with preserving regional unity. In the Eastern Caribbean, by contrast, identities have always been defined more in regional than national terms, institutionalized in a dense web of related political and economic agreements. From the start, the MA curve was seen as much lower, removing any incentive to alter strategy.

Conclusions and Implications

What, then, can we say about the future of monetary governance in a world of regional currencies? The working assumption, to repeat, is that economic globalization is driving states to reconsider their historical attachment to strictly national money. The question, once again, is: What delegation of authority, then, is most likely to emerge?

While firm predictions are difficult, four broad generalizations seem reasonable. First, while the deterritorialization of currency is clearly imposing growing constraints on traditional forms of monetary governance, it by no means dictates the choices that governments will eventually make. Many countries will consider some form of either dollarization or currency unification — but by no means all.

Second, we should expect to see relatively few *pure* cases of dollarization or currency unification. Few countries are apt to go the way of the Marshall Islands or Monaco, which willingly forgo any claim to a national money of their own. Likewise, even in the small handful of common integration projects now under way in the developing world — most notably, Mercosur and ASEAN — partnerships remain far from the degree of closeness that would be required to establish something as far-reaching as EMU or the ECCU. Regionalization may for many be a logical corollary of currency competition, but it does not follow that sovereign states will spontaneously delegate *all* of their monetary authority upward, either to a market leader or to a joint central bank. Most governments are likely to prefer somewhat more mixed models, involving a more limited element of regionalization.

Third, what those mixed models might in practice look like will vary considerably, depending very much on *bargaining context*. Practical experience demonstrates that many different degrees of regionalization are possible to accommodate the economic and political interests of participating states. No uniform outcome should be expected for either dollarization or currency unification.

Finally, bargaining context in turn will depend greatly on the key conditions of country size, economic linkages, political linkages, and domestic politics. Higher degrees of regionalization are more likely where states are small, economic and political linkages are strong, and domestic politics is heavily influenced by tradable-goods producers and financial interests. Conversely, lower degrees of regionalization may be expected insofar as countries are larger, economic and political linkages with others are weaker, and the domestic political setting is more pluralistic. In the largest states, with the weakest economic and political linkages and the most pluralistic politics, defense of national monetary sovereignty will remain the default strategy.

In short, there seems little doubt that a new geography of regional currencies is emerging as a byproduct of globalization. But as it evolves, the world's monetary map will in all probability come to look more like a messy, highly variegated mosaic than any simple structure of giant blocs and joint currencies. The essential elements of a positive theory of currency regionalization can be identified. What cannot be foretold is how these elements will work out in specific bargaining contexts. Standard microeconomic theory teaches that when monopoly yields to oligopoly, outcomes become indeterminate and multiple equilibria are possible. So, too, it would appear, is this true in matters of money.

Appendix to Chapter 6

TABLE 6A.1
Fully Dollarized Countries[1]

Country	Currency Used	Since
Andorra	euro	2002
Cyprus (Northern)[2]	Turkish lira	1974
East Timor	U.S. dollar	2000
Kosovo[3]	euro	2002
Liechtenstein	Swiss franc	1921
Marshall Islands	U.S. dollar	1944
Micronesia	U.S. dollar	1944
Monaco	euro	2002
Montenegro[3]	euro	1999
Nauru	Australian dollar	1914
Palau	U.S. dollar	1944
San Marino	euro	2002
Vatican City	euro	2002
TOTAL = 13		

Sources: International Monetary Fund, Europa World Year Book, various government sources.

[1]Independent states that extend exclusive legal-tender rights to a single foreign currency.
[2]De facto independent; under the protection of Turkey.
[3]Semi-independent; formally still part of Yugoslavia.

TABLE 6A.2
Near-Dollarized Countries[1]

Country	Currency Used	Since	Local Currency
Ecuador	U.S. dollar	2000	sucre
El Salvador	U.S. dollar	2001	colon
Kiribati	Australian dollar	1943	own coins
Panama	U.S. dollar	1904	balboa
Tuvalu	Australian dollar	1892	Tuvaluan dollar
TOTAL = 5			

[1]Independent states that rely primarily on one or more foreign currencies, but also issue a token local currency.

TABLE 6A.3
Currency Boards[1]

Country	Anchor Currency	Since	Local Currency
Bosnia and Herzegovina	euro (formerly deutsche mark)	1998	Bosnian marka
Brunei Darussalam	Singapore dollar	1967	Brunei dollar
Bulgaria	euro (formerly deutsche mark)	1997	lev
Djibouti	U.S. dollar	1949	Djibouti franc
Estonia	euro (formerly deutsche mark)	1992	kroon
Hong Kong[2]	U.S. dollar	1983	Hong Kong dollar
Lithuania	euro (formerly U.S. dollar)	1994	litas
TOTAL = 7			

[1]Countries with a formally irrevocable exchange-rate link to a foreign currency, both of which circulate domestically as legal tender and are fully interchangeable.
[2]Special Administrative Region of China.

TABLE 6A.4
Bimonetary Countries[4]

Country	Currencies Used	Since
Bahamas	Bahamanian dollar, U.S. dollar	1966
Belarus	Belarusian rubel, Russian ruble	1991
Bhutan	Bhutan ngultrum, Indian rupee	1974
Cambodia	Cambodian riel, U.S. dollar	1980
Guatemala	Guatemala quetzal, use of other currencies permitted	2001
Haiti	Haitian gourde, U.S. dollar	n.a.
Lao P.D.R.	Lao kip, Thai baht, U.S. dollar	n.a.
Liberia[2]	Liberian dollar, U.S. dollar	1982
Palestinian territories[3]	Israeli shekel, Jordanian dinar	1967
Tajikistan	Tajik ruble, use of other currencies permitted	1994
TOTAL = 10		

[1]Countries with one or more foreign currencies in circulation that are recognized legally but are subsidiary to the local currency as legal tender.
[2]Near-dollarized, with only token amounts of Liberian dollars in circulation, from 1944 until 1982.
[3]Occupied by Israel since 1967. The Israeli shekel is the exclusive legal tender in the Gaza Strip; both the shekel and Jordanian dinar are recognized in the West Bank.

TABLE 6A.5
Monetary Unions

Union	Member Countries	Institutional Arrangements	Since
Eastern Caribbean	Antigua and Barbuda, Dominica, Grenada, St. Kitts-Nevis, St. Lucia, St. Vincent and the Grenadines	Single currency (Eastern Caribbean dollar), currency union, single central bank	1965
Economic and Monetary Union (European Union)	Austria, Belgium, Finland, France, Germany, Greece, Ireland, Italy, Luxembourg, Netherlands, Portugal, Spain	Single currency (euro), single central bank	1999
CFA Franc Zone	Benin, Burkina Faso, Cameroon, Central African Republic, Chad, Comoros, Congo-Brazzaville, Côte d'Ivoire, Equatorial Guinea, Gabon, Guinea-Bissau, Mali, Niger, Senegal, Togo	Two regional currencies (both named CFA franc) and one national currency (Comorian franc); two regional central banks and one national central bank (Comoros)	1962–64
Common Monetary Area	Lesotho, Namibia, South Africa, Swaziland	Three currencies pegged to South African rand, four central banks (South African rand is legal tender in Lesotho and Namibia)	1986

TOTAL = 37

Chapter 7

GOVERNING GLOBAL FINANCIAL MARKETS

International Responses to the Hedge-Fund Problem

BARRY EICHENGREEN

THE EAST ASIAN FINANCIAL CRISIS did much to stimulate debate over the governance of global financial markets.[1] The crisis was unanticipated, its impact severe. It struck economies with superior records of macroeconomic performance, encouraging the perception that the events of 1997–1998 reflected flaws in the structure of the international system more than any shortcomings of policy in the crisis countries themselves. Malaysia's Prime Minister Mahathir bin Mohamed may have oversimplified when he assigned the blame for the crisis to rogue currency speculators whose actions, he alleged, had destabilized the Asian economies, but there is no question that, by pointing to the risks to national economies posed by the operation of international financial markets, he put his finger on a problem of concern to developing-country politicians and their constituents.

What this crisis did for the developing world in a consciousness-raising sense, the all-but-failure of the Greenwich, Connecticut–based investment fund Long-Term Capital Management (LTCM) did for the advanced industrial countries. It convinced officials that the international financial system as currently constituted and governed is dangerously volatile and that the presence of "highly leveraged institutions" (official argot for hedge funds) contributed significantly to that volatility.[2] It fueled a debate about how to better govern global financial markets — about how to "strengthen the international financial architecture," to use the now famous phrase coined by U.S. Treasury Secretary Robert Rubin in 1998.

A variety of proposals were then tabled in response to these prob-

---

[1] Prepared for the IGCC/UCSD Project on Governing the Global Economy. I thank Lee Hennesee of Hennessee Group LLC for permission to cite data from its 1999 hedge-fund survey, and Benjamin Cohen, Miles Kahler, and David Lake for helpful comments.

[2] The broader term is used to avoid creating the impression among hedge funds that they are being singled out and to indicate that, insofar as the problem for systemic stability is due to leverage (as the advanced industrial countries concluded in the wake of the Russia-LTCM crisis), it is not only hedge funds, but also other institutions using large amounts of leverage, that require scrutiny.

lems. Some officials and commentators, more often than not spokesmen for emerging markets, argued for tighter regulation of hedge funds and their activities with the goal of clamping down on the anti-competitive practices that had allegedly destabilized Asian markets in 1997 and jeopardized the stability of the global financial system in 1998. In opposition to this view, others — mainly officials of the advanced-industrial countries — proposed relying more heavily on financial markets to deal with the threat to stability.[3] One might say that they proposed "privatizing" what had previously been a public responsibility. Although governments were still part of the solution, their task was to be limited to allowing the exchange rate to be market determined in order to avoid creating one-way bets for currency speculators, upgrading the quality of domestic financial regulations and practices, and sharpening the incentives for market participants to more prudently allocate credit to their highly leveraged clients.

If one axis was defined by this public-private divide, the other was delineated by whether such regulation should be imposed at the national or international level. One view was that financial markets with global reach can be effectively supervised only by a global financial regulator, proposals for which began to circulate with the East Asian financial crisis (see Eatwell and Taylor 1999, 2000; Ocampo 2000; Soros 1998). These proposals emanated mainly but not exclusively from spokesmen for and commentators sympathetic to the problems of emerging markets. Others insisted that effective solutions could be found only at the national level, since supranational action required a degree of international consensus and a willingness to delegate regulatory prerogatives that did not exist. These officials came from both advanced industrial countries and emerging markets, although it was the former, and the large-country representatives in particular, who had the power to veto proposals for international action.

Not surprisingly, the initiatives taken subsequently lie in the interior of the space defined by these four extrema. They rely on both government regulation and market discipline, although the balance is heavily tipped toward the latter, reflecting the relative influence of the advanced industrial countries that favor market-based measures, as opposed to emerging markets that prefer official regulatory initiatives, the technical difficulty of directly regulating hedge funds in an otherwise liberalized financial environment, and the high mobility of financial capital, a phe-

---

[3] In what follows I adhere to convention by referring to the problem of market manipulation of special concern to emerging markets as that of "market integrity," and the problem of global financial volatility of particular concern to the advanced industrial countries as that of "systemic risk."

nomenon that hedge funds can be seen as epitomizing. They involve both national and international initiatives, although here, too, the balance is heavily tipped, this time toward national action. International initiatives are limited to promulgating codes for monetary, fiscal, and exchange-rate policies, internationally accepted frameworks for prudential supervision and regulation, and — importantly — internationally agreed-upon standards for *voluntary* disclosure by highly leveraged institutions (HLIs), while national governments are charged with implementing these reforms.

This chapter attempts to understand how this response to the hedge-fund problem was reached and to draw out its implications for efforts to strengthen the governance of global financial markets. Following an overview of the characteristics of the hedge-fund industry, I review the official reports on the hedge-fund problem issued by official bodies starting in 1998. These reports reveal the fault lines dividing the emerging markets from the advanced industrial countries. They distinguish those advocating direct regulation from those preferring more intense market discipline, and those advocating national responses from those favoring international solutions. Next I discuss why international agreement has proven difficult to reach and why the process of "strengthening the international financial architecture" has resulted in this particular approach to the hedge-fund problem. The concluding section draws out the implications for financial reform in a world of mobile capital and integrated financial markets.

Characteristics of the Hedge-Fund Industry

In part the difficulty of coming to grips with the hedge-fund problem is definitional: it is difficult to draw a line between hedge funds and other financial market participants, such as investment banks, mutual funds, and managed-futures funds, that engage in many of the same activities. In terms of legal distinctions, hedge funds are investment pools that are exempt from the disclosure requirements of the Investment Company Act of 1940 in the United States and its analogs in other countries.[4]

---

[4] Collective-investment vehicles are exempt from the investor-protection regulations of the Investment Company Act of 1940 if they have fewer than 100 accredited investors (or partners) and do not make a public offering of their securities. Accredited investors each must have a net worth of $1 million and an income of at least $200,000 in each of the last two years. Alternatively, joint spousal income must have been in excess of $300,000 in each of the last two years. Such firms are then exempt under Section 3(c)(1) of the Investment Company Act. The National Securities Markets Improvement Act of 1996 amended the Investment Company Act to provide a second exclusion (Section 3[c][7] which allows for as many as 499 investors, each with a net worth of at least $5 million). Not only are

They are narrowly held collective investment vehicles — they have a relatively small number of high-income institutional and individual shareholders — from which flow their other distinguishing characteristics (see table 7.1).

- *Hedge funds are exempt from regulation* on consumer-protection grounds, high-income investors being thought able to fend for themselves.
- *Hedge funds are mobile*, not requiring charters or licenses. Their overhead is light, allowing them to move their place of incorporation without having to relocate managers and staff.
- *Hedge funds are nimble*, since they are not bound by restrictive covenants or prospectuses that limit their ability to rapidly alter their portfolios (see table 7.2).
- *Hedge funds are leveraged*, although the extent of that leverage is not known with precision.[5] Surveys suggest that a third of hedge funds do not use leverage at all and that fewer than one in six lever their assets more than twice (See table 7.3). Such measures are highest for market neutral-arbitrage funds.[6] Macro funds of the sort that are likely to be active in

---

such entities exempt from disclosure and reporting requirements imposed on firms not meeting these conditions, but voluntary disclosure of positions and other investment information could be construed as soliciting business and thereby precipitate regulation under the Investment Company Act. (Offshore hedge funds are, by definition, exempt from even these limitations. Organized as private partnerships, they can offer unlimited numbers of accounts. Hence, many major hedge funds operating in the United States also have offshore vehicles.)

Hedge funds are also exempt from regulation under the Securities Act of 1933 because they offer their securities privately. But even exempt funds are still required under U.S. law to report information on their financial activities to their shareholders (as opposed to the regulators or the public). And hedge funds that trade on futures and option exchanges and accept investments from U.S. citizens must register as Commodity Pool Operators (CPOs) with the Commodity Futures Trading Commission (CFTC), the agency responsible for ensuring the integrity of U.S. futures and options exchanges; this makes them subject to disclosure, reporting, record keeping requirements, and fraud prohibitions under the provisions of the Commodity Exchange Act. Note that the CFTC does not impose capital requirements on CPOs, nor does it normally receive detailed information about their off-exchange trading of over-the-counter derivatives. See Eichengreen (1999a).

[5] In addition there is no consensus on the proper definition of, and therefore metric for, leverage. Be this as it may, there is evidence that the use of leverage has declined in the wake of the near failure of Long-Term Capital Management. This is discussed in more detail later in the chapter.

[6] Understandably so, since the volatility of an unlevered market portfolio would normally be low. This is, of course, the category in which LTCM is traditionally placed. This suggests that some hedge funds with exceptionally high investment-to-capital ratios may be lurking in the survey returns. LTCM normally leveraged its capital twenty to thirty times; the much higher ratios circa September 1998 that were reported in the press reflected the extraordinary losses of capital following Russia's default. The President's Working Group on Financial Markets (1999) reports that, as of September 1998, it was

TABLE 7.1
Registration of Hedge Funds (percent)

Investment Style	Broker Deal	Commodity Pool Operator	Registered Investment Advisor	3C7 Fund
Arbitrage	40	23	45	27
Distressed	0	0	29	33
Emerging markets	11	0	33	13
Event-driven	11	0	11	44
Financial equities	0	50	0	100
Growth	14	18	0	38
International	0	45	0	25
Macro	22	90	0	50
Market-neutral	16	29	26	16
Opportunistic	11	17	28	33
Technology	0	0	25	50
Value	7	24	39	22
Survey total	16	25	25	29

Source: Hennessee Group.
Note. 5 percent of respondents report more than one registration.

emerging markets typically use moderate leverage: nearly 70 percent claim to lever their capital less than two times. Estimates of industry-wide leverage range from 3–5 (President's Working Group on Financial Markets 1999) to 8 (Roach and Montgomery 1998).

This way of thinking about hedge funds explains why the industry has grown so rapidly.[7] With economic growth there develops a customer base of high-income individuals and institutional investors (such as CALPERS, charitable foundations, and Ivy League universities) who seek to balance their portfolios by including some high-risk assets man-

---

aware, on the basis of CPO filings, of ten hedge funds (out of the population with capital exceeding $100 million) with on-balance-sheet leverage of more than ten-to-one, and one hedge fund with leverage of more than thirty-to-one. Unpublished data from Hennessee Associates suggests that 12 percent of all hedge funds had leverage ratios greater than eight-to-one at the end of 1998, including 8 percent of macro funds, 33 percent of emerging-market funds, 25 percent of technology funds, and 71 percent of distressed securities funds. I thank Lee Hennessee for this information.

[7] There is no agreed metric of that growth, both because there is no reporting system and because there is no agreement on where to draw the line between hedge funds and other leveraged institutions. The President's Working Group (1999) estimates that hedge funds have grown from negligible levels in the early 1970s to their present (mid-1988) 2,500 to 3,500 funds with $200 billion to $300 billion in capital and perhaps $1 trillion in total assets.

Table 7.2
Portfolio Turnover Rate for 1998 (percent)

Investment Style	Under 100	101–200	201–300	301–400	401–500	501–600	601–700	Over 700	Other	Total
Arbitrage	7	10	14	28	17	3	3	3	14	100
Distressed	57	14	0	14	0	0	0	0	14	100
Emerging market	33	22	11	22	0	0	0	0	11	100
Event-driven	0	11	44	22	0	22	0	0	0	100
Financial equities	0	75	0	25	0	0	0	0	0	100
Growth	29	13	21	8	13	4	13	0	0	100
International	18	27	18	9	0	0	0	18	9	100
Macro	11	11	0	11	22	11	0	22	11	100
Market-neutral	5	20	5	25	15	0	0	30	0	100
Opportunistic	6	12	29	6	18	6	0	18	6	100
Technology	0	33	67	0	0	0	0	0	0	100
Value	39	19	26	0	0	3	0	0	13	100
Survey total	19	17	18	14	9	4	2	8	8	100

Source: Hennessee Group.

TABLE 7.3
Maximum Amount of Leverage in 1998 (percent)

Investment Style	Under 200	201–300	301–400	401–500	501–600	601–700	701–800	Other	Total
Arbitrage	45	12	18	6	6	0	0	12	100
Distressed	14	14	0	0	0	0	0	71	100
Emerging market	56	0	0	11	0	0	0	33	100
Event-driven	100	0	0	0	0	0	0	0	100
Financial equities	50	35	0	0	25	0	0	0	100
Growth	88	8	0	0	0	0	0	4	100
International	55	27	9	0	0	0	0	9	100
Macro	50	0	17	17	0	0	8	8	100
Market-neutral	45	23	14	5	5	5	0	5	100
Opportunistic	68	21	0	0	0	0	0	11	100
Technology	75	0	0	0	0	0	0	25	100
Value	84	6	0	0	0	0	0	9	100
Survey total	64	12	6	3	2	1	1	12	100

Source: Hennessee Group.

aged by professionals with high-powered compensation incentives (see table 7.4).[8] The existence of a demand for these services suggests that even concerted action by regulators will not make the corresponding supply go away.

This way of looking at the industry also suggests why hedge funds are of concern to emerging markets. $10 billion, the capitalization of the largest offshore hedge fund in mid-1998, is a large number relative to the reserves of most emerging-market central banks and the capitalization of most national stock and bond markets, even before taking the leverage available to such funds into account. (An estimate of the size distribution of hedge funds at the beginning of 1999 is shown in table 7.5.) A single fund can thus leave a large footprint when it enters and exits an emerging market, and the same is even more true when several do so simultaneously.

This perspective also suggests why hedge funds raise concerns among policymakers in advanced industrial countries. Given the size of their balance sheets, hedge funds engaging in uncollateralized or inadequately collateralized borrowing from their bank counterparties can pose a risk to the solvency of the latter if the market moves unexpectedly. High levels of leverage may also force the funds in question to sell into a falling market, amplifying volatility and threatening collateral damage to innocent bystanders. These were the concerns that led to the New York Fed–orchestrated rescue of Long-Term Capital Management in 1998.

EXISTING SITES FOR GLOBAL GOVERNANCE

Starting in 1998, the hedge-fund problem was considered in a variety of venues, by international organizations like the IMF, by intergovernmental organizations like the Basle Committee of Banking Supervisors and the Financial Stability Forum, and by national bodies like the Interagency Task Force of the U.S. President and the Standing Committee on Economics, Finance, and Public Administration of the Australian House of Representatives. Predictably, the participants in these reviews had different perspectives on the problem: while national committees and task forces adopted relatively narrow perspectives emphasizing national concerns, the reports and deliberations of the international and intergovernmental organizations reflected rather more diverse views, but found it difficult to agree on concrete recommendations. And—this is the key point—those participating in their deliberations instinctively

---

[8] Hedge-fund managers are typically compensated with 20 percent (sometimes less, sometimes more) of net profits once they surpass previous high-water marks.

TABLE 7.4
Sources of Capital (percent)

Investment Style	Individuals & Family Offices	Pensions & Retirement	Endowments & Foundations	Fund of Funds	Corporate	Other	Total
Arbitrage	46	11	6	16	20	2	100
Distressed	44	6	15	17	18	2	100
Emerging market	54	2	5	27	105	3	100
Event-driven	46	1	10	25	17	1	100
Financial equities	44	3	19	21	9	3	100
Growth	74	7	5	13	1	0	100
International	58	0	13	10	4	15	100
Macro	45	12	4	23	10	6	100
Market-neutral	33	12	5	30	12	8	100
Opportunistic	68	5	4	21	1	1	100
Technology	77	4	2	17	0	0	100
Value	64	9	3	14	7	4	100
Survey total	55	8	6	19	10	4	100

Source: Hennessee Group.

TABLE 7.5
Number of Hedge Funds by Asset Size

Asset Size	Number of Funds
Under 10 million	79
10–49 million	170
50–99 million	190
100–499 million	165
500–999 million	22
1 billion +	21
Total	647

Source: Hennessee Group.

preferred responses that fit within the framework of their existing pro-ceedings. The main achievement of the Basle Committee was to promul-gate international standards for the capitalization of international banks, and its main task when the hedge-fund issue arose was to com-plete its revision of those standards; naturally, it sought to address the hedge-fund problem by suggesting changes in the structure of those standards designed to intensify the oversight of HLIs by their bank counterparties. The Financial Stability Forum had been set up as a fo-rum for promoting cooperation and information sharing among regula-tors; logically enough, it sought to address the hedge-fund problem by promoting cooperation and information-sharing among regulators. These intergovernmental organizations possessed no power to override the decisions of national governments; it is no surprise that their re-sponse took the form of encouraging more systematic and effective cooperation among national regulators rather than a more ambitious supernational proposal. While the IMF possesses more extensive powers — by virtue of its status as an international organization with Articles of Agreement that impose obligations on its members and be-cause it is a lending institution with a budget of its own, it has no special competence in the regulation of financial institutions and part-nerships. While it could conceivably have encouraged the use of capital controls by emerging markets that felt themselves threatened by the hedge-fund problem, such encouragement would have cut against the grain of IMF policy and against the preference of its principal share-holders for capital account liberalization. It is hardly surprising that the Fund's directors did not come out strongly in favor of capital controls and, absent this, that its other recommendations for addressing the problem were limited. Hence, the nature of existing sites for global gov-ernance has important implications for the nature of outcomes.

The IMF Report and Directors' Conclusions

The hedge-fund issue came to the fore with Mr. Mahathir's famous speech (and Mr. Soros's equally famous response) at the Hong Kong meetings of the IMF and the World Bank in September 1997. A natural venue in which to pursue his claims, given their international nature, was the IMF. Malaysia's constituency thus asked the Fund to investigate Mr. Mahathir's charges. The result was a study conducted in the winter of 1997–1998 and a discussion in the IMF Executive Board in March of 1998.[9]

The staff report documented, on the basis of conversations with hedge-fund managers, their competitors, and their counterparties, that a small number of large hedge funds had been the main parties on the other side of the forward foreign exchange positions put on by the Bank of Thailand, but it concluded that the same was not true of other Asian central banks and currencies.[10] This is not surprising: while the Thai baht was pegged (creating the one-way bets that the managers of macro funds find so irresistible) and Thailand's problems were widely known (the Fund itself having warned of them in the course of the preceding year), other Asian countries were not thought to have similar problems and most had moved toward a more flexible exchange rate either before or soon after the outbreak of the Thai crisis. Both facts, but especially the first, made them less obvious targets.[11]

And even in Thailand, where hedge funds were active, they were not alone: international banks, with many more assets under management, utilized many of the same strategies and took many of the same positions as their hedge-fund customers and competitors. Some were said to have accumulated positions against the baht as large as any hedge fund. This raised the question of whether financial market outcomes would be changed in any significant way by tighter regulation of hedge funds alone, or whether initiatives designed to limit trades and positions would have to be designed to catch the entire universe of emerging-market investors in their net, implying a need for the wholesale re-regulation of financial markets.

[9] Full disclosure requires me to acknowledge that I was the lead author of this report.

[10] This is also the conclusion of Brown, Goetzmann and Park (1998), who regress the monthly returns of ten large hedge funds on changes in a vector of Asian exchange rates to infer hedge funds' underlying investment positions. The results do not indicate that hedge funds consistently had short positions against the Asian currencies that came under attack in 1997.

[11] As one hedge-fund manager explained to the IMF mission, "How do we decide which countries to take positions against? We just ask which ones have pegged exchange rates to blow up."

The IMF study did not focus on systemic stability, this not being the basis of Asian complaints or the task with which staff was charged. It commented only that "regulators in the United States and the United Kingdom, the countries in which banks and brokers are most active as counterparties and creditors to hedge funds, seem generally satisfied that these institutions are adequately managing their exposure to hedge funds, which therefore pose no special problems of systemic risk."[12]

The recommendations of the IMF report centered on fuller disclosure of information and stronger macroeconomic policies. More timely and regular disclosure of financial information by governments and market participants might, it was thought, limit the herding that takes place when the news or rumor of hedge-fund investments leads other market participants, assuming that the hedge funds have inside information, to take copycat positions. More information and greater transparency, in other words, might have some modest positive impact in limiting volatility. And better macroeconomic policies — sound and stable monetary and fiscal policies, plus more flexible exchange rates to avoid presenting hedge-fund managers with one-way bets — would avoid attracting the attention of hedge-fund managers in the first place.

The report suggested that countries concerned with market cornering and manipulation might consider installing a Large Trade and Position Reporting System of the sort in place in the United States, which requires entities with foreign exchange positions in excess of $50 million to report these to the authorities. This would give the authorities more information about market cornering and manipulation, and the knowledge that such information was available might discourage hedge funds and others from engaging in such practices. But the authors of the report questioned how much might be learned through such a system, given the ability of hedge funds to disguise their trades and positions by, inter alia, booking them through third parties. The report considered but rejected the idea of even more comprehensive reporting requirements because of the difficulty of drawing the line between hedge funds on the one hand and family groups and individual investors on the other (it hardly being feasible to ask individual investors to fully disclose their personal investment portfolios), and because of the ability of hedge funds to evade requirements they considered excessively burdensome by moving offshore. It discussed measures to limit position-taking,

<hr />

[12] The sentence continues, ". . . although they have been known to express concern that the difficulty of obtaining information on hedge funds complicates the efforts of the countries to assess the creditworthiness of potential hedge fund customers, and that not all banks have the expertise needed to evaluate the credit risk associated with some hedge funds' complicated derivatives holdings" (Eichengreen and Mathieson et al. [1998, 14]).

ranging from Chilean style capital-inflow taxes, which would increase the cost of putting on and taking off positions, to capital controls designed to prohibit certain kinds of portfolio flows, but concluded that while these might have some utility in limiting position-taking by hedge funds, they were unlikely to be effective in a full-fledged panic. And, in any case, these measures did not appeal to the majority of emerging markets, which by definition were seeking to finance domestic investment with the help of capital imports, since their imposition threatened to send an adverse signal about the credibility of their foreign investment policies.[13]

The IMF Executive Board's discussion of the report revealed predictable divisions between emerging markets and advanced industrial countries on the role of hedge funds in the Asian crisis and the appropriate policy response. While some directors, mainly from Asia, concluded that hedge funds had played an active role in the collapse of Asian financial markets, others, mainly from the advanced industrial countries, characterized them as mere symptoms of a problem caused by weak national policies. The discussion made clear that, on this issue like others, emerging markets were not a unified bloc. While Asian emerging markets were convinced that the risk posed by hedge funds to the stability and integrity of their markets was serious, Latin American governments, which had not shared the Asians' experience, saw the threat as less pressing. In the wake of the 1994–1995 Tequila Crisis they had sought to deepen their dependence on international financial markets, rather than turning away, and to use foreign finance as a lever for accelerating rates of investment and economic growth. Argentine and Brazilian officials, for example, saw hedge funds, which invested in their industries and real estate markets as well a speculating in their currencies, as more friend than foe.

While some officials, again generally from Asia, insisted on the need for more disclosure of hedge funds' trades, positions, and financial information to central banks and governments, others emphasized technical obstacles to making such disclosure mandatory. If the information disclosed was to reassure the governments concerned and be useful for detecting market cornering and manipulation, it would have to include detailed portfolio and position reporting and encompass commercial banks, investment banks, insurance companies and pension funds, warned some officials, echoing the staff report's conclusion that "the entire constellation of institutional investors, and not merely hedge funds . . . had

---

[13] This did not entirely prevent their adoption, the notable exception being Malaysia in 1998. See Kaplan and Rodrik (2001).

played a role in the market fluctuations of 1997."[14] And if mandatory disclosure was to convey information about positions and trades in emerging markets, it would have to occur on a real-time basis, not just annually or quarterly. In addition to obvious issues of technical feasibility, this raised concerns about the ability of regulators and the IMF itself to process and evaluate that information. Finally, to be effective such requirements would have to be implemented simultaneously in all countries if they were to prevent hedge funds that regarded such reporting requirements as onerous from evading them by simply booking their transactions offshore, and they would have to be imposed not only on organized exchanges, but also on the over-the-counter market, where many derivatives and foreign exchange transactions already took place. For all of these reasons it quickly became clear to the representatives of many of the countries involved in these discussions that compelling hedge funds to disclose the information needed to ascertain when they had large positions in particular emerging markets would be very hard to do in a liberalized financial environment and that effecting this might require large steps in the direction of re-regulating financial markets.

Thus, this first stab at addressing the hedge-fund problem led to no concrete action, due to disagreements between the emerging markets and advanced industrial countries over the severity of the problem as well as to technical obstacles to additional regulation.

The Basle Committee of Banking Supervisors

The LTCM affair rendered policymakers in the advanced industrial countries more receptive to warnings by emerging-market officials of the risks posed by HLIs. Russia's default precipitated a flight to quality and widening spreads between high– and low-risk financial instruments, creating distress among market participants with exposure to the former. The perception in official circles was that the sudden liquidation of LTCM's positions might seriously threaten the stability of global financial markets.[15] Placing the firm into receivership and forcing it to liquidate its positions could thus aggravate the volatility of already volatile financial markets. Suddenly, a phenomenon which had been seen as

[14] IMF 1998a, 20.

[15] Had the firm been forced to file for bankruptcy protection, repurchase and reverse-repurchase agreements containing acceleration clauses would have permitted its creditors to immediately sell the collateral securing those assets, since derivatives are exempt from the automatic stay provision of the bankruptcy code. A valid question is whether the counterparties to these repurchase agreements would have dumped the securities on the market when they foreclosed and took possession. For two views, see Mayer (1998) and F. Edwards (1999).

a problem for small, developing countries was recognized as a threat to all.

The obvious question was how an obscure investment firm based in Greenwich, Connecticut, with only a handful of employees could have accumulated positions of this magnitude. When news of its difficulties first became known, LTCM had a portfolio of $120 billion of securities and derivatives with a notional value of $1.3 trillion, backed by only $1 billion of capital. IMF (1998b) reports that as of Tuesday, 23 September 1998, LTCM's capital had fallen to just $600 million, which still supported balance-sheet positions in excess of $100 billion. Understandably, the concerns of advanced industrial countries and emerging markets coalesced around the issue of leverage — that is, how this firm had been able to take such large positions using incompletely collateralized credit from its bankers.

Given the threat posed by the collapse of LTCM to the hedge funds' international bank counterparties, the logical venue in which to pursue this problem was the Basle Committee of Banking Supervisors, the committee of supervisory authorities from the advanced industrial countries concerned with the regulation of international banks that meets regularly at the Bank for International Settlements in Basle to consider issues pertaining to the regulation of international banks and the stability of the global financial system.[16] The committee's report, issued in January 1999, criticized the banks for failing to adequately assess LTCM's creditworthiness and for relying on collateral in the form of government securities.[17] It recommended that the banks should more carefully monitor and control their exposures to hedge-fund customers and that regulators should intensify their scrutiny of the adequacy of that monitoring

[16] The Basle Committee, currently with thirteen OECD country members, was created to conduct ongoing reviews of the adequacy of oversight and capitalization of international banks in response to concerns raised by the impact on internationally active banks of the debt crisis of the 1980s. Its activities include the development and dissemination of policy papers on a wide range of supervisory matters (the management of banks' international lending, principles for the supervision of banks' foreign establishments, to take two examples), the creation of a network of worldwide supervisory authorities who meet in an international conference every two years, and the provision of supervisory training in Basel and at the regional and local level. See http://www.bis.org/bcbs.

[17] Credit to hedge funds is typically collateralized by the securities that the hedge funds purchase with the funds thereby obtained. Banks apply haircuts to the securities taken as collateral, discounting them relative to current market value to account for the possibility that their price may have fallen by the time they are liquidated in response to the default of the counterparty. The value of many of these securities fell sharply with the flight to quality, leaving collateral in practice worth less than collateral on paper. In addition, there were delays in identifying the need for additional margin and in rebalancing positions in rapidly moving markets.

and controlling. In addition it suggested giving consideration to revising the Basle Capital Adequacy Standards for International Banks to take into account the special risks associated with lending to hedge funds.

That the Basle Committee highlighted these problems and tabled these recommendations reflected its own particular structure and motivations. Its concern was with the threat to systemic stability epitomized by the collapse of LTCM, not with the market manipulation that preoccupied the emerging markets. This is not surprising, given that emerging markets were not represented on the Basle Committee. Nor was it surprising that the committee's recommendations fell squarely within the framework of its own previous activities, focusing as they did on stronger prudential policies by financial market participants themselves and stronger oversight by national supervisory authorities, and relying on international standards as the mechanism for encouraging such policies.[18]

The report of the Basle Committee also recommended that different departments within each financial institution should take into account one another's exposures vis-à-vis their hedge-fund customers. This idea had obvious attractions from the viewpoint of systemic stability, the committee's bread and butter, since it would encourage the large international banks to more closely manage their overall exposures. But, from the point of view of emerging markets, it had worrisome implications, because giving the proprietary trading desk information about how much credit a bank's dealers are giving their hedge-fund customers for particular transactions raised the clear danger of encouraging frontrunning by the prop desk. Emerging-market governments saw this measure as buttressing systematic stability at the price of further encouraging collusion and market destabilization.

Thus, while the crisis associated with LTCM expanded the range of countries concerned with the hedge-fund problem and brought together developed and developing countries around the issue of leverage and market stability, the two groups responded to different motivations — in one case market integrity, in the other systemic stability. Consequently, the recommendations to which they were led were fundamentally at odds.

---

[18] Specifically, the report contemplated revising the committee's Capital Adequacy Standards for International Banks (an accord reached in 1988 by the committee to establish uniform international standards to ensure that international banks were adequately capitalized), abolishing the maximum 50 percent risk weighting for nonbank over-the-counter (OTC) derivatives exposures and to encourage counterparties to impose an initial margin on repurchase transactions. Thus, the Basle Committee's previous activities, which focused on the development of international standards, led it to contemplate international standards as the obvious mechanism for addressing the hedge-fund problem.

The President's Working Group on Financial Markets

Yet another report was issued in April 1999 by an interagency task force consisting of senior staff of the U.S. Treasury, Federal Reserve, Securities and Exchange Commission, and Commodity Futures Trading Commission (CFTC). While this was only one of several reports issued by national governments in response to the hedge-fund problem, its significance was twofold. It defined the position subsequently adopted by the U.S. government in international discussions and negotiations. And it shifted discussions from the merits of disclosure to regulators to the merits of disclosure to the public.

The majority view was that information reported annually or even quarterly to the regulators would likely be of relatively little utility for detecting systemic risk.[19] Because hedge funds, not bound by restrictive covenants and prospectuses, can alter their portfolios so quickly and completely, information disclosed to the regulators on a periodic basis quickly becomes outdated.[20] In addition, given the heavy utilization by hedge funds of sophisticated derivative financial instruments, interpreting these data, even if they are available on a continuous basis, is likely to strain the analytical capacity of the regulators.[21]

This was the logic that led the President's Working Group to its principal departure from its predecessors, when it argued that hedge funds should be required to disclose aggregated financial information, not just to the regulators but also the public, so that market discipline could substitute for regulation. Requiring disclosure to investors would presumably strengthen the market discipline felt by managers.[22] Requiring disclosure to counterparties would allow the banks to better monitor and evaluate their exposures to their highly leveraged clients. And dis-

[19] The report and congressional testimony by officials of the agencies participating in the working group betray some disagreement among the agencies involved regarding desirable policy responses. It would appear that the CFTC, which is used to dealing with markets where market-cornering has been an issue (silver markets, for example), was more concerned than other agencies with issues of market integrity. It is to the CFTC that hedge funds report their large positions daily under the provisions of the U.S. Large Trade and Position Reporting System. And it is the CFTC that regulates hedge funds that are also commodity pool operators.

[20] It might be asked whether information on LTCM's positions, capital, and estimates of aggregate risk (VaRs) would have provided regulators with a useful warning had they last received it in May of 1998, much less August of 1997.

[21] Finally, disclosure to the regulators might create moral hazard by giving rise to the impression that the regulators had too much invested in their oversight of highly leveraged institutions to allow the latter to fail.

[22] For example, well-informed shareholders would presumably prevent managers preoccupied with regaining their previous high-water mark from taking on excessive risk.

closure to the public would impose market discipline on the banks, which historically have displayed a tendency to be overly generous with credit to hedge-fund customers. Disclosure could presumably be mandated by the passage of a bill requiring unregulated hedge funds to submit regular reports to the CFTC and/or the Board of the Governors of the Federal Reserve System similar to those already submitted by Commodity Pool Operators.

Questions could and were raised about these rationales for mandatory public disclosure. HLIs' disclosure of how much credit they have obtained in total will not tell investors how much credit they have from individual counterparties. Would information on individual hedge funds' assets under management and total leverage therefore tell individual investors what they need to know about particular counterparties' exposures to HLIs, leading them to sell shares in such financial institutions if such exposures were excessive? Would information on capital and assets under management, but not on positions in particular markets or instruments, really discourage HLIs from taking large positions in small markets for fear of being found out or significantly reduce the information asymmetries that lead to herding and market volatility? And if information disclosed quarterly is unlikely to be of much use to regulators, given the speed with which HLIs put on and take off positions, why then should one believe that it will impose effective market discipline? Thus, while the report of the U.S. President's Working Group shifted official discussions further from direct regulation and in the direction of disclosure, and away from disclosure to the regulators in favor of disclosure to the public, it was not clear that this response to the hedge-fund challenge would be successful in attracting the support of a broad international coalition.

Notwithstanding these uncertainties, the report of the President's Working Group opened up possibilities for coalition-building between advanced industrial countries and emerging markets. To the advanced industrial countries concerned about systemic stability, it offered disclosure and transparency as a way of strengthening market discipline on both hedge funds and their counterparties. And to emerging markets concerned with market integrity, it offered disclosure and transparency as a way of discouraging hedge funds from engaging in shady practices by exposing them to the light of day.

The Report of the Financial Stability Forum

The case for public disclosure was taken up by the Financial Stability Forum (FSF), the entity established in early 1999 as a venue for representatives of governments and regulatory agencies to discuss cooperation in the supervision and surveillance of financial markets. The FSF was created very much in the image of the Basle Committee of Banking Supervisors, but with a broader remit (encompassing securities markets as well as international banking).[23] It follows that its founders gave the FSF no official powers and almost no staff, and that they endowed it with no capacity to lend. They stipulated that most of its activities were to take place at the Bank for International Settlements in Basle, the host for the discussions of the Basle Committee of Banking Supervisors, another body with minimal in-house staff. The intent, in other words, was to create not a new international organization with supernational regulatory powers, but rather a venue for discussion along the lines of the Basle Committee. And this in turn suggested that the FSF would model its agreements on the Basle Committee's Capital Adequacy Standards for International Banks, an intergovernment agreement that commits its signatories to comply with those standards but gives no enforcement powers to the body promulgating them.[24] This "institutional agenda-setting" effectively dictated the parameters of the forum's subsequent report.

It succeeded in doing so despite the fact that members of the FSF Working Group on Highly Leveraged Institutions included representatives of the Monetary Authority of Hong Kong, an Asian country that had had prominent encounters with hedge funds and that had raised the issue of regulation in the past. (In addition, it included Australia, an Asia-Pacific economy that blamed hedge funds for the collapse of its currency in mid-1998.) The report of the Working Group (Financial Stability Forum 2000) was accompanied by an analysis by the "Market Dynamics Study Group," made up of staff seconded from the IMF, the Bank for International Settlements (BIS), and national central banks, which reviewed the activities of hedge funds in 1998 in Australia, Hong Kong, Malaysia, New Zealand, Singapore, and South Africa.

The FSF report drew arguments and recommendations from each of its predecessors. It imported several of the initiatives suggested in the

---

[23] The Basle Committee of Banking Supervisors, in contrast, lacks representation of dedicated securities market regulators, insurance market regulators, mutual fund regulators, and the like; its competence is limited to bank supervision, as its name suggests. In addition, the FSF includes representatives of the multilateral financial institutions (the IMF and the World Bank), of international regulatory organizations (the Basle Committee of Banking Supervisors, the International Organization of Securities Commissions, the International Association of Insurance Supervisors), and of committees of central bank experts (the Committee on the Global Financial System, the Committee on Payment and Settlement Systems). And it includes representatives of two emerging markets: Hong Kong and Singapore.

[24] See note 17, above.

IMF report (like large trade and position reporting systems and position limits for exchange-traded products) as ways for emerging markets to protect their markets against "anticompetitive practices." But the FSF also echoed this previous report in its skepticism about how much could be achieved through the application of such regulations. It embraced a key point of the IMF report—that investment banks, commercial banks, securities firms, and other market participants engage in many of the same practices as hedge funds—and therefore rejected hedge-fund regulation as a solution to the problems of emerging markets.

From the Basle Committee the FSF took its emphasis on the need for bank and nonbank counterparties to better manage their exposures to HLIs, and for national regulators to better scrutinize the risk-management systems of the counterparties for which they are responsible. Better risk management and regulation were thus seen as ways of addressing the systemic-stability problem of concern to the advanced industrial countries. And from the President's Working Group the FSF took its recommendation for disclosure by HLIs to the public (and not just the regulators) of aggregate financial and risk information, on the grounds that markets could do a better job than regulators of disciplining counterparties that failed to properly manage their exposures to HLIs, and that such information about the borrowers was necessary to invigorate market discipline.

The FSF offered no new recommendations for emerging markets, this despite complaints from Hong Kong and Australia about the anticompetitive and destabilizing practices of hedge funds. The Australian House of Representatives Standing Committee on Economics, Finance, and Public Administration held hearings on highly leveraged institutions, and the Australian Treasury made the case for requiring hedge funds "to provide more information so that those who are responsible for the regulation of markets have more information about the positions that are being taken by particular market participants."[25] The Hong Kong authorities presented evidence suggesting that hedge funds had been behind the 1998 "double-play," in which investors sold Hong Kong dollars, forcing the Hong Kong Monetary Authority to raise interest rates, while simultaneously shorting the Hang Seng stock exchange, which was then hammered down by the higher interest rates. Yet, despite the presence of representatives of Australia and Hong Kong on the Working Group on Highly Leveraged Institutions, its report did not endorse direct regulation. It offered large trade and position reporting systems and position limits as possible initiatives for emerging markets

---

[25] Hedgeworld, 13 March 2000, http://www.hedgeworld.com/news/. See also Rankin (1999).

desperate to do something but, as noted, questioned the effectiveness of such measures.[26] Those contributing to the report acknowledged the central point of the 1998 IMF study (repeated in the report of the Study Group on Market Dynamics), that privately held hedge funds, in terms of their trades and positions, are no different than the proprietary trading desks and in-house hedge funds of investment banks. Consequently, tight regulation of hedge funds would change little.

Rather, the FSF report embraced the market-discipline approach to systemic stability that features in the report of the U.S. President's Working Group. The FSF, like the working group before it, argued that while regulators lack the competence to evaluate banks exposures to HLIs, the resources of the markets are more extensive. Hence, market discipline should be more effective than regulatory scrutiny in preventing excessive exposures to HLIs that threaten systemic stability. But market discipline, to be effective, may require disclosure to be mandatory, since hedge funds, being large and valued customers, may otherwise have sufficient market power to withhold such information.

Although this was primarily an argument for public disclosure to limit threats to systemic stability, the report suggested reasons why disclosure requirements for HLIs should also appeal to emerging markets on market-integrity grounds. It argued that stronger pressure for stringent counterparty risk management may limit the leverage to which HLIs have access, in turn limiting their position-taking ability. Moreover, if market participants know that aggregate position data will be published, they might be further discouraged from taking large positions in small markets. And fuller disclosure of trades and positions would reduce the problems of asymmetric information that encourage herding into and out of asset markets by imperfectly informed investors and thereby limit the volatility of emerging financial markets. Thus, in highlighting fuller information disclosure as the most feasible solution to the hedge-fund problem, the FSF circled back to the original IMF report on dealing with the challenge posed by hedge funds for financial management.

One other initiative of the FSF and the Basle Committee was noteworthy in this context. Together with the Committee on the Global Financial System of the G-10 central banks, the International Association of Insurance Supervisors, and the International Organisation of Securities Commissions, it established in June 1999 a "Multidisciplinary

---

[26] Large trade and position–reporting because positions can be booked in a number of different national markets, and position limits on exchange-traded products because of the prevalence of over-the-counter transactions and danger of driving additional business into the OTC market.

Working Group on Enhanced Disclosure" (MWG). (While the Basle Committee was included in the group, the FSF released its report on its own website.) This group was charged with exploring whether hedge funds and other opaque financial entities could be induced to release more information on a voluntary basis and with developing guidelines for what kind of information was relevant. On its face, the notion of encouraging voluntary disclosure might seem naive, given the interest of hedge-fund managers and investors in keeping their cards close to the vest. But, against the background of threats of legislation to compel disclosure if the problem did not solve itself, there was an argument that a clearly defined list of minimum disclosure requirements might elicit a response.

Five major hedge funds in fact participated in the work of the MWG, which identified a list of specific items that should be disclosed to shareholders, creditors, and counterparties by financial institutions with material amounts of the relevant risk (MWG 2000). Its report urged hedge funds and others to quickly begin releasing the relevant information and regulators to provide suitable "encouragement" to those that proved reluctant. In response to this report and, presumably, to the threat of legislation mandating disclosure, a number of hedge funds moved quickly to meet the report's guidelines. Largely, in response to this initiative, the demand for legislation mandating disclosure receded in the United States and the other advanced industrial countries (Davies 2001).

Again, however, the kind of information whose disclosure was encouraged by the MWG was relatively aggregated in nature: it might tell investors, creditors, and counterparties how much portfolio risk, variously measured, a hedge fund had assumed, but without revealing particular positions in particular markets. This was the kind of disclosure that might speak to the concerns of a central banker or a financial regulator in an advanced industrial country concerned with systematic stability, but not to the concerns of the government of a developing country worried about the positions of hedge funds in its market. The composition of the working group, its charge, and the venue in which it undertook its study largely explain this outcome.

RESULTS

What, then, have been the results of all this conferring and reporting? Emerging markets have not been able to force hedge funds to release balance-sheet information as the price of doing business in their markets. Given the ease with which trades can be booked in different markets, any such initiative would be effective only if the governments of

the major financial centers signed up, something they are currently un-
prepared to do (see below). Some jurisdictions, Hong Kong for example, have tightened their reporting systems for investors making large
trades and booking large positions, but direct regulation has not been
relied upon. Emerging markets have not adopted the kind of capital-
inflow taxes used by Chile in the 1990s, which make it more costly for
hedge funds to take positions for short periods of time. Aside from
Malaysia in 1998–1999, they have not resorted to capital controls;
again, these measures would have to be coordinated internationally to
avoid their unilateral adoption from sending an adverse signal to investors. The large Latin American economies, hungry for capital and anx-
ious to avoid doing anything to avoid antagonizing foreign investors,
have shown no inclination to adopt such measures. In the absence of
universal agreement, it has not be possible to move toward a coordinated response.

Nor have new regulations affecting the hedge-fund industry been
adopted by the United States or the other advanced industrial countries
where hedge-fund investors and managers reside (Davies 2001). Their
governments have not passed legislation or adopted regulations requiring fuller disclosure of information on hedge-fund trades and positions.[27]
Although the United States contemplated legislative and regulatory provisions that would have mandated greater disclosure after the near collapse of Long-Term Capital Management, it abandoned those proposals
in response to industry initiatives increasing information flows to investors and counterparties.[28] Thus, the absence of more radical measures
by the U.S. and European governments can be understood as a response
to concessions by hedge funds intended in part to head off this threat.
Revealingly, it was public-private collaboration (the deliberations of the
Multidisciplinary Working Group on Enhanced Disclosure, involving
G-10 regulators and representatives of five major hedge funds) through
which this response was coordinated.

Thus, reliance has been staked not on mandatory disclosure through
legislation and regulation, but rather on promoting voluntary disclosure

[27] Two bills requiring additional disclosure were in fact submitted to the U.S. Congress
following the collapse of LTCM. The bill introduced to the Banking Committee by Representative Richard Baker, a Louisiana Republican, would apply to any fund with $3 billion
of capital (or with total assets under management of at least $20 billion), while the bill
introduced to the Commerce Committee by Representative Edward Markey of Massachusetts would require disclosure by any group with $1 billion in assets. At the time of
writing, neither has made much progress through the Congress.

[28] Davies 2001, 4. In addition, with recent structural changes in the hedge-fund industry, resulting in lower levels of leverage and uncollateralized credit, U.S. authorities have
come to see the need for disclosure as less pressing.

(admittedly, under legislative and regulatory threat) and encouraging banks and other credit providers to require more information from their hedge-fund customers as a way of ensuring that exposures to hedge-fund counterparties are more prudently managed (while requiring fuller collateralization as a way of minimizing the associated risks). The FSF, the Basle Committee, and IOSCO have issued reports recommending that international banks implement such controls and practices.[29] While there has been progress in this direction, the Basle Committee has acknowledged that it remains partial and incomplete. "Concerns about confidentiality still limit the adequacy of the information that HLIs are willing to share with regulated firms," it reported in the winter of 2001.[30] Despite healthier information flows between banks and hedge funds, "competitive pressures continue to affect firms' ability to insist on the full range of risk mitigants, including initial margin." In other words, concerns over systemic stability remain.

There has been little indication of a willingness to "shift the problem up" to a supernational authority. The role of multilaterals like the IMF has been limited to designing international codes that render monetary, fiscal, and exchange-rate policies more resilient to speculative pressures, and to promulgating international standards for financial supervision. While these codes and standards are promulgated by the multilaterals and by international committees of national financial supervisors, their implementation is left to national governments.

Governments, having reluctantly learned a lesson from the currency crises of the 1990s, have increasingly abandoned soft-currency pegs, which offered one-way bets to hedge-fund managers, in favor of hard pegs and more freely floating exchange rates. Stanley Fischer (2001), drawing on IMF staff's assessment of the de facto exchange-rate regime in IMF member countries, shows that the proportion with intermediate arrangements (neither hard pegs nor floats) was significantly lower in 1999 than 1991 (34 percent versus 62 percent for all countries, 42 percent versus 64 for percent for emerging markets). At the same time, emerging markets have accumulated international reserves in order to buttress the credibility of their remaining exchange-rate commitments. At the end of 1999, global reserves approached 5 percent of global GNP, almost 50 percent higher than at the start of the 1990s. South Korea doubled its reserve holdings between 1998 and 2000, while Taiwan increased its by more than 20 percent. Banks and brokers, for their

---

[29] For example, there is the report of the Basle Committee of Banking Supervisors on HLIs (2001) and that of the IOSCO Working Party on the Regulation of Financial Intermediaries.

[30] Basle Committee of Banking Supervisors 2001.

part, having learned a lesson from the collapse of LTCM now provide credit less freely to hedge-fund customers. It can be argued that fund managers learned the same costly lesson and, for their part, are demanding less bank credit.

These adjustments, while responding to the impetus provided by the hedge-fund problem, are at the same time broader responses by public– and private-sector entities to the explosive growth of domestic and international financial markets and transactions, of which hedge funds and their position-taking practices are only one manifestation. Governments have abandoned soft-currency pegs not simply because of hedge funds, in other words, but more generally in response to the difficulty of maintaining them in the face of high capital mobility. They have accumulated reserves in response to the realization that, in periods of volatility, more capital can now flow out over the capital account. International banks that were heavily exposed to LTCM have tightened up their collateralization practices in response, but they surely would have had to move in that direction in response to credit-market developments even if the LTCM crisis had not intervened.

These responses have had a noticeable impact on the hedge-fund industry.[31] Eliminating one-way bets in currency markets has made the "currency plays" that were the core investment strategies of macro funds less attractive and profitable, causing several of the leading macro funds to reorient their investment strategies or close up shop entirely. The decision in the second quarter of 2000 of two of the largest macro-fund managers, Julian Robertson and George Soros, to disband (in the first case) and scale back macro-related investing (in the second) can be understood in this light. As a result there are fewer hedge-fund "elephants" to disrupt emerging market "ponds." Currency crises have not disappeared, but when they occur they have not given rise as frequently to complaints about disruptions inflicted by rapacious hedge-fund managers.

Similarly, strengthened counterparty risk management has made it more difficult for hedge-fund managers to pursue the type of investment strategy utilized by "relative-value" funds like LTCM that involve using large amounts of credit to arbitrage small expected-return differentials between otherwise similar financial assets. While the new hedge fund started by John Merriweather of LTCM fame has not abandoned the relative-value approach entirely, the less liberal supply of credit being made available by hedge-fund counterparties has forced Merriweather's new fund to pursue a more conservative variant of the strategy. Systemic risk remains a concern, to be sure, but large highly leveraged

---

[31] These are the structural changes referred to in note 28, above.

institutions, having been placed on a stricter credit diet, would appear to pose less of a risk than before.

ANALYSIS

Interest-group politics undoubtedly supported the preference of the advanced industrial countries for dealing with the hedge-fund problem with a light hand. Investors in hedge funds are disproportionately concentrated in the high-income countries. Hedge-fund principals and employees are disproportionately residents of the high-income countries. Hedge-fund counterparties, who make money by extending the credit consumed by highly leveraged institutions, are headquartered in the high-income countries. None of these interests will find particularly appealing any measure whose intent is to limit the investment options of HLIs. Even emerging markets, when seeking foreign investment, have an interest in allowing HLIs freedom of operation if they perceive that their managers are pumping funds into their markets rather than taking them out, although it is still clear that interest groups in the two types of countries have, on balance, rather different attitudes toward giving hedge funds a free hand.

A further obstacle to concerted action, as alluded to above, is disagreement between emerging markets and industrial countries over what aspect of the problem matters most. Officials from emerging markets are concerned with the elephant-in-the-pond problem — the danger that large HLIs can corner the market in their currency (or in domestic-currency denominated financial assets), thereby destabilizing their markets and their economies. Officials of the advanced industrial countries are concerned instead with the threat to systemic stability posed by the large amounts of leverage and credit made available by hedge-fund counterparties. That their experiences have led officials from these two countries to focus on distinct, nonoverlapping aspects of the hedge-fund problem has not cultivated sympathy for the legitimacy of one another's complaints. Lack of shared experience has led to a lack of a common conception of the problem. And given their interests in different aspects of the problem, it would only be by the sheerest coincidence that they would agree on the common policy response.

In practice, these different concerns led policymakers from these two sets of countries to prescribe very different remedies. Emerging-market policymakers argue that the problems posed by hedge funds can be solved only by direct regulation of the leverage, trades, and positions of HLIs. Their advanced industrial counterparts recommend instead extending to the operations of hedge funds and their counterparties the same indirect measures, emphasizing market discipline, used to address counterparty risk management in other contexts. Because different policy responses are suited for addressing different aspects of the hedge-fund problem, the preoccupation of policymakers from advanced and emerging markets with different aspects of the problem leads them to different recommendations.

What prevents policymakers from these two parts of the world, both concerned with the threat posed by HLIs for financial stability, from embracing both sets of recommendations, or at least adopting elements of both? In principle, there is no reason why stronger counterparty risk management, invigorated by the market discipline that fuller disclosure of hedge funds' financial operations imposed, could not be combined with direct regulatory limits on hedge funds' trades and positions. The first set of reforms would address concerns over the implications for the global financial system, while the second would address the worries of small countries about large market participants.

The answer, in part, is that the first set of measures is compatible with the mind-set and terms of reference of the international community of financial supervisors while the second set of recommendations is not. The Basle Committee is moving away from direct regulation in favor of market discipline, reflecting doubts about the effectiveness of direct regulation in a world of highly developed, highly liquid financial markets. This is evident in the revision of the Basle Capital Adequacy Standards for International Banks: where the original Basle standards defined minimum capital ratios for different classes of financial assets by placing them into a set of separate risk buckets, the revision currently under consideration proposes allowing banks to estimate their own capital requirements using own their proprietary models of portfolio risk and relying on investors to apply discipline to bank management. This same perspective has led regulators in a number of countries to consider regulatory changes designed to heighten the sensitivity of financial intermediaries to market discipline, such as the requirement that banks issue fixed amounts of subordinated debt.

Initiatives designed around information dissemination and market discipline are consistent with this prevailing ethos, while those mandating additional direct regulation are not. This approach to prudential supervision reflects the rapid development of information, communication, and data-processing technologies. Advances in computing have made it easier for financial engineers to concoct and price derivative financial securities, in turn encouraging the development of liquid secondary markets in these assets. This has made it easier for portfolio managers to arbitrage regulatory requirements—in the case of the original Basle standards, to securitize assets subject to high capital charges and shift them off of the balance sheet without altering overall portfolio risk. This leads to the preference for market– and information-based discipline over direct regulation. It informs the belief that attempts to regulate the trades and positions of hedge funds in particular markets could similarly be evaded by clever financial managers (who booked their trades through third parties, for example).

Finally, neither emerging markets nor advanced industrial countries constituted a monolithic bloc when it came to attitudes toward and the regulation of hedge-fund activities. By the second half of the 1990s, the principal Latin American countries had moved further in the direction of (financial) market-led economic systems than their East Asian counterparts; they more enthusiastically accepted their dependence on international financial markets. Thus, they were more inclined to regard hedge funds as friend than foe — as suppliers of credit rather than manipulators of their markets. This rendered it difficult, if not impossible, to construct a united front of emerging markets committed to the tighter regulation of highly leveraged institutions. And, on the side of the advanced industrial countries, the United States was more fully committed than European and Japanese governments to relying on market discipline as a mechanism for discouraging excessive leverage and concentrated positions that might jeopardize systemic stability. Consequently it proved difficult to cultivate a coalition of advanced-industrial nations in favor of direct regulation.

Thus, interest-group politics; the growing difficulty of placing quantitative limits on positions and credit in a high-tech financial world; the movement of most regulatory authorities away from direct regulation of positions and portfolios in favor greater reliance on market discipline informed by publicly available information; and, finally, their very different diagnoses of the nature of the problem (shaped by the absence of shared experience) — all of these factors have allowed supervisors to agree on only limited international responses to the perceived threat of hedge funds for financial stability.

For all of these reasons, then, the response to the hedge-fund problem has taken place at the national rather than the international level, and through adjustments in exchange-rate policy, implemented unilaterally by national governments and central banks, rather than through the re-regulation of financial markets and transactions — something that would require very extensive international coordination, for which the preconditions do not presently exist. It has taken place at the level of markets rather than official institutions, through the adoption of stronger risk-management practices by financial intermediaries burned by their exposure to LTCM, again unilaterally as much as a result of official initiatives. That this "solution" has occurred at the national rather than the international level and has been undertaken by markets as much as governments reveals the difficulty the latter have encountered when attempting to agree on which aspect of the problem matters most and what responses are appropriate and feasible. And that the principal measures taken have been adopted in response to market pressures rather than in an effort to resist them is indicative of constraints that the market places on efforts at reform.

CONCLUSIONS AND IMPLICATIONS

It is the international mobility of capital that most strongly distinguishes financial markets today from financial markets fifty years ago. Capital mobility limits the effectiveness of efforts to regulate markets at the national level and creates a prima facie case for international cooperation. Hedge funds, allegedly the villains of the East Asian financial crisis and of the global financial instability of 1998, are probably the most footloose of international investors. Consequently, international efforts to respond to the hedge-fund problem provide an illuminating window onto the challenge of governing global financial markets.

In terms of the distinctions at the center of the present volume, responses to the hedge-fund problem have tended to rely more on market discipline than government regulation and more on national than international initiative. Responses to the problem of systemic stability, for their part, are mainly sited at the level of the markets and the nation-state. Banks are expected to demand additional information of their hedge-fund clients, to require more collateral when lending to highly leveraged institutions, and to more prudently manage the extension of credit. The role of governments is limited to agreeing on international standards for risk management by these private sector institutions and to using their powers of prudential supervision to sharpen the incentives for banks to carry out these tasks. In this respect, there is a parallel between this case and those considered by Mattli and Haufler in chapters 8 and 9, insofar as there is a tendency to privatize governance where globalization weakens the regulatory capacity of national governments. While it is often asserted that the globalization of economic activity creates an incentive to shift its governance "upward" to a supranational authority, this chapter, like others in the present volume, suggests that this is not the only, or, for that matter, even the most likely, response.

Responses to the problem of market integrity take a similar form. Again, the emphasis is on markets rather than governments and on national rather than international initiatives. With less credit at their disposal, it is hoped, a few hedge funds will be less able to destabilize a particular national financial market. In addition, since 1998 governments and central banks have accumulated additional international reserves with the goal of augmenting the resources they can throw into the battle with currency speculators. The majority of East Asian crisis countries have moved toward more flexible, market-determined exchange rates, eliminating the one-way bets that previously proved so irresistible to hedge-fund managers. Again, these are national rather than international responses. Again, they rely on market forces rather than government regulation to buttress financial stability. That is to say, several of these changes—more flexible exchange rates and more collaterization of lending to hedge-fund counterparties, for example—have occurred in response to market pressures rather than in an effort to resist them. This is indicative of the constraints that capital mobility and financial deregulation place on efforts at reform. There is a lesson here, in other words, for what kind of reform is feasible in a world where allocation decisions are, to an increasing extent, driven by the market.

Should we be surprised that governments have not come up with a more ambitious global approach to the problem of financial governance? This is hardly surprising when we recognize the preference of industrial-country policymakers (in particular, U.S. and U.K. regulators invested in the "Anglo-Saxon model") for market discipline and self-regulation, especially in a world of rapid financial innovation that increases the likelihood that government supervisors and regulators will always be one step behind the markets. It is not surprising when we observe that emerging markets are hardly a monolithic bloc; while most Asian countries continue to voice worries about hedge funds, the major Latin American economies have only sought to increase their reliance on, and access to, foreign funding. They tend to view hedge funds as suppliers of funding, as friends rather than foes. And this limits the viability of measures that must be pursued in concert by a large number of countries for the benefits to exceed the costs.

More generally, it is hardly surprising that governments have not agreed on an ambitious international response once one recalls how jealously they still guard the prerogatives of regulating their national economies, even in a world of globalized markets. There has been no call for the establishment of a new financial regulator with the ability to override national policies, in other words, not even by those emerging markets most concerned with the hedge-fund problem—who are as jealous of their national sovereignty as anyone.

International committees of national regulators charged with facilitating regulatory cooperation and information-sharing are then left as the obvious vehicles for coordinating the responses of these national entities to this international problem. Here, however, it is important to acknowledge the tendency to address new problems within the framework of existing institutions. The Basle Committee was an obvious venue for discussing the problems for supervision and regulation posed by highly leveraged institutions. And because its main achievement had been to promulgate international standards for the supervision and capitalization of international banks, and its main task when the hedge-fund issue arose was to complete its revision of those standards, it naturally sought to address the hedge-fund problem through limited changes in those standards designed to intensify the oversight of HLIs by their bank counterparties. Since the FSF had been set up as a forum for promoting cooperation and information-sharing among regulators, it naturally sought to address the hedge-fund problem by promoting cooperation and information-sharing among regulators. These intergovernmnental organizations lacked the power to override the decisions of national governments; it was thus predictable that their response to the hedge-fund problem should have been limited to encouraging more systematic and effective cooperation among national regulators rather than taking the form of some kind of more ambitious supernational proposal.

While the IMF possesses more extensive powers, it has no special competence in the regulation of financial institutions. In principle, it could have endorsed the use of capital controls by emerging markets feeling themselves threatened by the hedge-fund problem, but such encouragement would have cut against the grain of IMF policy and the preference of its principal shareholders, advanced industrial countries all, for capital-account liberalization rather than restriction. Financial markets and transactions are still dominated by institutional and individual investors who reside in the advanced industrial countries. It follows that these countries continue to play a disproportionate role in the decisions of the intergovernmental and international organizations that concern themselves with financial problems, and that their governments are responsive to the concerns and priorities of those investors.

If there are three lessons to be learned from this case, they are the following. First, globalization does not mean the "end of geography" in terms of political influence. Second, neither the advanced industrial countries nor the emerging markets are monolithic blocs when it comes to preferences and policies toward global financial markets. And, third, the nature and structure of existing sites for global governance have important implications for policy outcomes, as emphasized by the editors in their introduction to the present volume.

Chapter 8

PUBLIC AND PRIVATE GOVERNANCE IN SETTING INTERNATIONAL STANDARDS

Walter Mattli

In the preglobalization era, standards-setting used to be an internal matter for firms or the domain of designated technical organizations, many of them private. Government-mandated standards existed in areas of significant national security interest or high public policy salience.[1] Each country produced its own standards without much regard to what others were doing. International standards were few and far between; they originated, for the most part, in a handful of intergovernmental organizations.

Globalization has radically altered this picture. First, it has changed the technical needs and preferences of an ever-growing number of international producers and traders and has magnified the opportunity cost of incompatible national standards. This has triggered a rapid growth in the number of international and regional standards and a decline in the production of national standards (see figure 8.1). Second, globalization has laid bare some of the procedural inadequacies and organizational limits of traditional intergovernmental standards bodies, most notably the excruciatingly slow pace of standards production and, increasingly, their lack of technical expertise and financial resources to deal with ever more complex and demanding standards issues. This has lead to a much greater involvement of private sector actors in transnational standardization.

[1] I am grateful to Debbie Davenport, Virginia Haufler, Miles Kahler, David Lake, and Beth Simmons for excellent comments on earlier drafts. I also thank the other participants of the project and two anonymous reviewers for helpful suggestions. I have benefited greatly from discussions on international standards-setting with distinguished experts from Europe and the United Sates, including Aharon Amit (IEC), Christian Favre (ISO), Bruce Farquhar (ANEC), Manuel Gutierrez (ASME), Raymund Kammer (NIST), Anthony Kleitz (OECD), Florence Nicolas (AFNOR), Peter Parlevliet (CENELEC), Helmut Reihlen (DIN), Steward Sanson (CEN), James Thomas (ASTM), Evangelos Vardakas (EU Commission), Herve Vialle (EOTC), as well as Alessandra Casella, Henk De Vries, Giovanni Dosi, Christoph Engel, Josef Falk, Philipp Genschel, Christian Joerges, Adrienne Héritier, Wilfried Hesser, Manfred Holler, Rob Peters, and Raymund Werle. I am particularly grateful to the Center of International Studies at Princeton University and the Max Planck Institute in Bonn for generous fellowships that made this study possible.

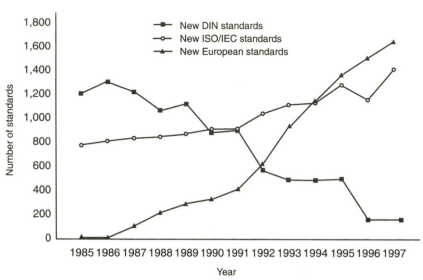

Figure 8.1. New International (ISO and IEC) and National (German, i.e., DIN) Standards per Year (1985–1997)

These trends raise the following questions: Are national standards organizations becoming obsolete, and is the authority of governments being undermined because of the growing importance of private sector actors? The answer to both questions, paradoxically, is no. The trend toward transnational standardization has strengthened national standards bodies institutionally. Much of international standardization is premised on strong national organizations. The international and national levels complement and reinforce each other. Demand for regional or international standards translates into more work for national standards bodies. Meanwhile, governments have not capitulated to private sector standardizers but have redefined their role in transnational standardization. Private standardization may fail to consider nonindustry interests or may revert to anticompetitive practices. Thus, in some cases, governments have been (re)asserting their authority by imposing upon private standardizers important organizational changes in order to encourage compliance with public interest safeguards. In other cases, governments have decided to work in tandem with transnational private standardizers, with each party contributing according to its comparative institutional advantage.

What emerges is a novel type of transnational standards governance, one that is neither primarily private nor public, but may best be captured by the term of "joint governance." It describes an arrangement that seeks to combine technical expertise, extensive resources, and market responsiveness with genuine openness, transparency, and legitimacy.

In sum, this study proposes a three-stage account of the evolution of standards governance in a globalizing world. The evolution is driven by externalities triggered by mismatches between (1) national standards and international markets, (2) limited public capabilities and expansive private sector needs, and (3) private rule-making and public policy goals. The first mismatch drives the site of governance upwards to the transnational level; the second causes a horizontal move from public (transnational) to private (transnational) governance; and the third drives the transfer from private governance to joint governance.

None of these transfers of the site of governance is automatic or inevitable, however. As Miles Kahler and David Lake note in the introductory chapter of the present volume, general efficiency gains alone do not explain governance change. In particular, I will show how the larger regional and international institutional contexts in which battles between potential losers and winners take place strongly influence the extent, nature, and pace of the move toward joint governance, contrasting the European case with trends at the international level.

The chapter is organized as follows. The next section discusses three traditional modes of standardization, while the one thereafter offers an account of the evolution of standards governance in a globalizing world. It examines how economic integration at the regional and international levels has been changing the relative weight of public and private actors in standardization. It also examines the nature of the shift of responsibilities in standards-setting between the national and the transnational levels and shows how institutions can shape the way actors with competing interests bargain over these interests. For illustrations, I draw on the European experience (the move from the Old Approach to the New Approach to Technical Harmonization and Standards), developments in international standardization, and governance changes in the information and telecommunications (IT) sector. The final section offers a summary of findings.

THREE TRADITIONAL MODES OF STANDARDIZATION

Traditionally, standards have been adopted by one of three modes, through market-driven standardization or through private or public standards-development organizations (SDOs). Market-driven or de facto standardization describes a situation where a firm produces a standard and then delivers it unilaterally for de facto ratification to the market. This process has several advantages, but market coordination on a single standard is notoriously difficult. Coordination difficulties and a variety of other problems with market-driven processes have led to the establishment of governance in the form of either private or public SDOs. SDOs provide forums for coordinating the choice between competing technological alternatives and for developing technical specifications. They support most of the world's standardization activity and operate across nearly all product areas, producing reference and measurement standards, safety, minimum quality, and performance standards, as well as compatibility standards (David and Shurmer 1996, 789). Private SDOs are based on the voluntary cooperation of primarily private actors, while public SDOs rely mostly on government participation and support.

Market-Driven Standardization

Market-driven or de facto standardization is the outcome of market rivalry. Market standards are typically decided on the basis of economic value and consumer demand rather than on purely technical grounds. De facto standardization can be quite speedy, yielding a single leading standard after as little as two or three years of intense market contest among competing standards. Cases in which markets have successfully set standards include video cassette recorders (VCRs), personal computers, compact discs, and audio cassettes.[2]

De facto standardization, however, is not without problems. Its performance can be evaluated by considering whether enough standards are supplied to meet the needs of users, whether markets select the right standards, whether inferior standards are abandoned when superior technologies become available, and whether the proper trade-off between variety and standardization is made (Besen and Saloner 1989, 194).

The economics literature on standards focuses primarily on compatibility issues, that is, an area where appreciable economic gains exist simply by achieving coordination among different agents (Besen and Farrell 1994; Besen and Saloner 1989; David and Greenstein 1990; David and Steinmueller 1994; Farrell and Saloner 1987). The distinctive feature of the models discussed in this literature is that standardization creates a demand-side economy of scale. Individual benefits — of expanding markets, scale economies, and reduced incompatibilities — increase with the number of users of the same standard; economists call this network effects, network externalities, installed base effects, or de-

---

[2] In personal computers, for example, the IBM PC with the DOS operating system, introduced in 1981, quickly trumped other operating systems and was dominant by 1984. Similarly, in VCRs, the VHS standard of 1978 had effectively won the contest against the Beta standard by 1980. See chapters 4 and 6 in Grindley (1995) for a detailed account.

mand-side economies of scale (Farrell and Saloner 1986; Katz and Shapiro 1985). Telephone, email, internet access, fax machines, modems, and operating systems all exhibit network externalities. Markets for such goods tend to be "tippy," that is, they tend to tip in favor of one standard or another and thus are sometimes called winner-take-all markets. This selection process is driven by the desire of users to acquire the standard that ultimately will prevail; that is, users want to be part of the network that has or is likely to have the largest number of users (i.e., the largest installed base).

Purely market-driven standardization processes in tippy markets, however, can fail to produce socially optimal outcomes. Several things can go wrong. For example, users that collectively would be better off with a new standard will switch to that standard if they know that everybody will switch. With incomplete information about others' preferences, however, no user can be sure that it would be followed in a switch to the new standard. This uncertainty can lead all users to remain with the old standards (even when they all, in fact, favor switching). In short, so-called "excess inertia" arises when not enough users are willing to go out on a limb by adopting the new technology; and if there are not enough early adopters, then the standard will never be adopted even though everybody would be better off if all switched (Farrell and Saloner 1985, 1987). Such an outcome may delay the development of markets and leave them fragmented with multiple technologically incompatible systems. Each standard will have fewer complementary goods and services, and the equipment costs may be high if the standards have not reached minimum efficient scale (David and Shurmer 1996).

Excess momentum, that is, the inefficient adoption of a new technology, can also occur. The decision of a user to adopt a new standard can impose a cost on users of the old standard if, for example, their network ceases to grow as a result of the adoption. For example, users of "Standard 8mm" movie cameras and projectors found that Standard 8-mm films became harder to find and delays in processing grew when "Super 8" equipment was introduced. Similarly, owners of Betamax VCRs had difficulties finding prerecorded tapes for rent after the introduction of the competing VHS standard. And owners of personal computers that are incompatible with DOS pay a relatively high price for software and have less software from which to choose. In all of these cases, users of old and losing standards suffer a loss from the introduction of a new standard. This loss is not taken into account by the sellers or users of the new standards. Thus excess momentum arises when a new standard is adopted but the harm imposed on users of the old technology, who are thereby stranded or "orphaned," exceeds the benefits to the adopters of the new technology (Besen and Saloner 1989, 198; Farrell and Saloner 1986).

A related problem occurs when a standard is chosen too early in the development of a new technology and the industry becomes locked into an inferior standard. Paul David, for example, has noted that the QWERTY typewriter keyboard, designed to prevent the keys from jamming by slowing down typing speed for the most frequently used letters, has been the dominant standard for over a century now, even though there exists a competing Dvořák keyboard, scientifically designed to be easier to learn and to allow greater speed (Arthur 1989; David 1985).[3] Nevertheless, we all learn to type on the QWERTY design because there are so few Dvořák typewriters, and there are so few Dvořák typewriters because almost no one knows how to type on them. This vicious cycle (a classic coordination failure), David argues, keeps us locked into an inferior standard.[4] In sum, reliance on markets provides no guarantee that standardization will be achieved or, if it is, that the right standard will be chosen.

A further problem with de facto standardization is that standards may be used as tools of competitive strategy, with firms seeking incompatibility or promoting their preferred standard to gain an advantage over their rivals. For example, a dominant firm may have an incentive to manipulate the interface between system components over which it has established proprietary control and other potentially complementary system components to prevent rivals from achieving compatibility; such compatibility could increase the value to consumers of rivals' products at the expense of the market share of the dominant firm.[5]

A final problem with market-driven standardization is that it can trigger standards wars, with competing firms spending exorbitant amounts seeking to establish and defend their technologies without a guarantee of winning. More generally, uncoordinated standardization, as is typical of market-driven standardization, gives rise to wasteful duplication in the development and promotion of standards. Time and money could

[3] The QWERTY design was patented by Christopher Sholes in 1868 and sold to Remington in 1873. Anton Dvořák obtained a patent for his layout in 1936.

[4] Stan Liebowitz and Stephen Margolis dispute many of the key facts in David's account and conclude that there is no evidence of lock-in in the case of QWERTY. See Liebowitz and Margolis (1990, 1994, and 1995).

[5] Claims about anticompetitive manipulations of interfaces have arisen typically in the context of antitrust litigation in the market for home photography products and automobiles. See David and Greenstein (1990); see also Besen and Saloner (1989); Gabel (1991); and Katz and Shapiro (1985). Two other anticompetitive practices associated with de facto standardization are predatory pricing and product preannouncements. For details, see Farrell and Saloner (1986); David and Greenstein (1990, 22–23); and Matutes and Regibeau (1996).

be saved if producers pooled their resources and developed a single standard (Grindley 1995, 58).

Private Standards Governance

The bulk of standardization in developed economies has traditionally been conducted in voluntary private organizations at the national level (Farrell and Saloner 1985, 70; Kindleberger 1983; Verman 1973). Though there is a wide range of organizational types, SDOs fulfill similar generic functions. First, they operate as information clearinghouses, providing essential data on the preferences and evolving needs of standards users in particular sectors and industries; such information facilitates the process of reaching consensus, unifying existing fragmented standards, and replacing entrenched standards once the underlying technology has become obsolete. Second, by encouraging deliberation, providing monitoring, and fostering trust, standardization organizations facilitate agreement on single standards before individual firms invest in competing standards. This process is helped by a set of principles that many SDOs share, including due process and transparency.

The organizational forms of private governance vary widely. In the United States, for example, private governance is highly decentralized, sector– and industry-oriented, and characterized by a high degree of competition among the many SDOs. In Europe, however, private governance is centralized in national standards monopolies that include many different economic groups.

In the United States, the first private standards organization was the Pharmacopial Convention of 1829, created to establish uniform standards for drugs. The American Iron and Steel Institute of 1855 was the first trade association to develop standards and the American Society of Civil Engineers, established in 1852, was the first scientific and technical society involved in the development of standards (Brady 1929; Cochrane 1966; Weber 1925). Today the private sector standards community comprises some 300 trade associations, 130 professional and scientific societies, 40 general membership organizations, and approximately 150 consortiums that together have set about 51,000 standards. It includes such influential and internationally respected SDOs as the American Society for Testing and Materials (ASTM), producer of the largest number of nongovernmental voluntary standards in the United States, the American Society of Mechanical Engineers (ASME), famous for its Boiler and Pressure Vessel Code, and the Institute of Electrical and Electronics Engineers (IEEE), which is responsible for the National Electrical Safety Code.

American SDOs have a long tradition of keeping government at arm's length. Attempts at governmental interference in the workings of the private standards system are few and have rarely lasted. During World War II, for example, the U.S. government assumed the role of coordinator of the system and also became involved in setting standards for consumer goods. It relinquished control, however, to private standardization organizations with the onset of peace and prosperity (Cochrane 1966). At a hearing held in 1996 by the National Institute of Standards and Technology (NIST; formerly the National Bureau of Standards, NSB) to determine whether the government should become more active in standards-setting, especially in the international arena, the response of standards bodies was an emphatic no.[6] Two years later at a conference on a similar topic, James Thomas, president of ASTM, echoed this view by noting that "U.S. industry is in a much better position than government agencies to determine whether and how well any particular standards development process works."[7]

In contrast to the American model, private standards governance in Europe is centralized, coordinated, and subsidized. Each country has a national standards organization (NSO) that adopts technical specifications and represents national interests at the regional and international levels.

As in the United States, the bulk of economic activity in Europe is conducted and organized in sectors such as engineering and materials technologies, transport and distribution of goods, information technology and telecommunications, agriculture and food technology, health and safety, construction, electronics, services, and many more. As is also similar to the U.S. case, standards experts are organized in private sector–specific bodies. Unlike their American counterparts, however, these bodies are not autonomous standardizers, but rather constituent elements of a much larger institutional structure represented by national standards organizations; examples are DIN, the German Institute for Standardization, and BSI, the British Standards Institution. Virtually all NSOs are private associations; membership includes trade associations, professional and scientific organizations, trade unions, consumer groups, and various other types of socioeconomic interest groups, as well as public agencies (De Vries 1999).

The drafting of standards is typically done by the technical committees and working groups of NSOs. In a few cases, the task is subcon-

---

[6] See NIST, Public Hearing Proceedings: "Improving U.S. Participation in International Standards Activities," cited in U.S. Congress 1992, 15. See also Krislov (1997, 124–133); and Dixon (1978).

[7] James Thomas, presentation during the 1998 conference "Toward A National Standards Strategy to Meet Global Needs"; see Leurtiz and Leight (1999, 53).

tracted to sectoral organizations; however, the NSO retains responsibility for the work. The standardization work is undertaken by technical experts from interested member-groups. The number of national experts involved in standardization at any given moment is in the thousands; it is about 36,000 for DIN and 20,000 for BSI. Generally, decisions about the content of draft standards are not taken by vote; instead, technical committees seek to reach consensus.[8] Draft standards then circulate for public comment before they are adopted and published as national standards.

The cost of participating in technical committees or working groups can be quite significant, not least because the work is nonremunerative. Thus representatives from consumer organizations, trade unions, and environmental groups may find it difficult to be active in the process. Most American standards organizations contend that willingness to pay is the best measure of interest in the process and see no need for financial assistance. In Europe, however, the need for subsidies to weaker groups is generally accepted and viewed as a prerequisite for genuine openness and due process. For this reason, governments tend to support private standardization, offering state subsidies that on average represent about 20 percent of the budget of private NSOs. The rest comes from membership fees and the sales of standards and related documents (Breuer 1989; Bundgaard-Pedersen 1997; Falke 2000; Falke and Schepel 2000; Lane 1996.)[9]

Private standardization organizations exist, of course, not only at the national but also at the transnational level. The most notable regional organizations are the European Committee for Standardization (or *Comité Européen de Normalisation*, CEN) and the European Committee for Electrotechnical Standardization (or *Comité Européen de Normalisation Eléctronique*, CENELEC). CEN produces voluntary standards in every sector of the European economy except the electrotechnical domain, which is reserved for CENELEC. The main members of these regional organizations are the national standardization organizations.

At the international level, the largest standardizers are the International Organization for Standardization (ISO) and the International Electrotechnical Commission (IEC). ISO was created in 1947 from the union of two organizations, the International Federation of National Standardizing Associations (ISA), established in 1926, and the United Nations Standards Coordinating Committee (UNSCC) set up in 1944

---

[8] Consensus does not mean unanimous consent but implies that objections have been reconciled, or are not sustained, or are considered to be of such minor significance as not to warrant further delay. See Schepel and Falke (2000, 107).

[9] For an interesting discussion of organizational differences among the main European NSOs, see also Tate (2001).

by the United States, the United Kingdom, and Canada to bring the benefits of standardization to bear on the war effort and the work of reconstruction (ISO 1997b, 15). The ISO covers all technical fields except electrical and electronic engineering standards, which are the responsibility of the ISO's sister organization, the International Electrotechnical Commission (IEC), founded in 1906 (IEC 1990). The membership of the ISO and IEC include national bodies "most broadly representative of standardization in their countries" (ISO 1994, art. 3.1.1). For the vast majority of industrialized countries, these bodies are private sector organizations.

All of these transnational organizations were relatively little known and had produced few standards until the 1980s; they clearly stood in the shadow of powerful national organizations such as DIN, BSI, or ASTM. This changed, however, when globalization catapulted them into prominence. This transformation, as well as a description of their operations, is discussed later in the chapter.

In conclusion, it is worth noting that private governance, despite its many virtues, is not flawless. Standardization in SDOs often operates on a fixed timetable and tends to be more time-consuming than de facto standardization; in some cases where technology is particularly fast-moving, decisions may be too slow for the market. Sometimes SDOs concentrate more on technical rather than commercial aspects, with the danger that the final product is not endorsed by market forces (Schmidt and Werle 1998). Further, SDOs facilitate but cannot guarantee cooperation. A difficulty is that the members of an SDO may have divergent preferences among competing standards, most likely because firms find that one standard is cheaper for them to meet than another. If side-payments are not forthcoming, deadlock is inevitable (Sykes 1995, 34). Finally, SDOs are forums where rivals meet to establish common standards; there thus exists the danger that the members of these organizations may engage in collusive and other anticompetitive activities (Austin and Milner 2001). This is more likely, of course, in small industry consortiums than in broad standards organizations with important public interest representation.

Public Standards Governance

Historically, governments and public agencies have dominated standardization in areas of significant national security interest and high public policy salience, such as health, safety, the environment, and consumer protection.

Government control is said to be necessary because of the "public goods" character of standards, or because of coordination and information failure of markets and private governance, inability of users to correctly assess risks (especially to life and limb), or capture by producer interests of SDOs (Berg 1987, 1989; Spruyt 2001; Sykes 1995).

In the United States, 52,500 standards, out of a total of 103,500, are governmental standards.[10] The Department of Defense is by far the largest producer of these standards, with a total of 38,000. Federal agencies such as the Environmental Protection Agency (EPA), the Food and Drug Administration (FDA), and the Occupational Safety and Health Administration (OSHA) have together produced about 8,500 standards (Cheit 1990; Hamilton 1978; Salter 1988; Toth 1991).

Telecommunications is another area where, until recently, standards were mandated by governments and set by state-owned national monopoly carriers (the PTTs). Government control was based on an understanding that telecommunications networks are "natural monopolies" and that control is necessary to secure certain functions essential to public interest, such as universal public telecommunications services and infrastructural support for military communications purposes (Genschel and Werle 1993, 205–6).

Standards issues in "sensitive" areas, such as telecommunications, arising at the international level have typically been tackled by governments through the creation of treaty organizations. A leading such organization is the International Telecommunications Union (ITU) which can trace its roots back to the International Telegraphy Union of 1865 (Blatherwick 1987; Codding and Rutkowski 1982). Its function was to facilitate international communications through the standardization of the technical, operational, and tariff aspects of international telegraphy and, later, telephony. Today, the ITU performs analogous duties for the range of wired and wireless communications.

The ITU has served as a governance model for subsequent intergovernmental collaborations in standardization. There are about twenty-five international treaty organizations that resemble the original ITU; they set standards in their own specialized areas and include the International Union of Railways, the International Atomic Energy Authority, the International Maritime Organization, and the Codex Alimentarius Commission (David and Shurmer 1996, 792).

As discussed in the next section, in Europe the institutional focal points of production and harmonization of technical standards until the mid-1980s were the Commission of the European Union (EU) and the Council of Ministers of the European Union. The approach consisted of regulating all technical product specifications at the highest political level in binding community directives.

---

[10] This number is unlikely to grow much given the recent trend among federal agencies to use voluntary standards whenever possible in both procurement and regulatory activities.

Other intergovernmental regional organizations for the harmonization of technical standards are the African Regional Standards Organization (ARSC) established in 1977, the Pacific Area Standards Congress
(PASC) of 1973, and, in Latin America, the *Comisión Panamericana de
Normas Téchnicas* (COPANT) of 1961 and the *Instituto Centroameri-
cano de Investigacion y Technologia* established in 1955.[11]

GLOBALIZATION AND STANDARDS GOVERNANCE

This section analyzes the dramatic impact of globalization on the main
sites of governance for standardization. It argues that standards governance has been evolving in three stages: (1) the internationalization
stage; (2) the privatization stage; and (3) the move from private to joint
private-public governance. The first stage describes a change in the level
at which most standardization occurs, from the national to the transnational, across all three traditional modes of standardization described in
the previous section. The second stage reveals the limits and failings of
transnational public governance under globalization, leading to a much
greater role for private transnational SDOs, but also boosting the importance of international market standards, especially in areas where
technology is fast-moving, such as the IT sector. The third stage, however, shows that transnational private rule-making and market processes
may have their own failings, triggering moves toward joint governance.
Joint governance can take on two forms: first, regulatory framing and
close supervision of private transnational SDOs by public authority to
ensure compliance with public interest safeguards; and, second, collaborative work between private and public standardizers, with each party
contributing according to its comparative institutional advantage. In the
discussion of the first type of joint governance, I will show how the
larger transnational institutional context in which battles between potential losers and winners take place may influence the extent and pace
of governance change. The contrast between the European and international cases is particularly revealing. The second type of joint governance will be illustrated in the concluding subsection on the IT sector.

The Internationalization Stage of Standards Governance

The onset of globalization has affected the main sites of standards governance in a predictable way, moving them upward to the international
level. This move has been driven by externalities triggered by a mismatch between national standards and increasingly international mar-

---

[11] See websites of these regional organizations, and Boli and Thomas (1999).

kets. Indeed, in the last two decades a series of revolutionary technological changes, combined with rapid economic integration at the regional and global levels, have altered the technical needs and preferences of an ever-growing number of international traders and producers and has magnified the opportunity cost of incompatible standards. These developments have boosted the demand for transnational standards and reduced the relevance of purely national standards; this is true not only for market standards and standards from private SDOs, but also for government-mandated standards.

For example, the explosive growth of the computer and telecommunications industries, and especially the recent convergence of information and telecommunications technologies, have given rise to new types of services and network functions in need of international standards. Similarly, growing levels of regional and international trade have increased the cost of differing product standards, testing procedures, and certification systems. As a result, export-oriented industries have been clamoring for "one standard, one test, accepted everywhere" (Atkins 1998; Pelkmans, Vos, and Di Mauro 2000).[12]

Transnational private SDOs have responded by increasing the production of technical specifications within their domains. Public authorities have also sought to accommodate some of these demands by harmonizing standards in intergovernmental organizations. The magnitude of this challenge, however, has been unprecedented and has quickly laid bare serious procedural inadequacies and organizational limits of public transnational governance, most notably the excruciatingly slow pace of standards production and, in some cases, lack of technical expertise and financial resources to deal with ever more complex and demanding standards issues. Examples discussed below include failed efforts by the EU to produce common standards for Europe and futile attempts by the ITU to keep up with the standards needs of actors in the IT sector. These failures ushered in a phase of privatization of standards governance in the 1980s, further boosting the importance of transnational private SDOs.

The Privatization Stage of Standards Governance

High economic costs attributable to a mismatch between limited public capabilities and expansive private sector needs have led to a much greater involvement of market actors in transnational standardization, in effect moving a key site of standards governance horizontally from

---

[12] Organized pressure for common standards is particularly high in sectors where the number of dominant export-oriented manufacturers is small and where economies of scale make it advantageous for firms to engage in regional or international trade.

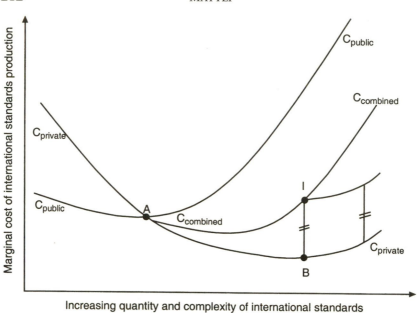

Figure 8.2. Marginal Costs of Standards Production

the transnational public domain to the private sphere. In some cases, market players have decided simply to bypass intergovernmental standards bodies, setting up rival standards consortiums or pursuing de facto standardization strategies. More typically, however, privatization has resulted from an act of delegation by governments of circumscribed regulatory authority to private sector transnational standards organizations; these organizations typically have greater resources and technical sophistication, as well as a better feel for market needs, than public officials and thus may be in a better position to produce complex international standards in a timely and cost-effective way.

This is represented in figure 8.2 by the lower marginal cost of private standards production ($C_{private}$) compared to the public cost (C_{public}) past point A, that is, with increasing quantity and complexity of required standards.

THE EUROPEAN CASE

The move by the EU from the traditional approach to the "New Approach to Technical Harmonization and Standards," introduced in the mid-1980s, is a particularly instructive case.[13]

For more than two decades, the EU had attempted to achieve market

---

[13] "New Approach to Technical Harmonization and Standards," Council Resolution, OJ 1985 C 136.1.

integration by harmonizing national technical rules. Governmental elites and supranational bureaucrats spent years on end drafting highly detailed directives and regulations in different areas.

In the early 1980s, the old harmonization approach had run its course; it had become excruciatingly slow and cumbersome with the increasing complexity of the subjects covered. Furthermore, with the quickening pace of technological change and the shortening of product cycles, the technical details in directives and regulations were often obsolete by the time the legal acts were finally promulgated. In the 1985 White Paper on the completion of the internal market, the Commission of the EU acknowledged that "relying on a strategy based totally on harmonization . . . would take a long time to implement, would be inflexible and could stifle innovation" (Commission of the European Communities 1985, 18).

A new approach was needed. Its cornerstone was the retreat of the EU legislature from the field of technical specification and the delegation of regulatory functions to private sector bodies, namely European standardization organizations. Under the "New Approach," EU legislation is limited to laying down in directives mandatory so-called essential requirements in issues of health, safety, environmental and consumer protection. These directives cover entire sectors rather than single products. The elaboration of the technical specifications that satisfy the essential requirements is delegated to the main European standardization bodies, namely CEN and CENELEC.[14] The national authorities are obliged to recognize that products manufactured according to the standards of these private organizations are presumed to conform to the essential requirements specified in directives (EU law); they must thus allow these products to circulate freely in the EU market. European standards, however, remain voluntary. Producers who come up with alternative technical solutions that meet the levels of safety or health specified in directives cannot be excluded from the market; however, these producers carry the burden of proving that their standards do indeed reach the required safety and health levels.

The New Approach has led to a sharp increase in the number of European standards and is generally considered much more successful in liberalizing trade than earlier approaches. As a result, the Commission has been eager to apply it more broadly. Indeed, in 1995, the Commission issued "Communication on the Broader Use of Standardization in Community Policy," announcing plans to extend the New Approach to areas such as biotechnology, environmental policy, and

---

[14] The Commission signed an agreement with CEN and CENELEC in 1984, recognizing them as "European Standardization Bodies."

telecommunications. More recently, it decided to begin applying the new technique in the areas of food safety, defense, and, services.[15]

THE INTERNATIONAL CASE

Transnational private sector standardization has been further boosted by the adoption of the Standards Code of GATT's Tokyo Round and, later, the Agreement on Technical Barriers to Trade (TBT Agreement), a refined and expanded version of the Standards Code that was adopted during the Uruguay Round.

The TBT Agreement is intended to tackle a new generation of trade barriers — technical barriers to trade — that the progressive elimination of tariffs, quantitative restrictions, and subsidies has uncovered. Technical barriers to trade arise from differences in domestic regulatory requirements that often reflect legitimate differences between countries in terms of taste, market and administrative culture, and risk assessment. According to a recent study, up to 80 percent of trade (equivalent to around $4 trillion annually) is affected by standards or associated technical regulation (OECD 1999, 4).

The TBT Agreement seeks to remedy the problems of incompatibility that these differences cause by achieving harmonization through appeal to international standards. The agreement states that "where technical regulations are required and relevant international standards exist or their completion is imminent, members shall use them, or the relevant parts of them, as a basis for their technical regulations, except when such international standards or relevant parts would be an ineffective or inappropriate means for the fulfillment of the legitimate objectives pursued."[16]

The obligation to use international standards extends not only to new regulations, but also to preexisting ones; that is, a signatory may ask another signatory to justify any regulation that it is "preparing, adopting, or applying," and such justification must include an explanation for a decision not to use international standards.[17] Further, when new standards or regulations depart from extant international standards or when international standards do not exist, and when the new measure "may have a significant effect on trade of other parties," signatories are required to go through a notice-and-comment period before the standard or regulation takes effect. Advance notice of the proposed measure has to be given to the WTO secretariat, and interested parties must have

---

[15] "New Areas of Standardization," CEN Newsletter 9 (December 2000), 1–3.

[16] GATT TBT Agreement, art. 2.4. The TBT Agreement concluded during the Uruguay Round is widely reprinted. It can be found, for example, in Sykes (1995, 169–214).

[17] GATT TBT Agreement, art. 2.5.

enough time to comment. Failure to use international standards may be found to constitute an "unnecessary obstacle" to trade.

These new international obligations have led to a rapid increase in the production of standards by the main international private sector standardizers, the ISO and IEC. By the end of 2001, the ISO had produced about 13,500 standards in a wide range of economic sectors, from agriculture and construction to mechanical engineering to the newest IT developments, such as the digital coding of audio-visual signals for multimedia applications; the IEC has produced about 4,800 standards. The two organizations account for about 85 percent of all known international standards and their annual output has almost doubled since the early 1980s.[18]

Does the move toward regional and international private sector standardization imply that national standards organizations are becoming obsolete? The answer is no. Paradoxically, the trend towards transnational standardization has not weakened national private organizations, but rather magnified their importance. These organizations constitute the veritable backbone of transnational standardization; they provide the resources, technical expertise, and main institutional infrastructure to support the production of European and international standards.

In the case of Europe, for example, national standards organizations select up to three national delegates to a given CEN technical committee; there are 274 CEN technical committees handling 8,842 standardization work items (CEN 1998/1999). At the same time, they establish so-called shadow– or mirror-committees at the national level that are open to all domestic groups interested in a specific standardization item. The shadow committees then brief the national delegates, ensuring that all national interests affected by European standardization are taken into consideration. During the public enquiry stage, the shadow committees debate the contents of draft standards and prepare comments that convey the national point of view. In the final stage of the process, the shadow committees decide on how the national delegates should vote. After the formal approval of a European standard, national SDOs

---

[18] The data are from interviews at IEC and ISO; see also ISO (1997a, 14); and David and Shurmer (1996, 792). Note that ISO standards are voluntary, that is, they are used only to the extent that people find them helpful. The ISO does not enforce their implementation. A growing number of ISO standards (especially those dealing with health, safety, and the environment) has, however, been adopted by countries as part of their regulatory framework or are referred to in legislation for which they serve as technical basis. The task of assessing whether an ISO standard has been implemented by users in conformity with the requirements of the standard is not the task of the ISO, but of suppliers and their clients in the private sector, and of regulatory bodies when an ISO standard is incorporated into public legislation.

implement the standards as national standards, either by publication of identical texts or by endorsement; conflicting national standards must be withdrawn (Schepel and Falke 2000, 135–50).[19]

In short, national SDOs produce hundreds of national consensus positions each year, and select and instruct thousands of individuals who serve in delegations to promote the national views in the various committees. Further, because CEN itself, with its small secretariat in Brussels, has neither the facilities nor the staff to house committees and working groups, the national bodies house and manage regional technical committees and working groups. For example, if the secretary of a CEN Technical Committee is a German, then the committee will be housed in the German National Standards Institute (DIN). In other words, the actual work of European standardization is done in a very decentralized way, with national bodies keeping a close eye on regional committees. Finally, national SDOs are the main financial supporters of CEN and CENELEC.

The mechanism of standards-setting at the international level closely resembles the European case. The technical work of the ISO, for example, is highly decentralized, carried out today in a hierarchy of 186 technical committees, 576 subcommittees, and 2,057 working groups. In these committees and working groups, representatives selected by national standards bodies, from industry primarily but also from research institutes and public organizations, gather to tackle standardization issues. Some 30,000 experts participate annually in ISO standardization.[20] They are advised throughout the standardization process by members of national shadow committees that operate similarly to the ones in European standardization. Their work is coordinated by the Technical Management Board and the ISO Central Secretariat in Geneva, which has a full-time staff of 165.

In sum, European and international standardization do not entail the obsolescence of national standards organizations; on the contrary, they are predicated on strong national bodies. These bodies select thousands of experts to promote national technical preferences in international committees. They also house and manage the various committees and provide funding for transnational standardization. In other words, the national and transnational levels work in tandem; they complement and reinforce each other. Demand for regional standards translates into

---

[19] The national transposition of European standards is an obligation for CEN members; however, the use of these standards remains voluntary and thus depends on their acceptability to firms and other users.

[20] This is an official estimate. Others have argued that the number is as high as 100,000; see, for example, Besen and Saloner (1989, 189).

more work for national standards bodies. Not surprisingly, many of these bodies have seen their staffs grow rapidly in the last decade.

Joint Standards Governance

The extraordinary growth of regional and international private sector standardization over the last two decades has been much applauded by the international business community; however, others have expressed concern, pointing out that private rule-making and public policy goals do not always go hand in hand. Indeed, private governance can fail in several ways. First, it may not succeed in producing genuinely common standards because of divergent technological preferences among market rivals; such divergence may even give rise to standards wars and deepen the fragmentation of markets. Second, poor coordination among private sector standards bodies can give rise to wasteful duplication in the development and promotion of standards. Third, participation in private standards-setting is costly and may thus exclude nonindustry actors, including consumer organizations, trade unions, and environmental groups. Finally, market players setting common standards may engage in collusive and other anticompetitive activities.

Where the mismatch between private rule-making and public policy objectives triggers significant externalities, pressure will develop for a move from private governance to joint governance. Joint private-public governance is an arrangement that seeks to combine technical expertise, extensive resources, and market responsiveness with genuine openness, transparency, and legitimacy.[21] It typically involves government intervention in the process of transnational private standardization with the aim of minimizing the risk of externalities, instituting checks and balances and ensuring broad societal representation.

In figure 8.2, the social and economic costs of externalities are represented by the area between lines $C_{private}$ and $C_{combined}$; $C_{combined}$ is the sum of the private marginal cost of standards production and associated externalities. At low levels of externalities, public intervention may not be worthwhile because of considerable organizational and economic costs of intervention. If we assume the marginal cost of intervention to be constant and equivalent to distance IB, then intervention will be socially desirable only when $C_{combined}$ reaches point I.[22]

Joint governance has important distributional implications, however,

---

[21] For a forceful argument in support of standardization that mixes private and public elements, see Abbott and Snidal, (2001, 361–67).

[22] In figure 8.2, intervention eliminates the cost of externalities; the new marginal cost of standards production past point B is $C_{private}$, which increases as a result of intervention, and the marginal cost of intervention, IB.

and thus is likely to trigger political battles between private sector standardizers, who may experience a rise in the cost of private rule-making
as a result of intervention, and those societal groups that stand to gain.
The course of such battles is rarely determined by economic factors
alone; it is also shaped by the broader transnational institutional setting, as well as accepted beliefs and practices. In the words of Kahler
and Lake, these other factors "refract and distort simple economic determinism, mediating and shaping political outcomes."[23] The following
two subsections offer illustrations of pressure for joint governance and
explain why joint governance has emerged in Europe, but not (yet) at
the international level.

THE EUROPEAN CASE

In the early years of the New Approach, many observers questioned its
legitimacy and even legality. It was argued that private standards
bodies, dominated by business interests, would be blind to broader social issues, and that the delegation of powers to these private actors
would render legislative control over their decisions impossible (Joerges,
Schepel, and Vos 1999). The following, offered by the leader of a major
European consumer group, is typical of the kind of concerns expressed
by nonindustry groups:

> It must be recalled that in placing . . . reliance on the use of standardiza-
> tion, the European and national public authorities have delegated enor-
> mous responsibility. Whereas governments and elected parliaments would
> have had the final say on consumer safety issues, considerable power has
> been delegated to what are effectively powerful national and European
> [standards] monopolies to interpret the broad requirements for safety con-
> tained in the European legislative framework. Consumer participation in
> this process then is no luxury but a necessity to counterbalance the enor-
> mous influence of industry . . . [and] ensure that the results of the European
> standardization process help meet legitimate public policy objectives.[24]

Demands by nonindustry groups for greater participation, accountability, and transparency in European standardization have been

---

[23] Kahler and Lake, chapter 1 in the present volume. This point is nicely illustrated in
the studies by Lisa Martin (chapter 2) and Barry Eichengreen (chapter 7), also in the
present volume. Martin finds that federal political institutions bias tourism policies in a
decentralized direction and Eichengreen finds that the response to the rapid growth of
potentially destabilizing hedge funds has been strongly conditioned by existing international institutions.

[24] Anne-Lore Köhne, President of BEUC (Bureau Européen des Unions des Consom-
mateurs), address at an international conference entitled "Standardization for the 21st
Century: Tackling the New Challenges," in Conference Reports (Brussels: Commission —
DG Enterprise 1999).

strongly supported by the EU Commission and European Parliament.[25] In addition, specific provisions in the Treaty of Rome guaranteeing high levels of consumer, health, and environmental protection added to the pressure for a change in standards governance. As a result, the member-state governments of the EU have been (re)asserting their authority over the last ten years or so by strengthening their control over standardizers and by engineering subtle but critical changes in the procedures and structure of private European SDOs. For example, they have forced these SDOs to accept the participation of consumer organizations and other societal groups. The member states issued a declaration in April 1992, emphasizing that the involvement of "social partners . . . at every stage of the standardization process and at every level of [European] Standardization Bod[ies] . . . — from Working Group to General Assembly — is a political precondition for the acceptability and further development of European standardization."[26] At the end of the same year, yielding to political pressure, CEN introduced a new category of membership, so-called Associate Members, to integrate into the CEN structure "social partners," such as the European Association of Consumer Representation in Standardization (ANEC),[27] as well as the European Trade Union Technical Bureau for Health and Safety (TUTB).[28]

Further, the member states have been improving control over standardization by changing the structure of their financial support to European standardizers, gradually cutting back on general lump-sum subsidies and switching to project-based financing. They also have increased the practice of employing independent experts to monitor regional standardization and determine whether European standards satisfy the essential requirements (Egan 1998a, 500; Joerges, Schepel, and Vos 1999; 23).

Last but not least, the member states have adopted a series of EU directives that provide for continuous supervision of the process of implementing standards. For example, the Directive on General Product Safety (Directive 92/59/EEC, 1992 OJ L 228/24) gives national adminis-

[25] See, for example, Commission Communication on Efficiency and Accountability in European Standardization under the New Approach, COM (1998) 291 final of 13 May 1998; and European Parliament Resolution of 12 February 1999 on the Report from the Commission, OJ 150, 28 May 1999.

[26] OJ C 96 of 15 April 1992, 23. See also Council Resolution of 28 October 1999 on the Role of Standardization in Europe, OJ C 141, 19 May 2000.

[27] ANEC stands for Association de Normalisation Européenne pour les Consommateurs.

[28] ITUTB was established in 1989 by the European Trade Union Confederation (ETUC) to monitor the drafting, transposition, and application of European legislation regulating the working environment.

trations considerable discretion to impose restrictions on the circulation of products that they find to be harmful to consumers notwithstanding conformity with European standards. Similarly, the Product Liability Directive (Directive 85/374/EEC, 1985 OJ L 210/29) offers national courts leeway to determine whether a product meets "legitimate consumer expectations" and whether standards reflect the latest scientific and technical knowledge.

In sum, "European standardization [today] . . . does not operate in a legal vacuum but is in varying intensity embedded into legal frameworks and constantly fed and controlled through networks of non-governmental and governmental actors" (Joerges, Schepel, and Vos 1999, 49–50, 59–61). This fusion of private and public elements in a joint form of governance has conferred upon European standardization a high degree of legitimacy that it lacked in the 1980s.

THE INTERNATIONAL CASE

As in the European case, representatives of consumer, health, safety, and environmental groups have been questioning the legitimacy of private international standards, particularly as the scope of standards in support of trade liberalization and public policy objectives has widened to include areas such as services, environmental protection, and the "information society." But, unlike in the European case, moves toward joint governance have not materialized at the international level. European-type checks and balances are conspicuous by their absence in international standardization and the participation of nonindustry groups is almost nonexistent.

Consider the following example: In Europe, ANEC is financially supported by the EU Commission and is accepted into the technical boards and general assemblies, and can even play a role in the administrative boards. At the international level, however, consumer participation is extremely weak. The only group that is allowed to represent consumer interests is Consumer International (CI), an umbrella organization representing over two hundred independent consumer organizations from almost one hundred countries.[29] Within the international standards bodies, CI representatives can serve on technical committees but not at any higher level, depriving CI of real influence at the critical technical-management and policy levels. Further, no funding is made available at the international level, which seriously hampers CI's ability to send observers to all important committees. Other social partners, notably

---

[29] CI's status as sole representative of consumers at the international level is a consequence of its observer status on the United Nations Economic and Social Committee.

trade unions, are similarly excluded from effective participation in international standardization.

The lack of progress toward joint standards governance at the international level is due, in part, to the absence of natural institutional allies that social partners could count on in their political battle against industry interests. Where is the international equivalent of the EU Commission or European Parliament? What binding international treaty guarantees high levels of consumer, health, and environmental protections? Further, consensus about the desirability of joint governance is bound to be weaker at the international level because of a much wider range of views on how standardization should be organized. As noted earlier, American standardization bodies vehemently oppose governmental intervention and contend that willingness to pay is the best measure of interest in standardization; they thus see little need for financial assistance. Not surprisingly, the WTO has been a timid voice at best in debates about change of international standardization practices. It is noteworthy that the type of transparency that it has promoted in its Code of Good Practice for the Preparation of Standards is aimed only at relations among governments; it includes no provision in support of social partners.[30]

Changing Standards Governance in the IT Sector

This concluding subsection offers a brief account of the transformation of standards governance in the IT sector over the past twenty years, highlighting elements of the three-stage account of the evolution of standards governance presented above: internationalization, failure of public governance and greater involvement of private sector actors in transnational standardization, and emergence of forms of joint governance.

Until very recently, telecommunications was divided into self-contained national systems controlled in Europe by monopoly network operators (the national post, telegraph, and telephone administrations) and in the United States by a tightly regulated corporation (AT&T).[31] "Hard-wired" technology was dominant and system growth was restricted to national markets. The ITU facilitated the process of finding interconnection points between national networks and agreeing on the administrative, technical, and legal rules of international cooperation (Genschel 1997, 604–5). Speed was not a pressing issue; indeed, the

---

[30] See Annex 3 of TBT Agreement.

[31] The monopoly extended from the operation of the national telecommuncations network to the provisions of telecommunications services and terminal equipment.

average time for producing an international standard was about seven years (David and Shurmer 1996, 795; Wallenstein 1990). Not surprisingly, the number of such standards was modest.

With the quickening pace of globalization, however, problems of compatibility became more urgent and triggered an unprecedented surge in the demand for transnational standards. This trend was further fueled by the combined effect of deregulation of telecommunications and the convergence of telecommunications with computer technology, which gave rise to new types of services and network functions in need of coordination (Aronson and Cowhey 1988; Cowhey 1990; Genschel and Werle 1993).

Multinational firms, long critical of international public governance organized exclusively according to nationalities, and myriad new firms that produced telecommunications equipment and provided transnational services now pressed institutions such as the ITU to offer them status equal to national operators and undertake deep structural reforms (Jacobson 1973; OECD 1988). Until then private sector experts had to be approved for participation by a member state of the ITU. The experts were allowed to take part in an advisory capacity only; that is, they could participate in the deliberations, but were not allowed to vote.

Reform within the ITU, however, was not forthcoming. It was blocked by veto-players, in particular developing countries fearing that organizational change would further marginalize them (Genschel 1997, 609; Macpherson 1990). Reform-minded groups responded to this impasse by establishing their own standards organizations. One such rival organization is the European Telecommunications Standards Institute (ETSI), formed in of 1988. Its distinctive institutional feature, which makes ETSI a prime example of the second type of joint private-public standards governance, is its unique membership structure and voting system. Its membership is highly diverse and includes public administrations (e.g., departments or ministries of transport and communications, ministries of post and telecommunications), network operators (e.g., France Telecom, Mannesmann, Vodafone), equipment manufacturers (e.g., Ericsson, Motorola, Matsushita), service providers, users, and others. These members adopt standards by consensus, utilizing weighted voting and a 71 percent rule for agreement; weights are proportional to size for both national delegations and firms.[32]

ETSI has grown over the years into an international institution with members from fifty-two countries. Its mission is to produce "telecom-

---

[32] Measure of size is GDP for national delegations, telecommunications-related revenues for firms.

munications standards that will be used . . . throughout Europe and beyond."[33] Some 3,500 experts are presently working for ETSI in 200 technical committees.[34] ETSI has produced about 5,000 standards.

ETSI, along with a few other successful start-ups, clearly threatened to undermine the ITU. This serious challenge finally broke the reform impasse in the ITU; and the ITU began to implement far-reaching reforms, widening the range of technical items covered and broadening the criteria for direct participation in ITU standards committees (Hawkins 1999, 163; Schmidt and Werle 1998, 50).

Not all private actors in the IT sector were attracted to the reformed ITU or to ETSI, institutions they deemed too slow given the speed of technological innovation in this sector. Instead, these firms pursued de facto standardization or chose to create new forms of private governance, namely consortiums that behave like individual firms in delivering their standards for de facto ratification to the market. The number of consortium grew rapidly from a handful in the late-1980s to about one hundred a decade later.

These consortiums vary greatly in character, size, and resources. They can range at one extreme from the comparatively compact collaborations typical of rival consortiums set up among large firms to develop standards for operating systems, computer network protocols, and the like, to organizations as extensive as the Object Management Group (OMG), the largest software development consortium (David and Shurmer 1996, 802; Mähönen 2000, 39–40).[35]

The advantage of these new consortiums is that they can offer great flexibility and speed as their membership, organization, and procedures are tailored to specific tasks. Further, the resources that some consortiums can mobilize often far exceed those of traditional SDOs, especially if they produce proprietary standards (David and Shurmer 1996, 802–3).

Consortiums, however, are not without problems. They may give rise

[33] See official website, http://www.etsi.org.

[34] Besides technical committees, ETSI has a general assembly, a management board, and a central secretariat with a small staff situated in Southern France.

[35] Other examples include the Asia Oceania Workshop (AOW), the Asymmetric Digital Subscriber Line Forum (ADSL-F), the Corporation for Open Systems (COS), the Cooperation for Open Systems Interconnection Networking in Europe (COSINE), the Digital Audio Visual Council (DAVIC), the Digital Video Broadcasting Project (DVB), the Electronic Document Interchange Group (EDIFACT), the International Multimedia Teleconferencing Consortium (IMTC), the Standards Promotion and Application Group (SPAG), the Telecommunications Information Networking Forum (TINA-A), the World Federation of MAP/TOP Users (MAP/TOP), the Internet Engineering Task Force (IETF), the Internet Society (ISOC), and the World Wide Web Consortium (W3C). See Genschel (1997, 606–7); and Hawkins (1999, 165); and Schmidt and Werle (1998).

to wasteful duplication of standardization efforts, or experience difficulties reaching consensus, especially as the diversity of interests increases with growing membership.[36] A more serious social risk is forsaken interoperability at the international or regional level. For example, the United States has three differing standards for personal communications systems (PCs): DAMPS, GSM, and CDMA. Each was brought to the market by rival consortiums. This diversity is hardly in the interest of consumers since it means smaller networks, inability to roam, and possibly higher prices due to lower scale economies in the production of equipment and phones (Pelkmans 2001, 447–51). In other words, consortiums may fail to take into consideration broader social interests because they often do not meet the standards of openness, transparency, and due process that are characteristic of more formal private or public SDOs (Anton and Yao 1995; David and Shurmer 1996, 803).

The risk of socially undesirable standards may have subsided somewhat due to a recent trend among consortiums to establish cooperation agreements with SDOs such as the ITU or ETSI. These agreements enable consortiums to submit their technical specification to the SDOs for consideration; SDOs may then decide to adopt them as official standards. The beauty of these arrangements is that they render formal standardization processes more efficient and responsive to industry requirements while maintaining some public interest safeguards; further, they enhance the legitimacy, and thus acceptability, of standards that have originated in consortiums. In sum, these cooperation agreements add further impetus to the move toward joint standards governance in the IT sector.

CONCLUSIONS AND IMPLICATIONS

Traditional international relations (IR) theory holds that states, which are assumed to be the key players, cope with the complexities of an increasingly interdependent world by establishing intergovernmental institutions; these institutions are said to correct "market failures" stemming from asymmetric information, moral hazard, risk, and uncertainty (Keohane 1984).

Standards-setting in an increasingly global world, however, teaches us that (1) the failure of intergovernmental institutional arrangements may be as pervasive as market failures; (2) international private sector actors may themselves be capable of remedying so-called market failures through the creation of private governance bodies (thus deserving a much more

---

[36] Some consortiums, such as the International Multimedia Association (IMA) or the Object Management Group (OMG), have over one thousand members.

central analytical place in IR theory);[37] (3) transnational private governance, in turn, may fail society because of capture and coordination dilemmas, necessitating public remedies; and (4) with regard to the level of governance, demands of globalization need not undermine national institutional arrangements, but may in fact strengthen them. These lessons suggest that only a comparative institutional analysis that weighs the costs and benefits of both private and public remedies of market or institutional failures across levels can provide a framework to address questions of efficiency, effectiveness, and optimal design of governance.

Transnational standards-setting in a globalizing economy is an intricate and complex matter for which traditional intergovernmental institutions were ill prepared and poorly fitted. As a result, governments have been delegating important powers *nolens volens* to transnational private standards bodies. The ensuing growth of private standards governance is a striking change in the institutional architecture of standardization and represents a remarkable development in governance more generally. The account, however, does not stop here. Equally striking is the recent trend away from purely private standards governance to joint private–public transnational governance, an arrangement that combines technical expertise, extensive resources, and market responsiveness with genuine openness, transparency, and legitimacy. This result is achieved through regulatory framing and close supervision of transnational private standardizers by public authority, or collaborative standards ventures between private and public actors. Joint governance does not imply an asymmetric relationship, with the public sphere dependent on the private one or vice-versa, but rather one of mutual dependency. As this chapter has shown, in transnational standardization the private often springs from the public and is framed, supported, and legitimized by it. And the public, in turn, feeds on the private, and is taught and challenged by it.

---

[37] For more evidence on the growing importance of nonstate actors in world affairs, see Carsten and Schneider (2000); Cutler, Haufler, and Porter (1999); Greenwood and Jacek (2000); Higgott, Underhill, and Bieler (2000); Knill and Lehmkuhl (forthcoming); and Mattli (2001).

Chapter 9

GLOBALIZATION AND INDUSTRY
SELF-REGULATION

Virginia Haufler

CRITICS ARGUE that globalization is shifting the patterns of authority and governance in the international system. Governance is moving upward to regional and international arenas, and downward toward local and subnational institutions. This chapter explores another option: that authority is moving "sideways," that is, out of the hands of governments and into the hands of nonstate actors. Many analysts argue that the state is retreating, and that other actors challenge the dominance of public authorities over public life (Strange 1996). One of the most prominent challenges to the sovereign state, according to many observers, is the increasing power and influence of the multinational corporation. Anticorporate criticism has heated up in recent years, animating much of the hostility to globalization visible in demonstrations in Seattle, Washington, D.C., Genoa, and at every international gathering addressing economic issues. This activism has not as yet led to extensive and comprehensive intergovernmental regulation of corporations. Instead, companies are proposing to regulate their own behavior through a variety of voluntary initiatives, many of them international in scope. Through these initiatives, the private sector may become an active participant in global governance.

The private sector has always been the primary source for some sorts of governance, particularly in the realm of technical standards-setting. (Cutler, Haufler, and Porter 1999; Mattli, chapter 8 in the present volume). But scores of multinational corporations in recent years have adopted a variety of policies that regulate their own behavior in social and environmental affairs. For example, Mattel established a global code of conduct setting labor standards for its suppliers, and DeBeers participated in the creation of a system to certify diamonds as "conflict-free." The private sector now engages in a range of activities that would have been unthinkable two decades ago. What has changed to make so many firms in so many different industries voluntarily limit their own behavior with regard to social, environmental, and political issues? Why are they willing to apply such limits without governmental coercion, apply those limits across national borders, and even enforce them outside the borders of the firm itself to apply to suppliers and partners?

Globalization has facilitated the rapid expansion of corporations abroad, bringing them into contact with people in countries with widely disparate standards and laws. At the same time, globalization has reduced the costs of organizing, allowing activists to build coalitions across national borders and launch global campaigns. Those activists, stymied in their reform efforts by intransigent and undemocratic governments in many corners of the world, increasingly have launched those campaigns against the activities of global corporations that are viewed as responsible for the ills wrought by economic change. Globalization also puts on the international agenda a range of transnational issues that can only be resolved through collective action by states, pushing them to negotiate new law in international political arenas that are alien to corporate managers more used to domestic lobbying. Corporate decision makers who perceive themselves to be under attack from both regulatory and reputational threats will be most likely to pursue a self-regulatory strategy in order to maximize their autonomy while responding to these twin pressures.

This chapter explores the changing role of the private sector in governance during the last few decades by analyzing a potentially significant change in corporate strategy: the move toward industry self-regulation. The following section discusses globalization and its general effects on corporations and activists. The next section introduces a framework for understanding the strategic choices facing corporate leaders and the conflicting pressures that push toward a variety of self-regulatory strategies. The chapter then provides a brief overview of industry regulation and self-regulation in two different periods of time, focusing particularly on environmental issues. The conclusion explores the challenges to accountability and democratic participation raised by industry self-regulation.

THE EFFECTS OF GLOBALIZATION

Globalization has been defined in a number of ways, but at heart it is an increase in economic integration among national markets, in which decreasing barriers to economic exchange and factor mobility gradually creates "one economic space from many" (Kahler and Lake, chapter 1 in the present volume). Since World War II, governments have progressively reduced the barriers to trade and capital flows, not just among the industrialized countries, but also, and significantly, in the developing world and former socialist-bloc countries (Simmons and Elkins, chapter 11 in the present volume). One of the main responses to this economic integration has been the entry of transnational corporations into markets in every corner of the world. More companies today do a larger share of their business abroad, they do it in more countries than ever before, and through a wider variety of commercial avenues. A second response to globalization is that political demands now are amplified internationally through the media and new information technologies. This facilitates transnational coalition-building among activists and the implementation of global advocacy campaigns coordinated with local activism. Those campaigns increasingly target international corporate behavior (and perceived misbehavior).

There are now well over 60,000 transnational corporations (TNCs) with more than 800,000 affiliates around the world (UNCTAD 2001). One of the largest corporations, General Motors, had revenue in 2000 of approximately $177.26 billion—greater than the national income of a small industrialized country such as Denmark (General Motors 2001). The top one hundred TNCs have steadily increased the percentage of their assets, employment, and sales abroad, becoming ever more transnationalized. In the past few years, a number of major firms have pursued a global corporate strategy through cross-border mergers and acquisitions, creating behemoth companies such as Daimler-Chrysler and AOL Time Warner. Corporations based in developing countries also have become more transnationalized, at a rate about seven times faster than that of the already transnationalized corporations from the OECD countries (UNCTAD 1998).

The mechanism of most of this transnational activity is through foreign direct investment (FDI). The largest proportion of FDI, both inward and outward flows, is concentrated in the developed countries, with more than two-thirds of inward FDI and 90 percent of outward FDI stocks occurring in those countries; however, the developing countries dramatically increased their share of inward foreign investment in the 1990s: from $34 billion in 1990 to $149 billion in 1997 (UNCTAD 1998). Direct investment in emerging markets has since declined from that high due to the East Asian financial crisis and the recent U.S. economic slowdown. Despite the downturn, $139 billion in direct equity went to emerging markets in 2001, and it is expected to rise in 2002 (Institute of International Finance 2002). At the same time, many developing countries are becoming linked into global markets through channels other than foreign direct investment. Local companies are linking up with transnational ones through complex, decentralized networks of joint ventures, strategic partnerships, long-term supplier relationships, and other ties between firms (Gereffi 1996; Gomes-Casseres 1994). For example in 2000—before the recent economic downturn—General Motors manufactured in over 50 countries and sold its products in about

200; it had a network of over 30,000 individual suppliers; and it had over 260 major subsidiaries, joint-venture partners, and affiliates around the world (General Motors 2000). Even without direct investment, developing country firms are increasingly tied into global production and marketing networks.

Globalization also has facilitated transnational ties among political groups, including activists critical of the expansion of global corporate activity. While the general statement that "all politics is local" remains true, what has changed is that the local political situation is now visible and of interest to political activists in other countries. Keck and Sikkink argue that transnational advocacy networks emerged between 1968 and 1993 (1998). They are activated when domestic political channels are blocked against reform. International pressure can often succeed where domestic activism cannot, bringing outside influence to bear on a government in a "boomerang" against it from the outside. Advocacy organizations today are better able to move information between developed and developing countries, linking issues between North and South. This has been facilitated by the introduction of new media and information technologies, which have lowered the costs of building transnational coalitions and launching global campaigns. The emergence of a "transnational civil society" and global social movements is a key feature of the recent phase of globalization. International nongovernmental organizations increasingly are engaged in "efforts to solve problems that span borders in the absence of border-spanning governments" (Florini 2000, 6).

GOVERNANCE AND CORPORATE STRATEGY

The expansion of TNCs abroad and the intensification of global activism have combined to bring more attention to the regulation of corporate activity. As Kahler and Lake point out, governance is politically contested — and one of the most contested issues today concerns the governance of corporate activity, both at home and abroad.(Kahler and Lake, chapter 1) There is no comprehensive international regulation of TNCs, and each nation has developed its own set of regulatory mechanisms within which the private sector must operate (Braithwaite and Drahos 2001). Regulatory systems vary widely in what activities are regulated and how stringently the rules are enforced. Diversity in national regulatory systems combined with economic competition under globalization leads many observers to worry about a "race to the bottom" in regulatory laxity, as discussed in other chapters in the present volume.

An overlapping system of nonstate actor–based governance has emerged alongside national and international regulatory systems. "Governance" concerns how groups manage their common affairs, and usually entails an authority relation between those who govern and those who are subject to that governance.(Cutler, Porter and Haufler 1999; Kahler and Lake, chapter 1) This definition excludes any reference to the actor doing the governing or the subjects being governed. As noted by Keohane and Nye in this volume, nongovernmental actors can produce authoritative outcomes either by their market power or their collective influence, and through this govern particular affairs (Keohane and Nye, chapter 15). This generic definition of governance also says nothing about the character of the output — the subject matter of collective decision making. Yet most people assume that governance is about specific kinds of issues, "public" ones that are typically addressed by governments, such as welfare or security. Contemporary discussions of the role of nonstate actors in global governance often focus on the issues they address and the functions they perform. Nonstate actors are said to "govern" not simply because they collectively manage their common affairs, or do so with authority over others, but because they choose to do so for issue areas that many people believe are the responsibility of governments.

In the past few decades, the private sector has created increasing numbers of global initiatives that establish voluntary rules, standards, decision-making procedures, and accountability mechanisms for corporations and their suppliers that cover a wide range of issues (Haufler 2001). This industry self-regulation is now a significant element of global governance. Technically, regulation is action or behavior that is required by governments — it is not voluntary, and the regulators are public authorities.[1] But it can be defined more generically as the formal rules or standards that dictate what is acceptable and even required behavior for the private sector, putting limits on what is permissible. *Government* regulations are developed through a political process, and implemented through bureaucratic agencies, with industry as the object of such regulation. Under industry self-regulation, official government agencies are not the main authors of the rules and are not the lead actors in developing and implementing regulatory systems.

Globalization has changed the regulatory environment for corporations in ways that often favor them as states implemented policies of deregulation, liberalization and privatization (Sassen 1996). But it has also significantly complicated their decision making. Global corporations now must operate in multiple arenas when they seek to influence their regulatory environment. They must bargain with each other; with

---

[1] Under GATT definitions, if it is voluntary, then it is labeled "standards."

a variety of national governments; and with transnational actors, including intergovernmental organizations and transnational activists. The negotiations in these multiple, overlapping arenas determine who will participate in governing corporate behavior, what the content of regulation will look like, and how regulations will be enforced. Different issues draw in different actors and generate different strategic choices among the participants.

Global corporations choose among a number of different strategies to manage this multifaceted political environment. These fall into four categories, which are not mutually exclusive.

1. *Stonewalling Strategies*: oppose all regulation in an issue area in order to protect markets, reduce costs, and eliminate government interference. This strategy is in opposition to traditional government authority.
2. *National Strategies*: oppose international regulation, but support national regulation in the expectation that it is easier to influence domestic political systems, and in order to gain competitive advantage in particular markets. This strategy is pursued simultaneously in multiple markets and essentially reinforces traditional sites of governance.
3. *Harmonization Strategies*: support international regulation but oppose national regulation, in order to reduce the costs of operating under multiple regulatory regimes and level the competitive playing field. This strategy strengthens international institutions as sites of governance.
4. *Global Self-Regulatory Strategies*: support voluntary limits on actions in order to benefit from collective goods, reduce the likelihood of national and/or international regulation, and reduce critical reaction from activists and consumers. This strategy shifts governance to nontraditional sites dominated by nonstate actors.

Over the course of the last few decades, there has been a notable shift by leading firms from stonewalling and national strategies to harmonization and especially new global self-regulatory strategies.

Self-regulatory strategies cover a variety of different forms adopted by the private sector: corporate governance, industry self-regulation, multistakeholder regulation, and co-regulation. Corporate governance applies within a single company, and establishes the framework for how the firm operates internally and how it defines the hierarchy of relationships among its owners, managers, and employees (see Gourevitch, chapter 12 in the present volume). As Gourevitch discusses, the United States has adopted a fairly narrow shareholder model of corporate governance, while other countries have more expansive definitions of what—or who—should be covered by corporate governance institutions. Because so many firms today are participants within larger networks, with long supply chains and numerous partners, traditional hierarchical authority relations can be hard to define. Standards established by major players may or may not apply to the last link in the supply chain. Firms also are embedded within a larger sociopolitical milieu that has led some to propose a "stakeholder" model of corporate governance in which all those affected by the activities of a firm have some voice in its decisions, including suppliers, the local community, the general public, and even nature itself (Donaldson and Preston 1995).

Industry self-regulation involves collective action by a group of firms, either sectoral (e.g., the American Petroleum Institute) or interest-based (the World Business Council for Sustainable Development). Industry associations and business groups establish standards for their members. These standards may cover technical or product standards, or reach further to address public concerns about how patterns of production affect social and environmental values.[2] These initiatives typically establish either a floor below which corporate behavior cannot go, or a benchmark standard toward which firms should progress. Monitoring and measuring compliance is done either internally, by the corporation and its auditors, or by the group itself. When noncompliance is detected, the group typically applies persuasion, offers training to bring the company into compliance, and, as a last resort, applies sanctions including expulsion from the group.

Multistakeholder regulation is a new phenomenon. It involves a negotiated partnership between corporations and nongovernmental groups that is designed to address the specific concerns raised by the NGOs. The partners collectively negotiate the rules that will govern corporate behavior, how compliance will be monitored and measured, and the consequences of noncompliance. This kind of negotiated partnership has emerged only in the past fifteen years, and often includes multiple actors, among them advocacy groups, local citizens, indigenous representatives, traditional governments, and international organizations. In a recent piece, Ottaway criticizes tripartite partnerships of international organizations, TNCs and NGOs as a form of global corporatism (Ottaway 2001).

Some industry self-regulation involves close coordination with traditional national governments, and can more accurately be described as co-regulation. In these cases, governance functions may be officially delegated to the private sector. This is often directly negotiated between industry and government regulators, and therefore has both voluntary

---

[2] An industry association is an organization whose members belong to a particular industry, such as the Canadian Chemical Manufacturers Association, while a business group such as the International Chamber of Commerce contains members from many different industries.

and coercive elements, as in many EU regulatory systems (Egan 1998b, 2001) In some cases, it may be difficult to distinguish whether the regulation is primarily private or public in nature, as Mattli (chapter 8) discusses with regard to international standards-setting.

Why have corporate executives chosen to pursue these strategies of global self-regulation in recent years, rather than the stonewalling and nationally based strategies of the past? Globalization has changed the calculation of the costs and benefits to TNCs of different strategic options. Although the choice of strategy depends on a variety of factors, two in particular stand out: regulatory and reputational threats. These may be reinforced by the diffusion of ideas about self-regulation, both within the business community and among those attempting to hold them accountable. As Simmons and Elkins point out, actor choices may be influenced by social emulation (Simmons and Elkins, chapter 11).

Most people would characterize the last twenty-five years as a period of time when regulatory threats to corporate actions actually declined due to the competitive forces unleashed by globalization. Governments have sought to liberalize, deregulate, and privatize their national economies, as Simmons and Elkins demonstrate (chapter 11). But this has been followed in many cases by re-regulation, although the exact nature of that re-regulation varies widely across countries (D. Vogel 1995; S. Vogel 1996). In some cases, the re-regulatory trend has been accomplished through mechanisms that either provide incentives for industry self-regulation or directly delegate government authority. The EU, for instance, delegates significant rule-making power to the private sector, and the government of the United States has sought to reduce or eliminate government action in favor of the market (Egan 1998b, 2001; Harrison 1999). After the East Asian financial crisis, some policymakers proposed delegating to the markets the responsibility for dealing with threats to financial stability, as Eichengreen describes (chapter 7).

Globalization can also increase the incentives for governments to develop multilateral regulatory regimes in order to address transnational issues that cannot be resolved by domestic action alone. As Keohane and Nye point out (chapter 5), "regulation by international organizations has become increasingly intrusive."[3] The pressures for regulation at the national and supranational levels varies across issues and industries, depending on factors that are explored in more detail by other authors in this volume. Despite an overall environment that appears to provide free rein to corporations, the threat of regulation — or the per-

---

[3] International regulation by the GATT/WTO or the World Bank and IMF is now perceived to be so intrusive that these organizations themselves have become the subject of activist campaigns. They are viewed as being too aligned with corporate interests.

ception of that threat—drives corporate decision making. Corporate leaders use self-regulatory strategies in large part for defensive reasons, believing their adoption may weaken support for government regulation.

As discussed above, globalization also has decreased the costs to activists of organizing widespread campaigns against corporate misbehavior. Globalization has created winners and losers, and the winners appear to be the corporations that are taking advantage of the integration of markets. The results, according to corporate critics, have been disastrous for the poor, the disempowered, and the unprotected, including the environment (Greider 1997). The demands of consumers, activists, and the media—all three of which are now active transnationally—have gained in force and influence. Nongovernmental advocacy organizations have become more effective in constructing transnational issue networks to press their causes in many different political arenas at once (Florini 2000; Keck and Sikkink 1998; Simmons 1998). In recent years, they have become adept at targeting corporations which have transgressed against common norms when they operate abroad, particularly in developing countries (Broad 2002; Broad and Cavanagh 1998). They use the media to expose corporate violators, organize protests, bring lawsuits against companies or entire industries, and generally raise the costs—economically and politically—of doing business.[4] Their actions mobilize both consumers and investors to use market choices about what products or investments to buy as tools to punish or reward corporate actions, and they do so on a global basis.[5] Consumers increasingly expect business to produce goods and services in ways that do not have negative externalities. Investors pressure corporate leaders by investing only in socially responsible companies and bringing shareholder resolutions to annual meetings; social investment funds now manage millions of dollars in investment from socially active investors. Through these tactics, NGOs can directly raise the costs of doing business, using attacks on corporate reputation as a point of leverage against them.

Globalization increases the value to a corporation of a positive reputation in relations with consumers, employees, and business partners. This is particularly true for corporations in industries with a high degree of asset-specificity, such as the extractive sector, whose assets are

[4] Business executives look upon this as affecting their "license to operate." Few firms actually have had their license to operate officially revoked. But anything that makes it too difficult for a firm to conduct normal business essentially takes away that license through informal means.

[5] Most transnational advocacy networks are based in the United States and Europe, but they have ties to local activist groups around the world. Recent public opinion polls indicate that publics in all countries, including the poorer ones, desire more socially responsible actions by the corporate community (Environics 2002).

tied to a particular place and thus are particularly vulnerable to concentrated advocacy campaigns. It is also especially true for companies that deal directly with consumers, as those consumers have become more sensitive to the social and environmental aspects of the products and services they buy. Once a firm loses its positive reputation, it is difficult to regain it; Nike is still associated with sweatshop labor ten years after the initial campaign against it. "Reputation management" is now integral to corporate decision making in a way it was not in the past, and it is a key area of leverage for transnational advocacy coalitions.[6]

We would expect that when the regulatory or reputational threats to industry increase, managers will pursue self-regulatory strategies. It is difficult, however, to disentangle the effects of these two factors. Anti-corporate advocacy campaigns generally include a large dose of traditional government lobbying. Most NGOs prefer government regulation to industry self-regulation on the issues they care about, and only support self-regulation as a second-best option. Furthermore, the impact of regulatory and reputational threats on corporate action is mediated by other factors, such as economic competition and social learning. Nevertheless, we can trace the evolution of changes in the effects of reputation and regulation on corporate strategies.

The following section explores these dynamics by comparing two periods of time. From 1972–1992, globalization was low compared to today, and transnational advocacy networks were rare and focused their efforts primarily on influencing national governments. This is in contrast to the period after 1992, when economic integration increased dramatically and activists began coalescing in a loose coalition against corporate abuses and some governments became more interested in issue-based international regulation. In the latter period we see an explosion in self-regulatory initiatives, particularly for the environment, which will be the main focus in the following section. Similar dynamics appeared for other issues, such as human rights and labor standards, and some observers describe these coalescing trends as a "corporate social responsibility movement" (Haufler 2001).

The Failure of International Regulation: 1972–92

The twenty-year period from 1972 to 1992 witnessed repeated attempts to construct a comprehensive interstate treaty governing the behavior of TNCs. Transnational corporations became more ubiquitous as barriers

---

[6] Recent corporate financial misdeeds — such as those of Enron or WorldCom — may make a positive reputation even more valuable. For a popular critical review of corporate reputation, see Naomi Klein (1999).

to trade and investment fell, particularly in the OECD countries. Their power and influence became an object of concern, especially in developing countries, where dependency theorists linked the penetration by TNCs of poorer countries to economic inequality, repression, and retarded development (Cardoso and Faletto 1979; Frank 1967). During this period, both advocacy groups and businesses generally pursued traditional pressure-politics strategies operating at the national level. Developing country governments sought to create new international law to restrain the actions of foreign corporations, and were supported in this by activists in the developed countries. The business community adopted traditional tactics of stonewalling and domestic lobbying against international regulatory action. All sides focused their efforts at the national level in an effort to influence international results.

In the 1970s, many developing nations banded together in an effort to construct a New International Economic Order that favored their interests over those of the industrialized world. One of the prime elements of their call for change was for a rebalancing of power between foreign investors and national governments. In 1972, after intense lobbying, the Economic and Social Council of the United Nations (ECOSOC) agreed to closely monitor the behavior of TNCs.[7] Two years later the UN established the Commission on Transnational Corporations with the mandate to negotiate an international code of conduct for transnational corporations. Under the proposed UN code, states would pledge to ensure that corporations met certain standards when investing abroad — for instance, that foreign investors would respect national sovereignty and human rights, disclose relevant information to the host governments, refrain from transfer pricing, and other points of contention.[8]

As deliberations began in 1976, scandals involving the role of ITT in Chilean domestic politics and Nestlé in improperly marketing infant formula in developing countries stimulated public pressure for a strong international regulatory response (Sikkink 1986). Developing countries insisted that the code be mandatory and cover only the activities of TNCs. The major industrialized nations, on the other hand, supported a purely voluntary code that addressed both host-government and corporate behavior. The business community, and those developed countries that often spoke in their defense, viewed the UN negotiations with a great deal of suspicion. They believed the UN intended to attack corporate power and limit the ability of foreign investors to operate on a

---

[7] This was also the year of the United Nations conference in Stockholm that first linked environmental issues to development.

[8] Transfer pricing is when a transnational corporation manipulates sales among its own far-flung operations in such a way that they minimize or evade taxes.

global basis. In the early stage of negotiations, the issues of nationalization with appropriate compensation and national treatment of foreign companies tied up the discussions.[9] The UN debate over a corporate code became a flashpoint for conflicts between the developing and industrialized countries, exacerbated by Cold-War tensions and the ideological fight over capitalism versus communism. The groups lined up against corporate power faced a business community inalterably opposed to international restraints. Both sides pursued traditional political strategies of pressuring their national governments, and remained intensely hostile to each other. No global campaign was launched by advocacy groups, and business representatives did not haunt the corridors of the United Nations. The negotiations dragged on for over a decade.

Throughout the 1970s, other efforts to negotiate international corporate codes met with slightly greater success, but these were much weaker initiatives. Both the OECD and the ILO successfully negotiated guidelines for government regulation of multinational enterprises. The OECD Guidelines for Multinational Enterprises were adopted in 1976, and the ILO Declaration of Principles Concerning Multinational Enterprises and Social Policy was adopted in 1977. The OECD guidelines were clearly designed to promote foreign investment, not hinder it. The guidelines were comprehensive, covering issues from taxation to environmental protection. Governments and the business community supported them, however, largely because they were voluntary, somewhat vague, and ultimately ineffectual. They represented either current practice for the OECD members, or else aspirations for the future. The ILO declaration also established voluntary guidelines for governments to adopt into law, focusing on employment, training, working conditions, and industrial relations. Unlike the UN negotiations, the representatives at the ILO knew from the start that these standards would be voluntary, and that their implementation rested entirely with the decisions of sovereign governments. The declaration provides the ILO with an instrument to explore and report on the activities of multinationals, but it does not have the force of law or the backing of a strong institution.

In a new development, some activists began to initiate strategies of directly targeting an industry for their behavior in non-OECD countries. The campaigns of the 1970s attempted to link activists in the North and South, typically on health-related issues (Broad and Cavanagh 1998, 6). The first of these was the action against Nestlé and other makers of infant formula, who were accused of abusive marketing

---

[9] The draft code did not contain anything too dangerous, and primarily addressed the need for corporations to respect their host-country governments and not subvert their policies.

practices in poor countries. This was a narrow issue, and it was relatively easy to generate international sympathy for starving children. Under pressure, the producers negotiated the WHO/UNICEF code on infant formula marketing in 1981 (Sikkink 1986).

Environmental groups had a harder time developing common cause with developing country partners. Sometime around 1976 a handful of major environmental NGOs began to support local opposition to the rash of big dam projects in developing countries, such as the Sardar-Sarovar Dam project in India (Khagram 2000). But, on this and many similar issues, the activists found themselves at odds with developing-country governments who were intent on pursuing development, even at the expense of the environment. The Group of 77 countries viewed environmental protection as a luxury for already developed countries. Throughout the 1970s and 1980s, there were relatively few global environmental campaigns (Keck and Sikkink 1998, 125). Although the "sustainable development" paradigm promoted in the 1980s sought to overcome these differing interests, it had only limited success.

A turning point in the dynamics of international regulation of corporate behavior came with the campaign against apartheid in South Africa. This was the first truly global campaign to pressure foreign investors in order to change a domestic political system. Activists pressured corporations to play a positive role in reforming or overthrowing the apartheid regime. In the mid-1970s, the Reverend Leon Sullivan proposed what became known as the Sullivan Principles, a set of voluntary guidelines for corporate practice in South Africa. The principles were launched in 1977 when twelve large U.S. corporations agreed to implement nonsegregation and nondiscrimination policies in their South African facilities. The Reverend Sullivan believed that apartheid could be changed and undermined from within, by companies committed to anti-apartheid principles. Despite the prominence given to them in international discourse, the Sullivan Principles alone could not fundamentally change an entrenched regime. Sullivan himself eventually repudiated the principles, since not enough corporations adopted them and even those that did never implemented them in their entirety. Sullivan then threw his support behind the growing international campaign for divestment — total withdrawal of foreign investors — from South Africa. Needless to say, business interests lobbied hard to avoid divestment and avert government sanctions against South Africa, and generally failed on both counts (Klotz 1995).

The campaign against apartheid in South Africa was the first sustained effort of this kind, in which activists formed an international coalition that pressured governments and corporations simultaneously. The key to the campaign was the use of the private sector as an instrument against the South African political regime, first by encouraging corporate resistance to apartheid policies within the country, then by withdrawal of investments and eventual sanctions. Both the Sullivan Principles and the divestment campaign played a role in the overthrow of apartheid by supporting the far more important efforts by South Africans themselves (Klotz 1995). But these efforts would be looked back upon as a model for the transnational activism that began to emerge in the 1980s and that picked up strength in the 1990s. The Sullivan Principles themselves would later be rewritten for this new era.

The decade of the 1980s was marked most of all by the sweeping turn to liberalism across a widening array of states. Reagan and Thatcher were elected in the United States and United Kingdom, respectively, and launched an attack on the interventions of government in the economy. In the early 1980s, both countries liberalized financial markets, stimulating the forces of globalization. Banks and other financial institutions joined in the rush to invest abroad, followed by the industries that serviced them most — the information industries, including, eventually, telecommunications (Simmons and Elkins, chapter 11).[10] The debt crisis in Latin America forced those governments to accept loans from the IMF and World Bank conditioned upon liberal reforms, spreading further the integration of markets. The so-called Washington Consensus emerged, favoring lower barriers to trade and investment, privatization of state-owned assets, and smaller governments.

These all affected the climate for international negotiations concerning corporate behavior. The UN negotiations over a code of conduct for transnational corporations dragged on throughout the decade, but gradually even those who had initially advocated it lost interest. The parties could agree on about 80 percent of the content of the code, but the final draft was never adopted and negotiations were terminated in 1992. The politicization and eventual failure of the UN code stigmatized any further consideration of comprehensive international regulation of TNCs for many years afterwards.

More narrowly tailored negotiations over specific policy issues did, however, produce significant international agreements. For instance, there was no slowdown in the negotiation and adoption of international environmental agreements. In the decade after 1972, sixty-four agreements were adopted, and in the following decades, numerous others

[10] Almost two decades later, the OECD would note a consensus on the need for regulatory reform to "eliminate unnecessary and obsolete regulations, soften excessively restrictive ones, replace 'command and control' measures with 'incentive-based' regulatory schemes, increase administrative transparency and reduce administrative burdens." (OECD 1999b, 179)

were negotiated and adopted (CIESIN 2001). These were traditional regulatory instruments, and not specifically directed at corporate actions, although they often had significant consequences for business.

Generally, throughout the 1980s, there was no self-conscious "corporate accountability movement," although there were scattered campaigns (Broad and Cavanagh 1998, 1). For instance, activism against major dam-building projects coalesced into a larger movement with the formation of the International Rivers Network in the mid-1980s. The network focused its attention on changing World Bank policies on funding for dams, and did not at first direct its attention to the corporations actually building them (Khagram 2000). In 1985, the Pesticides Action Network was created to work against the use of toxic chemicals. In the mid-1980s, campaigns involving both NGOs and UN agencies sought to limit tropical deforestation caused by unrestrained logging. As the tensions between environment and development were moderated by reframing environmental debates in terms of sustainable development, the number of international environmental networks grew, both in developed and developing countries (Keck and Sikkink 1998, 129).

Those campaigns that did target a company or industry were typically in response to industrial disasters. Some of the most high-profile corporate accidents occurred during this decade, and led to the development of some of the first voluntary codes by business. In 1984, a chemical plant owned by Union Carbide in Bhopal, India, spilled massive amounts of a toxic chemical, killing thousands of people, in one of the most horrific industrial accidents to date. American groups immediately attacked Union Carbide in the media, and many people filed lawsuits in both India and the United States. The industry as a whole, fearful of the specter of strict regulation, and suffering the ballooning costs of activism and litigation, initiated a voluntary program designed to strengthen and systematize the industry response to toxic spills and to allay public fears. The Canadian Chemical Producers' Association developed the Responsible Care program in 1987, which was adopted by the Chemical Manufacturers Association in the United States and eventually by similar associations in forty-six countries. Responsible Care lays out guidelines for how to construct internal lines of accountability, communicate relevant information to the local community, prevent accidents through industry best practice, and respond quickly and appropriately if an accident occurs. This is one of the most well-established examples of industry self-regulation today, and is credited by some with being an instrument for improving environmental standards in developing countries (Garcia-Johnson 2000). Many companies, not just in the chemical industry, began experimenting throughout this decade with corporate environmental codes and environmental-management systems. Much of this industry activity clearly responded to the possibility that governments would impose new environmental regulations, especially in Europe, where domestic environmental movements were growing in political influence.

In 1989, another disaster galvanized the environmental-activist community: the Exxon Valdez oil spill in Alaska. Millions of gallons of oil were dumped into the pristine waters and beaches of Prince William Sound, contaminating the area for decades to come. Public outcry was immediate and loud, and many lawsuits followed, with a major monetary settlement for Alaskans. But one group of activists chose an additional and different tactic. A group of investment managers and environmental groups developed the "Valdez Principles" that they promoted to corporations, now known as the CERES Principles. The CERES Principles lay out sound environmental-management practices, and include a checklist for corporate self-assessment. This was not a strong code when it was initiated, although over time it has gained more adherents, and in recent years the participants have begun to develop a monitoring system to assure compliance.

By the early 1990s, the number of international environmental networks had increased from about twenty-six in 1983 to about ninety in 1993 (Keck and Sikkink 1998, 11). Many activist groups had begun to develop guidelines, principles, and codes for multinational corporations to adopt. But their influence was weakened by the diversity of goals and strategies they chose. Some groups remained intensely hostile to the business community, while others were more willing to work with individual companies than with industry associations or business groups. Different groups busily advocated on separate and often narrow environmental issues, without sufficient coordination of their individual campaigns. They were more effective at stimulating consumer awareness of the importance of environmental protection than they were at developing common standards (Broad and Cavanagh 1998). In 1992, however, their individual efforts came together in a new way, driven by the preparations for the United Nations Conference on Environment and Development in 1992.

THE INCREASING ADOPTION OF SELF-REGULATORY INITIATIVES: 1992–PRESENT

In the last decade, national markets have become increasingly more integrated and corporations have spread their reach into the farthest corners of the world. Countries in the former Soviet bloc have joined much of the developing world in lowering barriers to trade and investment. Foreign investors have discovered the so-called emerging markets in the developing world, and capital flows from North to South increased dramatically (Simmons and Elkins, chapter 11). Large numbers of corporations began to participate in foreign markets, through trade, direct investment, and subcontractor relationships. At the same time, activism against the perceived downsides to this rapid globalization began to coalesce across national borders in shifting anticorporate and antiglobalization campaigns.

In 1992, the United Nations Conference on Environment and Development (UNCED) opened in Rio de Janeiro. For the first time, activist groups participated directly in developing the agenda of an international conference, and held a parallel conference to the official meeting. In meetings leading up to the conference, the NGOs drafted much of the agenda and established the main issues to be discussed. In order to be effective, the activists constructed transnational coalitions that would lay the foundation for further international activism in the decades to come. In general, the Rio conference emboldened the environmental community and strengthened its international ties (Wapner 1996).

Maurice Strong, chairman of the conference and a former business executive, vigorously urged the business community to participate in the conference lest the agenda be set entirely by the NGOs. Many of the proposals on climate change, tropical forestry, biodiversity, and other topics could have profound effects on business interests. In response, Swiss businessman Stephan Schmidheiny organized what became the World Business Council on Sustainable Development (WBCSD), composed of major TNCs. They committed themselves publicly to the principle of sustainable development while also working to ensure that the agreements that came out of Rio were not entirely hostile to business interests. This was one of the first significant efforts by TNCs to shape international negotiations by directly participating in the meetings, instead of only acting behind the scenes or in national capitals.

Twenty-seven international agreements were concluded at the Rio conference. The most significant were a number of framework agreements which would be the basis for international negotiations for the rest of the decade and beyond (CIESIN 2001; Peterson, forthcoming). During the next few years, international activists also pushed to link trade agreements to social and environmental standards and to corporate responsibility. Regional negotiations in the EU and in North America produced economic agreements that both opened up markets to foreign investment and established limited restrictions and standards for corporate behavior. The two major changes in this area were the Social Clause of the European Union, and the trade and environmental side agreements negotiated as part of the North American Free Trade Agreement (NAFTA). When the EU moved toward closer integration under the Maastricht Treaty, member-states included in the agreement new standards for workers in regional enterprises, and limitations on the environmental side effects of production. The NAFTA side agreements specifically addressed some of the social and environmental externalities of cross-border investment within North America. The effectiveness of these social and environmental agreements is a hotly debated topic, but it is significant that at the same time as governments opened markets and facilitated the regional expansion of business operations, they also negotiated these new limits on their activities.

From 1992 to the present, most international firms, and many smaller ones, have adopted a range of self-regulatory strategies in response to increased transnational activism and regulatory threat. The mechanism for their early efforts was the corporate code of conduct in which a company lays out its policy regarding specific social and/or environmental issues. An OECD report analyzed a sample of 233 corporate codes of conduct in 2001, which revealed that a growing number of companies either adopted a corporate code of conduct in the 1990s or revised the ones they already had (OECD 2001). Corporations that have adopted environmental codes now number in the hundreds if not thousands, although exact numbers are difficult to find. The consulting firm KPMG reported that, of one thousand large Canadian companies, 85 percent in 1999 had some sort of corporate code, which was a significant increase over the previous year (KPMG 1999). Attendance at the annual meetings of the U.S.-based membership organization Business for Social Responsibility has mushroomed in the last few years. In addition, membership in the U.S.-based Association of Ethics Officers went from only twelve in 1993 to over seven hundred seven years later, as more firms perceived the need to have ethics compliance officers (Ethics Officers Association 2000).[11] Apparently, the business community had acquired a new level of interest in corporate social responsibility by the middle of the decade.

Corporate codes of conduct are most often developed within the corporation itself, either by directive from the top (most common) or in a company-wide, bottom-up process (OECD 2001). Each individual code is unique to the corporation, although many firms imitate others. The wording in the codes may be relatively vague, simply committing the firm to be a good steward of the environment, for instance. Others are

---

[11] Many ethics officers were hired in the United States in response to changes in law, including sentencing guidelines that reduce penalties for companies and their officers if they had tried in good faith to prevent criminal conduct by employees. In many cases, these officers have also become responsible for broader issues of corporate social responsibility.

much more detailed, laying out requirements for meeting specific goals and targets, tailored to the character and concerns of that particular company. In a sample of codes analyzed by the OECD, about two-thirds state a commitment to comply with the law — which does not sound significant, but is a big improvement for those firms that operate in countries with little or no enforcement of the law. About one-third of these corporate-governance initiatives include measures that affect the firm's suppliers and business partners (OECD 2001). Many environmental codes also contain statements about providing education and training in environmental stewardship to their employees, working with local communities, producing environmentally friendly products and services, providing information to the public, and applying similar standards to suppliers and business partners and to its global operations in general. One of the leading corporations on environmental issues is the oil giant BP, led by Sir John Browne. Among other environmental initiatives, BP has made a commitment to reduce carbon emissions in its facilities worldwide. The company spent millions of dollars simply assessing the level of emissions at each and every one of its facilities, to use as a benchmark for future reduction efforts.[12] BP also organized a diverse group of companies to establish a private sector carbon emissions trading system, outside of government mandate, partly in response to the Kyoto Protocol on climate change.

The constant pressure of environmental activism and regulation throughout the 1980s stimulated a slow but steady development of environmental policy within the corporate community. Environmentalists were accusing companies of adopting codes that had no real implementation mechanisms and no real effect on the environment. In response to this, and in response to national-level environmental regulatory requirements, a number of companies began to develop and adopt "environmental-management systems" that established lines of accountability between the corporate-environmental code and the people who needed to implement it. These environmental management systems (EMS) had become so widespread that by the late 1980s and early 1990s many governments, especially in Europe, began to consider how to standardize them and incorporate them into official regulatory standards.

Partly in response to European interest, in 1992 (around the time of the Rio conference) the United States pushed the International Organization for Standardization (ISO) to consider developing an international voluntary standard for EMS.[13] The membership of the ISO is made up

[12] Unlike Exxon Mobil and other energy companies, BP supported the Kyoto Protocol to limit climate change.

[13] The United States feared that the Europeans would develop a standard that would

of national standards associations, and important decisions are dominated by industry representatives. Within the ISO, the participants negotiated a new standard for EMS, the ISO 14000; this is a process standard, not a product standard, unlike traditional ISO technical standards. ISO 14000 establishes guidelines for how the internal management of a company should be organized to implement an environmental code. Signatories are reviewed on a plant-by-plant basis by outside auditors, and violators are not certified as ISO-compliant (Haufler 1999).[14] The ISO 14000 standard is an odd mix of public and private regulatory initiative. The ISO itself is an international organization, but it is one in which industry representatives directly participate and design the standards. Unlike traditional international agreements, the standards do not apply to governments and do not require any change in domestic law and regulation. Instead, the ISO 14000 standard applies directly to corporations, and they can adopt it voluntarily — or not. Companies that adopt ISO 14000 do so in part to certify and "prove" the value of their environmental code of conduct and their ability to meet international "best practice" standards.

The ISO 14000 standard was negotiated in the shadow of environmental activism. Few activist groups had a say in the negotiations themselves, however, and they did not in the end support its adoption. Nevertheless, over the course of the next few years, the number of companies adopting ISO 14000 increased by about 50 percent each year (Haufler 1999). Many of the major buyers in world markets now require their suppliers to be ISO 14000-certified, and the European Union has adopted it into its own EMS system — in some ways shifting this from simple corporate governance to co-regulation. The ISO 14000 example demonstrates that the environmental movement need not single out one company for an intensive global campaign in order to influence a number of companies at once. Steady pressure over a long period of time, combined with the clear possibility that governments would step in, led many companies to try burnish their reputations, moderate the pressure for government intervention, and meet the expectations of the public through ISO certification.

Two of the main mechanisms for ensuring accountability that evolved throughout this decade were environmental-reporting requirements and certification systems. Firms that want to demonstrate their commitment

---

favor the competitive interests of European countries and harm the interests of U.S. business. The ISO was a more friendly forum to the United States and the American business community.

[14] ISO 14000 is controversial on many dimensions, from the process used to develop it to the substance of the standards themselves (Haufler 1999; Krut and Gleckman 1998).

to environmental improvement audit their own activities and report the results publicly. They hope (without much evidence) that environmentalists will mute their criticisms in response. Most companies have historically resisted any government requirement that they report relevant data, for instance, by their continuing efforts in the United States to dilute or eliminate the Community Right to Know Act, which requires companies to report the toxic chemicals they use on a particular site. Similar government requirements are being proposed in other OECD countries and in the OECD itself. Given these pressures, hundreds of companies now produce some form of environmental report. Individual reporting initiatives became so popular they became confusing, with each firm reporting different data in different ways. As a result, the United Nations Environment Programme, the International Chamber of Commerce, and a large number of activists and business representatives have been negotiating common reporting standards. The Global Reporting Initiative (GRI), as it is called, has involved the input of literally hundreds if not thousands of interested groups.[15] Despite early resistance, more than two thousand companies worldwide now report their social, economic, and environmental performance.

A number of major NGOs changed their own strategy, and sought a pragmatic way to achieve their particularly important goals. One of the most pressing concerns on the international environmental agenda was the rapid destruction of forests around the world, which was the subject of unsuccessful negotiations at the Rio conference. Despite continued pressure for governments to conclude an effective forestry agreement, in 1993 the World Wildlife Fund and Greenpeace for the first time joined together to negotiate directly with industry instead of with governments. The industry itself responded by supporting these negotiations to develop voluntary sustainable forestry codes. The negotiations brought together representatives from environmental and conservation groups, the timber industry, foresters, indigenous peoples, community forestry, wood products manufacturers, and certification companies from twenty-five countries. They created a new multistakeholder organization, the Forest Stewardship Council (FSC). The FSC established strict guidelines for managing forests in a sustainable manner. Independent third-party auditors evaluate implementation of the guidelines and certify forests as compliant, giving them the right to use the FSC seal. The FSC also certifies separately for "chain-of-custody" processes that assure that, at every step of the way from the forest to the store shelves, only FSC-

---

[15] The developers of the GRI standards circulated a number of drafts via the Internet and discussed the standards at numerous public meetings, creating a participatory process unlike the standards-setting processes of the ISO and other international institutions.

certified wood and wood products are used in anything that has the
FSC seal. By 2001, the FSC had granted 1,485 chain-of-custody certificates worldwide, and certified over 55.2 million acres of forests, with
the numbers increasing yearly (Forest Stewardship Council United
States 2001). The Home Depot, the largest wood and wood products
retailer in the world, threw its support behind the FSC when it came
under pressure from environmental activists and has made a commitment to carry FSC-certified products. In many countries, competing
sustainable forestry certification programs also have sprung up. The
American Forest and Paper Products Association, a purely industry-
based group, developed its own Sustainable Forestry Initiative — which
some activist groups such as the Rainforest Action Network criticized
as "greenwash." Today, over forty certification schemes in forestry exist
worldwide (Gereffi, Garcia-Johnson, and Sasser 2001; Meidinger 2001).

One of the most extensive multistakeholder partnerships, involving
industry, activists, intergovernmental organizations, and governments,
tried to overcome the controversies surrounding the construction of big
dams in developing countries. Around the time of the Rio conference,
the World Bank began to respond to criticisms that it funded projects
that were environmentally destructive, especially large infrastructure
projects such as major dams. By 1997, the campaigns against both dam-
building in general and the World Bank in particular had intensified to
the point that dams were no longer being built, and firms such as ABB
faced lengthy delays on these projects. The World Bank brought together antidam activists with the private sector in a grand meeting to
put together the World Commission on Dams. This commission, made
up of representatives of opposing — even hostile — groups, had the task
of reviewing all dams and their social and environmental effects, to assess alternatives, and develop criteria for decision making about dam
construction (Khagram 2000). It is, in the eyes of some, a new model of
"global public policymaking" and for others the prime example of "global
corporatism" (Ottoway 2001; Reinicke 1998a). The private sector participated in the negotiations in the expectation that, at the end, they
would be able to continue building dams, although under a new mix of
self-regulatory standards, World Bank rules, and, perhaps, government
regulations.

Throughout the 1990s, corporate self-regulatory strategies evolved in
tandem with activist pressure. Some activist pressure was brought to
bear in coordinated transnational campaigns, such as the campaign
against Shell Oil for its plans to dispose of an oil platform in the North
Sea. The resulting boycott of Shell gasoline in Europe and the damage
to its name led the company to reevaluate the costs and benefits of its
plans. Litigation strategies also evolved over the decade, as groups

pressed their claims in the U.S. court system, increasingly utilizing the Alien Tort Claims Act to hold companies accountable for the harm they did in other countries. Indigenous peoples in Ecuador, for instance, litigated against Texaco in New York courts over environmental destruction of their lands. Investors are also using their financial influence to put pressure on corporations. They impose costs by bringing shareholder resolutions on pressing issues to corporate annual meetings for a vote. They provide incentives through socially responsible investment (SRI) funds. In the United States, over $2 trillion is now managed by SRI funds, and over 120 institutions and mutual-fund families have used their ownership of assets to bring shareholder resolutions on social issues (Social Investment Forum 2000). The U.S.-based Interfaith Center on Corporate Responsibility (ICCR) coordinates the shareholder votes of 275 religious institutional investors and has submitted hundreds of shareholder resolutions at company annual meetings (OAPWBLF 2000). SRI was at a small scale in Britain until recently, but a recent survey of the top five hundred British occupational pension funds showed that 59 percent of them, representing 78 percent of assets, had some form of socially responsible investment policy (Moon and Thamotheram 2000). Another survey found that 71 percent of the financial community in London believes social and ethical considerations are more of a consideration for them today than five years ago, and 77 percent expect them to become more so in the coming five years (Opinion Leader Research 2000, 6).

These examples are just the tip of the iceberg when it comes to self-regulation for environmental and other issues. Almost every industry sector now has membership associations devoted to particular aspects of environmental self-regulation. Hotels have instituted a Green Seal program for recycling and conservation. The minerals sector has launched the International Mining Initiative to establish voluntary standards for sustainable mining. The issues they address are generally those that have made it into the headlines and given them a black eye. All of this has occurred under the twin threats of environmental activism that targets the public reputation of specific firms and industries, and continued negotiations among governments to conclude a variety of environmental agreements, from the Montreal Protocol on the Ozone Layer to the Kyoto Protocol regarding climate change.[16] A number of individual firms

---

[16] Industry played an interesting role in both of these negotiations, pursuing entirely different strategies. They played a positive role at Montreal, seeking international harmonization of standards. At Kyoto, significant industry players stonewalled while others sought more self-regulatory initiatives.

and industries chose self-regulation as the appropriate strategy to mediate among these pressures.

CONCLUSIONS AND IMPLICATIONS

A comparison of the two time periods, 1972–1991 and 1992–present, reveals the deep changes in strategies of both business and transnational activist groups. In the first period, political action centered on efforts to influence individual states as they negotiated a global framework for TNCs. Only a few activist campaigns were launched directly against a company or industry. Only the antiapartheid campaign represented a major departure—it was one of the first truly global campaigns that sought to leverage the private sector to resolve a societal problem. During the 1970s and 1980s, most OECD governments developed fairly extensive national environmental regulation systems. But as more companies began to internationalize their operations, they came under intense pressure from environmentalists and others concerned about how their operations affected people in distant locations. Environmental issues became an increasingly significant element of the international agenda, and a number of negotiations threatened to impose restrictions on industry. A handful of companies began to respond by adopting corporate codes of conduct as an experiment.

By the end of the 1980s and beginning of the 1990s, the level of regulatory and reputational threat, especially on environmental issues, had significantly increased. The private sector increasingly experimented with self-regulatory strategies, from individual corporate codes to industry programs such as Responsible Care. The real possibility that European governments might enforce environmental-management system standards pushed the private sector to ensure these standards were negotiated in a forum friendly to them—the ISO—and that the resulting standards would be purely voluntary. It was after the Rio conference in 1992 that these and other codes, standards, and voluntary initiatives became a significant and well-accepted instrument for both the private sector and the NGOs. Transnational activists began to launch global campaigns directly targeting a specific company or industry sector. They had more tools at their command than in the past, including new litigation strategies, financial leverage, and the information technology to conduct global campaigns. They had developed numerous ties among different groups, exchanging information and often planning strategy in concert. This activity was dominated by Northern advocacy groups, but they increasingly sought out partners in the developing world. Business leaders slowly became more sensitive to the costs of these campaigns,

both direct and indirect. Throughout the 1990s an increasingly pragmatic set of corporate leaders strengthened their corporate codes
through publishing environmental audits, implementing external monitoring of compliance, participating in certification programs, and partnering directly with advocacy groups and intergovernmental organizations.

Two factors not explored here but that appear to be significant are
leadership and learning. In many cases, policy entrepreneurs in the business and activist world changed the policy environment, reframing debates in ways that facilitated the adoption of self-regulatory strategies.
Sir John Browne of BP declared global warming to be real, and then
redefined the company as being in the energy-services business — not
oil — with plans to shift to gas and then renewable sources by the middle of the twenty-first century. Both the private sector and the advocacy
community learned to discover common ground in narrowly defined
areas, and redefined self-regulation itself through new partnerships.
Some of the learning on the part of the private sector involved knowledge about the real costs and benefits of action versus inaction on environmental issues (Prakash 2000). Some of the learning on the part of
activists involved the use of new instruments in leveraging their influence, including using the private sector to obtain policy goals blocked
by governments. Some of the learning had to do with how to deal directly with each other, instead of communicating only through media
broadsides.

At first glance, some might argue that industry self-regulation is another way of saying *no* regulation. But that is clearly not true, given the
growing sophistication and intrusiveness of some of these initiatives.
Industry self-regulation may also, at first glance, appear to be a sort of
death knell for the state. Who needs a government when the private
sector, with perhaps the help of advocacy groups, can regulate itself?
But it is clear from events that the state played a significant role in
creating conditions conducive to self-regulatory strategies. The threat of
national or international regulation hangs over most voluntary action
by the private sector. Corporate leaders view the threat of further regulation, especially the traditional "command-and-control" type, as having the potential to hobble them in international competition. They prefer to adopt voluntary mechanisms that would avoid legal liability and
preserve their flexibility in the face of rapidly changing technologies and
markets. While globalization may have shifted the sites of governance,
in this case to the side and away from public authorities, states still
wield significant power over outcomes. Fifty years ago, an industry
strategy of self-regulation would not have made sense. Today, many
corporations view it as a serious option with serious political and economic benefits.

Three points need to be made about this governance, however. First, self-regulation varies widely in the form it takes, from the corporate governance of a single firm to complex multistakeholder partnerships. Second, the various forms of self-regulation mean that effectiveness varies widely, too. Kathryn Harrison, in a review of environmental self-regulatory programs in the United States and Canada, comes to mixed conclusions about the effectiveness of the programs (Harrison 1999; but see also Garcia-Johnson 2000). In a recent paper, Kathryn Gordon argues that nonbinding agreements such as these have an important role to play in experimenting with new rules and creating consensus for eventual public regulation (Gordon 1999). In other cases, the self-regulatory initiatives have not been particularly effective without government enforcement. Third, most corporate executives point out that their operations are subject to a license to operate in every country in which they do business. The state has ultimate authority, or residual rights of control, and where government policy and self-regulation conflict, it is the former that has precedence.

Industry self-regulation does pose challenges to government capacity. On the one hand, relying on voluntary initiatives certainly lowers the cost of influencing and monitoring business behavior. In fact, they challenge governments to develop new institutional incentives for the private sector to expand these activities. On the other hand, these initiatives probably will not relieve the pressure on government to intervene, since in many cases the implementation of these codes is weak. The industrialized countries may view these voluntary private sector initiatives as a way to resolve the tensions between promoting foreign investment in developing countries while maintaining high environmental and social standards at the same time. To the degree citizens in developing countries turn more to the private sector for governance than to their own governments, it will undermine the strength and health of those governments. These initiatives may actually contribute to a backlash against globalization, since they can appear to be an abdication of government responsibility to the private sector.

Industry self-regulation also poses challenges to the advocacy community. There already appears to be a deep split between the moderate NGOs willing to form partnerships with business on specific issues (e.g., the World Wildlife Fund), and those that remain profoundly suspicious of corporate power and influence (e.g., Global Exchange). Individual NGOs often must tailor their activities to the sources of their funding, and partnering with business may lose them some support from those with a moral commitment that does not allow for this kind collaboration. Many NGOs have an inherent interest in maintaining a high profile with continuing campaigns against corporations, in order to gain publicity, membership, and money. Despite the tensions, however, some global NGOs have become more willing over time to sit down in dialogue with the private sector.

What are the implications of industry self-regulation for governance outside of government institutions, for democracy and accountability? Some critics might argue that collaboration between NGOs and corporations is simply a new form of collusion, a throwback to the "old" corporatism of Europe reincarnated at the international level (Murphy 2000; Ottaway 2001). Certainly, neither corporate executives nor leaders of NGOs are democratically accountable. Yet each is accountable to some constituency — consumers on the one hand, members on the other. Each is held up to "reputational" accountability, though in different ways (Keohane and Nye, Chapter 5). Self-regulatory initiatives themselves can become accountable to a broader public to the degree that they are transparent, monitored by independent external actors, and enforced through markets concerned with reputation. Recent scandals surrounding Enron and Arthur Anderson ultimately prove this point — the lack of transparency and the compromised independence of the auditors brought both companies down. Furthermore, new multistakeholder partnerships hold the promise of becoming deliberative institutions incorporating a diversity of perspectives. Through dialogue, debate, and contention, through a kind of "deliberative democracy," these partnerships may facilitate compromises that can become the basis for solutions to seemingly intractable problems (Kahane 2000).[17] On the other hand, there are many who hold a more pessimistic view about whether or not democratic values and accountable institutions are possible at the global level, beyond the nation-state (Greven and Pauly 2000; Murphy 2000).

We are still at the beginning of an era of experimentation in governance mechanisms at all levels. Social entrepreneurs are continuing to experiment with different forms and institutions for this nongovernmental form of governance. Their effectiveness and legitimacy are still being tested. It may be that their lack of democratic accountability will in the end undermine their efficacy too profoundly for them to continue as a significant mechanism of global governance. But in a time of upheaval and change, the principles and mechanisms developed by nonstate actors ultimately may form the basic building blocks of future international regulatory regimes.

---

[17] My sincere thanks to an anonymous reviewer who suggested looking at how self-regulation fits with theories of deliberative democracy.

PART 2

Convergence in National Governance

Chapter 10

INTERNATIONAL CAPITAL MOBILITY AND NATIONAL POLICY DIVERGENCE

RONALD ROGOWSKI

GLOBALIZATION, as Kahler and Lake note in their Introduction to the present volume, crucially involves easier movement of capital between nations; and, as Eichengreen cogently observes in chapter 7, "It is the international mobility of capital that most strongly distinguishes financial markets today from financial markets fifty years ago." (p. 115) In terms of governance and policy, easier international mobility of capital is commonly believed to have at least three consequences:

Policy convergence: all governments, to compete for mobile capital, are compelled to adopt similar, and similarly capital-friendly, policies. Specifically, differences in domestic policy preferences become irrelevant, and in this sense (polemicists often decry), democracy is "hollowed out."

Persistence of natural advantage: countries disadvantaged by nature, for example by distance, barriers (no or poor harbors, difficult terrain), or climate, will, when capital is mobile, converge also to highly capital-friendly policies, but will nonetheless attract less investment and grow more slowly, simply because, all else being equal, their higher costs and/ or risks imply lower returns to capital.

Wealth and growth convergence: convergence of policies permits, indeed entails, convergence in investment, wealth, and growth. Poor countries will adopt policies as capital-friendly as rich ones; and, having done so, will attract the lion's share of mobile capital, achieve sharply higher rates of investment and growth, and quickly become rich.[1]

Research on this chapter was supported in part by NSF grant 9819307. The author is grateful for superb research assistance from Mark Kayser and (at a later point) Eric Chang; and for particularly insightful comments and corrections from (in alphabetical order): Torben Iversen, Miles Kahler, Robert Keohane, David Lake, Eric Rasmussen, Beth Simmons, and Michael Wallerstein.

[1] Declining marginal productivity of capital implies that, in poor (i.e., capital-scarce) economies, capital will have higher marginal productivity and hence earn higher returns. If policies are as capital-friendly in, say, Brazil as in Belgium, returns to capital will be higher in, and investment will flow disproportionately to, Brazil; Brazil therefore grows more rapidly and—with allowance for stochastic differences in growth—converges rap-

I shall argue in this chapter that only the last of these assertions —
that poor and rich countries will converge in their policies — can be sustained by convincing logic; and even there the convergence is to a less
than fully capital-friendly policy. In both of the other cases, a simple
model implies almost the opposite of the conventional wisdom: countries that differ only in their preexisting friendliness to capital, or in the
advantages that nature has conferred, will *diverge* in their policies more
when capital is mobile than when it is not.

The crucial assertion of the whole trio is the first; and, as is probably
well known,[2] the evidence for it is surprisingly thin.[3] As one rough indicator, figure 10.1 compares 1996 with 2001 scores for 137 countries on
one widely invoked measure of capital-friendliness of governmental policy, the Heritage Foundation Index of Economic Freedom (O'Driscoll,
Holmes, and Kirkpatrick 2001, 18–22).[4] Convergence as usually understood would imply a relatively "flat" scatterplot, with most countries
moving toward capital-friendly policies over the five-year interval (with,
presumably, the initially most anticapitalist societies moving most). Instead we see mostly inertia (1996 scores correlate with those of 2001 at
$r = .93$), with about a quarter of the countries (36 of 137; in the scatterplot, those below the diagonal) having actually moved in a more *anti*capitalist direction over the five-year interval. Among the most star-
tling examples are Belarus (1996: 2.6 of a possible 5 points, 5 being
most procapital; 2001, 1.75, a net move of .85 in a less capital-friendly

---

idly to Belgium's level of wealth. Among the most compelling presentations of the argument is Lucas (1990); the authoritative technical treatment of neoclassical growth theory
is Barro and Sala-I-Martin (1995). For strong evidence that divergence, far more than
convergence, has characterized the last several centuries, see Pritchett (1997).

[2] A helpful overview of the argument and the evidence is Crook (1997); for an even
more skeptical view of the empirics, see Garrett (1998b, 2001). On the specific issue of
tax competition and convergence (or lack of convergence) in fiscal policy, the survey essay
of Schulze and Ursprung (1999) is invaluable.

[3] Simmons and Elkins (chapter 11, esp. table 11.1), find evidence that competition for
markets or capital may lead to convergence on specific proglobalization policies; this,
however, is not the same as convergence toward a broad array of policies that favor
capital. Nonetheless the panel approach that they adopt could be usefully pursued to
investigate measures of broader policy, including those employed here.

[4] The overall five-point scale summarizes fifty variables grouped into ten categories,
with each category weighted equally. The categories are: impediments to trade; fiscal burden of government (government share of GDP, income tax rates); extent of government
intervention in the economy; monetary policy and inflation; restrictions on foreign investment; reliability and efficiency of banking and finance; wage and price distortions; property rights; regulation; and extent of black market activity. See O'Driscoll, Holmes, and
Kirkpatrick (2001, chap. 4). The original scores are reversed in this presentation to provide a more reader-friendly format: where originally higher numbers meant a less capital-
friendly policy, here they indicate a more capital-friendly one.

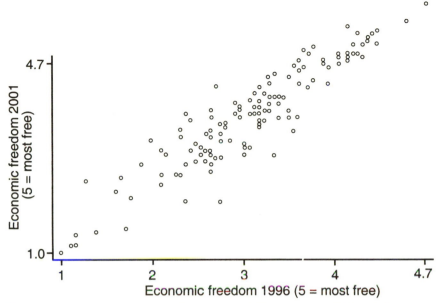

Figure 10.1. Overall Pro-capital Orientation of Governmental Policy, 1996 vs. 2001 (137 Countries)

direction); Indonesia (3.15 to 2.45, a net decline of .70); Paraguay (3.35 to 2.80, a net decline of .55); and Zimbabwe (2.25 to 1.75, a net decline of .50). While the average country became slightly more pro-capitalist (the mean score in 1996 was 2.91; in 2001, 2.96), the variance among countries certainly did not decline (standard deviation in 1996, .75; in 2001, .76). At the other extreme, many of the countries that were most procapital in 1996 had come to favor capital yet more in 2001. Ireland, for example, moved from a score of 3.9 to one of 4.35 (5, again, being most procapital); El Salvador, from 3.55 to 4.05; Estonia, from 3.5 to 3.95; and Chile, from 3.45 to 4.0.

Figure 10.2 presents the same data in perhaps a more transparent way, plotting net change in policy (positive numbers implying a more capital-friendly policy) over the five-year period against the 1996 rating; a lowess-smoothed regression line (bandwidth: 0.5 points) is superimposed. The very slight trend toward convergence appears in the downward-sloping line from about 2.0 on the horizontal (1996) axis; but we see also that the most anticapitalist countries in 1996 (those with scores below 2.0) actually became somewhat less friendly to capital.

In a different but perhaps even more telling context, there is little evidence that policy converges among the various jurisdictions (states, provinces, cantons) of federal systems, even when capital appears to be

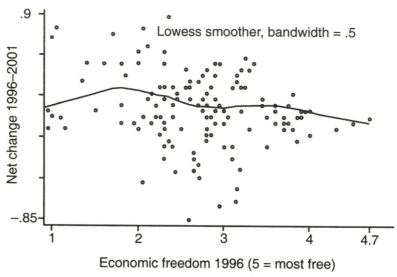

Figure 10.2. Net Change in Policy, 1996–2001, vs. 1996 Policy Score

perfectly mobile among them — or even, as McNamara (chapter 13 in the present volume) notes, when the central authorities are pressing for convergence. In the United States, for example, policy continues to diverge broadly among the "several states" on such issues as labor-union power (some states having "right-to-work" laws, others enforcing "closed" or "agency" shops) or levels of spending on education.

My concern here, however, will be to explore the logic that supposedly supports convergence. Rarely is that logic carefully laid out, let alone formally modeled. When one does so in even the simplest framework, I shall try to show here, rather different implications emerge, which are at least as well supported by the available evidence:

> *Policy divergence*: Under the likeliest circumstances, more mobile capital (assuming, as is done throughout this paper, total immobility of labor) means greater *divergence* of policy: governments that are capital-friendly at the outset adopt policies even more favorable to capital, while initially capital-hostile countries adopt policies even more inimical to capital (and, by assumption, policies closer to the "true" preferences of their (s)electorates). (In this sense policy in at least some countries becomes *more* "democratic" than it was under immobile capital.) Only where policy per se is an extreme kind of luxury good — that is, where it is weighted more heavily with increasing wealth — does policy converge.
>
> *Persistence of natural disadvantage*: All else being equal, a naturally disadvantaged country will, when capital is mobile but labor is not, adopt

markedly *less capital-friendly* policies than its better-situated rivals (and considerably less capital-friendly ones than it would have done when capital was immobile); and, partially because of its more hostile policy, will attract *less investment* than states advantaged by nature.

Wealth and growth divergence: Divergence of policy implies *divergence* in growth, investment, and wealth. The most capital-friendly countries attract the bulk of world investment, grow more rapidly, and increase the gap between the capital-friendly and capital-hostile states. Obviously, this trend increases incentives to migrate. On the other hand, ceteris paribus, and particularly between countries with equal policy preferences, capital will flow to the poorer (less capital-abundant) state; and, if countries differ only in their capital–labor ratios, policy will in fact converge, albeit to a rather capital-unfriendly position.

The basic approach of this chapter is readily outlined. I establish a simple model of two countries, a single technology of production, and a single policy dimension. The policy dimension could be, to echo issues addressed elsewhere in the present volume, the autonomy of domestic monetary policy (Cohen, chapter 6), the extent to which domestic governance is decentralized (Garrett and Rodden, chapter 4), the degree to which the domestic economy follows a "liberal" or an "organized" model (Gourevitch, chapter 12), or the deficits or surpluses that government spending incurs (McNamara, chapter 13); or it might be some broader measure, such as the index of "economic freedom" that was employed earlier in this chapter.

To simplify analysis, capital is assumed to have a single, cross-nationally ideal policy, defined simply as that which maximizes its returns. Voters (assumed also to be workers) prefer a different policy (otherwise no interesting problem arises), but rationally adjust policy toward capital's interests to improve wages.[5] Workers are assumed throughout to be totally immobile. If capital also cannot move, the problem is straightforward: voters concede to capital just until marginal benefit (from improved wage) equals marginal cost (from "ideological" loss of preferred policy); and the resultant concession to capital increases unambiguously with (a) the capital–labor ratio; (b) the voters' relative utility weighting of wages as against pure policy; (c) the share of social product that accrues to labor; and (d) the country's natural advantage in terms of location, climate, and accessibility.

We then permit capital to move between the two countries and sup-

---

[5] Nothing is assumed here about the number of voters: the analysis would go through under quite a restrictive franchise, or indeed an authoritarian "selectorate" (cf. Roeder [1993, esp. chap. 2, on the Soviet case]), so long as the decisive decision maker's bliss point differed from the policy that made capital maximally productive.

pose that a stylized capitalist (or, equivalently, the market) allocates available capital so as to equalize the rent of capital (assumed equal to its marginal product) in the two countries. After each such movement of capital, voters reequilibrate their optimal policy; after which markets reallocate capital, voters re-reequilibrate, and so on until an equilibrium is achieved. Under the simplifying assumptions invoked here, the resultant equilibrium is unique. Specifically:

> *If the two countries differ only in their voters' initial preferences*, under capital mobility more capital flows to the initially capital-friendlier country, which becomes friendlier still; while as capital deserts the less capital-friendly state, the marginal (wage) benefit of a policy concession declines, and consequently even less capital-friendly policies obtain in equilibrium.

> *If the countries differ initially only in their natural advantage*, then as capital becomes more mobile the disadvantaged country will adopt less capital-friendly policies and will attract even less capital; while the more advantaged country will gain capital and will move policy in a yet more capital-friendly direction.

> *If the countries differ initially only in their capital–labor ratios*, the bulk of mobile capital will normally flow to the one with the *lower* ratio, the rich and the poor country will adopt identical (albeit far from totally capital-friendly) policies, and existing inequalities between rich and poor states will diminish.

THE BASIC MODEL

We assume a standard unidimensional policy space, represented as a closed zero-one line. Each citizen's bliss point, as well as the policy most favorable to capital, can be represented as a point on this continuum. Without loss of generality, but to simplify some arithmetic, I assume throughout that "labor's" (i.e., the representative worker's) endowments and policies are to the "left" of capital's, that is, where x_L, x_K $\in [0,1]$ represent respectively the ideal points of labor and capital, we simply constrain $x_L < x_K$. The decisive voter is a worker, and we stylize her preferences in a way that will presently be specified.[6]

If, in a country of L workers, we denote x_M as the policy actually adopted (e.g., the one embraced by the decisive voter — or, if a non-democracy, the decisive decision maker) and D ($\in [0,1)$) as an index of the country's natural disadvantage (from, e.g., climate, poor access, paucity of natural resources), we can write the production function as

---

[6] Alternatively, we could stylize policy as some weighted average of the positions of capital and labor; I demonstrate below that such an approach would only strengthen this chapter's central result.

$$Y = [1 - (x_K - x_M)](1 - D)L^\alpha K^{1-\alpha} \mid \alpha \in (0,1). \qquad (10.1)$$

Obviously where capital gets both its optimal policy and its optimal natural endowments, this reduces to the classic Cobb-Douglas formulation (standardizing to unity the usual total factor productivity parameter, A) $Y = L^\alpha K^{1-\alpha}$. The total return to workers amounts — as also is standard in Cobb-Douglas models — to αY, that to capitalists is $(1 - \alpha)Y$.[7] For yet greater simplicity, we assume that the representative worker-voter earns exactly the marginal product of labor (equivalently: the average wage), that is, her income is $\alpha Y/L$. (We ignore, for both workers and capitalists, the effects of taxes and of governmental appropriations; and we also treat this as a single-period game, abstracting away from any issues of future returns or of the long-term effects of investment.)[8]

The representative voter cares about both policy per se (i.e., she has a most-preferred degree of centralization, budget surplus, monetary autonomy, or overall capital-friendliness) and wages; and we want to allow the possibility that the *extent* to which voters care about policy per se increases with income, that is, that policy is a "luxury good." One convenient way to capture this is to write the utility function of the representative voter as

$$U_L = g\,(K/L)^\beta[1 - a\,(x_M - x_L)^2] + \alpha Y/L \mid \beta \ge 0, g, a > 0 \quad (10.2)$$

where the first of the two summed terms captures the worker's utility from "pure" policy; the latter, utility from wages. The working assumption through most of the analysis will be that $\beta = 0$, but positive values of β admit precisely the possibility that voters value "pure" policy more as their income grows.[9] The product $g(K/L)^\beta$ (where g is simply some positive constant) captures the maximum utility from policy per se when $x_M = x_L$, while a expresses the slope of utility loss as policy diverges from the voter's ideal point.[10]

Substituting 10.1 into 10.2 gives us

[7] Across virtually all known societies, and indeed across sectors of the economy, the share of value-added that goes to workers seems to range between about 50 and 90 percent. (For representative U.S. data, see Salvatore [1994, 188].) In some illustrations below, we shall simply stylize α as 2/3.

[8] There is, however, no assumption of myopia: the representative worker optimizes at every point, and any equilibrium described must be Nash.

[9] This may be especially plausible in such policy areas as environmental protection and is, more generally, asserted by believers in "postmaterialist" political culture (notably Inglehart [1997] and earlier works).

[10] The inspiration here, albeit with considerable tinkering, is the utility function that Alesina and Spolaore (1997, 1030) employ.

$$U_L = g \, (K/L)^\beta \, [1 - a(x_M - x_L)^2] + \alpha[1 - (x_K - x_M)](1 - D)(K/L)^{1-\alpha}$$

(10.3)

and this is maximized (F.O.C.) by

$$x_M^* = x_L + \frac{\alpha(1 - D)}{2ag} (K/L)^{1-\alpha-\beta}$$

(10.4)

(Intuitively, each movement away from x_L and toward capital's optimal position entails a cost in utility from pure policy and a benefit in utility from wages; the representative worker of course moves just until marginal benefit equals marginal cost, and that point is specified by 10.4.)[11]

The crucial term in 10.4 is the second, that is, the degree to which the policy actually supported by the pivotal worker moves away from the one that she most prefers and toward what capital requires;[12] and its most important component is $(K/L)^{1-\alpha-\beta}$, indicating that — except when $\alpha + \beta > 1$ — the extent of accommodation *increases* with the capital/labor ratio, that is, with the wealth of the society. Only in a quite specific case — namely where a 1-percent increase in the capital–labor ratio produces a higher percentage increase in workers' utility from policy than it does in workers' wages — will the extent of workers' accommodation to capital decrease, rather than increase, with a rising capital–labor ratio.

The cross-national evidence suggests unambiguously, and despite widespread misapprehensions to the contrary, that policy becomes steadily friendlier to capital as per capita income (taken as a proxy for capital–labor ratio) rises. The average 1998 per capita income (in purchasing-power parity, or PPP) in the Heritage Foundation's most capital-unfriendly categories (scores below 3.0 in figures 10.1 and 10.2, above) was just over $2800. For countries with scores between 3.0 and 4.0, the average was over $11,000; for ones with scores above 4.0, over $21,200 (O'Driscoll, Holmes, and Kirkpatrick 2001, 2, 17). While the possibility remains that, over time in individual countries (e.g., Sweden), policy has

---

[11] Assuming, still, that the representative voter is a worker. If policy were instead some weighted combination of workers' and capitalists' preferences, and if capitalists also maximized some convex combination of their own bliss point and the rent to capital, as the K/L ratio grew (diminished), policy would move even more strongly toward (away from) capital's optimal point. Since the rent of capital is $(1 - \alpha)(L/K)\alpha$, any increase in the K/L ratio reduces the return to policy concessions by capital, leading capitalists to concede less while workers concede more; hence policy moves even more strongly in a procapital direction. Conversely, any decrease in the K/L ratio increases the return to policy concessions by capital and induces capitalists to concede more while workers concede less; overall policy departs even more strongly from capital's ideal point.

[12] Recall that, by assumption, $x_K > x_L$; hence we see that optimal policy almost always represents some accommodation to capital.

grown more inimical to capital as wealth has increased, the most reasonable assumption appears to be that $\alpha + \beta < 1$.

Three other useful comparative statics are revealed by 10.4. While we
might suppose ex ante that the most disadvantaged and poorly remune-
rated workforces would, under immobile capital, concede most to capital, in fact concessions normally increase — at least in this model — with:
(1) the economy's natural advantages (from location, climate, workforce, that is, with lower D); (2) the share of social product that goes to
labor (α); and (3) — no surprise here — workers' caring less about policy
per se (that is, with lower g or a). Taken together with the effect of the
capital–labor ratio, these points remind one, albeit by a quite different
route, of some of the standard arguments of twenty years ago about
"corporatism": the predilection of advanced, naturally advantaged
states (most of them in Northern Europe), and particularly of ones that
compensated labor generously, to accommodate capital and assure
prosperity.

We can go on to consider three further comparative statics that will
prove central to subsequent analysis, namely the effect of the capital–
labor ratio on (a) wages, (b) the rent of capital, and (c) workers' utility,
assuming that the representative worker-voter is optimizing according
to 10.4. Briefly, wages and workers' utility increase, and the rent of
capital normally decreases, with rising K/L.

> Wages, first of all, rise unambiguously with K/L. Intuitively, this should be
> apparent, since a higher ratio produces both a higher Y/L and a more
> accommodating policy. More formally, if we write (assuming for sim-
> plicity, and without loss of generality, that $x_K = 1$),
>
> $$w = \alpha Y/L = \alpha(1 - D)\, x_M{}^*(K/L)^{1-\alpha};$$
>
> and, recalling that $x_M{}^*$ is also a function of (K/L), we have the total
> derivative
>
> $$dw/d(K/L) = (\partial w/\partial x_M{}^*)(\partial x_M{}^*/\partial(K/L)) + \partial w/\partial(K/L), \qquad (10.5)$$
>
> all of whose component terms are plainly positive.
>
> Workers' utility rises also with K/L. Since $x_M{}^*$ is defined as maximizing U_L,
> the Envelope Theorem applies, and we can write
>
> $$d\, U_L/d(K/L) = \partial U_L/\partial(K/L); \qquad (10.6)$$
>
> and inspection of (10.3) reveals that this must be positive.
>
> Finally, the rent of capital decreases directly (in the sense that the marginal
> productivity of capital declines) with increasing K/L; but it is increased
> by the more accommodating policy that the representative worker
> adopts. To see which effect dominates, we write, under the same sim-
> plifying assumptions,

$$r = (1 - \alpha)Y/K = (1 - \alpha)(1 - D) \, x_M{}^*(K/L)^{-\alpha},$$

so that

$$dr/d(K/L) = (\partial r/\partial x_M{}^*)(\partial x_M{}^*/\partial(K/L)) + \partial r/\partial(K/L) = \alpha(1 - \alpha)(1 - D)$$
$$[(1 - \alpha - \beta)(1 - D)(1/2ag)(L/K)^{2\alpha+\beta} - x_M{}^*(L/K)^{1+\alpha}]; \quad (10.7)$$

and, substituting for $x_M{}^*$ from (10.4) and rearranging terms, this is equivalent to

$$\frac{(1 - 2\alpha - \beta)(1 - D)(K/L)^{1-\alpha-\beta}}{2ag} - x_L,$$

which is positive if and only if

$$(1 - 2\alpha - \beta)(1 - D)(1/2ag)(K/L)^{1-\alpha-\beta} > x_L \quad (10.8)$$

but, since all other terms on the lhs will be greater than zero, and since $x_L \geq 0$, the total derivative can be positive only if $1 - 2\alpha - \beta > 0$. But, as noted earlier, empirical estimates of α almost always show its value as greater than 1/2, implying that $1 - 2\alpha - \beta < 0$.

Hence we see that, except in highly abnormal cases, the direct effect overwhelms the indirect one and rents to capital decline with a growing capital–labor ratio. The converse, of course, is equally important: as a country loses capital, rents to capital in it normally increase.

A secondary point, intuitively obvious and trivially demonstrated, is that wages, rents, and worker utility all increase with x_L, assumed here to be exogenous, that is, with *decreasing* policy disagreement between labor and capital.

Immobile Capital and Labor

For tractability of analysis, assume initially an extreme Feldstein-Horioka world (Feldstein and Horioka 1980), in which each country has only (and all) of its domestically generated capital, which we take in each case to be one unit ($K = 1$). Then L simply expresses the labor–capital ratio and all the results of the preceding section go through: all else being equal (e.g., as between two countries), higher L (i.e., a lower capital–labor ratio) implies less policy accommodation, lower wages, higher returns to capital, and lower worker utility. Similarly, with all else being equal, an ex ante policy stance (x_L) more favorable to capital implies higher wages, higher returns to capital, and higher worker utility. Note particularly that, in a world of immobile capital, returns to that factor can (and, presumably, do) differ across national boundaries.

Suppose that two countries are identical in all relevant respects, except that one has a markedly higher capital–labor ratio. Then the more capital-abundant country will adopt a more accommodating policy and will offer higher wages and higher overall worker utility; if migration were possible — and I must reemphasize that in this model it is not — workers would want to move from the less to the more capital-abundant economy. On the other hand, returns to capital will normally be lower in the more capital-abundant country and investment would flow (if capital were mobile) to the poorer economy. Over time, these two economies would converge.

If, however, the two countries are identical in all respects save the representative worker's bliss point (x_L), then the one with the more accommodating electorate will offer higher wages, higher utility, *and* higher returns to capital. All else equal, both labor and capital would want to migrate to the more accommodating country, and over time the two countries would *diverge* in their economic paths, the rich one becoming richer and the poor one relatively poorer.

Mobile Capital, Fixed Labor

Now imagine "globalization" as follows: two states exist, and one capitalist must allocate the previous total endowment of both countries — two units of capital — between them. If $\gamma \in [0,1]$ is the share of total capital allocated to the first country (and, obviously, $1 - \gamma$ to the second), the rational capitalist chooses γ so as to maximize $Y_1 + Y_2$; and this entails equalizing marginal return between the two countries, that is, assuring that $\partial Y_1/\partial \gamma = \partial Y_2/\partial (1 - \gamma)$. Fairly straightforwardly, this implies

$$\gamma^* = \frac{L_1([1-(x_K - x_{M1})](1-D_1))^{1/\alpha}}{L_1([1-(x_K - x_{M1})](1-D_1))^{1/\alpha} + L_2([1-(x_K - x_{M2})](1-D_2))^{1/\alpha}} \quad (10.9)$$

This tells us, reasonably enough, that when the two countries are on balance equally attractive in terms of policy distance, natural advantages, and size, $\gamma^* = .5$, that is, the capitalist divides investment equally between the two locations. Where country 1 is inherently more attractive on these grounds, $\gamma^* > .5$; where it is less attractive, $\gamma^* < .5$.

Note however the effect that we have already established, for any case in which $\alpha + \beta < 1$: in the country that attracts more capital and thus achieves a higher capital–labor ratio, policy becomes *more* accommodating; in the other country, already less attractive to capital, x_M^* moves "left," that is, to a *less* capital-friendly position. In short, policy *diverges*, rather than converging, from what it had been in autarky. Moreover, wages and overall worker utility rise in the now more capital-abundant country; in the country that loses capital, both decline.

What remains, of course, is to establish what happens in equilibrium.

Since the amount of capital invested in country 1 is 2γ, we can rewrite 10.1 as

$$Y_1 = (1 - (x_K - x_{M1})](1 - D_1)L_1^\alpha(2\gamma^*)^{1-\alpha}; \qquad (10.10)$$

and then by an identical derivation as in the preceding section, we have

$$x_{M1}^* = x_{L1} + [\alpha(1 - D_1)/2a_1g_1](2\gamma^*/L_1)^{1-\alpha-\beta}. \qquad (10.11)$$

For Country 2, of course, we have analogously

$$x_{M2}^* = x_{L2} + [\alpha(1 - D_2)/2a_2g_2][2(1 - \gamma^*)/L_2]^{1-\alpha-\beta}. \qquad (10.12)$$

Only Preferences Differ

Suppose, for simplicity of analysis, that our two countries differ only in the policy preferences of their representative voter, and more specifically that $x_K = 1$, $x_{L1} > x_{L2}$ (i.e., country 1 offers the more capital-friendly policy). Since by assumption $L_1 = L_2$, $D_1 = D_2$, (10.9) reduces to

$$\gamma^* = \frac{x_{M1}^{*\,1/\alpha}}{x_{M1}^{*\,1/\alpha} + x_{M2}^{*\,1/\alpha}}; \qquad (10.13)$$

and, since this function is one-to-one, we can write its inverse as

$$x_{M2}^* = x_{M1}^*\left(\frac{1}{\gamma^*} - 1\right)^\alpha \qquad (10.14)$$

If, without loss of generality, we normalize $L_1 = L_2 = 1$, define $b = x_{L1} - x_{L2} > 0$, and specify $D = D_1 = D_2$, $a_1 = a_2 = a$, $g_1 = g_2 = g$, we can rewrite 10.11 and 10.12 as, respectively,

$$x_{M1}^* = x_{L2} + b + [\alpha(1 - D)/2ag](2\gamma^*)^{1-\alpha-\beta} \qquad (10.15)$$

and

$$x_{M2}^* = x_{L2} + [\alpha(1 - D)/2ag][2(1 - \gamma^*)]^{1-\alpha-\beta}. \qquad (10.16)$$

Substituting these into (10.14) gives us an equation only in exogenous variables, x_{L2}, b, and γ; and from this we can readily formulate

$$
F(x_{L2}, b, \gamma) = \left(x_{L2} + b + \frac{\alpha(1-D)}{2ag}(2\gamma^*)^{1-\alpha-\beta}\right)\left(\frac{1}{\gamma^*} - 1\right)^\alpha
$$
$$
- \left(x_{L2} + \frac{\alpha(1-D)}{2ag}[2(1 - \gamma^*)]^{1-\alpha-\beta}\right) = 0; \qquad (10.17)
$$

and can use the Implicit Function Theorem to determine $\partial\gamma/\partial b$. This turns out, under "reasonable" parameter specifications (i.e., ones that

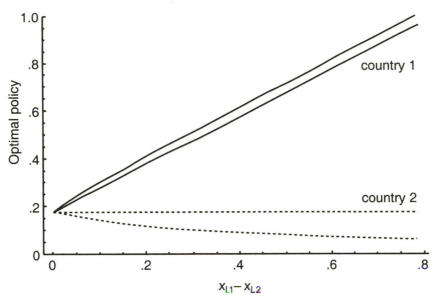

Figure 10.3. Policy as a Function of Distance between Two Otherwise Identical Countries, under Autarky (interior lines) and Capital Mobility (exterior lines)

$$(\alpha = 2/3, \beta = 0, D = .5, a = g = 1, x_{L2} = 0)$$

avoid the corner solution $\gamma^* = 1$), to be positive throughout the relevant domain.[13]

In short, when capital is free to move, it moves — in the sequential equilibrium just analyzed — ceteris paribus toward the country whose ex ante preferences are more favorable, and away from the one whose "true" preferences favor capital less. But, as is immediately apparent from 10.15 and 10.16, $\partial x_{M1}^*/\partial \gamma^* > 0$, $\partial x_{M2}^*/\partial \gamma^* < 0$ (assuming still that $\alpha + \beta < 1$); hence each such shift of capital moves actual policy in the already more favorable country yet closer to capital, in the less favorable one yet farther away.

To see what actually happens in a numerical example, we set $\alpha = 2/3$, $\beta = 0$, $D = 1/2$, $a = g = 1$, for both countries; and let $x_{L2} = 0$, $x_{L1} > 0$; then as x_{L1} moves away from x_{L2} the optimal policies of the two countries (x_{M1}^*, x_{M2}^*) vary as shown in figure 10.3, with the optimal policy in the more favorable country 1 becoming identical to capital's optimal position by the time that the bliss point of workers in country 1 approximates .8. (Interior lines represent optimal policy where capital is immobile, exterior lines where capital is mobile.)

[13] Calculated by iteration of Mathematica's FindRoot routine from the equations for γ, x_{M1}^*, x_{M2}^* given in the text (Wolfram 1999).

In addition, as we have seen in the earlier analysis, the country that loses capital winds up with lower wages and lower worker utility, while the one that gains capital improves on both fronts: thus *inequality* between the two states increases. Were migration possible, the easier movement of capital would also encourage greater mobility of labor.

This aspect of the model seems to find plausible real-world parallels in such downward spirals as Burma, Haiti, or many postcolonial African regimes. Hostile policy drives out capital, and the paucity of capital makes policy yet more hostile.

Only Natural Advantage Differs

Now alter our assumptions to permit the two countries to differ only with respect to their "natural disadvantage" parameter, D; specifically, we will say that $D_1 = 0$, $D_2 > 0$, that is, country 2 is disadvantaged relative to country 1. Otherwise, again for total simplicity of analysis, we suppose $x_K = 1$, $x_{L1} = x_{L2} = 0$, $L_1 = L_2$, $a_1 = a_2 = a$, $g_1 = g_2 = g$. By an analogous derivation as in (10.14) above, we now have

$$x_{M2}^* = \frac{x_{M1}^*}{1 - D_2}\left(\frac{1}{\gamma^*} - 1\right); \tag{10.18}$$

and, in place of (10.15) and (10.16), we can write

$$x_{M1}^* = (\alpha/2ag)(2\gamma^*)^{1-\alpha-\beta} \tag{10.19}$$

and

$$x_{M2}^* = (\alpha/2ag)(1 - D_2)[2(1 - \gamma^*)]^{1-\alpha-\beta}. \tag{10.20}$$

Substituting 10.19 and 10.20 into (2.6a) permits us to solve explicitly for optimal γ, which turns out after some algebra to be

$$\gamma^* = \frac{1}{(1 - D_2)^{-\frac{2}{1-2\alpha-\beta}} + 1} = \frac{1}{(1 - D_2)^{-\frac{2}{2\alpha+\beta-1}} + 1}; \tag{10.21}$$

which, under our by-now standard assumption that $\alpha > 1/2$, must be *increasing* in D_2: that is, the more *dis*advantaged is country 2, the *greater* the share of capital that flows to country 1 (and, by definition, the *less* the share of capital that locates in country 2). If, for example, $\alpha = 2/3$, $\beta = 0$, 10.21 reduces to

$$\gamma^* = \frac{1}{(1 - D_2)^6 + 1};$$

and this plots as shown in figure 10.4 over the domain $D_2 \in [0,1]$.

So far, the conventional wisdom is sustained, with capital fleeing the naturally disadvantaged country and flowing toward the advantaged

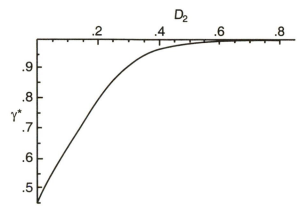

Figure 10.4.

one. But the optimal policy chosen by each country *diverges* more, with the advantaged country adopting a more capital-friendly position, the disadvantaged one a policy more hostile to capital, than would have obtained in autarky. If we substitute the optimal γ^* from 10.21 into 10.20 and plot the result for a representative case ($\alpha = 2/3$, $\beta = 0$, $ag = 1/2$), we see in figure 10.5 the contrast between x_{M1}^* and x_{M2}^* when capital is immobile (the straight, interior lines) and when it is fully mobile (the curved, exterior lines).

In the vicinity of $D_2 = .4$, for example, the "disadvantaged" country (country 2) would move as indicated by the downward-pointing arrow once capital became mobile, while the "advantaged" country (country 1) would move (as indicated by the upward-pointing arrow) to a considerably more capital-friendly position.

Just as policy diverges more under capital mobility when countries differ only in the extent of disagreement between labor and capital, it diverges also when countries differ only in the advantages that nature has provided, with the same result: mobility induces more capital to flow to the advantaged country, makes policy there more capital-friendly (but even less friendly in the disadvantaged country), and increases the disparity in wages and worker utility between the advantaged and the disadvantaged country.

What capital mobility does *not* do, somewhat counterintuitively, is raise returns to capital in the advantaged country.[14] In the advantaged country when capital is immobile, the rent of capital remains fixed under the parameter specifications adopted here at $(1 - \alpha)(\alpha) = (1/3)$

---

[14] Recall the earlier, more general analysis, which showed that the net effect of a capital inflow is (even allowing for the more accommodating policy that results) to decrease the domestic rent of capital.

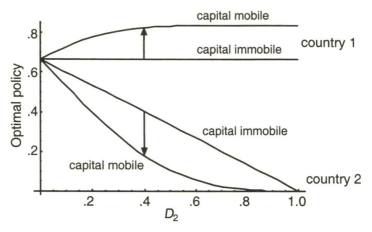

Figure 10.5.

$(2/3) = 2/9$. As capital becomes mobile and more of it flows to the advantaged country, the "world" rent of capital becomes, under these specifications,

$$\frac{2^{2/3}}{9}\left[1 + (1 - D_2)^6\right]^{1/3},$$

which plots as indicated in figure 10.6 (with the steady 2/9 return plotted as a benchmark) as D_2 varies from 0 to .75.

Capitalists in a country advantaged by nature would be better off if capital could be prevented from flowing to less advantaged areas. (Conversely, of course, capital in the disadvantaged country earns higher returns when capital is mobile.)

Only Wealth Differs

When the only difference between countries is that one is richer, we get rather more of what the conventional wisdom advertises: genuine policy convergence and a greater flow of investment to the poorer country; but policy hardly converges toward a totally capital-friendly stance. Assume, more specifically, that our two countries differ only with respect to their initial capital–labor ratio; at the outset $K_1 = K_2 = 1$, but $L_1 = 1$, $L_2 > 1$, that is, country 1 is the more capital-abundant (and thus, normally, the richer). Otherwise we assume $D_1 = D_2 = D$, $a_1 = a_2 = a$, $g_1 = g_2 = g$, $x_K = 1$, $x_L 1 = x_{L2} = 0$. By the now-standard parallel to 10.14 and 10.18 above, we have

$$x_{M2}{}^* = x_{M1}{}^*\left(\frac{1}{L_2}\right)^\alpha \left[(1/\gamma^*) - 1\right]^\alpha; \qquad (10.22)$$

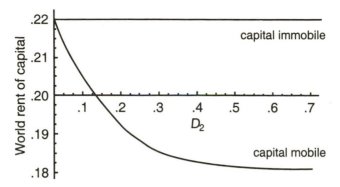

Figure 10.6.

but also

$$x_{M1}^* = \frac{\alpha(1 - D)}{2ag}(2\gamma^*)^{1-\alpha-\beta},$$ (10.23)

and

$$x_{M2}^* = \frac{\alpha(1 - D)}{2ag}\left[\frac{2(1 - \gamma)}{L_2}\right]^{1-\alpha-\beta}$$ (10.24)

Substituting 10.23 and 10.24 into 10.22 and performing some straightforward algebraic manipulation gives us the convenient expression

$$\gamma^* = \frac{1}{L_2 + 1},$$ (10.25)

which obviously is *decreasing* in L_2; that is, the poorer is country 2 (the lower its existing capital–labor ratio), the *less* the share of capital invested in country 1 (and the greater that invested in country 2).

In this case, however, we get genuine (and, indeed, total) *convergence*, for when we substitute the formula for γ^* from 10.25 into 10.23 and 10.24, we obtain

$$x_{M1}^* = x_{M2}^* = \frac{\alpha(1 - D)}{2ag}\left(\frac{2}{L_2 + 1}\right)^{1-\alpha-\beta}$$ (10.26)

If we recall that, under our assumptions here and with capital immobile, we would have

$$x_{M1}^* = \frac{\alpha(1 - D)}{2ag},$$

$$x_{M2}^* = \frac{\alpha(1 - D)}{2ag}\left(\frac{1}{L_2}\right)^{1-\alpha-\beta},$$

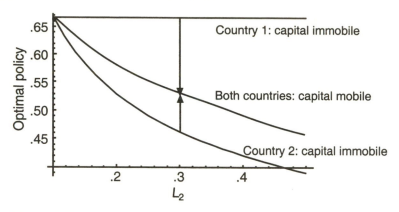

Figure 10.7.

it becomes obvious that country 1's concessions to capital diminish under mobility, while country 2's increase. Under our now-standard illustrative case ($\alpha = 2/3$, $\beta = 0$, $ag = 1/2$, $D = 0$), the respective policies plot as indicated in Figure 10.7 with increasing L_2, that is, increasing capital-scarcity of country 2.

The arrows indicate the kind of convergence that would occur, as capital became mobile, if one country were about three times as rich as the other: the poor country, (country 2), would adopt a more capital-friendly policy, the rich one (country 1) a markedly less capital-friendly one. We indeed get convergence, but hardly to the kind of completely capital-friendly policy that the conventional narrative posits.

Historically, such convergence to a less capital-friendly position has been observed even in the realm of tax competition: as Germany unified in the nineteenth century, and dropped all barriers to internal mobility of factors, individual state taxes on mobile factors converged, but to a higher level than had prevailed before unification (Hallerberg 1996).

Conclusions and Implications

That "Tiebout effects" (Tiebout 1956) entail greater diversity of policy among jurisdictions when *labor* is free to move among them is a commonplace (albeit one too frequently neglected in the literature). Yet it is widely believed that the contrary will hold when *capital* can move, but labor cannot. Working with fairly standard models of production and of policy choice by voters, I have shown that this intuition cannot generally be sustained: mobile capital also often implies greater diversity of policy, in a specific and troubling sense. Jurisdictions already more favorable to capital will become more so when capital can move, but jurisdictions already less favorable will turn even more away from the policies that capital requires. More specifically: more "leftist" countries will concede even less than before to capital, more "rightist" ones will concede even more. Only where policy per se displays strong characteristics of a luxury good, that is, where demand for it rises with income, will policy converge under pressure of capital mobility.

Convergence also occurs — and does so regardless of whether policy is a "luxury good" — when countries differ only in their capital–labor ratios, not in their underlying policy preferences or their natural advantage. When capital is mobile, poor and rich countries adopt identical policies, the poor ones moving in a somewhat more capital-friendly, the rich ones in a markedly more capital-hostile, direction. Investment flows disproportionately, just as standard growth theory would predict, to the poorer countries, which presumably grow more rapidly and converge toward the wealth levels of the already richer states.

Divergence of policy, however, is also the rule when countries differ only in their natural (dis)advantage: disadvantaged states, when capital is mobile, adopt policies more hostile to capital, advantaged ones more capital-friendly ones; and the lion's share of investment flows to the countries that nature has blessed. The disadvantaged country, all else being equal, becomes even poorer over time.

The model adopted here is, by design, extremely simplistic. That has the advantage of showing the holes in the conventional wisdom even under circumstances that would seem least complicated and most favorable to convergence. The disadvantage of such an approach, as Simmons and Elkins (chapter 11) note, is that a richer and more complex model might better capture some aspects of reality. To give three specific examples drawn from their critique:

Domestic decision makers might initially understand only poorly how policy affects output and wages and come to apprehend the true relationship only by diffusion or example. In terms of the model set forth in this chapter, such effects could be captured by making the values of the parameters a and g — the weights that policymakers attach to "pure" policy — decline as the link between policy and wages becomes better understood. Even more radically, x_L, the "bliss point" of the decisive voter, might be endogenized as an effect of social learning of neighboring-country examples. In other words, as voters better understand the world, they become less (or more!) "leftist."

State leaders, if modeled as separate from voters, might be especially concerned about economic growth or pressures for migration; and might therefore seek to alter voters' incentives or influence to assure policies friendlier to capital. As has been frequently observed, the provision of social insurance may make it easier for voters to accept integration into international markets (e.g., Rodrik 1998); but this could be modeled only as part of a longer time-horizon and some form of tax-smoothing. More straightforwardly, state leaders with these concerns might attempt to alter the identity of the decisive voter, either by expanding (Britain, 1832) or contracting (much of Latin America, the 1930s) the electorate.

Finally, one could imagine policy as decided not merely by domestic decision makers (assumed here to be workers), but by some weighted average of domestic preferences and those of capital, echoing the Marxist thesis of the state's "structural dependence" on capital (Simmons and Elkins, chapter 11). I have addressed this point directly (n. 11), showing that in such a case policy would diverge even more.

That said, the results of this admittedly simplistic model are perhaps even more troubling than the commonplace (but, in the view taken here, mistaken) vision of a "race to the bottom," or of "nothing left for the Left." For what they seem to foretell, if countries differ not only in their levels of wealth, but (as seems obvious) in their natural advantages and in their voters' "naive" policy preferences, is a world increasingly divided into two, probably hostile, camps: a set of countries that are extremely attractive to capital, and another that attracts it less and less.[15] A more immediate and practical extension will be to see whether the chief results of the present analysis hold up in more realistic models, particularly ones that include such aspects as taxation, investment, and deadweight costs. In the simplest model of policy, however, there seems little reason to believe that convergence should become the norm.

---

[15] A quite plausible conjecture is that countries abundant in human capital—owing to that factor's extraordinary complementarity with physical capital—will generally fall into the first category, while countries with less educated workforces will lose capital and adopt policies more hostile to it.

Chapter 11

GLOBALIZATION AND POLICY DIFFUSION
Explaining Three Decades of Liberalization

BETH A. SIMMONS AND ZACHARY ELKINS

WE LIVE IN A WORLD that is more fully integrated and globalized than at any other point this century.[1] What can account for the spread of liberal economic-policy choices by governments over the past three decades? The evidence suggests that economic-policy choice exhibits patterns of diffusion among countries: the decisions to liberalize by some governments impact the liberalization choices made by others. The purpose of this chapter is to try to understand these processes of policy diffusion. We argue that influences on policy are conditioned by competitive considerations; systematic evidence shows that what potential competitors do matters. Policy is also likely conditioned by foreign ideas and models to which governments are exposed. These two mechanisms are an important part of the explanation for the apparent diffusion of liberalization we have witnessed over the past three decades.

Unlike other contributions to the present volume, we focus on three policies that can be understood to intensify globalization — understood as the reduction of barriers to exchange and factor mobility (Kahler and Lake, chapter 1) — rather than on the effects of globalization per se. The first is liberalization of the current account. Increasingly, governments have committed themselves to refrain from interfering in foreign exchange markets for purposes of blocking or otherwise influencing current transactions (foreign debt repayment, payment for goods, services, or invisibles; see Simmons 2000). The second is liberalization of the capital account, or the removal of taxes, quotas, or other rules that would discourage the free movement of investment funds into and out of a country. The third is the unification of the exchange rate. Governments have, over the course of the past three decades, largely eschewed multiple or tiered systems, which were quite popular in the 1950s and 1960s in some regions, but that can be used to discriminate against particular kinds of transactions or particular trading partners. Together, these three policy areas constitute the major aspects of monetary and financial liberalization during the past three decades.

[1] The authors wish to thank to Aaron Staines, Monica Swanson, and Geoffrey Wu for research assistance.

Liberalization in these three policy areas has been significant. In 1967, for example, only 25 members of the IMF (23 percent) had capital accounts that were practically free from restrictions, 38 (32 percent) had fully liberalized current accounts, and 73 (68 percent) had unified exchange-rate systems. By 1996, more than 54 members (29 percent) had removed virtually all restrictions on capital account, while 79 (43 percent) had liberalized the current account and 158 (or 86 percent of the membership) had unified their exchange-rate systems.[2] Figure 11.1 illustrates the cumulative number of countries that are members of the IMF that have liberalized these three policy areas since the mid-1960s. In all three cases, there has been significant policy liberalization over time, set back somewhat by the economic difficulties of the early 1970s in the case of capital-account liberalization and in the mid-1990s in the case of the current account. Liberalization in all three policy areas seems to have accelerated in the early 1990s, but have been set back somewhat by the financial crises of 1997.

Economists have focused primarily on the growth and efficiency implications of these and other forms of economic policy liberalization,[3] while political economists and political scientists have focused primarily on domestic political explanations of liberalization, most recently with special attention to the capital account.[4] A close look at patterns of

[2] These figures come from the IMF's Annual Exchange Arrangements and Restrictions, Analytical Appendix, various issues. For a longer historical view of capital controls and the trade-off between liberal capital accounts and monetary-policy autonomy, see Obstfeld and Taylor (1998).

[3] See, for example, Obstfeld and Rogoff (1996, chap. 5), and Svensson (1988); for a critical view, see Bhagwati (1998). For a general discussion relating to the capital account, see S. Edwards (1999a, b). See also Dooley (1995). In a series of articles, Paul Krugman (1998b, c) argues in support of controls on capital, while Barry Eichengreen (1999b) argues in support of controls on inflows specifically. Edwards (1999a, b) argues that capital controls do not do much to reduce external vulnerability. On the effectiveness of controls on capital inflows, see De Gregorio, Edwards, and Valdes (2000). On the link between capital withdrawals and bank runs in developing countries, see Cole and Kehoe (1998) and Chang and Velasco (1998).

[4] Aizenman and Guidotti (1994); Alesina, Grilli, and Milesi-Ferretti (1994); Drazen (1989); Epstein and Schor (1992); Giovannini and de Melo (1993); Grilli and Milesi-Ferretti (1995); Quinn and Inclan (1997); Quinn and Jacobson (1989). Leblang (1997) is a partial exception to this domestic orientation since he purports to test the extent of a country's reliance on the global economy (operationalized as imports, exports, and investment as a proportion of GDP) and the global degree of financial integration (measured as the total size of yearly flows of bond or FDI lending across borders) as an explanation for liberalization of the capital account. See also Frieden (1991a, b) Goodman and Pauly (1993), and Encarnation and Mason (1990) for case studies that emphasize external pressures and linkages for capital-account liberalization. Garrett, Guisinger, and Sorens (2000) have found strong evidence that the proportion of countries in one's own "income category" (as defined by the World Bank) has a strong impact on the probability of liberalizing capital controls. They label this a "contagion" effect, but do little to expand on the mechanisms that might account for such an influence.

A. The current account

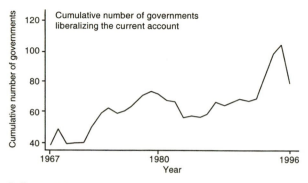

B. The capital account

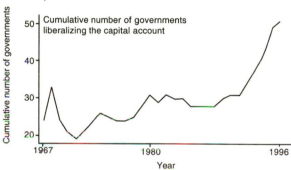

C. Exchange rates

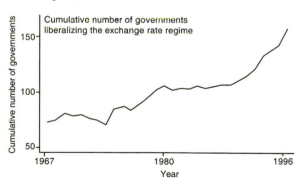

Figure 11.1. Cumulative Number of Governments Adopting Liberalization Policies

policy liberalization over the past three decades, however, provides strong prima facie evidence that liberalization is in some sense "contagious": choices in some countries seem to affect choices made by others. Figure 11.1 seems to suggest that something like contagion is likely to be at work:[5] Controls on the capital account, for example, accumulated quickly in the 1970s, while liberalization seems to have snowballed in the 1990s.

One statistical way to diagnose contagion is to compare the distribution of liberalizations across time to those predicted by a poisson distribution.[6] The poisson is a rare-events distribution that assumes events occur independently, and that the susceptibility of a particular event is homogenous across countries. None of these policy liberalization patterns fits the poisson very well. A chi-square test of equivalence of distributions suggests that, for each of the three policies, we can reject the null hypothesis that capital controls follow a poisson pattern (see appendix 11A). It is unlikely, therefore, that policy liberalization in these three areas is an independent choice taken across a set of governments that are equally susceptible to liberalization.

There are several distributions designed especially to detect contagion. King (1989) suggests that the negative binomial distribution is an appropriate candidate for diffusion processes. A crucial difference between the Poisson and the negative binomial is that the latter treats the dispersion of Y as a random variable to be estimated along with the other parameters. In fact, the estimate of sigma-squared will be a good estimate of the dispersion of Y_I, and therefore, the degree of contagion in the data. A reasonable way to proceed, then, is to compare the fit of the data with the negative binomial distribution to that with the Poisson. Again, in each of the three cases, a likelihood-ratio test reveals that the data fit a negative binomial distribution significantly better than they do a poisson, suggesting once again a process of contagion (see appendix 11A).

We cannot, however, tell whether these results are due to violating the assumption of independence or of homogenous susceptibility to a particular event. We have already explained why these decisions may not be independent. It is likely that the homogeneity assumption is violated as well. As Ronald Rogowski's model elsewhere in the present volume emphasizes, governments are likely to face different demands from their

---

[5] This cumulative curve of an event-count, when it demonstrates periods of sharp incline preceded and followed by relatively flat portions, is sometimes called the "contagion curve." See, for example, Rogers (1995), Valente (1995), and Coleman, Kate, and Menzel (1964).

[6] Most and Starr (1980); Siverson and Starr (1991).

domestic polities. Furthermore, national institutions are likely to aggregate these demands in very different ways (Garrett and Lange 1995), such that homogeneity with respect to liberalization seems an especially inappropriate assumption.[7] Since some heterogeneity is likely, we are in no position at this point to draw firm positive conclusions about contagion. What we *can* say is that our efforts to rule out contagion have failed.

The remainder of this chapter fleshes out and tests two plausible mechanisms that could explain why there appears to be some kind of policy diffusion with respect to monetary liberalization over the past three decades. The first is a model based on incentives created by international economic competition. The second is an ideational explanation that predicts emulation based on social networks. As with Rogowski's chapter, the arguments advanced here can account for partial, but by no means universal, policy convergence across countries. The explanations tested here, however, differ radically from those at work in his model. Rogowski's is an essentially domestic political account in which assumptions about heterogenous preferences distinguishing capital and labor drive outcomes; "the policy actually adopted" is that "embraced by the decisive voter" and this in turn reflects total returns to that voter. Capital-to-labor ratios, the economy's natural advantages, the share of social product that goes to labor, and the intensity of preferences are all relevant to policy choice.

While these domestic factors are important, we contend they cannot alone account for the patterns of diffusion in the data. In the Rogowski approach, governments respond to specified domestic preferences, and passively "sort" themselves into a relatively friendly or hostile policy stance vis-à-vis capital. Our research suggests that other dynamics are probably at play. First, we wonder about the appropriateness of the assumption of heterogenous preferences as between labor and capital given recent work that has argued for differences along sectoral lines, especially as globalization intensifies (Frieden 1991a). Second we would argue for a conception of the state that actively and strategically advances the policy agenda by defining options, anticipating other players' policies, and altering payoffs (through taxes and appropriations, for example) rather than one that passively responds to coalitional demands. This would seem an especially appropriate conception, given what Rogowski suggests is at stake, "Divergence of policy implies divergence in growth, investment, and wealth. The most capital friendly countries at-

---

[7] In the section that follows, we explicitly recognize that there are a host of "national-level" variables that could account for the observed patterns. Our tests try to distinguish between these effects and external mechanisms that could account for contagion.

tract the bulk of world investment, grow more rapidly, and increase the gap between the capital-friendly and capital-hostile states. Obviously this trend increases incentives to migrate." Even more obviously, anticipation of such an outcome should prompt a government that otherwise might be reluctant to do so to search for more competitive models of economic development. The evidence we analyze suggests that this is much more likely, and advances competitive and ideational mechanisms for understanding such international policy diffusion.

EXPLAINING THE APPARENT DIFFUSION OF POLICY LIBERALIZATION

How might we account for apparent contagion with respect to policy liberalization? Let us set aside models of the "ineluctable", "inexorable," or "inevitable" sort, and accept that there are *variations* in the patterns of policy convergence that require explanation across time and space.

Economic Competition

Patterns of diffusion might be most easily explained by *inter-state economic competition*. This is the mechanism of policy convergence that has been privileged by Miles Kahler and David Lake in the introductory chapter in the present volume. As they frame the discussion in the popular literature, "competitive economic pressures will produce institutional and policy homogeneity over time in a direction most favored by the mobile factors of production — footloose capital." In popular renditions, it is the mobile factors of production, not the "decisive" voter in Rogowski's model, that exerts influence on policy choice. In such a competitive model, there is room for recognizing what Marxists have traditionally referred to as a "structural dependence" on capital: the preference of the median voter is far less significant than the government's inability to rule without the cooperation and support of capital.

Key to a model of economic competition is that policies taken outside of one jurisdiction have negative spillover effects elsewhere. Access to international capital, or international business more generally, is assumed to be desirable for aggregate economic growth (Rogowski, for example, accepts this proposition), but the policies taken in foreign jurisdictions can negatively affect others' ability to enjoy such access. As a corollary, capital is assumed to be highly sensitive to the regulatory environment in which it potentially invests. When foreign competitors liberalize, trade and investment are drawn to those locations where they can more freely and securely do business. Capital and trade respond positively to the signal that policy liberalization sends (Bartolini and

Drazen 1997). This sets up the possibility of competition among jurisdictions, at least on the margins, for the location of international economic activity.

Most significantly, decision makers act strategically in this model in order to attract economic activity to their jurisdiction in order to boost aggregate growth. Pluralist renditions emphasize the preferences of electorally significant firms or groups in clarifying to leaders the interests they have in such policies (Goodman and Pauly 1993). In more statist versions, decision makers take such actions *regardless* of the preferences of domestic political groups; in the medium run, they are gambling on an aggregate growth payoff, for which, presumably, they will be rewarded by continuing to hold power. In each case, however, the government faces incentives to anticipate and counter decisions taken outside of their jurisdiction; they do not wait passively for these decisions to work their way through the international economy, the domestic economy, and the domestic electoral system. In an international environment that is assumed to be institutionally thin and nonhierarchical, the result is competitive pressure to implement capital-friendly policies when major competitors have done so (cf. McNamara, chapter 13).

Note that this model does not predict universal convergence on liberalization. It predicts convergence *among competitors*. The contours of convergence should trace the lines of economic competition. The task here is to map out competitive relations not only among trade partners, but also among economically similar countries that compete for trade or investment in third markets. Decision makers are assumed to have good information on who their competitors are, the policy choices they make, and the expected "payoff" attached to matching or failing to match the policies of competitors. In short, this is a model of rational competition for a scarce and desired resource (capital, trade), over which strategically sophisticated governments compete in an internationally unregulated setting.

Social Emulation

A distinct explanation for policy convergence focuses on the sociocultural ties among nations. This is an approach that has received no mention in the framing essay for this volume (Kahler and Lake, chapter 1), but which has strong roots in sociological research, and increasingly, in social constructivist theories of international monetary relations (see, for example, McNamara 1998a). In contrast to the theories delineated above, policy diffusion may have little to do with economic incentives based on competition or even on traditional measures of economic success. Social networks may complement or even supplant economic explanations in important ways, especially if we alter our assumptions about the nature of the information environment in which policy decisions are made. This approach assumes that the consequences of policy choice may not always be obvious, even after observing a number of "natural experiments" (i.e., liberalizations elsewhere). Policymakers may be capable, at best, of something akin to a *boundedly rational* search for policy guidance. The theoretical issue is then not strictly to determine the cost-benefit calculation underlying a specific policy choice, but to ask, *where do policymakers get the ideas and beliefs that inform such a choice in the first place?*

This question has long been at the core of sociological inquiry (Meyer and Rowan 1977; Powell and DiMaggio 1991; Scott and Meyer 1994) and it has recently entered international relations in the form of ideational or social constructivist theories of international politics (Checkel 1993; Haas 1992; Risse-Kappen 1994; Ruggie 1975). Sociologists begin with the assumption that "the transfer of ideas occurs most frequently between individuals . . . who are similar in certain attributes such as beliefs, education, social status, and the like" (Rogers 1995, 274). Axelrod (1997, 205) develops a model of the dissemination of culture that abstracts from this fundamental principle to say that communication is most effective between "similar" people. His theory of the diffusion of ideas specifies mechanisms of change for local actors in the absence of any coordinating central authority. In his model, actors are *adaptive rather than fully rational*: they follow simple rules about giving and receiving influence, but they do not necessarily calculate costs and benefits in a strategic, forward-looking way, in contrast to the approach described above. The result of Axelrod's model is pockets of ideational convergence, based on the number of features that two neighbors already share in common.

One can readily identify the kinds of network and communicative linkages that could contribute to social emulation with respect to monetary and financial liberalization. Contacts at the intergovernmental level may reflect network effects: frequent intergovernmental meetings at multiple official levels can transmit information to policymakers about "what works" in other settings. Where official contacts are infrequent, this information is less likely to be transmitted and less likely to become salient to decision makers in any case. Intellectual ties are also likely to be important. Anecdotal evidence suggests that links between the department of economics at the University of Chicago and Chile's economic ministry are not coincidentally related to that country's relatively liberal posture toward international market forces.

Social emulation may follow channels carved out by private actors, as well. Businesspersons may transmit ideas about appropriate economic policy by looking to the experiences of the countries with which they have especially intense trading contacts. Lessons drawn from these contacts may inform the shape of the demands they make on their own governments, thus feeding into the demand side of the policy equation. Transnational contact at the mass level can also prove important, although here the nature of the contact is less likely to contain precise policy-relevant information and more likely to be an indicator of the social salience one society attaches to the experiences of another.

Finally, social emulation may reflect subjective notions of identity contained in assumptions of commonly shared values and social purposes. In their search for relevant economic models, decision makers, consciously or not, may look to the experiences of those societies with whom they share an especially close set of cultural linkages. Such a tendency may be a cognitive short cut for an individual, or a focal point to limit cycling over alternatives in a group decision-making context. In either case, perceived cultural affinity assists in carving out the relevant models that inform policy development.

This model implies that given imperfect information about the consequences of policy choice, decision makers are likely to imitate the practices of nations with which they share linguistic, religious, historical, or social ties (see Friedkin 1993; Lerner 1964, see also Jacoby 2000). These common characteristics are likely to enhance the communicative mechanism central to Axelrod's model. Furthermore, there is strong evidence to suggest that policy contagion is more pronounced among actors that are structurally equivalent in that they share the same "kinds" of ties (e.g., Burt 1987). Axelrod's model is certainly consistent with the notion that agents are more likely to be influenced by other agents to the extent that they share a common social network.

In stark contrast to Rogowski's domestic political economy of the demand side of the policy-convergence question, this is an international sociological account of the supply side. To begin with, it assumes that many governments are not primarily inward-looking when seeking to design policy. In contrast to both Rogowski's model and the economic-competition model discussed above, information is poor and decision makers "satisfice" rather than maximize under constraints. There is no reason to expect universal policy convergence, even if these ideational influences are at work. In this case, convergence is expected among countries *within one's social network*, which certainly is conceptually distinct from one's economic competitors.

Controlling for Coincidence

It is important to control for explanations of observed policy convergence that cannot be attributed to processes of policy diffusion. Rogowski's model is an excellent starting point. His model suggests that where we do observe policy convergence (which is by no means a necessary outcome) it can be understood as an *uncoordinated response to common domestic political or economic conditions.* Facing similar domestic coalitional demands, governments find it *independently rational* to respond in similar ways. This is the tack taken by the bulk of the political-economy literature in the past decade.[8] In most cases, preferences are deduced from neoclassical economic models, and stand in for the "demands" the polity might make (Frieden 1991a; Magee, Brock and Young 1989; Milner 1988; Rogowski 1989).[9] Increasingly studies are addressing the importance of domestic political institutions in the liberalization process.[10] We do not propose to test a fully specified model of domestic policy choice, but feel it is critical to acknowledge the need for some domestic-level control variables. Three of these variables are suggested by Rogowski's model. Roughly capturing the capital-to-labor ra-

[8] The literature on capital controls is a surprising example of this domestic political-economy orientation. This literature has focused on the effects of capital controls on economic growth (Stockman and Hernandez 1988) and on income inequality within countries (Quinn 1997). Political economists have analyzed capital controls as a tool of economic repression (Giovannini and de Melo 1993), and reasoned that such controls could be explained by partisanship and the government's desire for seigniorage (Epstein and Schor [1992]; Grilli and Milesi-Ferretti [1995]; for an opposing view, see Quinn and Jacobson [1989]). Quinn and Inclan (1997) argue that domestic institutional arrangements also account for part of the differences in international financial regulation.

[9] Frieden (1991a, b) offers a sectoral explanation for financial openness, in which specific industries tied to the national economy oppose open capital regimes and internationally oriented financial and nonfinancial firms demand capital account openness. Leblang (1997) tests Frieden's explanation by including the extent of a country's reliance on the global economy (operationalized as imports, exports, and investment as a proportion of GDP) and the global degree of financial integration (measured as the total size of yearly flows of bond or FDI-lending across borders). He concludes that domestic forces play a more significant role in explaining the implementation and removal of capital controls. On the importance of transnational pressures to liberalize, see Goodman and Pauly (1993) and Encarnation and Mason (1990).

[10] Another cluster of research emphasizes the role of pegged exchange rates as a commitment technology for the control of domestic monetary inflation (Alogoskoufis, Lockwood, and Philippopoulos 1992). In this formulation, governments make exchange-rate commitments with an eye to the trade-off between monetary credibility and flexibility. Governments that are especially worried about inflation are believed to be willing to "tie their own hands" via a fixed exchange rate (which on average allows for much less inflation than do flexible regimes; Alogoskoufis and Smith [1991]). Fixed rates thus solve at least partially the time-inconsistency problem. Such commitments can be costly in the short run, however. Thus, Edwards (1996) argues that political stability and a strong governing majority make the choice of a fixed exchange-rate regime more likely (see also Simmons [1994]). Comparative political economists are now beginning to examine choice of exchange-rate regime and how it interacts with existing domestic political institutions, including central bank independence, democracy, and electoral timing and institutions (Bernhard and Leblang 1999; Broz 2002).

tio, we control for gross national product per capita. In an attempt to control for the demands of domestic constituencies, we control for the political strength of the export sector. We also control for two domestic institutional variables. The first is democratic governance. (This is assumed in all versions of Rogowski's model.) Garrett, Guisinger, and Sorens (2000) find that democracy is associated with a smaller probability that a developing country will liberalize the capital account. This may well be due to the difficulty of reconciling democratic politics with popular demands in the developing-country context. Finally we consider to what degree liberalization might be facilitated by the centralization of the governing structure. Our working hypothesis is that decentralization creates veto points that could prevent or slow the process of decisive decision making. Since the incidence of liberal policies is much lower in the early part of our sample than in the 1990s, in most cases this suggests that decentralization may drag down the process of liberalization. In addition to these domestic political variables, a battery of economic controls is included, as well.[11]

DATA, METHODOLOGY, AND EXPECTATIONS

In order to assess these contending explanations for policy diffusion, we have gathered yearly data for up to 180 countries since 1967. With country years as the unit of analysis, we have used logit analysis to model current-account, capital-account, and exchange-rate policy liberalization.[12] Because the data consist of observations across countries and over time, with a strong probability of temporal dependence among observations, a logit specification is used that takes explicit account of the nonindependence of observations (Beck, Katz, and Tucker, 1998).[13] Three cubic splines were generated and included in the results, but not reported here.

We want to examine hypotheses that not only would indicate that international-diffusion processes exist above and beyond the "sorting" effects attributable to domestic political and economic explanations; we

[11] Variation in world interest rates, for example could cause region-wide capital outflows, capital– and current-account deterioration, and exchange-rate pressure, with predictable effects on capital– and/or current-account deterioration (Bartolini and Drazen 1998). Similarly, robust growth rates or an improving balance of payments could increase policymakers' confidence in removing such controls (Goodman and Pauly 1993). Thus we control for world interest rates, volatility in the terms of trade, current-account balance as proportion of GDP, and GDP growth.

[12] As determined by the International Monetary Fund (see appendix 11B).

[13] A countervector was created using the STATA routine made available on Richard Tucker's website at http://www.fas.Harvard.edu/~rtucker/papers/grouped/grouped3.html, and three splines were included in the analysis, but their coefficients are not reported here.

also want to know whether economic competition or social emulation can account for the convergence patterns observed. Two indicators are constructed to capture the effects of competition for trade and capital. Trade competition is measured by an index of export similarity. This index is analogous to one developed by Finger and Kreinin (1979).[14] Using the bilateral trade data available from the International Monetary Fund, it captures the extent to which countries compete for the same export markets. We have taken each country's top ten competitors by this definition, and then taken the percentage of these countries that have liberalized in each of the three policy areas. Our hypothesis is that as the percentage of liberalizers in this group increases, the probability that the country for whom these are trade competitors will liberalize increases, as well. In short, trade competitors' policies should converge.

Competition for capital is conceptualized as the extent to which two countries compete for a particular pool of investment capital. Since investors have varying tastes for risk, it is reasonable to assume that countries that pose similar risks are, from an investor's point of view, close substitutes (the United States, for example, does not compete with Afghanistan for foreign capital; Angola might). "Similar risks" are gauged by the historical sovereign-risk rating assigned to each country by Standard and Poor's. We constructed this variable by calculating the percentage of countries within a country's own rating category that has liberalized in these three policy areas. Countries that are not rated at all are assumed to compete with other nonrated jurisdictions. If competition for international capital provides incentives to liberalize, then we expect a positive coefficient.

Next, we devise measures of some of the more sociologically oriented arguments that stress the role of social and information networks on emulation. One way in which these kinds of links can be forged is through economic relations. Trade means not only competition, but also contact, at both the private and official level. Governments are more likely to be influenced by countries with whom they, or, more likely, their citizens, trade very intensively. In order to capture this possibility, we use the yearly mean policy score of governments above the ninetieth percentile in their share of country A's total exports and separately, of country A's imports. If trade relations create a channel for the

---

[14] The index of export similarity we use is defined by:

$$S(ab,c) = \{\_\min[Xi(AC), XI(BC)]\}100$$

where countries A and B market to country C, and $Xi\ (ac)$ is the share of commodity I in A's exports to C.

transmission of policy influence internationally, we would expect coefficients on these two variables to be positive.

Institutional linkages may also create channels of policy influence. The process of negotiating and maintaining institutional affiliations may create opportunities to learn and persuade (Haas 1959, 1982). We test two kinds of institutional linkages: those forged via preferential trade arrangements and bilateral investment treaties. Again, the measure is the proportion of countries with which a particular state shares these kinds of arrangements that has liberalized. If these arrangements create opportunities for policy influence, then we would expect these variables to have a positive coefficient, as well. Finally we include two more variables, one that speaks to communication linkages and one that speaks to cultural linkages: we grouped countries by dominant religion and examine policy liberalization within one's religious reference group, and we examined data on telephone minutes between countries and coded the rate of liberalization for countries with very high levels of telephone communication. Once again, emulation along these channels of influence should return a positive coefficient.

We also control for a series of variables that could impact the decision to liberalize, but need not imply processes of policy diffusion. These include economic variables (world interest rates, using United States interest rates as a proxy; current account balance as a proportion of GDP, lagged two periods to minimize problems of endogeneity; each country's degree of volatility with respect to the terms of trade; GDP per capita; and GDP growth). Finally, we control for variables that potentially get at the nature of domestic demands (the significance of the trade sector and GDP per capita, a rough measure of the capital–labor ratio) and two institutional variables (democratic institutions and decentralization).

Findings

The full results of this analysis are presented in appendixes. Here we concentrate on examining the economic competition hypotheses and the social emulation hypotheses. In each of the tables that follow, two models are presented for each of the three dependent variables. The first is a model including variables for that particular diffusion mechanism only. The second provides ceteris paribus results, controlling for all other variables discussed in this chapter; as such it is simply a compression of each of the model 2s in appendix 11A.[15] All specifications in-

---

[15] Note that the current account is coded 1 for restriction, the capital account is coded 1 for liberalization, and the exchange-rate system is coded 1 for a multiple-rate system.

clude policies as a proportion of the countries in the region, a trend variable "year", and three cubic splines, which are not reported here.

International Economic Competition

Does economic competition spur policy convergence toward liberalization? If investors and traders prefer to do business where they are relatively sure of being able to export their capital and earnings and having contracts honored in the currency in which they were contracted at nondiscriminatory rates, then competition among potential business venues may be a spur to policy liberalization.

The results reported in table 11.1 suggest that this is indeed a strong possibility. Policies among a country's major export competitors (those that export most heavily to the same third markets) are likely to be positively associated in the case of exchange-rate unification and possibly in the case of current-account restrictions, as well. The relationship is, however, if anything, oddly reversed when it comes to capital-account liberalization. On the other hand, whether a country's capital competitors liberalize matters consistently across all specifications, all policies, and always in the correct direction. This points to an interpretation that competition for international capital is very likely to be a driver of the liberalization process.

The statistical strength and plausibility of these competitive mechanisms warrants a closer look at their substantive impact. Figure 11.2 graphs the marginal impact of export competition on exchange-rate unification. Using the results from model 1 (appendix 11A), which is the most fully specified model in which all included variables are statistically significant, the marginal probability of unifying the exchange rate clearly rises as the proportion of export competitors unify their rates. When about half of a country's export competitors unify their rates, the marginal probability of unifying is about 20 percent, controlling for a broad range of economic, political, and network variables. Export competition is both a statistically and substantively important part of an explanation for liberalization, at least when it comes to exchange-rate policies.

Figure 11.3 illustrates the marginal impact of policies among countries with a similar sovereign credit rating. The results here are even more dramatic. Once again using the results from model 1 for the capital account, this figure illustrates that when 25 percent of the countries

---

Thus, any control variable we would expect to contribute to liberalization should return a positive coefficient for the capital account and a negative coefficient for the current account and exchange rates. For our diffusion models, however, we always expect a positive coefficient.

TABLE 11.1
Competitive Explanations for Liberalization

Explanatory Variables	Current-Account Restrictions		Capital-Account Liberalization		Multiple Exchange Rates	
	Competitive vars. only	Ceteris Paribus	Competitive vars. only	Ceteris Paribus	Competitive vars. only	Ceteris Paribus
Constant	−70.81*** (9.39)	−99.15*** (19.55)	−181.61*** (14.84)	−217.89*** (36.5)	−71.80*** (10.01)	−66.26*** (.611)
Policies of export competitors	1.78*** (.591)	.180 (.992)	−7.90*** (1.02)	−1.83 (2.50)	2.75*** (.666)	4.68*** (1.27)
Policies of capital competitors	3.55*** (.338)	5.42** (.688)	7.38*** (1.08)	7.14*** (1.76)	4.93*** (.622)	3.68*** (.978)
Percentage of region liberalized	3.38*** (.200)	5.35*** (.435)	6.97** (.435)	5.39*** (.914)	4.33*** (.274)	5.37*** (.468)
Year	.034*** (.005)	.047*** (.010)	.091*** (.007)	.107*** (.019)	.034*** (.005)	.031*** (.010)
N	4361	2564	4133	2547	4319	2535
Log likelihood	−1858.87	−841.89	−756.14	−286.56	−1499.94	−743.97
Prob. > Chi²	0.00	0.00	0.00	0.00	0.00	0.00
Pseudo R^2	.38	.52	.65	.77	.40	.51

*$p > |Z| = .10$, **$p > |Z| = .05$, ***$p > |Z| = .01$.

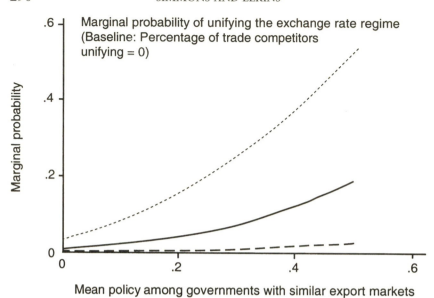

Figure 11.2. Impact of Export Competition on Exchange Rate Liberalization (within 95% confidence interval)

that are similarly rated have liberalized the capital account, the impact on liberalization is close to zero. But when 75 percent of the countries in this reference group liberalize, the probability of liberalizing is increased by nearly 30 percent, when all other variables are held constant. The impact on current-account liberalization is even more dramatic. When half of the similarly rated countries liberalize the current account, the probability of liberalizing is increased by about 20 percent. The curve rises steeply, though, so that when 75 percent of this group liberalizes, the marginal probability of liberalizing jumps to about 60 percent, once we have controlled for all the variables in model 1 (appendix 11A). This provides strong prima facie evidence that countries that compete for the same pool of capital — countries that offer investors roughly equal risk profiles — are under a degree of competitive pressure to liberalize when their competitors for capital do so.

Social Emulation

Next, we examine evidence that liberalization has a heavy ideational component that must be understood in terms of the social and information networks within which governments and their polities are situated. Table 11.2 presents the results of this analysis. The evidence is somewhat mixed regarding the strength of trade as a social network for in-

A. The capital account

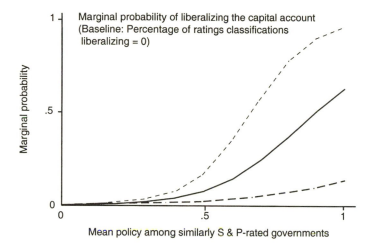

Marginal probability of liberalizing the capital account
(Baseline: Percentage of ratings classifications
liberalizing = 0)

Mean policy among similarly S & P-rated governments

B. The current account

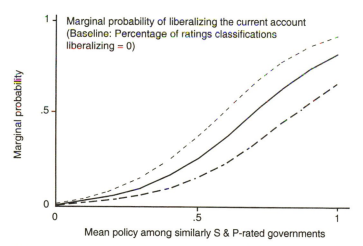

Marginal probability of liberalizing the current account
(Baseline: Percentage of ratings classifications
liberalizing = 0)

Mean policy among similarly S & P-rated governments

Figure 11.3. Impact of Capital Competition on Capital and Current Account Liberalization (within 95% confidence interval)

fluencing liberalization. And interestingly, these results suggest that it is the suppliers of a country's imports rather than the markets for its exports that may have the strongest and most consistent impact on policy orientation. The impact is not huge, but it is perceptible: when 25 percent of a country's major import suppliers liberalize the capital account, the marginal impact on liberalizing is less than 1 percent. On the other

TABLE 11.2
Social-Network Explanations for Liberalization

Explanatory Variables	Current-Account Restrictions		Capital-Account Liberalization		Multiple Exchange Rates	
	Network vars. only	Ceteris Paribus	Network vars. only	Ceteris Paribus	Network vars. only	Ceteris Paribus
Constant	-72.25 (.216)	-99.15*** (19.55)	-225.19 (16.18)	-217.89*** (36.5)	-91.04*** (10.65)	-66.26*** (.611)
Policies of major import suppliers	.725*** (.216)	-.031 (.372)	1.92*** (.401)	3.26*** (.869)	2.12*** (.338)	.688 (516)
Policies of major export markets	.053 (.202)	-.806** (.345)	.376 (.342)	-.906 (.572)	.843*** (.302)	1.09** (.449)
Policies of countries in shared PTAs	.446*** (.173)	-.220 (.251)	.131 (.352)	.673 (.559)	1.68*** (.234)	1.13*** (.297)
Policies of countries in BITs	.163 (.173)	.222 (.281)	-.673** (.293)	.077 (.631)	-.442 (.325)	-1.57*** (.484)

Policies of countries w/same dominant religion	2.32*** (.311)	2.28*** (.472)	10.55*** (1.06)	9.50*** (2.069)	1.37** (.609)	.600 (.864)
Policies of countries w/high phone minutes	.005 (.156)	.175 (.246)	−.323 (.262)	−.715* (.419)	−.466** (.196)	−.567** (.264)
Year	.035*** (.005)	.047*** (.010)	.112*** (.008)	.107*** (.019)	.045*** (.005)	.031*** (.010)
Percentage of region liberalized	3.71*** (.214)	5.35*** (.435)	5.56*** (.384)	5.39*** (.914)	4.23*** (.288)	5.37*** (.468)
N	4361	2564	4133	2547	4319	2535
Log likelihood	−1896.09	−841.89	−755.07	−286.56	−1499.37	−7432.97
Prob. > chi²	0.00	0.00	0.00	0.00	0.00	0.00
Pseudo R^2	.37	.52	.65	.77	.40	.51

$*p > |Z| = .10, **p > |Z| = .05, ***p > |Z| = .01.$

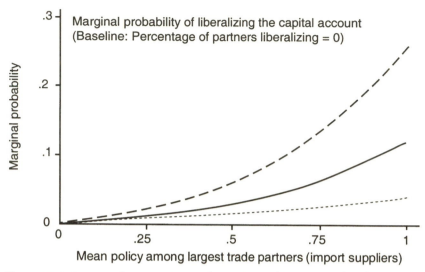

Figure 11.4. Impact of Import Networks on Capital Account Liberalization (within 95% confidence interval)

hand, when 75 percent of major import suppliers liberalize, the marginal impact on capital account liberalization is about 7 percent, which represents a large increase from an admittedly small base impact, as is illustrated in figure 11.4.

The policies of countries with which one has preferential trade arrangements appear to have a strong positive effect on policy, especially policies that can directly affect trade (current-account restrictions and multiple exchange-rate systems), though the relationship weakens in the more fully specified models. The policies of countries with whom a country has bilateral investment treaties (BITs) appears, if anything, to have a negative effect on policy, but this is probably due to the fact that BITs are usually signed precisely to establish a common legal framework between countries for whom this is lacking. It is very likely that the pool of countries with which a government would feel the need to sign a BIT comprises those whose policies raise questions about the protection of property rights; grossly speaking, these are likely to be countries that are low on mutual trust and shared values. A negative coefficient here is understandable in light of the purposes of negotiating BITs in the first place. The negative coefficient on telephone contacts is, however, probably due to missing data and should be taken very lightly.[16]

Much harder to dismiss is the impact of a common religion on the

[16] Telephone data were available only for very recent years and had to be estimated backwards, which might account for the negative coefficient.

tendency to emulate. The impact of a shared religion on policy similarity is consistent, positive, and extremely significant statistically and substantively for both capital-account and current-account liberalization (though not exchange rates in a fully specified model). This is astounding given the range of alternative explanations considered in the ceteris paribus model, which includes all of the economic variables, domestic political variables, and competition variables, as well as regional and time effects. Controlling for all of these factors, religious similarity is a strong predictor of economic policy convergence. Note that this is not an argument that a particular religion is more liberal than another; it merely shows that *countries that share the same religion are likely to share the same policy orientations* explored in this chapter. Why this should be is difficult to explain in the absence of some kind of cultural network in which governments look to the policies of those with whom they share the closest cultural ties in order to develop models of appropriate policy.

Figure 11.5 gives a sense of the magnitude of the effects attributable to common religion for the case of the current account. Once more than half of countries of the same religious heritage liberalize, the impact on liberalization becomes substantively significant, increasing the marginal probability of liberalizing the current account by about 20 percent when three-quarters of the group have liberalized. The magnitude of these effects is even greater for the capital account (not shown here).

Domestic Political and Economic Controls

None of this is to deny that domestic coalitions and institutions have something to do with policy choice in monetary and financial matters. The full results described in appendixes demonstrate that a domestic political-economy explanation is plausible; in particular, there is highly convincing evidence that publics residing in open economies demand and probably get greater policy liberalization, as Rogowski's model would lead us to expect. Every specification for trade openness is highly significant and in the correct direction. Of course, one reason this might be the case is the possibility of reverse causality, at least with respect to current-account restrictions and multiple exchange-rate systems (two-way causation may be less plausible, or at least much less direct in the case of capital controls). The impact of democracy washes out in more fully specified models, except in the case of exchange rates, where it is associated with unified systems. Democracy appears to be associated with capital controls in the simpler specification, though controlling for a wide range of explanations weakens this result significantly. Once again, this is not inconsistent with Rogowski's model, since he shows that, logically, democratic countries can diverge under certain conditions. Centralization of decision making seems largely marginal to the

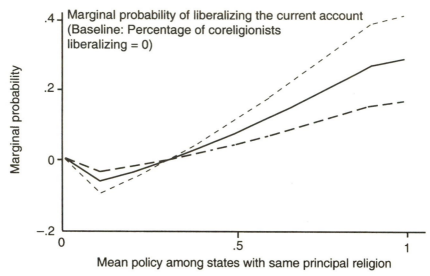

Figure 11.5. Impact of Religious Similarity on Current Account Liberalization (within 95% confidence interval)

liberalization process, with the exception of possibly contributing to policy liberalization with respect to the exchange-rate regime.

These domestic political variables are clearly insufficient on their own for explaining liberalization. Indeed, when the purely economic model is compared to the purely domestic political model, the former tends to explain more of the variance, especially in the case of capital-account liberalization. Moreover, evidence that there remains much to be explained can be found in the size of the regional coefficient in a purely domestic specification. "Region" (the proportion of countries in the region that have liberalized) soaks up a much larger share of the explanation in domestic models than in either the competitive or emulative specifications. Clearly, to black box external influences conceals important effects that our work has characterized as policy diffusion.

CONCLUSIONS AND IMPLICATIONS

There are good reasons to believe that governments are influenced by external conditions to liberalize their monetary and financial policies. The diagnostics performed in this chapter lent confidence to the proposition that something *systematic* must be driving states' policies in this area. From the simplest tests (a comparison of our data with the poisson distribution versus the negative binomial distribution) to the consistent finding that regional influences are positive, significant, and substantively important in every analysis, it is hard to reject the conclusion that there is not some kind of policy contagion involved in the liberalization of foreign economic policy.

It is extremely difficult, however, to pin down exactly the channels of policy transmission that account for the clustering in time and space of the decision to liberalize. We offer two plausible diffusion mechanisms — economic competition and social emulation — that might explain these patterns. In addition, we have controlled for a wide range of economic and domestic political variables. The control variables represent *alternatives* to contagion, assigning causation, as in Rogowski's model, instead to the economic and political conditions that are associated with essentially independent national policy-making. These domestic explanations found some support in our results, and corroborate the work of others. Economists will not be surprised at our finding that lower world interest rates, high GDP per capita, a strong balance of payments, and low volatility in the terms of trade are all very likely conducive to policy liberalization. Domestic political factors may also play a role, possibly in ways that are broadly consistent with Rogowski's model: economies that are structurally highly dependent on international trade are likely to generate political demands for liberalization. In every specification across all three policy areas, trade dependence was associated with liberalization. Also consistent with Rogowski's expectations, democracy is not associated in any clear and consistent way with foreign economic-policy liberalization; democracies can clearly diverge. Decentralization of decision making, as one way to think about veto points, did not yield convincing results, and certainly did not yield the impact (drag on liberalization) we expected.

Where this work begins to break new ground, and goes well beyond neoclassical models of the domestic political economy, is in the effort to model empirically mechanisms that explicitly deal with policy diffusion. The data cry out for an explicit examination of the external influences on policy choice, and a conception of the state that acts strategically (whether in ways best characterized as fully or boundedly rational) in response to its understanding of the possibilities for and constraints on liberalization. This volume has chosen to privilege explanations based on economic competition. We found some evidence of this possibility with respect to export competition. This mechanism is especially convincing with respect to exchange-rate liberalization — a policy that one can well imagine would be influenced by the policies of countries with which a country competes heavily for third markets. But even more convincing was the impact of policies among countries that arguably are the closest competitors for international capital: countries with similar bond ratings. Across all policy areas, and all specifications, policy choice is highly correlated with the orientation of other governments who are similarly rated. Could this simply be due to the fact that similarly rated countries are economically similar in a number of ways, and so have independently similar incentives to open their capital and current accounts? Such an interpretation would be consistent with Rogowski's expectations. We admit this is possible, though it is rendered much less likely by the inclusion of a battery of economic controls (wealth, growth, balance of payments, terms of trade volatility) that should to some extent control for this problem. Future research should explore other macroeconomic variables utilized by Standard and Poor's as criteria for their rating system, such as government deficits and inflation. The relationship is so strong and plausible in these tests that it provides a good point of departure for future research.

Finally we considered some of the arguments that have been inspired by more sociological approaches to policy diffusion. Focusing on the importance of models and social emulation rather than policy constraints, incentives, and competition, this approach suggests possibilities that scholars of political economy have not as of yet been willing to systematically explore. There may be good reasons for this: the conceptual problem of defining and defending a set of plausible "networks" that can generate the emulative behavior that we suspect lurks behind the patterns in the data is difficult. Nor is it trivial to gather the relevant data on these networks. These are daunting tasks, and when they are complete, one is left with a sense of where governments may have gotten their menu of possible policy approaches, but with very little theory about how and why certain approaches were actually chosen over others.

Yet it seems essential to probe somewhat more sociological arguments, especially since economic, political, and competition analyses failed to eliminate the large regional effects that resulted in each and every test. Just what do "regional effects" contain? Are they associational, informational, or cultural? This research has tested a few of the most plausible possibilities. Since business contacts may provide part of the answer, we looked at the policies of the major export and import partners. The latter seemed to have a fairly consistent positive effect on policy choice; there does seem to be a tendency to implement the policies of the countries that supply your imports. There seems to be no obvious competitive reason to do so. This leaves open the possibility of a process of socialization. Much more, of course, needs to be done to explore these ideas further.

Few political economists (though of course many more sociologists) would have nominated religion as a central explanation for policy diffusion. The results here, however, are difficult to ignore. Countries tend to liberalize along the lines of their co-religionists, controlling for several economic conditions, political conditions, trade relations, preferential trade agreements, and region. It seems intuitively as well as empirically plausible that shared cultural and value orientations are one important influence on policy convergence. Whether it is most plausible to view religious orientation as a filter on policymaking elites' search for acceptable alternatives, or whether values that cohere closely to religious orientations have an indirect effect through mass preferences, remains to be seen.

Overall, it is clear that economics and comparative political economy can take us only so far in understanding foreign economic-policy liberalization over the past three decades. The apparent diffusion of liberalization over this time cries out for an explicitly international theory and further testing. One thing is clear: we can only make theoretical and empirical progress if we drop the popular image of universal policy convergence as inherent in the process of globalization, and theorize a more subtle set of economic and social relationships that can explain observed variations in liberalization over time. As we think in these directions, we may uncover underemphasized sources of authority that structure competition and channel the search for appropriate models of foreign economic policy. Research into the dynamics of globalization and its underlying governance structures should push us to understand how and why this takes place.

Appendix 11A: Supplementary Tables

TABLE 11A.1
Analysis of Event-Counts, New Liberalizations

Null Hypothesis	Policy	Test Results	Conclusion	Indication
1. *Process of adoption fits a poisson distribution*	Liberalizing current account	Goodness of fit, Poisson regression (Chi^2 212.35 [30])	Reject	Process is not random
	Liberalizing capital controls	Goodness of fit, Poisson regression (Chi^2 77.74 [29])	Reject	Process is not random
	Liberalizing exchange-rate regime	Goodness of fit, Poisson regression (Chi^2 71.03 [30])	Reject	Process is not random
2. *Process of adoption fits a poisson regression better than it does the negative binomial*	Liberalizing current account	Likelihood-ratio test (Chi^2 136.02 [1])	Reject	Diffusion likely
	Liberalizing capital controls	Likelihood-ratio test (Chi^2 17.74 [1])	Reject	Diffusion likely
	Liberalizing exchange-rate regime	Likelihood-ratio test (Chi^2 11.11[1])	Reject	Diffusion likely

TABLE 11A.2

Explaining Policy Liberalization (Comprehensive Models)

Mechanism	Explanatory Variables	Current-Account Restriction		Capital-Account Liberalization		Multiple Exchange-Rate System	
		Model 1	Model 2	Model 1	Model 2	Model 1	Model 2
	Constant	−99.1*** (17.8)	−99.15*** (19.55)	−182.51*** (31.02)	−217.89*** (36.5)	−75.30*** (17.07)	−66.26*** (.611)
Economic controls	Real GDP per capita	.00058** (.00003)	.00005 (.00003)	.00010*** (.00005)	.00012** (.00058)	—	−.000041 (.000037)
	Terms of trade volatility	.307*** (.093)	.341*** (.102)	—	.008 (.190)	.200*** (.099)	.112 (.109)
	Policies of countries in shared PTAs	—	−.220 (.251)	—	.673 (.559)	1.19*** (.278)	1.13*** (.297)
	Policies of countries in BITs	—	.222 (.281)	—	.077 (.631)	−1.81*** (.471)	−1.57*** (.484)
	Policies of countries with same dominant religion	2.21*** (.452)	2.28*** (.472)	10.36*** (2.11)	9.50*** (2.069)	—	.600 (.864)
	Policies of countries in the region	5.25*** (.372)	5.35*** (.435)	5.38*** (.686)	5.39*** (.914)	5.64*** (.417)	5.37*** (.468)
	Centralization	−.010* (.006)	−.024 (.041)	.143*** (.039)	.089 (.072)	−.050*** (.017)	−.090 (.040)
International economic competition	Policies of export competitors	—	.180 (.992)	—	−1.83 (2.50)	5.09*** (1.14)	4.68*** (1.27)
	Policies of capital competitors	5.514*** (.633)	5.42*** (.668)	6.67*** (1.69)	7.14*** (1.76)	4.51*** (.878)	3.68*** (.978)

	International social emulation / Political controls					
Policies of major import suppliers	—	−.031 (.372)	3.32*** (.823)	3.26*** (.869)	.934* (.487)	.688 (.516)
Policies of major export markets	−.802** (.338)	−.806** (.345)	—	−.906 (.572)	.801** (.416)	1.09** (.449)
Current account balance/GDP (t-2)	−.021*** (.008)	−.021*** (.007)	.020** (.008)	.028*** (.008)	—	−.006 (.010)
World interest rates	.058*** (.024)	.057* (.024)	—	−.018 (.056)	.051*** (.024)	.058** (.026)
GDP growth	—	−.013 (.011)	—	.028 (.024)	—	−.002 (.011)
Openness (imports + exports/GDP)	−.106*** (.177)	−1.08*** (.180)	1.770*** (.347)	1.736*** (.363)	−.697*** (.170)	−.830*** (.198)
Democracy	—	.021 (.047)	−.054* (.029)	−.092 (.089)	.046*** (.016)	−.007 (.047)
Policies of countries with high phone minutes	—	.175 (.246)	−.673* (.416)	−.715* (.419)	−.646*** (.251)	−.567** (.264)
Year	.047*** (.010)	.047*** (.010)	.089*** (.016)	.107*** (.019)	.035*** (.008)	.031*** (.010)
N	2567	2564	2547	2547	2803	2535
Log Likelihood	−844.71	−841.89	−286.56	−286.56	−842.85	−743.97
Prob. > Chi²	0.00	0.00	0.00	0.00	0.00	0.00
Pseudo R^2	.52	.52	.77	.77	.49	.51

Note: Range of analysis: IMF members only 1967–1996. Results of a logit model with correction for time-dependence of observations coefficients (robust standard errors).

*$p > |Z| = .10$, **$p > |Z| = .05$, ***$p > |Z| = .01$.

Appendix 11B: Data

DEPENDENT VARIABLES

Capital Account Liberalization: A dichotomous variable coded 1 if a country's current account is free from restrictions and 0 if it is not. *Source: International Monetary Fund, Annual Exchange Arrangements and Restrictions, Analytical Appendix, various issues.*

Current Account Restrictions: Restrictions on current account; restrictions exist on payments in respect of current transactions. 1 if restrictions exist; 0 if they do not. *Source: International Monetary Fund, Annual Exchange Arrangements and Restrictions, Analytical Appendix, various issues.*

Multiple Exchange Rates: Whether 1 or not 0 the country has some form of multiple exchange-rate system. The case was coded as a multiple exchange-rate system if there were special rates for some or all capital transactions and/or some or all invisibles; import rates that differed from export rates; more than one rate for imports; or more than one rate for exports. *Source: International Monetary Fund, Annual Exchange Arrangements and Restrictions, Analytical Appendix, various issues.*

INDEPENDENT VARIABLES

Economic Competition Variables

Policy of Export Competitors: The yearly mean policy score of the 10 percent of governments whose export markets are most similar to country A's. Export similarity is calculated as the correlation of country A's share of exports to 150 countries with country B's. *Source: Based on Finger and Kreinin (1979) and calculated from the IMF Direction of Trade Statistics dataset.*

Capital Competitors: The yearly mean policy score of governments with similar sovereign bond ratings. *Source: Standard and Poor's Historical Sovereign Bond Ratings.*

Social Networks Variables

Policy of Major Export Partners: The yearly mean policy score of governments above the ninetieth percentile in their share of country A's total exports. *Source: IMF Direction of Trade.*

Policy of Major Import Partners: The yearly mean policy score of governments above the ninetieth percentile in their share of country A's total imports. *Source: IMF Direction of Trade.*

Policy of PTA Partners: The yearly mean policy score of governments with a preferential trade agreement with country A. *Source: Helen Milner and Edward Mansfield. Original source: World Trade Organization.*

Policy of BIT Partners: The yearly mean policy score of governments with a bilateral investment treaty with country A. *Source*: World Bank, http://www.worldbank.org/icsid/treaties/i-1.htm.

Policy of Telephone Partners: The yearly mean policy score of governments above the ninetieth percentile in their share of country A's total telephone minutes. *Source: AT&T.*

Policy of Countries with Shared Dominant Religions: The yearly mean policy score of nations who share the same major religion. The main religions coded were: Protestant, Catholic, Eastern Orthodox, Hindu, Buddhist, Muslim, Jewish, and Local/Traditional. *Sources: Countries of the World and Their Leaders Yearbook 2000; The Europa World Year Book 1999; The CIA World Factbook: http://www.odci.gov/cia/publications/factbook/*

Regional Liberalization: Proportion of current IMF members within each region who have liberalized in the policy area being analyzed (restrictions on current account, liberalization of the capital account, use of multiple exchange-rate systems). Classification of economies by region (East and Southern Africa, West Africa, East Asia and Pacific, Eastern Europe and Central Asia, Rest of Europe, Middle East, North Africa, Americas) are based on World Bank categories. *Source: International Monetary Fund, Annual Exchange Arrangements and Restrictions, Analytical Appendix, various issues.*

Economic Control Variables

Real GDP per capita: Source: Penn World Tables.

Current Account Balance/GDP: The current account balance (the sum of net exports of goods and nonfactor services, net factor income, and net private transfers as a percentage of GPD, before official transfers) as a proportion of GDP for each country for the period under observation. *Source: STARs database, indicators 223/38, World Bank.*

World Interest Rates: Annual average United States Treasury bill yield. *Source: International Monetary Fund, Time Series key 11160C . . . ZF . . . International Financial Statistics, May 1999.*

Terms of Trade Volatility: The log of the standard deviation of the terms of trade index, which is the relative level of export prices compared with import prices, calculated as the ratio of a country's index of average export price to the average import price (1987 = 100). *Source: STARs database, indicator 275, World Bank.*

GDP Growth: GDP average annual growth rate, for sum of GDP at factor cost and indirect taxes, less subsidies. *Source: STARs database, indicator 181, World Bank.*

Domestic Political Control Variables

Openness: Imports (total value of goods and services: sum of merchandise f.o.b., imports of nonfactor services and factor payments at market prices in current U.S. dollars) plus exports (total value of goods and services; sum of merchandise f.o.b, exports of nonfactor services and factor receipts at market prices in current U.S. dollars), as a proportion of GDP. *Source: STARs database, indicators (210 + 119)/38, World Bank; also Penn Wold Tables.*

Democracy: Democracy score (ranging from a low of 0 to a high of 10) denoting the degree of democratic institutions within each country. *Source: POLITY III data set. For a complete discussion of the conceptualization and coverage of this data set and comparisons with other measures of democracy, see Jaggers and Gurr (1999).*

Centralization of State Authority: Geographic concentration of decision-making authority. (1) = Unitary; (2) = Intermediate category; (3) = Federal. *Source: POLITY III data set.*

Chapter 12

CORPORATE GOVERNANCE
Global Markets, National Politics

Peter Gourevitch

A CENTRAL ISSUE in globalization debates is corporate governance—the way in which authority relations are structured within firms, linking their owners, managers, employees, and contractors. Market economies differ quite substantially in how they do this. The United States and the United Kingdom have strict rules against insider trading, limits on the concentration of shareholding in a firm, strong antitrust enforcement, and a vigorous market for corporate control. In Germany, shareholding is concentrated, banks own large numbers of shares and appoint members to the supervisory boards, there is little market for control, and insider-trading rules are lax. Japan's *keiretsus* have interlocking shareholding and control patterns that would violate American rules. The East Asian financial crisis brought into sharp relief the importance of the microinstitutions of corporate control; previously lauded for high growth rates, the Asian model was reclassified as "crony capitalism."

These differences in corporate-governance practices have important implications for the way economies function, the political relationships among states in the world trading system, and international institutions seeking to manage trade and dampen conflicts among trading partners. Corporate governance has traditionally been placed in the box of "domestic politics"—aspects of a nation beyond the reach of other countries. Now governance, like other aspects of domestic life, has become part of international politics, the object of disputes, treaties, efforts at harmonization, and international regulation. In so doing, corporate governance is now connected to global governance. How these issues are handled raises significant questions about the level of political action, international institutions, and the boundaries between the public and private, the national and domestic arenas.

The broadest form of the globalization discussion suggests a process

The author wishes to thank for advice and comment: Maria Estevez-Abe, Alex Gourevitch, Stephan Haggard, Peter Hall, Torben Iversen, Miles Kahler, Mikhail Klimenko, Lawrence Krause, David Lake, Jonah Levy, Ulrike Schaede, James Shinn, Matthew Shugart, Chris Woodruff, and Nicholas Zeigler.

of convergence. Open economic borders release market forces to operate around the world. As firms, and countries, compete, they are driven toward the most "efficient" modalities of economic activity. Competition presses all toward conformity around "best practice." In the field of corporate governance, that appears at present to be the Anglo-American model. The strength of the American economy is, so the argument runs, forcing its competitors to adopt American practices in corporate organization.

The business press suggests that some processes of this kind are at work. Germany, whose system represents the sharpest contrast from the American one, is sharply reducing its tax on the sale of shares; this, it is alleged, will break the high concentration of bank shares and the crossholding system that underlie the German model. Korea is reworking its laws on corporate governance. The European Union is developing a set of common standards in accounting, information, securities and exchange regulation. The World Bank and the IMF are helping to develop criteria for bank management. Japan has changed the way its firms relate to main banks (Hoshi and Kashyup 2001).

Are these press reports indicators of strong change, the beginnings of a convergence that leads to a common governance form (Dvořák et al. 2001)? Or are they indicators of "divergent" modernization—a process of constant change in which firms begin at different points and end at different points? Is it possible for a uniform force (the global market) to reward diversification, specialization—hence to encourage, or at least allow, divergence in this area? This chapter explores these questions as follows: first, a statement of the major differences in corporate-governance systems; second, an examination of the mechanisms at work that put pressure on these systems toward convergence; third, a study of the way these pressures are mediated by conflicting interpretations of the market and by political interests, processes, and institutions within each country; fourth, a look at the way international institutions mediate the impact of global pressures; and finally, an evaluation of these interactions.

The chapter argues that there is substantial reason to think divergent modernization continues to hold rather than convergence. Under the pressures of globalization, some convergence does occur, but in other areas sharp differences remain. Economic pressures are refracted through politics. Political processes, preferences, and institutions, domestic and international, structure the translation of economic pressures into policy outputs. There has always been considerable variance on policy output in the economy; there is reason to think this will continue.

Corporate-governance systems will evolve out of the interaction of political processes within three autonomous systems of decision making: the firm, the nation, and the international arena. Each experiences a common force — the global economy — and each processes that force differently. The firm integrates incentives from the market according to the existing structure of power within it. The nation aggregates preferences that arise from the economy through institutions that influence the outcome of that aggregation mechanism. The international system, institutionalized or anarchic, aggregates in turn the preferences of states and of private actors. The interaction of these systems mediates the common force of the global economy to produce outputs that are varied, not uniform. Corporate governance as an issue-area thus becomes an object of global governance, but also an influence upon its evolution. (Shinn and Gourevitch 2002).

Corporate-Governance Systems

Definition

Corporate governance refers to the authority structure of firms — the distribution of power in the firm, shaping who makes decisions, who monitors the decision makers, and what measures are used. Discussions of governance often look only at the board of directors, but this is incomplete. Shinn (2001) has identified the key features of a governance system:

> *Information institutions*: accounting rules, audit procedures, standards-settings, and third-party analysis.
>
> *Oversight institutions*: boards of directors and the rules governing their fiduciary responsibilities.
>
> *Control institutions*: the degree of voice minority shareholders have in the case of contested control and the rules that govern such contests, including the rules for hiring, compensating, and firing senior managers.

These parameters of corporate control can vary, comprising alternative models of corporate governance.

Alternative Models

Among the several typologies (Albert 1992; Boyer 2002; Dore 1987, 2000) that describe differences in governance models, I use here the labels employed by Hall and Soskice (2001), Iversen (1999), and Iversen and Soskice (2001a): Liberal Market Economies (LME) and Organized Market Economies (OME). The systems differ in the way they monitor and reward the individuals who make them function. As Kester (1992) phrases it, LME systems see the core managerial problem as agency, and solve it by stressing the monitoring powers of external shareholders; the OME systems see the core managerial problem in terms of transaction pcosts, and solve it with strong internal linkages. Writers in law and

economics focus their distinction on diffuse shareholding versus concentrated blockholding; the overlap with LME and OME is substantial
(Gourevitch 2003; La Porta, Lopez-de-Silano, Shleifer, and Vishny
2000, 2002; Shleifer and Vishny 1999; Roe 2002).

LIBERAL MARKET ECONOMIES (LME)

This model overcomes moral hazard through monitoring the behavior
of agents (the managers) by principals (the public stockholders). To prevent managers from abusing their privileged position, regulations require the public disclosure of information about the firm to outsiders
and forbid the formation of special relationships between managers and
selected shareholders. LME systems have strong antitrust regulations.
Concentration of ownership is prohibited. Banks and other institutions
cannot own substantial chunks of firms or name their representatives to
firm boards. Cross-shareholding, rotation of managers, tight bonds to
suppliers or sellers up and down the supply chain—these are limited to
prevent collusion.

Managers are monitored by the stock market. A vigorous market for
corporate control limits moral hazard by the threat of takeovers, hostile
or friendly. "Patient" capital may exist—shareholders who stress value
over the long haul and are thus less responsive to short-term fluctuations, but these shareholders interact with many whose values are more
short-term. Since stockownership cannot be concentrated, shareholders
own small shares of the whole. Monitoring thus encounters a collective-
action problem: no one can have enough leverage over the whole to
have much incentive to pay the costs of gathering substantial information. Instead, shareholders monitor through relatively "cheap" (low
search-cost) information provided by the quarterly reports.

By protecting the interests of external shareholders, this system encourages the mobilization of savings through shareownership; LME
economies are substantially more capitalized than are OME ones. Conversely, the LME system incurs substantial transaction costs. The mechanism of coordinating at arm's length inhibits information-sharing
among the members of the production network. LME systems seem to
do well with venture capital (a good balance to the charge that it discourages long-term horizons) and with transferring capital away from
declining sectors. They do less with modernizing of stable industries and
with certain activities that reward close relationships—very high-quality
volume manufacturing, for example.

ORGANIZED MARKET ECONOMIES (OMEs)

OMEs stress the problem of reducing transactions costs and building
long-term relationships. Where the LMEs pay a price in higher transac-

tions costs for stressing agency problems, the OMEs lower these at the cost of agency problems. Instead of rewarding external shareholders using cheap information indicators, LMEs reward patient shareholders with long-term investments. Other stakeholders, workers, suppliers, sellers — the participants in a productive system — have more voice than is the case in LMEs.

Shareholding resides with banks, trusts, or other firms in a network with the firm. Ownership is concentrated. These institutions own very large percentages of the stock. Share turnover is low. External shareholders are small in number and weak in voice. Cross-shareholding is substantial.

These systems may reflect cultural values but these values, are backed up quite strongly by rules, regulations, and regulatory institutions. Laws allow concentration of ownership and cross-shareholding and may even reward it — for example, until recently German law taxed share sales quite heavily. Antitrust law is weak and/or poorly enforced. Securities regulation does not punish insider information. In the LME system, manufacturing is buffered by overinvesting in capital stock or other protections from disruption. This has been called "buffered manufacturing," rather than "lean production," a feature of the OME system.

Indeed, insider information is the essence of the system because its advantages lie with the incentives to share information. In the LME system, manufacturers and suppliers have every incentive to conceal information and not to invest too far in the specific assets of each other's business. By contrast, the OME system encourages information-sharing because the economic fates of the firms lie together, and various forms of cross-ownership and rotation of managers prevent the opportunism that sharing of information can provoke.

Creditors sit on the boards of firms in the OME system. As major long-term shareholders, they have incentives to pay the costs of obtaining substantial information. Fights for corporate control are rare, as are antitrust suits and insider-trading cases. Stocks are held for very long periods. Firms are able to invest in long-term relationships and share extensive information.

OME systems appear to do better at modernizing existing industries and improving on manufacturing systems. The quality of German and Japanese manufacturing is linked to the incentives their systems provide to invest substantially in the specific assets that correlate with excellence in these activities. Conversely, LME systems may have more flexibility in globalizing production. American firms in the hard-disk-drive industry moved early to learn the techniques of disaggregating the components of a product, scattering their production to the most advantageous site, and making final assembly again in an appropriate location

(Gourevitch, Bohn, and McKendrick 2000; McKendrick, Doner, and Haggard 2000). OME firms have had more difficulty doing this.

The disadvantage of the OME system lies in overinvestment in existing sectors and underinvestment in radically new technologies and processes. Venture-capital systems are weak. Capital is generated from within each network, but is then limited in its allocation to the interests of that network. At times this generates productivity in quality processes; at other times, when technological change is rapid, these systems pay a price for that advantage.

CORPORATE-GOVERNANCE STRUCTURES
AND NATIONAL PRODUCTION SYSTEMS

Strictly speaking, corporate governance consists of a firm's authority structure. Recent research notes that internal authority sits in a broader social framework (Gourevitch 2003; Roe 2002). Corporate-governance structures interact with other features of a nation's political economy: industrial relations (wages, labor markets), union and management-association structure, educational and worker-training systems, welfare and social-services models (Garrett 1998a; Hall and Gingerich 2001; Hall and Soskice 2001; Kitchelt et al. 1999; Stephens and Stephens 2001). For some researchers, the interactions are very powerful, so that it is hard to change one piece of the system without changing the others. Hall and Soskice, for instance, speak of them as "National Production Systems."

LME systems encourage all parties to invest in general assets, transferable to other activities (Iversen and Soskice 2001a, b). The OME models, conversely, allow actors to invest in specific assets particular to specific situations. For example, the German training system links workers to specific jobs, while labor-market regulations make it difficult to discharge workers, and the welfare system is tied to employment, discouraging workers from leaving. The British system trains workers more generally, labor markets are fluid, and the welfare system universal. Facing a common stimulus, such as an exchange-rate appreciation, firms in the two systems respond differently: British firms pass along the price increase to customers to maintain profitability—they can sustain loss of market share because they can lay off workers if necessary; German firms can sustain a decline in profit because their relationship with creditors allows for it and labor markets make lay offs difficult (Knetter 1989).

IMPACT OF THE DIFFERENCES

What impact do these differences in governance structures have on economies and societies? Kester (1992) argues that in LME countries investors move faster into new activities and abandon old ones, while in

OMEs the movement is less rapid, though investors may help modernize older sectors more thoroughly.

Iversen and Wren (1998) find strong differences among groups of countries, and these differences correlate with variance in their governance systems. They posit that governments are able to obtain only two of three goals together (employment, balanced budgets, and equality) and must therefore choose which to sacrifice. Liberal economies sacrifice equality, Social Democratic systems sacrifice budgets, and Christian Democratic systems sacrifice employment. Collapsing the categories to two, Hall and Soskice (2001) find relatively small differences between models: the OMEs have slightly lower unemployment than LMEs, lower inflation rates, and greater equality. Both have similar growth rates, which Hall and Soskice take as confirmation that different systems can be effective. Other differences include:

- *Patents*: Hall and Soskice (2001) find that firms in Germany take more patents in mechanical engineering, product handling, transport, consumer durables, and machine tools, generally in incremental innovation, while firms in the United States innovate disproportionately in fields where radical innovation is important, such as medical engineering, biotechnology, semiconductors, and telecommunications.
- *Unionization*: Trade unions have been weakened in LMEs by deregulation and business initiatives, but remain strong in CMEs, as measured by percentage of the workforce in unions (Hall and Soskice 2001; Hemerijck and Visser 2000; Lange et al. 1995; Visser, 1998).
- *Deregulation*: Deregulation has been far-reaching in the LMEs of Britain, the United States, New Zealand, Canada, and Australia, but much less extensive in the OMEs of Northern Europe and East Asia (Hall and Soskice 2001).

Does globalization threaten the survival of this kind of ecological heterogeneity, or can diversity survive? To evaluate this question, it is important to examine the mechanisms of pressure, that is, to look at the actors who cause the convergence or nonconvergence to take place and identify the incentives they have in order to make the predicted changes. The next sections of the chapter examine the mechanisms of convergence, the mechanisms of mediation of those pressures, and the mechanisms of resistance or modification of them.

GLOBALIZATION: MECHANISMS OF CONVERGENCE

In examining the mechanisms, which link globalization to corporate governance, it seems useful to begin with a focus on managers who have the formal authority to structure the firm.

Market Pressures

The economy can press firms in a variety of ways: costs of capital, levels of sales, profits, employment, and growth. Getting capital for less than its rival gives a firm, and a country, a competitive advantage. Shinn (2000, 2001) postulates that external investors prefer corporate-governance models that provide protection to all shareholders: open, transparent systems, that protect them from agency and expropriation risk—thus they prefer LME firms to OME ones. He estimates that preference (the premium on return that investors demand of OME firms to match the returns from LME ones) to be between 20–40 percent. Shinn then argues that this kind of premium is a pressure on countries to adjust their systems in the LME direction, and explores ten countries to see if regulatory changes are taking place in that direction. He finds a mixed pattern—change in some places, not in others; the reasons for the difference are explored in the next section.

Another mode of market pressure derives from falling profits, sales, and revenue that derive from technological development, manufacturing processes, marketing, labor relations, design, and sales. American auto firms have been hurt by the perception among some consumers that their defect rate was high in comparison to that of Japanese producers. Those defects gradually came to be understood by researchers as being located in a system of relationships between manufacturer and suppliers that in turn was closely connected to governance systems (Hall and Soskice 2001; Womack 1991). Conversely, OME firms have been slower to absorb new communications technologies. Thus shifts in the global economy reward some of these specific features of production and punish others—as these shifts occur, managers feel pressure on their firms to lower costs, improve design, reduce product defects, and squeeze inventory. Some of these changes may require alteration in firm structure, which may put pressure on corporate-governance models. How managers respond to these pressures will vary according to the incentive structure they face; that is how the various elements of the firms authority system are able to pressure or reward them.

POLITICIANS AND REGULATORS

Whatever they may wish to do, managers are constrained in various ways by national regulatory systems. In order to alter corporate organization, regulations would have to change. That in turn means the politicians and regulators have to feel some incentive to carry these out. What makes some politicians more or less responsive to such pressure will be considered in the next section. Here, we consider the mechanisms that cause a demand for change.

A simple lobby model would identify interest groups that think they would benefit from a change of the rules and then demand policies to produce it. Lobbies of this kind could be investors seeking greater protection of their interests as outsiders, or they could also be economically strong groups, competitive in the world economy, who seek freedom from rules they think restrict their ability to take advantage of opportunities. Lobbying against altering the regulations could be groups with high investment in specific assets based on existing rules.

A more complex interest model would connect more general problems in the economy to pressure for structural change. Unemployment, stagnant growth, poor social services, money-losing public enterprises, and/or deficits in national budgets could all provide general support for policy change (Carey and Shugart 1995; Haggard and McCubbins 2001). If voters, politicians, and administrators came to see the national production system as somehow the cause of these structural negatives, they could become responsive to efforts for system reform. Shinn (2001) suggests it is this kind of pressure—the fiscal crisis of the state and EU requirements on deficits, rather than focused shareholder-oriented interest groups—that is driving reform efforts. Businesses are being privatized, pension plans shifted to individuals, and public firms pressed to be more efficient. This has increased the level of securitization in the economy, which increases the pressure of shareholding interests on the firm. Public sector pension funds, for example, have been among the leaders in shareholder activism, and investor groups in various countries have emerged, forming a network in the "civil economy" (Davis 2002).

Whether the demands come from specific interest groups or from more generalized pressure for economic reform, the mechanism for change flows through the political system. "Citizens"—voters, employees, managers—indicate to politicians (by voting, lobbying, investing, spending) a desire for reform, specific or general; politicians, for their part, see a political opportunity to organize, or oppose, those demands.

As with managers, the connection for politicians and regulators between general incentives from the world economy and the specific issues of corporate governance are not transparent or obvious. Diffuse pressures can be interpreted in quite different ways, some of which have to do with corporate organization, some not at all. Thus the response of countries to similar pressures can vary substantially.

INTERNATIONAL INSTITUTIONS AND REGULATIONS

A third mechanism for change in corporate governance comes from international institutions, treaties, and legislation. The leading trading countries are all deeply embedded in a network of regimes that formulate general principles to which counties must conform. Corporate governance, seen as part of the sphere of domestic national economies, used to play very little role in such institutions. As economic integration has deepened, these regulations have come to be understood as key components of a unified market, and have entered the arena of inter-state relations.

The European Union has gone the farthest of any international institution in doing this. Starting in the 1960s, and accelerating after the Unified European Act of 1987, it set out to harmonize all aspects of company law (Wymeersch 2001). The range of topics included in that framework was quite broad: accounting, shareholders' rights, mergers, financial institutions, the flow of investments. The Commission of the European Communities has created committees of experts who generate reports and recommendations on each item that influences governance (insurance, securities, finance, banking), producing such important measures at the 1989 EU Solvency Ratio Law and the Second Banking Co-ordination Directive (Crane and Schaede 2001). These committees are supposed to explore areas of concordance on policies and standards (European Union Commission 2001).

In general, while in effect saying, "There is no single model of good corporate governance," EU positions call for the "equitable treatment of shareholders and the transparency and accountability of the corporate process" (Wymeersch 2001). The same report calls for a European Company Statute (ECS) as a priority of the Single Market Plan, and then notes that "it is important that any ECS model be neither unduly rigid nor inflexible" (Wymeersch 2001). The tone of commission reports on this topic is generally in the direction of neoliberal concepts of governance: transparency, flexibility, ease of flow of funds, incentives to shareholders, and so on. The core model is an LME one (Wymeersch 2001). Other international institutions have also generated processes of harmonization. The "OECD Principles of Corporate Governance" (OECD 1999a) is one example, while various international finance agencies have been developing governance guidelines as conditions for granting loans.

So one source of pressure for change comes from international institutions. These have a process of their own, interacting with, but different from, the national policy processes in each country. Countries are then led to change their rules on corporate organization because of their membership in organizations and/or their treaty commitments.

NGOs, ASSOCIATIONS, "PRIVATE AGREEMENTS"

A fourth mechanism for change lies outside the formal regulatory apparatus and in the hands of specialized associations and NGOs. Associations of specialists formulate international standards, enforceable only by agreement, in the shadow of the state, but outside it. The International Accounting Standards Board develops rules for assessing corporate balance sheets and the presentation of information. The International Organization of Securities Commissions develops criteria for stock regulations. The Bank for International Settlements sets criteria for bank inspection. This sort of regime governance is common in many issue-areas beside corporate governance: airlines and product standards (the International Organization for Standards) among others. These organizations can develop standards only if there is consensus on what they should be. That puts the mechanism back on issues of power and politics: which standards have market and political power behind them?

International agreements, formal and informal, have to be internalized by each country and enforced by them. That leaves a lot of room for slippage and the possibility of a significant gap between formalized rhetoric versus actual practice. Many countries have regulations that look quite strong but which are not enforced. What actually happens—what gets adopted and what is enforced—is shaped strongly, then, by political variables, to which we now turn more directly.

FROM PRESSURE TO POLICY:
MEDIATING GLOBALIZATION VIA MARKETS AND POLITICS

The logic of the convergence position is that globalizing market forces pressure firms into conforming on uniform best practice. If investors prefer firms with LME systems, managers of OME firms will experience higher costs of capital, which, by weakening their competitiveness, forces managers to change corporate-governance structures. This assumes a very direct causal sequence from general pressures to specific changes. It assumes the market pressures are strong, direct, and uniform, that they will be understood as caused by corporate-governance models, and that the response will be to converge to the LME model. Conversely, it is possible that the market signs are not strong against OME structures, that they are not clear in their signal, that they can be understood in different ways, and that a variety of responses can be chosen.

The market is, moreover, but one force shaping the rules, albeit an important one. Since national regulatory rules shape corporate governance, we need to see how gobalization influences the politics that shapes those rules. Pressures in politics are also open to different interpretations and a range of responses.

Mediating Market Pressures: Conflicting Market Signals

IS THERE "BEST PRACTICE"?

Central to the convergence hypothesis is the notion of a clear best practice, the way of doing things that is so efficient that, under the Darwin-

ian selection mechanism of competition, all economic actors will have
to adopt.

The literature on OME-LME comparisons challenges this. In the view
of these authors, more than one system can be efficient at the same
time. Each system may have its own efficiencies — its own characteristic
strengths along with its own characteristic weaknesses. If so, then competition will not drive all but one system out, but rather will provide
rewards to each according to its comparative advantage and may even
accentuate differentiation. Taken together, production systems are a
form of specialization — a technology of organization at the national
level. By rewarding specialization, international competition will thus
intensify the division of labor (Berger and Dore 1996; Bhagwati 1996).

The behavior of firms in globalizing production networks confirms
this logic of efficient but divergent national production systems. As
firms disaggregate production into components, they can then spread
the location of these activities around the world, according to the comparative advantage of each country (Gourevitch, Bohn, and McKendrick 2000; McKendrick, Doner, and Haggard 2000). Hall and Soskice
(2001) provide an excellent example of this: GM picks Germany for a
motor factory, despite the high costs there, because of the extremely
high quality of precision manufacturing it wants for that component. It
locates items requiring less precision in other countries with lower costs
of other kinds. Seeing the choice as alternative forms of efficiency,
which can coexist, allows us to find reasons to be cautious about the
idea of convergence — there can instead be division of labor.

DIFFERENT CUES FROM THE SAME PRESSURE

Globalization arguments assume not only "best practice" but "unifor-
mity of cues." When firms experience pressure from competition, the
convergence argument supposes that they will experience those pressures in the same way and respond to them in the same way. This is not
likely. Managers and firms operate in varied institutional contexts that
structure incentives and costs in different ways. In the costs of capital
argument, for example, various institutional arrangements can influence
the cost and the pressure managers feel to respond to it. The whole
tissue of OME cross-holding and favoritism of insiders weakens the immediate impact of any market signal when compared to what happens
in LME systems, where managers are monitored by visible external
indicators.

The market cost of capital may be an insufficient indicator of external
pressure from finance issues. In the early 1990s much was written about
the difficulties American firms had in raising capital because of the
problems in its LME system: investors were held to be oriented around

the short term, having higher trigger points for making loans or investments, demanding faster rates of return. LME systems lacked patient capital, a willingness to make investments whose payback may take some time (Porter 1992; Tyson 1992). Japanese firms have been thought to have cheaper capital than U.S. firms because the institutions of savings there favored corporate borrowers over savers. For the shareholder premium noted by Shinn to have a strong impact on managers, a range of regulations and practices would have to change.

Germany provides a case in point. "Although the large German banks are seeking a global role, they are still engaged with German industry and regional banks maintain important Hausbank relationships" (Ziegler 2000). Many German firms have embraced international accounting standards, but there are still few independent directors on their boards and "shareholder value" has been used mainly as a slogan to justify reorganizations that would have been dictated in any case. Although hostile takeovers have become more common in France, they remain rare in Germany, where regulatory regimes and cross-shareholding militate against them. The market for corporate governance is changing, but at a pace that may allow firms to retain many aspects of their longstanding strategies (Crane and Schaede 2001; Hall and Soskice 2001; Shinn 2001).

ALTERNATIVE UNDERSTANDINGS

The logic of a market-pressures approach to explaining changes in corporate governance assumes firms will understand that the problems are caused by that variable. But market pressures, while surely powerful, can be understood in quite different ways. Faced with stiff competition from Japanese manufacturers in the 1970s, for example, Ford and GM interpreted their problems quite differently. GM thought Japan's success derived from the use of reprogrammable machines, able to produce multiple items. Ford thought it had to do with supplier relationships, an organizational issue. GM spent a lot of capital on machine tools, but did little in reorganizing the structure of the firm and the supply system; Ford put its energy into organizational issues (Womack 1991).

Within the limits of their national regulatory system, managers can alter structures. Some American firms absorbed important aspects of the Japanese supplier model to create just-in-time manufacturing processes; Boeing leads an American style keiretsu. Japanese and German firms are undertaking substantial changes toward outsourcing and geographically dispersed production networks. Nonetheless, substantial variety of structure remains, even among firms in the same industry. At the same time, nationally specific rules constrain managerial choices: American firms are constrained by antitrust rules from using various OME techniques. In OME countries, firms may have little incentive to pay the costs of transition to another system and may well encounter regulatory obstacles in trying to do so. Since rules are set by national politics, the way globalization hits the firm will turn on the interaction of two processes: the way that pressure is refracted through the national political system as it shapes regulatory policy and the way managers interpret the meaning of the changes.

Mediation via Politics

Culture, history, and accidents may all have had some influence on the evolution of governance systems, but nowhere are they without an extensive tissue of regulations to protect them — everywhere they depend on the shadow of the state. We need, therefore, some political models to explain how politics preserves or undermines one or another of these governance models. Two alternative models seem most relevant: a demand-centered model, focusing on interest-group preferences and their influence on partisanship and parties; and an institutions-centered model, focusing on the mechanisms of preference aggregation. The U.S. case provides a vivid example of the way politics, interest-group pressure, and institutions together combined to produce a major change in American policy and practice, moving it from on OME-type model to its current status as the prime example of the LME one.

THE U.S. CASE: THE POWER OF POLITICS

In several ways the United States of 1890 resembled the current German model more than the LME system toward which it has moved. At least in 1890 it looked far more like the Germany of 1890 than either does one hundred years later. How did this divergence take place?

In the late nineteenth-century United States, large banks and insurance companies owned large blocs of shares in specific companies and played a supervisory role in their management. The industrial economy was in many areas structured around trusts, which dominated their sector, regulating competition. The United States thus had a governance model at the corporate level that resembled the OMEs of the time, that is, Continental European patterns, not British ones. While the banking system was decentralized geographically, it did have concentrated share-ownership in individuals or financial institutions.

Then American politics got to work: The Sherman Anti-Trust Act (1890) set the framework for a commitment to competition, sustained by the Supreme Court's 1906 decision against Standard Oil. Regulatory structures were legislated to protect consumers from railroad price-gouging and harmful food and drugs. In the years before World War I,

insurance companies, then the largest shareholders of stocks, were prohibited from buying shares (Roe 1994). Between the wars, Congress
passed several major bills: the McCarren Act, which sharply limited
inter-state banking; the Glass Steagal Act forced the separation between
commercial and investment banks; the Securities and Exchange Commission was authorized to apply strict rules to protect external shareholders from stock manipulation and insider trading; the Wagner Act
recognized union rights in collective bargaining; the Social Security laws
obligated employers to contribute to a national retirement system
(Gourevitch 1996). This series of legislative acts, among others, and
their enforcement gradually pushed the United States toward the LME
model.

The American experience shows the importance of politics in shaping
the regulations, which shape managerial incentives. Of course, laws and
regulations interact with other forces: technology, the marketplace, international agreements, and the behavior of other governments. These
forces interact with domestic politics to change or preserve the rules
that shape governance structures, and it is to this that we now turn.

POLITICAL INSTITUTIONS AND THE CHOICE OF SYSTEMS

Why has the American system developed so differently from those of
Europe and Japan? Why do the United States, United Kingdom, and
British Commonwealth models differ from the German-Japanese one?
One important line of research calls attention to political institutions as
a way of explaining public-policy divergence in general, regulatory politics in particular. For any set of preferences, the outcome of a process
can be strongly influenced by its structure (Cowhey and McCubbins
1995; Haggard and McCubbins 2001). Noll and Rosenbluth (1995),
for example, explain differences between Japanese and American regulations on telecommunications as a function of different institutions.
Similarly, Hall and Soskice (2001) suggest that OME systems rest on the
ability of a government to make a credible commitment to maintain the
regulatory system, which the dense investment in specific assets of the
OME system requires. If a government cannot credibly commit to preserving these specific assets, economic actors will shift toward the LME
system because it gives them the flexibility to deal with shifting economic conditions. OME systems can exist where the "relevant producer
groups have enough structural influence to punish the government for
any deviations from such agreements" (Hall and Soskice 2001).

What political system will do that? Political systems that protect producer groups through coalition governments, multiple veto-points, and
group-dominated parties (Hall and Soskice 2001). Conversely governments that concentrate power inhibit credible commitment to producer

groups because such governments can produce substantial swings in policy.

There is some evidence to support these ideas. In a comparison of political systems of the countries Hall and Soskice examine, Gourevitch and Hawes (2002) show that types of national production systems do correlate with the type of electoral system, party cohesion, and the number of political parties (Beck et al. 1999; Lijphart 1999). Institutions that drive countries toward two-party systems and distort the relationship between vote percentage and total seats in the legislature predicate that a shift of a relatively small number of voters can produce a large shift in the party in power and in the size of its majority. Thus small shifts of voters can produce a large swing in policy orientation by changing majorities or size of majority bloc. So the electoral-system variable supports the argument. Political cohesion and number of effective political parties produce similar effects.

The effects of institutions depend on care in specifying the key relationships. The number of veto players and political-regime type (Presidential vs. parliamentary) do not show a pattern with respect to OME-LME corporate governance. The key explanatory relationship is consensus versus majoritarian regimes. Majoritarian institutions allow a single party to dominate the legislature (the United Kingdom) or divided government (the United States). These systems have low credibility to commit to the policy constancy OMEs desire. Consensus systems by contrast have multiparty coalitions, which provide policy protection to all groups (Gourevitch and Hawes 2002). The LME countries (United States, United Kingdom, Canada, Australia) have majoritarian systems; the OME countries (Germany, Scandinavia, Austria) have consensus regimes.

In sum, political institutions do seem to favor one regulatory outcome over another. These structures refract the impact of globalization on corporate governance. A common pressure, from the world economy, will be processed differently in each country as a function of its political institutions.

POLITICS AND INTEREST-GROUP PREFERENCES

An alternative way of explaining policy choices looks at the preferences of the population, at those who make demands on governments and on whom governments rely for support. Institutionalist analyses hold preferences constant and vary institutions to examine the consequences. The contrasting tradition begins with interests and preferences. It assumes that these vary with economic conditions, geography, history, resources, and culture. Institutions themselves express actor preferences. Lobbies are often able to find ways through most political systems to apply pressure on governments (Frieden 1999; Gourevitch 1999; Rogowski 1999). There are two major versions of this argument: the first calls attention to differences in the economies of countries that influence the preferences of actors, which in turn influence policy choices. The second measures the balance of partisan political forces: Left versus Right.

A classic version of the first argument is Gerschenkron's (1962) late development model. Britain, as the first industrializer, was able to develop a highly decentralized economy without strong coordinating institutions. Germany and Japan industrialized under quite different conditions: a strong advanced rival, the United Kingdom, and high capital costs in steel and railroads, rewarded centralization. This has a first-cut plausibility to it: the middle and later industrializers are more likely to fall in the OME category than the early ones, including the United Kingdom. Yet, there was only one first industrializer, and several of the later ones did become LMEs.

One way to read the U.S. shift to an LME system lies in some distinctive features of the American economy. The United States was from the beginning very heterogeneous: large farmers and small, dispersed geographically, in quite different climates with varied crops; manufacturers of all kinds, large and small, again widely dispersed; workers of many kinds, employed in a range of industries. Under these conditions, it is not surprising the United States failed to develop highly centralized structures.

It is interesting to note that Gerschenkron says very little about the politics of how the choice was actually made to move down a particular development path; his analysis is a correlation explained by a functionalist logic — the late industrializers made use of institutions to solve problems (1962). He does not examine what produced the politics in Germany and Russia that led to this choice. By inference, we can construct the argument to suggest an interest-institutions interaction: Early industrialization spawned interest groups in the United Kingdom that wanted LME, while in Germany the logic of late industrialization did the reverse. In the United Kingdom, interest-group preferences found a resonance with the liberal institutions already in existence, which gave them voice. In Germany, state leaders made decisions, which the institutions allowed them to do, that favored the late-industrializing interests.

LEFT VERSUS RIGHT

Another version of an interests approach looks at partisan conflict, in particular the balance of Left versus Right as mediated by political parties. As Left and Right have conflicting positions on key items of political economy, the mix of policies in a particular country expresses the relative balance of political forces. Thus Scandinavian political economy reflects the strength of Social Democracy parties and their union allies there, and conversely, the neoliberalism of U.S. policies expresses the corresponding weakness of Social Democracy in that country (Roe 2000). Substantial research of this kind has been done on a wide range of dependent variables, with Hibbs (1977) in the 1970s, to Garrett and Lange (1995) and others in the 1990s.

Roe has recently (2002) applied this approach directly to the issues of corporate-governance. Since corporate governance forms do correlate highly with other features of the economy (national production models), it can, by extension, be linked with them. There is indeed a rough correlation: the Social Democratic and the Christian Democratic versions of OMEs reflect the strength of those political forces in each country, and the "historical compromise" between Left and Right after the bitter experiences of the 1930s—the reaction against fascism, the fear of communism, and the commitment to democracy.

An important critique of this line of reasoning comes from analysts who challenge the adequacy of a Left-Right model of cleavages. At times labor and business interests can converge, so that policy alliances cut across class lines (Frieden 1991a; Rogowski 1989). When factor specificity is high, as in a Ricardo-Viner model, the different factors in an industry have a common interest in protecting it; when factor mobility is high, class conflict prevails. Hiscox (1999, 2001) argues both conditions are theoretically possible, and vary in place and time.

The Hall and Soskice national production–system approach extends this reasoning to a wide range of elements of the economy. Swenson (1991), Thelen (2001), Estevez-Abe (1999), Mares (2000, 2002), and others have shown in detail how these cross-class alliances work in a number of issue-areas, from the welfare state to training to labor-market regulation, and so forth. Governance systems have again not been one of the dependent variables explicitly examined, with the exception of the German *mitbestimmung* arrangement, but by extension they can be: labor and capital in the OME systems share an interest in the status-quo governance model that shields all players from the uncertainties of a strong competitive, neoliberal market (Streeck 1997). In LMEs, labor would probably like structures that give it more voice and limited the neoliberalism of the system, so there one would expect conflict. But little research has been done on labor views of corporate-governance issues directly.

The national production–systems approach generally questions the traditional assumptions about cleavages along political-economy lines within each country and the implications of international competition for political cleavages insofar as it argues the existence of a different set of preferences. It can be seen as a highly extended specific-actors approach. For governance, it predicts the defense of OME models will be substantial. As such, it conflicts somewhat with research that shows a divergence of interests within OME systems: some sectors seek to weaken the system because it constrains them from taking advantage of new opportunities in liberalizing world markets (Esping-Anderson 1999; Pontusson 2000).

Internationalization of Governance Disputes and Domestic Politics

The previous section examined the way domestic politics mediates the influences of economic globalization upon economic behavior in general and corporate governance in particular. Similar processes of mediation by domestic political processes are also at work in dealing with the pressures that come from international agreements. Governance forms have become objects of trade conflict and have entered the arena of international negotiations. Countries now discuss governance-related issues bilaterally (U.S.-Japanese disputes over the functioning of Japanese keiretsu in trade-related areas such as parts purchasing and supplier networks) or multilaterally, as with the European Union, where efforts are underway at harmonization of the rules on corporate governance. So one source of pressure for change comes from international obligations: countries are led to change their rules on corporate organization because of their membership in organizations or treaty arrangements. This produces a complex interactive pattern between domestic and international processes. Nations participate in shaping international agreements that in turn pressure them to comply. Nations, to paraphrase Rousseau, are "forcing themselves to be free," that is, they impose obligations on themselves. Are these institutions able to shape what countries do independent of what these countries may prefer out of their own domestic politics? What shapes national positions in negotiations? How does the process influence the outcome? How are agreements enforced?

These questions show that aspects of corporate governance lead directly to issues of global governance. If harmonization is purely voluntary, no international structure of governance is necessary. If rules require mechanisms of enforcement, then a structure is needed to determine standards, monitor compliance, and direct punishment. The EU provides an interesting test case of these issues on the most institutionalized end of a continuum of international structures.

It appears that at the EU level, representatives of each nation support more neoliberal policies on corporate governance than the government of each country could get adopted by its own legislature if proposed directly. Did those who agreed to have the community deal with governance issues understand that the agents of the countries would form neoliberal agreements? Or is this an example of democratic deficit (Scharpf 1999), where the agents of countries are doing things that would not be democratically supported if openly discussed?

Countries belong to international institutions voluntarily. They are not compelled to join, to stay, or to comply. Thus, it could be argued that the agreements are an extension of the wishes of each independent sovereign. This is the model of the EU advanced by Moravscik (1998), wherein the EU expresses intergovernmental bargains made by the agents of national governments. Countries are influenced by external pressures insofar as the desire to adhere to the treaty imposes the need to accept whatever compromises were allowed to have it come about or keep it. In this way, countries may come to accept terms of regulation, which they would not independently have generated internally. It must still be the case that there exists a support coalition in each country for adherence to the larger treaty, despite the cost — what Kahler calls compliance constituencies (2001).

Other views of the EU give even more importance to the impact of the institution and its processes on members. It is argued that various constituent parts of the EU have grown in power: the European Court of Justice, for example, has through its decisions been able to build a set of common obligations upon members to which they must conform. The EU executive and legislature may also have gained in power. As a result, engagement in the EU leads members to accept obligations they may never have generated at home via internal political factors alone.

The issues of harmonization at the European level are reproduced at the global level, with much weaker institutions to manage the problems (Gourevitch 1999). The EU has committed itself to a single market and harmonization and designed procedures to which the members are committed, even if there can be disputes about them. Nothing like this exists at the world level. The OECD discusses these issues but cannot enforce commitments to them. NAFTA does not include corporate governance, nor do the other regional-trade arrangements. The WTO has not integrated corporate governance into its treaties. Will this happen? That is, can global-governance institutions be structured that can handle corporate-governance issues?

No institution has gone as far the EU in this regard, but the example still holds as a way of grasping another mechanism for change: international-treaty commitments and international organizations. After the East Asian financial crisis, the IMF became quite interested in regulations on banks, securities, and financial markets. As in the European case, however, international institutions have not been able to get the authority to handle corporate-governance regulations unless states want them to do so. That, in turn, will depend on state preferences. Harmonization implies convergence on a standard, but that raises the issue of whose standard. Countries are likely to prefer an agreement that most closely resembles what they already have internally. Shifting to a different governance model will create costs, so interest groups and politicians will prefer to project the national model onto the world. The Anglo-Americans like principles that are clear, uniform, external. The Japanese prefer a networked pattern and thus are skeptical about the need for rules. The Americans will thus be the leaders for standards and convergence provided they are LME. The Japanese will resist such rules, as will other OME countries.

What shapes the preferences of developing countries? These may tend toward the system of their major trading allies. Many East Asian countries follow a Japanese model of corporate governance, though this could also be read as arising out of similar preceding structures in the economy. The economic leaders certainly encourage countries to adopt their respective structures and policies. That could itself be a component of trade conflict — the attempt at getting your trading partners to resemble you.

Conclusion: Globalization, the Convergence Debate, and Corporate Governance

Corporate governance is a critical arena in which to watch the interaction of domestic politics, the private sector, and global governance. Among market economies, substantial divergence exists in the ways of structuring firms, as well as in the relationships of managers to various stakeholders, such as shareowners, banks, employees, and suppliers. Can these persist? The argument of this chapter has been that global market forces are mediated by market institutions and by political processes, so that the direction of their influence can vary by country. Market signals provide different incentives in contrasting contexts; one firm may find reason to increase its concentration in an expensive production area, while another may outsource. At the same time, the force of the market is mediated by politics and political systems, which aggregate these diverse incentives and preferences into policy outputs. The combination of economic situation, national institutions, and politics produces national production systems, complex patterns of corporate governance, linked to macro and micro policies affecting welfare, education, labor relations, and taxes. These national production systems are likely to continue to find ways of diverging. As a result, we need to rethink our vocabulary in discussing globalization — convergence-divergence is an inadequate distinction by which to measure change. Three

alternatives are suggested here: first, the shifting "terms of trade" between alternative production systems; second, divergent modernization,
patterns of change that are nonetheless not identical; and third, the
evolving international institutions for managing corporate governance.

Comparative Advantage and the "Terms of Trade" between Alternative National Production Systems

Instead of convergence, it might be more useful to think about shifting
"terms of trade" between alternative national-production systems. Each
system may have a comparative advantage in some process or mode of
economic activity. These can coexist, indeed even deepen, through specialization. Likewise, they can do better or worse in relation to each
other. If they can have a comparative advantage, we can speak of "shifting terms of trade" between systems.

National production systems are socially constructed factors of production. The pioneers of trade theory examined natural endowments to
demonstrate the law of comparative advantage. Later theorists saw that
societal variables could influence their factor endowments: education,
infrastructure, savings rates, macro and micro policy. The concept of
national production systems can be seen as another step in this process
of expanding our notion of societal construction of factor endowments.
It now includes the tissue of institutions, the web of interconnections,
that influence the specificity, mobility, and relative productivity of the
factors of production. The national production system can be seen as a
process innovation—analogous, though on a larger scale, to the assembly line or just-in-time systems, which improve efficiency by the organization of the parts of the system.

With this idea in mind, we can speak of the terms of trade between
different production systems. That is, if OME and LME are highly aggregate composites of the socially constructed elements of factors, then
we can speak of the exchange of products or product components between them in the same way we discuss coffee traded for autos. OMEs
specialize in those products, or components of products, that benefit
from the high investment in specific assets (i.e., auto engines). LMEs
specialize in those products that benefit from general unspecific assets—
new computerized applications, for example.

We can then suppose that the terms of trade between these families of
products—hence between the national production systems—will shift
back and forth as they do with coffee and autos. In some periods, comparative advantage may lie with rapid innovation and the absorption of
new technologies: thus the fluidity of the LME systems. At other times,
it may favor precision manufacturing and systematic improvement of

known technologies: thus the OME systems. The balance may shift back and forth over time.

This may well describe what has happened in recent decades. With new technologies after World War II, the United States did well (though this period is also obscured by the war-time damage to Germany and Japan). Then, at about the time that Germany and Japan recovered, technological change slowed down. The advantage shifted to precision manufacturing, moving down the cost of stable technologies. This favored the OME systems. In the 1980s and 1990s, many observers of comparative capitalism wrote about American weaknesses. Michael Porter's "America's Failing Finance System" (1992) is but one example.

Then the economy shifted ground. Technological change picked up, new processes and products emerged. Rapid change now tilted advantage back to the fluid systems (LME). The United States sloughed off to Japan and Germany, or to developing countries, the production of standardized manufacturing products, seeing that the rate of return to these sorts of products was stagnating compared to new products and processes. The money in computers was not in making the desktop machines; those rapidly went the way of shoes and clothing. High value-added lay in design, research, software, applications, marketing, and in managing global production networks. With the East Asian financial crisis of 1997, the Japanese-Asian model got relabeled "crony capitalism." Now writing in the United States speaks triumphally about the Washington Consensus, while German and Japanese writers question their systems.

Is this pattern fixed forever? Will the United States retain its dominance? Other countries could converge on the U.S. model, adopting and adapting its technology and methods. Conversely, countries could retain their own models, but the advantage could shift again, from the LME, and rapid change toward the OME, and stable development.

If there are, then, these shifting terms of trade, then changes are mistakenly attributed to convergence when they should be seen more accurately as shifting terms of trade—where from advantage can shift back. Rather than think of sequences in economic development, in the Gerschenkronian logic, we may think instead of "alternatives" in patterns of economic activity (Gourevitch 2001).

Divergent Modernization

The forces of globalization will certainly cause change in corporate governance. The logic of the market forces a constant process of destruction and innovation—as Schumpeter ([1942] 1962) argued a century ago. So we should not expect things to stay the same.

The business press reports many stories of change, especially in Japan and Germany, the core adherents to the OME model and the main rivals to the U.S. LME system. (Dvořák et al. 2001). How are these to be interpreted? Are they harbingers of basic transformations leading to convergence, or to modernizations of each system, which continue to have striking differences?

We should not confuse change with convergence (Berger and Dore 1996; Shinn 2001). Systems may change, but each may evolve into something different. The arguments about convergence require some specification in advance of deciding which change would amount to convergence, and which would not. If communist and capitalist economies both produced high levels of education, health services, and the like, does that mean they have converged? Countries can change without converging. Convergence literature needs to specify more clearly ahead of time what kinds of change constitute a test of convergence theory and which not.

Corporate governance is a good place to start a measurement process: if the OME countries adopt LME rules on shareholding, mergers, concentration of shares, reporting, and accounting, then the the systems will have converged. If the LME countries create rules that allow LME firms to develop OME governance forms (for example, concentrated shareownership, investment-bank involvement in firm management, and active use of proxies by pension and investment funds), that will also indicate convergence. If countries deregulate labor markets, or all have universal health plans, but allow different rules pertaining to shareholder powers and manager responsibility, they remain quite different. And, alternatively, if corporate-governance models converge, but policies concerning welfare, the labor market, and training systems remain different, these will be shown to be far more independent than some theorists are currently arguing. A key indicator on the governance side is the concentration of shareholders and existence of blocks that play a substantial role in management. We will need to track these developments systematically to understand just how autonomous or integrated these components of a production system are.

Interactive Change Processes

To understand the rate and direction of change in corporate-governance patterns, we need models of change that provide for the interaction of causes and structures. We can see contradictory processes at work. Existing structures have ways of perpetuating themselves. Once patterns of corporate governance are formed, groups acquire interest in their preservation (Kitschelt 1991). The costs of change are substantial. Reformers have to see a gain great enough to pay the costs of political action in order to desire to change the rules. The institutions of the political system may strengthen the status quo by institutionalizing the power of existing groups. An equilibrium of different elements develops — interests, ideas, institutions — that reinforces all of them: the various elements of the German system that protect asset-specific investment may indeed "need" each other (Gourevitch 2001; Hall and Soskice, 2001). This may provide a better explanation than culture and/or legal tradition of the observation that the LMEs tend to be part of the British cultural sphere: it is not just that the common law produces this economic form, but the structures spawned by British control of its former colonies created a network of interests that perpetuated that system (Rajan and Zingales 2001).

If one element is dismantled, does this destabilize the equilibrium? Or can politics preserve these differences, isolating areas of change from one another, so that change in one area does not drive changes in others. That equilibrium can be disrupted by a number of forces. A crisis — war, depression — can "puncture" the balance. A shift in political institutions — a new constitution, changing electoral laws, new political parties — may alter the power matrix. Technological change and economic competition alter the profitability of different approaches. Geopolitical changes may alter the flow of money, goods, and strategic interests. For Japan and Germany, defeat in war changed the role of labor, weakened authoritarian elites, and altered the political structure. Despite these changes, neither country shifted radically its system of corporate governance. Mitbestimmung in Germany and lifetime employment in Japan were interesting developments, important for democracy and the rights of labor, but they were integrated into a coordinated mode of governance, rather than transformative of it. In Japan, U.S. occupiers sought to break up the *zaibatsu*, but many of the regulations demanded by the United States were either revoked or rendered meaningless by nonenforcement. The keiretsu soon recreated many of the same linkages in some modified form to continue the Japanese version of an OME model.

The processes of change and persistence suggest that while global market forces may be uniform, creating a kind of pressure to which all are subjected, they are experienced in varying ways and produce different results. Market pressures are experienced differently, mediated through politics within countries and mediated by international organizations.

Global-Governance Institutions for Corporate Governance

Convergence on corporate governance cannot happen without rather full harmonization of rules and a mechanism for their enforcement. This will require an international-governance structure for corporate governance. What sorts of institutions would be required to promote and defend rules of corporate governance? Would the mechanism be police patrols or fire alarms (McCubbins 1985)? Here the content of the issue of corporate governance interacts with the global governance issue directly (Kahler and Lake, chapter 1). Corporate governance enters a realm of detail in which international institutions so far have not been very deeply engaged.

Many elements of corporate governance are so complex that it is hard to imagine a global bureaucracy able to enforce rules. Decentralized mechanisms are likely — for example, in arenas of accounting. Even private or self-enforcing systems often rely upon some "shadow of the state" as a court of last resort. But this is an area where political institutions themselves will have trouble enforcing harmonization without substantial backing among the very groups that are to be regulated (Levy 1999). After the East Asian financial crisis, we have seen calls for "better regulation" of financial institutions in developing countries. These calls do not specify what politics will actually produce enforcement of regulations, however intelligently crafted.

Some work is likely to take place through the various professions and standard-setting institutions. They will try to develop technical versions of shareholder rules, accounting, capital requirements, and the like. Judges and administrative courts may try to do the same. These will pretend to be apolitical, but can only be enforced if there is political backing to do so. It is possible that standard-setting is itself more neoliberal and pro-LME in impact: OME systems prefer particularistic, localized relationships, general principles applied to specific situations. Codifying and systemizing turns cases into codes, an approach that LME economic actors prefer.

In the end, privatized voluntaristic mechanisms will have their limits. The trade regime moved from the loose arrangements of GATT to the stronger ones of the WTO because the desire for expanded trade brought with it a need for stronger modes of monitoring and enforcing trade agreements. Corporate governance, similarly, will require some formalized regulatory oversight. The existing trade system may become the prototype, or the instrument whose competencies are expanded — in much the same way that the European Coal and Steel Community became the framework for the Treaty of Rome, with all of the attendant problems of democratic deficit.

Thus the evolution of corporate governance involves the interaction of three sorts of "politics." First, there is the politics of the corporation, its internal struggles to make sense out of the changing market environment — the conflicts among different constituencies of the "firm." Second, there is the politics of the nation, as it responds to these changes in shaping the regulatory structure of corporate governance. And third, there is the politics of international institutions, shaping the global or regional regime for corporate governance. In this way, the issue-area of corporate governance becomes a variable in the story of global governance.

Chapter 13

GLOBALIZATION, INSTITUTIONS, AND CONVERGENCE

Fiscal Adjustment in Europe

Kathleen R. McNamara

Globalization, according to some, is forcing states to converge across a range of policy areas.[1] The increasing integration of markets across the globe allows firms and investors to take their business anywhere they like, unimpeded by restrictions on the flow of goods, services, and capital. Logically, this exit option means that governments will, in a globalized world, be required to either offer market-pleasing, business-friendly policies or sacrifice growth and employment to states more congenial to the needs of capital. Such policies are presumed to be those that call for very limited government intervention, regulation, and taxation, resulting in a convergence of policies across national settings.

The logic of this globalization thesis is compelling. It seems intuitive that if firms and investors are "footloose," surely the threat of exit, even if not exercised, will exert a powerful force on policy choice, producing convergence (Andrews 1994; Cerny 1990; Kurzer 1993; McKenzie and Lee 1991; Strange 1996). The convergence argument is not airtight by any means, however. Both its general logic and empirical validity have come under question (Drezner 2001; Kahler 1998; Gourevitch, chapter 12 in the present volume) as has its theoretical basis in Tiebout models of factor mobility (Rogowski, chapter 10). Early empirical work has demonstrated continuing heterogeneity in a range of policy areas (Berger and Dore 1996; Hall and Soskice 2001; cf. Simmons and Elkins, chapter 11). Nonetheless, the convergence argument is omnipresent in political debates and newspaper stories, viewed with approbation in corporate

[1] An earlier version of this chapter was presented at the American Political Science Association Annual Meeting, September 2000, Washington, D.C. I thank Miles Kahler, David Lake, Steve Krasner, James Caporaso, the Globalization and Governance project participants, as well as Orfeo Fioretos, Mark Hallerberg, and Mark Pollack for their help with this project. The Institute on Global Conflict and Cooperation, Princeton University's Woodrow Wilson School, and the Russell Sage Foundation Visiting Scholar's Program all provided financial support for this research.

boardrooms and the financial press, while demonized at antiglobalization rallies as a "race to the bottom."

To investigate the validity of these different claims about the causal effects of market integration, I evaluate fiscal policy convergence in the European Union (EU). Policy adjustments taken in the context of increasing levels of capital mobility under the EU's Economic and Monetary Union (EMU) project provide a unique natural experiment for assessing the convergence argument. I examine how national-level policies regarding taxing, spending, and borrowing changed in the run-up to EMU as a way of shedding light on the bigger question of how much room for maneuver governments actually have under conditions of constraint, be it the rule-based constraint of EMU or the market-based constraint of the global economy. What policy choices can, and will, governments make in an era of globalization?

My findings in this case are twofold. First, convergence did indeed occur in Europe, as monetary policies converged prior to the start of EMU, and, on the fiscal side, as the majority of states met the 3-percent EMU budget-deficit target. Yet this overall convergence in budget-deficit levels has produced neither a race to the bottom nor a convergence in the composition of fiscal policy. My results depict a range of divergent policy adjustments, including tax increases, tax cuts, and tax reforms, as well as both spending cuts and spending increases in a variety of areas. Pension reform is the area where the most long-term adjustment has been made, but even reforms there have been more modest than dramatic, and the level of social spending has remained quite stable in the EU. In short, policy heterogeneity persists despite the constraint of EU-level budget rules.

My second conclusion is equally important. In the EMU story, convergence around the 3-percent deficit figure resulted from political choices and formal institutional rules, rather than being the product of markets penalizing profligate states. Indeed, financial markets played a serendipitous role in *facilitating* adjustment to those politically determined rules. Specifically, in most EU countries, interest rates on government debt fell early in the process, *before* significant policy adjustments were made, thus facilitating the reduction of national deficits. Apparently, perceived national commitment to the entry rules of EMU carried enough weight with capital markets to reduce the costs of borrowing, allowing states the room to meet the criteria.

In sum, this chapter argues that the EU and its Maastricht treaty, not global capital markets, were the definitive site of authority and governance in the area of fiscal policy, promoting convergence along some dimensions while leaving ample room for policy diversity, as well. This conclusion serves to remind us that market integration, and globalization more broadly, does not occur in a vacuum. Rather, markets are inextricably shaped by politics, and globalization has the potential to produce shifting levels of governance and a demand for authoritative institutions rather than a race to the bottom.

The argument is developed in four sections. The first section of the paper discusses the parallels and differences between market integration in the EU and globalization. I argue that if globalization is defined as high levels of market integration across national borders, the EU is an example of states under the conditions of globalization and is thus a particularly important case for examining the interaction between market integration and policy convergence. I then outline in more detail how economic and political factors have interacted historically in the case of EMU. The next section focuses on fiscal policy and globalization and outlines the conventional wisdom on policy convergence. The following section presents my empirical materials. I provide a summary description and interpretation of the policy adjustments taken prior to EMU, focusing on three "laggard" states that were perceived as being least likely to meet the convergence criteria: Belgium, Italy, and Portugal. I also provide some comparative evidence from the French case. In the concluding section, I argue that the evidence on fiscal convergence presents a more mixed and contingent picture than portrayed in the majority of globalization debates, and call for further research on the role of international institutions as a key intervening source of governance in a globalized world.

Globalization and European Integration

Why should the taxing, borrowing, and spending choices of EU states in the run up to EMU tell us anything about the effects of globalization? How comparable are the conditions governing the situation under Maastricht to globalization dynamics more broadly? I argue that the European experience is an instance of deep cross-national economic integration, albeit one that occurs in a regional setting, and thus may provide a sort of laboratory for examining the dynamics of globalization. The fact that the EU is also a highly institutionalized setting with well developed supranational governance structures is analytically separate from the fact of market integration, although the two facts are likely to be causally related, as will be discussed below.

In this volume's introduction, globalization is defined as "economic integration at the global level" created by the reduction of cross-national barriers to economic exchange and factor mobility (Kahler and Lake, chapter 1). High levels of trade and capital flows between states signify substantial market integration and openness to international economic forces—globalization, as we understand it. The question that concerns us in the present volume is how increased market integration across different states may change levels and forms of governance. These phenomena are not necessarily dependent on the number or geographic spread of countries involved: African states, for example, are largely shut out of today's international market exchange, yet we still view the world as globalized.

The EU states are very clearly some of the most open in the world and their national economies are heavily dependent on economic exchange with other states in the region as trade and investment flows within the single European market continue to grow at a rapid rate. Intra-European trade is extremely high: in 1997, intra-EU trade in industrial products was valued at 31.5 percent of GDP as an average across the EU, rising from 26.5 percent in 1993 (European Commission 2000, 5). For the smaller states, such as Belgium, that figure is astoundingly high, almost 94 percent of GDP. Although the majority of trade occurs within the EU, the EU's trade linkages with the rest of the world are also significant and rising: the EU's import-GDP ratio for trade with external partners has risen from below 10 percent in 1988 to above 12 percent in 1999 (European Commission 2001).

More potentially consequential for policy convergence is the increase in capital mobility in the EU. Financial integration, in the sense of the removal of barriers to capital mobility and the liberalization of financial services, has proceeded apace in Europe over the past decade. Capital controls became the target of the European Commission's efforts in the 1980s as it tightened prohibitions against their use in 1984 and then proposed a timetable in 1986 for their complete eradication. The member states adopted into law the proposals for financial-market liberalization in 1988 and the majority of states had fully lifted their controls by mid-1990, with a few states (Greece, Portugal, Ireland, and Spain) allowed several extra years to comply (Gros and Thygesen 1998, 92). Today, formal capital controls do not exist within the EU, and informal barriers are subject to legal challenges under EU law.

Market integration is the basic permissive condition for the operation of the policy convergence thesis with which this chapter began: the easier it is to move factors of production across borders, the more readily businesses can credibly threaten to exit if government policies do not suit them. The level of market integration across the EU is unique, outstripping any other regional or bilateral cross-border exchanges in the world. Looking solely at the key variable of market integration, then, the EU appears to be a case that should give us leverage over broader questions of globalization and policy convergence.

Two other dimensions of the EU, however, are critical factors to consider when assessing the impact of market integration: the density of governance structures at the supranational level, and the degree of social safety-net programming that exists in tandem with integration. These institutional developments clearly have a reciprocal relationship with market integration. Political decisions established the setting for the single European market in the early postwar years of the European Coal and Steel Community. In turn, economic flows and the political coalitions they create provided further impetus for political action promoting integration (Sandholtz and Stone Sweet 1998). These dynamics have also caused political actors to build institutions to stabilize and maintain those markets and provide social safety-nets for the citizens who participate in them (Fligstein, Sandholtz, and Stone Sweet 2001).

The EU has a well-developed set of supranational institutions governing over a wide range of issues, not only those regarding market integration, but those in realms such as foreign policy, the environment, and human rights. An executive (the European Council), a bureaucracy (the European Commission), a representative body with some capacity to legislate (the European Parliament), and a judiciary (the European Court of Justice) govern over the EU. Market integration has occurred through a political process channeled through these institutions.

The second unique quality of the EU, in terms of broader questions about globalization, is the level of redistributive social insurance within the European states and the level of regulation at the European level (Garrett 1998a). Again, this may be both a cause and consequence of economic openness: these "embedded liberalism" measures may be necessary to maintain political support for market integration (Cameron 1978; Katzenstein 1985; Ruggie 1982). Democratic societies need to provide socioeconomic cushioning against market vicissitudes and the risks associated with increased economic competition, and thus will provide for regulatory and/or redistributional protections.

The EU therefore can be taken as one example of a highly globalized setting that has amply demonstrated the tendency of market integration to occur in tandem with political and institutional developments. The difference between the EU and the international-market setting is one of degree; both economic integration and political action have proceeded much further in the EU than in the world as a whole.[2] The EU therefore is indeed an appropriate case study for those interested in the effects of

---

[2] Verdier and Breen (2001) offer a valuable alternative assessment of the relationship between globalization and European integration. Their account fundamentally differs from mine, however, because it equates globalization with deregulation or the absence of institutions, whereas I separate out market integration and institutionalization as distinct analytical and empirical variables.

globalization, keeping in mind the particularities of the EU's political setting. The level of market integration in the EU should create a logic of constraint and convergence as hypothesized in the globalization thesis. In fact, the EU case, as it is an extreme example of the economic conditions purported to force convergence, is a "most likely case" for convergence. The fact that political leaders in Europe have created a host of unique supranational institutions to manage interdependence does not make the EU case sui generis, but rather makes it a powerful example of how political institutions may interact with globalization dynamics to produce outcomes of both market integration and political action.

Markets and Institutions in EMU

The movement towards Economic and Monetary Union is a particularly significant demonstration of the recursive qualities of globalization and governance. EMU is both product and cause of capital mobility and market integration in the EU, and provides an opportunity to unwind the effects of globalization on policy choice and the mixture of political and economic factors shaping the level and form of emerging governance structures. In this section, I briefly outline the causes and consequences of EMU and summarize the stages of European monetary integration and their relationship to increasing financial-market integration.

Monetary union and a single currency for Europe has long been a dream of certain political leaders, as much for geopolitical reasons as for its economic benefits (Sandholtz 1993). A single money for the EU, it was hoped, would irrevocably tie together European states with a mutual interest in peace and cooperation. In addition, a critical necessary condition for the movement towards EMU was the significant convergence in monetary policies across the EU beginning in the mid-1970s and solidifying in the 1980s (McNamara 1998a). The costs of moving to a single currency are substantial, however, particularly as the EU does not constitute an "optimal currency area" (Eichengreen 1992). Yet increasing capital mobility within Europe played a role in pushing states toward EMU by raising the costs of exchange-rate stabilization. The removal of capital controls and deepening financial-market integration in the mid– to late 1980s, the signing of the Maastricht treaty in 1992, and the exchange-rate crises of 1992–1993 all contributed to the Euro's eventual introduction, as described below.

The removal of capital controls across Europe in the 1980s was the first key turning point influencing the path to EMU. The difficulties of maintaining the EU's fixed exchange-rate system (the European Monetary System) as capital mobility increased after the Single-Market program began in the 1980s made consolidation into a single currency attractive, as EU policymakers noted in an influential 1987 report (Padoa-Schioppa 1987, chapter 12). With capital mobility, member states found it difficult to defend their exchange-rate parities. National monetary policies had to be geared exclusively toward upholding these parities, rather than directed at internal domestic concerns. Macro-economic coordination and intensified multilateral exchange rate–inter-vention procedures adopted in the late 1980s helped somewhat, but the only solution, in the eyes of some central bankers and finance ministers, was to move to a single currency (McNamara 1998a, 169–70).

The Treaty on European Union, agreed to in Maastricht in December 1991, set out a timetable for the move to a single currency and EMU, requirements for participation in EMU, and a design for a European Central Bank to govern the new EU money (Commission of the European Communities 1992). Exchange-rate values were sorely tested on the heels of Maastricht in the summers of 1992 and 1993. Exchange-rate crises cast doubt on the viability of EMU in some eyes, while causing others to advocate moving directly to a single currency to avoid a long destabilizing period of financial flows and uncertainty over who would participate, which would offer currency traders wide latitude for speculation.[3] While this did not occur, some officials held the view that a fixed–exchange rate regime could not last under levels of very high financial integration. The possibility of floating currencies was never seriously considered, as Europeans have long shunned exchange-rate volatility despite the rest of the world's tolerance for flexibility even under high levels of trade and investment (Giavazzi and Giovannini 1989).

The links between capital-market integration and monetary integration came full-circle with the start of EMU on 1 January 1999. Financial-market integration has proceeded apace since that time, with the bond markets quickly embracing the Euro. EU money markets have been relatively swift to integrate, as well, assisted by the TARGET payment system, although equities markets have remained more segmented (BHF Bank 2000). In terms of foreign direct investment (FDI), Europe has long been host to significant investment and cross-border mergers and acquisitions, particularly in the banking sector, increased in conjunction with the lifting of capital controls and the run up to EMU (European Commission 2000, figs. A.10, A.11, A.12). Further integra-

---

[3] Apparently, at a meeting of the ECOFIN (Council of Economic and Financial Ministers) during the height of the exchange-rate crises, there was a proposal to move immediately to an "overnight EMU" so as to outwit the markets. Interview, European Commission official, Brussels, 1994.

tion of markets is planned, as Europe's leaders endorsed the European Commission's Financial Services Action Plan (FSAP) at their Lisbon summit in March 2000. The FSAP recommends forty-two measures to streamline the regulation of retail and wholesale financial markets by 2005, many of which are already being implemented.

Thus, rising capital mobility, in conjunction with the other perceived benefits of EMU, has helped push the single currency forward, while the introduction of the Euro has further deepened financial-market integration. Given the degree of trade and capital-market integration outlined above, the EU therefore represents one of the most globalized regions of the world and demonstrates the complexity of the interaction between market integration and political institutions. We are now ready to turn to the central question of this chapter: the degree to which this market integration has prompted convergent fiscal policies.

EMU, Deficits, and the Convergence Criteria

The rules of entry into EMU stated, among other goals, that governments should have budget deficits of 3 percent per year or less, making concrete and specific one of the logics of fiscal constraint that is purported to operate in a globalized world. The challenge that governments faced in the run-up to the Euro matches the widely held belief that high levels of integration into world markets limits national authorities' ability to run large budget deficits and thus reduces their ability to pursue divergent policies. Even a skeptic of globalization's effects, Geoff Garrett, has stated that "one can certainly point to examples where globalization constraints on national policy choices are readily apparent. The mobility of financial capital, for example, has tended to put downward pressure on budget deficits" (Garrett 1998b, 788).

The convergence criteria set out in the Treaty on European Union set out goals regarding inflation rates, interest rates, exchange rates, deficits, and public debts for states wishing to enter EMU. The fiscal criteria spelled out targets of 3 percent of GDP for government deficits and 60 percent of GDP for public debt, and the treaty further specified that members must avoid "excessive government deficits" once EMU begins. If the numerical targets were not met, a nation still could be considered eligible if "the ratio has declined substantially and continuously and reached a level that comes close to the reference value; or, alternatively, the excess over the reference value is only exceptional and temporary and the ratio remains close to the reference value" (Article 104c).[4] Im-

---

[4] Although there was an assumption in the treaty that these criteria would remain operative once EMU began, the specific nature of the rules and enforcement of the deficit

portantly, the criteria did not specify, however, how states should reach those targets.

The EU leaders were to meet before 1 July 1998 to determine which states fulfilled the necessary conditions to join EMU, based on recommendations from the Council of Economic and Finance Ministers (ECOFIN), drawing on two separate convergence-criteria assessments by the European Commission and the European Monetary Institute, as well as the opinion of the European Parliament. The statistics on national economic conditions would be gathered and reported by Eurostat, the statistical agency of the European Union.[5]

It is important to note that the fiscal constraint imposed under EMU was the result of a series of political bargains: the overwhelming majority of observers have argued that the convergence criteria are not economically necessary, or even desirable, as initial or sustaining conditions for monetary union (De Grauwe 1996; Eichengreen 1992; Eichengreen and Wyplosz 1998). Rather, the convergence criteria and continuing Excessive Deficit Procedure performed a variety of political functions. Some have argued that the criteria were designed so as to allow Germany to restrict the number and nature of participants in EMU so as to ensure a dominant position and macroeconomic policies more closely in line with Bundesbank tradition (De Grauwe 1993; Moravcsik 1998). Other national negotiators knew that for the German government to agree to give up the mark, the Bundesbank and the German public had to be reassured about the fiscal and monetary sobriety of their partners. Setting up strict standards in the convergence criteria was the political bargain struck to move forward with EMU. Finally, the criteria served another political function because of their symbolic value to both market participants and other EMU governments (McNamara 1998b). Undertaking the policy adjustments necessary to stay within the convergence-criteria targets might be read as an important political signifier of the willingness to commit to price stability and whatever policy adjustments might be necessary in the coming years of monetary union, despite potential costs in terms of unemployment and slow growth.

Most observers believed that EMU would have significant and profound effects on economic policymaking in the EU long before Euros actually filled pocketbooks and cash registers in January 2002. Given the logic of globalization's convergence thesis, the budgetary rules of

---

procedures after EMU was to begin were not initially established. European leaders agreed in Amsterdam in 1997 to a "Stability and Growth Pact," which detailed the provisions of the Excessive Deficit Procedure that would be in place once EMU began. In practice, the operation of this Stability Pact has proven highly political, with much negotiation between national leaders over its application in particular cases.

[5] See Savage (2000) for a valuable account of Maastricht's budgetary politics.

EMU, operating in a context of high market integration, might be hypothesized to produce policy convergence in the fiscal realm at the very least. In this view, national programs of taxing, spending, and borrowing should start to move in the direction of policies designed to capture and retain mobile firms and investment. The next section spells out these predictions more fully.

FISCAL POLICY AND GLOBALIZATION

Taxing, spending, and borrowing policies are at the center of the modern state and a key battleground in the debate over globalization's effects. Fiscal policy both reflects and shapes public values, influencing what sort of society we have by way of its impact on redistribution of resources and on the size and activities of the public sector relative to the private economy. Fiscal policy also is intimately linked to the external face of the state through its relationship to war-fighting capabilities and international leadership. These are deeply political dynamics that mark profound national differences: if a true convergence is occurring under globalization, it would be a profound development.

What are the hypothesized effects of increased market integration on fiscal policy? Capital mobility and financial-market integration are generally thought to have the most impact on such policies. Under the Mundell-Fleming model, capital mobility is supposed to increase the efficacy of fiscal policy if exchange rates are fixed, but diminish it if rates float. In the European case, largely fixed (but adjustable) rates have dominated over the postwar era. The conventional view, however, is that mobile capital will undermine certain types of policy choices, for example in the area of taxation on mobile assets (Steinmo 1993, chapter 6; Strange 1996).

Although the literature does not precisely address the mix of policies more likely to occur in a tightly integrated environment, we can make some general predictions drawing on work on policymaking under economic openness. The basic logic relates to the idea of asset specificity (Frieden 1991a; Rogowski 1989). When borders open up, actors whose assets are mobile will have an advantage in pressing governments for their favored policies insofar as they can credibly threaten to exit that locality in favor of a more congenial one. This should create an advantage for people whose wealth comes from capital investments as opposed to being generated from their labor, as capital is more readily mobile than labor. Within these categories, we might further identify some heterogeneity. Portfolio capital, such as bonds, will be more mobile than FDI, which is more tied to specific assets such as factories and firms. Within labor, as well, we might expect that those whose skills are particularly marketable and transferable across sectors, such as managers or certain types of technology workers, and those viewed as generating significant wealth and having exit options, would be favored by policy.

Given the hypothesized ability of capital to disproportionately dictate policy preferences, the next question is *what does capital want* in terms of fiscal policy? The conventional wisdom suggests that capital should seek low taxes, so, when borders are open, we should see reductions in the level of corporate taxation, the taxation of financial instruments, and taxation of wealthy individuals. In contrast, taxes should remain unchanged or increase on those tethered to the domestic economy, such as unskilled workers or public sector employees, or those in the agriculture or extractive industries who have significant sunk costs and limited relocation options.

Beyond the specific linkages between sectoral interests and policies, there is a broader assumption that capital will favor a reduced public sector that diverts only limited resources to the social safety-net or welfare state while spending its revenues on a limited number of public goods. Borrowing by the government should be limited, in this model, as business will prefer lower public debt and the lower interest rates that might be expected to follow.

A wave of scholarship has made some headway in examining patterns of fiscal policy making in light of such ideas about globalization. The largest area of research has asked specifically about the future of the welfare state given possible fiscal constraints (Pierson 1994, 2001; Ross 1997; Scharpf and Schmidt 2001; Schwartz, 2001; Swank 2002). Another strand has carried out a series of large-*n*, statistical studies that have attempted, among other things, to determine the degree to which internationalization correlates with downward fiscal convergence: the results so far have been inconclusive (Clark 1998; Garrett 1998a; Rodrik 1997).[6]

The literature in comparative and international political economy has, however, some analytical and empirical limitations. First, research tends to focus on singular aspects of the fiscal stance of the state, such as taxation levels, the welfare state, or budgetary rules. Very few scholars have tried to see the overall picture of budgetary politics as a multidimensional one of critical *trade-offs* across programs.[7] A second related problem plaguing the literature has been a focus on the aggregate

---

[6] Of course, this literature had important precursors, notably Cameron (1978) and Katzenstein (1985), among others.

[7] This appears to be a more general problem with the literature on fiscal policy. Commenting on the public opinion literature, Mark Hansen also notes that most authors "have neglected *the* essential aspect of the problem: the tradeoffs inherent in public budgeting" (Hansen [1999, 2, italics in original]).

levels of spending, taxing, and borrowing, without attention to the substantive programmatic decisions being made by governments. Finally, the third lacuna in the literature is the lack of attention to the role of institutions, particularly those at the international level, in shaping the ways in which national governments respond to globalization. The role of domestic institutions has begun to be addressed (Hallerberg and Basinger 1998; Swank 2002). The role for formal international organizations, however, such as the IMF or the EU, remains to be fully explored.[8] The next section attempts to redress some of these shortcomings by evaluating the overall fiscal stance of selected European governments, their programmatic choices, and the role of EU rules in producing policy outcomes in the context of market integration.

EMPIRICAL EVIDENCE FROM THE EU CASE

The Overall Numbers: Deficit and Debt Ratios in the EU

The states most observers initially viewed as facing the biggest battle in qualifying for EMU were Belgium, Spain, Italy, and Portugal.[9] States viewed as likely to participate included France, Germany, the Netherlands, Austria, Finland, Ireland, and Luxembourg. The United Kingdom, Sweden, and Denmark were viewed as not likely to be first-round participants in EMU by their own political choice. Figure 13.1 presents a schematic representation of perceptions in the press, as well as academic and official statements regarding various states' chances of qualifying for EMU.

Remarkably, however, all of the EU members, save Greece, were deemed in 1998 eligible to participate in EMU (Greece reached the targets by 2000) despite the initially quite wide gap between the convergence-criteria targets and the macroeconomic positions of many of the EU states. EMU was made possible because of the dramatic decline in deficit ratios of the EU states in the period from the signing of the Maastricht treaty in 1992 to the 1998 decision on participation in EMU. The most dramatic declines were in Greece and Sweden (roughly 10 percent each), Italy (7 percent), the United Kingdom and Finland, (6 percent) and Belgium, Spain, and Portugal (5 percent). The exceptions to this trend were those fiscally prudent states who were never very far from the criteria:

---

[8] An important exception in the EU realm is Cowles, Caporaso, and Risse (2001). The role for informal institutions, or ideational regimes, in globalization's effects is also important and has received some study (see Drezner [2001]).

[9] Greece was seen as being out of the running for the first round, because, in addition to its fiscal situation, it had not participated in the EU's fixed exchange-rate system, the Exchange Rate Mechanism (ERM) of the European Monetary System (EMS).

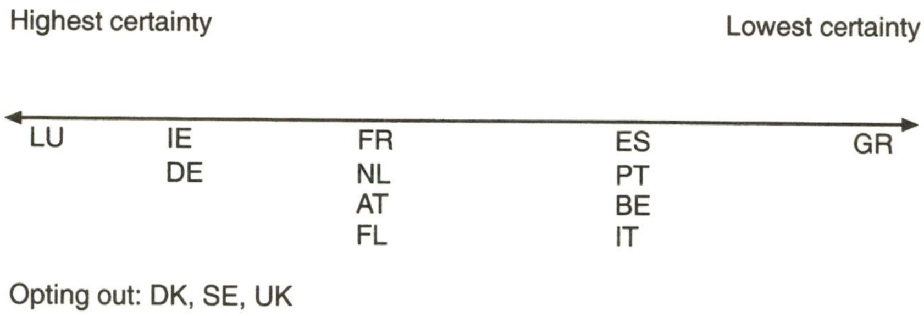

Highest certainty   Lowest certainty

LU	IE	FR	ES	GR
	DE	NL	PT	
		AT	BE	
		FL	IT	

Opting out: DK, SE, UK

Figure 13.1. Initial Views on EMU Participation

Germany, Ireland, Luxembourg, and the Netherlands. Figure 13.2 details the fiscal trajectory for each EU state.

These deficit trajectories were of course influenced by the national public debt situation of the EU states, which varied greatly as shown in figure 13.3. The high public debts faced in the first half of the 1990s by Belgium (137 percent of GDP at its highest) and Italy (125 percent) made deficit reduction a particular challenge, as a substantial amount of funds had to be budgeted for debt payments. Other states facing sustained debts significantly in excess of the 60 percent of GDP Maastricht figure included Greece, Ireland, and Sweden.

The Policy Choices: Fiscal Adjustments on the Way to EMU

What policies did the EU states pursue on the way to this remarkable convergence in overall deficit levels? The brief policy narratives that follow highlight the major initiatives undertaken in the area of fiscal policy in several of the "excessive-deficit" states.[10] I survey Italy and Belgium as they were seen as being in the most problematic positions to qualify, yet were also viewed as politically central to the EU project. The pressures for adjustment on their part should therefore have been extremely strong, so they are the most likely cases for evidence of some sort of convergence effect. Portugal is also examined as it, too, was viewed as one of the "Club Med" countries least likely to meet the

---

[10] The empirical information is drawn primarily from the annual country-by-country OECD Economic Surveys. Further information was drawn from a private client publication by Deutsche Bank, EMU Watch, with some information from the European Monetary Institute's convergence reports, as well as *Financial Times* and *Economist* reports. Because of the complexity of fiscal policy and the possible motivations of observers to spin out their own interpretations, I have tried to confirm the information and remained aware of the potential for subjective bias in these accounts. The European Commission's convergence reports, in particular, put fiscal consolidation efforts in the EU in the most positive light, as did the national convergence–program planning documents.

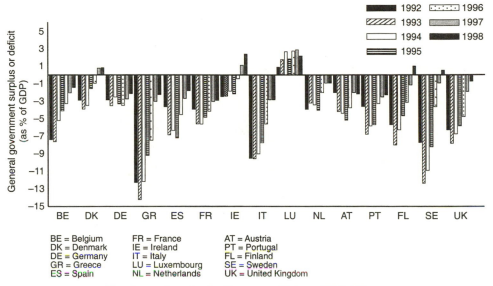

Figure 13.2. Fiscal Positions in the European Union, 1992–98

criteria. France is also examined, in less detail, for comparative purposes as a state nearer to the deficit criteria.

There are three major categories of policy adjustments that may occur when governments are attempting to meet deficit targets. The first category of action is to increase revenues to make up the shortfall, which can be done through the imposition of new or increased taxes, direct or indirect, through the sales of nationally owned assets, or through borrowing. The second option is to decrease spending through discretionary cuts or changes in entitlement or other program definitions. Finally, administrative and accounting changes can be undertaken, for example to redefine national accounts in such a way as to improve the numerical budget balance.

I draw two major analytical conclusions from my assessment of these categories across the cases that follow. First, the EU states approached the goal of meeting the fiscal criteria using a mixture of different policies spanning the three categories above, demonstrating continuing heterogeneity in national policymaking even under quite significant constraint. Second and relatedly, the majority of policies chosen did not reflect the conventional wisdom about convergence to a lowest common denominator of public sector activity. Some areas of traditional welfare-state activity, such as pensions, were subject to reforms and ongoing debates about their structure and sustainability. But in no way did

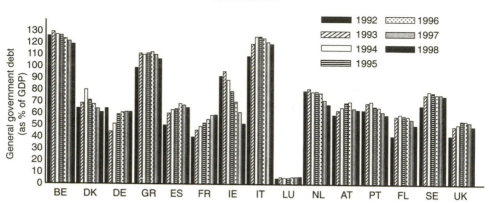

Figure 13.3. Public Debt in the European Union, 1992–98

spending cuts produce the majority of progress in the deficit-reduction programs. For example, during this period, the Portuguese government was able to increase revenues through efficiency reforms and tax collection improvements while simultaneously increasing public spending on infrastructure. Other governments, such as France and Italy, increased taxes on corporations and high-income earners to make up some of the budget shortfalls. Importantly, the challenges facing the most highly indebted countries were significantly reduced after interest rates began to fall in expectation that these states would in fact participate in EMU, lessening the costs of borrowing. Falling interest rates made long-term adjustments less necessary and created more room for shorter-term strategies.

A summary of policy adjustments on the way to EMU follows, as does an evaluation of the general findings in terms of the policy-convergence hypotheses.

ITALY

At the time of the Maastricht signing, Italy was not in a position favorable to entry into EMU.[11] Successive governments had increased public spending during the 1980s, with general government expenditures increasing 11 percent from 1979–1991, a rate twice the European average. Despite several changes of government after Maastricht, however, as well as a period of recession and exchange-rate crisis in 1992–93, Italy's budget deficit dropped dramatically over the 1992–1998 period, from a high of 9.5 percent of GDP to 2.7. This decline in the deficit was

---

[11] The section on Italy draws on the OECD Country Surveys (Italy). See also Sbragia (2001) for an account of the shift in fiscal institutions within Italy that occurred during this time.

brought about by a mixture of structural changes and cuts, improved interest-rate conditions, privatizations, and special one-time taxes including the "Euro tax." Reforms included improved planning and control of expenditures, rationalization of the tax system and tax collection, decentralization of fiscal policymaking, rebalancing of social-welfare provisions, and reform of the pension system. These initiatives created virtuous-circle effects vis-à-vis the markets, as decreasing interest rates eased the path toward a balanced budget. I provide some highlights of these adjustments below.

Revenue Adjustments. Tax changes have played an important role in Italy's fiscal-policy adjustments. The most visible revenue increase occurred with the 1997 establishment of a one-time "Euro" or "Europa" tax measure that produced revenue equivalent to approximately 1 percent of GDP.[12] The Europa tax was a progressive income tax ranging from 1.5 percent on a minimum salary of L23.4 million (about $15,000) to 3.5 percent on incomes over L100 million ($65,000). For the self-employed, the minimum annual tax was set at L17.2 million. (OECD 1996–1997I, 65). An increase in the VAT was believed to make up about half of the total revenue increases in 1997.

The 1998 budget focused to a large extent on tax reform. Taxation on corporate income was reduced from 37 percent to 19 percent (on retained profits), provided the average rate for the individual company did not fall below 27 percent. This change was meant to stimulate investment. Personal income taxes have been simplified, from seven to five tax-rate categories, with the top rate being reduced from 51 to 46 percent while the minimum rate increased from 10 to 19 percent. Various central-state corporate taxes were eliminated and replaced by a single regional tax of 4.25 percent. Taxation on capital income was reduced to two rates (12.5 percent and 27 percent) while the tax base was broadened by making capital gains and income from derivative trading taxable. VAT taxes were harmonized with EU norms by reducing the number of rates from four to three, keeping the minimum rate at 4 percent but increasing the top rate from 19 to 20 percent. Most goods and services moved from the previous rate of 16 percent to the new top rate of 20 percent. The stated goals of these reforms were to reduce their disproportional impact on corporate decision making, and to have a uniform effect on labor and capital costs in line with OECD recommendations. The overall thrust was "to reduce personal and corporate income taxes as well as employers' social security charges, while raising

---

[12] The government promised to pay 60 percent of the Europa tax back, and did so by mid-1999.

indirect taxes, broadening the tax base and reducing tax discrimination against labor income and equity capital. . . . EU harmonization has also entailed a simplification, and rise, in the VAT." (OECD 1999I, 14.)

These recent reforms were purported to be revenue neutral as the changes widened the tax base, reducing tax avoidance while reducing tax rates. Administratively, the reforms also shift more taxing powers to local authorities, doubling from about 5 percent of general government revenue in 1997 to 10 percent in 1998. This spurred the creation of new systems of public administration and control on the local level to carry out the devolution of policymaking.

Privatizations also helped generate significant revenue, as Italy led the OECD in privatizations in 1997 with revenues equal to nearly 2 percent of GDP. Several state banks were sold off, as well as the energy conglomerate (ENI), Telecom Italia, and SEAT. Plans were drawn up to offer further enterprises for sale; however, the state retained "golden share" in many important enterprises. The Italian government attempted to count the sale of central bank gold reserves toward the deficit-reduction efforts, but this tactic was rejected in a ruling by the EU statistical agency, Eurostat, which also rejected similar attempts on the part of Spain and Belgium.

Spending Adjustments. Many observers point to the importance of the pension reforms approved in August 1995 under the Dini government as an early indication of serious efforts at structural reform that bolstered market confidence and reduced domestic interest-rate risk premia. Further reforms were predicated on a subsequent compromise between the Prodi government and Communists (the Prodi Agreement) regarding welfare-state reforms. Although the social-insurance reforms were less ambitious than originally planned, pension-system reforms were notable. Italy's pension system has taken up one of the largest shares of GDP in the OECD at 15 percent. This has been to some degree at the expense of other forms of welfare-state protections, such as those for individuals and families in distress, which constitute less than 4 percent of GDP, low by EU standards (OECD 1999I, 14). Pension reforms included increasing the age limit for retirement pensions from 53 to 54, and to 57 by 2002, while ending generous early-retirement benefits. New 1998 pensions were to be paid with a time lag of three months, some pensions would not be indexed, and self-employed contributions were to increase. The reforms were viewed as a step toward making the pension system sustainable, while not radically changing its nature.

These policy adjustments produced a dramatic drop in the deficit from 6.7 in 1996 to 2.7 percent in 1997, one of the largest annual retrenchments recorded in the OECD area. This was accomplished in no small part by the drop of over 1 percent in Italian interest-service payments as a percent of GDP, as well as another economic upturn in 1997 after unexpectedly low growth in 1996. The interest-rate drop was a product both of the low level of interest rates worldwide, as well as financial markets also rewardeding the Italians in light of their budget-consolidation efforts.

Administrative Adjustments. During the pre-EMU period, an important development toward increasing the credibility of the Italian effort at reform came with the November 1993 move of the Bank of Italy away from the Treasury, as a moratorium was called on the granting of credit or overdrafts by the bank. On the accounting side, reclassifications in public accounts in line with EU rules on comparability and transparency, particularly in the crucial 1997 budget, had the effect of reducing the public debt.

The impact of each change is difficult to measure precisely. The crucial 1997 budget that would determine Italy's fate regarding EMU contained about half "ordinary" fiscal adjustments and half supplementary "*Intervento per l'Europa*" adjustments, and four-fifths of the ordinary adjustments were "structural" in nature according to the OECD (OECD 1996–1997I, 6). Around half of the supplementary budget adjustments consisted of tax measures such as the Europa tax, discussed above. The balance of the deficit reduction came from accounting-rule changes.

EU finance ministers commended Italy in early 1998 for hard work on its austerity programs, leading observers to believe that prevailing opinion in the EU would allow Italy to qualify for EMU despite its persistently high public debt figures. Finance Minister Ciampi presented the 1999 budget very early, in April 1998, in order to put Italy in the best possible light before the May meeting to decide on entry. Despite Italy's reliance on short-term adjustment strategies to reduce the deficit, the commitment of its leaders and its public to moving toward the convergence criteria and the positive reaction of the markets to the budget-consolidation efforts combined to make Italy a plausible candidate for entry into the single currency.

BELGIUM

Belgium shared some of Italy's challenges in meeting the convergence criteria, but benefited from its reputation as a more politically and economically stable state at the center of the EU's integration project. At 7.5 percent, Belgium's deficits were not quite as high as Italy's in the wake of the Maastricht treaty, but at over 130 percent its public debt was much worse—the highest in the EU. The Belgian franc had been tightly linked to the German mark for over a decade, however, and interest rates had closely tracked those of Germany since 1988. This curious blend of fiscal insolvency and political and market confidence made Belgium a difficult country to judge under the strictures of the convergence criteria. Over the years after Maastricht, and particularly in the 1994 budget, the government successfully brought about significant reduction in budget deficits, in conjunction with a formal policy program called the "The Global Plan," introduced by the government to meet the convergence criteria while attempting to promote employment and competitiveness. The high debt had created a negative "snowball effect" where the payment on the debt made deficit reductions particularly difficult without serious reforms and cuts.

Revenue Adjustments.   On the revenue side, there was a small increase in Belgian withholding taxes on Belgian bonds in 1994. The general government receipts increased to over 48 percent of GDP, but this level was still less than in the mid-1980s before tax reforms. Government policy in the Global Plan moved to more "alternative financing" of the social security system, which shifted the relative importance of different types of receipts. To reduce nonwage labor costs and promote employment, the Belgian government moved to indirect taxation and taxes on revenue from capital rather than labor and decreased employers' contributions on lower-wage salaries. Specific policy examples included the increases in withholding taxes on interest income (from 10.3 percent to 13.39 percent), and an increase in taxes on some commercial-property income. As in other EU states, the VAT was increased, to 19.5 percent from 10.5 percent in 1994. In addition, a variety of one-time revenue measures, including privatizations and an attempt to include proceeds from the sale of gold reserves (which was declared ineligible for inclusion against the deficit by Eurostat) allowed Belgium to record a deficit of just under 2 percent in 1997, and to move its debt downward to 123 percent.

Spending Adjustments.   At the start of the run up to EMU, emphasis was placed on long-term planning for structural reform of the economy and concurrent fiscal adjustments, and policy adjustments in 1994, in conjunction with an improving economy, did a lot to put Belgium on a firmer footing vis-à-vis the criteria. The November 1993 Global Plan implemented structural measures, including a change in the wage-indexation system, alternative financing of some nonwage labor costs, and curbs on social security spending. This effort contributed to budget reduction of 5.3 percent of GDP in 1994, and stabilization of the debt-GDP ratio at over 130. Government investment, however, increased by

6.8 percent in 1994 as local authorities increased public spending before local elections. The Belgian *Accord interprofessionel* of 1995–1996 lowered the early-retirement age to 55 for two years. A health index was introduced, restraining the growth of the pension program (the largest portion of social expenditure), and unemployment-benefit transfers were leveled off.

According to the OECD, 60 percent of the Belgian budget savings from 1992–1995 came from new direct and indirect taxes, and, to a lesser extent, social security contributions, 30 percent from cuts in expenditure, and 10 percent from other sources, including the proceeds of some privatizations (OECD 1995B, 31). The 1995 budget needed only minor changes as the benefits of renewed economic growth, increasing revenues and decreased expenditures from the 1994 measures began to improve Belgium's public finances. Falling interest rates, as the markets passed positive judgment on the Belgian government's actions, further contributed to the improving fiscal situation and put Belgium squarely on the path to EMU.

PORTUGAL

Portugal initially was viewed as an unlikely participant in EMU. It has traditionally been lumped together by EU observers with Italy and Spain as a "Club Med" country, with suspicious finances and an erratic economic record. This despite the fact, as its central bank president has repeatedly stated, "not one inch of its coastline" is on the Mediterranean. Portugal's budget deficit went from a high of almost 7 percent of GDP in 1993 to just over 2 percent in 1998. On balance, Portugal has followed a distinctive path in meeting the criteria, relying on revenue increases while simultaneously expanding its public expenditures.

Revenue Adjustments.   A series of thoroughgoing reforms in tax collection, the reduction of widespread tax evasion and fraud, and tax-amnesty programs (the "Plano Mateus") allowed for an increase in revenues without significant tax hikes. In fact, corporate tax rates were reduced from 40 to 36 percent in 1998. Privatization played a part in reducing the Portuguese government debt, as in other EU states. The privatization program was projected to bring PTE 400–500 billion into government coffers from the sale of corporate holdings.

Spending Adjustments.   There were also efforts at budget consolidation, though government spending in the economy, excluding interest payments, actually rose in Portugal more than in any other OECD state (from 36.1 percent in 1994 to 43. percent in 1997). In part this may be due to the very high level of public investment in infrastructure projects that Portugal has pursued in tandem with the convergence program. These investments, aided by EU structural or development funds, have spurred high GDP growth levels. The longest bridge in Europe, the Vasco da Gama 18 km bridge, opened in Spring 1998, and other big infrastructure projects include a new Metro railway in Oporto, a second Lisbon airport, and very large hydroelectric dam project at Alqueva.

A key factor in achieving the convergence criteria and lowering public debt was the fall in interest rates that Portugal enjoyed when markets became convinced that the country was serious about entering EMU. Antonia Sousa Franco, the Finance Minister in the new Socialist government in October 1995, was viewed as a disciplinarian by financial markets, which contributed to their favorable view of Portugal's performance.

FRANCE

At the time of the Maastricht treaty, the French were thought to be in a reasonably good position for qualifying. The recession of 1993 caused the budget to balloon, however, as it did in most of the EU states, and the subsequent election of a more expansionist and activist Socialist government raised doubts in some quarters about French prospects. To reach the 3-percent target in 1997, from a high of 5.6 percent in 1993, the French government relied on increases in corporate taxes, privatization schemes, and one-time revenue increases, with relatively little structural reform or reduction in expenditures. At the time of Maastricht, the public debt level was a relatively low 40 percent, which made it easier for the Jospin government to heed its campaign promises about employment and growth. By 1998, however, debt had crept up to near 60 percent, although it was still under the qualifying standard for EMU.

Revenue Adjustment. French budget deficit–reduction efforts rested on substantial hikes in corporate taxation. The tax burden on corporations increased, in part as the result of a special 15 percent surcharge, increasing the tax rate to 41.6 percent from the previous rate of 36.6 percent. The overall rate was made up of a basic 33.3-percent rate plus a special 10-percent supplementary levy imposed by Prime Minister Juppe in May 1995. A raise in the capital gains tax increased rates from 20.9 percent to 41.6 percent, although the rates only applied to companies with annual revenues exceeding FRF 50 million, and the special corporate tax surcharge was to be reduced by 5 percent in 1999. The capital gains tax was also modified in August 1997 to exempt licenses, patents, and other intellectual property, which were added to previously exempted profits on the sales of shares.

Other tax policy changes included tax increases on mineral oil; the ending of commercial shipping tax credits; the reduction of tax breaks for investments in French overseas departments; the reduction of tax breaks for domestic help and the child allowance; means tests for family allowances; and higher taxation on income from savings. Changes were also being made to social security taxes: the CSG social tax was raised from 3.4 percent to 7.5 percent, but employee contributions for health insurance were lowered from 5.5 percent to .75 percent. On balance, the tax burden on households will increase in the short term by FRF 4.5 billion, and will be used to decrease deficits in the social security area.

Deficit savings also resulted from measures designed to heavily tap the resources of state-owned companies such as CDC, Caisse des Depots et consignations, and Electricité de France, with privatization plans for Thompson CSF, France Telecom, Air France, and GAN-CIC. Finally, a one-time transfer of pension funds from France Telecom was undertaken, reducing the deficit in 1997 by approximately 0.5 percent of GDP. This action was ruled acceptable by Eurostat and the Commissioner in charge of Economic and Monetary Affairs, over criticism in the press and the protests of Germany and other states.

Spending Adjustments. Adjustments on the expenditure side were minor, and tended to increase, not reduce, spending. The Jospin government carried out some significant spending increases after coming into office, including increases in the minimum wage (SMIC) by 4 percent (costing approx. FRF 2 billion); a fourfold increase in assistance to families at the start of the school year (FRF 6 billion); jobs for young people in the public sector (FRF 2 billion); and various other education and welfare measures (FRF 2 billion).

Summary of Findings

The empirical record, presented in stylized form below in table 13.1, indicates the mixture of choices the case-study states made to reach the 3-percent Maastricht budget targets. There certainly were some efforts taken along the lines of the downward-convergence hypothesis, as delineated in the "Capital-Friendly Policies" category. Structural reforms in the area of pensions (e.g., raising the retirement age), reducing corporate taxes, and raising VAT taxes all might be in line with the hypothesized vision of stripped-down governance under capital mobility. On the other hand, many reforms undertaken to increase revenues contradict the downward-convergence hypothesis. In particular, increased corporate taxation and infrastructure-spending binges are hard to square with the capital-friendly policies hypothesized as necessary in a context of

TABLE 13.1
The Composition of Fiscal Adjustment in Four EU Member-States, 1992–1997

Strategic Budgeting/One-time Measures	Prolabor Policies	Procapital Policies	Exogenous Factors Aiding Deficit Reduction
Transfer of pension funds, privatizations sales (IT, BE, FR, PT)	Corporate tax increases (FR)	VAT raises (IT, BE)	Interest-rate reductions on public debt (IT, PT, BE, FR)
Tax-amnesty programs (PT)	Short-term "Euro taxes" on high-income earners (IT)	Pension reform and other welfare-state adjustments (IT, BE)	
Accounting changes to EU standards (IT)	Increased taxation of financial instruments (BE)	Corporate tax reductions (PT, IT)	
Improved tax collection and fraud reduction (PT, IT)	Increased social spending (FR)		
	Increased public infrastructure spending (PT)		

BE = Belgium; FR = France; IT = Italy; PT = Portugal.

highly integrated financial and trade markets. Neither did the convergence criteria spell the end of welfare-state programming. Over the period of adjustment, in fact, one recent cross-national study of social dumping found "in contrast to the idea of a race to the bottom, almost all countries examined . . . continued to increase the level of social spending at a faster rate than economic growth so that their social expenditure ratios kept growing" (Alber and Standing 2000, 107; quoted in Rhodes 2001).

More important, perhaps, than the more conscious programmatic and structural reforms that sought to rationalize public spending were one-time policy changes, which constituted the majority of the deficit reduction. These "strategic budgeting" exercises demonstrated the creativity of the EU states in achieving budget reductions without sacrificing key welfare-state programs, challenging the race-to-the-bottom thesis.

Finally, the role played by financial markets also departed dramatically from the conventional wisdom about the disciplinary effects of mobile capital. In all of the high-deficit–high-debt countries, a virtuous circle occurred whereby a commitment to deficit reduction under the

EMU process was rewarded by the markets even if the stated commitment far outstripped actual deficit reduction. The easing of interest rates, already significant by 1996 in advance of the actual deficit reductions, made it possible for states like Italy, Belgium, Portugal and Spain to meet the criteria. This snowball effect was a critical factor that allowed for EMU to go forward. The markets viewed these governments as credibly committing to deficit reduction despite their reliance on "creative accounting" and one-time measures to reach the EMU target of 3-percent deficits. The markets acted in advance of policy changes, responding to political messages being sent by politicians about their commitment to EMU. The decrease in interest rates charged to governments subsequently allowed for the eventual meeting of the EMU deficit targets.

These findings indicate that national differences, and continuing creativity on the part of policymakers, will persist in the face of even quite stringent economic constraints. A rough general indicator of the persistence of this diversity in the presence of government in the economy is figure 13.4, which shows the standard deviation among the EU fifteen for general government expenditures as a percentage of GDP during the postwar era. The degree of divergence in government activity in the economy has fluctuated over time, increasing particularly in periods of economic hardship, such as in the mid-1970s and early 1990s. But there does not appear to be strong convergence along this particular dimension, despite an extremely high degree of market integration within Europe and increasing globalization more generally.

Conclusion: The Institutionalist Logic of Market Integration

This chapter has outlined how some of the most free-spending, highly indebted states of Europe achieved an astonishing reduction in their budget deficits in the run up to EMU, resulting in a remarkable convergence around a 3-percent budget-deficit figure. Yet I also demonstrate that they achieved convergence without substantially scaling back their historic commitments to government intervention in the economy, and without conforming neatly to the conventional wisdom about globalization as a race to the bottom.[13] Moreover, financial markets were willing to give even these highly indebted states the benefit of the doubt regarding their participation in EMU, and to reward them with interest-rate

---

[13] In his exhaustive cross-national evaluation of the effects of the move to EMU on the welfare states of Europe, Rhodes goes further, arguing that his evidence shows that, in fact "EMU became part of the solution for enhancing the welfare state sustainability rather than a force for destruction" by politically allowing for needed reforms (Rhodes [2001, 33]).

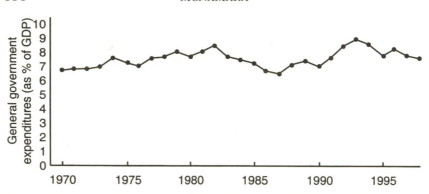

Figure 13.4. General Government Expenditure (% GDP), Standard Deviation in EU 15, 1970–1998

reductions at the same time as their governments pursued a variety of short-term, sometimes dubious measures designed to meet the convergence criteria. This evidence, surprising in what should have been a "most likely case" for the globalization thesis, should give us pause when assuming that financial markets are a punishing force, promoting downward convergence in national spending policies.

Although going against the grain of conventional wisdom, my findings in this EU case are congruent with Rogowski's observations in the present volume about the logic of divergence and specialization under globalization, as well as Gourevitch's account of the continued importance of national differences in the area of corporate governance despite high levels of financial integration. But this should not, of course, imply that we should never expect convergence in policies: the chapter by Simmons and Elkins demonstrates that there has been a significant global convergence on policies of financial liberalization. Rather, the outcomes of fiscal adjustment in the EU case should remind us of the contingent nature of policy change under globalization and the need to specify very closely the processes and factors at work before we can judge likely outcomes.

The EMU case should also remind us of the dynamic and recursive interaction between globalization and governance. The 3-percent budget deficit, an EMU benchmark, was created through negotiation and embodied in institutional and legal rules at the European level; it was not forced on states by markets. Only after the Maastricht treaty did the 3-percent rule become a rubric that financial-market participants used in assessing the creditworthiness of national governments. The European budget constraint was created in a political process that then boomeranged back to shape financial markets' perceptions of fiscal orthodoxy. Although one case can only be suggestive, the EU experience underlines the importance of political institutions in shaping the progress of globalization and its outcomes.

A further lesson we might take from this case relates to how globalization relocates the site of authoritative policymaking. Market integration across European borders has provoked movement in authoritative institutions upward, to the EU level, while demonstrating the continued importance of national institutions and policy trajectories. EU governance structures have been the embodiment of convergence and a source of constraint, even as EU rules have been interpreted in diverse ways by member states, in the case of EMU as in Gourevitch's findings on European corporate governance. The role for a variety of regional and international institutions, such as the International Monetary Fund, to mediate market forces, in tandem with national political structures, is ongoing and a critically important area for further systematic study.

Political authority will continue to be a necessity, even with globalization. While the EU states have reduced their budget deficits significantly, they continue to make important choices about the way they tax, spend, and borrow, even under the twin constraints of EMU and high levels of market integration. More generally, European political actors have chosen to build institutional capacity at the EU level even as they dismantle barriers to cross-national economic exchange. Instead of viewing the EU as an anomaly in its high levels of cross-border market integration and its governance capacity, I have suggested that it be viewed as a laboratory within which to learn about the causal relationships between markets and politics. The lessons are clear. Convergence is not a foregone conclusion in a globalized world, and its occurrence may stem more from political choice than market dictates. Moreover, governance structures must keep pace with market integration. In all, the EU's experience has much to teach us about the relationship between globalization and governance in today's interdependent world.

PART 3

Democratic Deficits and the Problem of Accountability

Chapter 14

DEMOCRACY, ACCOUNTABILITY, AND RIGHTS IN SUPRANATIONAL GOVERNANCE

James A. Caporaso

DOES DEMOCRACY stop at the water's edge? Realist theory, with its spare division between hierarchy and anarchy, would confine the logic of democracy to domestic politics. In "Why Is There No International Theory?" (1966), Martin Wight explains that pursuit of the good life — as opposed to survival — is confined to relations within the polis. The external realm of relations among states is characterized by balancing and arms'-length strategic relations. Democratic politics is not transposed to international organizations. Instead, states bargain in these organizations through agents who are carefully instructed by principals in the constituent states. A conceptual firewall is set up between domestic and international politics in which democracy is confined to the domestic realm.

The background for this chapter, indeed for the project as a whole (Kahler and Lake, chapter 1), accepts the relationship between globalization and governance structures as the starting point. It may therefore be useful to define some terms to relate this chapter to the book. I define globalization as increases in the velocity and magnitude of economic exchange, factor mobility, transmission of symbols, and diffusion of political practices. This formulation differs somewhat from the definition used in the introduction, which emphasizes the "reduction of barriers to economic exchange and factor mobility." For my purposes, reduction of barriers to exchange is a proximal cause of globalization, not an expression of it, per se.

I define international governance as the institutions and processes that regulate collective problem solving internationally. This definition is broadly consistent, in its focus on collective problem solving, its distinction between governance and government, and its inclusion of authoritative and nonauthoritative relations, with the one offered by Keohane and Nye (2000b, 12) and used in this volume (Kahler and Lake chapter 1).

Europeanization is a more difficult concept to define. Aside from obvious differences — the regional as opposed to global focus — I define

Europeanization and globalization in similar fashion. Europeanization involves increasing factor mobility, trade in goods and services, and movement of symbols and political practices on a regional scale. Changes in the share of intra-European exchange, compared to the world at large, reflect Europeanization also. To be sure, Europe is distinct in some ways, especially on the dependent-variable side (governance). The EU has institutions, decision-making procedures, and political practices that may not be duplicated in other places. I conceptualize these differences as ones of degree (of discretionary authority, institutional autonomy, rules to protect sovereignty) so as to preserve the possibility of comparison with other sites of international governance.

To the extent that the relationship between Europeanization and globalization is an empirical rather than definitional matter, we can ask how closely aligned they are in practice. Verdier and Breen attempted to distinguish between the effect of market integration, a global force, and political integration, a regional phenomenon. They found "no significant instances of political voluntarism [effect of political institutions] in the integration of factor markets" (2001, 258). In fact, corporatism declined more rapidly inside the EU than outside and there was little evidence that state-correcting policies took hold in the capital markets of the EU (2001, 259). On other measures, however — dealignment of the electorate and partisan loyalty — the EU's institutions did have an impact, lending some support to Europeanization as "globalization plus." Thus, while Europeanization and globalization are not replicas of each another, they are closely related processes, and the divergences between them can be examined by focusing on European political institutions.

I will proceed as follows. In the first section I will situate the EU within the context of broader debates about globalization, governance, and democratic control. Second, I will set forth the criteria used to assess democracy in the EU. Since democracy is a set of procedures as well as a relation between rulers and ruled, this is not a straightforward task. In the third section, I will analyze the EU as a system of democratic (or nondemocratic) governance, using the criteria alluded to above. Fourth, I will offer some conclusions.

EUROPE AND GLOBAL GOVERNANCE

Since the 1950s, Europe has progressively integrated in economic and political terms. The sixties saw completion of the free-trade area and customs union, while the eighties witnessed the liberalization of capital controls and restrictions on the movement of labor. By 1993, the EU had achieved substantial liberalization of trade in goods and services as well as factor markets. As part of the Treaty on European Union, a plan to integrate the currencies and monetary policies of the member states replaced the less demanding European Monetary System (EMS).

How is this transnational market governed? Many feel that states have lost control (Sassen, 1996) in the face of mobile capital. Because of the liquidity of transnational capital, its capacity to exit a country on very short notice, national policymakers are pressured to convince not only voting publics but also foreign investors (Cerny 1995; Strange 1996). Further, this loss of control may not be politically innocent. Mobile capital may be gaining relative to fixed factors, such as labor. While Garrett and Lange (1991) insist that there is still a substantial amount of policy discretion available to Left-oriented governments, and Mosley (2000) argues that international financial markets offer "room to move," one can also see a shrinking of the range of feasible public policies. It is difficult to interpret the convergence of preferences among the major states of the EC during the eighties in any other way (Cameron, 1998; Moravcsik 1991): Are we examining smaller and smaller political variations under more and more powerful microscopes?

One interpretation of the problems created by globalization is framed in terms of externalities.[1] This framework treats globalization as a process that contributes to an increased demand for governance—global, national, and subnational. In today's world, many externalities are not just external to transacting parties, but also external to the borders of different countries. If externalities are viewed dyadically, as having an origin and destination, then many exchanges that originate in country A have effects (uncompensated) on actors in country B. Even if governance were solely limited to identifying, managing, compensating, and controlling externalities, the demand created by increased interdependence would be great.

One model of governance is provided by the Westphalian state. The effectiveness of this model is based on a variable coincidence of territory, public authority, citizenship, and identity. The Westphalian model works best to the extent that (a) economic transactions can be sufficiently contained within territorial borders, (b) cross-border externalities can be readily identified and internalized, and (c) decentralized coordination among governments can manage the effects that are not corrected by private parties. That is, where transaction costs are high

---

[1] The language of external effects is not the only one available to analyze problems of interdependence and governance. The externality paradigm assumes a given definition of property rights and goes on to ask whether nonparties to the exchange are affected. But assume that the system of rules governing the movement of capital are changed so that capital moves more freely and sensitively from country to country. Even on the assumption that costs and benefits are fully internalized, the environment of domestic policymaking is likely to be substantially altered.

and the Coase theorem does not provide the solution, governments will be able to step in and solve the problem.

To a considerable degree, the Westphalian model is breached in Western Europe. Ratios of foreign trade to gross domestic product are extremely high, and an increasing share of the foreign sector is made up of other EU member states (Grieco 1997). Externalities, far from perfectly correlated with cross-border transactions, are doubtlessly high, since transactions have a high rate of "leakage" in all economies, even ones with well-developed systems of property rights and legal liabilities. In addition, externalities are not as objectively given as we might think. The internationalization of gender-equality policies in the EU has been partly reasoned as a defense against social dumping — an externality — (Caporaso 2000, 22–23; Hoskyns 1996), and compensation by the French government to a British citizen who was mugged while on vacation in Paris has been defended by the European Court of Justice (ECJ) as necessary to preserve free movement of services (tourism).

Further, the impacts of globalization go beyond externalities. The crises of the 1990s — in Brazil, Asia, Russia, and Mexico — involve macroeconomic policies and conditions in the broadest sense. There are problems of liquidity, debt, and exchange rates. Requirements for domestic policy (and structural) changes have been large and invasive, and not just in the less-developed world. In the United Kingdom, domestic welfare legislation (e.g. the Sex Discrimination Act of 1970) had to be redrafted in the face of constant pressure by the European Court of Justice (ECJ) and Commission (Caporaso and Jupille 2001). France has had to break up industries as a result of the Competition Directorate in Brussels. Italy has had to undertake painful reforms of its pension system. Several countries have had to undertake institutionally costly reorganizations of domestic banking structures so as to bring them more in line with the requirements of the EMU. France, Belgium, and Spain have all passed legislation to strengthen the independence of their banks, some even altering the banks' ministerial (hence political) status in order to bring them more closely into line with the Bundesbank (Elgie 1998, 1).

For a while, as Keohane and Nye (2000b) point out, the club model worked in a satisfactory way. Pressing problems confronted states, mass publics were not really aware in detail and across issue-areas, so a "permissive consensus" to manage the effects of globalization sufficed. To be sure, the smaller countries felt the press of globalization more acutely and voiced their concerns. Within Europe, Ireland, Spain, Portugal, and Denmark have had a lot to say about loss of economic sovereignty as well as structural policy. The club model works well when it is possible to draw together the elites from a limited number of countries, within a well-defined issue-area that does not sit within the fishbowl of world wide public attention.

But as Keohane and Nye (2000b) note, the very success of the club model to some extent undermines it. Successful management leads to increased interdependence as well as greater linkage across issue-areas. To take just one example, foreign direct investment is today increasingly tied to merger policy, competition policy and anticompetitive behavior, company law, and demands for more open and uniform accounting principles. In turn, these changes have led to increased pressure for higher levels of participation, accountability, and transparency. This brings us to the issue of democratic governance.

CRITERIA FOR ASSESSING GOVERNANCE

Discussions of democracy and the democratic deficit often proceed without explicit definitions and criteria of democracy. Yet democracy is not a self-evident concept, does not vary along a single continuum, and does not necessarily imply a homogenous set of operational indicators. The following have been offered as important components of democracy: government responsiveness to citizen preferences, representation, participation, openness, rights, legitimacy, accountability, political competition — especially party and electoral competition — and separation of powers. As has been mentioned, effective democracy does not imply that all good things go together. Tensions and dilemmas may be present in the democratic process, such as between participation and efficient problem solving or between independence (of government institutions) and accountability. It may be better to recognize these tensions as inherent parts of the concept, and to explore them empirically, rather than to rule them out as part of a "coherent" measurement strategy. Increased participation may increase subjective satisfaction (and legitimacy) but worsen effective problem solving in the long run. Openness (e.g., lobbying) may be a good thing but may result in the unequal access of privileged interests, thus resulting in welfare-reducing outcomes from the standpoint of the society as a whole. In addition, independent agencies, far removed from public opinion and direct political control, may lead to policies that are closer to the median voter than majoritarian arrangements.

In the remainder of this section, I will address two democratic criteria: accountability and rights. Accountability is a highly general characteristic of democratic governance that cuts across various other indicators of democracy; for example, elections, political competition, representation, judicial review, and legislative hearings could all be justified in the name of accountability. To hold government officials and leaders accountable for their actions, especially their positions on public policies, would seem fundamental to any notion of democracy. I choose also to examine the place of rights in democratic institutions precisely because rights are not logically entailed by the general notion of accountability. The idea of rights is somewhat separate and is in some ways a modification of majoritarian processes.

Accountability and Transparency

To be accountable means to be held responsible for a state of affairs: the way a department is run, a budget is spent, a soccer team performs, and a transnational system is governed. Accountability is a central criterion because it is the meeting place for numerous other yardsticks of democracy, among them transparency. A government can be secretive only at the cost of denying the information required to bring rulers to account. For preferences to reflect interests, people have to be informed. To be informed requires information, and not just the kind handed out by those who are being evaluated. In fact, evidence that government leaders can shape public opinion to view actions they have taken in a more favorable light (Maravall 1999; Page and Shapiro 1983) works against accountability in some ways, though not in all. If government leaders are the only ones who know the negotiating position of a foreign leader, where the nuclear waste is situated, or whether mad cow disease is a hoax or a real threat, citizens can't form the relevant preferences to exercise political control (Przeworski, Stokes, and Manin 1999, 11).

The accountability criterion immediately suggests the principal-agent perspective (McCubbins, Noll, and Weingast 1987). Democratic theory raises the issue of agency. Democracy is a system of governance in which there is a certain relation between rulers and ruled in which the former are agents of the latter. Dahl (1971, 1) notes that "a key characteristic of democracy is the continued responsiveness of the government to the preferences of its citizens." Along similar lines, Schmitter and Karl (1991, 76) argue that "modern political democracy is a system of governance in which rulers are held accountable for their actions in the public realm by citizens."[2] Actors and institutions do not come, however, with the labels "principal" and "agent" on their foreheads. These are role designations that can only be contextually defined and this difficulty is compounded at the transnational level where exact structural and functional equivalents of legislatures, courts, and executives do not exist.

---

[2] As cited by Przeworski, Stokes, and Manin (1999, 4).

Rights

It may seem awkward, even misdirected, to use rights as a criterion of transnational democracy. Rights adhere to citizenship, which in turn implies membership in a polis. Rights and responsibilities are badges of citizenship, "emblems of public understanding" (Shklar 1991) that seem recognizable only with an established political order. Can we think of rights at all outside of the state? Is it possible to imagine rights as part of a transnational market? Most transnational-governance arrangements are based on international treaties, compacts among states that do not create rights for individuals. The Treaty of Rome was no exception. It was an agreement among six sovereign states to secure certain ends, for the purpose of which they accepted certain constraints. Thus, individuals had, for all practical purposes, no standing under the Treaty of Rome. If a piece of national legislation infringed on a person, individuals did not have recourse to courts. Only institutions of the EEC or another member-state could bring proceedings (Mancini and Keeling 1994, 182). Simply put, individuals could not defend their rights under the Rome treaty.

GOVERNANCE IN THE EUROPEAN UNION

Accountability

In an age of mass politics, nearly all policy is made by elites. Democracy may be "for" the people but it is not generally "by" the people. In a democratic system, elites are authorized and accountable to the public and to other institutions. Democracy, in other words, is almost necessarily delegated democracy. We should expect this to be more rather than less true at the international level.

Policymaking by elites, limited and costly information in mass publics, and organizational difficulties involved in translating individual interests into coherent social demands have led many to the cynical conclusion that democracy is nearly impossible. If "the people" do not have information, how can they make reasoned choices about alternative political programs and leaders? This is the heart of the democratic dilemma identified by Lupia and McCubbins (1998, 12). This dilemma would seem to be even more sharply posed at the European level if Lupia and McCubbins are right that conflicting interests and asymmetrical information are the two biggest reasons for the gap between principals and agents.

Two complications must be mentioned before examining accountability in the EU. The first stems from the fact that the EU is a multi-level polity. There is a parliament, an executive or executives, a council, a court, and various advisory committees. There are interest groups, policy networks, experts, and so on. Many of the European-level institutions also exist at the national level. Thus, the same question often must be asked twice; first addressed to the European level and second to the relation between national and European level. For example, in asking about parliamentary control of executive actions, the analyst can ask about the control exercised by the European Parliament and by various national parliaments.

The second complication runs deeper. We do not know what kind of animal the EU is, nor is it obvious that what is emerging follows the structural template of familiar political forms. Many analysts assume that what is taking shape is a classic federation, but it is not easily situated on a continuum that points in this direction. Yet an answer to the question, "What is the EU an instance of?" would seem to be important when assessing accountability.

I will simplify the following discussion by assuming two basic political forms, that of Europe as an emerging parliamentary system (Dehousse 1998) and, alternatively, an emerging regulatory state (Majone 1999). In the former model, parliamentary control, oversight of the executive, and popular checks on the governing structures of the EU (including the EP) are central. In the latter, majoritarian mechanisms of control are less important. Instead, administrative oversight, standard-setting, making information available, and the coupling of targeting of goals with administrative discretion are more relevant criteria.

THE EU AS EMERGING PARLIAMENTARY DEMOCRACY

By probing the EU with the standards of parliamentary democracy, I enter a thicket that Keohane and Nye seem to discourage. As they rightly point out, the phrase "democratic deficit" rests on an implied domestic model (chapter 15). Without arguing that the EU is a full state, based on a distinctive demos, fitted with its own sinews of war and taxation structures, I argue that the evolving EU does display institutional features that are comparable to existing states. The legislative process in the EU involves interaction among the Council of Ministers, the European Commission, and the European Parliament. In addition, the heads of state and government meet twice per year in the European Council to provide overall political direction. Acting on the initiative of the European Commission, and in cooperation with the European Parliament, the Council of Ministers makes laws (regulations and directives) by unanimity and qualified majority vote (QMV). Members of the Council of Ministers are national government ministers, appointed by the chief of government.

Councils of Ministers and the European Commission are organized on a sectoral basis according to specialized subject matter and expertise. There are general directorates on agriculture, transport, energy, social affairs, competition, and so on. The Ministers of Foreign Affairs provide overall coordination in the General Affairs Council and are also responsible for overall direction of foreign policy. The rules of legislation vary with each sector but the two most commonly used voting rules are unanimity and QMV. The role of the EP has progressed from the simple right to be consulted by the Council on proposed legislation (Treaty of Rome), to the right to a second reading of legislation (cooperation, Single European Act), and finally to the right to co-decision (Treaty of European Union [TEU]).

The broad sectoral organization of the Council and Commission generates the first criticism of the lawmaking process. The departmentalization of Community business and the taking of decisions sector by sector work against the creation of broad coalitions that put forth comprehensive agendas. Focusing attention on sectoral policy experts and organized constituencies serves to minimize interest among electorates and political parties. The Commission's various general directorates act as magnets for lobbyists and arguably favor narrow concentrated interests — different in degree but not in kind from the pattern of lobbying at the national level. Individual members of the Council of Ministers can be removed through national elections and changes of cabinet posts but there is no mechanism for removal of an entire cabinet — in short, no overall ministerial responsibility.

If we conceive of the Commission as executive, subject to accountability by the Council of Ministers acting as the upper house of a legislature, one reading suggests that the Commission has a great deal of autonomy.[3] Ironically, many defenders of the process of European integration are quite enthusiastic about Commission autonomy, seeing it as necessary to get beyond the gridlock generated by the veto in the Council of Ministers. But within the context of an assessment of the democratic nature of EU institutions, such autonomy becomes more problematic. This autonomy becomes understandable when one recalls that one hat worn by the Commission involves playing a neutral (or nonpolitical) administrative role. Here individual commissioners are closer to national civil servants than to elected politicians. Indeed, commissioners are appointed by the chief executives of the member states, along with

[3] The Commission has several roles, but among the most important are the power to initiate legislation and to implement the laws of the EU. The Commission is entrusted with being guardian of the treaty and is given power to investigate compliance and bring infringement proceedings against recalcitrant member-states.

approval of the EP. They have no political mandate and "they are solemnly sworn to an oath of independence; and they do not take their decisions in the shadow of electoral retribution" (Lord 1998, 82).

In addition, the Commission does most of its work in small committees, and delegates a great number of specialized tasks to even smaller committees composed of experts, national administrators, and Commission members (the comitology procedure). This serves to make the process by which the Commission drafts legislation and amendments less visible, and to mix its activities with networks that cross Council and Commission lines. While this mixing of structures and functions is praised by "new governance theorists" as creating task-oriented networks based on expertise and problem-solving ability, it also makes it more difficult to trace relations through a line of command. As the organizational hierarchy flattens, it becomes more difficult to assess accountability.

Let us turn to the transparency issue. How visible are the proceedings and even conclusions of the legislative process? Until recently, Council proceedings have been quite secret, taking place *in camera*, with little information provided on how decisions were reached. When Shirley Williams first launched her critique of the democratic deficit, the lack of transparency in Council proceedings was a big part of it (1991, 159). Williams argued that while both houses of the British Parliament have committees to examine EU legislation, debates rarely attract much attention since ministers will rarely commit themselves before Council meetings. Commission proposals are themselves not within the jurisdiction of the British Parliament, and hence are not debated there. Since the Council's meetings are closed sessions, it is very difficult to monitor, let alone control, the Community's legislative process.

To a certain extent, the secrecy of the Council is understandable. The Council's position lies uncertainly between intergovernmental diplomacy and domestic policymaking. Whether the EU is better described as a treaty-based, intergovernmental arrangement involving intense coordination and interdependence, or a political arrangement where the separate parts (member states) make policy directly effective on individuals, is difficult to say. Treaties are traditionally treated as horizontal compacts among states rather than constitutions; yet most everyday policymaking comes closer to the polity model. In any case, when the Council acts more in its diplomatic capacity, secrecy seems more appropriate. We expect our diplomats to guard information that may advantage a particular national constituency. While Williams's critique may have been valid in the early nineties, since then procedures have changed in a direction more favorable to transparency and democratic accountability.

Scholars of European integration have recently borrowed from the American-politics literature on delegation of authority. As Simon Hix (1999b, 48) argues, the administrative and legislative tasks of the European Commission and Council of Ministers are regularly monitored by the EP, much as the U.S. Congress monitors activities of administrative agencies in the United States. The rotating president of the Council of Ministers presents the aims and agenda of this minister for the upcoming six months. Ministers often appear not only before their own parliaments but also in front of the EP and its committees. It is also the case that heads of EU agencies, modeled after independent regulatory commissions in the United States, appear before these committees on a regular basis (Hix 1999b, 48).

In addition, the Commission has made progress in the direction of greater transparency. In 1994 the Commission presented a "transparency package." This involved several things. First, the work program of the Commission would henceforth be published in October instead of January, allowing more time for debate of the initiatives by the Council and EP before the adoption of the legislation in January (Hix 1999b, 49). In addition, the Commission was to take greater care to circulate its ideas early, and widely, so that broad and meaningful discussion could take place when the issues were still malleable: thus, the emphasis on greater use of "Green Papers" and "White Papers" as vehicles of making legislative initiatives available to a wider constituency (Hix 1999b, 49).

Another way of viewing the accountability relationship is to ask how well the interests of member states are preserved. The existence of the veto provides a procedural guarantee of the Pareto principle, that no change in the status quo will take place that leads to a deterioration in the position of any member. Even when votes are taken by qualified majority, members make an effort to reach consensus. We can use the voting records of the Council of Ministers to examine how frequently positions of national ministers are overridden by majorities of other ministers. Data on Council votes are available for December 1993–December 1994. According to information reported by Hix (1999b, 73), there were 261 votes taken by the Council during this period. Of these 261, 197 were by unanimity (no vetoes or abstentions), 28 were made with abstentions (but no vetoes), and 36 votes were taken with one or more countries in opposition. This breakdown suggests a strong emphasis on consensus, since, even when voting is technically by QMV, there is an urge not to override the interests of opposing states(Hix 1999b, 73).

Meetings of the sectoral Councils provide a second piece of indirect evidence in favor of preservation of national positions. Since the Councils meet when decisions cannot easily be made routinely in the Committee of Permanent Representatives (COREPER, the staff and secretariat of the Council of Ministers), we can take the frequency of Council meetings as an indicator of conflict in that area. We thus expect to see more meetings in those areas where there is the greatest conflict and where these conflicts cannot be resolved through delegation to administrative committees. Again, relying on data provided by Hix (1999b, 67), we can see that the bulk of the meetings of the Council of Ministers were taken up by the General Affairs Council (Foreign Ministers), Agriculture, and EcoFin (Economics and Finance Ministers). Agriculture is one of the few areas of redistributive politics in the EU, Foreign Affairs is legendary for being both conflictual and a preserve of nation-states, and the EcoFin Councils deal with the tough questions of monetary politics. If it is true that principals delegate less (or rein in more tightly) when important issues are at stake, this is the pattern we expect to see.

To underline the above point about ministerial responsibility, it is important to observe the logic of Council decision making. Members of the Councils are national ministers who have full-time jobs in their own countries. They do not sit in Brussels on a daily basis. How, then, do they guard the interests of their national constituencies and prevent capture of the decision-making process by EU experts? How, indeed, do they manage to deal with the load of work required by governance of two interrelated political systems?

Much of the work of the Council is completed by the Committee of Permanent Representatives, an ongoing body of experts made up of national delegations in Brussels. The COREPER meets at least once a week at the levels of ambassadors COREPER and deputies COREPER and continually again as working groups. On many issues the COREPER is able to come to full agreement. These matters become "A points" and are generally adopted by the Council at the beginning of their sessions. While the decisions taken are sometimes important, their character, as Noel and Etienne put it, "is more technical than political" (1969, 44). Essentially this same procedure is followed by the Special Committee on Agriculture, to which the Council refers Commission proposals on agriculture. According to estimates (Hayes-Renshaw and Wallace 1995, 562), approximately 70 percent of the business of the Councils is decided by working groups and deputies in COREPER I. The higher level body (COREPER II) then tackles more controversial issues (another 10–15 percent) that are handed up to the Ministers as "A points" (meaning they have been decided by the COREPER but need ministerial approval). Perhaps only 10–15 percent of the overall work is left for the Council of Ministers to deal with themselves.

Given the absence of strong central authority, as well as a large bureaucracy, the EU is faced with a problem of overload. The "A" procedure described here was instituted in 1962 as a way to manage this overload and to prune the number of items that the Councils had to eventually tackle. Another crucial function, however, was to identify what was truly important. This filtering process, by which routine issues are decided by expert groups with the greatest autonomy, leaving a smaller subset of items to be dealt with by political actors who are more accountable, fits with what we expect from a principal-agent perspective. Hard-wired into the organizational design relating working groups, COREPER, and Council of Ministers is a system of fire alarms rather than police patrols (McCubbins and Schwartz 1984). The procedures are designed to detect levels of controversy in the work of the Council and to separate what is routine from what is politically charged.

Accountability of ministers to national leaders is important but so is accountability of the Council of Ministers and European Commission to parliaments, both national and EU parliaments. It is not surprising that the earliest charges of a democratic deficit in the EU centered on the weak role of the European Parliament and national parliaments. Indeed, when Williams launched her attack on the nature of the EU's institutions, it was based on the expanding power of the Council of Ministers (national executives acting as a supranational legislature) synchronized with the declining power of national parliaments and weak role of the EP (Williams 1991, 155). Williams concluded that "the loss of accountability to national parliaments has not been compensated [for] by increased accountability to the European Parliament" (1991, 155).

How accurate is this picture of weak accountability to parliaments? This question has two parts. First, what role does the European Parliament (EP) play? Second, what role do national parliaments play?

The EP was not set up as a strong institution, or one designed to engage public opinion and attract legitimacy. Both Gaullist and Monnet visions of Europe discouraged the construction of influential popular assemblies as part of the institutional design of the EEC, for different reasons. Members of the EP were not directly elected, something that did not change until 1979. Further, the EP was given only the power to consult in the legislative process, a power that itself was not always fully respected until the European Court of Justice (ECJ) established it in the Roquette Freres case (1979).[4] Further, legislative power was con-

---

[4] The case was *Roquette Freres v. Council* (1979, reported 1980), ECR, 3333. The Council of Ministers adopted a regulation fixing production quotas for isoglucose without giving the EP adequate time to respond to its proposal. A dissatisfied French company, Roquette Freres, challenged the regulation before the ECJ, and used as one of its argu-

centrated (indeed monopolized) in the hands of national executives operating as a supranational legislature through the Council of Ministers. The same executives who appoint the ministers sitting on the Councils also hold the power to appoint members of the ECJ and the executive (the European Commission). Overall, it could not be denied that power was heavily concentrated in the executive branch when the EEC came into existence.

One obvious way to strengthen the EP would be to further increase its legislative powers and responsibilities. The institutional imbalance among the European Parliament, Council, and Commission was noted earlier. The Commission enjoys the right of initiative as well as its role as "guardian of the treaty" while the Council of Ministers has the final word with regard to most legislation. Prior to the Single European Act (SEA), the EP found itself in an institutional no-man's land. For the passage of most legislation, the cliché according to which "the Commission proposes and the Council disposes" was largely accurate, and the European Parliament usually had only opinion-giving power. With the entry into force of the SEA in 1987, of the Maastricht treaty in 1993, and the Amsterdam treaty in 1999, however, the modest powers of the European Parliament have increased tremendously.

The SEA took the first steps by introducing two new procedures for the adoption of legislation. The "assent procedure" applies to a narrow range of issues (essentially some areas of external relations). The SEA also created a "cooperation procedure" for legislation needed to complete the internal market. While the early stages of this procedure resemble the traditional legislative procedure (Commission proposal, nonbinding EP opinion, Council decision), in later stages the EP gains the right to propose amendments that stand a good chance of gaining adoption by the Council. In effect, if the Commission agrees with the EP amendments, it becomes easier for the Council to adopt those amendments (because adoption requires only a qualified majority agreement) than it is to change or reject them (both of which require unanimity). The cooperation procedure, which was extended to new areas in the 1993 Maastricht treaty but which was largely abolished (in favor of co-decision) at Amsterdam, gave the Parliament substantial "conditional agenda-setting power" (Tsebelis 1994) and enabled it for the first time to exert meaningful legislative influence.

The 1993 Maastricht treaty extended the assent and cooperation procedures and, most importantly, created a "co-decision procedure" that bestowed additional powers on the EP. What this procedure entails, es-

---

ments the fact that the Council had failed to obtain an opinion of the EP (see Mancini and Keeling 1994, 178).

sentially, is a limited form of joint legislative power with the Council of Ministers. This power is limited by domain to areas such as the internal market, free movement of persons, rights of establishment, and education, culture, and public health. In effect, if the EP and the Council of Ministers cannot agree on a policy, a conciliation committee is convened that tries to iron out their differences. At the end of the procedure, the EP can veto any policies that the Council might try to impose on it. Skeptics suggested that co-decision actually exacerbated the EU's democratic deficit because it replaced the EP's highly effective "conditional agenda-setting power" under cooperation with an absolute veto that it would almost never wish to use (Tsebelis and Garrett 1997). Further analysis has belied this expectation (Tsebelis and Kreppel 1998), and the 1999 Amsterdam treaty has continued the trend toward increasing EP power by simplifying the procedure and by more than doubling the number of treaty articles that employ it (Caporaso 2000, 65–66).

The thesis of parliamentary decline extends to the national level. Defenders of the EU's institutions often point to the fact that critics of the EU adopt as a reference point a heavily idealized image of the powers of national parliaments. These critics point out that national parliaments are also in decline and they are not the heroic bastions of deliberative and representative democracy often assumed by EU analysts (Raunio and Hix 2001, 148–49).

Recent research suggests that the role of national parliaments is not as weak as imagined, nor is the relationship between the pace and depth of European integration and the strength of national parliaments necessarily negative. The first part of the salvage operation is to question and modify the divided-government view of the relation between executives and parliaments. The divided-government view sees the relationship between executive and legislatures as basically conflictual (Martin 2000, 4). As Martin argues, the relationship between parliaments and executives can be modeled in a different way: as a game in which both parties can exploit large mutual gains. Often, one branch can only succeed with the help of the other. Martin argues that this cooperative arrangement is important when the implementation of results of international negotiations is at issue (2000, 166).

A second move in this reconceptualization of executive-legislative relations involves moving away from the question of "how much influence parliaments wield" in some absolute sense toward identifying the variables on which such influence depends. Once the appropriate variables have been identified and the relations specified within a comprehensive model, we can ask which causal pathways are most important, and under what conditions.

To motivate this reconceptualization, it is useful to place the discussion within the context of two different models: abdication versus delegation (Martin 2000, 148). The abdication model asserts that parliaments have basically relinquished their policymaking authority to governments (executives), leaving them unable to influence policy. One weakness of this model lies not in its empirical accuracy or inaccuracy, but more in the nature of the claim itself. It is a straightforward descriptive assertion that is stated in an unconditional way. Its truth or falsity lies in our assessment of a set of facts, not in the empirical evaluation of a causal structure. It is possible that parliaments were passive during the eighties and activist during the nineties. We then must conclude that the abdication model is accurate for the former period but not for the latter. By specifying the conditions under which we are likely to see parliamentary activism, we might derive a general model that can produce both outcomes as special cases.

As Martin argues, the weakness of the abdication model is that it treats a host of actors as either exogenous or in systematic secular decline (e.g., party discipline, strength of majority party, capacity for oversight). By contrast, delegation models "predict systematic variation in the institutional structures that allow parliaments to exercise influence over government actions" (2000, 149). Several hypotheses suggest themselves.

First, as the stakes increase (i.e., as the importance of the negotiations increases), so will the concern and oversight activity of national parliaments. Second, as conflict between the executive and legislature goes up, so will the incentives for oversight and control increase. Third, as the margin of political control of the dominant party decreases, parliaments will be less inclined to make broad delegations of authority to supranational institutions. Fourth, as international institutions move from unanimous voting rules to majority voting — QMV for the EU — we are likely to see heightened concern about legitimacy of these institutions, and along with this, greater demand for parliamentary involvement.

The delegation model fits the broad differences between the eighties and nineties — weaker national parliaments during the eighties and stronger oversight and control during the nineties. The Single European Act spanned the latter part of the eighties and the early part of the nineties. Its major objectives were to perfect and complete the internal market (for factors as well as goods and services). The TEU initiated major institutional reforms such as the three-pillar architecture, expanded the competencies of the EU, and established minimum citizenship rights. These innovations, as well as the important changes in the area of monetary policy, altered the "permissive-consensus" environment within which regional integration took place and increased the incentives for parliamentary control. During the nineties, all members of the EU set up committees specializing in EU affairs. These committees appeared to be strongest in those countries with narrow majorities or in some cases (e.g., Denmark), minority governments (Martin 2000, 160). In short, the changes in parliamentary oversight follow quite well the predictions of the delegation model.

THE EU AS REGULATORY STATE

Efforts to categorize the EU as a political system generally move across a continuum ranging from decentralized state system to federal union. The special cases of anarchy, regimes, and regional government all take up different positions on the same continuum. Analysts differ on where to locate the EU but they usually share the presumption that the gap between the EU's observed position on the continuum and the federal location is due to the EU's youthful state. In short, the EU is a primitive political system that will develop as a full political entity, given a sufficient amount of time.

But what if the EU lies on a different continuum? Suppose its developmental DNA contains different instructions. A casual look at the EU tells us that Tilly's sinews of war are absent, as is Weber's central and continuous administrative staff with lines of authority extending throughout a well-marked territory. In addition, the EU has weak extractive capabilities. Its tax powers are weak and are constitutionally limited to less than 2 percent of the combined GDPs of the member states. In the area of citizen rights, the normal Marshallian sequence of political rights, participation rights, and socioeconomic rights appears to be reversed, with economic rights coming first and maybe last, too (Marshall 1973). Yet, despite these limitations, the EU is generally recognized as an important actor.

One answer to this paradox lies in conceiving of the EU not as a full-fledged Westphalian state, but rather as an international regulatory state (Caporaso 1996).[5] A regulatory state is (in this case) essentially an international state (or polity if you prefer) specializing in the control and management of international externalities. Because this state does not engage substantially in the redistributive, stabilization, and symbolic functions of government, and because it relies on the administrative structures of member states to carry out policies, it can get by with a small revenue base.[6] In this sense, the tax limit on the EU's expenditures is a misleading indicator of its real strength.

The EU as a regulatory state rests on both a supply-side and demand-

---

[5] There is a paradox in the sense that the EU has limited extractive capacity but well-developed lawmaking and regulatory capabilities.

[6] The stabilization functions of the EU have increased substantially with the establishment of the European Monetary Union.

side analysis (Majone 1992, 1993, 1994, 1999). Briefly, the supply side rests on the notion that the Commission is a bureaucracy with limited powers that faces an environment in which the member states carefully guard most important areas: security politics, the welfare state, and most redistributive programs. Rather than compete with the member states to become a rival center for what states already provide, the Commission specializes in what it is permitted to do: the elaboration of regulatory structures to manage distinctively international problems.

The demand side is also important. What motivates international regulatory policy? Market transactions create externalities that often cannot be managed by countries acting alone through national regulations. When national attempts fail, we can speak of national regulatory failure. The conditions under which this is likely to happen include lack of information (or asymmetric information), problems of credibility, and the existence of incentives for strategic use of regulations (Majone 1994). Information problems arise when regulators do not have adequate knowledge of the behavior of those whom they are attempting to regulate, especially across borders. Credibility problems exist when, because of opportunism, there is the possibility that agreements among countries will not be enforced, or enforced in a lax manner. Strategic use of regulatory policy — from laws for brewing German beer, to making pasta only from durum wheat, to setting nationally convenient standards in health and safety — are not only numerous but have actually been attempted. If regulating faithfully in compliance with national standards and national regulatory bodies disadvantages home-country firms, an international regulatory body is called for.

If the EU is seen as a regulatory rather than a parliamentary state, this has implications for the assessment of democracy (Dehousse 1998). Many of the regulated areas are complex and do not lend themselves to ex ante legislation. Instead, a logic of delegation is implied in which specialized agencies are granted broad mandates to make and implement rules.

Delegation of course implies independence, so as to avoid political pressure and possibly capture. Here is where the democratic concerns emerge. On the one hand, independence is necessary for agencies to be credible. If the Competition Directorate of the Commission were strongly politicized, so as to make policy outcomes the resultant of group pressures, cartel policy would not be socially optimal. On the other hand, removal of agencies' work from direct political control runs another type of risk, namely that agencies will become fiefs of their own not responsive to any principal, or develop a cozy relationship with those whom they are to regulate.

Reconciling independence with accountability is a major task for regulation theorists but the mechanisms on which they rely are somewhat different from the traditional methods of legislative and political oversight. Among the methods suggested are clear statutory objectives, judicial review, transparency, budgetary discipline, and monitoring by interest groups. Providing clear standards is important but not enough by itself. The actual operation of specialized agencies is often opaque, even if objectives are spelled out. Thus, publication of documents and access to records are important mechanisms for controlling the activities of the regulatory state. In this regard, it is interesting that the Treaty of Amsterdam (1999) introduces a number of innovations. It establishes in clear terms the right of citizen access to documents of the EP, the Council, and the Commission. Since much of the work of the Council and Commission is done in specialized committees (comitology), information related to activities of regulatory bodies becomes available in principle. Of course, rights of access are only effective if they work on the ground. In any case, in the post-Amsterdam period, public access has become the rule, and secrecy and confidentiality are to be interpreted narrowly (Dehousse 1998, 19).

As the EU develops, it becomes clearer that it contains elements of both the parliamentary and regulatory templates. The struggle for democratic accountability will continue along the several paths suggested by parliamentary democracy and the regulatory state. The Amsterdam treaty extends co-decision (a parliamentary mechanism) at the same time that it develops new transparency procedures. While both sets of controls may be judged weaker than desired, the movement is clearly in the direction of more rigorous accountability.

Rights

Few would deny that the existence of rights is important for the working of a democracy. What many are skeptical of is the relevance of rights for international governance. For rights to be meaningful, some form of state must exist. Arguments about what qualifies as a state are not likely to get us far but what can be more readily agreed upon is that a structure of political authority must ensure such rights. But a stable authority structure, partly insulated from the changing powers and interests of states, is exactly what the international system most lacks.

My focus on the extension of rights represents one aspect of democratic development. Rights are important in any democracy, though in some (the United States, Germany) they are formalized and entrenched while in others (the United Kingdom) they are closely associated with parliamentary legislation (hence less entrenched). Rights provide a layer of protection against arbitrary government interference and a buffer against movements of public opinion. Rights may identify the proper kinds of participation in markets and the state. They may be generous and entrenched, or thin and nonentrenched. The thesis that rights are narrowly attached to market-creation and perfection is the "thin citizenship" view (Caporaso 2002). The alternative, that rights are robust and have breadth beyond what would be required to oil market exchanges, implies "thick citizenship."

The Rome treaty, however, did not provide for individual rights. Individuals had no status under EU law, could not sue a member state, an EU institution, or a private body in light of EU law. Thus, before the Rome treaty and the European Court of Justice could play a meaningful role in the lives of ordinary citizens, indeed before the idea of citizen rights could have much meaning at all, the ECJ had to overcome two rather large obstacles. The first obstacle was that citizens of member states had no legal standing. The basic documents of the EU, the legal texts that the ECJ was to interpret, were international treaties, not constitutions outlining a series of basic rights and obligations for people. The Rome treaty was a classic compact among states, a legal agreement entered into by sovereign powers to secure certain ends, and for the purpose of which states accepted certain constraints. The "Community" of which the Rome treaty spoke was a horizontal community of states, not of individuals (Mancini and Keeling 1994, 183).

The second obstacle had to do with the relationship between domestic and EU law. In the event that domestic and EU law conflicted, the question arose as to which legal order would be superior? While this question has no simple answer, in parliamentary systems Acts of Parliament are supreme. The metanorm that the more recent rule applies can work to the favor of domestic parliaments in that the force of treaty law can be overturned by an Act of Parliament. So, in parliamentary systems, domestic law trumps international law if it is more recent.

The process by which the ECJ altered this compact among states is today referred to as "constitutionalization" (Stone Sweet 1995, 1). Constitutionalization describes a process by which an international treaty becomes relevant for individuals within those states. In more elaborate terms, it "refers to the process by which the EC treaties have evolved from a set of legal arrangements binding upon sovereign states into a vertically integrated regime conferring judicially enforceable rights and obligations on all legal persons and entities, public and private, within EC territory" (Stone Sweet and Caporaso 1998, 102). If this process of constitutionalization accurately describes what has taken place, the EC has been transformed from a traditional international organization into "a multi-tiered system of governance founded on higher law constitutionalism" (Stone Sweet and Caporaso 1998, 102).

How did this process of constitutionalization take place? Simplifying greatly, the Court of Justice progressively made the treaties relevant to individuals, firms, and other private actors. The historic case came in 1963. In *Van Gend en Loos*, the ECJ established the doctrine of direct effect. That is to say, the ECJ asserted that provisions of the Rome treaty created rights and responsibilities for individuals even without supplementary actions by national institutions to translate treaty doctrine into domestic law. Before the *Van Gend* case, it was possible for member states to sue one another. But individuals had no legal standing. They could not sue other individuals for breaches of European Community law, or sue their employer, or bring legal proceedings against a public authority in their home country. It is precisely this gap that the Van Gend case addressed. The ECJ propounded a radical doctrine, broke down a standing partition between international and domestic law, and created a mechanism by which individuals could claim judicial remedies before international courts.

Important as the doctrine of direct effect was, it could not very well work by itself in the face of contrary domestic law. It is not surprising that in the year following the direct-effect doctrine, the Court of Justice grasped the nettle and confronted the issue of the relationship between municipal and international law. In *Costa v. E.N.E.L.*, the Italian courts first heard the case in which an Italian law of parliament, passed after the Rome treaty, was used by the Italian Constitutional Court to over-rule provisions of the Rome treaty. The case then was appealed under the Article 177 procedure, and the ECJ, while supporting the ruling of the Italian Constitutional Court, cited offhandedly that European law constituted a separate legal order that was supreme over national law. This has become known as the "supremacy doctrine."

It is difficult to exaggerate the importance of direct effect and supremacy. Indeed, they make up what many now think of as the constitutional pillars of the EU system. In announcing direct effect, the ECJ provided individuals with legal standing under an international treaty, and by so doing, it considerably closed the gap between treaty law and municipal law. A transnational legal space was created within which individuals could seek redress for complaints before domestic courts relying on European Community law. One area in which direct effect took root was gender equality. It is not the only area (free movement of individuals, of goods and services, nondiscrimination are others) where progress has been made, but it provides one good illustration of the basic principle at work.

EQUAL PAY FOR EQUAL WORK, ARTICLE 119

Article 119 of the Treaty of Rome states that each member state shall ensure and maintain "the application of the principle that men and women should receive equal pay for equal work," going on to define pay as "the ordinary basic or minimum wage or salary and any other consideration, whether in cash or in kind, which the worker receives, directly or indirectly, in respect of his employment from his employer." The article was based on, but narrower than, earlier International Labor Organization (ILO) standards calling for equal pay for work of "equal value." Its narrowness and the relatively tenuous foundations of EU law in the late 1950s made it difficult to imagine how this provision would have practical effect.

The absence of aggressive testing of the equal-pay principle throughout the sixties is not surprising (Hoskyns 1996, 60–68) given the lack of direct effect until 1963. Even then, it was far from clear which provisions would have direct effect. By the mid-sixties, however, the legal basis for testing Article 119 was in place. In 1968, a Belgian woman, Gabrielle Defrenne, initiated legal proceedings in domestic courts against Sabena Airlines, which wrote into their contracts that female airline stewardesses must retire at age forty, while male stewards were required to retire at age fifty-five.

Having reached the age of forty, Ms. Defrenne, a Belgian national and airline stewardess for Sabena Airlines, was asked (i.e., told) to take another job with Sabena or be "let go" (fired). After working through the national judicial system unsuccessfully, Ms. Defrenne brought her case to the European Court of Justice. The ECJ ruled in Defrenne's favor, pointing out that a male steward in the same position was not required to switch jobs. It went on to say that Article 119 imposed a duty on states to ensure application of the equal-pay principle and that, given the precise nature of that obligation, domestic courts could use the provision to enforce individual rights. While the particulars of the case were important enough, the ECJ's language (rights, duties, obligations, autonomous legal order) is evocative of fundamental rights.

The Defrenne case was the start of a long line of equal-pay cases. An institutional thickening of rules took place in which the ECJ interpreted the treaty, as well as directives, expansively, despite the opposition of some member states. In doing so, it extended the logic of equal pay to areas that might not have been included under the original meaning of the term. The ECJ's jurisprudence took two routes. First, the ECJ expanded the substantive meaning of "pay." Second, it gradually broadened the idea of discrimination to include indirect as well as direct forms.

To summarize radically, the ECJ extended the "equal pay" provisions of Article 119 to include indirect discrimination, pensions, company perquisites, vacations, and equal work for equal value. On the procedural level, the ECJ allowed for more generous standards regarding use of comparators (a male standard) and shifted the burden of proof in some cases in favor of female claimants. The European standard is often higher than the national standard, providing an additional layer of protection against labor-market inequality. In such cases, domestic institutions must revise their laws to bring them into line with the European yardstick.

Few would argue with the proposition that the ECJ has pioneered a gender-equality jurisprudence. But in what sense does this add up to citizenship rights? First, the gender-equality provisions of the EU have been brought under the highest interpretation of rule of law at the European level. A transnational space has been carved out at the transnational and intergovernmental level, in which individuals can press their claims for certain rights. While there are certainly other cases where individuals have been given status in legal forums beyond the nation-state, the regular taken-for-granted way in which women and domestic courts use the ECJ as a legal forum suggests that the institutionalization of rights has proceeded quite far.

A second point relating to the institutionalization of rights is that the rights established by the ECJ do not stand on their own, but rather are entangled with legislation enacted by the Council of Ministers, an institution with indirect albeit strong links to popular national constituencies. Between 1975 and 1979 three major pieces of legislation were passed, clarifying, implementing, and broadening the goals set out in Article 119 (Cichowski 2000, 11). These were the Equal Pay Directive (1975), the Equal Treatment Directive (1976), and the Equal Treatment in Social Security Directive (1979). While subsequent directives were passed, most of the Article 177 litigation in the area of gender equality is based on Article 119 and these three directives. Indeed, Cichowski reports that 98 percent of the 177 cases between 1970 and 1998 were invoked using rules supplied by one of these four provisions (Cichowski 2000, 14).

I have argued that rights require something more than a policy resulting from a momentary (or even durable) alignment of preferences. In Shepsle's terms (1989), the entrenchment of rights comes closer to a structure-induced equilibrium than a preference-induced equilibrium. That is, when rights are guaranteed, the equilibrium is stable — if it is stable at all — because of the way the rules are arranged. In a sense, the very notion of citizenship rights requires some institutional insulation between rights and popular preferences. If national parliaments could pass laws to overturn rights, we would not think of them as secure. But national parliaments are not as free to do this as they would be in the absence of the judicial scrutiny associated with European law. On the contrary, national legislation, such as the British Sex Discrimination Act, is continually under pressure to conform to the standards of EU law.

My third and final point relating to the deep institutionalization of rights has to do with path dependence and judicialization. (Stone Sweet and McCown 2000) The path-dependence literature tells us that institutions can and often do create self-reinforcing processes that make reversals costly, and increasingly so the longer the system operates. We can think of the entrenchment of rights as follows: If we arrange preferences, policies, and rights on a continuum, surely preferences would be easiest to change, extant policies next, and rights would be the most resistant. By integrating rights into a pattern of precedents, it becomes more difficult to erode one right without calling many others into question. If justices take consistency seriously, it follows that the corpus of judicial precedent — the judicial *acquis* — will provide an additional constraint on how they make decisions. Equal pay and equal treatment are now thickly institutionalized in a pattern of precedents covering pay, vacation allowance, pregnancy, maternity, indirect discrimination, bonuses, and social security. In addition, ECJ cases in these areas sit on an overall judicial architecture provided by the *Van Gend* and *Costa* cases. While it is not impossible to erode rights at the margins, it is difficult to unravel a pattern of rights that is entrenched not only by the doctrine of the ECJ, but also by a powerful structure of state-society relations. In the United Kingdom, feminist groups, legal experts, and public bodies such as the Equal Opportunities Commission (EOC), form a state-society complex that constantly exerts pressure on the private and public bodies suspected of discrimination.

Conclusion

Globalization has often been treated primarily as an economic phenomenon. As globalization deepens, it creates problems that generate demand for political control. Hence international governance structures have emerged to coordinate separate actions of states. Sometimes these governance structures have become institutionalized on a global basis, sometimes regionally. As they become institutionalized, it is natural to inquire about their democratic nature (Curtin 1997).

The EU is one case of a thickly institutionalized regional organization operating within an overall global environment. Since ongoing institutionalized governance has advanced so far in the EU, it allows us to ask questions that would be more difficult to investigate in other contexts. In this sense I attempt to make methodological virtue out of necessity, even vice, taking an institution that many consider as sui generis, and hence not good material for comparison, as the leading edge of the globalization-and-governance movement. The rationale for studying the EU is not that it is typical, but rather that it embodies tendencies toward which other organizations are moving. Questions about uniqueness and generality do not have factual answers. At some level of abstraction, the EU is unique. Its observed institutional structure does not have a counterpart in any other international organization of which I know. Yet it differs from other collections of state and nonstate actors in the degree of economic integration, the voting rules of its decision-making bodies, and the extent to which authority has been delegated to its institutions. These are surely comparable properties.

I have posed some questions about the democratic (or nondemocratic) nature of the EU in this chapter, applying two standards of democracy — accountability of EU institutions and the emergence of rights. With regard to the accountability criterion, conceiving of the EU as an emerging parliamentary democracy versus a regulatory state shaped subsidiary standards for the evaluation. Scholars disagree vigorously about what the EU is becoming, what emergent political form it represents. Those who see the EU as a system of delegated powers to solve international problems will not find the model of EU parliamentary democracy convincing. The chains of delegation starting at the national level, including national parliaments, will suffice. The international regulatory state may provide a more convincing model. Others see the struggle to democratize the EU through national controls taking place simultaneously with the emergence of fledgling democratic institutions at the European level. However inefficient, the struggle to understand the nature of the beast that is the EU will proceed simultaneously with our efforts to democratize it.

Chapter 15

REDEFINING ACCOUNTABILITY
FOR GLOBAL GOVERNANCE

ROBERT O. KEOHANE AND JOSEPH S. NYE, JR.

GLOBAL INSTITUTIONS are under challenge.[1] One of their problems is a lack of legitimacy. Legitimacy implies that those subject to a governance process accept it as properly authoritative. The legitimacy of institutions can rest on tradition, symbols, or effectiveness. In democratic societies, legitimacy can also rest on procedures that are regarded as sufficiently fair and participatory.

International institutions have little prospect of benefiting from symbolic, affective, or traditional legitimacy. Their defenders tend to justify them in terms of their apparent efficacy: the essential role they play in promoting international cooperation and providing global public goods. Such a justification is important, but rarely sufficient in a democratic era. In today's world, there is also a widespread demand for accountability. For international institutions to be legitimate, the challenge of accountability must be confronted. This chapter explores issues of accountability in global governance.

Issues of accountability have frequently been framed in terms of the so-called democratic deficit afflicting global governance. The leading democratic political theorist of our era, Robert A. Dahl, has recently declared (1999, 32) that "international organizations are not and are not likely to be democratic." In this view, chains of delegation are too long, there is too much secrecy, and much international organizational activity does not take place even in the shadow of elections. It has been argued, furthermore, that democracy requires a demos — in Joseph Weiler's words, "a polity with members by whom and for whom democratic discourse with its many variants takes place" (1999, 337). Observing

[1] The authors are grateful, for comments on previous versions of this paper, to Craig Borowiak, Jessica Einhorn, Barbara Koremenos, Lisa Martin, Dan Nielson, and Dani Rodrik, as well as to the editors, other participants at the La Jolla conference, 23–24 March 2001, and members of the Visions of Governance Project at the John F. Kennedy School of Government, Harvard University. We have also benefited from conversations on this topic with Francesca Bignami, Ruth Grant, and David Soskice. We are particularly indebted to Kal Raustiala for calling our attention to the significance of administrative law for our subject.

this lack of a democratic community and agreed-upon procedures at the global level, Dahl suggests that political scientists should treat international organizations as bureaucratic bargaining systems rather than as democratic institutions (1999, 32).

Three quite different reactions to this alleged democratic deficit can be identified. The first is to decry the lack of democracy in international organizations, and to urge caution, as a result, in their use. In Dahl's view, international organizations are never likely to be democratic, and we should therefore be cautious in expanding their authority. "In weighing the desirability of bureaucratic bargaining systems in international organizations, the *costs to democracy* should be clearly indicated and taken into account. Even if we concluded that the gains, or expected gains, outweigh these costs, that is no reason to ignore them entirely" (Dahl 1999, 34; italics in original).

A second view, exemplified by David Held, is to agree that existing international governance is undemocratic, but to urge more democracy. Held argues that we should think more seriously about "cosmopolitan democracy," which would "seek to entrench and develop democratic institutions at regional and global levels as a necessary complement to those at the level of the nation-state" (1996, 354).

A third, quite different reaction to the democratic deficit is to accept its reality but deny its relevance for policy. Among "realist" students of world politics, it seems self-evident that global governance cannot come close to meeting democratic standards. At the core of realism is the strong distinction between politics within states, where political communities exist, and among them, in politics characterized neither by community nor hierarchy, but by anarchy (Waltz 1979). International institutions are seen essentially as instruments that states use to achieve common purposes. To hold them to domestic standards of democratic procedure is to engage in what philosophers call a "category mistake." It makes no more sense to ask whether an inter-state organization is "democratic" than it does to ask if a broom has a nice personality. One should ask merely if the instrument works well. One might ask about the personality of the janitor handling the broom, and one might ask about democratic procedures in the states using an inter-state institution. In this realist view, world politics is inherently undemocratic and there is little point in lamenting the obvious.[2]

---

[2] Commenting on the creation of the World Bank and the International Monetary Fund in 1946, John Maynard Keynes implicitly offered a fourth alternative. This view rejects democratic accountability as an ideal in favor of technocracy. Keynes said that he hoped these two organizations would not be affected by the "bad fairy's curse that 'you two brats will grow up politicians.'" If this should happen, Keynes declared, "then the best

We agree with the realists up to a point. In the absence of a global political community (which is not imminent), it makes little sense to hold global institutions to domestic democratic standards. Their ultimate democratic legitimacy rests in substantial part on the extent to which they are faithful instruments of the (mainly) democratic states that created them. Their electoral accountability is derivative, and depends on whether they are faithful agents of democratic principals. But we are not prepared to let the matter rest there. Both Dahl and Held have valid points, as well. As governance moves increasingly toward the global level — as documented by other chapters in the present volume — maintaining a realist dichotomy between "domestic" and "international" politics becomes increasingly untenable. Transnational relations and globalization cross borders to the point where boundaries become, to a certain extent, blurred. Insofar as decisions that affect ordinary citizens — from trade to environmental standard-setting — are made through international, transnational, and transgovernmental processes, relying on nominal sovereignty is no longer reassuring to advocates of democracy.

Those who raise the issue of democratic procedures are asking the right question, but phrasing it in a confusing way. The phrase "democratic deficit" is based on an implied domestic model. The issue is not, "How close do international organizations and regimes come to meeting the model of a democratic community with a demos and institutionalized means of representation and accountability?" If we ask that question, the answer is clear: "Not very close." And the prospects for closing the gap between global reality and democratic utopia are not good. A better way of putting the question is to ask about different *types* of accountability. Even in well-ordered democratic polities, some institutions are not subject to direct electoral accountability: witness the Supreme Court or the Federal Reserve Board of Governors in the United States. Rather than making a judgment about how far global institutions deviate from an ideal standard of domestic democratic accountability, we propose to investigate how different forms of global governance create potentials for various kinds of accountability.

The key to our analysis is the assertion that accountability can take multiple forms. Direct electoral representation is not the only relevant form for contemporary international governance. Accountability can be

---

that could befall would be for the children to fall into an eternal slumber, never to waken or be heard of again in the courts and markets of mankind" (Gardner 1980, 266). Our view, on the contrary, is that international institutions that are significant for allocating values will necessarily be political — and, on grounds of direct or indirect democratic accountability, ought to be.

created through actions "in the shadow of elections." It can also be created by rules and monitored by independent organizations and by courts. Accountability can also be accomplished through markets, and as the result of publicity. We seek in this chapter to consider how various forms of accountability — not merely electoral accountability — could be instituted in ways that give publics more influence on policy and that enhance the legitimacy of international governance. We hope that our analysis will enrich the mental models of colleagues in international relations and political economy who focus on positive questions of description and explanation, and that it will also promote a productive exchange with political philosophers.

ACCOUNTABILITY: CONCEPT AND TYPES

Webster's dictionary defines accountability as "liable to be called to account; responsible." Accountable actions are explainable and sanctionable. Principals can require agents to give reasons so that they can make judgments about agents' actions and can also directly or indirectly sanction their agents if displeased with their actions (Schedler 1999).

Notice, however, that accountability does not necessarily imply democratic accountability. A minister could be accountable to a king or a dictator. Private firms are accountable to investors in the equity markets; governments may be accountable to investors in bond markets (Mosley 2000), or to other elites with sources of power not derived from electoral strength. For an agent to be accountable, the agent must face adverse consequences if his or her actions are inconsistent with the values and preferences of the principals. Since principals require information to hold agents accountable, measures to assure accountability require mechanisms for transmission of information as well as enforcement.

In this chapter we identify five different sets of processes through which this accountability can occur:

1. Electoral accountability is familiar to citizens of democracies. Ideally, democratic accountability means that processes of governance are responsive broadly to those who are affected by them, giving everyone a fair opportunity to be heard and providing procedures that correct inequalities of wealth and access among individuals. Electoral responsibility is fundamental to democratic accountability. "The democratic method," declared Joseph Schumpeter in 1942, "is that institutional arrangement for arriving at political decisions in which individuals acquire the power to decide by means of a competitive struggle for the people's vote" (Schumpeter [1942] 1962, 269). In practice, of course, accountability is far from perfect: governing elites can sometimes manipulate pub-

lics by controlling the agenda, through campaign spending, or otherwise. But the competition of elites provides some assurance that, in the long run, governments cannot defy the strongly felt will of a majority.

2. Hierarchical accountability is typical of most domestic governmental systems. Principals can remove agents from office, constrain the agents' room for discretion, and adjust the rewards for services. Internationally, heads of agencies can be removed (or not renewed); rules can be developed to restrict discretion, and governments can hold back their budgetary contributions.

3. Legal accountability through judicial or quasi-judicial processes is common in domestic polities. Agents can be sued, fined, and jailed. Furthermore, administrative law in democratic countries provides for procedures such as "notice and comment," by which parties that are not hierarchically superior to the agents promulgating rules can appeal to legal processes to request changes. Legal accountability is a somewhat less prominent mechanism internationally, but it can be observed in international civil litigation, and, recently, in the operation of international criminal tribunals. Moreover, corrupt agents of international institutions can be tried in national courts. In chapter 14, James Caporaso discusses the development of legal accountability in the European Union as the founding treaties have been constitutionalized and individual legal rights have been established through rulings by the European Court of Justice.

4. Reputational accountability occurs through publicity. The media enhance necessary transparency, and can also produce the sanction of embarrassment and damage to reputation. Judges have to write opinions that are scrutinized by the public and fellow members of the Bar. Federal Reserve decisions are criticized both by Congress and by professional economists. Internationally, organizations are subject not only to press criticism, but also to transnational professional judgments by members of epistemic communities. Transnational corporations are subject to naming and shaming campaigns by NGOs, and market-rating organizations can help police the credibility of companies, banks, and countries. Given the importance of credibility as a key power resource in an information age, reputational measures may become increasingly important in the future.

5. Market accountability works through the information that markets provide and the rewards and punishments they bestow. It is important to emphasize that this form of accountability is not to an abstract force called "the market," but to specific principals, whose influence on their agent is exercised in whole or in part through markets. In centrally planned systems, accountability of managers is hierarchical. Hierarchical accountability also operates within capitalist firms. Investors and boards of directors exercise direct political control, through elections of board members and selections of CEOs. For these principals, market responses are signals of performance. In competitive markets, however, firms are also accountable to investors and consumers, whose responses can reduce market share and stock prices. Hence market accountability is an important

category of its own — although its effects are both indirect (signaling to boards of directors and shareholders) and direct (punishment by affecting stock prices). Market accountability is hardly democratic, since influence in unequally distributed by wealth. Yet undemocratic markets can have unintended side-effects, some of which can reinforce democratic accountability. Global markets may undermine entrenched domestic monopolies, and international investors may demand transparency in public policy as a condition for entering a domestic market.

Accountability is sometimes treated as a good, per se, but it is an instrumental value, subject to being traded off against other values. Making decisions about trade-offs is a complicated problem even in well-ordered domestic polities. Processes without accountability can become corrupted and costly. On the other hand, processes designed to enhance democratic legitimacy and efficiency may turn out to be counterproductive in terms of effectiveness. In the United States, for example, progressive efforts to enhance bureaucratic accountability on issues of finances or fairness have diminished bureaucratic accountability for performance (Behn 2001). Hammers costing $600 in the Pentagon are the product not of corruption, but rather of congressionally imposed regulations to prevent it.

Electoral accountability is insufficient within modern democracies because many tasks are delegated to nonelected agents, from bureaucratic agencies to courts. The increasing intensity of regulation during the twentieth century fostered delegation of powers from Congress to its agents (Epstein and O'Halloran 1999; Shapiro 1988). Delegation can provide flexibility and bring expertise to bear on problems, but it raises difficulties with respect to accountability. Trade-offs need to be recognized and dealt with. Speaking of delegations of powers to administrative agencies by Congress, one expert declares that "broad delegations recognize that tight accountability linkages at one point in the governmental system may reduce the responsiveness of the system as a whole" (Mashaw 1997, 155). In chapter 14, James Caporaso discusses delegation models as they apply to the various components of the European Union and to relationships on EU issues between national executives and national parliaments.

To maintain more than nominal accountability by administrative agencies, elections are insufficient. The chains of delegation are too long, and voters cannot be expected to make their decisions contingent on agency actions. Hence, countries such as the United States, which have separate institutions sharing legislative and executive authority, have developed administrative law to make agencies genuinely accountable to the people they serve. In the United States, an extensive body of administrative law has been created both by Congress and by the courts (Shapiro 1988). It has been impossible for more than a century for Congress to specify, in statutes, contingencies that regulators might face. Seeking to do so would be burdensome for Congress, and politically unpalatable since specific choices will necessarily antagonize some groups of voters. From the standpoint of Congress, it makes more sense to enact general legislation and to build in provisions for notice and comment, as well as judicial review, that will enable affected interest groups to appeal adverse rulings. These appeals will serve as "fire alarms," alerting Congress to dissatisfaction with agency rulings and the possibility that agency policies are diverging from congressional intent (McCubbins, Noll, and Weingast 1987).

Without broad delegation of authority to agencies, deadlock would often result. Such deadlock would be normatively problematic, since it would maintain the status quo even when there is a winning coalition favoring a general direction of policy change. Advocates of broad discretion for agencies argue that it is best for the legislature to grant broad authority to agencies, which can be responsive to particular situations, and to control the risk of arbitrariness through procedural requirements and judicial review (Mashaw 1997, 148–56; see also Epstein and O'Halloran 1999). Such requirements have been elaborated in American administrative law, which requires advance public notice; that affected interests be allowed to comment on proposed rules; that agencies respond to such comments; and judicial review of both adjudication and rule-making by agencies (Shapiro 1988, chapters 2–4).

Not only can accountability be implemented through nonelectoral means in democratic countries, but also it can be deliberately limited. The public may hold inconsistent time-horizons and preferences, and may deliberately establish nonresponsive institutions as a means of "tying itself to the mast" as it sails by the Sirens of public or interest-group demands. Most judges are appointed for a fixed term to insulate them from direct democratic accountability. Central bank independence in many democracies is based on the belief that bankers are more likely than politicians to take the long view required for a monetary policy that accomplishes the public's preference for a stable price policy. Similarly in trade policy, Congress sometimes chooses to restrain its individual members by adopting a fast-track procedure as a way to deal with collective-action problems related to ratifying agreements.

None of these limitations on electoral accountability implies absolute lack of accountability to electorates. High-level executive-branch officials must be confirmed by the Senate. Congress can, and often does, change its laws in response to agency or court decisions of which a winning coalition disapproves. The vaunted independence of the Federal Reserve remains subject to the approval of Congress, and should the Fed lose its effectiveness in producing a successful economy, Congress could change the rules. The structure of lower federal courts, and even the number of members of the Supreme Court, can be altered by Congress. Impeachment serves as a safety net to insure ultimate democratic accountability, but it is not the most important way. The important general point is that in constitutional systems with division of powers—as in the United States and the European Union—institutions incorporating various forms and degrees of accountability are constructed. The accountability systems are variegated and nuanced, rather than unitary and uniform.

International organizations typically have weaker legitimacy than comparable domestic institutions: they often have shorter records of accomplishment, and they do not benefit from being within the framework of a legitimate sovereign state. The result, ironically, is that they may be more accountable than their formal provisions imply precisely because they are more vulnerable to outside pressure. For instance, the European Central Bank (ECB), partially modeled on the U.S. Fed, is, in formal terms, less accountable, although it makes quarterly reports to the European Parliament and holds monthly press conferences. Yet if the ECB were to fail at its task of maintaining stability without throttling economic growth, it would surely be held accountable by the governments that are its ultimate masters, and that could reduce its autonomy.[3]

Democratic political theory emphasizes that government should be "responsive and accountable to the demos, a sovereign authority that decides important political matters either directly in popular assemblies or indirectly through its representatives" (Dahl 1999). By this definition, no global governance arrangements could pass muster as democratic, since it is impossible to identify the demos in the absence of a sense of global political community. But we have seen that, even within democratic countries, accountability is more varied than this description would imply. Administrative law is all about procedures to decide important political matters outside of popular assemblies or legislative bodies. In our view, international organizations are here to stay because they are needed to promote international cooperation. Rather than offer a counsel of despair, we argue for more imagination in conceptualizing, and more emphasis on operationalizing, different types of accountability. It is better to devise pluralist forms of accountability than to bewail the the "democratic deficit."

---

[3] This point was suggested to one of the authors by David Soskice in a conversation on 2 March 2001.

In the United States Constitution, fragmentation of power and indirect accountability were designed not to promote effectiveness or democracy, but rather to protect liberty. Internationally, as well, accountability involves trade-offs among values. In both domains, it is a reasonable response to construct varied instruments that provide a measure of accountability while limiting its costs. Tennyson's "parliament of man" made great nineteenth-century poetry, but, despite proposals to the contrary, it is not the most feasible means of accomplishing global accountability in the twenty-first century.

Accountability and Models of Governance

Governance can occur in a variety of ways. At a global level there is no world government, so we need not discuss hierarchical forms of governance in which rules are authoritatively enforced by an entity called the "state." Putting world government aside, four quite distinct ideal-typical models can be elaborated:

1. A "statist" model of governance. The classic political-science model of governance revolves around the state, as in the Janus-faced concept of sovereignty. Sovereignty is a shield against external interference by other states. Hence, at the international level this statist model focuses, as realists do, on competition among states in an anarchic environment lacking common government. Governance occurs when inequality of power allows some states additional constraint over others. Sovereignty also connotes authority over internal governance, hence autonomy. In this model, therefore, the state is autonomous internally and externally, and the autonomy of the state is the essential basis for democratic governance.

2. An "international-organization" model of governance. Governance is viewed in terms of "sites of authority" and the relationships between them. The key questions are those of delegation. How much ultimate authority do principals retain when they delegate tasks to agents such as international organizations? Who has the rights of residual control? The guiding idea here is that the ability authoritatively to allocate values, in David Easton's (1965) phrase, is located in particular entities, or shared between them.

3. A "transnational-actors" model of governance. Nongovernmental actors can produce authoritative outcomes by wielding market power or by acting in concert within issue-areas over which they have influence. Examples include the decisions of multinational corporations on employment and investment, and decisions of industry organizations on standards. Such a model does not stand alone, since nongovernmental actions take place within a framework created by state action. For example, capital markets in East Asia rest on a security structure that rests on a long-term American military presence. Private actors can

produce authoritative outcomes in wide areas of global activity—witness the
East Asian financial crisis of 1997—and they can also affect the patterns of
public governance as exemplified by the fall of the Suharto government in Indonesia. But many of the most important activities of transnational actors—from
the Landmine Coalition to banking practices—exert effects by prompting actions by governments.

4. A "policy-networks" model of governance. In this model, outcomes are not
seen as the decisions of organizational entities, but rather as negotiated results
of bargaining among actors in networks. In *Understanding Governance*, R.A.W.
Rhodes has reinterpreted British governance in terms of networks. "Network
governance" refers, in Rhodes's terms, to *"self-organizing, interorganizational
networks* characterized by interdependence, resource exchange, rules of the
game, and significant autonomy from the state" (Rhodes 1997, 15; emphasis in
original). The key features of network governance are: (1) interdependence between organizations; (2) continuing interactions between network members; (3)
game-like interactions, "rooted in trust and regulated by rules of the game negotiated and agreed by network participants; and (4) a significant degree of autonomy from the state.[4] More recently, Wolfgang Reinicke has applied a variant of
this model to international governance (1999–2000).

It is important to emphasize that these four models should not be
seen as alternatives. It is more helpful to see them as "layered," with
each successive model introducing new layers of complexity. The state-
autonomy variant of statism brings domestic politics into the picture.
The delegation model introduces international organizations, with some
degree of agency, into the statist framework, within which the organizations operate. This model also incorporates domestic politics, since publics and legislatures serve as "principals" with respect to agents in executive branches, and executives serve as principals with respect to
international organizations. The transnational-actors model explicitly
introduces multinational firms and nongovernmental organizations. Finally, the policy-networks model takes into account the facts of state
power and chains of delegation to analyze how horizontally organized
networks affect outcomes along with the hierarchies of states and international organizations.

These four models of governance—all ideal types—have quite different implications for how we should conceptualize issues of accountability under conditions of globalization. Indeed, since the very nature
of accountability depends on the model of governance that one em-
ploys, we turn now to the question, *What would accountability mean*

---

[4] Rhodes's formulation is designed to help understand contemporary British government, and, as will be shown, requires some modification as the basis for a discussion of
the policy-networks model of global governance.

when processes of global governance are thought of as operating as each model specifies?

The Statist Model

In the statist model, emphasis is placed on the activities of territorially bounded states, internally and externally. Two sets of questions about governance arise within the context of this model.

INTERNATIONAL CONSTRAINTS

In traditional realist interpretations of world politics, international constraints are constructed by powerful states on the basis of their interests — geopolitical and economic. In the phrase of the Athenians quoted by Thucydides, "the strong do what they can and the weak suffer what they must" (Thucydides 1962, book 5, para. 89). Or, to use a modern economic example, capital flows to where it is welcome and flees when it is threatened. A democratic global organization that tried to allocate private flows of capital would not likely be effective. Even a World Bank and IMF with equally weighted votes would not be effective. Public development organizations not controlled by the major donor countries — such as the African Development Bank and the United Nations Industrial Development Organization — command scant resources. For realists, democracy is not an issue at the inter-state level since governance is otherwise organized. Hence, as we noted in our Introduction, issues of accountability at the inter-state level are largely irrelevant to realists.

STATE AUTONOMY

Issues of state autonomy under conditions of globalization raise more complicated issues for governance. A necessary condition for accountability in this classic comparative-politics model is that state agents have the ability to take effective action since if they lack such authority their principals can hardly demand that they achieve results. Hence, within this framework the most important barrier to accountability would be a process by which the capacity of the state was undermined or overwhelmed by globalization. If effective national control over important outcomes were lost, accountability through nationally based hierarchies and legal systems would be unattainable. Thus, the focus of recent literature on state policy and globalization is on whether states have been strengthened, weakened, or merely changed by forces of globalization acting upon them (Garrett 1998b; Kitschelt et al. 1999; Rodrik 1997).

Developing countries can be severely buffeted by global capital mobility, as the World Financial Crisis of 1997–1999 — which began in

East Asia but also affected Latin America — demonstrates. These countries lack the economic resources and governance capabilities to manage globalism on their own (Grindle 2000). The poorest countries, which depend on international financial institutions for funding, sacrifice considerable autonomy in return for loans. For developed countries, however, the pressures of globalization are more manageable and the state-autonomy model more relevant. For these countries, national economic integration remains strong, maintaining the relevance of borders. For example, John Helliwell's studies show that in North America national boundaries have a powerful effect on economic activity. Toronto trades ten times as much with Vancouver as it does with Seattle (Helliwell 1998), controlling for the relative size of these two cities.

For highly developed countries, the constraints imposed by financial markets are, in general, strong but narrow. "Despite financial globalization, the motivations for many government policies remain rooted in domestic politics and institutions"(Mosley 2000, 766). Furthermore, states, prodded by their leading firms, can be seen as seeking "comparative institutional advantage," emphasizing those activities that are favored by the institutionalized structures — liberal or coordinated — that have evolved within them (Soskice 1999). Globalization interacts with domestic politics. It is neither true that globalization produces the same effects everywhere (much less destroys the welfare state, or destroys state power), nor that globalization is irrelevant (Sen 1999; Weiss 1998). Governments of rich countries can find multiple feasible paths for dealing with the effects of globalization, depending on history, structures, and attitudes. Tom Friedman's "golden straitjacket" is an arresting phrase rather than an accurate description (Friedman 1999).

Since governments in highly developed countries retain policy choices, traditional democratic accountability remains possible on many issues. The key obstacle to effective accountability, at least for advanced industrial states, is not that the state is overwhelmed by globalization, but that governments have to make difficult trade-offs between autonomy and welfare-enhancing efficiency. As interdependence increases, incentives increase to submit to the rules of international regimes — as in the World Trade Organization (WTO) — in order to gain assurance that others will also behave in a predictable, rule-driven fashion. From the state-policy perspective, the problem for governments is that successful policy must meet the demands both of their own publics and of international politics. Successful foreign economic policy requires that domestic and international "win-sets" be made to overlap (Evans, Jacobson, and Putnam 1993; Putnam 1988). The state needs to act strategically in the international arena, building coalitions and making deals that advance its interests; and these bargains must be consistent with the preferences of publics at home, and not easily overturned by opposition political parties.

The International-Organization Model

The international-organization model builds on the statist model: it assumes the existence of states as the most important sites of authority in the contemporary global system. This model, however, introduces international organizations operating within the framework of public international law, which recognizes the nominal equality of states. Hence, in contrast to the realist world of untrammeled state power, the international organization model builds in a set of restraints—however weak they may be—on the exercise of power. Power has to be exercised through sets of procedures that, at least in formal terms, respect the independence of states, although they may (as in the UN Security Council) institutionalize inequalities in certain respects.

The key question of accountability in this model becomes one of delegation. Can the principals design institutions that ensure that their agents act as they wish? Do the nominal principals retain residual rights of control if they wish to retain them? At what cost can they reclaim such control? Can the principals remove leaders (their agents) from power? Most generally, do principals retain the ability to control, within relatively narrow limits, the actions of their agents—national executives or international organizations?

As we have done throughout this chapter, we have to distinguish, in this model, between accountability per se and democratic accountability. If we focus on accountability per se, international organizations clearly have more of it than the classic realist model of inter-state relations. The head of state of a hegemonic power is accountable to no one outside of his country, while the executive heads of international organizations are accountable to states through a regularized process of election and reelection. In reality, heads of international organizations may be accountable, through a hierarchical process, to one or a few powerful states. Boutros Boutros-Ghali was denied a second term as Secretary-General of the United Nations as a result of opposition from the United States, and many other leaders of international organizations have found their reelections contested. When one state alone is able to ensure the defeat of an executive head's candidacy for reelection, there is indeed a form of what could be called "hierarchical accountability," although it is hardly democratic. On the other hand, neither was it democratic when the inept head of UNESCO was kept in office by one-state–one-vote majority composed principally of small nondemocratic countries. In that case, the United States and some other democracies withdrew from the organization. Since almost all international organizations lack taxation sources of their own, they are typically dependent on states for revenue, and thus subject to the formal controls that accompany these subventions. When only a few states with relatively consistent preferences wield ultimate control over appointments and finances, international organizations are subject to accountability from member states, as new work on the World Bank has begun to show (Nielson and Tierney 2002a, b).

Democratic accountability is more elusive. In principle, as James Caporaso argues in the present volume, democratic accountability could be enhanced by increasing legislative control over policy at the supranational level, either by giving national legislatures a direct oversight role with respect to international institutions or by creating supranational legislatures. Only in the European Union has either of these two mechanisms been developed: the first in countries such as Denmark, the second (somewhat haltingly) with the European Parliament, whose powers have gradually been increased. In Denmark it is not the Parliament as a whole but only the European Committee of the Parliament that exercises oversight, and this oversight is inhibited by poor access to timely information, and generates a lack of flexibility for Danish negotiators in Brussels (Hegeland and Mattson 1996). Since generalizing Danish oversight to fifteen or twenty-seven countries could easily lead to deadlock, expanding the powers of the European Parliament is more promising.

What may be true in Europe does not generalize easily at a global scale. Since all members of the EU are democratic, the EU is hardly an appropriate model for a diverse world in which many states are undemocratic, or only marginally democratic. Even the European Parliament has confronted serious problems of voter disinterest. A global legislature in a world of six billion people, many of whom do not live within national democracies, could hardly be expected to be representative.

An experiment in 2000 by the Internet Corporation on Assigned Names and Numbers (ICANN) indicates how difficult global elections would be, even among the high-tech professionals who live on the Internet. When ICANN decided to elect five directors worldwide by direct vote of Internet users, fewer than 35,000 individuals voted (of hundreds of millions of Internet users), and groups that organized better than others — often organized on the basis of national affiliation — were able to capture the process (Kennedy School 2001). Hence, fully democratic accountability on a global scale is likely to remain elusive.

Yet despite the lack of direct electoral accountability of actual international organizations, they may operate indirectly in the shadow of electoral accountability. As we have pointed out, states — especially powerful states — act as the principals, supervising the behavior of inter-

national organizations and instructing their representatives at such organizations. It is not inherently any more undemocratic for the U.S.
president to delegate authority to the U.S. trade representative to negotiate at the WTO than for the president to delegate authority to the
attorney general to deal with organized crime. As long as the public
knows what actions the delegated agent took, it can reward or punish
the president, and his party, for its deeds. In such situations, transparency is critical. Affected interests need to be notified and given the op-
portunty to participate in the process — which may mean engaging in
political activity at the domestic or at the international and transnational levels. It is not surprising that recent criticisms of the IMF, World
Bank, and European Commission have often centered not only on their
distance from democratic voters, but on their alleged lack of transparency and the insufficient procedural legitimacy of the processes by
which they are claimed to have taken decisions affecting governments,
private firms, nongovernmental organizations, and individuals.

The normative issues become more serious when the agent is not a
representative of a democratic government but an anonymous World
Bank or IMF bureaucrat, or a panel, or Appellate Body, at the WTO.
The absence of a legislative body in the WTO, apart from periodic
meetings of the parties, means that rule-making takes place largely
through adjudication. The lack of a legislature — and the unanimity requirement for action when WTO-member governments meet — ensures
considerable freedom of action for the Appellate Body in particular.[5]
When agents have this much freedom to make binding rules, transparency may not be sufficient to assure adequate accountability.

The Transnational-Actors Model

In the transnational-actors model, accountability principally takes the
forms of market and reputational accountability. Legal issues may also
be important because most markets are embedded in legal systems providing, more or less, for protection of contracts (though in some circumstances kinship structures may be functional equivalents). Established firms rely for their success on their reputations with a variety of
constituencies, including financial analysts, customers, and their own
employees (Kreps 1990). Markets and NGOs provide a form of nonelectoral accountability. Corporations and governments that fail to perform well are held accountable by principals acting through markets.
Rating agencies help to consolidate and publicize a number of market

---

[5] Unanimity provisions make it hard to overrule or modify the interpretations of agents
and courts. See Tsebelis and Garrett (2001, especially 369).

judgments about firms. Governments that are closed and corrupt find it more difficult to attract capital and maintain the confidence of transnational investors. In the aftermath of the East Asian financial crisis, accountability to markets may have led to more increases in transparency than did any formal intergovernmental agreements.

The most important threats to the efficacy of accountability in the transnational-actors model lie in a breakdown of legal or market mechanisms. On the legal side, corruption and "mafias" turn attention from productive activity to rent– or protection-seeking behavior. On the market side, monopoly power by definition reduces the accountability of dominant firms, who need no longer fear "exit" by their customers (Hirschman 1970). Severe informational problems, and collective-action problems involving panic, can also adversely affect the efficacy of accountability in the market model.

There is no necessary connection between accountability in the transnational-actors model and democratic accountability. Obviously, people have unequal votes in markets depending upon the wealth they bring to the table. And NGOs are self-selected, not elected. Indeed, if resources, and effective demand, are distributed in highly unequal fashion, market accountability may well be at odds with democratic accountability. At the same time, by pressing for transparency and legality, private investors and NGOs can sometimes reinforce democratic accountability.

The Policy-Networks Model

The policy-networks model assumes the existence of the other three models: markets and states are important, and policy is made largely through international organizations, acting as the (imperfectly controlled) agents of states. In the policy-networks model, however, crosscutting networks and mixed coalitions, sometimes involving actors from all three sectors, are important forces in shaping the policies pursued by states and international organizations. Furthermore, networked coalitions may themselves make policy through arriving at agreements that are then implemented within bureaucracies, by corporations, or by nongovernmental organizations (NGOs). Accountability becomes more problematic, since sites of governance are more dispersed. As Rhodes discusses with reference to his network model of British government, "The system of accountability focused upon institutions and their processes of decision making and implementation. Here lies the fundamental problem: to call one institution to account for how it has operated is to disregard key features of the differentiated polity. *Policy is the responsibility of no one institution but emerges from several*" (1997, 21; emphasis added).

In this model, outcomes result from the interactions of independent political entrepreneurs rather than from the decisions of hierarchical organizations. Rhodes contrasts such networks with the formal Westminster model of ministerial accountability to the electorate. In the international analogue, states and international organizations — acting as principals and agents linked by delegation — are replaced by transnational networks that may involve one or several sectors.

The most important forms of accountability in the policy-network model are nonelectoral. In this model, decision-making elites are accountable to other elites with which they have ongoing relationships. Hierarchical and legal accountability are not very important. Reputational accountability is crucial: without credibility, organizations and groups cannot become accepted as participants in the ongoing bargaining processes that produce outcomes. Well-informed participants in networks have the ability to pull "fire alarms" — including "false alarms" — when outcomes do not meet with their approval (Lupia and McCubbins 1994; McCubbins and Schwartz 1984). A related form of accountability consists of the responsiveness of the elites who belong to these networks to professional norms. As Arthur Applbaum has argued, professional ethical standards can be used to hold adversaries accountable (1999). Lawyers care about the opinion of the bar; academic economists about their standing in the eyes of some colleagues. Epistemic communities increasingly take the lead in raising the issues and constructing the domestic and transnational conversations necessary to create a public space (Haas 1992; Keck and Sikkink 1998). Their activities, at least to some limited extent, may keep governing elites accountable, corresponding to the way in which networks of legal scholars or economists make the Supreme Court or the Federal Reserve accountable: through reasoned criticism and discussion, rather than through elections.

In the absence of hierarchy, the efficacy of any form of accountability in the policy-networks model depends first of all on the diffusion of power. If power is diffused, specific actors need to bargain with others to attain their objectives. As in the United States Constitution — which incorporates elements of the policy-networks model even within a hierarchical sovereign state — power checks power.

The second essential condition for accountability in the policy-networks model — which is also important in the other models — is the availability of information: *transparency*. The media play a particularly crucial role in this model because hierarchical controls between principals and agents are weak or nonexistent. In networks, the efficacy of actors depends on their credibility, and on their reputations, more generally. Accountability is achieved not through legal actions, hierarchy, or markets, but through the effects of one's actions on one's reputation, and therefore on one's future effectiveness and influence.

Even if accountability is secured in the policy-networks model through the operation of reputation, there is no guarantee of *democratic* accountability. Indeed, networks are by definition elitist. To be an active player, an organization or group must devote resources to being informed. In the absence of formal hierarchy, much less elections, there are no regularized ways of assuring that public reactions — as a result, for instance, of media publicity — will have focused effects. Formal governmental institutions provide such a focus and in democratic societies give competing politicians incentives to publicize errors and corruption by those in power; such institutions are lacking in global governance. In the absence of such institutions, the collective-action costs of publics making their wishes known — even if they have sufficiently well-formed attitudes to regard them as "wishes" — may be prohibitive. Hence, policy-network forms of accountability are unlikely to be democratic.

ACCOUNTABILITY IN "CLUBS" AND "CONTESTED NETWORKS"

Reality under conditions of complex interdependence *blends* all four abstract models that we have discussed above. The models we sketched are useful for highlighting the features of actual regimes that are likely to generate certain types of accountability, and difficulties of accountability. But they cannot be transferred one-to-one to real situations, all of which incorporate some combination of the features highlighted by the abstract models.

For this analysis of accountability, however, we do not purport to offer a rich description of all of the varieties of transnational and international governance that are appearing at the beginning of the twenty-first century. Instead, we propose to stylize the range of real situations along a dimension that is directly relevant to accountability: that is, the *degree of informational transparency and openness to new groups* of a given network or cluster of networks. In this descriptive conceptualization, the "blends" of states, international organizations (IOs), and networks can run from *IO-based clubs* to *contested issue networks*. IO-based clubs (Keohane and Nye 2001) involve a closed, selected group of actors — units of states, international organizations, and transnational actors — focused around an international regime: a set of rules, standards, organizations, and procedures established to govern a set of issues. Contested issue networks, by contrast, are open to new entrants, whether the established participants welcome them or not. Contested issue networks are likely to be more transparent to nonparticipants through the media.

It is important to recognize that we do *not* assume that more openness necessarily means more accountability, much less more legitimacy. If all other features of situations were held constant, transparency certainly would increase accountability. But transparency and openness may have other effects. For example, they could enable new groups, whose internal arrangements are less transparent than those of established groups, to play more important roles. Openness to new groups could cause the breakdown of established, publicly known procedures for decision making, complicating the process so much that few outsiders could understand it, even if information were, in principle, available. Finally, openness could lead to deadlock — to Fritz Scharpf's "joint-decision trap" (Scharpf 1988) — that makes it difficult to know whom to hold responsible for *nondecisions*.

Accountability in IO-based Clubs

Transgovernmental relations seem to have been expanding rapidly in recent years, but they are not necessarily new (Keohane and Nye 1974; Slaughter 2000). Indeed, many of them seem to have emerged from the international regimes that were created during the 1940s and 1950s. In the club-like institutions that emerged, cabinet ministers or the equivalent, working in the same issue-area, initially from a relatively small number of relatively rich countries, got together to make rules. They negotiated in secret, then reported their agreements to national legislatures and publics. Until recently, they were largely unchallenged. Their members constructed rules — either in the form of traditional international law or as sets of established, but less obligatory, practices known as "soft law" — to govern their relationships within the issue-area.[6] As James Caporaso points out in chapter 14 in the present volume, such clubs worked satisfactorily in the European Community as long as mass publics were not involved in the issues being discussed.

IO-based clubs were very convenient for officials negotiating agreements within issue-areas since they kept outsiders out (Keohane and Nye 2001). Indeed, in IO-based clubs a *lack of transparency to outsiders* was a key to political efficacy. Protected by this lack of transparency, ministers could make package deals that were difficult to disaggregate or even sometimes to understand. For instance, after the United States Congress deconstructed the trade agreements made during the Kennedy Round (1967), implementing unilateral modifications to bar-

---

[6] Our IO-based clubs resemble what Rhodes refers to as "policy communities." We regard "community" as inappropriate language for world politics, in view of the divergences of interest that persist even among members of clubs.

gains that had been reached, America's trade partners demanded modifications in internal U.S. practices as a condition for the next trade round. Congress agreed to use a "fast-track" procedure that limited its power to pick apart agreements. In effect, Congress agreed to "tie itself to the mast" as it sailed past specific protectionist Sirens. Cooperation on international trade was enhanced. but labor and environmentalist interests, whose power was reduced by the practice have reacted strongly against it and the associated international institutions.

In terms of hierarchical delegation, IO-based clubs can meet some requirements in democratic theory for accountability, but often in such an indirect way that the delegation is highly attenuated. Banking policy, securities coordination, and insurance policy do not often make the front pages even of the business section. The networks in these areas, as Slaughter recognizes, are often closed; the Basle network of central bankers is a case in point (Slaughter 2000, 182). Their activities take place largely in secret. The agents in these networks cannot easily be removed or sanctioned by publics through democratic processes. The World Bank and the IMF may seem far removed from publics, but at least their actions can be identified (and made more transparent) and a chain of delegation can be identified with governments as the principals and the international organizations as the agents. Such identification is in many cases impossible with respect to transgovernmental networks. "The informality, flexibility, and decentralization of networks means that it is very difficult to establish precisely who is acting and when" (Slaughter 2000, 193–94).

The pattern of accountability in IO-based clubs is mixed. They do not meet traditional democratic standards of accountability, and are therefore normatively questionable insofar as they seek to make binding policies on issues of general significance. The strongest lines of accountability within the club model are to interest groups within issue-areas, and only indirectly to legislatures influenced by a broad range of interest groups. Yet the normative implications of policy-making through clubs depend on whether the issues are technical or involve a broad range of values. The more technical the task, the more legitimate these clubs may be. If clubs make effective policy, they may be justified on output grounds (Slaughter 2000).[7] Indeed, publics are "rationally

---

[7] Fritz Scharpf (1999, chapter 1) has distinguished between "input-oriented" and "output-oriented" legitimization, but he limits "input-oriented legitimization" to participatory processes involving strong collective identities and consensus. Hence, his category of "output-oriented legitimization" merges together what we wish to separate: accountability and effectiveness.

ignorant" about many issues and do not expect or even desire to be consulted about everything.

Accountability in Contested Issue Networks

In some respects the broader issue networks that are now emerging on trade and development issues arguably allow for greater accountability than the old policy communities did. The issue networks are open, if raucous; the policy communities were closed and sedate. But the rough accountability that is emerging is very rough indeed, and partial.

In the first place, the new contested issue networks are also dominated by elites. What has changed is not so much public participation — the number of demonstrators is tiny relative to the electorates of developed countries — but the resources that are effective in the network. In the old clubs, effective resources included access to government policy processes and resources that would enable political entrepreneurs to affect policy. Such resources included economic resources that could be translated into political power at home. On the obscure issues, political power was exercised discreetly. Only on major issues such as trade were public appeals important. In the new contested issue networks, by contrast, the ability to appeal to individuals worldwide on the Internet and to catch the attention of the media become major political resources. Demonstrators chanting democratic and environmental slogans are visually more telegenic than technocrats discussing arcane policy issues or seeking to defend themselves with complex justifications of policies that seem pernicious to many.

The collapse of the proposed OECD Multilateral Agreement on Investment (MAI) illustrates the shift from clubs to issue networks in dramatic fashion. More than 600 organizations in nearly 70 countries formed an Internet-based network of opposition to this agreement, which had been negotiated secretly within the OECD. In the phrase of the *Financial Times*, "network guerillas" ambushed the negotiations (Kobrin 1998). From the perspective of the OECD negotiators, these new participants in the political process came out of nowhere. They helped to create a contested issue network where earlier there was only a policy community.

Contested issue networks are much more transparent than IO-based clubs. Hence, what we referred to as the "informational mechanisms" of issue networks are much more conducive to democratic accountability than the informational mechanisms of relatively closed policy communities; however, procedures for rewards and sanctioning — in which agents can be provided with consistent sets of incentives by principals — are bedeviled, in contested-issue networks, by uncertainty. When new actors "ambush" negotiations, incentives change dramatically: the MAI, for instance, while still not agreed-upon by governments was a dead letter soon after it was leaked and publicized. Anticipating adverse publicity and activism in response to complex negotiations, governments and other organizations in the old policy community or club may decide that it is not worthwhile to make the effort.

A major problem with policy processes both of policy communities and contested issue networks is that they are *disarticulated*; that is, they lack a focal set of institutions in which interests are aggregated, bargains are struck, trade-offs are made, and authoritative decisions are taken (Bignami and Charnovitz 2001). The *structural stability* that one observes in domestic constitutional systems is lacking at the international level. As we have seen above, those intergovernmental organizations that do make binding rules often lack the democratic legitimacy that comes from having transparent procedures, institutional arrangements that facilitate accountability, and activities by politicians seeking reelection by appealing to publics. Their delegated decisions are less authoritative, at the best of times, than those of legitimate national governments. Furthermore, as IO-based clubs have given way, at least in part, to more open contested issue networks, the stability of decisions has been further threatened. Established processes are subject to sudden invasion by new actors with populist appeals, effective networking skills, and media savvy. Recently, such invasions have been particularly evident in the issue-area of food safety. Processes governing acceptance of genetically modified foods have been removed from a principally technical and industry-dominated set of organizations to the forum of public debate and media discussion of "Frankenstein foods" (Pollack and Shaffer 2001). These new actors find international organizations a much easier target than the governments of established democracies, run by politicians with direct ties to their publics, and able to call on national symbols, as well as electoral procedures, for legitimacy.

The disarticulation of contested issue networks seems to have a bias. It is relatively easy to defeat proposals but difficult to negotiate cooperation. Hence, transparency and openness may lead to a one-sided accountability. Governments and international organizations may be held strictly, and rather rudely, accountable for their *actions*, but may not be held equally accountable for *inaction*. The result would be a bias against policy change, and against cooperation. Ironically, contests mounted in the name of "civil society," or "the people," lack even the semblance of democratic accountability that delegation theory provides, and may prevent cooperation that would benefit "the people" if they were consulted. In an era of extremely rapid technological and economic change, gridlock in the policy process could create serious inconsistencies between policy and practice.

The Missing Element: Intermediating Politicians

The key element that is missing both from the IO-based clubs and from expanded issue-networks is the presence of intermediating politicians, communicating both with each other and with their publics. The absence of effective political leadership may have mattered less in the club model when most issues were less publicized, and linkages between issues were weaker. On the minor issues, publics did not demand strict accountability. On major ones such as trade, accountability to legislatures and publics could be maintained through institutionalized arrangements as discussed above. But linkages between major issues, such as trade and environment or labor, and the publicity associated with many policies dealt with by contested issue networks, create a stronger need for the involvement of politicians who can articulate policy themes in ways that are attractive to domestic and transnational constituencies.

Politicians, furthermore, are needed to create the political conditions under which decision-making organizations — as in the principal-agent model — face stable incentives from their principals. International organizations need to know the parameters that define the limits of political feasibility in their policy areas; and they need assurance that leaders of national governments who support the idea of negotiations will not leave them in the lurch when advocates in issue networks publicize their objections. Someone has to take responsibility for making judgments about the relative importance of issues, and how to manage the trade-offs between them. In a democratic society, politicians who take this responsibility are held accountable for their actions. Indeed, their very accountability is a source of credibility and strength, since policy pronouncements, for accountable officials, are potentially costly, rather than being mere "cheap talk." If constituents have confidence in their elected officials, they are more likely to support policies endorsed by those officials, even if they do not understand the specifics of those policies. Politicians intermediate between organizations and constituencies in civil societies, strengthening the legitimacy of organizations in return for ensuring that constituencies have influence over the organizations' policies.

In the international, transnational, and transgovernmental politics that we are describing, politicians have rarely played this role. We conjecture that this is not because they are ignorant of what might be required to make these networks operate more effectively, but rather because the structure of the situation creates insufficient interests to play entrepreneurial roles. At home, heads of government reap rewards for risky and costly political efforts. But at the international level, the benefits of success will be widely diffused, while the costs and risks of taking an initiative may remain specific to the politician and his political organization. In other words, due to classic collective-action problems, one should expect systematic underinvestment by politicians in making contested issue-networks operate. These problems will be compounded by the pervasive uncertainty already discussed: in such a turbulent environment, the likelihood of misjudgment, hence failure, is relatively high. UN Secretary General Kofi Annan's efforts to create a global compact of transnational corporations and NGOs could be considered the apparent exception that "proves" (or tests) the rule. The fact that even the most articulate and charismatic UN Secretary-General lacks close ties to democratic publics makes it very difficult for him to connect publics with policy. Without a political community, it is hard to be an effective political entrepreneur.

CONCLUSION: LEGITIMACY AND ACCOUNTABILITY IN GLOBAL GOVERNANCE

A potentially debilitating problem for international governance is lack of legitimacy. Critics of contemporary law and institutions, from both the Right and the Left, argue that international institutions suffer from accountability deficits.

These critics have a point, but their conception of accountability tends to be limited to hierarchical, and especially electoral, accountability. Legal accountability (as in administrative law), reputational accountability, and market accountability are also important in the policy networks in which the business of international governance is actually conducted. Recognizing the role of networks, particularly the contested issue-networks that we have described, makes it clear that the problem is more complex than one of a democratic deficit, with its implied domestic analogy. If we think clearly about other forms of accountability than traditional electoral accountability, we may be able to design international institutions that meet our needs for effective cooperation without handing our fates over to unelected technocrats.

The international problem is structural. In a well-functioning constitutional democracy, the various aspects of political inputs—popular activity, media attention, pluralist interest-group lobbying, parties, elections, and formal legislation—are articulated together. There is a clear pathway by which laws can be created; and when laws are enacted, regular procedures and organizations exist to implement, amend, and change those laws. *Actions*, broadly consistent with the public will, can be taken. Ideally, then, both the input-oriented and output-oriented requirements for legitimacy can be met. In transnational and international relations, by contrast, IO-based clubs accomplish tasks at the expense of direct accountability, jeopardizing input-oriented legitimacy. Contested issue-networks increase transparency and therefore awareness by outsiders of what is happening; but they diffuse responsibility. They may enhance reputational and market accountability, but diminish delegated democratic accountability. They may produce deadlock, in which there is lack of focus and no effective decisions for which to hold policymakers accountable. Output-oriented legitimacy, based on effective action, therefore suffers.

International governance does not benefit from affective or symbolic legitimacy — as in Max Weber's traditional or charismatic forms of legitimacy. Hence, its legitimacy must rest principally on its apparent efficacy as an instrument. The justification may be that rational-bureaucratic organizations are devoted to purposes that cannot be accomplished effectively at a national or local level (Barnett and Finnemore 1999); or that networks are flexible and effective in responding to the complex challenges of globalization (Slaughter 2000). Nonetheless, procedural legitimacy matters because of democratic values as well as for reasons of efficacy. Neither government in backrooms, nor government by demonstration, would meet the tests of democratic legitimacy.

We need a more sophisticated normative theory of accountability. Delegation theory is necessary but not sufficient given the distance between democratic principals and their international agents, and given the plurality of principals that allows for considerable agency slack. We have argued that democratic electoral accountability can be supplemented by other forms of accountability — hierarchical, legal, reputational, and market — that, while not democratic per se, can help to ensure some responsiveness of international agents to publics (and thus be more consistent with democratic principles). International organizations as agents may be distant from the shadow of direct elections, but they should not be held to a higher standard of democratic accountability than are such instruments as domestic regulatory agencies or monetary authorities.

Global governance today lacks a sufficient role for politicians, intermediating between policy and publics. Even leaders such as the United Nations Secretary-General and the head of the European Commission cannot effectively play this role, much less the executive heads of the International Monetary Fund or World Bank. They simply do not have sufficiently strong links with elites or broader publics in democracies, or sufficient credibility with those nationally based audiences.

A major normative implication of this argument is that the governance of globalization will depend in significant measure on *national* political leaders in democratic states. Political support for coherent governance will require that these leaders look beyond their borders as they devise their strategies. For example, rather than hide behind and blame international agencies such as the IMF for unpopular actions, they would have to help shoulder the political burden. But as we have pointed out, national political leaders have incentives to do exactly the opposite: appeal to their own national publics and blame international organizations for failures. As political scientists, therefore, we expect global political leadership from domestic politicians to be rare, and the governance of globalization to remain disarticulated and disjointed.

In view of the inadequacies of accountability in global governance, more experimentation would be desirable. Contested issue-networks are relatively transparent, due to the competition among the actors, but lack focus, and often capacity for decision. IO-based clubs are threatened with a loss of legitimacy, partly because they often rely on secrecy; but at least the international organizations provide focal points for assessing actions, and assigning responsibility. New combinations of issue networks with international organizations are needed, to combine openness and contestability with the capacity to make decisions. Transnational representation needs further institutional work, as the difficulties with ICANN elections shows; but the idea is promising. As NGOs become more important, they will need to become more transparent about their membership and finances to ensure internal accountability. It may be that more involvement of parliamentarians in international networks would help to broaden their horizons.

In judging whether the problems of democratic accountability, both of organizations and networks, are justified by their results in terms of efficacy of global governance, we need to assess the trade-offs. As Dahl says, "the *costs to democracy* should be clearly indicated and taken into account." How we evaluate international-governance processes depends both on their accomplishments and on the extent to which their procedures approximate ideals of democratic accountability. We have not sought in this chapter to provide a net assessment of the legitimacy of all such instruments, but instead to offer a framework that helps us to make relevant normative judgments as we confront the complexity of international and transnational governance in the twenty-first century.

Chapter 16

GLOBALIZATION AND CHANGING PATTERNS OF POLITICAL AUTHORITY

Miles Kahler and David A. Lake

In the heated debate surrounding globalization, its effects on governance are especially controversial. Remote authorities that are not democratically accountable lie at the core of many anxieties. Others fear a more far-reaching erosion of the nation-state as a unit of governance. National capitals may lose influence recently gained from imperial masters to economic centers of power; the social protections of the welfare state could be eroded by impersonal markets. Increased regionalism might cause nation-states to fracture into smaller units. Treasured national differences, and perhaps even national identity itself, might be lost in the homogenizing pressures exerted by global market integration.

In contrast, we find the effects of globalization on governance to be more heterogeneous and contingent than the most vocal proponents and opponents claim. Globalization is a fact of contemporary life, and its effects on daily economic activities are profound. It is also a process whose endpoint is not yet clear. Small changes in governance occur constantly, and they may later cumulate in a more profound transformation. At this point in history, however, globalization has not yet produced a fundamental change in the structure of political authority. The chapters in this volume are neither a systematic sample of issue areas nor a set of carefully selected critical cases that would allow us to reach a definitive conclusion on the extent and magnitude of changes in the sites of governance. Our findings, as a result, must be treated cautiously. Nevertheless, changes in governance engendered by globalization appear to be neither universal nor uniform.

In the areas of international finance and monetary affairs, where globalization has extended furthest, no clear trend toward supranational (regional and global) governance is apparent. Cohen (chapter 6) finds important instances of delegation of monetary authority both to other governments, particularly dollarization, and to regional currency arrangements, most notably Europe's Economic and Monetary Union (EMU). He nonetheless concludes that most states are likely to settle for more limited forms of currency regionalization that transfer some monetary authority to other states or supranational entities but stop short of delegating complete authority. Despite an expansion of international co-ordination after the East Asian financial crisis, Eichengreen (chapter 7) finds that government responses to the growth of highly leveraged and potentially destabilizing hedge funds have been strongly conditioned by existing international institutions and dependent on national political institutions for enforcement. Mattli (chapter 8) finds greater transna-tional governance in standards-setting, but that, at the same time, this development reinforces the position of national authorities.

If delegation of political authority to the supranational level is far from clear, there is also no obvious trend toward decentralization of national authority. Martin (chapter 2) finds a tendency for tourism pol-icy to decentralize as the industry develops and expands, especially in federal states. Likewise, Hiscox (chapter 3) finds that globalization, through its effect on incomes and income distributions within states, may encourage disintegration of existing political units. Garrett and Rodden (chapter 4), on the other hand, conclude that the greater vul-nerability of regions in a global economy actually increases the fiscal role of central governments. Without denying the importance of de-mands for greater regional autonomy, in turn, Van Houten (chapter 5) finds little direct evidence that globalization actually stimulates de-mands for autonomy; rather, globalization is mediated heavily by politi-cal parties and institutions.

Mattli (chapter 8) and Haufler (chapter 9) document an increase in international standards and industry self-regulation in response to glob-alization. What is less clear, however, is whether such private actions are substitutes or complements for actions by national governments. In both cases, industry actions depend on public authority, which channels private demands and represents firms at the international level in the case of standards, and creates leverage for disaffected citizens and trans-national NGOs in the case of self-regulation. Although the number of national standards and regulations may appear to decline, the coercive power of the state remains an important actor in the background, one which can be invoked if private initiatives at the international level fail in the eyes of powerful political actors. In this sense, private governance may complement rather than replace the regulatory power of states.

States and governments are not uniformly converging in institutional form or policy. Simmons and Elkins (chapter 11) demonstrate clearly a strong diffusion of policies of economic liberalization in recent decades, but even this trend is influenced by the actions of economic competitors. Rogowski (chapter 10), Gourevitch (chapter 12), and McNamara (chap-ter 13) argue on both theoretical and empirical grounds that a logic of specialization and differentiation follows from globalization and that states retain considerable discretion in how they respond to international markets. Rather than strong convergence toward a neoliberal ideal, they predict continuing, and perhaps increasing, diversity of state institutions and policy in the global economy.

Finally, despite concerns over the so-called democratic deficit, the new sites of global governance have not slipped entirely from the control of democratic electorates. Caporaso (chapter 14) argues that, at least in the European Union, traditional mechanisms and standards of democratic accountability still apply. More generally, as both Caporaso and Keohane and Nye (chapter 15) explain, there are multiple instruments of accountability that continue to constrain authority within a globalized economy. Electorates must exercise the same vigilance over delegated authority that is required in the domestic arena. Globalization, however, does not imply the exercise of authority by faceless bureaucrats or corporate managers free from public scrutiny.

These variegated and contingent findings should not be misread. Authority has diffused to other sites within the world system, and patterns of governance have become more subtle and complex. The structure of global governance is evolving. Our evidence of evolutionary rather than revolutionary governance change does not mean that the state has been rendered ineffective, as anti globalists charge, nor that it will forever be the locus of political activity within the international system, as realists expect. Our conclusions may not satisfy those who view globalization as either a remorseless juggernaut crushing existing practices and policies or a benign process that automatically reinforces democracy and economic development. Understanding how, when, and where globalization affects governance becomes an even more important and daunting challenge.

Many treatments of globalization describe it as an environmental transformation, a possibly irreversible and increasingly binding constraint on national governments. Friedman has labeled these constraints, which accompany the economic benefits of globalization, as the "golden straitjacket." In his view, the benefits of economic openness bring a narrowing of political choice: "your economy grows and your politics shrinks" (Friedman 1999, 87). Andrews (1994) has argued that international financial integration — the sphere in which globalization is most pronounced — should be treated as a structural feature of international politics. This view of globalization as a competitive environment underlies the functionalist and efficiency arguments described in chapter 1 that are examined by some of the authors in this volume. In this view, shifts in the global economic environment create demands for change in governance location, typically to a larger — supranational — jurisdiction. Governance gravitates toward the level at which public goods are produced most efficiently. Globalization viewed as environmental change produces both activism and fatalism. Activists protest the constraints that globalization is believed to impose on societies and press to retain democratic control of policy at the national or local level. Fatalists may admit some remaining degrees of freedom for national policy, but assert that governments and electorates in the long run must learn to live with globalization and its consequences.

In contrast to this emphasis on globalization as a competitive and unforgiving environment, the authors in the present volume emphasize the significant strategic choices that remain with political actors. Globalization changes the policy preferences of some actors, mobilizes new transnational actors into the political arena, increases the bargaining power of others, and opens new institutional options for still others. Individually and collectively, we reintroduce agency into the story of globalization and its effects. As a result, the prevailing view of residual political choice here is decidedly less pessimistic than elsewhere. Indeed, in some cases, as the preceding chapters demonstrate, the range of political choice remains broad and may even be enhanced by globalization.

Analytically, the authors in this volume trace and explain the effects of globalization through changes in actors and the strategic environment that they create, rather than assuming fixed actors and the tightening constraints of a globalized environment. This actor-oriented approach leads to contingent and often tentative conclusions. In contrast to a public debate about globalization that is often framed in yes-no, good-bad dichotomies, the questions that frame the present volume typically begin with "under what conditions?" and the answers with "it depends." Those answers deal with three changes in governance that have often been attributed to globalization: shifts in the site of governance away from public and national authority toward international institutions, subnational units, and private or nongovernmental actors; convergence or divergence in the institutions of governance and the policies that they promote; and more or less accountability to democratic electorates.

GLOBALIZATION AND THE SITES OF GOVERNANCE: TOWARD A POSITIVE THEORY OF SUBSIDIARITY

Many link globalization to a migration of governance away from the nation-state. Governance transfer in three directions is possible. The most familiar from long-standing debates over international economic integration is an apparently inevitable push for supranational governance wider in scope than the nation-state. Throughout the twentieth century, theorists and statesmen have pondered the need for political structure to align itself with the wider domain of an integrated world economy. Carr (1942) pointed out the contradiction between a world based on self-determination and small political units and economic trends toward greater global interdependence. The dilemmas of governance centered on nation-states have grown as the number of sovereign territorial units has dramatically increased over the last half-century.

Running counter to this older view of the tension between political self-determination, small-scale units, and globalization is a more recent claim that globalization encourages the decentralization of governance to subnational political jurisdictions and may even stimulate demands for secession or national disintegration. (These arguments are reviewed in the chapters [3–5, respectively] by Hiscox, Garrett and Rodden, and Van Houten.) To the degree that global economic integration reduces threats of military conflict and conquest, the need for the security provided by large-scale units declines. More importantly, the reduction in economic barriers among nation-states reduces the value of large national markets: the effective market is now the world economy. As a result, smaller political units demand more autonomy and are encouraged to "go it alone" in a liberal international economy.

Finally, a third migration, from public to private, has also been associated with globalization. What Reinicke (1998b) has labeled horizontal subsidiarity is linked to an increase in the bargaining power of private actors, who are assumed to prefer self-governance. Increasingly mobile corporations, in this view, demand a greater voice in their own regulation and may press for self-regulation, in which public authority is minimized (discussed in Haufler, chapter 9). The ability of private actors to pick and choose among jurisdictions increases the weight of their demands. In addition, technological change may inhibit the abilities of national governments to maintain regulatory or other governance functions in a more open economic environment.

Although migration of governance may occur in any of these three directions, all point away from national governments. The combined image is one of national governance at risk of "hollowing out," stripped of many core functions that are dispersed to international and regional institutions, local authorities, or private corporations. Whether this pattern of governance transfer is accurate must be established and, as already described, each of the authors in the first section of this volume assesses a piece of this larger puzzle. The second aim is explanation, constructing a positive theory of subsidiarity. In the European Union, subsidiarity denotes a normative guide: for reasons of democratic accountability, governance should take place at a level closest to the governed, unless positive benefits can be demonstrated to result from its transfer. Here we are not suggesting where governance *should* be sited. Rather, we seek to explain how, when, and why deepening economic integration produces movement in the location of governance.

Economic Models of Governance Change

Models drawn from economics offer one starting point for the construction of such a positive theory. In chapter 1, we summarize those models under the heading of functionalist and efficiency theories. In chapters 2 and 3, Martin and Hiscox, respectively, describe their underlying logic in greater detail. The assumed starting point or baseline is governance at the national level. Change in governance results from a tug of war between two powerful variables. Heterogeneous preferences over public-goods provision bias governance toward levels closer to an electorate. Externalities and economies of scale in public-goods provision encourage movement of governance to a supranational level. As preferences become more heterogeneous, governance on a smaller scale will provide public goods that are closer to the ideal points of the fragmented electorate. The pull toward larger units of governance assumes that political principals will act on the basis of increased efficiency in public-goods provision. Politics in these models balances public-goods provision closer to any given elector's preferences against possibly higher-cost (less efficient) provision of public goods.

As Martin describes, the international tourism industry, which expanded rapidly during the last decades of the twentieth century, has not seen dramatic shifts in governance. Nonetheless, the economic model is useful in explaining a governance life cycle in this sector. Initial infrastructure projects and marketing may have large economies of scale, and thus benefit from central provision early in the development of a tourist destination. But since tourism tends to be differentiated at the local level, the public goods demanded also tend to be specialized (ski resorts versus theme parks) and are often provided most efficiently at lower levels of governance. Decentralization and privatization (horizontal subsidiarity) become more pronounced within national tourist policies over time — a trend magnified in states with more federal political institutions. Intervention at the national level only reappears if and when tourism becomes overdeveloped and externalities demand intervention. For the most part, in mature tourist destinations governance at the supranational level remains limited to relatively shallow regional cooperation. As later discussion suggests, issue-area matters: the pattern of limited upward transfer of governance may not be characteristic of other economic sectors. Nevertheless, the example of tourism suggests that even a sector that is highly internationalized may not require extensive public-goods provision or international collaboration beyond the nation-state.

Hiscox (chapter 3) calls into question the familiar assumption that policy preferences are exogenous, fixed, and necessarily heterogeneous. Instead, he argues that globalization may well affect preferences over public goods because of its influence on income distribution within and between societies. (Globalization might also create more homogeneous preferences through processes of competition or emulation.) By drawing attention to the redistributive effects of globalization, Hiscox lays the foundation for a political theory of governance. The greater the income differential between regions within a state, he finds, the greater are the pressures for regional autonomy.[1]

Testing Economic Models of Governance Change

Testing functionalist and efficiency models of governance change is difficult. As Hiscox (chapter 3) suggests, measurement of externalities resulting from global economic integration (as compared to those perceived to result from that integration) is imprecise at best. The proverbial smokestack belching its quantifiable pollutants that cross national borders is seldom replicated for other cross-border externalities. Economies of scale in the provision of public goods are also hard to document. Heterogeneity of preferences is subject to estimation over time, but comparison across issue-areas is more demanding. As a first step at testing, however, one can advance rough estimates of "more or less" on these dimensions.

As already described, Martin (chapter 2) finds little regional or global collaboration in the tourism industry. She attributes this to the diversity of public goods demanded in this sector, the absence of many cross-

[1] Nonetheless, the effects of changes in income distribution remain very indirect in Hiscox's model. They play out in the political process through their implications for public-goods provision. Other, more direct distributional effects of globalization may swamp these more indirect influences. The political power of particular interests that are threatened by further integration may be more significant than a realignment of political preferences over public-goods provision. For example, Hiscox predicts a reduction in resistance to political integration if income distributions in industrialized and developing countries converge. Further integration is likely to widen income inequality in labor-scarce industrialized economies (as it has already done), and labor's political clout in those economies is far greater than it is in the labor-abundant developing world. The attitudes of U.S. labor toward further integration with Mexico or those of European labor toward integration with Turkey (both hostile) are more likely to be reflected in policy than those of the median voter whose preferences over the mix of public goods provided converge. As other contributors to the present volume confirm, institutions matter.

border externalities, and limited economies of scale in the provision of public goods beyond the level of national government. By implication, one would expect to find more reliance on supranational governance among small countries that cannot efficiently produce public goods such as tourist infrastructure and that might engage in beggar-thy-neighbor policies without regional coordination. Geographical proximity and small size might also produce less heterogeneity in the types of public goods demanded to support tourism. The relatively high degree of regional collaboration in such areas as the Caribbean appears to confirm such predictions.

Changes in governance that result from financial integration provide an excellent test of these economic models. International finance demonstrates economic globalization at its most advanced. The large number of national currencies certainly suggests that economies of scale in the production of stable currencies have not been fully exploited, although the EMU may be a step in this direction. Externalities, particularly the effects of large-country monetary policies on smaller economies, are also significant drivers in the push for currency regionalization. Consistent with this prediction, the most advanced forms of delegation, particularly dollarization, have been more characteristic of small economies. As Cohen's account in chapter 6 suggests, however, financial globalization has elevated both externalities and economies of scale far beyond any contemporary increase in currency regionalization. Preferences have also become more homogeneous. Among the industrialized economies in particular, monetary policies have targeted low inflation and stable exchange rates as a central monetary goal. The symbolic hold of national currencies has also eroded. Despite these changes, delegation of monetary authority by national governments is arguably far lower than would be predicted by a purely economic model. Outside Europe, no significant trend toward currency regionalization among larger states has occurred. As Cohen describes, national politics shapes this pattern in important ways. A politically motivated desire for policy autonomy, the symbolism of a national currency, and the mobilization of prospective losers from deeper economic integration have slowed movement toward supranational delegation.

Eichengreen (chapter 7) documents even less movement toward new global governance in the sphere of financial regulation. The spillover effects of inadequate financial supervision and regulation have been evident since a series of crises in the Euromarkets in the early 1970s. Hedge funds, a class of financial institutions that were virtually unregulated, received close scrutiny from emerging-market countries during the East Asian economic crisis and its aftermath. Despite vivid demonstration of the risks posed by inadequate regulation, emerging-market and industrialized countries failed completely in their efforts to reach agreement on a new global regulatory regime. One could attribute this outcome to heterogeneous preferences, since the two groups diverged on whether regulation should be primarily intergovernmental or market-based and whether national governments should be its principal locus. The case of hedge-fund regulation points to two additional shortcomings in economic models of governance transfer, however. First, the mere existence of externalities may not produce a change of governance to capture those externalities. Second, asymmetries in externalities may be critical in determining whether governance remains at the national level or shifts to the supranational. As Eichengreen describes, the financial crises were more severe for emerging-market economies than for the larger industrialized economies. When hedge funds entered and exited an emerging market, they left "a large footprint." Although the failure of Long-Term Capital Management in 1998 seemed a fairly large footprint for even the United States, the activities of highly leveraged institutions rarely seemed to pose the same level of threat to macroeconomic management in the industrialized world. The G-7 governments felt little pressure to increase regulation through new global agreements and institutions.

The economic models deployed to explain transfers of governance to regional and global levels can also be tested against patterns of decentralization to the subnational level in a more integrated global economy. Hiscox (chapter 3), Garrett and Rodden (chapter 4), and Van Houten (chapter 5) review arguments drawn from existing economic models that link decentralization with the advance of globalization. Economic integration may influence bargaining and decentralization itself by changing the preferences of key actors, shifting their calculus of costs and benefits, or altering their capabilities.

Globalization may produce more heterogeneous preferences over policy and public goods in contrast to the conventional view that it induces homogeneity. Global economic integration may produce cultural and political backlash, reinforcing local identities and claims for political recognition. Hiscox adds a second important driver of heterogeneous preferences that has been overlooked in existing models: the effects of globalization on incomes and income distribution. In cases where globalization has such effects, the positive benefits of political integration decline and political conflict and demands for dis-integration rise. Once again decentralization or even the dismantling of existing states is the predicted outcome.

An open world economy may reduce the costs of political separation by producing what Van Houten labels new "opportunity structures" for subnational groups. These may be economic or institutional. The advantages of a national market without barriers declines as international barriers to economic exchange fall (Alesina and Spolaore 1997). Threats of secession become more credible, since "going it alone" appears to be a more plausible economic option. The bargaining leverage of subnational groups may increase as a result, producing greater decentralization or fiscal redistribution. In certain regional contexts, such as Europe, new institutional routes for self-assertion may also be opened.

A final causal link between globalization and decentralization lies in changing capabilities at the national level. Pressure from foreign investors may create incentives for federalism, particularly of the "market-preserving" variety. National budgets may be placed under pressure by capital mobility, leading the center to "off-load" government responsibilities onto local governments that may have fiscal resources less influenced by global financial integration. National policies may simply be seen as less effective under conditions of globalization, in light of spillover effects on macroeconomic management. (Why smaller, local jurisdictions would be more effective, however, is not clear.) A combination of rising international and subnational demands and a perception of declining national-level capabilities could produce decentralization or even the creation of new jurisdictions.

Garrett and Rodden (chapter 4) argue, however, that globalization produces other demands from local jurisdictions that outweigh these potential pressures for decentralization. In particular, Garrett and Rodden emphasize economic specialization within an integrated market and the risks that it imposes on the constituent jurisdictions. (The competing dynamics of specialization and homogenization also figure in the analysis of convergence, discussed later in this chapter.) Specialization increases demands for risk-sharing from local jurisdictions; fiscal centralization, rather than decentralization, is the likely outcome. In similar fashion, globalization's effects on income distribution might also produce fiscal centralization at the national level, rather than inevitable decentralization. In contrast to Hiscox's (chapter 3) emphasis on the convergence or divergence in income distribution within and between jurisdictions and its consequent effects on preferences over public-goods provision, Garrett and Rodden emphasize the need to strike new redistributive bargains at the national level in order to counter globalization's effects. Their empirical evidence does, indeed, confirm their expectations, indicating that globalization produces fiscal centralization rather than decentralization.[2]

---

[2] Their analysis raises several questions, however. A willingness to centralize fiscal risk-sharing in national hands implies that the risks from globalization are evenly distributed across jurisdictions. If certain localities are more subject to such risks than others (more

Van Houten (chapter 5) also finds little evidence to support a causal connection between regional assertiveness, measured by demands for revenue-raising authority, and global or regional (European) economic integration. None of the economic models described earlier are particularly powerful explanations for this dimension of regional political action. Instead, Van Houten attributes differences in regional assertiveness to preexisting cultural distinctiveness, relative economic position within the national economy, and especially the institutions of party competition. Rather than a redefinition of globalization's effects — the demands for macroeconomic stabilization and risk-sharing suggested by Garrett and Rodden — Van Houten finds only weak effects of globalization on the production of far-reaching regional political demands.

Although they seem to be at odds, the results of Hiscox, Garrett and Rodden, and Van Houten are not entirely inconsistent. First, they use different proxies for decentralization. Hiscox measures increased regional autonomy primarily through expanded elections for municipal, state, and provincial governments. Garrett and Rodden focus on the distribution of spending (not the authority to tax) between central and local governments. Van Houten concentrates on subnational pressures for decentralization, not policy or institutional outcomes. He also limits his analysis to a sample of highly industrialized societies in Europe, which enriches his data but may also limit the applicability of his conclusions. As Hiscox suggests, for example, region-specific economic assets may become less important with industrialization. Following the arguments of Garrett and Rodden, industrialized societies with highly developed welfare states may also have a wider array of instruments to compensate for distributional conflicts.

As they suggest, the differences among these authors can only be resolved with research that will extend their actor-oriented models. These valuable, first-stage efforts to construct political models that will explain the effects of globalization on decentralization of political authority must be succeeded by a second stage. Those revised models will

---

likely to benefit from fiscal insurance), then the willingness of other, less risk-prone jurisdictions to support centralization would be doubtful. Second, if risk-sharing favors national level policymaking, a strong case could be made that a regional or even global level of governance could more effectively deal with these effects of globalization. Why the delegation stops at the central government rather than some higher level is unclear. Finally, the ability of any given national government to accumulate the resources for redistributive bargains in the face of demands from subnational groups and governments depends on agreement among those groups and governments on the terms of the final bargain and the attractiveness of outside options (such as secession). Demands for redistribution in the face of economic integration may easily lead to political conflict and breakup rather than centralization and a new federal fiscal bargain.

move beyond changes in actor preferences, cost-benefit calculations, and capabilities to the bargaining and institutional contexts of the key political actors. For example, as Garrett and Rodden point out, an alteration in the calculus of costs and benefits on the periphery may produce different results depending on the institutional parameters of bargaining. Credible threats of secession may produce either decentralization or fiscal centralization to "buy off" those threats (or a combination of the two). An "explicit model of bargaining" (Hiscox) and a better understanding of "the political institutions through which such battles are fought" (Garrett and Rodden) are required for more definitive conclusions. Van Houten's emphasis on systems of party competition as a key variable only reinforces these directives for the future.[3]

A Political Model of Changes in the Site of Governance

Although the present volume does not provide a fully developed political model that connects globalization to shifts in governance, the components of such a model are clear. First, a political model concentrates on the distributive and asymmetric effects of globalization: economic interdependence creates winners and losers within and between societies. The definition of those winners and losers has been a centerpiece of research in political economy over the past decade.[4] The insights developed there can be applied in a relatively straightforward way to the analysis of governance structures. Winners try to preserve favorable institutions or alter governance structures to further "lock in" their winnings. Losers try to shift decisions to governance structures more amenable to their influence and pressure.

Economic integration has not produced governance shifts that match its global reach. One political explanation for this lack of fit lies in the search for political influence by both winners and losers. Political actors may respond to efficiency concerns over time, but they are more likely to concentrate on assigning governance functions to venues in which their political influence is maximized, and thus their policy preferences best served. Strategies of capture on the part of particular actors will often trump broader concerns over public-goods provision or externalities. Issue-area will also influence the strategies of actors, particularly whether they are intent on restraining national governments or influencing their conduct. The contrast between currency regionalization and financial regulation, both driven in large measure by globaliza-

---

[3] Hiscox nonetheless also finds that regions with site-specific assets (primarily ores and metals) increase their share of state and local government spending.

[4] See Bates (1997); Frieden (1991b); Frieden and Rogowski (1996); Hiscox (2001); and Rogowski 1989.

tion, illustrates the importance of such forum-shopping. An internationalist coalition, made up of financial and manufacturing interests with strong links to the world economy, plays an important political role in both of these issue-areas. In the case of currency regionalization, internationalists typically favor movement of monetary policy to the supranational level (or into the hands of another national central bank) as a means of constraining national authorities. Loss of influence at the national level is compensated for by the creation of supranational entities that are more likely to pursue policies that internationalist business interests prefer. In the case of financial regulation, however, the issue of political influence is more significant. Financial institutions cannot be certain that any international entity created for regulatory purposes will offer the same reliable channels of influence as national regulatory authorities. In addition, any global entity will award some voice to their chief critics in the emerging-market capitals. Although global regulation might well be more "efficient," it is not the politically favored outcome in this case.

Second, in a political model, institutions matter. Most of the economic models are institution-free. Political influence is closely associated with economic weight: the economic winners from globalization are typically the political winners. Yet institutions refract and distort that simple economic determinism, mediating and shaping political outcomes. Federal political institutions tilt policies toward international tourism in a decentralized direction (Martin, chapter 2). Existing global institutions bias outcomes in the international regulation of hedge funds (Eichengreen, chapter 7). The outcome of bargaining over redistributive and risk-sharing policies is partly determined by political institutions (Garrett and Rodden, chapter 4). Political party systems prove to be critical intervening variables in amplifying or dampening demands for regional autonomy (Van Houten, chapter 5). Institutions and the bargaining context that they create are critical intervening variables linking actors and governance outcomes. The battle over distributional outcomes often becomes a battle over institutions.

Finally, a political model of globalization and its effects on governance location must take into account the mobilization of new political actors. Economic models assume a fixed cast of actors whose preferences are easily specified. Martin's (chapter 2) description of globalization's political effects, however, includes the emergence of new NGOs that are driven by nonmaterial externalities, in this instance, the exploitation of children in the sex-tourism industry in other countries. Haufler (chapter 9) describes the growing activism of NGOs around environmental issues. Predicting the preferences of these new actors over sites of governance relies on the same calculus of winners and losers and forum-shopping versus efficiency. Although NGOs in the sex-tourism case may prefer a global institution with enforcement powers, they recognize that this is unrealistic under current conditions and therefore choose to lobby national governments for enforcement against violators in other jurisdictions. This "lateral" extension of enforcement by national authorities — exercising jurisdiction over nationals while they are resident in other countries — is yet another example of the ambiguities in global governance.

Governance across the Public-Private Divide

Globalization constrains the array of policy instruments available to states. This consequence of globalization is particularly important in explaining shifts of governance across the public-private divide. Regulation or standards governance by national political authorities may become less effective in a global economy. Capital can too easily evade national regulations. Incompatible national standards become barriers to trade, raising consumer prices and engendering discord between firms and states. New activist groups promoting the environment or human rights seek to politicize and ultimately regulate the behavior of both foreign producers and subsidiaries of home-country multinationals. Underlying these trends is the same fundamental mismatch between national jurisdictions and a global market that predicts transfers of authority to the supranational level. At the same time (or as an alternative) globalization may also expand the regulatory role of private actors. As discussion of the vertical dimension of governance transfer confirmed, however, prospective gains from new governance structures alone are insufficient to explain many of those changes. A political theory of globalization and governance change is required once again to explain horizontal change across the public-private divide.

With the exception of the European Union, intergovernmental cooperation has produced little supranational regulation of international corporations. Rather, the principal response to growing cross-border investment has been an increase in self-regulation by corporations and new forms of joint public-private regulation. In the latter case, rules may be developed by private or public-private international bodies but enforced by national authorities. In international finance, as Eichengreen (chapter 7) describes, governments have collaborated at the international level on new standards of transparency that are then enforced by the markets and by national governments. Standards governance, discussed by Mattli (chapter 8), witnessed a shift to transnational processes under conditions of globalization, whether the primary actors were public or private. (The precise mix varied by region and by sector.)

Globalization simply and sharply increased the costs of purely national standards-setting. The inefficiencies of intergovernmental standards-setting, however, led to a greater role for private actors through market-driven adoption of standards or private transnational standards-development organizations (SDOs).

Purely private regulation or standards governance may not be a stable political equilibrium, however, even under conditions of globalization. As Mattli argues, private competitors may find it as difficult to agree on common standards as governments; the failure of coordination results in wasteful and duplicative outcomes. Collusive and anticompetitive practices—an excess of cooperation—may produce equally undesirable outcomes. The exclusion of key political actors from such arrangements provides one of the principal motivations for moving from private governance to joint standards governance. Renewed government intervention is most likely in response to evident failures of private coordination or demands by those who have been disadvantaged by private standards governance. The pattern of joint governance is most pronounced in the European Union, where such groups have greater access to regional policymaking. As Mattli describes, a similar model is now being adopted in global standards governance.

The mobilization of new groups into the political arena is also likely to explain increased regulation—public or private. Globalization produces better information about economic and political practices in other countries, lower transactions costs for organizing groups within and across borders, and a fledgling global civil society. As transnational activist groups arise, they make new demands for corporate responsibility—not only in how firms themselves act within countries, but also for how the governments of host countries act (Ottaway 2001). As issue-groups grow in number and size, firms come under increasing pressure to reform corporate practices. The failure of intergovernmental efforts at such regulation leads to direct pressure on corporations operating across national boundaries. As Haufler (chapter 9) shows, firms that rely upon reputation or that are easily targeted because of brand recognition are especially likely to adopt self-regulation in response. Domestic political institutions play an important role in determining the site and nature of regulation. In the case of industry self-regulation, unresponsive authoritarian governments block access for their citizens who, in league with transnational activists, then target reputationally sensitive firms in the private sector. Pressure on such firms aims either to alter the firm's behavior directly or to initiate pressure on the local government. Following a similar logic, activists will attempt to mobilize citizens in democratic societies with more decentralized and permeable institutions, like the United States, where they have the easiest access (Risse-Kappen 1995). The United States becomes a focus of transnational activity, not only because of its central role in international markets, but also because of its easily penetrated state institutions.

As a central part of the strategic environment, governments continue to play an important role in governance even when they are not themselves actively issuing regulations or setting standards. Since they retain residual rights to enact policy — to regulate business practices, to license new plants, to tax corporations — states are a feature of the bargaining process. When pressed by transnational activists, firms regulate themselves because of the possibility that states might regulate their behavior. Self-regulation by firms may be intended to preempt tougher public regulations. The corporations may tie their hands just enough to diffuse pressure on governments to take public regulatory action. Although often represented by firms as exercises in corporate citizenship, the expressed motivation for self-regulation omits an important reason — avoiding public regulatory oversight — that may prompt corporations to subordinate short-term profits in order to bolster their reputation or maintain future freedom of action.

Private governance does not stand independent of public governance. Governments help define the institutional arena in which bargaining between private actors occurs, and, through their continuing regulatory power, set one of the possible outcomes should bargaining break down. They play a central role in enforcement even when bargaining takes place in a private context. And in a joint public-private context, such as standards-setting, national bodies that aggregate interests within states are central to the success of the international bodies. States that do this well may have a leg up in international negotiations, encouraging firms to work with, rather than outside of or against, public authorities.

Private governance is not only shaped by the possibility of government action, it is often complemented by public governance. The case of standards-setting is illustrative. National standards are no longer adequate, but governments retain authority in this important area — authority is delegated to private SDOs or to the international level, not permanently transferred, a distinction that we make in chapter 1. A new level of governance is created alongside the old without (at least in the near term) weakening existing national governance structures. A more complex system may provide more and deeper governance rather than simply shifting the site of a fixed quantity of governance toward the private sphere.

THE CONVERGENCE HYPOTHESIS: CONTENDING MODELS

Perhaps the most controversial effect of globalization is its alleged ability to homogenize national politics and culture. The image of an unstoppable cultural juggernaut creating "McWorld" pervades contemporary polemics and inspires political action to protect national cultures and institutions. Equally serious is the claim that the competitive pressures of globalization will induce societies to give up hard-won regulatory gains. In this view, the leveling effects of globalization will force a race to the bottom that weakens national regulatory protections.

We challenge this view of convergence on two grounds. First, rather than inducing only conformity, the logic of globalization may also promote specialization and differentiation.[5] Indeed, divergence rather than convergence is perhaps the more typical result. At the very least, the constraints of the global economy are compatible with many different national governance structures and policies. Even Simmons and Elkins (chapter 11), who find greater convergence than others in this volume, conclude that the spread of monetary and financial liberalization occurs within groups of countries related by similar market positions, geography, and cultural ties. General movement toward external liberalization over the last decades has occurred along highly differentiated and contingent paths.

Second, the process of convergence or divergence is the product of highly strategic and political choices by national governments. Far from being driven by inexorable market forces toward some neoliberal nirvana or hell, depending on one's perspective, governments retain room for maneuver, weigh the costs and benefits of alternative actions, respond to domestic political pressures and interests, and arrive at different destinations. Politics and choice remain central at all levels.

Rogowski (chapter 10) makes the strongest case that globalization contains a logic of divergence as well as convergence. His model parallels that of Charles Tiebout, in which voters "shop" jurisdictions for bundles of public goods that most closely match their preferences. In Rogowski's model, however, only capitalists are mobile, and both capital and workers (voters) are assumed to have fixed policy preferences. Capital mobility discourages voters in jurisdictions with policies unfriendly to capital from adjusting those policies in order to improve wages. Capital mobility, in effect, drains away the incentive for policy adjustment rather than imposing uniform competitive pressures on governments to converge on capital-friendly policies. Policy divergence ensues as some countries move toward policies more attractive to mobile capital and others move further away. Policy convergence occurs only as a special case under limited circumstances.

Gourevitch (chapter 12) and McNamara (chapter 13) argue that capital mobility permits governments and societies considerable room for

---

[5] We are not the first to reach this conclusion. See, for example, Berger and Dore (1996).

maneuver, thereby allowing existing policy and institutional differences to persist. Although Gourevitch notes several channels through which globalization could exert pressure for convergence in corporate governance — capital markets, political demands for reform in the face of declining economic performance, international institutions, and either governmental or nongovernmental regulatory standards — he contends that international market signals are filtered by corporations and by domestic political institutions in ways that reduce pressure to converge on a single international "best practice." Gourevitch argues that market integration implies wider market scope, creating incentives for specialization, an ecological effect that may produce successful, differentiated niche strategies. Framing this effect in terms of institutional comparative advantage and the shifting "terms of trade" between national production systems, Gourevitch argues that this specialization may also be reinforced by the production strategies of international investors. Rather than simply offering cost-of-capital premiums to corporations that change their governance practices (as indicated in a model based on competition for scarce capital), a firm's multinational production strategy may award value to locational specialization. Under conditions of globalization, that specialization may occur at the level of national economies.[6] Finally, given that corporate governance structures are themselves deeply embedded in national governance structures, and that different combinations of corporate and political governance structures may thrive at different times in an integrated global economy, there appear to be at most weak pressures for convergence.

McNamara notes that the most significant forces for convergence in fiscal policies within the European Union were political, generated by the decision to form the EMU and embodied in the fiscal convergence criteria agreed in the Treaty on European Union. Those criteria, however, did not specify how the targets should be reached, and McNamara discovers considerable diversity in the policy choices made. Most significant is her analysis of the composition of fiscal policies, which fails to demonstrate a bias toward "procapital" initiatives. Mobile capital rewarded deficit reduction with interest-rate declines, but appeared relatively indifferent to the mix of policies that achieved the fiscal targets. Surprisingly, then, even in this most likely case of convergence — where national leaders agreed on a common goal and committed themselves to

---

[6] A different parallel can be found in the new economic geography, in which agglomeration and dispersion effects (the degree to which spatial units specialize economically) depends on industry characteristics (increasing returns to scale) and trade costs (Krugman 1991; Ottaviano and Pugo 1998). Refining the determinants of institutional convergence and divergence (specialization) over time requires a similar research strategy.

substantial policy alterations to reach it—different paths presented themselves, and countries chose their own routes.

In their investigation of the striking convergence on external liberalization since 1970, Simmons and Elkins (chapter 11) draw attention to policies that promote further global economic integration and take issue with those who argue for policy and institutional inertia in the face of globalization. By controlling for domestic political and economic variables that would support independent decisions for policies of financial and monetary liberalization, Simmons and Elkins conclude that policy diffusion through two different mechanisms is an important explanation for the advance of liberalization (and globalization). The first mechanism is the familiar one of economic competition: governments liberalize to improve aggregate economic performance (with accompanying political benefits for those implementing the policies). The second is a sociologically grounded model of policy emulation. Transnational networks of information and belief support policy choices for liberalization in an environment of imperfect information regarding the consequences of those choices.

Different models of political action underlie these different conclusions regarding policy convergence, divergence, and inertia. Once again, globalization's consequences for governance reflect its effects on political actors. As before, the core question is a contingent one: under what conditions will each of these models dominate? Rogowski (chapter 10) posits governments that are passive registers of the preferences of voters who choose how much of their preferred policy they will give up in the interests of a higher wage. Governments ignore the prospective behavior of other governments. As Simmons and Elkins suggest, however, most convergence models rely on strategic interaction among governments, which face "incentives to anticipate and counter decisions taken outside of their jurisdiction." Strategic behavior, in turn, is more likely to occur among governments that see themselves as similar on certain dimensions, and therefore in competition for mobile capital, export markets, or, possibly, skilled labor. Simmons and Elkins demonstrate that countries with similar export markets and investment risk profiles converge on policies of financial and monetary liberalization. The effects of competition for mobile capital appear to be stronger. Nevertheless, persistent, strong regional effects are more difficult to explain using a competitive model. They appear to confirm the importance of other, noncompetitive avenues of influence that also underpin convergent policies.

Mobile capital plays a central role in models that emphasize jurisdictional competition, such as Rogowski's and the economic-competition model of Simmons and Elkins, and those that do not. Contingent models of convergence-divergence might therefore differentiate more fully among policies that are of highest priority to capital and those of lesser importance. In this respect, Rogowski's treatment of the electorate's policy preferences remains abstract, and Simmons and Elkins deal only with a limited range of policies (financial and monetary liberalization). Mobile capital is unlikely to hold homogeneous policy preferences: a multinational manufacturing firm will sort countries according to different policy criteria than a portfolio investor. As Gourevitch (chapter 12) suggests, even different multinationals may hold different policy preferences depending on how their production chain can be disaggregated and optimized across countries with different national production profiles. In a model based on competition for scarce international capital, how governments (and the electorates behind them) read those preferences will strongly influence the breadth of policy convergence.

In attempting to discern the conditions under which a particular model holds, a key difference should be emphasized between Simmons and Elkins, on the one hand, and the other chapters in this section, on the other. Simmons and Elkins find a contingent convergence among similar countries on external liberalization, which is itself one of the key drivers of globalization. Without monetary and financial liberalization, capital flows across national borders are impeded. At this level, there may be stronger pressures to take advantage of the gains from foreign investment, and thus greater convergence. The other chapters in this section suggest that, *given* monetary and financial liberalization, there may be few pressures for convergence in other sectors of policy. Mobile capital and globalization more generally may reward specialization and diversity (Gourevitch, chapter 12), or at least not demand it (McNamara, chapter 13), and electorates may have few incentives to alter their policies to cater to fleet-footed capitalists (Rogowski, chapter 10). Here, as elsewhere, issue-area matters. Pressures for open monetary and financial liberalization may not require similar convergence on other policy dimensions.

A final variable that appears in these accounts of convergence and nonconvergence is regional and global institutions. As McNamara's description of fiscal convergence suggests, the European Union's Maastricht treaty imposed obligations for fiscal convergence on those countries that wished to join the EMU. This membership incentive for convergence has also been deployed effectively by the European Union for those countries negotiating to join the the organization. Institutional membership is valuable, as McNamara confirms, for the credibility that it imparts to government policies — credibility that rewards governments and their economies with lower interest rates. The European Union and other regional arrangements produce policy harmonization through agreement among existing members. They may also act to *prevent* convergence through policy competition, distinguishing between market-influenced convergence with positive consequences and competition that risks socially undesirable deregulation. Gourevitch documents the role of the EU in formulating corporate governance rules and suggests that other regional and global institutions may intervene in similar fashion. Elkins and Simmons suggest that regional institutions (preferential trade arrangements) may provide a means for inducing similar, trade-promoting policies among economic partners through the elaboration of networks of information and social interaction. These regional effects are yet another demonstration of the contingent nature of globalization's effects on governance and the importance of actor preferences and institutions in understanding those effects.

GLOBALIZATION, DEMOCRACY, AND ACCOUNTABILITY

If globalization transfers governance to new sites or leads to a convergence in national policies, questions of accountability naturally follow. Democracy has only been realized at the level of the nation-state and its subordinate units, and even there it is by no means universal. By moving key governance functions to supranational institutions or private actors, globalization may weaken the accountability of policymakers to democratic electorates. Fears of a democratic deficit are based on both an absence of direct electoral accountability in key decision-making units as well as long chains of delegation from democratically elected governments to the newly authoritative bodies. Caporaso (chapter 14), in the case of the European Union, and Keohane and Nye (chapter 15), more generally, examine the concept of accountability and conclude that it is more robust at the global level than many critics have allowed.

Focusing on structures of delegation, the ability of principals to create incentives for agents, and degrees of transparency, Caporaso argues that accountability within the European Union can be considered using two templates. If one considers the European Union as a parliamentary state, it appears that traditional institutions of democracy are simply being rebuilt at the supranational level. If so, applying standards and practices of democratic accountability to the EU may be appropriate. Considered as a regulatory state, the European Union is a different kind of polity, one with limited powers to deal with the externalities that follow from market integration. Here, European institutions are more similar to administrative agencies — such as an independent central bank — where some degree of autonomy may be required for the adoption of socially optimal policies. In this case, the instruments of accountability rest not on direct elections but on clear statutory objectives, judicial review, budgetary discipline, and monitoring by interest groups. In both templates, Caporaso concludes, accountability has recently become a more important objective, and the European Union has responded by tightening the mechanisms of accountability.

Caporaso also argues that rights, embodied in law, are a key foundation for holding both national and supranational procedures and policies to account. In the European Union, he argues, economic integration has produced an extension of rights through actions of the European Court of Justice that have constitutionalized European law and extended it directly to individuals and other nonstate actors. In certain areas, such as gender equality, the judicial confirmation of rights occurred first at the European level, not at the national level. In this institutional context, at least, political responses to economic integration have produced an extension of rights that might not have occurred independently among a collectivity of national states. This extension, in turn, creates a new basis for ensuring that politicians and procedures at all levels must respond to citizen demands. Although standards of accountability in either a supranational parliamentary or a regulatory state may be unique to the European Union, the extension of rights may be a process that opens up new and more general routes of accountability in different sites of governance.

Keohane and Nye disaggregate accountability and ask how the differing mechanisms, deployed within national democracies, fare under conditions of globalization. Outside the European Union and certain issue-areas such as trade, Keohane and Nye see no increase in electoral accountability or accountability to national representative bodies, which they argue are impractical in the absence of a global political community. Nonetheless, they argue that other forms of accountability may more than compensate for an imperfect reflection of national democratic governance at the supranational level. Hierarchical accountability, central to delegation models, and legal accountability, similar to Caporaso's emphasis on rights, are central to statist and international organization models of governance. In a globalizing world, Keohane and Nye argue, reputational and market accountability can be enforced by actors within transnational and policy-network models of governance. The mix of mechanisms that ensures accountability varies, in their view, as international governance changes. The growing importance of transnational actors in international governance, for example, may enhance accountability through increased transparency.[7]

---

[7] The accountability of new participants in this form of governance (NGOs, multinational corporations) is often questionable, however. Not only are NGOs themselves sometimes less than entirely democratic, but a multiplication of principals with conflicting

The relationship between sites of governance and accountability is subtle and deserves greater analysis. For example, throughout the debate over democratic deficits and accountability, one assumption is pervasive: governance is more accountable when it is "closer" to its principals, particularly electorates. The normative principle of subsidiarity—that power should be decentralized whenever possible—incorporates this assumption (CEPR 1993). Even when formally democratic, however, decentralized governance may also be liable to capture (Bardhan and Mookherjee 1999). Long recognized in theories of trade policy, concentrated interests may be able to dominate policymaking at local levels. The trade-off between the risk of capture and increased information that may enhance accountability must be considered. Governance at the supranational level may provide a means of breaking the hold of local interests, albeit at the cost of a longer chain of delegated authority.

In similar fashion, regulatory institutions at the supranational level may be more vulnerable to pressure from their national "owners" than analogous national institutions since they lack direct channels of popular support. The European Central Bank (ECB), for instance, appears to have more formal (legal) independence than any national monetary authority in history. Nevertheless, if central bank independence ultimately rests on the preferences of democratic electorates, as has been argued at the national level (Posen 1993), then the nominally more independent ECB may actually be less immune from political interference than its national counterparts.

More generally, as part of the larger political framework that guides this project, the debate over democratic accountability can be profitably understood as part of a larger struggle over policy outcomes. Institutions are contested by groups and countries who are dissatisfied by existing or expected outcomes. Winners seldom complain about the political rules and procedures that produced their policy success. Losers seek to change the rules, often through appeals to larger normative principles, like democracy. Calls for democratic accountability can be seen as attempts to alter institutions in order to change policy. By including additional interests and voices in the policy process, advocates of democratic accountability hope to alter the action of supranational institutions or private actors who have assumed potentially public responsibilities (e.g., international standards governance; see Mattli, chapter 8). Some advocates urge greater accountability because of a sincere

---

preferences may allow enhanced and undesirable autonomy for those engaged in international governance. Accountability under contested-issue networks, in the absence of political entrepreneurs who can use the new networks for forging cooperative bargains, is likely to create large incentives for inaction and stalemate.

attachment to democratic values, but other advocates criticize the capture of global institutions by corporate interests because they believe more direct citizen involvement and shorter chains of delegation would shift policy in directions that they prefer. The demand for greater accountability is itself political — and the construction of more accountable governance is the product of changing preferences and existing institutions.

Conclusions and Implications

The differentiated portrait of globalization and governance presented by the authors of this volume points to at least two strong conclusions. First, globalization defined as economic integration is not global. Integration remains uneven and spatially differentiated. The European experience in economic integration and governance change is particularly pertinent, both as an instance of long-standing and deep regional economic integration and an example of particular political and institutional responses to that integration. Most authors have taken Europe as an example of advanced globalization. Whether its responses to economic integration will be imitated elsewhere is far from clear. Strong regional effects on liberalization, discovered by Elkins and Simmons (chapter 11), suggests that geographical proximity and regional differentiation remain important elsewhere. Equally important is differentiation by issue-area. Finance, the ever-advancing frontier of global economic integration, illustrates upward pressure on governance as regional currencies and dollarization become more popular. Even in this sphere, however, upward pressure is uneven, as the variation in currency arrangements and failure of supranational regulatory initiatives demonstrate.

Second, globalization has affected national political authority, but its influence has seldom matched simple claims of diminished governance and the hollowing out of the state. Although they were never the self-contained billiard balls of past imagination, nation-states have clearly grown more porous over the last decades. Producers, consumers, and citizens are more exposed to, and affected by, decisions made by actors outside of their national borders. Governments, in turn, respond to the demands of their constituents to either reinforce or block the direction of international change. In some ways, governments are more constrained, since successfully confronting externally induced change often requires collaboration with other governments. Globalization by its very nature tends to lie beyond the effective control of any single government.

At the same time, globalization has not sharply reduced or limited national capabilities. In some cases, in fact, globalization has reinforced national political authorities and institutions that are necessary to implement international bargains, such as those forged in the sphere of financial regulation or fiscal policy, described in the European case by McNamara (chapter 13). As Mattli (chapter 8) suggests, national standards bodies remain important for aggregating local firms and effectively representing their interests in international forums. Indeed, to the extent that states with stronger national bodies more often succeed in getting favorable standards adopted at the international level, this will create additional pressure for states to expand their national capabilities and practices. Shifts in governance to the supranational level often continue to rely on the capabilities of national governments.

In other cases, globalization has expanded national capabilities through new opportunities for extrajurisdictional reach on the part of more powerful states. The same avenues of commerce and capital that constrain states also create opportunities for more powerful and less dependent governments to manipulate the preferences and policies of others. Martin's (chapter 2) discussion of national and international responses to child-sex tourism illustrates the importance of this "lateral" extension of national governance. Similarly, as money becomes, in Cohen's term (chapter 6), deterritorialized, some states are weakened while others expand their influence. As small or economically mismanaged states either adopt the currency of another or peg their currencies to it, the currency and policy domain of the currency issuer expands well beyond its national boundaries.

Analytically, the authors of the present volume advance agent-centered theories of globalization and governance. Rather than seeing globalization as an inexorable force, we see it as part of an evolving environment to which political actors at all levels must choose how to respond. Although perhaps more constrained than in the past, political actors still have a considerable range of choice. How they choose is a function of their preferences, especially whether globalization makes them winners or losers, and the institutions within which they bargain.

The future of national political authority will in large measure lie in the response of two sets of actors: transnational economic and political actors, on the one hand, and national electorates, on the other. Although governance shifts have expanded opportunities for forum-shopping on the part of various actors, nation-states remain central sites of political contestation. Multinational corporations (MNCs) are the engines of economic globalization, and their preferences over the sites and substance of governance are influential. Having prospered within the interstices of national political authorities, they are reluctant to see an expansion of public regulation at any level (see Lake 1999b) and would prefer to govern themselves when necessary (Haufler, chapter 9). Yet, when public authority is required to either solve market failures or constrain other actors, MNCs have tended to rely upon national governments — and especially those of their home states. Indeed, even the vaunted Multilateral Agreement on Investment — advocated by the MNCs themselves and sponsored by the investor-friendly OECD — did not create a new supranational authority, apart from a quasi-judicial dispute-resolution procedure. Instead, the agreement sought primarily to constrain state encroachments on the privileges of foreign investors and depended entirely on national means of enforcement, elements that produced overwhelming opposition by the developing countries.

NGOs, despite their transnational scope and ambition, also remain highly dependent on state authorities for their effectiveness. As Haufler (chapter 9) and Martin (chapter 2) indicate, NGO influence relies largely on an ability to threaten legal or regulatory action through national governments and to affect corporate reputations through consumers in their home countries. The attitudes of NGOs toward global and regional governance have often been mixed. An international convention to curb child-sex tourism exists, but it has had little direct effect. The convention has been more successful in legitimating national measures. If NGOs become more global in their transnational activities and more influential in the developing countries, in particular, their present bias toward exercising influence through national governments in the industrialized countries may shift, with profound implications for governance choices.

The electorates of the most powerful (and democratic) nation-states are also central to the future of political authority. Although electorates have shown surprising willingness to delegate their control of some governance functions (as in the construction of regional currencies or dollarization), democratic accountability remains a criterion of governance that they are unwilling to forgo in many other domains. The European Union will remain a bellwether in assessing the response of democratic electorates to expanded governance that does not immediately acquire the form of a national parliamentary democracy. For other global and regional institutions, the task of demonstrating politically acceptable levels of accountability is even more difficult.

Overall, there is little evidence of a hollowing out of governance at the national level. National governments remain effective and necessary players in the global economy. Globalization does require, however, that national institutions adapt to the new environment if they are to succeed in meeting the demands of their constituents. For those countries that do not give up their national currencies under conditions of financial integration, a strengthening of central banks with greater delegated authority or a shift to a fixed exchange rate seems to be required for effective monetary policy (Bernhard and Leblang 2002; see Broz 2002). Standard-setting negotiated by national governments has proven ineffective under conditions of globalization; joint governance by both public and private entities has proven more efficient (Mattli, chapter 8). As financial regulation becomes more market-based, as advocated by most developed countries (Eichengreen, chapter 7), governments must give up direct, command-and-control regulatory rules in favor of practices designed to enhance transparency and provide better information to investors. Rather than the wholesale shift in the location of governance or competitive convergence on similar institutions, national adaptation and an expansion of governance alternatives constitute our most likely future.

REFERENCES

Abbott, Kenneth, and Duncan Snidal. 2001. "International 'Standards' and International Governance." *Journal of European Public Policy* 8 (3): 345–70.

Ades, Alberto, and Edward Glaeser. 1995. "Trade and Circuses: Explaining Urban Giants." *Quarterly Journal of Economics* 110 (1): 195–227.

Aizenman, Joshua, and Pablo E. Guidotti. 1994. "Capital Controls, Collective Costs, and Domestic Pubic Debt." *Journal of International Money and Finance* 13 (February): 41–54.

Alber, J., and G. Standing. 2000. "Social Dumping, Catch-up or Convergence? Europe in a Comparative Global Context." *Journal of European Social Policy* 10 (2): 99–119.

Albert, Michael. 1992. *Capitalism against Capitalism*. London: Whurr.

Alesina, Alberto, R. Baqir, and William Easterly. 1999. "Public Goods and Ethnic Divisions." *Quarterly Journal of Economics* 112 (November): 1243–84.

Alesina, Alberto, and Robert J. Barro. 2001. "Dollarization." *American Economic Review* 91, 2 (May): 381–85.

———. 2002. "Currency Unions." *Quarterly Journal of Economics* 117, 2 (May): 409–36.

Alesina, Alberto, Vittorio Grilli, and Gian Marie Milesi-Ferretti. 1994. "The Political Economy of Capital Controls." In *Capital Mobility: The Impact on Consumption Investment, and Growth*, edited by Leonardo Leiderman and Assaf Razin. Cambridge: Cambridge University Press.

Alesina, Alberto, and Enrico Spolaore. 1997. "On the Number and Size of Nations." *Quarterly Journal of Economics* 112, 4 (November): 1027–56.

Alesina, Alberto, Enrico Spolaore, and Romain Wacziarg. 2000. "Economic Integration and Political Disintegration." *American Economic Review* 90, 5 (December): 1276–96.

Alesina, Alberto, and Romain Wacziarg. 1998. "Openness, Country Size and Government." *Journal of Public Economics* 69 (3): 305–21.

Alogoskoufis, G. S., B. Lockwood, and A. Philippopoulos. 1992. "Wage Inflation, Electoral Uncertainty, and the Exchange Rate Regime: Theory and U.K. Evidence." *Economic Journal* 102 (415): 1370–94.

Alogoskoufis, G. S., and R. Smith. 1991. "The Phillips Curve, the Persistence of Inflation, and the Lucas Critique: Evidence from Exchange-Rate Regimes." *American Economic Review* 81 (5): 1254–75.

Alter, Karen J. 1998. "Who Are the 'Masters of the Treaty'? European Governments and the European Court of Justice." *International Organization* 52, 1 (winter): 121–47.

Amin, Ash, and Nigel Thrift, eds. 1994. *Globalization, Institutions, and Regional Development in Europe*. Oxford: Oxford University Press.

Anderson, Jeffrey J. 1990. "Skeptical Reflections on a Europe of the Regions: Britain, Germany, and the ERDF." *Journal of Public Policy* 10: 417–47.

Andrews, David M. 1994. "Capital Mobility and State Autonomy: Toward a Structural Theory of International Monetary Relations." *International Studies Quarterly* 38 (June): 193–218.

Anonymous. 1998. "Asia's Booming Sex Business." *The UNESCO Courier* 51 (11): 39.

———. 2000. "Asia: A Walk on the Depraved Side." *The Economist* 355 (8164): 39–40.

Ansell, Christopher K., Craig A. Parsons, and Keith Darden. 1997. "Dual Networks in European Regional Development Policy." *Journal of Common Market Studies* 35: 347–75.

Anton, James, and Dennis Yao. 1995. "Standard-Setting Consortia, Antitrust, and High-Technology Industries." *Antitrust Law Journal* 64: 247–63.

Applbaum, Arthur. 1999. *Ethics for Adversaries: The Morality of Roles in Public and Professional Life.* Princeton, N.J.: Princeton University Press.

Arellano, Manuel, and Stephen Bond. 1998. "Dynamic Panel Data Estimation." Unpublished manuscript, Institute for Fiscal Studies, London.

Aronson, Jonathan, and Peter Cowhey. 1988. *When Countries Talk: International Trade in Telecommunications Services.* Cambridge, Mass.: Ballinger.

Arthur, Brian. 1989. "Competing Technologies, Increasing Returns, and Lock-in by Historical Events." *The Economic Journal* 99: 116–31.

Arts, Bas. 1998. *The Political Influence of Global NGOs: Case Studies on the Climate and Biodiversity Conventions.* Utrecht: International Books.

ASEAN. 1998. "Plan of Action on ASEAN Cooperation in Tourism." Available at *http://www.aseansec.org/economic/poa_tour.html.*

Atkeson, Andrew, and Tamim Bayoumi. 1993. Private Capital Markets in a Currency Union." In *Policy Issues in the Operation of Currency Unions,* edited by Paul Masson and Mark Taylor. Cambridge: Cambridge University Press.

Atkins, W. S. 1998. *Technical Barriers to Trade.* Luxembourg: Office for Official Publications of the European Communities.

Auerbach, Nancy Neiman. 2001. *States, Banks, and Markets: Mexico's Path to Financial Liberalization in Comparative Perspective.* Boulder, Colo.: Westview Press.

Austin, Mark, and Helen Milner. 2001. "Strategies of European Standardization." *Journal of European Public Policy* 8 (3): 411–31.

Axelrod, Robert. 1997. "The Dissemination of Culture: A Model with Local Convergence and Global Polarization." *Journal of Conflict Resolution* 41: 203–26.

Baldwin, Richard E., and Philippe Martin. 1999. "Two Waves of Globalisation: Superficial Similarities, Fundamental Differences." NBER Working Paper 6904. National Bureau of Economic Research, Cambridge, Mass.

Baliño, Tomás, J. T., Adam Bennett, and Eduardo Borensztein. 1999. *Monetary Policy in Dollarized Economies.* Washington, D.C.: International Monetary Fund.

Barber, Benjamin R. 1996. *Jihad Versus McWorld.* New York: Ballantine Books.

Bardhan, Pranab, and Dilip Mookherjee. 1999. "Relative Capture of Local and Central Governments: An Essay in the Political Economy of Decentralization." Unpublished manuscript, University of California, Berkeley.

Barke, Michael. 1999. "Tourism and Culture in Spain: A Case of Minimal Conflict?" In *Tourism and Cultural Conflicts*, edited by Mike Robinson and Priscilla Boniface, 247–67. New York: CABI Publishing.

Barnett, Michael N., and Martha Finnemore. 1999. "The Politics, Power and Pathologies of International Organizations." *International Organization* 53, 4 (autumn): 699–732.

Barro, Robert J., and Xavier Sala-I-Martin. 1995. *Economic Growth*. New York: McGraw-Hill.

Bartolini, Leonardo, and Allan Drazen. 1997. "Capital Account Liberalization as a Signal." NBER Working Paper W5725. National Bureau of Economic Research, Cambridge, Mass.

———. 1998. "When Liberal Policies Reflect External Shocks, What Do We Learn?" NBER Working Paper W5727. National Bureau of Economic Research, Cambridge, Mass.

Basle Committee of Banking Supervisors. 2001. "Review of Issues Related to Highly Leveraged Institutions." Basle Committee Publication no. 79 (March). Basle: Basle Committee of Banking Supervisors.

Bates, Robert H. 1997. *Open-Economy Politics: The Political Economy of the World Coffee Trade*. Princeton, N.J.: Princeton University Press.

Beck, Neal, Jonathan N. Katz, and Richard Tucker. 1998. "Taking Time Seriously: Time-Series-Cross-Section Analysis with a Binary Dependent Variable." *American Journal of Political Science* 42 (4): 1260–88.

Beck, T., G. Clarke, A. Groff, P. Keefer, and P. Walsh. 1999. "New Tools and New Tests in Comparative Political Economy: The Database of Political Institutions." Unpublished manuscript, World Bank.

Beddoes, Zanny Minton. 1999. "From EMU to AMU? The Case for Regional Currencies." *Foreign Affairs* 78, 4 (July/August): 8–13.

Behn, Robert. 2001. *Accountability*. Washington, D.C.: Brookings Institution.

Beirich, Heidi, and Dwayne Woods. 2000. "Globalisation, Workers, and the Northern League." *West European Politics* 23 (1): 130–43.

Benabou, Roland. 1993. "Workings of a City: Location, Education, and Production." *Quarterly Journal of Economics* 108: 619–52.

Berg, Stanford. 1987. "Public Policy and Corporate Strategy in the AM Stereo Market." In *Product Standardization and Competitive Strategy*, edited by Landis Gabel. Amsterdam: North Holland.

———. 1989. Technical Standards as Public Goods: Demand Incentives for Cooperative Behavior." *Public Finance Quarterly* 17: 29–54.

Berger, Suzanne, and Ronald Dore, eds. 1996. *National Diversity and Global Capitalism*. Ithaca, N.Y.: Cornell University Press.

Bernhard, William, and David Leblang. 1999. "Democratic Institutions and Exchange-Rate Commitments." *International Organization* 53 (1): 71–97.

———. 2002. "Political Parties and Monetary Commitments." *International Organization* 56, 4 (autumn): 803–30.

Besen, Stanley, and Joseph Farrell. 1994. "Choosing How to Compete: Strategies and Tactics in Standardization." *Journal of Economic Perspectives* 8 (2): 117–31.

Besen, Stanley, and Garth Saloner. 1989. "The Economics of Telecommunications Standards." In *Changing the Rules: Technological Change, International*

Competition, and Regulation in Communications, edited by Robert Crandall and Kenneth Flamm. Washington, D.C.: Brookings Institution.

Besley, Timothy, and Stephen Coate. 1999. "Centralised Versus Decentralized Provision of Public Goods: A Political Economy Analysis." NBER Working Paper 7084. Cambridge, Mass.: National Bureau of Economic Research.

Bhagwati, Jagdish. 1996. "The Demands to Reduce Domestic Diversity Among Trading Nations." In *Fair Trade and Harmonization*, edited by Jagdish Bhagwati and Robert Hudec , 9–40. Cambridge, Mass.: MIT Press.

———. 1998. "The Capital Myth: The Difference Between Trade in Widgets and Trade in Dollars." *Foreign Affairs* 77: 7–12.

BHF Bank. 2000. "Euro Accelerates Consolidation of Financial Market Infrastructure." *Economics Review* 1485, 23 May.

Bignami, Francesca, and Steve Charnovitz. 2001. "Transatlantic Civil Society Dialogues." In *Transatlantic Governance in the Global Economy*, edited by Mark A. Pollack and Gregory C. Shaffer, 255–84. Lanham, Md: Rowman and Littlefield.

Bishop, Ryan, and Lillian S. Robinson. 1998. *Night Market: Sexual Cultures and the Thai Economic Miracle*. New York: Routledge.

Blatherwick, David. 1987. *The International Politics of Telecommunications*. Berkeley, Calif.: Institute for International Studies.

Boix, Carles. 1998. *Political Parties, Growth and Equality: Conservative and Social Democratic Economic Strategies in the World Economy*. Cambridge: Cambridge University Press.

Boli, John, and George Thomas, eds. 1999. *Contracting World Culture: International Nongovernmental Organizations Since 1875*. Stanford, Calif.: Stanford University Press.

Bolton, Patrick, and Gérard Roland. 1997. "The Breakup of Nations: A Political Economy Analysis." *Quarterly Journal of Economics* 112, 4 (November): 1057–90.

Bolton, Patrick, Gérard Roland, and Enrico Spolaore. 1996. "Economic Theories of the Break-up and Integration of Nations." *European Economic Review* 40: 697–705.

Bookman, Milica Z. 1992. *The Economics of Secession*. New York: St. Martin's Press.

Boonchalaksi, Wathinee, and Philip Guest. 1998. "Prostitution in Thailand." In *The Sex Sector: The Economic and Social Bases of Prostitution in Southeast Asia*, edited by Lin Lean Lim, 130–69. Geneva: International Labour Office.

Bordo, Michael, Barry Eichengreen, and Douglas A. Irwin. 1999. "Is Globalization Today Really Different than Globalization a Hundred Years Ago?" NBER Working Paper W7195. National Bureau of Economic Research, Cambridge, Mass.

Borrus, Michael, Dieter Ernst, and Stephan Haggard, eds. 2000. *Rivalry or Riches: International Production Networks in Asia*. London: Routledge.

Börzel, Tanja, and Thomas Risse. 2001. "Private-Public Partnerships: Effective and Legitimate Tools of International Governance?" Prepared for the Workshop on Global Governance, RSCAS, 6–7 April, Florence, Italy.

Boyer, Robert. 2002. "Variété du capitalisme et théorie de la regulation." In *L'Année de régulation 2002*, vol. 6. Paris: Presses de Sciences Po.

Brady, Robert. 1929. *Industrial Standardization*. New York: National Industrial Conference Board.

Braithwaite, John and Peter Drahos. 2001. *Global Business Regulation*. Cambridge: Cambridge University Press.

Breuer, Rüdiger. 1989. "Die internationale Orientierung von Umwelt-und Technik Standards im deutschen and europäischen Recht." *Jahrbuch des Umwelt-und Technikrechts* 9: 1–20.

Briassoulis, Helen, and Jan van der Straaten. 1992. "Tourism and the Environment." In *Tourism and the Environment: Regional, Economic and Policy Issues*, edited by Helen Briassoulis and Jan van der Straaten, 1–9. Dordrecht: Kluwer Academic Publishers.

Broad, Robin, ed. 2002. *Global Backlash: Citizen Initiatives for a Just World Economy*. New York: Rowman and Littlefield.

Broad, Robin, and John Cavanagh. 1998. *The Corporate Accountability Movement: Lessons and Opportunities*. Washington, D.C.: World Resources Institute.

Brown, Stephen J., William N. Goetzmann, and James Park. 1998. "Hedge Funds and the Asian Currency Crisis of 1997." NBER Working Paper 6421. National Bureau of Economic Research, Cambridge, Mass.

Broz, J. Lawrence. 2002. "Political System Transparency and Monetary Commitment Regimes." *International Organization* 56, 4 (autumn).

Brustein, William. 1988. *The Social Origins of Political Regionalism: France, 1849–1981*. Berkeley: University of California Press.

Buiter, Willem H. 1999. "The EMU and the NAMU: What is the Case for North American Monetary Union?" *Canadian Public Policy/Analyse de Politiques* 25, 3 (September): 285–305.

Bundgaard-Pedersen, Torben. 1997. "States and EU Technical Standardization: Denmark, the Netherlands and Norway: Managing Polycentric Policy-making 1985–95." *Journal of European Public Policy* 4: 206–24.

Burt, Ronald S. 1987. "Social Contagion and Innovation: Cohesion Versus Structural Equivalence." *American Journal of Sociology* 92: 1287–1335.

Cameron, David R. 1978. "The Expansion of the Public Economy: A Comparative Analysis." *American Political Science Review* 72 (4): 1243–61.

———. 1998. "Creating Supranational Authority in Monetary and Exchange Rate Policy: The Sources and Effects of EMU." In *European Integration and Supranational Governance*, edited by Wayne Sandholtz and Alec Stone Sweet, 188–216. Oxford: Oxford University Press.

Caporaso, James A. 1996. "The European Union and Forms of State: Westphalian, Regulatory, or Post-Modern?" *Journal of Common Market Studies* 34, 1 (March): 29–52.

———. 2000. *The European Union: Dilemmas of Regional Integration*. Boulder, Colo.: Westview Press.

———. 2002. "Transnational Markets, Thin Citizenship, and Democratic Rights in European Union: Can the Market Generate Rights?" Paper presented at the European Community Studies Association—Canada, 30 May–2 June, Toronto.

Caporaso, James A., and Joseph Jupille. 2001. "The Europeanization of Gender Equality Policy and Domestic Structural Change." In *Transforming Europe: Europeanization and Domestic Change*, edited by Maria Green Cowles,

James A. Caporaso, and Thomas Risse, 21–43. Ithaca, N.Y.: Cornell University Press.

Cardoso, Fernando and Enzo Faletto. 1979. *Dependency and Development in Latin America*. Berkeley: University of California Press.

Carey, John M., and Matthew S. Shugart. 1995. "Incentives to Cultivate a Personal Vote: A Comparative Analysis." *American Political Science Review* 72: 1243–61.

Carr, E. H. 1942. *Conditions of Peace*. New York: Macmillan.

Carsten, Ronit, and Volker Schneider, eds. 2000. *Private Organizations in Global Politics*. London: Routledge.

Casella, A., and J. Feinstein. 1990. "Public Goods in Trade: On the Formation of Markets and Political Jurisdictions." Working Paper in Economics E-92-12. The Hoover Institution, Stanford University, Stanford, Calif.

Castells, Manuel. 1997. *The Power of Identity*. Oxford: Blackwell.

Castles, Stephen, and Mark J. Miller. 1993. *The Age of Mass Migration: International Population Movements in the Modern World*. New York: The Guilford Press.

CEN. 1998/1999. *Memento*. Brussels: European Committee for Standardization, Central Secretariat.

Center for Economic Policy Research (CEPR). 1993. *Making Sense of Subsidiarity: How Much Centralization for Europe?* London: Center for Economic Policy Research.

Center for International Earth Science Information Network (CIESIN). 2001. *Environmental Treaties and Resource Indicators (ENTRI)*. Available at *http://sedac.ciesin.org/entri/*.

Central Intelligence Agency. 1999. *The CIA World Factbook*. Available at *http://www.odci.gov/cia/publications/factbook/*.

Cerny, Philip G. 1990. *The Changing Architecture of Politics*. London: Sage.

———. 1995. "Globalization and the Changing Logic of Collective Action." *International Organization* 49, 4 (autumn): 595–625.

Chang, Roberto, and Andres Velasco. 1998. "Financial Crises In Emerging Markets: A Canonical Model." National Bureau of Economic Research Working Paper No. 6606 (June).

Checkel, Jeffrey. 1993. "Ideas, Institutions, and the Gorbachev Foreign Policy Revolution." *World Politics* 45: 271–300.

Cheit, Ross. 1990. *Setting Safety Standards: Regulation in the Public and Private Sectors*. Berkeley: University of California Press.

Chiotis, George, and Harry Coccossis. 1992. "Tourist Development and Environmental Protection in Greece." In *Tourism and the Environment: Regional, Economic and Policy Issues*, edited by Helen Briassoulis and Jan van der Straaten, 133–43. Dordrecht: Kluwer Academic Publishers.

Choksi, A., M. Michaely, and D. Papageorgiu. 1991. "The Design of Successful Trade Liberalization Policies." In *Foreign Economic Liberalization*, edited by A. Koves and P. Marer. Boulder, Colo.: Westview Press.

Cichowski, Rachel A. 2000. "Judicial Rulemaking and the institutionalization of EU Sex Equality Policy." Paper presented at European University Institute, San Domenico di Fiesole, Italy, 31 March–1 April.

Clark, William Roberts. 1998. Structuring Strategies: Capital Mobility, Central Bank Independence, and the Political Control of the Economy. Unpublished manuscript, New York University.

Cochrane, Rexmond. 1966. *Measures for Progress: A History of the National Bureau of Standards*. Washington, D.C.: National Bureau of Standards.

Codding, G. A., and A. M. Rutkowski. 1982. *The International Telecommunications Union in a Changing World*. Dedham, Mass.: Artech.

Cohen, Benjamin J. 1998. *The Geography of Money*. Ithaca, N.Y.: Cornell University Press.

———. 2000a. "Beyond EMU: The Problem of Sustainability." In *The Political Economy of European Monetary Integration*, 2d ed., edited by Barry Eichengreen and Jeffry A. Frieden. Boulder, Colo: Westview Press.

———. 2000b. "Life at the Top: International Currencies in the Twenty-First Century." In *International Economics* 221. Princeton, N.J.: International Economics Section.

Cole, Harold, and Timothy Kehoe. 1998. "A Self-fulfilling Debt Crisis." Federal Reserve Bank of Minneapolis Staff Report 221 (July).

Coleman, James S., Elihu Katz, and Herbert Menzel. 1966. *Medical Innovation: A Diffusion Study*. Indianapolis, Ind.: Bobbs-Merrill.

Collier, Paul, and Anke Hoefler. 2000. "Greed and Grievance in Civil War." Unpublished manuscript, World Bank.

Commission of the European Communities. 1985. *Completing the Internal Market: White Paper from the Commission to the European Council*. Brussels: COM.

———. 1992. *Treaty on European Union*. Luxembourg: Office for Official Publications of the European Communities.

Commission on Global Governance. 1995. *Our Global Neighborhood*. New York: Oxford University Press.

Connor, Walker. 1994. *Ethnonationalism: The Quest for Understanding*. Princeton, N.J.: Princeton University Press.

Cooper, Richard. 1972. "Economic Interdependence and Foreign Policy in the 1970s." *World Politics* 24 (2): 159–81.

Cowhey, Peter F. 1990. "The International Telecommunications Regime: The Political Roots of Regimes for High Technology." *International Organization* 44 (2): 169–99.

Cowhey, Peter F., and Mathew D. McCubbins. 1995. *Structure and Policy in Japan and the United States*. Cambridge: Cambridge University Press

Cowles, Maria Green, James Caporaso, and Thomas Risse, eds. 2001. *Transforming Europe*. Ithaca, N.Y.: Cornell University Press.

Cox, Gary W. 1997. *Making Votes Count: Strategic Coordination in the World's Electoral Systems*. New York: Cambridge University Press.

Crane, Dwight, and Ulrike Schaede. 2001. "Changing Corporate Governance: the Financial System of Germany." Unpublished manuscript, Harvard Business School.

Cremer, Jacques, and Thomas Palfrey. 1999. "Political Confederation." *American Political Science Review* 93: 69–93.

Crook, Clive. 1997. "The Future of the State: World Economy Survey." *The Economist*, 20 September.

Curtin, Deirdre M. 1997. *Post-National Democracy: the EU in Search of a Political Philosophy.* The Hague: Kluwer Law International.

Cutler, A. Claire, Virginia Haufler, and Tony Porter, eds. 1999. *Private Authority and International Affairs.* Albany: SUNY Press.

Dahl, Robert A. 1971. *Polyarchy: Participation and Opposition.* New Haven, Conn.: Yale University Press.

———. 1999. "Can International Organizations Be Democratic? A Skeptic's View." In *Democracy's Edges,* edited by Ian Shapiro and Casiano Hacker-Cordon. Cambridge: Cambridge University Press.

Dardanelli, Paolo. 2001. "The Europeanisation of Regionalisation: European Integration and Public Support for Self-Government in Scotland 1979/1997." *Queen's Papers on Europeanization,* 5/2001 (available at *http://www.qub. ac.uk/ies/onlinepapers/poe5-01.pdf*).

David, Paul. 1985. "CLIO and the Economics of QWERTY." *American Economic Review* 75: 332–37.

David, Paul, and Shane Greenstein. 1990. "Economics of Compatiblity Standards: An Introduction to Recent Research." *Economics of Innovation and New Technology* 1: 3–41.

David, Paul, and Mark Shurmer. 1996. "Formal Standards-Setting of Global Telecommunications and Informations Services: Toward an Institutional Regime Transformation?" *Telecommunications Policy* 20 (10): 789–815.

David, Paul, and Edward Steinmueller. 1994. "Economics of Compatibility Standards and Competition in Telecommunication Networks." *Information Economics and Policy* 6: 217–41.

Davies, Howard. 2001. "Progress in Implementing the Recommendations of the Working Group on Highly Leveraged Institutions (HLIs)." Basle: Financial Stability Forum.

Davis, Donald. 1996. "Trade Liberalization and Income Distribution." Discussion Paper Number 1769. Cambridge, Mass.: Harvard Institute of Economic Research.

Davis, Lance E., and Robert A. Huttenback, 1986. *Mammon and the Pursuit of Empire: The Political Economy of British Imperialism, 1860–1912.* Cambridge: Cambridge University Press.

Davis, Stephen. 2002. "The 'Civil Economy'." Forum 2000, mimeograph. Prague.

De Grauwe, Paul. 1993. "The Political Economy of Monetary Union in Europe." *The World Economy* (November).

———. 1996. "Reforming the Transition to EMU," in Peter B. Kenen, ed., "Making EMU Happen: Problems and Proposals," *Princeton Essays in International Finance,* No. 199. Princeton: International Finance Section, August)

De Gregorio, Jose, Sebastian Edwards, and Rodrigo O. Valdes. 2000. "Controls on Capital Inflows: Do They Work?" NBER Working Paper No. W7645. National Bureau of Economic Research, Cambridge, Mass.

De Vries, Henk. 1999. *Standards for the Nation: Analysis of National Standardization Organizations.* Boston: Kluwer Academic Publishers.

De Winter, Lieven. 1998. "Conclusion: A Comparative Analysis of the Electoral, Office, and Policy Success of Ethnoregionalist Parties." In *Regionalist*

Parties in Western Europe, edited by Lieven De Winter and Huri Türsan. London: Routledge.

De Winter, Lieven and Margarita Gomez-Reino Cachafeiro. 2002. "European Integration and Ethnoregionalist Parties." *Party Politics* 8: 483–503.

Deeg, Richard. 1996. Economic Globalization and the Shifting Boundaries of German Federalism. *Publius: The Journal of Federalism*, 26 (1): 27–52.

Dehousse, Reynaud. 1998. "European Institutional Architecture After Amsterdam: Parliamentary System or Regulatory Structure?" European University Institute Working Papers, RSC no. 98/11. San Domenico di Fiesole, Italy, 1–25.

Delamaide, Darrell. 1994. *The New Superregions of Europe*. New York: Penguin.

Dixon, Robert. 1978. *Standards Development in the Private Sector: Thoughts on Interest Representation and Procedural Fairness*. Boston: National Fire Protection Association.

Dollar, David, and Aart Kraay. 2001. "Trade, Growth, and Poverty." Unpublished manuscript, World Bank.

Donaldson, Thomas, and Lee Preston. 1995. "The Stakeholder Theory of the Corporation: Concepts, Evidence, and Implications." *The Academy of Management Review* 20 (1).

Donovan, Mark, and David Broughton, eds. 1999. *Changing Party Systems in Western Europe*. London: Pinter.

Dooley, Michael P. 1995. "A Survey of Academic Literature on Controls over International Capital Transactions." NBER Working Paper W5352. National Bureau of Economic Research, Cambridge, Mass.

Dore, Ronald Philip. 1987. *Taking Japan Seriously: A Confucian Perspective on Leading Economic Issues*. London: Athlone.

———. 2000. *Stock Market Capitalism, Welfare Capitalism: Japan and Germany Versus the Anglo-Saxons*. Oxford: Oxford University Press.

Dornbusch, Rudi. 2001. "Fewer Monies, Better Monies." *American Economic Review* 91, 2 (May): 238–42.

Drazen, Allan. 1989. "Monetary Policy, Capital Controls, and Seigniorage in an Open Economy." In *A European Central Bank? Perspectives on Monetary Unification After Ten Years of the EMS*, edited by M. de Cecco and Alberto Giovannini, 13–32. New York: Cambridge University Press.

Drezner, Daniel W. 2001. "Globalization and Policy Convergence." *International Studies Review* 3 (spring): 53–80.

Dupoirier, Elisabeth. 1998. *Régions: la croisée des chemins*. Paris: Presses de Sciences Po.

Dvořák, Phred, Robert A. Gut, Jason Singe, and Todd Zaun. 2001. "Loose Ends: Frayed by Recession, Japan's Corporate Ties are Coming Unraveled." *Wall Street Journal*, 2 March, A-1.

Eade, John, ed. 1997. *Living in the Global City: Globalization as Local Process*. London: Routledge.

Easterly, William, and Richard Levine. 1997. "Africa's Growth Tragedy: Policies and Ethnic Divisions." *Quarterly Journal of Economics* 112 (November): 1203–50.

Easterly, William, and S. Rebelo. 1993. "Fiscal Policy and Economic Growth: An Empirical Investigation." *Journal of Monetary Economics* 32: 417–58.

Easton, David. 1965. *The Political System*. New York: Knopf.

Eatwell, John, and Lance Taylor. 1999. "Capital Flows and the International Financial Architecture." Unpublished manuscript, New School for Social Research.

———. 2000. *Global Finance at Risk: The Case for International Regulation*. New York: New Press.

Edgell, David L., Sr. 1990. *International Tourism Policy*. New York: Van Nostrand Reinhold.

Edwards, Franklin R. 1999. "Hedge Funds and the Collapse of Long-Term Capital Management." *Journal of Economic Perspectives* 13: 189–210.

Edwards, Sebastian. 1996. "Exchange Rates and the Political Economy of Macroeconomic Discipline." *The American Economic Review* 86, 2 (May): 159–63.

———. 1999a. "Crisis Prevention: Lessons from Mexico and East Asia." NBER Working Paper W7233. National Bureau of Economic Research, Cambridge, Mass.

———. 1999b. "How Effective Are Capital Controls?" NBER Working Paper W7413. National Bureau of Economic Research, Cambridge, Mass.

Egan, Michelle. 1998a. "Regulatory Strategies, Delegation, and European Market Integration." *Journal of European Public Policy* 5 (3): 487–508.

———. 1998b. "Mutual Recognition and Standard-Setting: Public and Private Strategies for Regulating Transnational Markets." Seminar Papers/Policy Papers 10. American Institute for Contemporary German Studies, Washington, D.C.

———. 2001. *Consructing a European Market: Standards, Regulations and Governance*. London: Oxford University Press.

Eichengreen, Barry. 1992. "Is Europe an Optimum Currency Area?" In Silvio Borner and Herbert Grubel, eds., *The European Community After 1992*. Basingstoke: MacMillan.

———. 1994. *International Monetary Arrangements for the Twenty-First Century*. Washington, D.C.: Brookings Institution.

———. 1996. *Globalizing Capital: A History of the International Monetary System*. Princeton, N.J.: Princeton University Press.

———. 1999a. "The Regulator's Dilemma: Hedge Funds in the International Financial Architecture." *International Finance* 2: 411–40.

———. 1999b. *Toward a New International Financial Architecture: A Practical Post-Asia Agenda*. Washington, D.C.: Institute for International Economics.

Eichengreen, Barry, and Tamim Bayoumi. 1999. "Is Asia an Optimum Currency Area? Can It Become One? Regional, Global, and Historical Perspectives on Asian Monetary Relations." In *Exchange Rate Policies in Emerging Asian Countries*, edited by Stefan Collignon, Jean Pisani-Ferry, and Yung Chul Park. London: Routledge.

Eichengreen, Barry, and Donald Mathieson, with Bankim Chadha, Anne Jansen, Laura Kodres, and Sunil Sharma. 1998. "Hedge Funds and Financial Market Dynamics." IMF Occasional Paper no. 166 (May).

Eichengreen, Barry, and Nathan Sussman. 2000. "The International Monetary System in the (Very) Long Run." In *World Economic Outlook Supporting Studies*. Washington, D.C.: International Monetary Fund.

Eichengreen, Barry, and Charles Wyplosz. 1998. "The Stability Pact: More than a Minor Nuisance?" *Economic Policy* 26 (April): 65–114.

Elgie, Robert. 1998. "Democratic Accountability and Central Bank Independence: Historical and Contemporary, National and European Perspectives." *West European Politics* 21 (3): 1–15.

Encarnation, Dennis J., and Mark Mason. 1990. "Neither MITI nor America: The Political Economy of Capital Liberalization in Japan." *International Organization* 44, 1 (winter): 25–54.

Environics International. 2002. *Corporate Social Responsibility Monitor 2002*. Toronto: Environics International.

Epple, Dennis, and Thomas Romer. 1991. "Mobility and Redistribution." *Journal of Political Economy* 99 (4): 828–58.

Epstein, David and Sharyn O'Halloran. 1999. *Delegating Powers: A Transaction Cost Politics Approach to Policy Making Under Separate Powers*. New York: Cambridge University Press.

Epstein, Gerald A., and Juliet Schor. 1992. "Structural Determinants and Economic Effects of Capital Controls in OECD Countries." In *Financial Openness and National Autonomy: Opportunities and Constraints*, edited by Tariq Banuri and Juliet Schor. Oxford: Clarendon Press.

Esman, Milton J. 1977a. "Perspectives on Ethnic Conflict in Industrialized Societies." In *Ethnic Conflict in the Western World*, edited by Milton J. Esman. Ithaca, N.Y.: Cornell University Press.

———, ed. 1977b. *Ethnic Conflict in the Western World*. Ithaca, N.Y.: Cornell University Press.

Esping-Anderson, Gosta. 1999. *Social Foundations of Postindustrial Economies*. New York : Oxford University Press.

Estevez-Abe, Margarita. 1999. "Welfare and Capitalism in Post-War Japan." Ph.d. diss., Department of Government, Harvard University.

Ethics Officers Association. 2000. "Member Survey 2000." *EOA News* 2 (3): 1.

Europa. 1999. *Europa World Year Book 1999*. London: Europa Publications.

European Commission. 1999. *Sixth Period Report on the Social and Economic Situation and Development of the Regions of the European Union*. Brussels: European Commission.

———. 2000. *Economic Reform: Report on the Functioning of Community Product and Capital Markets*. Presented by the commission in response to the conclusions of the Cardiff European Council.

European Commission. Directorate-General XXIII—Tourism Unit. 1996. *Tourism and the European Union: A Practical Guide*. Chap. 4. Brussels.

European Commission. Directorate-General Trade. 2001. Available at *http://www.europa.eu.int/comm/trade/pdf/wto_imgdp.pdf*.

European Union Commission. 1999. Economic Reform: Report on the Functioning of Community Product and Capital Markets.

———. 2000. Institutional Arrangements for Regulation and Supervision of the Financial Sector.

———. 2001. Financial Services: Building a Framework for Action. Available at *http://www.europa.eu.int/scadplus/leg/en/lvb/l24050.html*.

Eurostat. 1996. *Regions: Statistical Yearbook*. Brussels: Eurostat.

Evans, Peter B., Harold K. Jacobson, and Robert D. Putnam. 1993. *Double-Edged Diplomacy: International Bargaining and Domestic Politics*. Berkeley: University of California Press.

Falk, Richard, and Andrew Strauss. 2000. "On the Creation of a Global People's Assembly: Legitimacy and the Power of Popular Sovereignty." *Stanford Journal of International Law* 36 (summer): 191ff.

Falke, Josef. 2000. *Rechtliche Aspekte der Normung in den EG-Mitgliedstaaten und der EFTA: Deutschland*. Vol. 3. Luxembourg: Office for Official Publications of the European Communities.

Falke, Josef, and Harm Schepel, eds. 2000. *Legal Aspects of Standardisation in the Member States of the EC and of EFTA: Country Reports*. Vol. 2. Luxembourg: Office for Official Publications of the European Communities.

Färber, Gisela. 1996. "Regions in Europe — The Economic Perspective." In *The Regions: Factors of Integration or Disintegration in Europe?*, edited by Gisela Färber and Murray Forsyth. Baden-Baden: Nomos.

Farrell, Joseph, and Garth Saloner. 1985. "Standardization, Compatibility, and Innovation." *Rand Journal of Economics* 16 (1): 70–83.

———. 1986. "Installed Base and Compatibility: Innovation, Product Pre-announcements, and Predation." *American Economics Review* 76 (5): 940–55.

———. 1987. "Competition, Compatibility, and Standards: The Economics of Horses, Penguins, and Lemmings." In *Product Standardization and Competitive Strategy*, edited by Landis Gabel, 1–21. Amsterdam: Elsevier Science Publishers.

Faulkner, H. W., and D. J. Walmsley. 1998. "Globalisation and the Pattern of Inbound Tourism in Australia." *Australian Geographer* 29 (1): 91–106.

Fawcett, Louise, and Andrew Hurrell, eds. 1995. *Regionalism in World Politics: Regional Organization and International Order*. Oxford: Oxford University Press.

Fearon, James D. 2002. "Why Do Some Civil Wars Last So Much Longer Than Others?" Unpublished manuscript, Stanford University.

Fearon, James D., and Pieter Van Houten. 1998. "The Politicization of Cultural and Economic Difference: A Return to the Theory of Regional Autonomy Movements." Paper presented at the Annual Meeting of the American Political Science Association, Boston.

———. 2002. "The Politicization of Cultural and Economic Difference." Paper presented at the Fifth Meeting of the Laboratory in Comparative Ethnic Processes, Stanford University, May.

Feenstra, Robert C. 1998. "Integration of Trade and Disintegration of Production in the Global Economy." *Journal of Economic Perspectives* 12 (4): 31–50.

Feldstein, Martin, and Charles Horioka. 1980. "Domestic Saving and International Capital Flows." *The Economic Journal* 90: 314–29.

Financial Stability Forum. 2000. "Report of the Working Group on Highly Leveraged Institutions." Basle: Financial Stability Forum.

Finger, J. M., and M. E. Kreinin. 1979. "A Measure of 'Export Similarity' and Its Possible Uses." *Economic Journal* 89, 356 (December): 905–12.

Finkelstein, Monte S. 1998. *Separatism, the Allies, and the Mafia: The Struggle for Sicilian Independence, 1943–1948.* Bethlehem, Pa.: Lehigh University Press.

Fischer, Stanley. 2001. "Exchange Rate Regimes: Is the Bipolar View Correct?" *Journal of Economic Perspectives* 15, 2 (spring): 3–24.

Fitzmaurice, John. 1996. *The Politics of Belgium: A Unique Federalism.* London: Westview Press.

Fligstein, Neil, Wayne Sandholtz, and Alec Stone Sweet, eds. 2001. *The Institutionalization of Europe.* New York: Oxford University Press.

Florini, Ann, ed. 2000. *The Third Force: The Rise of Transnational Civil Society.* Washington, D.C.: Carnegie Endowment for International Peace.

Forest Stewardship Council United States. 2001. "Forest Stewardship Council— What It Is." Available at *http://www.fscus.org/html/index.html.*

Fornasari, Francesca, Steven Webb, and Heng-fu Zou. 1999. "The Macroeconomic Impact of Decentralized Spending Deficits: International Evidence." Latin American and Caribbean Sector, Poverty Reduction and Development Economic Research Group. Washington, D.C.: World Bank.

Frank, Andre Gunder. 1967. *Capitalism and Underdevelopment in Latin America.* New York: Monthly Review Press.

Frieden, Jeffry. 1988. "Sectoral Conflict and Foreign Economic Policy, 1914– 1940." *International Organization* 42, 1 (winter): 59–90.

———. 1991a. "Invested Interests: The Politics of National Economic Policies in a World of Global Finance." *International Organization* 45, 4 (autumn): 425–51.

———. 1991b. *Debt, Development, and Democracy.* Princeton, N.J.: Princeton University Press.

———. 1999. "Actors and Preferences in International Relations." In *Strategic Choice and International Relations,* edited by David A. Lake and Robert Powell. Princeton, N.J.: Princeton University Press.

Frieden, Jeffry A., and Ronald Rogowski. 1996. "The Impact of the International Economy on National Politics: An Analytical Overview." In *Internationalization and Domestic Politics,* edited by Robert O. Keohane and Helen V. Milner. New York: Cambridge University Press.

Friedkin, N. E. 1993. "Structural Bases of Interpersonal Influence in Groups: A Longitudinal Case Study." *American Sociological Review* 58: 861–72.

Friedman, Thomas L. 1999. *The Lexus and the Olive Tree.* New York: Farrar Straus Giroux.

———. 2000. *The Lexus and the Olive Tree: Understanding Globalization.* New York: Anchor Books.

Friedrich, Carl J., ed. 1958. *Authority: NOMOS I.* Cambridge, Mass.: Harvard University Press.

Gabel, Landis. 1991. *Competitive Strategies for Product Standards: The Strategic Use of Compatibility Standards for Competitive Advantage.* London: McGraw-Hill.

Gale Group. 1999. *Countries of the World and Their Leaders Yearbook 2000.* Cleveland, Ohio: Eastword Publications Development.

Garcia-Johnson, Ronnie. 2000. *Exporting Environmentalism: U.S. Multinational Chemical Corporations in Brazil and Mexico*. Cambridge, Mass.: MIT Press.

Gardner, Richard N. 1980. *Sterling-Dollar Diplomacy in Current Perspective*. New York: Columbia University Press.

Garrett, Geoffrey. 1998a. *Partisan Politics in the Global Economy*. Cambridge: Cambridge University Press.

———. 1998b. "Global Markets and National Politics: Collision Course or Virtuous Circle?" *International Organization* 52, 4 (autumn): 787–824.

———. 2002. "The Distributive Consequences of Globalization." Unpublished manuscript, Yale University.

Garrett, Geoffrey, Alexandra Guisinger, and Jason P. Sorens. 2000. "The Political Economy of Capital Account Liberalization." Unpublished manuscript, Yale University.

Garrett, Geoffrey, and Peter Lange. 1991. "Political Responses to Interdependence: What's 'Left' for the Left." *International Organization* 45 (4): 539–64.

———. 1995. "Internationalization, Institutions, and Political Change." *International Organization* 49, 4 (autumn): 627–55.

General Motors. 2000. General Motors website. Available at *http://www.gm.com*.

———. 2001. *Annual Report*.

Genschel, Philipp. 1997. "How Fragmentation Can Improve Co-ordination: Setting Standards in International Telecommunications." *Organization Studies* 18 (4): 603–22.

Genschel, Philipp, and Raymund Werle. 1993. "From National Hierarchies to International Standardization: Modal Change in the Governance of Telecommunications." *Journal of Public Policy* 13 (3): 203–25.

Gereffi, Gary. 1996. "Global Commodity Chains: New Forms of Coordination and Control Among Nations and Firms." *Competition & Change* 1 (4): 427–39.

Gereffi, Gary, Ronnie Garcia-Johnson, and Erika Sasser. 2001. "The NGO-Industrial Complex." *Foreign Policy* 125 (July/August): 56–65.

Gerschenkron, Alexander. 1962. *Economic Backwardness in Historical Perspective A Book of Essays*. Cambridge, Mass.: Belknap Press.

Giavazzi, Francesco, and Alberto Giovannini. 1989. *Limiting Exchange Rate Flexibility*. Cambridge, Mass.: MIT Press.

Giddens, Anthony. 1999. *Runaway World*. London: Profile Books.

Gilg, Andrew W. 1991. "Switzerland: Structural Change within Stability." In *Tourism and Economic Development: Western European Experiences*, edited by Allan M. Williams and Gareth Shaw, 130–52. London: Belhaven Press.

Giovannini, Alberto, and Martha de Melo. 1993. "Government Revenue from Financial Repression." *American Economic Review* 83, 4 (September): 953–63.

Golden, Miriam. 2001. International Sources of the Collapse of Rent-Seeking Regimes: Hypotheses Drawn from the Italian Case. Paper presented at the ECPR Joint Sessions, Grenoble.

Gomes-Casseres, Benjamin. 1994. "Group Versus Group: How Alliance Networks Compete." *Harvard Business Review* (July/August): 62–73.

Goodman, John, and Louis Pauly. 1993. "The Obsolescence of Capital Controls? Economic Management in an Age of Global Markets." *World Politics* 46: 50–82.

Gordin, Jorge P. 2001. "The Electoral Fate of Ethnoregionalist Parties in Western Europe: A Boolean Test of Extant Explanations." *Scandinavian Political Studies* 24: 149–70.

Gordon, Kathryn. 1999. Rules for the Global Economy: Synergies between Voluntary and Binding Approaches. Paper presented at the conference Corporate Citizenship: Linking CSR Business Strategies and the Emerging International Agenda. Royal Institute of International Affairs, London.

Gourevitch, Peter A. 1979. "The Re-Emergence of 'Peripheral Nationalisms': Some Comparative Speculations on the Spatial Distribution of Political Leadership and Economic Growth." *Comparative Studies in Society and History* 21: 303–22.

———. 1996. "The Macro Politics of Micro-Institutional Differences in the Analysis of Comparative Capitalism." In *Convergence or Diversity? National Models of Production and Distribution in a Global Economy*, edited by Suzanne Berger and Ronald Dore. Ithaca, N.Y.: Cornell University Press.

———. 1999. "The Governance Problem in International Relations." In *Strategic Choice and International Relations*, edited by David A. Lake and Robert Powell. Princeton, N.J.: Princeton University Press.

———. 2001. "Comparative Capitalism in the Globalized Economy: Understanding National Production Systems." Unpublished manuscript, University of California, San Diego.

———. 2003. "The Politics of Corporate Governance Regulation." Review of Mark Roe, *Political Determinants of Corporate Governance*, *Yale Law Journal* 112 (7): 1829–80.

Gourevitch, Peter A., Roger Bohn, and David McKendrick. 2000. "Globalization of Production: Insights from the Hard Disk Drive Industry." *World Development* 28 (2): 301–17.

Gourevitch, Peter A., and Michael B. Hawes. 2002. "The politics of choice among national production systems." L'Annèe de la règulation 2002. Paris: Presses de Sciences. Paper presented at the Annual Meeting of the American Political Science Association, San Francisco, 30 August–2 September.

Green, Howard, and Colin Hunter. 1992. "The Environmental Impact Assessment of Tourism Development." In *Perspectives on Tourism Policy*, edited by Peter Johnson and Barry Thomas, 29–47. London: Mansell Publishing.

Greenwood, Justin, and Henry Jacek, eds. 2000. *Organized Business and the New Global Order*. New York: St. Martin's Press.

Greider, William. 1997. *One World Ready or Not: The Manic Logic of Global Capitalism*. New York: Touchstone/Simon and Schuster.

Greven, Michael, and Louis Pauly, eds. 2000. *Democracy Beyond the State? The European Dilemma and the Emerging World Order*. New York: Rowman and Littlefield.

Grieco, Joseph M. 1997. "Systemic Sources of Variation in Regional Institutionalization in Western Europe, East Asia, and the Americas." In *The Political Economy of Regionalism*, edited by Edward Mansfield and Helen V. Milner, 164–87. New York: Columbia University Press.

Grilli, Vittorio, and Gian Marie Milesi-Ferretti. 1995. "Economic Effects and Structural Determinants of Capital Controls." *International Monetary Fund Staff Papers* 42 (3): 517–51.

Grimes, Arthur, and Frank Holmes. 2000. *An ANZAC Dollar? Currency Union and Business Development*. Wellington: Victoria University of Wellington, Institute of Policy Studies.

Grindle, Merilee S. 2000. "Ready or Not: The Developing World and Globalization." In *Governance in a Globalizing World*, edited by Joseph S. Nye, Jr., and John D. Donahue, 178–207. Washington, D.C.: Brookings Institution.

Grindley, Peter. 1995. *Standards Strategy and Policy: Cases and Stories*. Oxford: Oxford University Press.

Gros, Daniel, and Niels Thygesen. 1998. *European Monetary Integration*. 2d ed. Longman: London.

Guillén, Mauro F. 2001. *The Limits of Convergence: Globalization and Organizational Change in Argentina, South Korea, and Spain*. Princeton, N.J.: Princeton University Press.

Haas, Ernst B. 1958. *The Uniting of Europe: Political, Social, and Economic Forces, 1950–1957*. Stanford, Calif.: Stanford University Press.

———. 1959. *The Future of West European Political and Economic Unity*. Santa Barbara, Calif.: Technical Military Planning Operation, General Electric Company.

———. 1982. "Words Can Hurt You; Or, Who Said What to Whom About Regimes." *International Organization* 36: 207–43.

Haas, Peter M. 1992. "Introduction: Epistemic Communities and International Policy Coordination." *International Organization* 46, 1 (winter): 1–36.

Haggard, Stephan, Chung H. Lee, and Sylvia Maxfield, eds. 1993. *The Politics of Finance in Developing Countries*. Ithaca, N.Y.: Cornell University Press.

Haggard, Stephan, and Sylvia Maxfield. 1996. "The Political Economy of Financial Internationalization in the Developing World." In *Internationalization and Domestic Politics*, edited by Robert O. Keohane and Helen Milner, 209–39. Cambridge: Cambridge University Press.

Haggard, Stephen and Matthew D. McCubbins, eds. 2001. *Presidents, Parliaments, and Policy: The Political Economy of Institutions and Decisions*.

Hall, C. Michael. 1998. "The Legal and Political Dimensions of Sex Tourism: The Case of Australia's Child Sex Tourism Legislation." In *Sex Tourism and Prostitution: Aspects of Leisure, Recreation, and Work*, edited by Martin Oppermann, 87–96. Elmsford, N.Y.: Cognizant Communication Corporation.

Hall, Colin Michael. 1994. *Tourism and Politics: Policy, Power, and Place*. New York: Wiley. (02)

Hall, Peter A., and Robert J. Franzese, Jr. 1998. "Mixed Signals: Central Bank Independence, Coordinated Wage Bargaining, and European Monetary Union." *International Organization* 52 (3): 505–35.

Hall, Peter A., and Daniel Gingerich. 2001. Varieties of Capitalism and Institutional Complementarities in the Macroeconomy: An Empirical Analysis. Paper presented at the Annual Meeting of the American Political Science Association, San Francisco, 30 August–2 September.

Hall, Peter A., and David Soskice, eds. 2001. *Varieties of Capitalism: The Institutional Foundations of Comparative Advantage*. New York: Oxford University Press.

Hallerberg, Mark. 1996. "Tax Competition in Wilhelmine Germany and Its Implications for the European Union." *World Politics* 48: 324–57.

Hallerberg, Mark, and Scott Basinger. 1998. "Internationalization and Changes in Tax Policy in OECD Countries." *Comparative Political Studies* 31 (3): 321–53.

Hamilton, Robert. 1978. "The Rate of Non-Governmental Standards in the Development of Mandatory Federal Standards Affecting Safety of Health." *Texas Law Review* 56: 1329–1484.

Hansen, Mark. 1999. "Thinking about the Budget: Public Opinion and Trade-offs over Spending, Taxes and Deficits." Unpublished paper, Department of Political Science, University of Chicago.

Harrison, Kathryn. 1999. "Talking with the Donkey: Cooperative Approaches to Environmental Regulation." *Journal of Industrial Ecology* 2 (3): 51–72.

Hartmann, Jürgen, ed. 1997. *Handbuch der deutschen Bundesländer*. 3d ed. Frankfurt: Campus.

Harvie, Christopher. 1994. *The Rise of Regional Europe*. London: Routledge.

Haufler, Virginia. 1999. "Negotiating International Standards for Environmental Management Systems: ISO 14000 Standards." Global Public Policy Network Report to the United Nations Secretary General. Washington, DC.

———. 2001. *The Public Role of the Private Sector: Industry Self-Regulation in a Global Economy*. Washington, D.C.: Carnegie Endowment for International Peace.

Hausmann, Ricardo. 1999a. "Should There Be Five Currencies or One Hundred and Five?" *Foreign Policy* 116 (fall): 65–79.

———. 1999b. "Why the Interest in Reform?" In *Rethinking the International Monetary System*, edited by Jane Sneddon Little and Giovanni P. Olivei, 94–96. Boston: Federal Reserve Bank of Boston.

Hawkins, Richard. 1999. "The Rise of Consortia in the Information and Communication Technology industries: Emerging Implications for Policy." *Telecommunications Policy* 23: 159–73.

Hayes-Renshaw, F., and Helen Wallace. 1995. "Executive Power in the European Union: The Functions and Limits of the Council of Ministers." *Journal of European Public Policy* 2 (4): 559–82.

Hearl, Derek J., Ian Budge, and Bernard Pearson. 1996. "Distinctiveness of Regional Voting: A Comparative Analysis Across the European Community (1979–1993)." *Electoral Studies* 15: 167–82.

Hechter, Michael. 1975. *Internal Colonialism: The Celtic Fringe in British National Development, 1536–1966*. Berkeley: University of California Press.

Hegeland, Hans, and Ingvar Mattson. 1996. "To Have a Voice in the Matter: A Comparative Study of the Swedish and Danish European Committees." *The Journal of Legislative Studies* 2, 3 (autumn): 198–215.

Held, David. 1996. *Models of Democracy*. 2d ed. Stanford, Calif.: Stanford University Press.

Held, David, Anthony McGrew, David Goldblatt, and Jonathan Perration. 1999. *Global Transformations: Politics, Economics and Culture*. Stanford, Calif.: Stanford University Press.

Helleiner, Eric. 1998. "National Currencies and National Identities." *American Behavioral Scientist* 41, 10 (August): 1409–436.

Helliwell, John F. 1998. *How Much Do National Borders Matter?* Washington, D.C.: The Brookings Institution.

Hemerijck, Anton, and Jelle Visser. 2000. "Change and Immobility: Three Decades of Policy Adjustment in the Netherlands and Belgium." *West European Politics* 23 (2): 229–41.

Henderson, Vernon. 2000. "The Effects of Urban Concentration on Economic Growth." NBER Working Paper W7503. National Bureau of Economic Research, Cambridge, Mass.

Hibbs, Douglas. 1977. "Political Parties and Macroeconomic Policy." *American Political Science Review* 71, 4 (December): 1467–87.

Higgott, Richard, Geoffrey Underhill, and Andreas Bieler, eds. 2000. *Non-State Actors and Authority in the Global System*. London and New York: Routledge.

Hilpert, Ulrich, ed. 1991. *Regional Innovation and Decentralization: High Tech Industry and Government Policy*. London: Routledge.

Hirschman, Albert O. 1970. *Exit, Voice and Loyalty: Responses to Decline in Firms, Organizations, and States*. Cambridge, Mass.: Harvard University Press.

Hiscox, Michael J. 1999."The Magic Bullet? The RTAA, Institutional Reform, and Trade Liberalization." *International Organization* 53 , 4 (autumn): 669–98.

———. 2001. "Class Versus Industry Cleavages: Inter-Industry Factor Mobility and the Politics of Trade." *International Organization*. 55, 1 (winter): 1–46.

Hiscox, Michael J., and David A. Lake. 2002. "Democracy, Federalism, and the Size of States." Unpublished manuscript, University of California, San Diego.

Hix, Simon. 1999a. "Dimensions and Alignments in European Union Politics: Cognitive Constraints and Partisan Responses." *European Journal of Political Research* 35: 69–106.

———. 1999b. *The Political System of the European Union*. New York: St. Martin's Press.

Holder, Jean S. 1996. "Maintaining Competitiveness in a New World Order: Regional Solutions to Caribbean Tourism Sustainability Problems." In *Practicing Responsible Tourism: International Case Studies in Tourism Planning, Policy, and Development*, edited by Lynn C. Harrison and Winston Husbands, 145–73. New York: Wiley.

Holton, Robert J. 1998. *Globalization and the Nation-State*. London: Macmillan.

Honohan, Patrick, and Philip Lane. 2001. "Will the Euro Trigger More Monetary Unions in Africa?" In *EMU and Its Impact on Europe and the Developing Countries*, edited by Charles Wyplosz. Oxford: Oxford University Press.

Hooghe, Liesbet. 1995a. "Belgian Federalism and the European Community."

In *The European Union and the Regions*, edited by Barry Jones and Michael Keating. Oxford: Clarendon Press.

———. 1995b. "Subnational Mobilization in the European Union." *West European Politics* 18: 175–98.

———. ed. 1996. *Cohesion Policy and European Integration: Building Multi-Level Governance*. Oxford: Oxford University Press.

Hooghe, Liesbet, and Gary Marks. 1996. " 'Europe with the Regions': Channels of Regional Representation in the European Union." *Publius: The Journal of Federalism* 26 (1): 73–91.

———. 2001. *Multi-Level Governance and European Integration*. Lanham, Md.: Rowman and Littlefield.

Hopkins, A. G. 1973. *An Economic History of West Africa*. London: Longman.

Horowitz, Donald L. 1985. *Ethnic Groups in Conflict*. Berkeley: University of California Press.

Hoshi, Takeo, and Anil Kashyup. 2001. *Corporate Financing and Governance in Japan: The Road to the Future*. Cambridge, Mass.: MIT Press.

Hoskyns, Catherine. 1996. *Integrating Gender: Women, Law, and Politics in the EU*. London: Verso Publications.

Huntington, Samuel. 1993. "The Clash of Civilizations?" *Foreign Affairs* 73 (2): 22–50.

IMF. 2000. "Global Portfolio Investment Survey." Available at *http://www.imf.org/external/np/sec/nb/2000/NB0008.HTM*.

Inglehart, Ronald. 1997. *Modernization and Postmodernization: Cultural, Economic, and Political Change in 43 Societies*. Princeton, N.J.: Princeton University Press.

Inman, Robert, and Daniel Rubinfeld. 1997. "The Political Economy of Federalism." In *Perspectives on Public Choice*, edited by Dennis Mueller. Cambridge: Cambridge University Press.

Institute of International Finance (IIF). 2002. "Moderate Recovery Seen in Private Capital Flows to Emerging Markets." April release. Available at *http://www.iif.com/press/pressrelease*. Accessed July 2002.

Inter-American Development Bank (IADB). 1997. "Fiscal Decision Making in Decentralized Democracies." In *Latin America After a Decade of Reforms: Economic and Social Progress in Latin America Report*. Washington, D.C.: Johns Hopkins University Press.

International Electrotechnical Commission (IEC). 1990. *Inside the IEC*. Geneva: IEC Central Office.

International Labor Organization. 1998. "Sex Industry Assuming Massive Proportions in Southeast Asia." Available at *http://www.ilo.org/public/english/bureau/inf/pr/1998/31.html*.

International Monetary Fund (IMF). 1997. *World Economic Outlook*. Washington, D.C.: International Monetary Fund.

———. 1998a. Annual Report. Washington, D.C.: IMF.

———. 1998b. Interim World Economic Outlook and International Capital Markets Report. Washington, D.C.: International Monetary Fund.

International Standards Organization (ISO). 1994. *ISO Statutes and Rules of Procedure*. 13th ed. Geneva: ISO.

———. 1997a. *ISO in Brief*. Geneva: ISO.

———. 1997b. *Friendship Among Equals: Recollections from ISO's First Fifty Years*. Geneva: ISO Central Secretariat.

International Tribunal for Children's Rights. n.d. "International Dimensions of the Sexual Exploitation of Children: Global Report." Montreal: International Bureau for Children's Rights.

Irwin, Douglas A. 1996. "The United States in a New Global Economy? A Century's Perspective." *American Economic Review* 86: 41–46.

Iversen, Torben 1999. *Contested Institutions*. New York: Cambridge University Press.

Iversen, Torben, and David Soskice. 2001a. Asset Specificity, Trade and Politics: An Argument for Divergence. Paper presented at the Annual Meeting of the American Political Science Association, 30 August–2 September, San Francisco.

———. 2001b. "An Asset Theory of Social Policy Preferences." *American Political Science Review* 95, 4 (December): 875–94.

Iversen, Torben, and Anne Wren. 1998. "Equality, Employment, and Budgetary Restraint: The Trilemma of the Service Economy." *World Politics* 50 (4): 507–46.

Jacobson, Harold. 1973. "ITU: A Potpourri of Bureaucrats and Industrialists." In *The Anatomy of Influence*, edited by Robert Cox and Harold Jacobson. New Haven, Conn.: Yale University Press.

Jacoby, Wade. 2000. *Imitation and Politics: Redesigning Modern Germany*. Ithaca, N.Y.: Cornell University Press.

Jaggers, Keith, and Ted Robert Gurr. 1999. *Polity III*. Ann Arbor, Mich.: Inter-university Consortium on Political and Social Research. Available at *http://www.bsos.umd.edu/cidcm/inscr/polity/index.html*.

Jeffery, Charlie. 2001. "Sub-National Mobilization and European Integration: Does it Make Any Difference?" *Journal of Common Market Studies* 38: 1–23.

Joerges, Christian, Harm Schepel, and Ellen Vos. 1999. The Law's Problems with the Involvement of Non-Governmental Actors in Europe's Legislative Processes: The Case of Standardization Under the "New Approach." EUI Working Paper Law No. 99/9. Florence: European University Institute.

Jun, Jong S., and Deil S. Wright, eds. 1996. *Globalization and Decentralization: Institutional Contexts: Policy Issues, and Intergovernmental Relations in Japan and the United States*. Washington, D.C.: Georgetown University Press.

Kahane, David. 2000. "Pluralism, Deliberation, and Citizen Competence: Recent Developments in Democratic Theory." *Social Theory and Practice* 26, 3 (fall): 509–26.

Kahler, Miles. 1996. "Trade and Domestic Differences." In *National Diversity and Global Capitalism*, edited by Suzanne Berger and Ronald Dore, 298–332. Ithaca, N.Y.: Cornell University Press.

———. 1998. "Introduction: Capital Flows and Financial Crises in the 1990s." In *Capital Flows and Financial Crises*, edited by Miles Kahler. Ithaca, N.Y.: Cornell University Press.

———. 1999. "Modeling Races to the Bottom." Unpublished paper, University of California, San Diego.

Kaplan, Ethan, and Dani Rodrik. 2001. "Did the Malaysian Capital Controls Work?" NBER Working Paper no. 8142. National Bureau of Economic Research. Cambridge, Mass.

Katz, Michael, and Carl Shapiro. 1985. "Network Externalities, Competition, and Compatibility." *American Economic Review* 75: 424–440.

Katzenstein, Peter J. 1977. "Ethnic Political Conflict in South Tyrol." In *Ethnic Conflict in the Western World*, edited by Milton J. Esman. Ithaca, N.Y.: Cornell University Press.

———. 1985. *Small States in World Markets*. Ithaca, N.Y.: Cornell University Press.

Keating, Michael. 1988. *State and Regional Nationalism: Territorial Politics and the European State*. New York: Harvester Wheatsheaf.

———. 1995. "Europeanism and Regionalism." In *The European Union and the Regions*, edited by Barry Jones and Michael Keating. Oxford: Clarendon Press.

———. 1997. "The Political Economy of Regionalism." In *The Political Economy of Regionalism*, edited by Michael Keating and John Loughlin. London: Frank Cass.

———. 1998. *The New Regionalism in Western Europe: Territorial Restructuring and Political Change*. Cheltenham: Edward Elgar.

———. 2001. *Nations Against the State: The New Politics of Nationalism in Quebec, Catalonia, and Scotland*. 2d ed. London: Palgrave.

Keating, Michael, and Liesbet Hooghe. 1996. "By-Passing the Nation State? Regions and the EU Policy Process." In *European Union: Power and Policy Making*, edited by Jeremy J. Richardson. London: Routledge.

Keck, Margaret E., and Kathryn Sikkink. 1998. *Activists Beyond Borders: Advocacy Networks in International Politics*. Ithaca, N.Y.: Cornell University Press.

Kellas, James G. 1991. "European Integration and the Regions." *Parliamentary Affairs* 44: 226–39.

Kennedy School of Government. 2001. ICANN draft case study.

Keohane, Robert O. 1982. "The Demand for International Regimes." *International Organization*, 36: 325–56.

———. 1984. *After Hegemony: Cooperation and Discord in the World Political Economy*. Princeton, N.J.: Princeton University Press.

———. 2002. "Political Accountability." Unpublished manuscript, Duke University.

Keohane, Robert O., and Stanley Hoffman, eds. 1991. *The New European Community*. Boulder, Colo.: Westview Press.

Keohane, Robert O., and Helen V. Milner, eds. 1996. *Internationalization and Domestic Politics*. New York: Cambridge University Press.

Keohane, Robert O., and Joseph S. Nye, Jr. 1974. "Transgovermental Relations and World Politics." *World Politics* 27, 1 (October): 39–72.

———. 1977. *Power and Interdependence: World Politics in Transition*. Boston: Little Brown.

———. 2000a. "Globalization: What's New? What's Not? (And So What?)" *Foreign Policy* 118 (spring).

———. 2000b. "Introduction." In *Governance in a Globalizing World*, edited by Joseph S. Nye, Jr. and John D. Donahue, 1–41. Washington, D.C.: Brookings Institution.

———. 2001. "The Club Model of Multilateral Cooperation and Problems of Democatic Legitimacy." In *Efficiency, Equity, Legitimacy: The Multilateral Trading System at the Millennium*, edited by Roger Porter, Pierre Sauvé, Arvind Subramanian, and Americo Beviglia Zampetti. Washington, D.C.: Brookings Institution.

Kester, W. C. 1992. "Industrial Groups as Contractual Governance Systems." *Oxford Review of Economic Policy* 8, 3 (autumn): 24–44.

Keynes, John Maynard. 1923. *A Tract on Monetary Reform*. London: Macmillan.

Khagram, Sanjeev. 2000. "Toward Democratic Governance for Sustainable Development: Transnational Civil Society Organizing Around Big Dams." In *The Third Force*, edited by Ann Florini. Washington, D.C.: Carnegie Endowment for International Peace.

Kiewiet, D. Roderick, and Mathew D. McCubbins. 1991. *The Logic of Delegation: Congressional Parties and the Appropriations Process*. Chicago: University of Chicago Press.

Kindleberger, Charles. 1983. "Standards as Public, Collective, and Private Goods." *Kyklos* 36: 377–95.

Kirshner, Jonathan. 1995. *Currency and Coercion: The Political Economy of International Monetary Power*. Princeton, N.J.: Princeton University Press.

Kitschelt, Herbert. 1991. "Industrial Governance Structures, Innovation Strategies, and the Case of Japan: Sectoral or Cross-National Comparative Analysis?" *International Organization* 45, 4 (autumn): 453–93.

Kitschelt, Herbert, Peter Lange, Gary Marks, and John Stephens, eds. 1999. *Continuity and Change in Contemporary Capitalism*. New York. Cambridge University Press

Klein, Naomi. 1999. *No Logo: Taking Aim at the Brand Bullies*. New York: Picador Press.

Kletzer, Kenneth, and Jürgen von Hagen. 2000. "Monetary Union and Fiscal Federalism." Working Paper B1. Bonn: Zentrum fur Europaische Integrationsforschung.

Klotz, Audie. 1995. *Norms in International Relations: The Struggle Against Apartheid*. Ithaca, N.Y.: Cornell University Press.

Knetter, Michael M. 1989. "Price Discrimination by U.S. and German Exporters." *American Economic Review* 79 (1): 198–210.

Knill, Christoph, and Dirk Lehmkuhl. Forthcoming. "Private Actors and the State: Internationalization and Changing Patterns of Governance." *Governance*.

Kobrin, Stephen. 1998. "The MAI and the clash of globalizations." *Foreign Policy* 112 (fall): 97–109.

Kohler-Koch, Beate. 1996. "Regionen im Mehrebenensystem der EU." In *Das europäische Mehrebenensystem*, edited byThomas König, Elmar Rieger, and Hermann Schmitt. Frankfurt: Campus.

KPMG. 1999. "Ethics and Integrity:Business Ethics Survey." Available at *http://www.audit.kpmg.ca/ethics/vl/00ethicse.html*. Accessed June 1999.

Krasner, Stephen D. 1983. "Structural Causes and Regime Consequences: Regimes as Intervening Variables." In *International Regimes*, edited by Stephen D. Krasner. Ithaca, N.Y.: Cornell University Press.

Kreps, David M. 1990. "Corporate Culture and Economic Theory." In *Perspectives on Positive Political Economy*, edited by James E. Alt and Kenneth A. Shepsle. Cambridge: Cambridge University Press.

Krislov, Samuel. 1997. *How Nations Choose Production Standards and Standards Change Nations*. Pittsburgh, Pa.: University of Pittsburgh Press.

Krueger, Anne. 1978. *Liberalization Attempts and Consequences*. Cambridge: Ballinger.

Krueger, Russell, and Jiming Ha. 1996. "Measurement of Cocirculation of Currencies." In *The Macroeconomics of International Currencies: Theory, Policy, and Evidence*, edited by Paul D. Mizen and Eric J. Pentecost. Brookfield, Vt.: Edward Elgar.

Krugman, Paul R. 1991. *Geography and Trade*. Cambridge, Mass.: MIT Press.

———. 1993. "What Do We Need to Know about the International Monetary System?" In *International Finance* 190. Princeton, NJ: Princeton University, International Finance Section.

———. 1998a. "The Confidence Game." *The New Republic*, 5 October, 23–25.

———. 1998b. "Saving Asia: It's Time to Get Radical." *Fortune*, 7 September, 74–80.

———. 1998c. "Heresy Time." Available at *http://www.mit.edu/krugman/www/heresy.html*.

Krut, Riva, and Harris Gleckman. 1998. *ISO 14001: A Missed Opportunity for Sustainable Global Industrial Development*. London: Earthscan Publications.

Kurzer, Paulette. 1993. *Business and Banking*. Ithaca, N.Y.: Cornell University Press.

———. 1997. "Decline or Preservation of Executive Capacity? Political and Economic Integration Revisited." *Journal of Common Market Studies* 35: 31–56.

Laitin, David D. 1997. "The Cultural Identities of a European State." *Politics and Society* 25: 277–302.

———. 2000. "What Is a Language Community?" *American Journal of Political Science* 44: 142–55.

Laitin, David D., and Daniel Posner. 2000. "The Implications of Constructivism for Constructing Ethnic Fractionalization Indices." *APSA-CP* 12 (1): 13–17.

Lake, David A. 1999a. "Global Governance: A Relational Contracting Approach." In *Globalization and Governance*, edited by Aseem Prakash and Jeffrey A. Hart. New York: Routledge.

———. 1999b. *Entangling Relations: American Foreign Policy in its Century*. Princeton, N.J.: Princeton University Press.

Lake, David A., and Angela O'Mahony. 2002. The Incredible Shrinking State: Explaining Change in the Territorial Size of Nations. Paper presented at the 98th Annual Meeting of the American Political Science Association, 29 August–1 September, Boston, Mass.

Lake, David A., and Robert Powell, eds. 1999. *Strategic Choice and International Relations*. Princeton, N.J: Princeton University Press.

Lane, Christel. 1996. "The Role of Technical Standards in the Social Regulations of Supplier Relations in Britain and Germany." Working Paper 39. ESRC Center for Business Research , Cambridge, U.K.

Lange, Peter, Michael Wallerstein, and Miriam Golden. 1995. "The End of Corporatism? Wage Setting in the Nordic and Germanic Countries." In *The Workers of Nations*, ed. Sanford Jacoby, 76–100. New York: Oxford University Press.

La Porta, Rafael, Florencio Lopez-de-Silanes, Andrei Shleifer, and Robert W. Vishny. 2000. "Legal Determinants of External Finance, Investor Protection, and Corporate Governance." *Journal of Financial Economics* 58.

———. 2002. "What Works in Securities Laws?" Working Paper.

Laws, Eric, Bill Faulkner, and Gianna Moscardo. 1998. "Embracing and Managing Change in Tourism: International Case Studies." In *Embracing and Managing Change in Tourism: International Case Studies*, edited by Eric Laws, Bill Faulkner, and Gianna Moscardo, 1–10. New York: Routledge.

Le Galès, Patrick. 1998. "Conclusion—Government and Governance of Regions: Structural Weaknesses and New Mobilizations." In *Regions in Europe*, edited by Patrick Le Galès and Christian Lequesne. London: Routledge.

Le Galès, Patrick, and Alan Harding. 1998. "Cities and States in Europe." *West European Politics* 21 (3): 120–45.

Le Galès, Patrick, and Christian Lequesne, eds. 1998. *Regions in Europe*. London: Routledge.

Leblang, David A. 1997. "Domestic and Systemic Determinants of Capital Controls." *International Studies Quarterly* 41, 3 (September): 435–54.

Leontidou, Lila. 1991. "Greece: Prospects and Contradictions of Tourism in the 1980s." In *Tourism and Economic Development: Western European Experiences*, edited by Allan M. Williams and Gareth Shaw, 84–106. London: Belhaven Press.

Lerner, Daniel. 1964. *The Transfer of Institutions*. Durham, N.C.: Duke University Press.

Leurtiz, Krista Johnsen, and Walter Leight, eds. 1999. *Conference Report*. Washington, D.C.: U.S. Department of Commerce.

Levy, Jonah D. 1999. *Tocqueville's Revenge: State, Society, and Economy in Contemporary France*. Cambridge, Mass: Harvard University Press.

Levy Yeyati, Eduardo, and Federico Sturzenegger. 2000. "Is EMU a Blueprint for Mercosur?" *Latin American Journal of Economics* 110 (April): 63–99.

Lichbach, Mark I., and Paul Almeida. 2001. "Global Order and Local Resistance: The Neoliberal Institutional Trilemma and the Battle of Seattle." Unpublished manuscript, University of California, Riverside.

Liebowitz, Stan, and Stephen Margolis. 1990. "The Fable of the Keys." *Journal of Law and Economics* 1: 1–26.

———. 1994. "Network Externality: An Uncommon Tragedy." *Journal of Economic Perspective* 8: 133–50.

———. 1995. "Path Dependence, Lock-In, and History." *Journal of Law, Economics, and Organization* 11: 205–26.

Lijphart, Arend. 1999. *Patterns of Democracy Government Forms and Performance in Thirty-six Countries*. New Haven, Conn.: Yale University Press.

Lim, Lin Lean. 1998. "Child Prostitution." In *The Sex Sector: The Economic and Social Bases of Prostitution in Southeast Asia*, edited by Lin Lean Lim, 170–205. Geneva: International Labour Office.

Lindsay, James M. 1994. *Congress and the Politics of U.S. Foreign Policy*. Baltimore, Md.: Johns Hopkins University Press.

Lipset, Seymour M., and Stein Rokkan. 1967. "Cleavage Structures, Party Systems, and Voter Alignments: An Introduction." In *Party Systems and Voter Alignments: Cross-National Perspectives*, edited by Seymour M. Lipset and Stein Rokkan. New York: Free Press.

Liu, Zhen-Hua. 1998. "Tourism and Economic Development: A Comparative Analysis of Tourism in Developed and Developing Countries." In *Tourism and Development: Economic, Social, Political, and Environmental Issues*, edited by Clement A. Tisdell and Kartik C. Roy, 21–37. Commack, N.Y.: Nova Science Publishers.

Lockwood, Ben. 2002. "Distributive Politics and the Costs of Centralization." *Review of Economic Studies* 69: 1–25.

Lord, Christopher. 1998. *Democracy in the European Union*. Sheffield: Sheffield Academic Press.

Loriaux, Michael, Meredith Woo-Cumings, Kent E. Calder, Sylvia Maxfield, and Sofía A. Pérez. 1997. *Capital Ungoverned: Liberalizing Finance in Interventionist States*. Ithaca, N.Y.: Cornell University Press.

Loughlin, John. 1996. "'Europe of the Regions' and the Federalization of Europe." *Publius: The Journal of Federalism*, 26 (4): 141–62.

Lucas, Robert E., Jr. 1990. "Why Doesn't Capital Flow from Rich to Poor Countries?" *AEA Papers and Proceedings* 80: 92–96.

Lupia, Arthur, and Mathew D. McCubbins. 1994. "Learning from Oversight: Fire Alarms and Police Patrols Reconstructed." *The Journal of Law, Economics and Organization* 10, 1 (April): 96–125.

———. 1998. *The Democratic Dilemma: Can Citizens Learn What They Need to Know?* Cambridge: Cambridge University Press.

Lynch, Peter. 1996. *Minority Nationalism and European Integration*. Cardiff: University of Wales Press.

Macpherson, Andrew. 1990. *International Telecommunication Standards Organizations*. Boston: Artech House.

Magee, Stephen P., William A. Brock, and Leslie Young. 1989. *Black Hole Tariffs and Endogenous Policy Theory: Political Economy in General Equilibrium*. Cambridge: Cambridge University Press.

Mähönen, Petri. 2000. "The Standardization Process in IT: Too Slow or Too Fast?" In *Information Technology Standards and Standardization: A Global Perspective*, edited by Kai Jakobs. Hershey, Pa.: Idea Group Publishing.

Mair, Peter. 1997. *Party System Change: Approaches and Interpretations*. Oxford: Clarendon Press.

Majone, Giandomenico. 1992. "Regulatory Federalism in the European Community." *Environment and Planning C: Government and Policy* 10: 299–316.

———. 1993. "The European Community: Between Social Policy and Social Regulation." *Journal of Common Market Studies* 31 (2): 153–70.

———. 1994. "The European Community: An 'Independent Fourth Branch of

Government'?" In *Verfassungen fur ein ziviles Europa*, edited by G. Brug-gemeier, 23–43. Baden-Baden: Nomos.

———. 1999. "The Regulatory State and Its Legitimacy Problems." *West European Politics* 22 (1): 1–19.

Mancini, G. Federico, and David T. Keeling. 1994. "Democracy and the European Court of Justice." *The Modern Law Review* 57, 2 (March): 175–90.

Mansfield, Edward D., and Helen Milner, eds. 1997. *The Political Economy of Regionalism*. New York: Columbia University Press.

———. 1999. "The New Wave of Regionalism." *International Organization* 53: 589–628.

Maravall, Jose Maria. 1999. "Accountability and Manipulation." In *Democracy, Accountability, and Representation*, edited by Adam Przeworski, Susan C. Stokes, and Bernard Manin, 154–96. Cambridge: Cambridge University Press.

Mares, Isabella. 2000. "Strategic Alliances and Social Policy Reform: Unemployment Insurance in Comparative Perspective." *Politics and Society* 28 (2): 195–223

———. 2002. "Social Protection around the World." Paper presented at the Annual Meeting of the American Political Science Association, Boston.

Marks, Gary, and Liesbet Hooghe. 2000. "Optimality and Authority: A Critique of Neoclassical Theory." *Journal of Common Market Studies* 38, 5 (December): 795–816.

Marks, Gary, François Nielsen, Leonard Say, and Jane E. Salk. 1996. "Competencies, Cracks, and Conflicts: Regional Mobilization in the European Union." *Comparative Political Studies* 29: 164–92.

Marks, Gary, and Carole J. Wilson. 2000. "The Past in the Present: A Cleavage Theory of Party Response to European Integration." *British Journal of Political Science* 30: 433–59.

Marshall, T. H. 1973. *Class, Citizenship, and Social Development*. Westport, Conn.: Greenwood Press.

Martin, Lisa L. 1999. "Delegation, Accountability, and Efficient Governance." Memorandum prepared for the meeting on Globalization and Governance, University of California, San Diego, La Jolla, Calif.

———. 2000. *Democratic Commitments: Legislatures and International Cooperation*. Princeton, N.J.: Princeton University Press.

Mashaw, Jerry L. 1997. *Greed, Chaos, and Governance: Using Public Choice to Improve Public Law*. New Haven, Conn.: Yale University Press.

Mathews, Jessica T. 1997. "Power Shift." *Foreign Affairs* 76 (1): 50–66.

Matthews, Harry G., and Linda K. Richter. 1991. "Political Science and Tourism." *Annals of Tourism Research* 18: 120–35.

Mattli, Walter. 1999. *The Logic of Regional Integration*. Cambridge: Cambridge University Press.

———. 2001. "Private Justice in a Global Economy: From Litigation to Arbitration," *International Organization* 55: 919–47

Mattli, Walter, and Anne-Marie Slaughter. 1998. "Revisiting the European Court of Justice." *International Organization* 52: 177–209.

Matutes, Carmen, and Pierre Regibeau. 1996. "A Selective Review of the Economics of Standardization Entry Deterrence, Technological Progress, and International Competition." *European Journal of Political Economy* 12: 183–209.

Mauro, Paulo, Nathan Sussman, and Yishay Yafeh. 2001. "Emerging Market Spreads: Then Versus Now." Paper presented at the All-UC Group in Economic History Conference, 27–29 April, Berkeley, Calif.

Maxfield, Sylvia. 1990. *Governing Capital: International Finance and Mexican Politics.* Ithaca, N.Y.: Cornell University Press.

Mayer, Martin. 1998. "The Big Bailout." Unpublished manuscript, Brookings Institution, Washington, D.C.

McCubbins, Mathew D. 1985. "The Legislative Design of Regulatory Structure." *American Journal of Political Science* 29 (4): 721–48.

McCubbins, Mathew D., Roger G. Noll, and Barry R. Weingast. 1987. "Administrative Procedures as Instruments of Political Control." *Journal of Law, Economics, and Organization* 3, 2 (fall): 243–87.

McCubbins, Mathew D., and Thomas Schwartz. 1984. "Police Patrols Versus Fire Alarms." *American Journal of Political Science* 28: 165–79.

McGillivray, Fiona, and Nathan Jensen. 2000. "The Political Determinates of Foreign Direct Investment." Paper presented at the Annual Meeting of the American Political Science Association, Washington, D.C.

McKendrick, David, Richard Doner, and Stephan Haggard. 2000. *From Silicon Valley to Singapore: Location and Competitive Advantage in the Hard Disk Drive Industry* Palo Alto, Calif.: Stanford University Press.

McKenzie, Richard, and Dwight Lee. 1991. *Quicksilver Capital.* New York: Free Press.

McNamara, Kathleen R. 1998a. *The Currency of Ideas: Monetary Politics in the European Union.* Ithaca, N.Y.: Cornell University Press.

———. 1998b. "Globalization is What We Make of It: The Political Construction of Market Imperatives." Unpublished manuscript, Princeton University.

Meadwell, Hudson. 1991. "A Rational Choice Approach to Political Regionalism." *Comparative Politics* 23: 401–21.

Meidinger, Errol. 2001. "Governance and Forest Certification." In *The Social and Political Dimensions of Forest Certification.* Freiburg, Germany.

Meltzer, A., and S. Richards. 1981. "A Rational Theory of the Size of Government." *Journal of Political Economy,* 89: 314–27.

Meyer, John W., and Brian Rowan. 1977. "Institutionalized Organizations: Formal Structure as Myth and Ceremony." *American Journal of Sociology* 83: 340–63.

Micklethwait, John, and Adrian Wooldridge. 2000. *A Future Perfect: The Challenge and Hidden Promise of Globalization.* London: Heinemann.

Milner, Helen V. 1988. *Resisting Protectionism: Global Industries and the Politics of International Trade.* Princeton, N.J.: Princeton University Press.

Montinola, Gabriella, Yingyi Qian, and Barry R. Weingast. 1995. "Federalism, Chinese-Style: The Political Basis for Economic Success in China." *World Politics* 48: 50–81.

Moon, Peter, and Ray Thamotheram. 2000. "Corporations Become 'Socially Responsible.'" *The Independent* (London).

Moravcsik, Andrew. 1991. "Negotiating the Single European Act: National Interests and Conventional Statecraft in the European Community." *International Organization* 50 (1): 19–56.

———. 1998. *The Choice for Europe: Social Purpose and State Power from Messina to Maastricht.* Ithaca, N.Y.: Cornell University Press.

Mosley, Layna. 2000. "Room to Move: International Financial Markets and National Welfare States." *International Organization* 54, 4 (autumn): 737–74.

Most, B., and H. Starr. 1980. "Diffusion, Reinforcement, Geopolitics, and the Spread of War." *American Political Science Review* 74: 932–46.

Mowforth, Martin, and Ian Munt. 1998. *Tourism and Sustainability: New Tourism in the Third World.* New York: Routledge.

Multidisciplinary Working Group on Enhanced Disclosure. (MWG) 2000. Final Report. Basle: MWG.

Mundell, Robert. 1961. "A Theory of Optimal Currency Areas." *American Economic Review* 51 (September): 657–65.

———. 2000. "A Reconsideration of the Twentieth Century." *American Economic Review* 90, 3 (June): 327–40.

Muntarbhorn, Vitit. 1995. "Child Prostitution: International and National Perspectives." A study for the U.S. Department of Labor's Seminar on Child Prostitution, 29 September, Washington, D.C.

Murphy, Craig. 2000. "Global Governance: Poorly Done and Poorly Understood." *International Affairs* 76, 4: 789–803.

Musgrave, Richard. 1959. *The Theory of Public Finance: A Study in Public Economy.* New York: McGraw-Hill.

Nagel, Klaus-Jürgen. 2001. "The 'Europe of the Regions' and the Identity Politics of Nations Without States." *Scottish Affairs* 36: 48–72.

Nairn, Tom. 1977. *The Break-Up of Britain: Crisis and Neo-Nationalism.* London: NLB.

Newman, Saul. 1996. *Ethnoregional Conflict in Democracies: Mostly Ballots, Rarely Bullets.* Westport: Greenwood Press.

Nielson, Daniel, and Michael Tierney. 2002a. "Principals and Interests: Agency Theory and Multilateral Development Bank Lending." Unpublished manuscript.

———. 2002b. "Principles or Principals? Agency Theory, Organizational Reform, and Multilateral Development Bank Lending." Unpublished manuscript.

Nijkamp, Peter. 1993. "Towards a Network of Regions: The United States of Europe." *European Planning Studies* 1: 149–68.

Noel, Emile, and Henri Etienne. 1969. "Quelques Aspects Des Rapports et de la Collaboration entre le Conseil et la Commission." In *La Decision dans les Communautes Europeennes,* edited by Pierre Gerbet and Daniel Pepy, 40–48. Brussels: University of Brussels Press.

Noll, Roger, and Frances Rosenbluth. 1995."Telecommunications Policy: Structure, Process, and Outcomes." In *Structure and Policy in Japan and the United States,* edited by Peter Cowhey and Mathew McCubbins. Cambridge: Cambridge University Press.

Nye, Joseph S., and John D. Donahue. 2000. *Governance in a Globalizing World*. Washington, D.C.: Brookings Institution.

O'Brien, Robert, Anne Marie Goetz, Jan Aart Scholte, and Marc Williams. 2000. *Contesting Global Governance: Multilateral Economic Institutions and Global Social Movements*. New York: Cambridge University Press.

O'Driscoll, Gerald P., Jr., Kim R. Holmes, and Melanie Kirkpatrick. 2001. *2001 Index of Economic Freedom*. Washington, D.C., and New York: The Heritage Foundation and Dow Jones.

O'Niell, Kathleen. 2000. Changing Decentralization in Bolivia: Electoral Incentives and Outcomes. Paper presented at the conference "Decentralization in Latin America," University of Minnesota, 11–12 February.

O'Rourke, Kevin H., and Jeffrey G. Williamson. 1999. *Globalization and History: The Evolution of a Nineteenth-Century Atlantic Economy*. Cambridge, Mass.: MIT Press.

Oates, Wallace E. 1972. *Fiscal Federalism*. New York: Harcourt Brace Jovanovich.

———. 1999. "An Essay on Fiscal Federalism." *Journal of Economic Literature* 37 (3): 1120–49.

Obstfeld, Maurice. 1995. "International Capital Mobility in the 1990s." In *Understanding Interdependence: The Macroeconomics of the Open Economy*, edited by Peter B. Kenen. Princeton, N.J.: Princeton University Press.

———. 1998. "The Global Capital Market: Benefactor or Menace?" *Journal of Economic Perspectives* 12 (4): 9–30.

Obstfeld, Maurice, and Giovanni Peri. 1998. "Regional Non-adjustment and Fiscal Policy." *Economic Policy* 26.

Obstfeld, Maurice, and Kenneth Rogoff. 1996. *Foundations of International Macroeconomics*. Cambridge, Mass.: MIT Press.

Obstfeld, Maurice, and Alan M. Taylor. 1997. "The Great Depression as a Watershed: International Capital Mobility over the Long Run." National Bureau of Economic Research Working Paper 5960. National Bureau of Economic Research, Cambridge, Mass.

———. 1998. "The Great Depression as a Watershed: International Capital Mobility over the Long Run." In *The Defining Moment: The Great Depression and the American Economy in the Twentieth Century*, edited by Michael D. Bordo, Claudia Goldin, and Eugene N. White, 353–402. Chicago: University of Chicago Press.

Ocampo, Jose Antonio. 2000. "Recasting the International Financial Agenda." Working Paper, Group of Twenty Four (November).

Ofreneo, Rene E., and Rosalinda Pineda Ofreneo. 1998. "Prostitution in the Philippines." In *The Sex Sector: The Economic and Social Bases of Prostitution in Southeast Asia*, edited by Lin Lean Lim, 100–29. Geneva: International Labour Office.

Ohmae, Kenichi. 1995. *The End of the Nation State: The Rise of Regional Economies*. New York: Free Press.

Olson, Mancur. 1965. *The Logic of Collective Action: Public Goods and theTheory of Groups*. Cambridge, Mass: Harvard University Press.

Opinion Leader Research. 2000. Does the City Have a Conscience? London: Control Risks Group, London, 22 May.

Organization for Economic Cooperation and Development (OECD). 1988. *The Telecommunications Industry: The Challenges of Structural Change.* Paris: OECD.

———. 1991. "Inventory of Measures Perceived as Obstacles to International Tourism in the OECD Area." Paris: OECD.

———. 1997. "Tourism Policy and International Tourism in OECD Countries." OCDE/GD(97)173. Paris: OECD.

———. 1999a. *Principles of Corporate Governance.* Paris: OECD.

———. 1999b. *Economic Outlook.* Paris: OECD.

———. 2000a. "The OECD Tourism Committee." Available at *http://www. oecd.org/dsti/sti/transpor/tourism/news/committee.html.*

———. 2000b. "Liberalisation of International Tourism Services." Available at *http://www.oecd.org/dsti/sti/transpor/tourism/act/liberalisation.html.*

———. 2000c. "Performance of OECD Tourism Policies." Available at *http:// www.oecd.org/dsti/sti/transpor/tourism/act/policies.html.*

———. Various years. *OECD Economic Surveys,* selected countries.

Organization for Economic Cooperation and Development (OECD). Working Party of the Trade Committee. 1999. *Regulatory Reform and International Standardization.* Paris: OECD.

———. 2001. *Codes of Corporate Conduct — An Expanded Review of Their Contents.* Paris: OECD.

Ottaviano, Gianmarco I. P., and Diego Pugo. 1998. "Agglomeration in the Global Economy: A Survey of the 'New Economic Geography.'" *The World Economy* 21 (August): 707–31.

Ottaway, Marina. 2001. "Reluctant Missionaries." *Foreign Policy* 125 (July/ August): 44–55.

———. 2002. "Corporatism Goes Global: International Organizations, Non-governmental Organization Networks, and Transnational Business." *Global Governance* 7, 3: 265–93.

Oxford Analytica and Prince of Wales Business Leaders Forum. (OAPWBLF) 2000. *Changing Corporate Roles and Responsibilities: Business and Socially Responsible Investment.* London: Oxford Analytica and PWBLF.

Padoa-Schioppa, Tommaso. 1987. *Efficiency, Stability, and Equity: A Strategy for the Evolution of the Economic System of the European Community.* London: Oxford University Press.

Page, Benjamin I., and Robert Y. Shapiro. 1983. "Effects of Public Opinion on Policy." *American Political Science Review* 77: 175–90.

Panizza, Ugo. 1999. "On the Determinants of Fiscal Centralization: Theory and Evidence." *Journal of Public Economics* 74: 97–139.

Parliament of Australia. House of Representatives. Standing Committee on Legal and Constitutional Affairs. 1994. *Advisory Report on Crimes (Child Sex Tourism) Amendment Bill 1994.* Canberra: Commonwealth of Australia.

Pastor, Manuel, and Carol Wise. 2001. "From Poster Child to Basket Case." *Foreign Affairs* 80, 6 (July/August): 60–72.

Pauly, Louis W. 1988. *Opening Financial Markets: Banking Politics on the Pacific Rim.* Ithaca, NY: Cornell University Press.

Pearce, Douglas. 1992. *Tourist Organizations*. Essex, England: Longman Scientific and Technical.

Pelkmans, Jacques. 2001. "The GSM Standard: Explaining a Success Story." *Journal of European Public Policy* 8 (3): 432–53.

Pelkmans, Jacques, Ellen Vos, and Luca Di Mauro. 2000. "Reforming Product Regulation in the EU: A Painstaking, Iterative Two-Level Game." In *Regulatory Reform and Competitiveness in Europe*, edited by G. Galli and J. Pelkmans, 1–55. Cheltham: Edward Elgar.

Pennings, Paul, and Jan-Erik Lane, eds. 1998. *Comparing Party System Change*. London: Routledge.

Pennock, J. Roland, and John W. Chapman, eds. 1987. *Authority Revisited: NOMOS XXIX*. New York: New York University Press.

Pérez, Louis A., Jr. 1974. "Aspects of Underdevelopment: Tourism in the West Indies." *Science and Society* 37: 473–80.

Persson, Torsten, and Guido Tabellini. 1996a. "Federal Fiscal Constitutions: Risk Sharing and Redistribution." *Journal of Political Economy* 104 (5): 979–1009.

———. 1996b. "Federal Fiscal Constitutions: Risk Sharing and Moral Hazard." *Econometrica* 64.

———. 2000. *Political Economics: Explaining Economic Policy*. Cambridge, Mass.: MIT Press.

Peters, R. S. 1967. "Authority." In *Political Philosophy*, edited by Anthony Quinton. New York: Oxford University Press.

Peterson, M. J. Forthcoming. "International and Transboundary Accords: Environmental." In *International Encyclopedia of Social and Behavioral Sciences*. Amsterdam: Pergamon.

Pierson, Paul. 1994. *Dismantling the Welfare State?* New York: Cambridge University Press.

———, ed. 2001. *The New Politics of the Welfare State*. New York: Oxford University Press.

Pinelli, Dino, Rosella Giacometti, Richard Lewney, and Bernard Fingleton. 1998. "European Regional Competitiveness Indicators." Discussion Paper 103, Department of Land Economy, University of Cambridge.

Pollack, Mark A. and Gregory C. Shaffer. 2001. "The Challenge of Reconciling Regulatory Differences: Food Safety and Genetically Modified Organisms in the Transatlantic Relationship." In *Transatlantic Governance in the Global Economy*, edited by Mark A. Pollack and Gregory C. Shaffer, 153–78. Lanham, Md.: Rowman and Littlefield.

Pontusson, Jonas. 2000. "Social Europe Versus Liberal America: Inequality, Employment, and Social Welfare in the Global Economy." Unpublished manuscript, Cornell University.

Porter, Michael. 1992. "Capital Disadvantage: America's Failing Capital Investment System." *Harvard Business Review* (Sept./Oct.)

———. 1998. *The Competitive Advantage of Nations*. London: Macmillan Press.

Posen, Adam. 1993. "Why Central Bank Independence Does Not Cause Low

Inflation: There Is No Institutional Fix for Politics." In *Finance and the International Economy*, edited by Richard O'Brien, 7. New York: Oxford University Press.

Pou, Pedro. 2000. "Is Globalization Really to Blame?" In *Rethinking the International Monetary System*, edited by Jane Sneddon Little and Giovanni P. Oliveri, 243–50. Boston: Federal Reserve Bank of Boston.

Powell, Walter W., and Paul DiMaggio. 1991. *The New Institutionalism in Organizational Analysis*. Chicago: University of Chicago Press.

Prakash, Aseem. 2000. *Greening the Firm: The Politics of Corporate Environmentalism*. Cambridge: Cambridge University Press.

Prakash, Aseem, and Jeffrey A. Hart. 2000. *Coping with Globalization*. New York: Routledge.

President's Working Group on Financial Markets. 1999. Hedge Funds, Leverage, and the Lessons of Long-Term Capital Management, Washington, D.C.: President's Working Group (April).

Pritchett, Lant. 1997. "Divergence, Big Time." *Journal of Economic Perspectives* 11: 3–17.

Przeworski, Adam, Susan C. Stokes, and Bernard Manin, eds. 1999. *Democracy, Accountability, and Representation*. Cambridge: Cambridge University Press.

Putnam, Robert D. 1988. "Diplomacy and Domestic Politics: The Logic of Two-level Games." *International Organization* 42, 3 (summer): 427–60.

Quinn, Dennis. 1997. "The Correlates of Change in International Financial Regulation." *American Political Science Review* 91, 3 (September): 531–51.

Quinn, Dennis P., and Carla Inclan. 1997. "The Origins of Financial Openness: A Study of Current and Capital Account Liberalization." *American Journal of Political Science* 41, 3 (July): 771–813.

Quinn, Dennis P., and Robert Jacobson. 1989. "Industrial Policy Through the Restriction of Capital Flows: A Test of Several Claims Made About Industrial Policy." *American Journal of Political Science* 33, 3 (August): 700–36.

Rajan, Raghuram G., and Luigi Zingales. 2001. "The Great Reversals: The Politics of Financial Development in the Twentieth Century." Unpublished manuscript, University of Chicago.

Rankin, Bob. 1999. "The Impact of Hedge Funds on Financial Markets: Lessons from the Experience of Australia." In *Capital Flows and the International Financial System*, edited by David Gruen and Luke Gower, 151–63. Sydney: Reserve Bank of Australia.

Raunio, Tapio, and Simon Hix. 2001. "Backbenchers Learn to Fight: European Integration and Parliamentary Government." In *Europeanized Politics: European Integration and National Political Systems*, edited by Klaus H. Goetz and Simon Hix, 142–68. London: Frank Cass.

Regional Conference for Africa and the Mediterranean. 1991. "Food Safety and Tourism." Tunisia, 25–27 November. Madrid: World Tourism Organization.

Reinicke, Wolfgang. 1998a. "Global Public Policy." *Foreign Affairs*.

———. 1998b. *Global Public Policy*. Washington, D.C.: The Brookings Institution.

———. 1999–2000. "The Other World Wide Web: Global Public Policy Networks." *Foreign Policy* 117 (winter): 44–57.

Rhodes, Martin. 2001. "Why EMU Is (or May Be) Good for European Welfare States." Unpublished manuscript.

Rhodes, R. A. W. 1997. *Understanding Governance: Policy Networks, Governance, Reflexivity and Accountability*. Buckingham: Open University Press.

Richter, Linda K. 1983a. "Political Implications of Chinese Tourism Policy." *Annals of Tourism Research* 10: 395–413.

———. 1983b. "Tourism Politics and Political Science: A Case of Not So Benign Neglect." *Annals of Tourism Research* 10: 313–35.

———. 1989. *The Politics of Tourism in Asia*. Honolulu: University of Hawaii Press.

Richter, Linda K., and William L. Richter. 1985. "Policy Choices in South Asian Tourism Development." *Annals of Tourism Research* 12: 201–17.

Risse-Kappen, Thomas. 1994. "Ideas Do Not Float Freely: Transnational Coalitions, Domestic Structures, and the End of the Cold War." *International Organization* 48: 185–214.

———, ed. 1995. *Bringing Transnational Relations Back In: Non-State Actors, Domestic Structures, and International Institutions*. New York: Cambridge University Press.

Roach, Steven, and John Montgomery. 1998. "Hedge Funds—Scale, Scope and Impact." Morgan Stanley Dean Witter Equity Research Briefing Note, 13 October. New York: Morgan Stanley Dean Witter.

Robbins, D. 1996. "Trade, Trade Liberalization, and Inequality in Latin America and East Asia." Unpublished manuscript, Harvard Institute for International Development.

Robinson, James A. 2000. "Where Does Inequality Come From? Ideas and Implications for Latin America." OECD Development Centre, Paris (December).

Robinson, Mike. 1999. "Cultural Conflicts in Tourism: Inevitability and Inequality." In *Tourism and Cultural Conflicts*, edited by Mike Robinson and Priscilla Boniface, 1–32. New York: CABI Publishing.

Rodden, Jonathan. 2002. "The Dilemma of Fiscal Federalism: Grants and Fiscal Performance Around the World." *American Journal of Political Science* 46 (2): 670–87.

———. 2003a. "Federalism and Decentralization: On Meaning and Measurement." Forthcoming. *Comparative Politics*.

———. 2003b. "Federalism and Soft Budget Constraints in Germany." In *Decentralization and the Challenge of Hard Budget Constraints*, edited by Jonathan Rodden, Gunnar Eskeland, and Jennie Litvack. Cambridge, Mass.: MIT Press.

Rodrik, Dani. 1997. *Has Globalization Gone too Far?* Washington, D.C.: Institute for International Economics.

———. 1998. "Why Do More Open Economies Have Bigger Governments?" *Journal of Political Economy* 106 (5): 997–1032.

Roe, Mark. 1994. *Strong Mangers, Weak Owners: the Political Roots of American Corporate Finance*. Princeton, N.J.: Princeton University Press.

———. 2000. "Political Preconditions to Separating Ownership from Corporate Control." *Stanford Law Review* 53(3): 539–606.

———. 2002. *Political Determinants of Corporate Governance*. Oxford: Oxford University Press.

Roeder, Philip G. 1993. *Red Sunset: The Failure of Soviet Politics*. Princeton, N.J.: Princeton University Press.

Rogers, E. M. 1995. *The Diffusion of Innovations*. 3d ed. New York: Free Press.

Rogoff, Kenneth. 2001. "Why Not a Global Currency?" *American Economic Review* 91, 2 (May): 243–47.

Rogowski, Ronald. 1989. *Commerce and Coalitions: How Trade Affects Domestic Political Alignments*. Princeton, N.J.: Princeton University Press.

———. 1999. "Institutions as Constraints on Strategic Choices " In *Strategic Choice and International Relations*, edited by David A. Lake and Robert Powell. Princeton, N.J: Princeton University Press.

Rokkan, Stein, and Derek W. Urwin, eds. 1982. *The Politics of Territorial Identity: Studies in European Regionalism*. London: Sage.

———. 1983. *Economy, Territory, Identity: Politics of West European Peripheries*. London: Sage.

Roller, Elisa. 1999. "Catalan Nationalism Within a Europe of the Regions: The Development of a Dual Strategy." Working Paper 1/99, European Policy Research Institute, University of Manchester.

Roller, Elisa, and Pieter Van Houten. 2002. "National Parties in Regional Party Systems: The PSC-PSOE in Catalonia." Paper presented at the Third Mediterranean Social and Political Research Meeting, Florence.

Rose, Andrew K. 2000. "One Money, One Market: The Effect of Common Currencies on Trade." *Economic Policy* 30 (April): 7–45.

———. 2002. "The Effect of Common Currencies on International Trade: A Meta-Analysis." paper prepared for a conference on the Euro and Dollarization, Fordham University, New York, 5–6 April.

Rosecrance, Richard. 1996. "The Rise of the Virtual State." *Foreign Affairs* 75 (4): 45–61.

Ross, Fiona. 1997. "Cutting Public Expenditures in Advanced Industrial Democracies: The Importance of Avoiding Blame." *Governance* 10 (April): 175–200.

Rubinfield, D. 1987. "The Economics of the Local Public Sector." In *Handbook of Public Economics II*, edited by A. Auerbach and M. Feldstein. Amsterdam: North-Holland.

Ruggie, John Gerard. 1975. "International Responses to Technology: Concepts and Trends." *International Organization* 29: 557–83.

———. 1982. "International Regimes, Transactions, and Change." *International Organization* 36 (spring): 195–231.

Sachs, Jeffrey, and Xavier Sala-I-Martin. 1992. "Fiscal Federalism and Optimum Currency Areas.," in Matthew Canzoneri, Paul Masson, and Vittorio Grilli, eds., *Establishing a Central Bank: Issues in Europe and Lessons from the U.S.* Cambridge: Cambridge University Press.

Sachs, Jeffrey, and Andrew Warner. 1995. "Economic Reform and the Process of Global Integration." *Brookings Papers on Economic Activity* 1: 379–416.

Salter, Liora. 1988. *Mandated Science: Science and Scientists in the Making of Standards*. Dordrecht: Kluwer Academic Publishers.

Salvatore, Dominick. 1994. *Microeconomics*. 2d ed. New York: HarperCollins College.

Samuels, David, and Richard Snyder. 2001. "The Value of a Vote: Malapportionment in Comparative Perspective." *British Journal of Political Science* 31,4: 651–71.

Sandholtz, Wayne. 1993. "Choosing Union: Monetary Politics and Maastricht." *International Organization* 47: 1–39.

Sandholtz, Wayne, and Alec Stone Sweet, eds. 1998. *European Integration and Supranational Governance.* New York: Oxford University Press.

Sassen, Saskia. 1994. *Cities in a World Economy.* Thousand Oaks, Calif.: Pine Forge Press.

———. 1996. *Losing Control? Sovereignty in an Age of Globalization.* New York: Columbia University Press.

———. 1998. *Globalization and Its Discontents.* New York: The Free Press.

Savage, James D. 2000. "Budgetary Collection Action Problems: Convergence and Compliance Under the Maastricht Treaty on European Union." *Public Administration Review.*

Sbragia, Alberta. 2001. "Italy Pays for Europe." In *Transforming Europe,* edited by Maria Green Cowles, James Caporaso, and Thomas Risse. Ithaca, N.Y.: Cornell University Press.

Scharpf, Fritz W. 1988. "The Joint-Decision Trap: Lessons from German Federalism and European Integration." *Public Administration* 66: 239–78.

———. 1994. *Optionen des Föderalismus in Deutschland und Europa.* Frankfurt: Campus.

———. 1999. *Governing in Europe: Effective and Democratic?* Oxford: Oxford University Press.

Scharpf, Fritz W., and Vivian Schmidt, eds. 2001. *Welfare and Work in the Open Economy: From Vulnerability to Competitiveness.* New York: Oxford University Press.

Schedler, Andreas. 1999. "Conceptualizing accountability." In Andreas Schedler, Larry Diamond and Marc F. Plattner, eds., *The Self-Restraining State: Power and Accountability in New Democracies.* 13–28. Boulder and London: Lynne Rienner.

Schepel, Harm, and Josef Falke. 2000. *Legal Aspects of Standardisation in the Member States of the EC and EFTA: Comparative Report.* Vol 1. Luxembourg: Office for Official Publications of the European Communities.

Scheppele, Kim Lane, and Karol Edward Soltan. 1987. "The Authority of Alternatives." In *Authority Revisited: NOMOS XXIX,* edited by. J. Roland Pennock and John W. Chapman. New York: New York University Press.

Scheve, Kenneth F., and Matthew J. Slaughter. 2001. *Globalization and the Perceptions of American Workers.* Washington, D.C.: Institute for International Economics.

Schmidt, Susanne, and Raymund Werle. 1998. *Coordinating Technology: Studies in the International Standardization of Telecommunications.* Cambridge, Mass.: MIT Press.

Schmitter, Philippe, and Terry Lynn Karl. 1991. "What Democracy Is . . . and What It Is Not." *Journal of Democracy* 2: 75–88.

Schnell, Peter. 1991. "The Federal Republic of Germany: A Growing International Deficit?" In *Tourism and Economic Development: Western European Experiences,* edited by Allan M. Williams and Gareth Shaw, 207–24. London: Belhaven Press.

Schulze, Günther G., and Heinrich Ursprung. 1999. "Globalization and the Economy of the Nation State." *The World Economy* 22: 295–352.

Schumpeter, Joseph S. [1942] 1962. *Capitalism, Socialism, and Democracy.* New York: Harper Torchbooks.

Schwartz, Herman. 2001. "Round Up the Usual Suspects! Globalization, Domestic Politics, and Welfare State Change." In *New Politics of the Welfare State*, edited by Paul Pierson. New York: Oxford University Press.

Scott, Allen J. 1998. *Regions and the World Economy: The Coming Shape of Global Production, Competition, and Political Order.* Oxford: Oxford University Press.

Scott, W. Richard, John W. Meyer, and associates, eds. 1994. *Institutional Environment and Organizations: Structural Complexity and Individualism.* Thousand Oaks, Calif.: Sage.

Sellers, Jefferey M. 2002. *Governing from Below: Urban Regions and the Global Economy.* Cambridge: Cambridge University Press.

Sen, Amartya. 1999. *Development as Freedom.* New York: Knopf.

Shankar, Raja, and Anwar Shah. 2000. "Bridging the Economic Divide Within Nations: A Scorecard on the Performance of Regional Policies in Reducing Regional Income Disparities." World Bank, Policy Research Working Paper 2717.

Shapiro, Martin. 1988. *Who Guards the Guardians? Judicial Control of Administration.* Athens: University of Georgia Press.

Sharpe, L. J. 1993. "The European Meso: An Appraisal." In *The Rise of Meso Government in Europe*, edited by L. J. Sharpe. London: Sage.

Shaw, Gareth, Justin Greenwood, and Allan M. Williams. 1991. "The United Kingdom: Market Responses and Public Policy." In *Tourism and Economic Development: Western European Experiences*, edited by Allan M. Williams and Gareth Shaw, 173–90. London: Belhaven Press.

Shepsle, Kenneth A. 1989. "Studying Institutions: Some Lessons from the Rational Choice Approach." *Journal of Theoretical Politics* 1 (2): 131–47.

Shinn, James. 2000. "Nitwits in Pinstripes Versus Barbarians at the Gate: Capital Market Integration and Corporate Governance Convergence in Japan, Germany, and South Korea." Unpublished manuscript, Princeton University.

———. 2001. "Private Profit or Public Convergence?" Unpublished manuscript, Princeton University.

Shinn, James, and Peter Gourevitch. 2002. "How Shareholder Reforms Can Pay Foreign Policy Dividends." New York: Council on Foreign Relations.

Shklar, Judith. 1991. *American Citizenship: The Quest for Inclusion.* Cambridge, Mass.: Harvard University Press.

Shleifer, Andrei and Robert W. Vishny. 1999. "Corporate Ownership around the World." *Journal of Finance* 54.

Shugart, Matthew Soberg, and John M. Carey. 1992. *Presidents and Assemblies: Constitutional Design and Electoral Dynamics.* New York: Cambridge University Press.

Sikkink, Kathryn. 1986. "Codes of Conduct for Transnational Corporations: The Case of the WHO/UNICEF Code." *International Organization* 40 3 (fall): 815–40.

Simmons, Beth A. 1994. *Who Adjusts? Domestic Sources of Foreign Economic Policy During the Interwar Years*. Princeton, N.J.: Princeton University Press.

————. 2000. "The Legalization of International Monetary Affairs." *International Organization* 54, 3 (summer).

Simmons, P. J. 1998. "Learning to Live with NGOs." *Foreign Policy* 112: 82–96.

Sinclair, M. Thea, and Mike Stabler. 1997. *The Economics of Tourism*. London: Routledge.

Siverson, Randall, and Harvey Starr. 1991. *The Diffusion of War: A Study of Opportunity and Willingness*. Ann Arbor: University of Michigan Press.

Slaughter, Anne-Marie. 2000. "Governing the Global Economy Through Governance Networks." In *The Role of Law in International Politics: Essays in International Relations and International Law*, edited by Michael Byers, 177–205. Oxford: Oxford University Press.

Smith, Anthony D. 1995. *Nations and Nationalism in a Global Era*. Cambridge: Polity Press.

Smith, Ginger, and Abraham Pizam. 1998. "NAFTA and Tourism Development Policy in North America." In *Embracing and Managing Change in Tourism: International Case Studies*, edited by Eric Laws, Bill Faulkner and Gianna Moscardo, 17–28. New York: Routledge.

Social Investment Forum. 2000. "SIF Research: 1999 Trends Report." Available at *http://www.socialinvest.org/Areas/ research/ trends/1999-trends.html*. Accessed January 2001

Sorens, Jason. 2002a. "The Cross-Sectional Determinants of Secessionism." Unpublished manuscript, Yale University.

————. 2002b. "Globalization, Autonomy, and the Politics of Secession." Unpublished manuscript, Yale University.

Soros, George. 1998. *The Crisis of Global Capitalism*. New York: Public Affairs Press.

Soskice, David. 1999. "Divergent Production Regimes: Coordinated and Uncoordinated Market Economies in the 1980s and 1990s." In *Continuity and Change in Contemporary Capitalism*, edited by Herbert Kitschelt, Peter Lange, Gary Marks, and John Stephens, 101–34. Cambridge: Cambridge University Press.

Spruyt, Hendrik. 2001. "The Supply and Demand of Governance in Standards-Setting: Insights from the Past." *Journal of European Public Policy* 8 (3): 371–91.

Steinmo, Sven. 1993. *Taxation and Democracy*. New Haven, Conn.: Yale University Press.

Stephens, John, and Evelyn Huber Stephens. 2001. *Development and Crisis of the Welfare States: Parties and Policies in Global Markets*. Chicago: Chicago University Press.

Stiglitz, Joseph E. 2002. *Globalization and Its Discontents*. New York: W. W. Norton.

Stockman, Alan C., and Alejandro Hernandez. 1988. "Exchange Controls, Capital Controls, and International Financial Markets." *The American Economic Review* 78, 3 (June): 362–74.

Stolper, Wolfgang, and Paul Samuelson. 1941. "Protection and Real Wages." *Review of Economic Studies* 9, 1: 58–73.

Stone Sweet, Alec 1995. "Constitutional Dialogues in the European Community." European University Institute WP 95/38. Robert Schuman Centre, EUI, Florence, Italy.

Stone Sweet, Alec, and James A. Caporaso. 1998. "From Free Trade to Supranational Polity: The European Court and Integration." In *European Integration and Supranational Governance*, edited by Wayne Sandholtz and Alec Stone Sweet, 92–133. Oxford: Oxford University Press.

Stone Sweet, Alec, and Margaret McCown 2000. "Path Dependence, Precedent, and Judicial Power." Unpublished manuscript, Nuffield College, Oxford University.

Storper, Michael. 1997. *The Regional World: Territorial Development in a Global Economy*. New York: The Guilford Press.

Strange, Susan. 1996. *The Retreat of the State: The Diffusion of Power in the World Economy*. New York: Cambridge University Press.

Streeck, Wolfgang. 1997. "The German Economic Model: Does It Exist? Can it Survive?" In *The Political Economy of Modern Capitalism: Mapping Convergence and Diversity*, edited by Colin Crouch and Wolfgang Streeck. London: Sage.

Svensson, Lars E. O. 1988. "Trade in Risky Assets." *American Economic Review* 78 (June): 375–94.

Swank, Duane. 2002. *Global Capital, Political Institutions, and Policy Change in Developed Welfare States*. New York: Cambridge University Press.

Swenson, Peter. 1991. "Bringing Capital Back In or Social Democracy Reconsidered: Employer Power, Cross-Class Alliances, and Centralization of Indusrialization in Denmark and Sweden." *World Politics* 43 (4): 513–44.

Sykes, Alan. 1995. *Product Standards for Internationally Integrated Goods Markets*. Washington, D.C.: Brookings Institution.

Tate, Jay. 2001. National Varieties of Standardization. In *Varieties of Capitalism: The Institutional Foundations of Comparative Advantage*, edited by Peter Hall and David Soskice. Oxford: Oxford University Press.

Taylor, C., and M. Hudson. 1972. *World Handbook of Political and Social Indicators*. New Haven, Conn.: Yale University Press.

Taylor, Keith. 1995. "European Union: The Challenge for Local and Regional Government." *Political Quarterly* 66: 74–83.

Thelen, Kathleen. 2001. "Varieties of Labor Politics in the Developed Democracies." In *Varieties of Capitalism*, edited by John A. Hall and David Soskice. Cambridge, Mass: Harvard University Press.

Thorsten Beck, George Clarke, Alberto Groff, Philip Keefer, and Patrick Walsh. 1999 "New Tools and New Tests in Comparative Political Economy: The Database of Political Institutions." Washington, D.C.: World Bank.

Thucydides. 1962. *The Peloponnesian War*. Translated by T. E. Wick. New York: Modern Library.

Tiebout, Charles M. 1956. "A Pure Theory of Local Expenditures." *Journal of Political Economy* 64, 5 (October): 416–24.

Tisdell, Clem. 1998. "A Review of Tourism Economics with Some Observations on Tourism in India." In *Tourism and Development: Economic, Social, Political, and Environmental Issues*, edited by Clement A. Tisdell and Kartik C. Roy, 7–17. Commack, N.Y.: Nova Science Publishers.

Tomaney, John. 2000. "Review of Keating 1998." *International Journal of Urban and Regional Research* 24: 498–99.

Tossutti, Livianna S. 2002. "How Transnational Factors Influence the Success of Ethnic, Religious and Regional Parties in 21 States." *Party Politics* 8: 51–74.

Toth, Robert. 1991. *Standards Activities of Organizations in the United States.* Gaithersburg, Md.: U.S. Dept. of Commerce, National Institute of Standards and Technology.

Treisman, Daniel. 1999. *After the Deluge: Regional Crises and Political Consolidation in Russia.* Ann Arbor: University of Michigan Press.

Tribe, John. 1995. *The Economics of Leisure and Tourism.* Oxford: Butterworth-Heinemann.

Tsebelis, George. 1994. "The Power of the European Parliament as a Conditional Agenda-Setter." *American Political Science Review* 88: 128–42.

———. 2000. "Veto Players and Institutional Analysis" *Governance* 13: 441–74.

Tsebelis, George, and Geoffrey Garrett. 1997. "Agenda-Setting, Vetoes, and the European Union's Co-Decision Procedure." *Journal of Legislative Studies* 3 (3): 74–92.

———. 2001. "The Institutional Foundations of Intergovernmentalism and Supranationalism in the European Union." *International Organization* 44, 2 (spring): 357–90.

Tsebelis, George, and Amie Kreppel. 1998. "The History of Conditional Agenda-Setting in European Institutions." *European Journal of Political Research* 33 (1): 41–71.

Tuppen, John. 1991. "France: The Changing Character of a Key Industry." In *Tourism and Economic Development: Western European Experiences*, edited by Allan M. Williams and Gareth Shaw, 191–206. London: Belhaven Press.

Turner, Louis. 1976. "The International Division of Leisure: Tourism and the Third World." *World Development* 4 (3): 253–60.

Tyson, Laura. 1992. *Who's Bashing Whom? Trade Conflict in High-Technology Industries.* Washington, D.C.: Institution for International Economics.

U.S. Congress. Office of Technology Assessment. 1992. *Global Standards: Building Blocks for the Future.* TCT-512. Washington, D.C.: U.S. Government Printing Office.

U.S. House of Representatives. 2000. "Bill Proposing Enactment of the Derivatives Market Reform Act of 1999." HR 3483 IH, 106th Congress, 1st sess.

UNCTAD. 1998. *World Investment Report 1998: Trends and Determinants.* New York: United Nations.

———. 2001. *World Investment Report 2001: Promoting Linkages.* Geneva: UNCTAD.

United Nations Commission on Sustainable Development. 1999. *Commission on Sustainable Development Holds High-Level Meeting on Tourism.*

Valente, T. W. 1995. *Network Models of the Diffusion of Innovations.* Cresskill, N.J.: Hampton Press.

Van Houten, Pieter. 2000. "Regional Assertiveness in Western Europe: Political Constraints and the Role of Party Competition." Ph.D. diss., University of Chicago.

———. 2001. "Regional Assertiveness in Western Europe: A Statistical Exploration." Paper presented at the ECPR Joint Sessions, Grenoble.

Verdier, Daniel. 1998. "Domestic Responses to Capital Market Internationalization Under the Gold Standard, 1870–1914" *International Organization* 52, 1 (winter): 1–34.

Verdier, Daniel and Richard Breen. 2001. "Europeanization and Globalization: Politics Against Markets in the European Union." *Comparative Political Studies* 34, 3 (April): 227–62.

Verman, Lal. 1973. *Standardization: A New Discipline.* Hamden, Conn.: Archon Books.

Visser, Jelle. 1998. "Two Cheers for Corporatism, One for the Market: Industrial Relations, Wage Moderation, and Job Growth in the Netherlands." *British Journal of Industrial Relations* 36 (2): 269–93.

Vogel, David. 1995. *Trading Up: Consumer and Environmental Regulation in a Global Economy.* Cambridge, Mass.: Harvard University Press.

Vogel, Steven. 1996. *Freer Markets, More Rules: Regulatory Reform in Advanced Industrial Countries.* Ithaca, N.Y.: Cornell University Press.

Von Furstenberg, George. 2000. "A Case Against U.S. Dollarization." *Challenge* 43, 4 (July/August): 108–20.

Von Hagen, Jürgen. 1998. "Fiscal Policy and Intranational Risk-Sharing," Working Paper B13. Bonn: Zentrum für Europäische Integrationsforschung.

Wallenstein, Gerd. 1990. *Setting Global Telecommunication Standards.* Norwood, Mass.: Artech House.

Waltz, Kenneth N. 1979. *Theory of International Politics.* Reading, Mass: Addison-Wesley.

Wapner, Paul. 1996. *Environmental Activism and World Civic Politics.* New York: SUNY Press.

Weber, Gustavus Adolphus. 1925. *The Bureau of Standards: Its History, Activities, and Organization.* Baltimore, Md.: John Hopkins University Press.

Weber, Steven. 2001. *Globalization and the European Political Economy.* New York: Columbia University Press.

Wei, Shang-Jin. 1991. "To Divide or to Unite: A Theory of Secessions." Unpublished manuscript, University of California, Berkeley.

Weiler, Joseph H. H. 1999. *The Constitution of Europe.* Cambridge: Cambridge University Press.

Weingast, Barry. 1995. "The Economic Role of Political Institutions: Market-Preserving Federalism and Economic Development." *Journal of Law, Economics, and Organization* 11: 1–31.

Weiss, Linda 1998. *The Myth of the Powerless State.* Ithaca, N.Y.: Cornell University Press.

Wight, Martin. 1966. "Why Is There No International Theory?" In *Diplomatic Investigations*, edited by Herbert Butterfield and Martin Wight. London: George Allen and Unwin.

Williams, Colin H. 1997. "Territory, Identity, and Language." In *The Political*

Economy of Regionalism, edited by Michael Keating and John Loughlin. London: Frank Cass.

Williams, Phil. 1997. "Trafficking in Women and Children: A Market Perspective." *Transnational Organized Crime* 3 (4): 145–70.

Williams, Shirley. 1991. "Sovereignty and Accountability in the European Community." In *The New European Community: Decisionmaking and Institutional Change*, edited by Robert O. Keohane and Stanley Hoffmann, 155–76. Boulder, Colo.: Westview Press.

Williamson, Jeffrey G. 1998. "Globalization, Labor Markets and Policy Backlash in the Past." *Journal of Economic Perspectives* 12 (4): 51–72.

Wolfram, Stephen. 1999. *The Mathematica Book*. 4th ed. New York: Cambridge University Press.

Womack, James P. 1991. *The Machine That Changed the World*. New York: Harper.

Wood, A. 1994. *North-South Trade, Employment, and Inequality: Changing Fortunes in a Skill-Driven World*. New York: Oxford.

World Bank. 2000. *World Development Indicators*. CD-ROM. Washington, D.C.: The World Bank.

World Congress Against Commercial Sexual Exploitation of Children. 1996. "Declaration and Agenda for Action," 27–31 August, Stockholm.

World Tourism Organization. 1994. "Seminar on GATS Implications for Tourism." 2–3 December, Milan, Italy.

———. 1999a. "Global Code of Ethics for Tourism." Santiago.

———. 1999b. "Yearbook of Tourism Statistics." Yearbook of Tourism Statistics.

World Tourism Organization Business Council. 1998. "Tourism Taxation: Striking a Fair Deal." Madrid: World Tourism Organization.

World Travel and Tourism Council. 1999a. "Travel and Tourism's Economic Impact."

———. 1999b. "Travel and Tourism: North America Economic Impact."

———. 1999c. "Travel and Tourism: European Union Economic Impact."

———. 1999d. "Travel and Tourism: Caribbean Economic Impact."

———. 1999e. "Travel and Tourism: Middle East Economic Impact."

Wright, Vincent. 1998. "Intergovernmental Relations and Regional Government in Europe: A Sceptical View." In *Regions in Europe*, edited by Patrick Le Galès and Christian Lequesne. London: Routledge.

WTO Commission for the Americas. 1995. "Preliminary Report on Tourism Legislation in the Americas Region." Buenos Aires.

WTO/CEU-ETC Joint Seminar. 1997. "Faced with Worldwide Competition and Structural Changes: What Are the Tourism Responsibilities of European Governments?" 9–10 April, Salzburg, Austria. Madrid: World Tourism Organization.

Wymeersch, Eddy. 2001. "Current Company Law Reform Initiatives in the OECD Companies: Challenges and Opportunities." Workpaper 2001-4. Financial Law Institute, University of Ghent.

Young, Oran. 1999. *Governance in World Affairs*. Ithaca, N.Y.: Cornell University Press.

Ziegler, Nicholas. 2000. "Corporate Governance and the Politics of Property Rights in Germany." *Politics and Society* 28 (2): 195–223.

Zimmerman, Friedrich. 1991. "Austria: Contrasting Tourist Seasons and Contrasting Regions." In *Tourism and Economic Development: Western European Experiences*, edited by Allan M. Williams and Gareth Shaw, 153–72. London: Belhaven Press.